To Margaret S. (Peggy) and Cy Nathan –

Every good wish,

Natalie Ornish

Nov. 1989

PIONEER JEWISH TEXANS

PIONEER JEWISH TEXANS

THEIR IMPACT ON TEXAS AND AMERICAN HISTORY

FOR FOUR HUNDRED YEARS

1590 - 1990

Natalie Ornish

TEXAS HERITAGE PRESS, PUBLISHERS, DALLAS, TEXAS

Texas Heritage Press, Dallas 75225-6490

FIRST EDITION

Library of Congress Cataloging-in-Publication Data

Ornish, Natalie.
Pioneer Jewish Texans.

Bibliography: p.

Includes index.
1. Jews—Texas—Biography.
2. Texas—Biography.
I. Title.

F395.J5076 1989 920'.00929240764 88-50885

ISBN 0-9620755-0-7

Printed in the United States of America
Design: Tom McBride
This edition printed on acid-free paper.

To my Father and Mother
in appreciation
and to my ancestors
who first came to
Texas to visit and trade in
1843 and who came to
settle in 1863.

The long and dramatic story of the Jews in Texas history has never been told.

- The first Jew set foot in Texas in 1590.
- There was a Jewish buccaneer in the Galveston Island camp of pirate Jean Laffite.
- A Jewish seaman from Holland helped form the Texas Navy.
- A London-born Jew died at the Alamo with Davy Crockett.
- The soldiers who died at Goliad included a nineteen-year-old Jewish lad from Cincinnati named Ed Johnson.
- A Jewish physician, who came to Texas after living in London, Philadelphia, and Richmond, Virginia, served as surgeon-in-chief of the Texas Volunteers in the battles for Texas independence.
- The sister of composer Jacques Offenbach became a pioneer Texas housewife.
- A Jewish Texan helped blaze the Chisholm Trail. His family's cattle ranches embraced a million Texas acres and some as far as Wyoming.
- When Texas joined the Union, a Jew who graduated from Princeton University became the first person from Texas elected to the House of Representatives of the U.S. Congress.
- A West Texas Jew who wildcatted on University of Texas lands struck oil, providing the University Fund with billions of dollars.

They may seem incredible, but all these statements are true. Even before Texas existed, Jews numbered among the Spanish conquistadors. Later, in its days as a Republic, then a state, Texas boasted a robust land whose farms and ranges attracted many persons from Europe who sought greater freedom and more opportunity for economic development. Among those earliest pioneers who risked Indian raids, blizzards, and droughts was a surprisingly large number of ambitious Jews. Most historians have overlooked the contributions of Jews to the growth of the Lone Star State, perhaps because of the tendency to lump them with other immigrants from countries from which they originally came such as Spain, Portugal, England, Holland, Jamaica, France, and Germany.

True, the Jews who settled in Texas did not form separate colonies as did some of the French and the Germans. Instead, they penetrated every section, every occupation and profession. Of course, not every Jewish cowboy became a cattle baron, and not every Jewish peddler became a merchant prince; but a surprising number, by industry and perseverance, made envious names for themselves in the new land.

In the days of the conquistadors, Jewish explorers came to Texas representing the Spanish Crown. A Spanish Jew traveled on horseback with a group of men, women, and children across western Texas in 1590, following the Pecos River as far north as present Santa Fe, New Mexico. He literally became "The Law West of the Pecos" in the sixteenth century. He served as lieutenant governor and his friend served as governor of an incredible area that included twenty-five percent of present-day Texas and fifty percent of Northern Mexico.[1]

Later, Jewish pioneers settled in the colony of Stephen F. Austin, "Father of Texas." When Texas fought to throw off the Mexican yoke, Jews served on the front lines in all the principal battles.

Among those attracted to Texas in the Republic era was a Jew of Jamaican birth, Jacob De Cordova, who arrived in 1837 after living in Philadelphia. His father had been president of Philadelphia's Congregation Mikveh Israel and his great uncle had been the great rabbi of Amsterdam, and later Curacao and Kingston.[2] In Kingston the family published the *Gleaner*, "the best known newspaper in the entire Caribbean area."[3] In Texas, Jacob De Cordova published newspapers, and he traveled to Philadelphia to publish books on Texas. He lectured on Texas extensively in New York and Manchester, England, and boosted the cotton trade between Texas and England.[4] De Cordova explored more Texas territory than did its first European traveler, Cabeza de Vaca, and brought more settlers than did its first colonizer, Stephen F. Austin.[5]

The Lone Star State acted as a magnet also for Henri Castro, a Jew descended from nobility who lived in Paris, France. In the 1840s he contracted with Sam Houston to form a colony near San Antonio and brought from France more than two thousand settlers (mostly Catholics, interestingly enough). This empresario spent much of his personal fortune to provide his colonists with seed, implements, and livestock, but in spite of setbacks, his settlement survived. It made valiant progress in taming the wilderness and moving the frontier west.

The Sanger family, of Bavarian Jewish ancestry, moved to the frontier before the Civil War, then followed the advancing railroads and established stores in several Texas towns in an era when chains of stores were unheard of, selling such items as groceries, dry goods, crockery, harnesses, saddles, and plows, making it easier for frontier people to acquire items that they could not produce. In a later day, Neiman-Marcus helped to make Dallas a center of high fashion and good taste.

Jewish Texans cannot be stereotyped. Not all lived and worked like Stanley Marcus. Many peddled goods or owned small shops and lived in poverty. However, many reached high positions in education, government, journalism, and the arts. Others excelled as merchants or bankers.

With banks far away, some frontier merchants kept large safes in which farmers and ranchmen left valuables for security, including gold received for cattle sent up the trails. Occasionally this practice evolved into merchants establishing banks to serve their customers. Among Jews who became prominent in banking, a Dallasite led in financing the exploration of the great East Texas Oil Field, which added much to the wealth of America.[6]

One of the most famous Jewish Texans was an outstanding humanitarian, Rabbi Henry Cohen of Galveston. Born in London, Rabbi Cohen came to Galveston in 1888 after pulpits in Jamaica and Mississippi. He is best remembered for spearheading the Galveston Immigration Movement. At the turn of the century, many of New York's pioneer Jews were embarrassed at the plight and sight of their Yiddish-speaking coreligionists recently escaped from the pogroms in Russia's ghettos, who appeared in shocking contrast to such elegant Jewish families as the Guggenheims and Schiffs, New Yorkers for generations. Jacob Schiff of New York wanted to divert these immigrants away from crowded New York, where they slept in halls, and donated $500,000 to his project. He selected Galveston because Cohen was there to coordinate finding jobs for the new Americans in towns all over the United States. Galveston offered a Gulf port with direct steamship service to Europe as well as direct railroad connections with the country west of the Mississippi, including Denver, Kansas City, St. Louis, and points farther north where newcomers could be distributed. Of the first thousand immigrants, one hundred went directly to Kansas City, Missouri. During the seven years (1907-1914) of Project Galveston, Jews came through the port of Galveston to fifteen states — Texas, Iowa, Missouri, Minnesota, Nebraska, Louisiana, Colorado, Illinois, Oklahoma, Kansas, Tennessee, Arkansas, Wisconsin, Mississippi, and North Dakota. Iowa received 1,225 immigrants, second only to Texas, and Kansas City alone received more than a thousand immigrants.[7]

This book's limited scope makes it impossible to list all the Jewish Texans who have prospered or failed and shared their uniqueness with the people of Texas. Even a mere listing could fill another chapter. However, too few history books have included the names of Castro, De Cordova, Cohen, and other Jewish pioneers. This book hopes to fill that important gap in Texana.

Traveling thus with his people in order, with his banner high, and arriving in sight of the pueblo, he ordered the trumpets that they brought to be blown.

Castaño Journal, *December 31, 1590*

Chapter 1

The Adventurers

Conquistadors and the Search for Freedom

Those conquistadors who rode north, with banners and trumpets, to carry the rule of their king to the farther reaches of New Spain, included Jews whose role in American exploration, adventure, and settlement often has been overlooked.

They came to the New World to escape torture and death. Some became horse ranchers or cattle ranchers in northern Mexico, and a few crossed the Rio Grande and established themselves in what became Texas. They rode their stallions as far north as the present San Antonio.

Some of the earliest of those Jews — the ones who landed with conquistador Hernando Cortés — became victims of the Inquisition.[1]

In 1528, ninety-two years before the Pilgrims landed at Plymouth Rock, members of the Spanish Inquisition in Mexico City burned a Jew, Hernando Alonso, at the stake.[2] They charged him with being a "Judaizing heretic," a Spanish legal term then used to describe one who officially belonged to the Catholic Church but who allegedly practiced Jewish rituals or rituals that were allegedly Jewish. Conquistador Cortés had hired Alonso, a carpenter, to build bridges for Cortés' march across Mexico. It was Cortés and his men who defeated Emperor Montezuma II and ended the Aztec nation, capturing Mexico for Spain. Jewish history in North America, replete with dark tragedies such as Alonso's, also boasts of triumphs in settling the land and building industries and opportunities for new generations.

This continent's Jewish history began, not in New England, but with adventurers in Mexico and Texas, known as New Spain. Alonso lived in the New World one hundred years before Manhattan Island was acquired from the Indians. One hundred twenty-six years after his death — in truth, murder — the *St. Charles* sailed into New Amsterdam in 1654 with the first group of Jews to land on the soil of what is now the United States of America. Both Alonso and the newcomers to New Amsterdam shared the common experience of persecution by the Inquisition. It punished Protestants, Muslims, and Jews. This work deals with only one aspect of the Inquisition, its handling of the Jews.

In the late 1400s, Spanish Jews became increasingly hated because of their commercial successes and because they allegedly assisted the Moors. The Dominicans called for the introduction of the Inquisition, and in 1492 the Inquisitor General in Spain issued an edict expelling all Jews. Many Jews accepted Baptism, which produced a large group of "New Christians," although many other Jews remained loyal to their faith and practiced Judaism in secret.[3] The Inquisition continued wherever the Spanish landed and conquered, in this instance in New Spain, which included Mexico and what is now called Texas. Besides Alonso, others kept their Jewish ancestry secret in New Spain during the 1500s, and a few traveled on horseback north into Tejas territory.[4]

The story of the earliest Jewish adventurers in Texas embraces the lives of four men: two conquistadors, Gaspar Castaño de Sosa and Luis Carvajal II; one professional soldier, West Point graduate Samuel Noah; and a member of Jean Laffite's colony on Galveston Island with the Karankawa Indians, a pirate named Jao de la Porta. Each of their lives ended in tragedy. Though many other early Jews lived and traveled in Mexico/Texas, these four Jews became historically the most significant.

Conquistador Castaño is credited as being the first Jew to set foot on Texas soil. He served as the mayor (*alcalde*) of what is now called Monterrey, Mexico.[5] He led a group of 170 colonists north into Texas looking for the Pecos River in 1590. Thus a man of Jewish descent acted as "the law west of the Pecos" in the sixteenth century. Consumed by political jealousy, his enemies ousted him from control and then exiled him: He sailed toward the Far East, where he died a grisly death in the Philippines in a mutiny on a Chinese junk.[6]

Carvajal II, also called Carvajal the Younger (*el Mozo*), anticipated succeeding his uncle, Luis de Carvajal y de la Cueva, a great captain and explorer almost the equal of Cortés, in governing a vast area of northern Mexico that included parts of Texas territory. The spacious empire sprawled from Tampico, Mexico, north all the way to San Antonio, Texas. Set up by charter May 31, 1569, from the Spanish Crown, the empire covered land 600 miles square and embraced both sides of the Rio Grande. It encompassed one of the largest, yet most dangerous, Spanish land grants. Later, Spanish authorities stripped young Carvajal of rights to his uncle's empire and burned him at the stake for following what he called "the law of Moses." He died a martyr's death in 1596, ending an unmatched Texas dynasty.

Two hundred years later, we find in Texas Samuel Noah, the first Jewish graduate of West Point. To help a college friend, he traveled to Texas and fought a major battle in Texas' earliest struggle for independence from Spain. When their Magee-Gutierrez Expedition failed, he fled Texas and returned to New York, weary and disillusioned from the animalistic slaughter of humanity he had witnessed.

The fourth adventurer, Jao de la Porta, a pirate-patriot, rode the high seas as a free spirit with bands of adventurers. He worked as an official with Luis Aury, first governor of Texas under Mexico.

When Aury left Galveston, de la Porta served as secretary and trader under the swashbuckling Jean Laffite. When the pirates expanded assaults on Spanish ships in the Gulf of Mexico to include American ships, the U.S. government pressured them to leave the Bay at Galveston.

These are the men, the adventurers, who began to make Jewish history on Texas soil.

We know more about these men who walked on Texas soil 400 years ago — how they thought, whom they loved, why they made war, how they sold slaves and lived with the Indians — than we do about most modern-day Texans. Spanish ordinances, including the Laws of Settlement of 1573, required all explorers to keep "a journal account of the expedition's day to day travel" for the governor who had dispatched the entourage.[7]

Castaño, Great Captain in New Spain and explorer in West Texas in 1590.

Art from Twelve Travelers by Tom Lea.

Castaño kept a most detailed journal of his mobile colony. Carvajal, the sixteenth century's Anne Frank, kept a poignant diary as he languished in jail at the hands of the Inquisition.

GASPAR CASTAÑO DE SOSA

. . . the Padres came
Upward from Mexico and the great river the Bravo
Over the many rivers, bruising the shallow land
Into a path for the king.

A Letter From Texas, *Townsend Miller*

Jews followed the rivers, too. They adventured west of the Sabine, west of the Trinity, west of the Brazos, west of the Colorado, west of the Pecos, and west of the Rio Grande.

In 1590 Castaño, a Portuguese by birth and by religion a Catholic, converted from Judaism, set forth on an expedition looking for the Pecos River in Texas— and silver as well.

Castaño was as rugged as Coronado, as idealistic and sometimes even as comic as Don Quixote. He guided his actions by chivalry, magnanimity, and morality, sometimes bordering on the ridiculous. When betrayed, framed, and captured, he embraced his traitor and remained loyal to his king. His brief life covered three continents and generated robust excitement and violence.

Castaño attained the rank of lieutenant governor of a vast province 600 miles north-south and 600 miles east-west, the New Kingdom of Leon (*Nuevo León*). This area, from the Gulf of Mexico to Mexico's Pacific coast, north to the state of Chihuahua, and east to San Antonio, Texas, became known as "Carvajal's Tragic Square."[8] Castaño received his appointment as lieutenant governor from Governor Luis de Carvajal. Castaño and Carvajal had founded settlements together. Carvajal founded, and Castaño became mayor of, a village in Mexico called *San Luís*, renamed Monterrey. There Castaño owned a farm called The Enchanted Lady (*La Encantada*).[9]

He later moved to the silver-mining town of Almaden (meaning *mine*), now renamed Monclova. When the silver ran low, he told the people in Almaden of mines to the north, appealing to the citizens personally, luring them by showing a large ingot. Equally, his desire to move may have been motivated by the knowledge that on April 13, 1589, Spanish officials arrested Governor Luis de Carvajal in Almaden, and charged him with being a secret Jew. On Monday, February 26, 1590, the governor began his sentence in the Royal Prison, where he died in a matter of months.[10]

On July 27, 1590, Castaño set out to cross Coahuila in Northeast Mexico and West Texas, seeking silver in New Mexico. The entire town enlisted to move with him.

That morning in late summer of 1590, the adventurers loaded a large supply of corn and wheat and located several Indian interpreters. The company of 160 or 170 men and women — together with their beef on the hoof, goats, and at least ten carts — marched north, seeking glory and silver for themselves and for the king of Spain, their sovereign.

Gaspar Castaño de Sosa traveled in the manner of a true conquistador. One of his men documented in their official journal, "He traveled along with his people in [military] order with flag flying high, and on gaining sight of the village he ordered the trumpets sounded which they had with them."[11]

. . . Here is most Spain
Here they the wanderers, the slow marchers northward
Remembering Spain in the long afternoons
Toledo, dusty Salamanca.

A Letter From Texas, *Townsend Miller*

It took forty-five days — a full six weeks — from July 27 to September 9, just to get from Almaden (Monclova) to the Rio Grande, now the Mexico-Texas border. (Monclova to Del Rio is approximately 175 miles.) The final three weeks in September Castaño and company encamped on the low sandy hills and lush greenery on the banks of the Rio Grande, near modern Del Rio, Texas. Castaño had sent an urgent message to the viceroy, formalizing his request for permission to colonize the New World. He waited at the Rio Grande for a response, crossing the great river and moving camp to the east bank. This move stands as the first documentation of a Jew setting foot on Texas soil.

On October 1 the group broke camp and headed north-northwest, and two days later reached Devil's River. The crossing presented a supreme challenge; it took the party all day to ford San Pedro creek, a little north of what is today Texas Highway 90.

The journey continued during the month of October, with endless marching by foot, ox, and horse across West Texas. On past Cow Creek and Dead Man's Creek near present-day Comstock. They continued north-northwest between Devil's River and the Pecos, toward Live Oak Creek. The expedition finally sighted the waters of the Pecos River on October 26. They crossed the Pecos fifteen to twenty miles below present-day Sheffield, Texas.

No roads or towns existed in this rugged, rocky terrain. They used more than 300 horseshoes as they penetrated the Indian territory between the Rio Grande and the Pecos. When the ordeal's obstacles mounted, several dissenters protested and wanted to turn back from the steep passages. Castaño in his own way became like Moses in the wilderness during the Exodus from Egypt. Castaño's top aide who always agreed with him to take the route he selected was Juan de Carvajal, once arrested by Captain Juan de Morlete at Almaden.[12]

They moved five to eight miles a day. Women, children, and cattle walked in the moving colony. Castaño led his group up the lower Pecos across what became these West Texas towns: Sheffield, Iraan, Abel City, Grandfalls, Pecos, Arno, and Orla.[13] They journeyed across the Davis Mountains and the Delaware Mountains of Texas. Waters they passed had colorful names later such as Independence Creek, Comanche Creek, Cottonwood Draw, Salt Creek, and finally Red Bluff Lake on the Texas-New Mexico border.

Here Castaño climbed a bluff and saw in the distance the Guadalupe Mountains, which straddle the present Texas-New Mexico line. On November 29, 1590, the colony-on-the-move reached Willow Lake and crossed the present New Mexico border at Dark Canyon and Carlsbad. The expedition continued to present-day Santa Fe before it aborted.[14]

While on the move, Castaño refused to allow his men to rape the land or the women. This great captain contrasted with other governors of the era, who indulged in their own trading ventures and enslaved Indians.[15] Castaño brought the Indians meat, maize, ornaments, small knives, and other gifts as gestures of goodwill.

The journal entry for January 2 to 5, 1591, reads in part, "The Lieutenant Governor ordered . . . that no harm should be done [the Indians' belongings], but that search should be made in the houses to see if some things that belonged to us could be found. This was done without any harm being done them."[16] Castaño's insistence that nothing be taken from the Indians nor

Detail of the first part of Castaño's trip: Monclova, Mexico, to the Rio Grande.

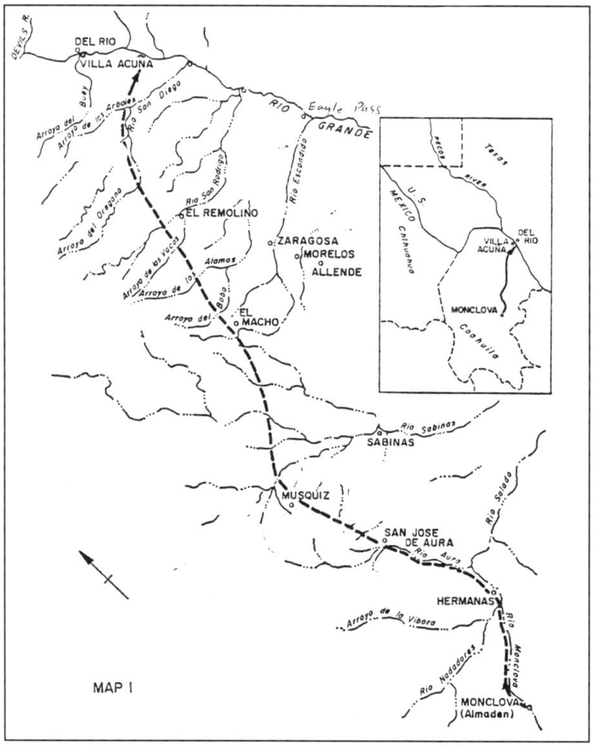

Detail of the second part of Castaño's trip: from the Rio Grande to the Pecos River.

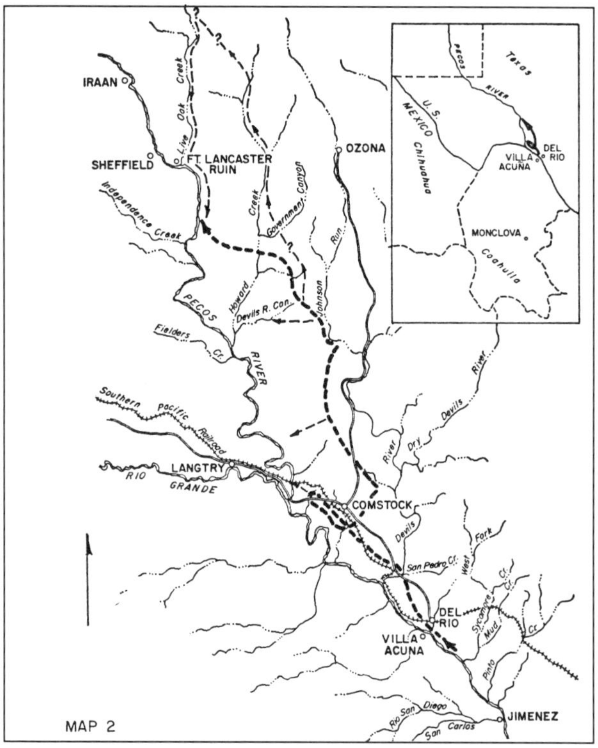

any of them molested almost led to a mutiny near the end of the expedition's exploration on the Rio Grande.[17]

The Indians' fear of the Spaniards seemed understandable, especially where there had been earlier slave expeditions. The journal describes one scene in detail:

> They showed great fear at seeing us, especially the women, who wept very much. One [Indian] came to us with much fear, and the Lieutenant, in order to reassure them all, dismounted and embraced the Indian. And when he (Castaño) saw that there was a band of Indians in another place, he went to them, and they waited for him, and he embraced them. While they were touching him and placing their hands on the face of the Lieutenant and on his clothing, he kissed them, while they all caressed him and touched him with their hands.

At one point a horseman notified Castaño that one of the Indians in a pueblo wore much jewelry of precious stones; he suggested Castaño go see him and take it. The journal reads: "He [Castaño] replied that it was not then convenient to do so as he did not wish the Indians to think that they coveted their things or believe that they came to their land for what they had. . . . The lieutenant governor only wished to see it and went to the Indian who had it. The said Indian was covered with beautiful buffalo hide. He reached him [the Indian] wishing to see it as has been said, but he [the Indian] did not want to show it. So the matter was dropped."[18]

Castaño's expedition was unique. Unlike all other expeditions into the Southwest, his had no friars traveling with the party. Although it began hurriedly without advance sanction of the viceroy and without undergoing an inspection, the expedition complied with the Laws of Settlement.[19] The Laws permitted expeditions "in parts already discovered . . . provided that notice of the settlement made in the discovered area be forwarded to us immediately."[20]

After Castaño sent notice to the viceroy, his impatience caused him to start the trip without advance official sanction, hoping these papers would catch up with him. He had waited three weeks at what became Del Rio, Texas, on the banks of the Rio Grande.

But his hidden problem centered on an enemy he had made. Long before the trip, he had had a falling out with Captain Juan Morlete. Envious of the lieutenant governor, Morlete had written to the high court of Mexico requesting a commission to go and seize him. Previously, Morlete had acted as a scribe for the Inquisition.[21]

Juan de Carvajal, previously arrested by Morlete and released before Castaño led the expedition out, and two other of Castaño's men were the first to warn him.

They "had come to call the lieutenant governor because Captain Juan Morlete with fifty men had arrived in camp."[22] When Castaño heard who they were, "this caused him to worry greatly." However, he did not heed his men's advice to flee but rode rapidly back to his camp. Several historians agree that jealousy and Castaño's "adherence to the ordinance" forbidding the infliction of injury on the Indians caused Morlete's conspiracy.[23]

Throughout his expedition Castaño had sent detailed, documented messages to the viceroy and king. He had done what no conquistador had done before: he had conquered the Pecos and pacified the New Mexico Indians. Instead of a garland of laurels, a warrant for his arrest awaited "by order of his majesty and the viceroy Don Luis de Velasco."[24] "He was arrested, not on the charge of having led an unauthorized expedition into [Texas and] New Mexico, but on the accusation that he had attempted to raise rebellion in New Mexico and to make himself an independent ruler."[25]

Castaño did not resist arrest. When presented with the warrant for his arrest and put in irons, "he placed the irons over his head first kissing them in the presence of said Juan Morlete and his camp as well as his own. All rejoiced greatly to see the great humility and obedience which the lieutenant governor manifested. The said Captain Juan Morlete, seeing the

The third part of the trip: in Texas along the Pecos River.

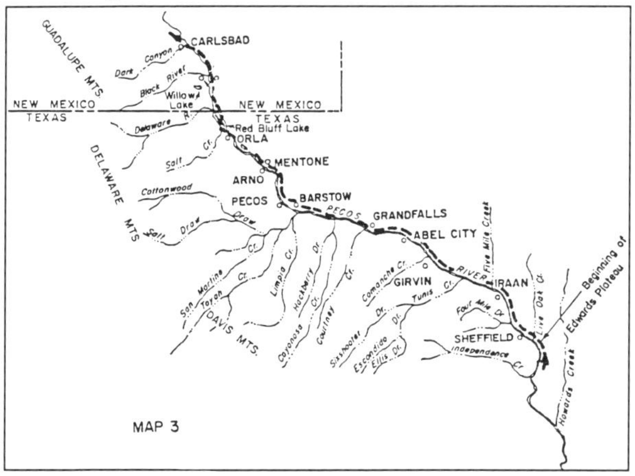

Maps prepared by Albert H. Schroeder.
Published with permission of The School of American Research

humility of the said Gaspar Castaño, praised him as was due to his character and merit. Both camps rejoiced."[26]

On the return route, Morlete led the way down the Rio Grande. A court in Mexico City found Castaño guilty and exiled him. He appealed, and more than a year later higher courts in Spain reviewed his case and reversed the earlier verdict. He was exonerated and ordered home from exile to become the first royally authorized governor of New Mexico.[27]

Tragically, the acquittal arrived too late. Word came that mutineers had killed Castaño months before on a Chinese junk in the Philippines. This venture demonstrates the long arm of the viceroy in 1591, which reached out to arrest him more than 600 miles from his point of departure. It was a violent end for this adventurer of Portuguese-Jewish descent.

Castaño's presence had far-reaching significance. Juan de Oñate, colonizer of New Mexico, reported eight years later that the ruts of the carts of Castaño's expedition were still visible in the El Paso region. Castaño found more mineral deposits than any other Spanish explorer.[28] The area in Texas that Castaño crossed is known today as the West Texas Permian Basin, famous for its rich oil reserves. Castaño was looking for minerals in the right place — more than 350 years ahead of his time.

LUIS DE CARVAJAL II

"Carvajal the Younger"

The contemporary Mexican writer Fernando Benítez called Carvajal II (1566-1596) "the most exciting personage in New Spain."[29] Conquistador Carvajal I groomed his nephew to succeed him as governor of an incredible area of real estate that included twenty-five percent of present-day Texas and half of present-day Mexico. The land grant extended from Tampico, Mexico, to what is now called San Antonio, Texas. It ran 600 miles westward from the Gulf of Mexico and was one of the largest sections of land ever granted by the Spanish Crown.

Young Carvajal aborted his future when he openly declared himself a Jew and circumcised himself by the bank of the Pánuco River.[30] One of the world's greatest martyrs, Carvajal the Younger was burned at the stake on Saturday, December 8, 1596, in Mexico City, for following what he called "The Law of Moses." His mother and three sisters suffered this heinous death, but his uncle of Jewish origin who did not practice Judaism, was imprisoned and died behind bars.

Carvajal I, the uncle, explored and searched for minerals in Taxco in 1576, 200 years before the American Revolution. Carvajal I founded Almaden, the city from which Lt. Governor Castaño's expedition emanated. The governor was Carvajal himself.

Carvajal I, a conquistador, achieved only lesser fame than Cortés. His track record as an explorer rivaled Cortés. As a teen-ager, he was given command of a Spanish armada in the waters off Flanders and built a spectacular career as a naval warrior in Europe.

Born in 1539, he was only twenty-two years old when he returned to Lisbon in 1561. In 1566 he married a young lady of aristocracy who secretly "unabashedly discharged her energies in the clandestine practice of Judaism."[31] She was the daughter of a wealthy New Christian. In the sixteenth century in Spain and Portugal, "Old Christian" meant no Jewish ancestors on the family tree. "New Christian" meant descended from Jews who had accepted Christianity in the wake of the massacres of Jews that swept Spain. At first the converts (*Conversos*) were accepted and married into many noble families of Spain. However, when the economy of the nation soured, the ruling classes sought out the "New Christians" as their scapegoat. Luis I presented himself publicly as an "Old Christian" and had not been told of his Jewish background. His parents had zealously clung to the church, never giving him reason to doubt an Old Christian descent. He had married Guiomar de Ribera because she was the wealthy daughter of his business associate.[32]

He made his first trip to the New World in 1568, setting sail from Seville that summer with several important officials and a precious cargo that included Spanish wine and 873 quintals of mercury to use in refining silver. He left Spain as an admiral in a fleet of eleven vessels. Ironically, Carvajal was one of the first explorers to extract silver from the mines of Mexico; he greatly enriched a monarch who later turned on him.

The twenty-nine-year-old admiral and his fleet first landed on the island of Jamaica, where they captured three English pirate vessels carrying stolen hides. He then landed on the North American mainland and governed first as the local judge or magistrate of the port of Tampico, Mexico.

Like most conquistadors, Carvajal I desired the territory he pacified as his own, so ten years after his first trip he returned to Spain to seek a charter, which was granted May 31, 1579. It named Carvajal I governor of the entire expanse of land he had traversed which became known as the "New Kingdom of Leon." The charge gave him the privilege of passing on his holdings to an heir. He and his wife had no children, and he claimed no illegitimate heirs.

The governor, however, had many nephews and nieces and named his nephew, Luis Rodriguez, to be his heir and successor. The teen-ager Luis Rodriguez changed his name and became Luis Carvajal the

Younger (*el Mozo*). His mother was Francisca and his father, Francisco Rodriguez. The governor named Luis II's older brother, Baltasar Rodriguez, treasurer of the kingdom in New Spain (*Nueva España*).

Although school books show Isabella selling her jewels to finance Columbus' expedition, later missions like Carvajal's were funded by the explorers themselves and not by the Crown. Carvajal had to accumulate the *ducats* and *pesos* to pay for forts, troops, provisions, and tools. Nonetheless, the mother country received royalties from all of the gold or silver discoveries.

Right before the voyage, Señora Carvajal assigned her niece, Luis II's older sister Isabel, to help try to convert her husband, the governor, to Judaism once they settled in the New World. The conquistador's wife admonished, "If he wants to succeed in his endeavors, he should cleave to the Law of Moses, for not to do so would lead him to failure."[33] However, Carvajal I was not a Jew, although of Jewish descent. His parents had died while he was a small boy, and he was raised by an uncle in the Catholic faith, from which he never swerved. He lived his life as a devout Catholic. The fact that he was raised by an uncle may have motivated him to adopt his own nephew, Carvajal II.

In June of 1580 this wing of the Carvajal family set sail for New Spain. The seventy-five men of *Converso* background who joined the expedition aided in supplying funds to outfit the expedition.[34]

A trans-Atlantic trip in the 1500s took nearly three months. The convoy departed in early June, spent four days in the Canary Islands near Africa and arrived in the Gulf of Mexico the end of August. Luis II, then fourteen, remained ill during much of the voyage. The close contact aboard ship caused some of the passengers to suspect the family of being secret Jews since they dressed in their finest clothes on Saturday, their sabbath, and abstained from eating pork during the long trip. The governor's sister and her daughter Catalina spent much time fasting and praying to God that, just as He had freed the children of Israel from the Red Sea and set them on their path, so might He now guide them from danger.

When the ship finally arrived at Tampico, the Carvajals suffered a severe cultural shock. They viewed a few shanties in a barren wilderness. A hurricane hit the city, and soon mosquitoes and snakes appeared. The affluence promised was nowhere to be seen, and the family of Carvajal the Younger lived in despair and poverty. His father, Francisco, took up peddling to eke out a living. He peddled blankets, linens, confections, and furniture between the mining regions, the capital, and the Gulf coast.[35]

Francisco tried to give Luis' brother Gaspar a good education by enrolling him in a monastery. When this son converted to Catholicism and rejected Judaism, the father suffered a great sadness and now looked to young Luis to carry on the family's Jewish tradition.

Luis studied in great secrecy, learning about Passover and the Day of Atonement. Passover symbolized deliverance from persecution. The secret Jews also identified with the story of Esther, who kept her Jewish identity a secret.

There were many secret Jews in their community—physicians, merchants; men and women. The story goes that young Luis once came upon Gaspar Castaño de Sosa's relative Manuel de Herrera slaughtering a rooster according to Jewish ritual. He engaged him in conversation and discovered he was a secret Jew.[36]

Luis kept his religion a private affair. When Luis' father died in 1584, the governor invited his nephew to accompany him on a long expedition into the wild territories of the Chichimec Indians. The invitation coincided with the governor's wish to educate and train young Luis in his future duties in government. Luis remained with his uncle a year and a half.

By this time the governor and his expeditions had founded the town of Leon (now Cerralvo), approximately fifty miles from present Texas, and the town of Almaden (now Monclova) in Coahuila. They made settlements along the Rio Grande and traveled over much of their territory, and extensively in the area around what is now called Laredo and other parts of present-day Texas.[37]

The governor boasted years later at his Inquisition trial there was so much silver in the mines of Almaden that the King's share of a fifth of the silver already exceeded 2,000 pesos per year, and he predicted that the Crown's share would rise to over 50,000 pesos annually.[38] But for the time, the silver mines of Almaden ceased to produce.

When silver became scarce, Luis I and Luis II joined other adventurers from various European countries in rounding up Indians and selling them for slaves. A healthy Chichimec male could bring at least eight gold pesos in the markets around Mexico City and a young female, up to one hundred pesos. Perhaps it was the slave-trading that made sensitive young Luis decide to leave

Carvajal I.

Art by Jose Cisneros.

his uncle. After much soul-searching, he decided to become a merchant.

It also was becoming doubtful whether Luis II would have the opportunity to succeed his uncle in his high position as governor because the viceroy in Mexico City had a running conflict over sovereignty of areas. When the governor won a case in the courts, the viceroy decided to get revenge.[39]

The Crown's policy, almost from the moment of the discovery of the Americas, was to induce high-spirited private adventurers to take all the risks of exploration, but once their tasks were successfully completed, to swoop down and replace them with bureaucratic servants who were easily controlled. It was a continuing reconquest of the New World from the conquistador. The Carvajal arrests were politically inspired acts using the facade of religion. The ax fell on the night of April 13, 1589, when officials arrested the governor. On March 13, 1589, his niece Isabel (Luis II's older sister) had been arrested in the unfolding drama of desertion. On May 9, Luis II came under arrest.

The governor's arrest came at Almaden, the former mining town. The cycle now completed itself. Guards bound the governor in chains and took him to the Royal Prison in Mexico City. At first, the viceroy pressed no charge against the governor. Then he was accused of "observing the law of Moses." After several hearings, the Inquisition reduced his charge to being an "aider, abettor, and harbourer and concealer of Jewish apostates from the Holy Catholic faith." The Court sentenced him to serve one year in jail and then to be exiled for six years. He died during the year of his imprisonment in 1591, the same year as Castaño's betrayal by Morlete.

Luis II was convicted of heresy and sentenced to four years in a monastery, where he was to be re-indoctrinated into Catholicism. He was arrested a second time and subjected to an *auto da fe,* or sentencing. From the Inquisitorial prison, Luis de Carvajal the Younger wrote in May 1595 the following in a letter to his sisters, "This is the road to the glory of paradise... and there is none other. And the journey is better than the one to Castile."[40] On December 8, 1596, Luis the Younger was ceremoniously burned at the stake with his mother (sister of the Governor Luis I) and three sisters because they had "relapsed" to Judaism.[41]

Four and a half years later, on March 25, 1601, a sister Mariana Núñez de Carvajal, was garroted and her body set afire at the stake. The last years of her life had alternately been spent in lucidity and insanity.[42] The Jews in Mexico then enjoyed a respite from persecution from 1605 to 1642, except for an *auto da fe* in 1635.[43] Another sister Ann (*Ana* or *Anica*), the youngest in Luis' family, was murdered in a similar fashion as

Governor Carvajal's land grant: Tampico to San Antonio and westward in a square.

Conquistador. *Art by Jose Cisneros.*

Doña Isabel de Carvajal, sister of Luis the Younger, before the Inquisitors.

her brother and sisters, in 1649, fifty-three years later.[44]

Genealogist Malcolm Stern said that other early Carvajals whose destiny propelled them into being adventurers were likely in the same clan as Luis' family.[45] Before these Carvajals came to Mexico-Texas, Francisco de Carvajal gained fame as one of the conquistadors of Peru, where he died in 1548. His portrait is in the National Library at Lima.

In 1655, when Manassah ben Israel petitioned for the return of Jews to England, Antonio F. Carvajal, a Portuguese secret Jew there, emerged as founder of the Anglo-Jewish community.

Bernardo de Carvajal served as an officer at St. Augustine, Florida, in 1723 and 1724.

Geronimo Carvajal died in San Antonio at an early date, leaving a widow, Maria, who married again in 1722. I. Mateo Carvajal died in San Antonio in 1748.

José M. J. Carvajal came as one of the original forty-one families to settle on the Guadalupe grant of his father-in-law, Martin de Leon. A surveyor, Carvajal laid out the town of Victoria. Highly educated, he was granted a license to publish (in English and Spanish) the laws of the state of Coahuila and Texas. While living in Victoria he became a delegate from that city to the signing of the Texas Declaration of Independence. He witnessed the signing, although his signature does not appear on it. His brother-in-law Placido Benavides, an intrepid fighter in the cause of Texas, gathered a company of thirty native Mexicans, rancheros from Victoria, superb horsemen and stalwart frontiersmen, and assisted materially in the Storming of Bexar, December of 1835, in that battle for Texas Independence.

Most of the descendants of these adventurers are Catholics today.[46] A Mexican citizen who read this chapter in manuscript form told an anecdote about the time he visited in Monterrey, Mexico, a highly industrialized city. He said that as he jested with an official, kidding him about being so industrious, the man who wore a cross on a chain around his neck laughed and said, "Of course we're persevering people; we're Jews." He and his family had been church-going Catholics for generations, yet they still talked about their Jewish heritage, going back to the sixteenth century conquistadors.[47]

When Luis de Carvajal II met a martyr's death at the stake in 1596 at the age of thirty, he left behind not only the renown he attained as an exemplary secret Jew but also a valuable literary legacy; Luis II is considered the first Jewish writer in the New World.[48] He left his memoirs, his last will and testament, and his letters to his mother and sisters in the Inquisitorial prison.

The authorities in Spain allowed the Inquisition to continue in Spain and in the colonies until 1813, when a decree was issued, but the Inquisition did not end until 1820. In the two and a half centuries of its existence in Spain and New Spain, the Inquisition had done its work efficiently against the children of Abraham, sending many to their deaths, frightening others into conformity with the church, and sending others to flight.[49] When Governor Carvajal died, his kingdom, which extended to San Antonio, again saw men brutally killed, Indians enslaved, Indians revolt, and people forced to leave their homes. During the 1600s, the Texas Indians became so difficult to deal with that in 1693 the Spanish missionaries abandoned the country, and they did nothing toward its occupation for over twenty years.

In 1715 descendants of the Carvajal family led a group of five families from northern Mexico to settle on the banks of the San Antonio River.[50] This was the beginning of the Spanish occupation of Texas. The city council (*cabildo*) presented a petition to Governor Rafael Martinez Pacheco stating, "It is certainly evident and clear that the settlement of this province of Texas was begun in the year 15 of our present century," thus establishing 1715 as the beginning date for Bexar, now called San Antonio. Expeditions of soldiers had surveyed the province, but this marked the first official civil settlement. "Then, some bold citizens, from the two neighboring provinces — Nuevo Reyno de Leon or Monterey [*sic*] and Nueva Estremadura Monclova or Coahuila — . . . the last and frontier provinces. . .

Doña Mariana de Carvajal as Inquisitors set fire to her in Mexico City in 1601.

desirous of renown or wishing to advance their own private interests, had well-authenticated and individual information that the many gentile [Indian] nations living in these two provinces and in their principal districts about this time were at peace . . . conceived the idea, and with manly courage set out to seek the famous and much lauded river of San Antonio, on whose banks they formed a settlement very near the point at which our villa San Fernando is planted today. They brought with them not only their wives and children, but all their goods, cattle, horses, goats, sheep, and such other things as they thought necessary for their sustenance. . . . They had no troops for their defense except the guard they themselves formed from their own number. . . . The names of the most prominent men among them — they were Don Mateo Carabajal, Cristobal Carabajal, and Don Francisco Hernandez — and of the survival and increase of the cattle they brought. This memory exists in the minds of their descendants — our relatives, but it is not such as those men deserve as first settlers."[51]

These earliest settlers in 1715 came at their own expense. Sixteen years later the King of Spain wanted to populate Texas to fortify it against the French, so the Crown paid expenses for a group of families from the Canary Islands, who founded the villa of San Fernando de Bexar. Numerous Jews who had fled Spain during the Inquisition had settled in the Canary Islands off the coast of Africa. However, it cannot be documented whether these later 1731 families were Jewish. It is possible they were not. Historian Seymour B. Liebman, whose area of expertise is Jews in Europe and Latin America during the Inquisition, 1493-1825, said he believes they were Jews.[52] Around fifty Islanders from fifteen families made up the group of immigrants who had volunteered to come to Texas. The arduous journey by sea and land took a year, and they reached Bexar on March 9, 1731.[53]

The Mexican viceroy then issued a decree forbidding these Canary Island settlers from leaving the province; they lived in the San Antonio area in a state of captivity, while unsponsored settlers who came to the area after their arrival were free to travel.[54] The king feared they would leave if free to choose, to escape the hard times in Texas. They suffered from Indian raids and economic deprivation.

By 1806 San Antonio had become the capital of this Mexican-Spanish province and the town had around 5,000 persons, all Mexicans.[55] The Anglo-American infiltration of Texas began, and it took on importance with the Magee-Gutierrez Expedition in which Samuel Noah, a Jew, served as an officer.

SAMUEL NOAH

Samuel Noah, born in England in 1779, is believed to be the first Jew ever to graduate from West Point Military Academy. Noah joined a group of adventurers hoping to set up Texas as a new country, independent of Spain. The adventurers included Americans, Mexicans, Frenchmen, and Indians. Among the Americans numbered Augustus W. Magee, a native of Massachusetts and a graduate of West Point's class of 1809. Noah had graduated in the class of 1807.[56] They became a part of the Magee-Gutierrez Expedition that sought to liberate Texas from Spain. Possibly it should be called the Gutierrez-Noah-Magee Expedition, because Noah graduated two years ahead of Magee at West Point, and Noah had been a first lieutenant and Magee a Second Lieutenant in the U.S. Army. Noah spent only two years in Texas, but these evolved into his and Texas' most grisly and hideous years.

He had spent the first decades of his life in England. When he turned twenty, he sailed to New York City and a few years later was awarded the appointment to West Point. This may have been possible because his distant cousin Manuel Noah had fought as an officer in the American Revolution under George Washington, who attended Manuel Noah's wedding.[57]

From the very beginning of his career, Samuel's goals seemed diverted. Originally, he aspired for a midshipman's appointment, but accepted that of a cadet instead. Having good penmanship, he acted as judge advocate or recorder of courts at West Point. When he graduated in 1807, he was one of a class of five cadets.

His career began at Fort Adams, Mississippi, where he devoted his leisure hours to the study of the early campaigns of Napoleon, then the military prodigy of the world. Noah took an assignment to police for pirates and smugglers along the Florida frontier. His life remained unglamorous as he marched from one camp to another along the mosquito-ridden Gulf Coast. During these trips he met many famous officers, including Captain Winfield Scott just after his duel near Natchez, and General James Wilkinson, who presided over the Sabine River on Texas' east border.

Although Noah reached the rank of first lieutenant in the army, he resented that often civilians received job appointments that outranked him. He resigned his commission at age thirty-two, in 1811, the year that served as an important one in the history of Mexico and inevitably changed Noah's life. In that year the Spanish Royalists shot a Catholic priest, Father Miguel Hidalgo y Costilla, who two years previously had launched a movement to liberate Mexico of Spanish rule. The

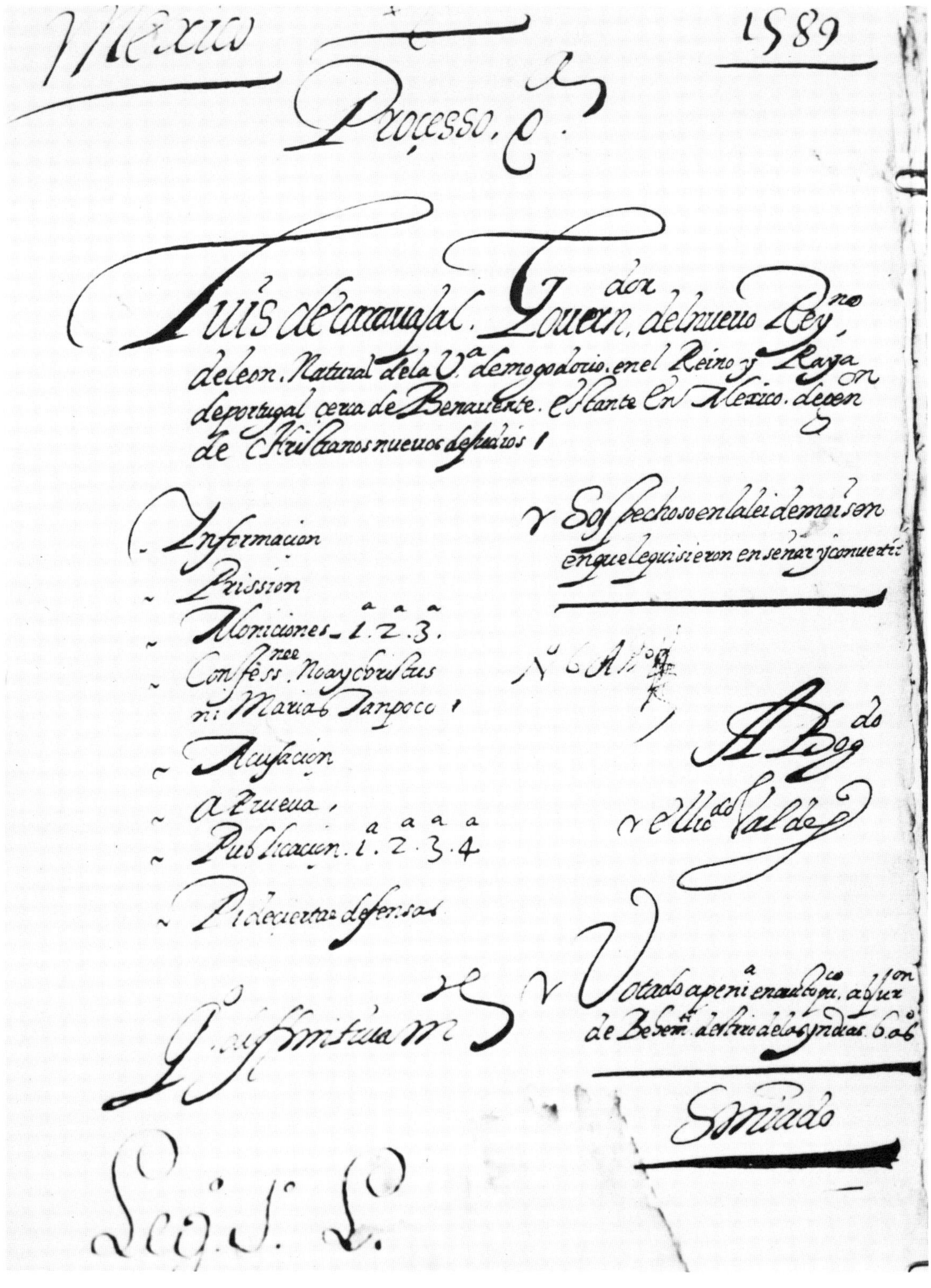

Mexico 1589

Processo. C.

Luis de carvajal. Gouern.dor del nuevo Reyno de leon. Natural de la V.a de mogodorio. en el Reino y Raya de portugal cerca de Benavente. estante en Mexico. de xpianos nuevos de judios

Informacion

Prission

Moniciones 1.a 2.a 3.a

Confess. nee Noay christus ni Marias tampoco

Acusacion

a prueva

Publicacion 1.a 2.a 3.a 4.a

Pide ciertas defensas

Sospechoso en la lei de moisen en que le quisieron enseñar y conuertir

Votado a peni.a en auto pu.co

Processo (prosecution), 1589, against Luis de Carvajal, Governor of the New Kingdom of Leon (Nuevo Leon).

Courtesy American Jewish Historical Society.

Samuel Noah

Art by Jose Cisneros.

movement for Mexican independence had its roots with Father Hidalgo, who had raised money, munitions, and an army. Anyone who challenged the authorities risked being accused of Jewish ancestry, an accusation that could lead to imprisonment and death. Even Father Hidalgo, a Catholic priest who raised the standard of revolt against Spain, was falsely charged with being a Jew.[58]

In the uprising of 1811 the Spanish authorities finally captured Hidalgo and shot him as a rebel. Many of his followers deserted. The Spaniards put to death any of his followers they found. They captured one of them, a Colonel Delgado, in San Antonio, where they executed him and stuck his head on a pole. A ghastly description of this capture: "Among his adherents, Colonel Delgado was apprehended at San Antonio, executed, and his head stuck on a pole at the crossing of the river between the Alamo and the town. Another, Bernardo Gutierres [*sic*], effected his escape and took refuge at Natchitoches."[59]

Bernardo Gutierrez de Lara fled to Louisiana near the Shreveport area, where he picked up aid to continue the dream of freeing Mexican Texas. There he met an American who, like Noah, had been assigned to police for smugglers and who then also held the rank of lieutenant. Augustus Magee "drank with eagerness the marvelous tales of Bernardo."[60] They planned the conquest of Texas from Louisiana to the Rio Grande.

Carefully they mapped each detail. They published notices to recruit men, promising to each volunteer forty dollars per month and a league of land.[61] It is in this way the plight of the Texans and Mexicans became known in America, and in 1812 Noah joined the expedition.

While the West Point men raised recruits and supplies, Gutierrez got anxious and set out to attack the Spaniards. The time for successful invasion of Texas was at hand. The people of the province did not oppose it, and the Spaniards could not stop it. Gutierrez and his men set out the middle of June, and easily took Nacogdoches, an important east Texas town.[62]

Magee collected his friends — including Noah — and set out to join the headquarters of the invading army. The entire ragged group traveled on horseback more than 250 miles across rugged Texas terrain, and ended their march near Goliad, then called La Bahia, a crumbling town and fort 100 miles downstream from present-day San Antonio. By the time they reached this site, their troops numbered nearly 800

For almost a month the Americans (or *filibusters*, as soldiers who came to Texas to fight against the Spanish authorities were called) held their position against a siege inflicted by the Spanish commander, who finally invited Colonel Magee to dine with him. Magee agreed to deliver the fort and send the Americans home. When he presented this idea to his men, Noah and the others became indignant, striking the butts of their rifles against the ground. They voted down the treaty. The confusion was great; Magee retired to his tent, never to return. Some say he committed suicide; others say he died from an attack of "consumption."

When the time came for surrender, the group sent the flag back with no reply. The angered Spanish governor vowed to kill the whole rebel army, which then consisted of 800 Americans, 325 Indians, and 180 Mexicans.[63] Noah served with the right wing that marched in the rear with Colonel Sam Kemper, who after Magee's death, had taken command of the so-called American Volunteers.

The viceroy continued to send troops until the Spanish force held 1,500 men strong, around 200 more than the rebels.

The Spanish made an intense assault, took the town of Goliad, and advanced to the walls of the fort with the same name. The Americans drove them from the walls, and then out of town, fighting furiously until darkness.

When the Spaniards retreated toward San Antonio, the gutsy rebels decided to take them on and marched in pursuit. About nine miles from the city, the battle occurred, with the Royalists killed in great numbers, many cruelly butchered by the Indians in a sharply fought battle. New recruits came to aid the victorious volunteers.

The next day Noah and the volunteers rode into the town of San Antonio and demanded surrender. The Spanish governor presented his sword to General Gutierrez. He would not hand it to him, but surrendered by sticking it into the ground in front of the general, who took it up.

Noah and the Americans then marched into the Alamo and released seventeen of their imprisoned countrymen. These battles in 1813 could be called Goliad I and Alamo I. They were the reverse of the infamous Alamo II and Goliad II fought twenty-three years later, in which sympathizers of the Mexican cause massacred the Texans. These early events at the

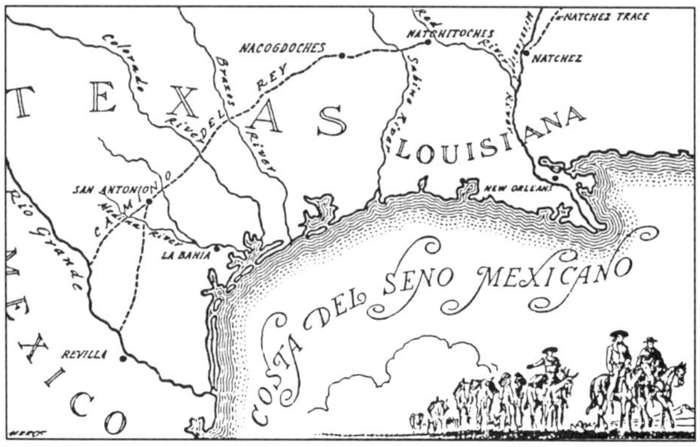

Route of West Point graduate Samuel Noah during the Magee-Gutierrez Expedition in 1812

Map by Jose Cisneros

Alamo and Goliad, hardly remembered, were military triumphs for the Texans.

At the Alamo the spoils were distributed, and each man received his wages, a fifteen-dollar tip, a suit of clothes, and two horses or mules. The Spanish soldiers taken as prisoners were set at liberty, and some joined the ranks of the rebels while others went home.[64]

The next day, April 1, 1813, dawned as an April Fool's Day of great magnitude. General Gutierrez read a letter informing his men that two vessels on the Gulf were about to sail to New Orleans, and he proposed sending the captured Spanish governor and his staff there to remain on parole until the war ended. The governor, who had been at liberty on his honor in San Antonio, began the march under the guard commanded by Captain Antonio Delgado, son of Colonel Delgado who had been executed two years prior and whose head had been displayed on a pole in a ghastly scene. Delgado marched the prisoners about a mile below the town, and there he stripped and tied the prisoners and cut their throats. This group of fourteen included not only foot soldiers, but also the Governor Manuel de Salcedo and former General Simón de Herrera, Governor of Nuevo León.[65]

Lieutenant Noah, Colonel Kemper, and the other officers were shocked. Having pledged their honor for the safety of the victims, they arrested Delgado. At his trial, he defended himself, saying that he wanted to avenge his father's gruesome death and had been given permission to put the prisoners to death by Gutierrez. They released Delgado and put Gutierrez on trial. Gutierrez explained that young Delgado had implored him on bended knees to avenge his father's death. The other officers found Gutierrez guilty of treachery and deprived him of his command. The American officers had become disgusted with the barbarity and began to leave the service. A mass exit of officers followed.

With his West Point friend Magee dead and America having declared war in 1812 on Great Britain, his native country, Noah left Texas to fight for his adopted land. He chose to fight in the New York area because he still had roots and family there. His distant cousin, Mordecai Manuel Noah (son of Manuel Noah, friend of George Washington), was an editor of several New York newspapers, a U.S. Consul to Tunis, and later a founder of New York University.[66] Samuel Noah felt bitterly disappointed when President James Madison refused to recommission him into the U.S. Army. Undaunted, he volunteered as a private. Noah became instrumental in defending Brooklyn and Harlem, New York, in the final years of the War of 1812, which ended in January 1815. Noah served in the militia from August 1814 until February 1815. National Archives in Washington, D. C. state Noah "was stationed at Brookleine Heights, Long Island, New York" and at "Haerlem" in a company of light infantry commanded by Captain (later Brigadier General) Benjamin Dunning.[67]

In a letter dated 1862 to a member of the U.S. Senate requesting pension, Noah wrote, "I am truly thankful to Hon. Joseph Barrett for his very liberal remarks relative to my services in the War of 1812." This is about the only complimentary or laudatory item in Noah's turbulent life.

When Noah's military service halted, he taught

Signature of Samuel Noah on document dated 1851.

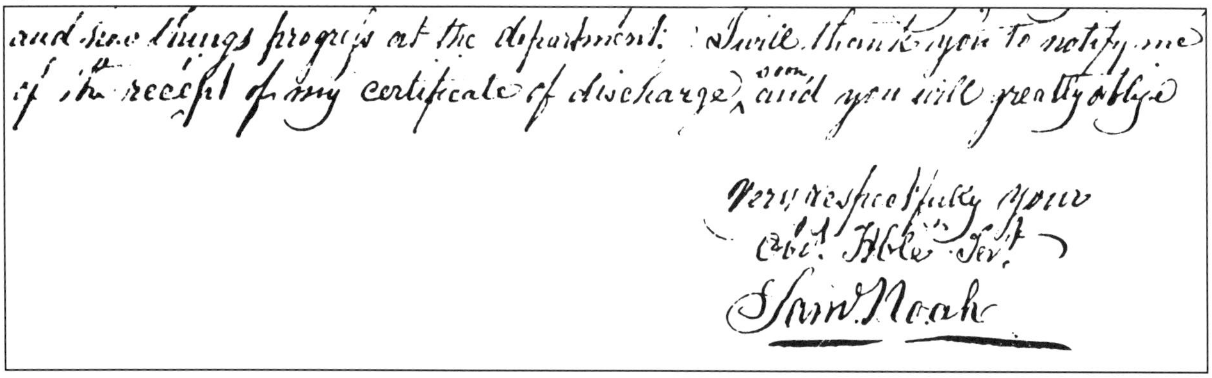
and see things progress at the department. I will thank you to notify me of the receipt of my certificate of discharge, and you will greatly oblige

Very respectfully your
Obt. Hble Servt.
Saml Noah

Jao de la Porta, second in command at the Laffite headquarters on Galveston Island.

school near Goshen, New York, until 1820, then spent two years in his native England, where he attended the coronation of King George IV. Noah resumed teaching in the United States, mostly at academies in Virginia, until 1848, at which time he resided with a friend in Mount Pulaski, Logan County, Illinois, where he died March 10, 1871, at the age of ninety-two.[68] His old age ended in poverty, a sharp contrast to his wild adventure in Texas, where he marched into the Alamo to liberate the seventeen Americans in 1813.

What happened to the invasion of Texas after Noah left? It ended when 2,000 Spanish soldiers arrived and crushed the rebel army.[69] At least, it ended temporarily. Soon a new brawl began to ferment. The exiled General Gutierrez joined Dr. James Long in his 300-man Long Expedition to conquer Texas and liberate it. Needing more men, Long visited the pirate Jean Laffite on Galveston Island, where Laffite plundered ships laden with gold and silver mined in Spanish Mexico and intended for Spanish ports.

Although he had sent men to fight at the Battle of New Orleans in the War of 1812, Laffite refused to fight to liberate Texas from the Spanish. He said he felt he did more to destroy Spain's influence by attacking her treasury, than by direct combat. Laffite had gathered more than 1,000 men and this swashbuckling Frenchman reigned as king or "governor" of Galveston Island. A Jew of Portuguese descent, Jao de la Porta, served as secretary of the Jean Laffite encampment in Texas, Jao having known this privateer in New Orleans and having arrived in Galveston before Laffite. He sold Laffite his camp.

THE DE LA PORTA BROTHERS

Jao (also called Joseph) de la Porta and his older brother Moses de la Porta (also called simply Morin), financed the first settlement of white men on Galveston Island, which included the man who would become the first governor of Texas.[70]

The de la Portas found their way to Texas in a circuitous route from Portugal. The brothers were born in Portugal and were secret Jews.[71] At a young age they moved to Paris, where they received their education. They later joined the European immigration of Jews to Brazil, where they worked in the sugar, coffee, rubber, and chocolate industries. But their Jewishness forced them out of Brazil. The brothers accumulated enough money to set sail for New Orleans.

Moses was known simply as "Morin," a French corruption of the Spanish word *Marrano*, which signifies pig, a term of contempt applied to Jews who underwent forcible baptism to escape the Inquisition. Joseph O. Dyer, a historian who has written extensively on the de la Porta brothers, believed that their Jewishness got them charged with dealing in slaves and contraband. They decided to leave New Orleans.

In planning their departure, Morin conceived of a way to finance their way out of New Orleans and possibly build a new business.[72] He had watched the successful exploits of the buccaneer Jean Laffite and decided to simulate Laffite's financially successful business of privateering — legalized seizing of Spanish ships. Laffite ran his buccaneer camp on Grand Terre Island off the coast of Louisiana (fifty miles south of New Orleans). He also leased vessels to South American countries rebelling against Spain.

Laffite's ships in the Gulf of Mexico were making terrible inroads on Spanish commerce.[73] In 1814 the United States moved in and took possession of Laffite's Louisiana buccaneer camp, accusing him of smuggling merchandise and resisting revenue officers. When Laffite and his men joined U.S. General Andrew Jackson, fighting the British in the Battle of New Orleans, Morin began to set up his new business.[74]

Morin met with two individuals who shared the goal of his proposed venture, but for different reasons. José Manuel de Herrera and Luis Aury signed on with Morin.[75] De Herrera, a priest, had come to the United States on behalf of Mexican patriots to encourage others to run the Spanish out of Mexico and Texas. De Herrera had contacted Commodore Aury who, after having broken the Spanish blockade of Cartagena, the principal seaport of the northwest coast of Colombia, had escaped with fourteen small vessels with refugees.

Aury and his fleet stopped in Haiti, headquarters of many South American insurgents who were in arms against Spain. While in Haiti, Aury received de Herrera's invitation to come to New Orleans with the idea of invading Texas. De Hererra had already induced several ship owners to operate as privateers against Spain. Aury went to New Orleans.

But Aury had no money. His small vessels lacked the speed, size, and armaments required for privateer cruisers. In New Orleans he met with de Herrera and the de la Porta brothers and reached an agreement

Jean Laffite, shipowner and head of Commune. Sketches of members of Laffite Commune made by Lacassinier, c.1818.

whereby the brothers would finance and furnish cruisers for a privateering camp on San Luis Island, later called Galveston. Aury enlisted South Americans who owned small vessels to join his expedition, now composed primarily of two of Morin's large trading brigs, converted into war brigs.

Another who sent men to the de la Porta fleet was Henry Perry who had started the first buccaneer camp in the Galveston area. He was one of the more durable survivors of the Magee-Gutierrez Expedition, and although many Anglos returned to the United States, he elected to stay in Texas, coming to Galveston, or "Snake Island" as it was called then. He made camp on the Texas mainland and named his campsite Bolivar Point in honor of President Simón Bolívar of Venezuela, who had given him letters of marque, which gave him license to hunt Spanish ships on whose captured goods he need not pay custom duty.When Perry lost his fleet of three vessels in Texas Gulf storms of 1815 and 1816, he transferred his men to the de la Porta brigs, one renamed *Don Luis Aury.*

Commodore Aury arrived in Galvez Bay September 1, 1816, with a small fleet. Like Perry, he held a commission from President Bolívar on behalf of South American republics Venezuela, New Granada, and la Plata. He brought from Haiti to Galveston 200 men, 130 of whom were Santo Domincan negroes. On September 12 the Aury camp formed a government and hoisted the Mexican patriot flag in the presence of de Herrera, who had accompanied the expedition from New Orleans in the name of the President of Mexico. De Herrera appointed Commodore Aury civil and military governor of the Galveston Island and the country to the north, M. Rousselin treasurer of the first government on Galveston Island, and Jao de la Porta secretary of state.

The privateers brought in a number of prize cargoes during October and November. In December General Francisco Xavier Mina arrived in a magnificent war brig and joined the command of Aury, who was intent on invading Mexico. Morin opposed military operations and threatened to withdraw his vessels, but during his absence in the United States (where he had trouble in disposing of captured prize vessels and their cargoes), the three militant leaders sailed for the Santander River in spite of the objections of Jao, whom Morin had left behind to guard their interests. Early in 1817 the combined fleet, (which included the ships of Morin de la Porta, Aury, and Mina), with land forces of about 100 men commanded by Commodore Perry, set out for a campaign against Spanish forces in Mexico.

Morin lost many ships in the privateering enterprise and sailed for New Orleans. Here he became ill and died. Jao took over his brother's interests on San Luis Island, where Jao and Rousselin remained with seven men to oversee the island camp.

By now, Jean Laffite had received a pardon from President James Madison, forgiving his smuggling and resisting U.S. revenue officers. Laffite traveled to Washington, where he was honored for his fight against the British. In 1816 he went to Savannah, where relatives advanced him the money to build a new privateer-cruiser, the *Jupiter.* In the spring of 1817 the *Jupiter* set sail for the Texas Coast. Laffite found that the Morin expedition under Commodore Aury had gotten ahead of him and occupied San Luis Island and its bay of Galvez.

The *Jupiter* sailed down the coast and opened a camp on an island in Matagorda Bay. Here several shipowners joined him with their small vessels and they formed a stock company. Shipowners and the crews of the vessels shared in the profits of the company, known as the Laffite Commune. All moneys derived from prizes and their cargoes went into the common treasury to be divided *pro rata.*

On May first a felucca — a fishing boat rigged with two masts — arrived in Matagorda Bay with Jao de la Porta and M. Rousselin, the treasurer of the Aury camp, on board. Jao offered to sell the interest of his brother, Morin, to the Laffite Commune. Jao sold the Morin-Aury expedition's camp fixtures and supplies to recover part of Morin's investment, and the Laffite Commune took possession of the island on May 5, 1817.

Both Jao de la Porta and Rousselin remained with the commune established by Laffite. Jao acted as secretary and Rousselin as treasurer. As secretary, Jao issued shipowners, who docked to trade, a letter of marque from Venezuela, still at war with Spain, thus legalizing the privateering seizures. Jao also provided credentials to the various traders, who sold articles captured in the cargoes of seized vessels to the Karankawa Indians and the few white settlers nearby.

In July of 1817 Commodore Aury returned from Mexico with two vessels and requested to join the Laffite Commune. His expedition into Mexico had failed. General Mina had been killed, Perry had committed suicide, and Aury had lost everything except two ships and one hundred men. Laffite refused Aury's request to join his camp, and Aury sailed to Amelia

Island, Florida.

Laffite remained on Galveston Island three years. On the night of May 5, 1820, Laffite boarded his ship the *Pride* and sailed out of the bay on his way to the Yucatan Peninsula of Mexico.[76]

Laffite had urged Jao to join him in the Yucatan, but Jao chose to stay in Galveston.

Now Jao became a full-time trader. The Karankawa Indians on Galveston Island held him in such esteem for his integrity as a trader that they made him a blood brother of the clan. The Indians had another name for the middle-aged Jao — Old Blanco — because of white patches of pigmentary degeneration scattered over his face, hands, and arms. Jao made his way back to New Orleans to purchase a new stock of goods and a small vessel.

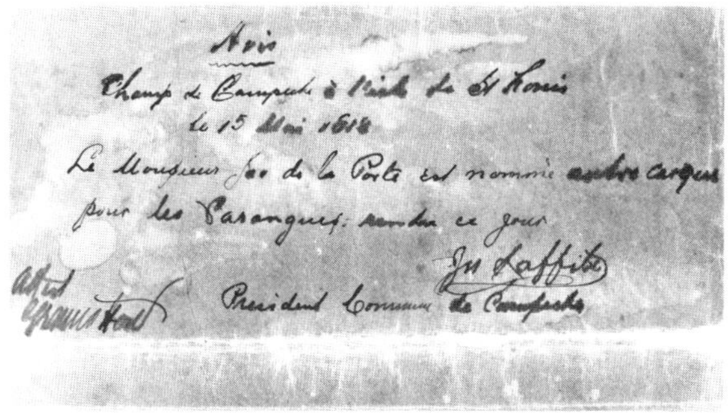
Avis
Champ de Campeche à l'aile de St Louis
le 15 Mai 1818
Le Monsieur Jao de la Porta est nommé cargueur
pour les Parangues ce jour
Jn Laffite
President Commun de Campeche

Notice regarding de la Porta showing Jn. Laffite signature, 1818. Courtesy Rosenberg Library.

In 1823 hostilities erupted between the Stephen F. Austin colonists and the Karankawas over the white men's mistreatment of the native women. However, Blanco entered Matagorda Bay at this time to resume business and to trade.

About the time that Jao, or Blanco, arrived, the tribe needed a mascot to change their luck. Albinos were occasionally born to Indians, who considered them supernaturally endowed persons capable of interceding with the spirit world. Blanco's mottled skin marked him at that time as the man they needed. The Karankawas detained him and placed him in the charge of the shaman, or priest, and a huge bond brother guarded him. When the dangers of battle approached, the Indians took him with the women and children across the San Bernard River. During his period of detention, Blanco noted the ethnological characteristics of the Karankawa tribe, which he discussed years later when he became a resident of New Orleans.[77] The Jao de la Porta adventures became of special interest to Gershom Kursheedt, son of a famous rabbi and a resident of New Orleans in 1835, who possessed one of the finest libraries in the South and avidly sought out persons he considered of historical interest.[78] In his pursuit of history, Gershom met and interviewed Jao de la Porta who had moved back to New Orleans and told him about life in the buccaneer camps on the Texas coast.

Jao de la Porta trading with the Indians.

Gershom also met another Jew, Adolphus Sterne of Nacogdoches, who at the time was in New Orleans with James Bowie to further the cause of the independence of Texas. Leon Dyer, of a prominent Jewish family from Baltimore, had arrived in New Orleans in 1834 to open a branch of the packing house owned by his father, John Maximilian Dyer, and numbered among the persons Sterne and Bowie enlisted. Leon Dyer became an officer in the Texas army.

Leon's son, Dr. J. O. Dyer, also an avid historian, later presented himself to Gershom Kursheedt with a letter of introduction and obtained Gershom's unpublished materials on the de la Porta brothers. Dyer's articles on the buccaneers in Laffite's camp and other adventurers appeared in early Texas newspapers. These writings cover New Orleans residents such as brothers Rezin and James Bowie (for whom the Bowie knife is named), as well as Jewish leaders such as Adolphus Sterne and Major Leon Dyer.

Dr. J. O. Dyer wrote, "The material concerning the buccaneer camps commenced to be collected in 1874. At that time there were still a number of survivors of the Laffite commune (aged of course) and of Austin's colony. . . . In the summer of 1874 the writer, bearing a letter of introduction from his father, Colonel Leon Dyer, met Mr. Gershom Kursheedt in New Orleans and obtained from him a great deal of historical material . . . which was mainly derived from Joseph Morin (Jao de la Porta). . . . In 1835 Gershom Kursheedt made New Orleans his home and became interested in Texas and its history. He befriended Joseph Morin, then an aged man who, poor and in ill health, had returned a few years previously from Austin's colony, where he was well known as 'old man Blanco.' . . . From this source we have inherited much information of the buccaneer camps on the Texas coast and also of the Karankawai [*sic*] clans, for Jao de la Porta . . . was a member of three of these camps and became a trader with the native tribes.

"Gershom Kursheedt became acquainted with Adolphus Sterne who lived at Nacogdoches, Texas, and prior to 1835 was postmaster for the Mexican government. The two brothers, Rezin and James Bowie, with Adolphus Sterne, were in 1835 active in New Orleans in furthering the cause of the independence of Texas."[79]

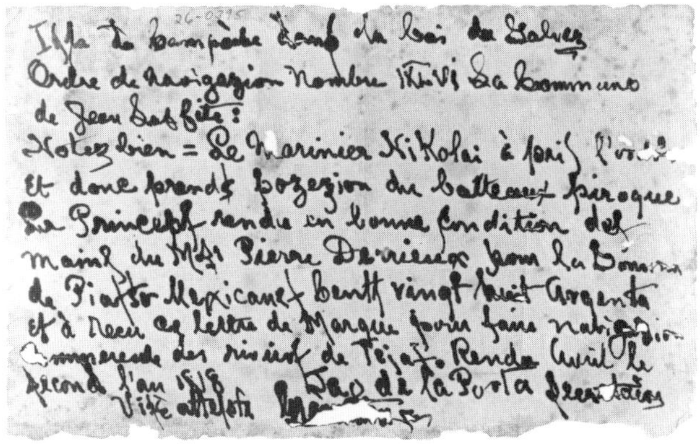

Order signed by Jao de la Porta at "The Commune of Jean Laffite" giving a mariner possession of a boat and "this letter of marque to carry on commercial navigation of the rivers of Texas," 1818.

Courtesy Rosenberg Library.

Gershom Kursheedt, New Orleans historian who furnished first hand information on adventurer Jao de la Porta to Dr. J.O. Dyer of Galveston. Kursheedt's son married the niece of Dr. Albert Moses Levy.

Courtesy Jewish Museum.

Adolphus Sterne helped bring Sam Houston from Tennessee to Texas, and Gen. Houston lived in Sterne's home.

Chapter 2

The Soldiers

Jews in the Battles for Texas Independence

1826-1842

Jews were among the first and the last to fight in the Texas War for Independence. They participated in battles for sixteen years (from 1826 to 1842), including the climactic battles in 1836 — the Alamo, Goliad, and San Jacinto. Jews, whose ages ranged from twelve to fifty-one, fought at the Alamo with Travis, Crockett, and Bowie.

The few Jews already in Texas in this colonial era joined the armies in large proportion to their numbers.[1] Some volunteered for purely idealistic reasons, to fight for liberty, but most journeyed to Texas to take advantage of the offers of Texas land to those who fought. Posters and broadsides posted in New Orleans announced the acreage to be earned by serving the cause of the Texians. Although many came in hopes of receiving new lands, others had hopes of alleviating their grievances against Mexico regarding immigration and commerce.[2]

Most of the brave "men of Texas" who fought in its battles for independence were barely men and were newly arrived Texans. They were in reality youths — many of them mere teen-age boys — from Cincinnati, Ohio; New Orleans, Louisiana; Charleston, South Carolina; Philadelphia, Pennsylvania; Alabama; New York; and Tennessee.

ADOLPHUS STERNE

Nicholas Adolphus Sterne, a German-Jewish immigrant, is called "an historical character of much complexity. He was an urbane, sophisticated man of the world who was a mover and a shaker in the early period of Texas history." Sterne spoke English, French, Spanish, German, Yiddish, Portuguese, and Latin. As historian Archie McDonald wrote, "Living in Nacogdoches during the years when it was both an important town and a port of entry, the panorama of Texas unfolded around him. He was therefore in a position to see, to understand what he saw, and his character and intelligence qualifies him as a reporter who could incisively and accurately chronicle his surroundings. Sterne emerges . . . as much more than the 'rosy little Jew' that he is so often called by Houston biographers [i.e. Marquis James, M.K. Wisehart]. He was a man . . . who met his times with a powerful force for accomplishment. But above all, he was a man."[3]

Sterne was elected a member of the Texas House of Representatives in the Second and Third Legislatures and was elected to the Texas Senate in November, 1851, holding his Senate seat at the time of his death in New Orleans the following year.[4]

Old Stone Fort where Sterne was imprisoned.

One of the earliest Jewish settlers in Texas, Sterne fought for Texas' freedom ten years before David Crockett did. He participated in the Fredonian Rebellion, the Texas Revolution, and the Cherokee War. He lived in Nashville and New Orleans several years before moving to Nacogdoches, near the Louisiana border, and in December of 1826 and January of 1827, he helped smuggle supplies and munitions in bales of dry goods and barrels of coffee to the small band of thirty men trying to declare themselves "Fredonians," free of Mexico.[5]

Friction between settlers near Nacogdoches triggered the Fredonian Rebellion in one of the oldest settled sections of Texas. The fight pitted the squatters against the legal settlers. Brothers Haden and Benjamin W. Edwards had an empresario (land agent) contract from Mexico on this land and ordered old settlers to produce title or secure title from them. Haden Edwards appealed to the *alcalde* (mayor), Jose Antonio Saucedo, who charged him with declaring himself military commandant and with ordering the old settlers to produce titles, both punishable offenses.

While Haden was in the U.S., his brother launched the Fredonian Rebellion, rode with his men into Nacogdoches under a flag inscribed "Independence, Liberty, and Justice," seized the Old Stone Fort, and proclaimed the Republic of Fredonia. They could unify neither the citizens in Austin's colony nor the Indians for help, and when the Mexican militia, including members of Austin's colony, reached Nacogdoches, the revolutionists fled across the border to Louisiana on January 31, 1827. Sterne sided with Benjamin W. Edwards.

Sterne was arrested and imprisoned. A Mexican military court sentenced him to be shot. However, Sterne had been a leading Mason in New Orleans and was the first known Scottish Rite Mason to make his home in Texas. The grand master of the Grand Lodge of Louisiana interceded in his behalf with Mexican Masons in Mexico City, and Sterne was released on parole on condition he never again bear arms against Mexico.[6]

After Stern's release from prison, his loyalty to his oath prevented him from other military battles, but nine years later he assisted with financing, organizing, and issuing propaganda for the Texas Revolution. Like Haym Solomon during the War for Independence against Great Britain in 1776, Sterne helped by raising funds. But he was more than a financier. He recruited troops for the new Texian army.

Adolphus Sterne had been a Texan for at least six years before Sam Houston arrived. The date of Sterne's coming to Texas is usually given as 1824, although on a land application made in Nacogdoches August 7, 1835, Sterne wrote he had come in 1826.[7] Sam Houston came December of 1832.

DAVID LEVI KOKERNOT

Another Jew, David Levi Kokernot, also arrived in Texas prior to Sam Houston. Kokernot was born in Holland December 12, 1805. In 1817 his father, Levi Moses Kokernot, brought him to New Orleans.[8] For many years he and members of his family lived in New Orleans, where they engaged in the mercantile business. Young Kokernot was an accomplished seaman. For five years, from ages twelve to seventeen, he apprenticed as a pilot on the Mississippi River. Then he went to school for one year. At age eighteen he began life as a seaman on commercial ships between Haiti, New York, and Bremen.

On March 12, 1831, he received orders from the New Orleans collector of customs to cruise down the Gulf Coast as far as Galveston Bay in search of smugglers. His schooner wrecked on the beach of Galveston during a storm.[9] The children of Galvestonian Burrel Franks, one of Jean Laffite's huntsmen, rescued him. A week later Kokernot and his men caught a ride back to New Orleans in a small schooner.[10] Kokernot, who later wrote of his adventures, said that he returned to Texas from New Orleans on April 6, 1832, with his

David Levi Kokernot

wife, one child, and his mother-in-law with her two sons. "I brought with me a thousand dollars worth of merchandise, and opened a store." It was here at Anahuac, on Galveston Bay, that Kokernot helped form the first Texas navy, with three tiny five-ton schooners with four or five men aboard each. He commandeered one ship in an effort to rescue several Texans — among them William B. Travis (afterwards martyr of the Alamo) — who had been imprisoned by Col. Juan Davis Bradburn, a Kentuckian in the Mexican service in charge of the Anahuac garrison.[11] The ensuing battle was the first skirmish leading to the Texas Revolution.[12]

When Col. Bradburn put the prisoners aboard a schooner to send them to Mexico, the Texans decided to stage a rescue operation. Francis W. Johnson, (who after the death of Col. Ben Milam commanded the triumphant Storming of Bexar), approached Kokernot:

"He asked me if we had any boats. I told him we had three fine small schooners — the *Stephen F.Austin*, the *Water Witch*, and the *Red Rover*. He then ordered us to fit them out with men, arms, and provisions, for the purpose of blockading the town. . . . The *Red Rover* was commanded by Capt. D.L. Kokernot; was of five tons, with five men and five guns. Now, this was the first Texas navy. . . .

"After some fighting the enemy surrendered, Bradburn making his escape by night and fleeing into Louisiana. Then we had great pleasure in liberating our friends from the prison.

"Our fleet then sailed for Galveston Island to capture the custom house with its officers and stores. We ran in after dark and captured everything without sustaining the slightest loss. Having loaded our vessels, we set sail for Anahuac and home."[13]

Kokernot in 1834 had been hired by a friend to get land titles for himself and others in Nacogdoches. Kokernot's description of Sam Houston is one of the most vivid ever recorded.

"On the 15th of May I arrived at the town, and as I walked up the street I noticed the finest looking man I ever saw, seated on the steps of Col. [Frost] Thorn's storehouse. He was dressed in a complete Indian costume made of buckskin and ornamented with a profuse variety of beads, and his massive head was covered with a fine broad beaver hat. When he arose I stopped and looked at him with both surprise and admiration and bid him good morning. He asked me whence I had come. I told him from Galveston Bay, Middle Texas. Then he invited me to sit down and have a chat with him in reference to land matters, which I did for a considerable time. Our conversation ended. He invited me into the store to take a glass of wine with him, which I readily accepted. He then told me he owned some land on Cedar Point, Galveston Bay, as also on Goose Creek. I remarked that the Goose Creek land was located by one Dr. Wightin, and that I had the field notes with me with a view to getting a patent on the land. He said, 'All right, if you can get it.' But, sure enough, I never did, as a patent had already been issued to the General.

"'Now, my friend,' said the General, 'tell me the news.'

"I replied the news is war; that it was rumored that Santa Anna was gathering troops to send into Texas to disarm the inhabitants. But said I, we are determined not to surrender our arms.

"'Well, my friend,' said he, 'how will you act in that case?'

"I replied: We will fight them to the last, or die in the attempt.

"'That is right,' said he, 'they shall never drive us out so long as we can fight them.'

"As he made this remark his eyes sparkled with lightning, and another bottle of wine was ordered on the strength of it.

"'Now,' said he, 'the people ought to organize and get ready to meet them.'

"I told him I was of the same opinion.

"'Who will command the army?' he asked.

"I replied: My dear sir, if I had the authority to make the appointment, you are the man; for you are the

Adolphus Sterne home. *Courtesy Sterne-Hoya House Library & Museum.*

finest looking man I ever laid eyes on.

"He immediately replied, 'Well, my dear sir, if I get the appointment as commander I will give you a commission.'

"Then he pulled out a small pocketbook and asked my name, which he wrote in his book, and then wrote his own name and handed it to me. After talking a while longer we shook hands and bade each other farewell. From that day I loved Sam Houston. He proved a friend indeed in times of need, as many letters in my possession will show."[14]

STERNE AND THE NEW ORLEANS GREYS

In December 1832 Sam Houston had come to Texas, attracted partly by his friendship with Adolphus Sterne. Sterne had an enormous zest for living, and he was described as the life of the lobbies, inns, and stagecoach parties. As one historian has described Sterne:

"As a peddler and storekeeper prospecting for a better location, he had visited Nashville and there, a member of the tavern's afternoon whiskey-drinking coterie, he had made the acquaintance of attorney Houston when Houston's star was rising."[15] Sterne and Houston had become friends in Nashville and the friendship continued after Houston became governor of Tennessee, and long after Houston moved to Texas.[16]

Houston planned to spend only a few months in Texas and had hopes for financial gains that would enable him to return to Tennessee. When he first came to Texas, Sam Houston boarded with the amiable Sterne and his wife in Nacogdoches, and their home was the seat of East Texas hospitality. Sam Houston presented to Sterne's wife Eva, a woman of superior intelligence, a beautiful diamond ring.[17]

The Mexican law that only Catholics could be landowners and serve as lawyers may have had something to do with the conversion to Catholicism of both Sterne and Houston.[18] Mrs. Sterne served as Houston's godmother in his "conversion." One historian stated Sterne was not the godfather because the baptism at the mission occurred on *erev Yom Kippur*.[19]

At one point Sterne saved Sam Houston's life. Sterne wrote in his diary, "General Houston was attacked by Col. [S.W.] Jordon of the late Federal Army, and had it not been for my interference, Jordon would have killed him with an axe."[20]

Sterne personally carried orders signed by General Houston to expedite delivery to men in high places in the U.S.A. who would set up committees and raise funds for two companies of infantry. Sterne rode to New Orleans, bringing the first news of the Texan revolution. He met with prominent citizens and then had the town of New Orleans plastered with posters shrieking the announcement he and Houston had composed:

"War in defence of our rights . . . is inevitable, in Texas! If volunteers from the United States will join their brethern in this section, they will receive liberal bounties of land. . . . Let each man come with a good rifle and one hundred rounds of ammunition, and to come soon. Our war cry is: 'Liberty or Death.' Our principles are to support the constitution, and down with the Usurper!!!"

Excitement permeated New Orleans as Sterne stepped on the platform at Bank's Arcade October 13, 1835.[21] Sterne felt at home in New Orleans, having lived there in his twenties, working as a clerk and law student and making valuable friends.[22]

Sterne made it known that Texas wanted men as well as money and that, as a Texan agent, he had that day purchased fifty muskets to be given to those who would go with him to Texas. Young Herman Ehrenberg bragged he was the third boy to volunteer in the

Albert M. Levy's name on Muster Roll, New Orleans Greys at Seige of Bexar, 1835.

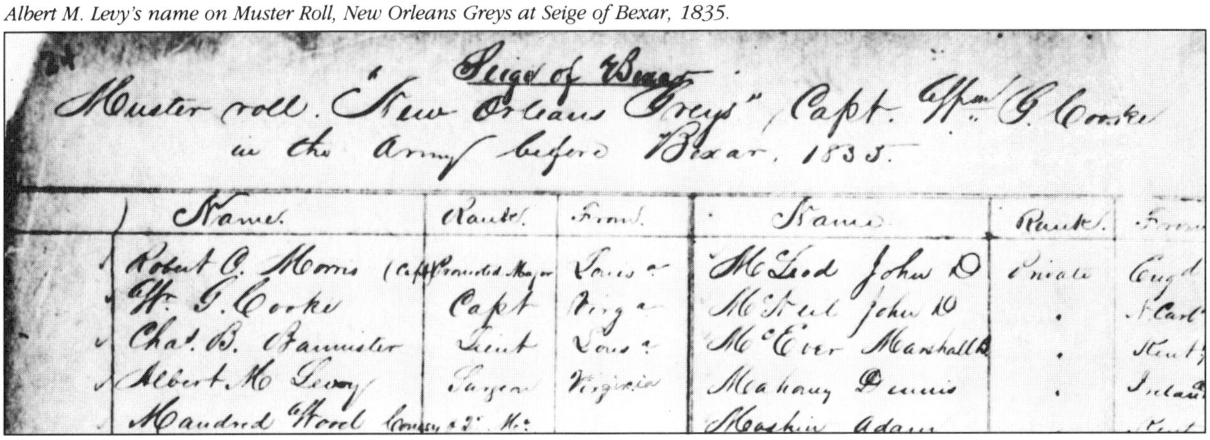
Seige of Bexar
Muster roll. "New Orleans Greys", Capt. Wm. G. Cooke in the Army before Bexar, 1835.

Name	Rank	From	Name	Rank	From
Robert C. Morris (Capt)	Promoted Major	Louis	McLeod John D	Private	Engd
Wm. G. Cooke	Capt	Virga	McNeil John W	"	N Carl
Chas. B. Bannister	Lieut	Louis	McEver Marshall	"	Kent
Albert M. Levy	Surgeon	Virginia	Mahoney Dennis	"	Ireland
Maurice Wood			Mashin Adam		

New Orleans Greys.

Sterne called for more volunteers and two companies were raised, one commanded by Captain (later Colonel) Robert C. Morris and the other by Captain Thomas H. Breese. The Texan committee dressed them in grey uniforms, and they departed for the theatre of war, one company by way of sea and one by land — known as the New Orleans Greys. The 118 men came from twelve states and six foreign countries. The First Company sailed from Louisiana to Texas in several ships via the Gulf of Mexico (arriving at the mouth of the Brazos River). The Second Company traveled on horseback.[23]

"Adolphus Sterne spent $820 to buy rifles for the first fifty recruits from the United States, and the rifles were claimed by the N[ew] O[rleans] Greys who arrived in Nacogdoches on foot. These men had to be entertained and fed while they remained in or camped near the town, and young [Herman] Ehrenberg of their number describes one sumptuous banquet given in their honor on the eve of their departure for the front. . . . Some of the horses and money for the equipment of the New Orleans company were furnished by the most wealthy of the Mexicans in Nacogdoches."[24]

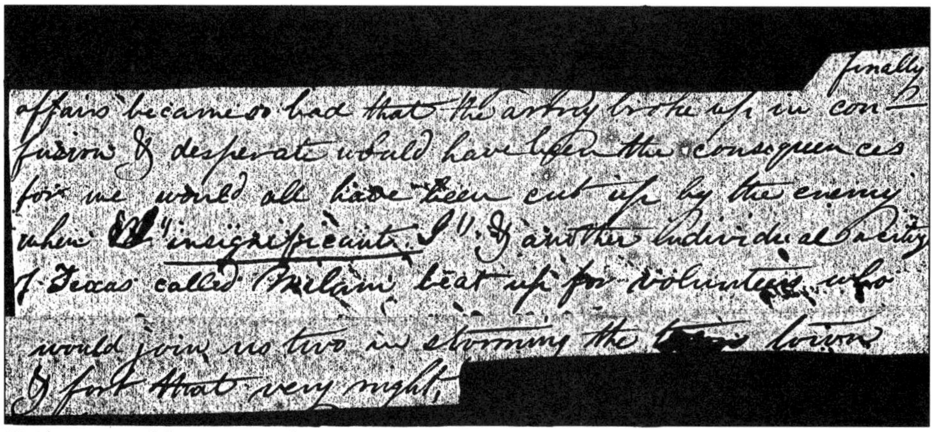
finally
affairs became so bad that the army broke up in con-
fusion & desperate would have been the consequences
for we would all have been cut up by the enemy
when the insignificant I [illegible] & another individual a citizen
of Texas called Milam beat up for volunteers who
would join us two in storming the [illegible] town
& fort that very night,

Vivid account of the Storming of Bexar, December 1835, written by participant Dr. Albert Moses Levy. Excerpt mentions Ben Milam. Courtesy Saul Viener.

While Sterne had been in New Orleans raising funds and troops, the battles of the Texas Revolution already had begun. David Levi Kokernot had joined Stephen F. Austin's small army of patriots and fought at Cibolo Creek; he also fought at the Battle of Concepcion, where over a thousand Mexicans attacked a troop of eighty-two Texans on October 28, 1835. Concepcion was a former mission along the river to the south of San Antonio. Historian Barker described this as "a sharp battle" led by James Bowie and James Fannin.[25]

"The attack was made on us at sunrise, by at least one thousand against eighty-two," Kokernot wrote.[26] "We reserved our fire until the enemy came within forty yards of us. Then we let fly at them, and, as the Kentuckian said, it would have done you good to have seen us drop them. Our officers, Bowie and Fannin, exhibited the utmost coolness and bravery by going up and down the line and exhorting us to keep cool and not to fire until we saw the eyes of the enemy. About half past two. . . the cannon was seized and turned upon the enemy. At three o'clock the enemy retreated, leaving 120 dead on the field, besides many that were thrown into the river."

The next month Kokernot participated in what became known as "The Grass Fight," a skirmish a mile from San Antonio. On the morning of Nov. 26, 1835, Mexican General Martín Perfecto Cos sent a party of more than 100 men to cut grass for their horses. Having supplied themselves with forage, they were on their way back when discovered by Texans, who thought the Mexicans were bringing silver to pay their troops. Word reached Colonel James Bowie, who sent 100 mounted men in galloping pursuit. One of Bowie's men was Kokernot.[27] Reinforcements came to aid both sides. In the confused running fight that followed, the Mexicans lost fifty men; the Texans had no losses and two wounded. The Grass Fight, although a skirmish, is the first engagement of sizeable importance in the first major battle for Texas independence, the Storming of Bexar. Kokernot served as a private for three days, until November 29, 1835, when the General Council of the Provisional Government of Texas at San Felipe de Austin elected him second lieutenant in the Regiment of Infantry of the Army of Texas. He was age thirty at the time.

DR. ALBERT MOSES LEVY

In the meantime, the New Orleans Greys, the "two notable companies,"[28] reached San Antonio in time to participate in its capture. The Texans had no large artillery and decided on a siege, which lasted more than a month. Among the Greys was Dr. Albert Moses Levy who had lived in Amsterdam, Holland; London, England; Philadelphia, Pa., and Richmond, Virginia. Dr. Levy served as Surgeon General in Sam Houston's army. He enlisted October 22, 1835, the same day another member of the Greys, Julian Harby, enlisted. Harby, from Charleston, South Carolina, was the son of Issac Harby, father of American Reform Judaism. Born in 1815, he was age twenty when he came to Texas and served as a private.Their fighting began with the siege or storming of Bexar in 1835 at the Alamo. It is possible that David Levi Kokernot, Dr. Levy, Julian Harby, and a fourth Jewish volunteer, Herman Ehrenberg (believed youngest member of the Greys), met in this battle, in which they all participated.

After the long siege of Bexar, or San Antonio, the Texans decided to attack the town and also the Alamo, which had been fortified by the Mexican troops. At four o'clock the morning of December 4, the storming began and lasted five days with negotiations on the sixth day. House by house, the work took place. It was like guerrilla warfare. Three of the Jewish volunteers, Kokernot, Dr. Levy, and Ehrenberg, recorded their experience. Kokernot wrote:

"That night we took possession of the Veramendi house, situated in the northern part of the place. This gave us a fair chance to fire upon the Mexicans as they came to the cannon, which were placed across the street. From this house we broke through one house after another until we reached the Plaza. In this movement no little work and much hard fighting was

Republic of Texas certificate awarding Dr. Albert M. Levy land for "having fought at Bexar from the 5th to the 10th of Dec. 1835 with exemplary bravery."

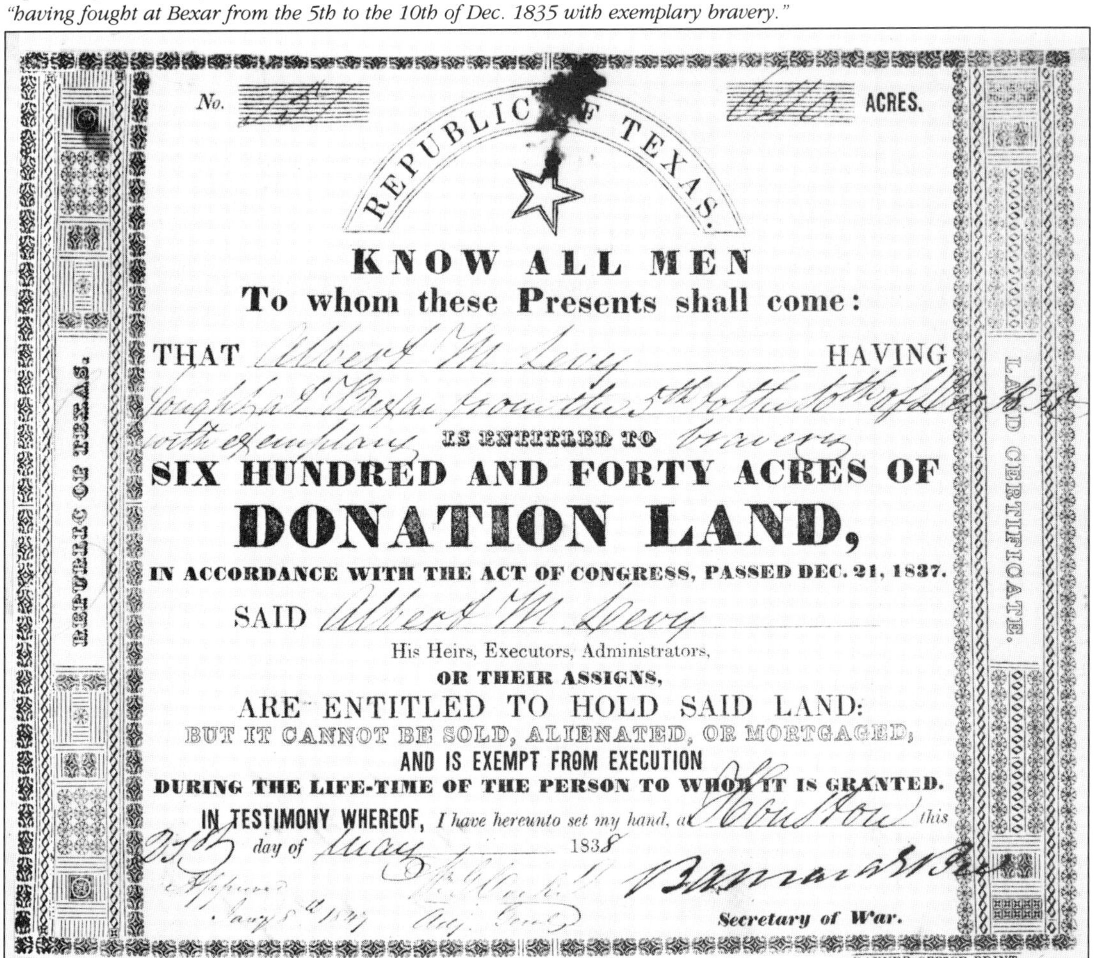

No. 137 — 640 ACRES.

REPUBLIC OF TEXAS.

KNOW ALL MEN

To whom these Presents shall come:

THAT Albert M Levy HAVING fought at Bexar from the 5th to the 10th of Dec 1835 with exemplary IS ENTITLED TO bravery

SIX HUNDRED AND FORTY ACRES OF

DONATION LAND,

IN ACCORDANCE WITH THE ACT OF CONGRESS, PASSED DEC. 21, 1837.

SAID Albert M Levy

His Heirs, Executors, Administrators,

OR THEIR ASSIGNS,

ARE ENTITLED TO HOLD SAID LAND:

BUT IT CANNOT BE SOLD, ALIENATED, OR MORTGAGED;

AND IS EXEMPT FROM EXECUTION

DURING THE LIFE-TIME OF THE PERSON TO WHOM IT IS GRANTED.

IN TESTIMONY WHEREOF, I have hereunto set my hand, at Houston this 25 day of May 1838

Approved Aug 8th 1847 Adj. Genl

Barnard E. Bee

Secretary of War.

REPUBLIC OF TEXAS.

LAND CERTIFICATE.

BANNER OFFICE PRINT.

done. Col. [Ben] Milam, one of the noblest and bravest officers fell in this heroic struggle, greatly lamented by all."[29]

The most vivid account of the battle comes from a letter Dr. Levy wrote to his sister:

"Address me as
Surgeon in Chief of the
volunteer army of Texas

San Antonio de Bexar
Dec. 20th, 1835

Dearest Sister:

. . . After suffering a thousand deaths in traveling through and sleeping in the cold bleak prairies night after night without a tree or shrub to shelter us from the cold rain and wind (of which we had an abundance) we found the greatest state of confusion and dissatisfaction. . . . Finally affairs became so bad that the army broke up in confusion, and desperate would have been the consequences for we would all have been cut by the enemy when I, *insignificant* I, and another individual a citizen of Texas called Milam [Colonel Ben R. Milam], beat up for volunteers who would join us two in storming the town and fort that very night, (I should mention that from my mixing about a great deal with the soldiers and chatting and joking with them I had acquired some popularity among them). Our company, called the Grays, [*sic*] immediately and to a man signed their names, and mounting one of the baggage waggons [*sic*] (for we, as I have observed, were just ready for a hasty retreat) I harangued them for a few minutes and thus succeeded in getting 3 hundred men. We laid our plans appointed our leaders, and about daylight marched up to the enemy's halls got into some strong houses in town and after a regular storm of five days and nights duration, during the whole of which the enemy kept up an incessant firing, we forced them to surrender, thus atchieving [*sic*] a victory perfectly unparalleled in history, a victory obtained by 225 disorganized and undisciplined men armed with muskets and bayonets in a well fortified fort. . . . Our men fought like devils, (even I fought). I worked in the ditches, I dressed the sick and wounded, I cheered the men, I assisted the officers in their counsels, for five days and nights I did not sleep that many hours, running about without a coat or hat, dirty and ragged but thank God escaped uninjured. I received a slight wound on the forehead the first day which was entirely well before we took the town. I was much exposed to the fire of the enemy and all our men wondered how I escaped with my life. I have crossed a street when more than two hundred muskets were shot at me, our men begging me not to expose myself as I was a double man, being both soldier and surgeon."[30]

Art by Charles Brannon, copyright © by Natalie Ornish.

In his official account of the Storming of Bexar, Colonel Francis W. Johnson wrote on Dec. 14, 1835, "Doctors Levy and Pollard also deserve my warmest praise, for their unremitted attention and assiduity."[31] Levy received on May 27, 1838, a "Donation certificate" #151 signed by General Barnard Bee, Secretary of War, for 640 acres "having fought at Bexar from the 5th to the 10th of Dec. 1835 with exemplary bravery."[32]

HERMAN EHRENBERG AT THE ALAMO BATTLES

Soldier Ehrenberg also wrote of his experiences in the storming of Bexar, and described how he and his men worked from "a small entrenchment . . . fortified with only two small cannons with which my comrades thundered on the old Alamo. We could in fact see pieces of the old walls roll down from time to time. . . Our friends were attacking the Alamo. Instantly the enemy drums began to roll and the bugles pealed in motley confusion. From the fort there was an incessant booming . . . our people with their little guns challenged the whole Mexican army. The glances of our leader, the Mexican lieutenant, hung constantly on the Alamo, which we could see to our left as a black colossus.[33]

"The bugles whirred wildly out of the quadrangle and the drums rolled for battle. The profanity of the enemy and the incessant musket fire was completely drowned by the cannon of the Alamo, which now in short intervals thundered through the darkness. But there was something inspiring in this powerful roaring through the night . . . we considered ourselves invincible, a conclusion that later caused us deep wounds and almost caused the destruction of the new republic. The fifth day was closed gloriously and we were looking eagerly for the sixth, the tenth of December [1835]. The fire of the enemy had died down. . . . The humble white flag of submission was waving from the ruins of the Alamo. . . . The Mexicans were to be allowed to march away unmolested. As a protection against the Comanches they were allowed 150 guns. . . . The officers were obliged to give their word of honor never again to fight against Texas. The officers and troops were to leave the town at once, the Alamo on

Led by a Mexican lieutenant, the Texans, including Ehrenberg, attacked the Mexican army inside the Alamo in 1835, winning a six-day war. The victorious Texans let the Mexicans go free, after which Ehrenberg and others lived in the Alamo until spring.

the twelfth of December, and to evacuate the whole country on this side of the Rio Grande as speedily as possible. On the designated day Cos marched away with his troops, and by virtue of conquest, we took possession of the magazine and the Alamo. Forty-eight cannons, approximately 4,000 muskets . . . fell into our hands. . . .[34]

"Soon after the departure of the enemy troops, most of my comrades and I set up our living quarters in the ruins of the Alamo . . . a retreat offering protection against the cold and storm of the winter."[35]

Ehrenberg, who found himself living in the Alamo, served the Texas army by scouting the area and obtaining much needed corn and other provisions in enemy areas, often risking his life.

Mexican forces had occupied the Alamo, an abandoned mission, as a barracks from 1821 to December, 1835, when the Texas forces won the mission. There were two battles at the Alamo in San Antonio. The first, also known as the Storming of Bexar, as San Antonio was then called, was a great victory for the Texans, who occupied the mission and the entire city. Less than three months later, the more famous fall of the Alamo began.

The worst was still to come — Alamo — Goliad — San Jacinto. Houston anticipated that Santa Anna's invasion would come with "the rise of grass." The first green of spring is usually seen around March first in Texas, when trees begin to leaf out and dormant grass becomes alive. To be prepared for this anticipated assault, Houston requested the conscription of a regular army, not just volunteers. Houston was to command only the regular army, which had yet to be created. The volunteer army then operating in San Antonio was not subject to regulation by the new provisional government, resulting in great confusion, as no standing army of any size ever came into being.

It was not even clear what the Texans were fighting for: A majority had voted to fight for the restoration of the Mexican constitution; a minority voted in favor of a declaration of independence. While great confusion took place in Texas, the opposite was happening south of the Rio Grande. There Santa Anna was preparing an army of more than 6,000 men for the purpose of forcing the Texans to submit. The "Napoleon of the West" did not wait until the grass turned green. On February 12, 1836, he led his army across the Rio Grande and proceeded directly to San Antonio. Part of this force reached San Antonio on February 23, to the great surprise of the Texans, who were poorly prepared. The siege of the Alamo began.

The Alamo was not even supposed to be there. On January 17th General Houston ordered Bowie to the Alamo to blow it up and to remove any guns to Goliad and Gonzales. Bowie decided to defend it and was joined on February 2 by Travis and on February 8 by Davy Crockett with his twelve Tennessee Mounted Volunteers. Crockett had been a member of Congress from Tennessee, and when defeated in 1834, he reportedly said his constituents could go to hell and he would go to Texas. Crockett reached Nacogdoches, home of Adolphus Sterne, on the fifth of January, 1836, and attended a banquet there for two high Mexican officials sympathetic with the Texan principles, before marching on to war. Crockett was one of the few mature fighters, most of the volunteers being teen-agers. He arrived in Texas just in time to die two months later.

The Texas defenders of the Alamo struggled thirteen bloody days before their tragic end. General Travis wrote his famous letter during this time. When the garrison finally fell and the Mexicans climbed the ladders to scale the wall and view the death scene, it appeared all the defenders were dead. When the *alcalde* (mayor) of San Antonio looked over the bodies with Mexican General Santa Anna and pointed out Crockett's, he then added it to the funeral prye with colonels Jim Bowie and Buck Travis — and a young Jew named Anthony Wolf.[36]

A. WOLF AT THE ALAMO'S FALL

The Alamo as published in Baker's Texas Scrap Book, 1875.

Avram Wolf, a documented Jewish Englishman who anglicized his name to Anthony Wolf, had come to Texas in 1835, shortly after his wife Sarah died in England.[37] He had brought with him his two sons Benjamin and Michael, who were around the ages of twelve and eleven. Wolf had heard of Adolphus Sterne and settled in Sterne's Nacogdoches area. He later traveled to San Antonio as part of the Texan army.[38]

The curator of the Alamo, Charles J. Long, said, "Wolfe, a widower, came to San Antonio with two children, twelve years old. According to [Enrique] Esparza in an article in 1907, a twelve year-old boy was killed in a room with the survivors, which I assume may have been one of Anton Wolfe's boys."[39] [Wolf's name has been spelled many ways.] Wolf served as a private in the artillery. "Gunner Antony Wolfe's boys — they looked less than twelve — were ruthlessly slaughtered, but Enrique somehow was missed in the crush," wrote Walter Lord in *A Time to Stand.*

Ralph Elder, head of public services, Barker Texas History Center of the University of Texas, discovered unpublished material on Wolf in the Kemp Papers, as follows: "WOLFE, Anthony - Killed at the Alamo. Mrs. Dickinson, whose life was spared, stated that Wolfe was the only man who begged for quarter [clemency] of the Mexicans. His two boys aged eleven and twelve years went to the room where Mrs. Dickinson was, and, with a man named Walker, were killed and their bodies carried out on bayonets."[40]

In 1851 D.S. Kaufman (see chapter 4), on behalf of Wolf's heirs, filed "A claim for Services in the Army in 1835 & 1836" for the sum of twenty-four dollars — three months' service at eight dollars a month.[41]

Although Wolf and his two sons are the only Jews who died at the Battle of the Alamo, there may have been eight Jews at the Alamo in the fighting for Texas independence. Kokernot, Dr. Levy, Harby, and Ehrenberg fought at the Alamo's first battle in December of 1835 when Ben Milam was killed. The Wolf family brings the total to seven.

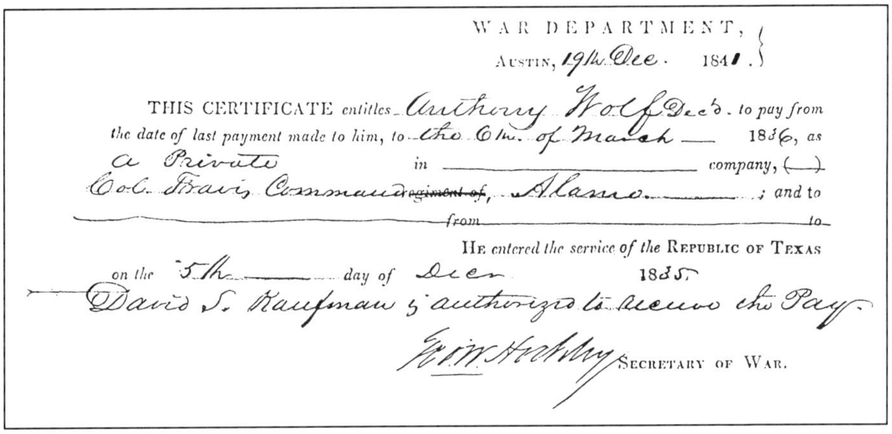

WAR DEPARTMENT,
Austin, 19th Dec. 1841.

THIS CERTIFICATE entitles Anthony Wolf Dec'd. to pay from the date of last payment made to him, to the 6th. of March 1836, as a Private in ______ company, (—) Col. Travis Command, ~~regiment of~~, Alamo ; and to ______ from ______ to ______

He entered the service of the Republic of Texas on the 5th day of Dec 1835.

David S. Kaufman is authorized to receive the Pay.

G. W. Hockley Secretary of War.

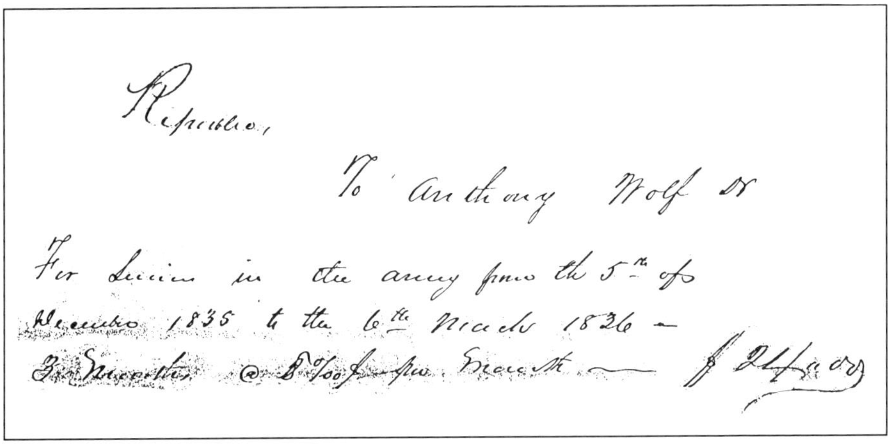

Republic,

To Anthony Wolf Dr

For Services in the army from the 5th of December 1835 to the 6th March 1836 — 3 months @ $8.00 per month — $24.00

(Top): War Department certificate and (center): hand-written promissory note entitling Anthony Wolf, deceased, payment for service as a private under Colonel Travis at the fall of the Alamo on the 6th of March 1836. Wolf entered the service of the Republic on the 5th of December 1835. Certificate authorizes David S. Kaufman, attorney for Wolf's heirs and later Texas' first congressman, to receive the pay. Wolf earned $24.00 (three months at eight dollars per month).

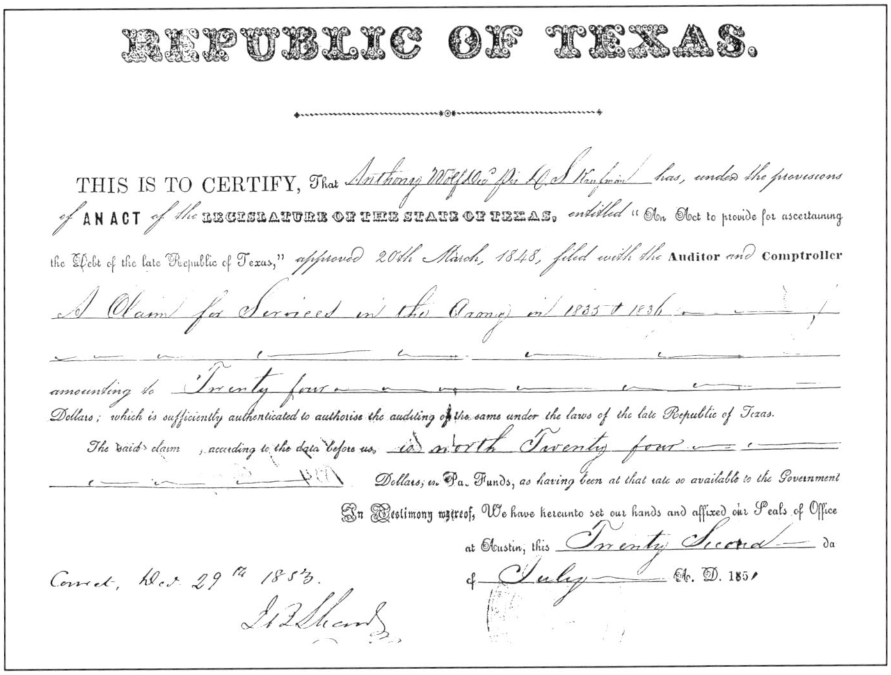

REPUBLIC OF TEXAS.

THIS IS TO CERTIFY, That Anthony Wolf dec'd by D. S. Kaufman has, under the provisions of AN ACT of the LEGISLATURE OF THE STATE OF TEXAS, entitled "An Act to provide for ascertaining the Debt of the late Republic of Texas," approved 20th March, 1848, filed with the Auditor and Comptroller A Claim for Services in the Army in 1835 & 1836

amounting to Twenty four

Dollars; which is sufficiently authenticated to authorise the auditing of the same under the laws of the late Republic of Texas.

The said claim, according to the data before us, is worth Twenty four Dollars, in Pa. Funds, as having been at that rate so available to the Government

In Testimony whereof, We have hereunto set our hands and affixed our Seals of Office at Austin, this Twenty Second day of July A. D. 1851

Corrd, Oct 29th 1853.

Ten years later, Wolf's claim still had not been paid to Kaufman. However, Kaufman could not have received the funds during his lifetime as he died Jan. 31, 1851, prior to this claim being filed on July 22, 1851.

MOSES ROSE'S FIGHTING TEN DAYS AT THE ALAMO AND HIS ESCAPE TO TELL THE STORY

The eighth person who likely was of the Jewish faith at the Alamo was Louis (Moses) Rose.[42] He also was a contemporary of Adolphus Sterne. They had fought together in two of the earliest battles for Texas independence, the Fredonian Rebellion and the Battle of Nacogdoches.[43] Rose was a warm friend of Col. James Bowie and accompanied or followed him to the Alamo in the fall of 1835 and continued with him till within three days of the fall of the fort. Rose was at both battles at the Alamo — the Storming of Bexar and the battle that preceded the fall.

Both Sterne and Rose had business relations together — both witnessed legal land documents for applicants.

Moses Rose never married, but his nephew Isaac Rose of Lexington, Kentucky, had eleven children. The wife of a descendant of Isaac Rose reported Jewish lineage.[44]

It is said he was called "Moses" because he was an older man, being age fifty-one at the time of the Alamo.

In regard to Rose's ethnic background, Alamo curator Long said, "I have had that brought up to me several times, that he was a French Jew. I don't have any theories as to whether he was Jewish or not. . . . He has been put down a lot; he deserves more credit than he gets. He served honorably in the French army. He sold his property in Texas to buy equipment to fight with at the Battle of Bexar. When he decided to leave the Alamo, he was jumping from the frying pan into the fire."[45] Long referred to Rose escaping the Alamo after fighting there ten days, three days before the fall. Of the soldiers who witnessed the battle, he was one of the few survivors.

Rose was not the only person to survive the Alamo. History records sixteen surviving non-combatants — women, children, and slaves who remained behind closed doors. Less known is the questioned report that Santa Anna called an armistice for three days, giving the Texans time to deliberate on surrendering. Approximately ten men are said to have walked out the front door during this time, but no one ever reported doing so. Enrique Esparza said, at age eighty-two in 1907, "Rose left after this armistice had expired. Rose went out after Travis drew the line with his sword. He was the only man who did not cross the line. Up to then he had fought as bravely as any man there. He had stood by the cannon. Rose went out during the night. They opened a window for him and let him go. The others who left before went out of the doors and in the daytime."[46] Enrique Esparza had been a child, age eleven, at the Alamo. Esparza and his family entered the Alamo through a window when the fighting began, jumping inside via a cannon placed in the window.

Louis Moses Rose owes his place in Texas history to the fact he escaped from the Alamo and related the famous tale about Colonel Travis' drawing the line with his sword. It is his legacy to Texas history. This legacy has stayed alive with controversy since he first told the story. Did Travis actually take out his sword during the most dismal day at the Alamo and ask all who were ready to die with him to cross a line, and give others the chance to escape? Did men carry the cot, on which Jim Bowie lay, over to Travis' side? Was Louis Moses Rose really the only man in the Alamo who preferred to live? Did he really vault the wall or go through a window and escape?

There are different versions of this legend.[47] However, more important to this particular work is the fact that Rose probably was Jewish. He came from Alsace-Lorraine, and records show he fought in Russia as a member of Napoleon's army. Rose was, curiously, a soldier of fortune, and it is now fairly well established that he was not a coward at the Alamo as he was originally accused of being. He may have been illiterate, but he was not stupid. Rose was a mature fifty-one years by the time he got to the Alamo, a veteran soldier. During his life he had fought for love of country, love of money, love of adventure, and love of battle — but never for love of death such as the Alamo promised.[48]

He lived to act as a witness for numerous heirs to get land for families of martyrs of the Alamo.[49] Rose's testimonies to the Board of Land Commissioners included such items: JOHN BLAIR — Rose testified, "left him in the Alamo 3rd of March, 1836." CHARLES HASKEL — "knew him four years; suppose him killed in the Alamo." DAVID WILSON — "knew him before 2nd May, 1835; was in the Alamo when taken." MARCUS SEWELL — "knew him in the Alamo, and left him there three days before it fell." Louis Moses Rose appeared as witness in at least sixteen cases before the Board. In no instance was the testimony of Rose rejected as lacking credibility.[50]

For almost forty years after the Alamo (1836 to 1873) the histories of Texas contained no mention of either Rose or the speech made by Travis or of the line drawn by his sword. But in 1873 the *Texas Almanac* published "An Escape from the Alamo" by W.P. Zuber, whose parents took Rose in after he left the Alamo.[51] Zuber wrote that Rose escaped, although Rose's name was on the first partial list of fallen heroes published soon after the fall of the Alamo in the *Telegraph and Texas Register* at San Felipe and later in Richardson's *Texas Almanac* for 1860. He pointed out that Rose's name erroneously had been inscribed on an Austin monument to the Alamo dead "on the fourth pillar, the first name after that of David Crockett." Zuber observed, "We must pronounce Rose's account of that [Travis'] speech and of that mutual pledge reasonable and credible.

"Is it incredible that, when all the other men in that little garrison covenated to stay there and fight to the death, Rose alone declined to do so, and resolved on an attempt to escape? I believe that a majority of men will admit that, if similarly situated, they might do as Rose professes to have done. Is it incredible that, to disencumber himself from descending from the top of the wall on the outside, he threw down his wallet of clothes, which fell into a puddle of blood, part of which adhered to some of his garments, and on drying glued them together? My mother saw her black servant-girl, Maria, take those garments out of the wallet and find them so glued. On leaving the fort, he did not attempt to go east through the Mexican army, by which he would have been killed or captured, but went west, through San Antonio; then south, down the San Antonio river, about three miles; then east through open prairie, to the Guadalupe river, carefully avoiding roads."[52]

Moses Rose, after fighting at the Alamo ten days, climbed the wall and left three days before it fell.

In the open prairie, Rose encountered rugged terrain, and thorns of hundreds of large cactus inflicted wounds on his legs. He did not take time to remove the thorns until they had worked so deeply into his flesh that he could not bear the pain of drawing them out. Zuber said, "My parents drew those thorns from his legs with nippers."[53] Rose crossed rivers by rolling logs into the streams, sitting on them, and paddling across with his hands. During his escape, all the homes he encountered were abandoned except one, where he spent a night. Two Nacogdoches men also spent the night there, and when they heard of Rose's escape, told the landlord they felt Rose was an imposter who had never seen the Alamo. The landlord later boasted to Zuber that he had sent Rose away. Zuber wrote that Rose was so embarrassed by this treatment that "he resolved never again to say that he had been in the Alamo. . . his reticence on this subject was what prevented his statement from being inserted in the early histories of Texas." Rose moved on to Grimes County, where he stayed in the Abraham Zuber home. He told his tale only to the Zubers, who related it to their son who wrote it down.[54] "My writing down of Rose's narrative was incidental to a more important purpose, which was to preserve the substance of Colonel Travis's speech to his fellow-heroes of the Alamo, on March 3rd, 1836. Rose's disconnected recitals of that speech, my mother's repetition of them to me, and my many rewritings of the same, by which I compiled the disconnected parts into a discourse, all are explained in my account of the adventures of Rose."[55]

For years, few scholars took Zuber's account seriously. Then in 1939 came a thunderbolt. R. B. Blake of Nacogdoches uncovered the "amazing evidence" in the Nacogdoches County Courthouse which showed convincingly that there was indeed a Louis Rose, that he had been in the Alamo during the siege, and that his testimony was accepted in deciding claims for Alamo victims.[56]

After leaving the Zuber ranch in 1836, Rose went to Nacogdoches, where he previously had resided for more than ten years. He operated a butcher shop until late 1842. He moved to Logansport, Louisiana, where he made his home with the Aaron Ferguson family, where he died in 1851 at age sixty-six. His death was attributed to the thorns imbedded in his legs.

Rose, like many of his Jewish counterparts, had been a wanderer. He was born around 1785 in France.[57] He served in Napoleon's army in the invasion of Russia and in the retreat from Moscow.[58] One writer questions Rose's Russian service, adding that Rose fought in campaigns in Naples of 1806 through 1810, in Portugal in 1811 and 1812, in the Spanish campaign of 1813, and in 1814 named to the Legion of Honor.[59] Rose was a common man who came up through the ranks.

No one knows his port of entry into the United States. But, unlike Travis, Bowie, and Crockett, Rose was a long-time resident of Texas. He had lived in East Texas almost ten years before the war and was issued Texas certificate of entry #580 in 1827. In Nacogdoches he was employed as a log cutter and hauler for John Durst's and then Frost Thorn's sawmill, as well as a messenger between Nacogdoches and Natchitoches, La., and became a paymaster for a cargo company.[60] John Durst's relative, Mary Victoria Durst, married A. Wolf. At the Battle of Nacogdoches, Rose was one of seventeen daring Texans to capture an entire enemy garrison three and a half years before the Alamo massacre. When asked, "Mose, why didn't you stay there in the Alamo with the others?" his invariable reply was, "By God, I wasn't ready to die."[61] Had Rose died an Alamo martyr, the writing of history would have been poorer.

Walt Whitman was wrong when he wrote "Not one escaped to tell the fall of the Alamo."[62] Rose was more like the messenger to Job who said, "I only am escaped alone to tell thee."[63]

While the grim Battle of the Alamo raged, Texas leaders met on March 2 (at Washington-on-the Brazos) and issued a declaration of independence from Mexico, whose dictator had offered "either to abandon our homes . . . or submit to the most intolerable of all tyranny, the combined despotism of the sword and the priesthood." Jewish scholars have cited the Texas Declaration of Independence as a significant step in securing religious rights of Jews in the United States.[64] The Texians had charged they were denied "the right of worshipping the Almighty according to the dictates of our conscience, by the support of a national religion calculated to promote the temporal interest of its human functionaries rather than the glory of the true and living God."

Hardware store stands where Moses Rose had his meat market in the Republic era, Commerce and Church streets, Nacogdoches.

On March 17, the Constitution of the Republic of Texas was established, and it included in its declaration of rights the statement that "no preference shall be given by law to any religious denomination or mode of worship over another, but every person shall be permitted to worship God according to the dictates of his own conscience." In this constitution nothing disqualified a man on religious grounds from holding office and exercising full political rights in the Republic except the provision denying "Ministers of the gospel" and "priests of any denomination whatever" the right to hold the presidential office or a congressional seat. After the forced Catholicism of Mexico, religious freedom was foremost on the Texans' minds.

Only three weeks after the Alamo fell, another tragedy struck: Goliad![65] In a mop-up action, Santa Anna ordered about 330 Texas prisoners including their leader, Colonel James W. Fannin, Jr., shot to

Descendant (P.E. Baimbridge, Jr.) at Moses Rose's burial site in Louisiana.

death. A nineteen-year-old Jewish lad from Cincinnati, Edward I. Johnson, died at Goliad. According to Lawrence P. Johnson of Cincinnati, who in 1981 was age seventy-five, Edward Isaac Johnson, his grandfather's brother, "went to Texas in 1835 because he was promised eight hundred acres if he lived and sixteen hundred acres if he was killed in the battles for Texas Independence."[66]

Of the four known Jews at Goliad, three escaped: Ehrenberg, Benjamin M. Mordecai, and M. K. Moses.[67]

Goliad was an old stone fort encircled by a stone wall, covering three and a half acres on a rocky height above the San Antonio River. Of nearly 400 men there, only a fourth were Texans. Santa Anna's forces in Texas numbered 6,000 men and were advancing. Ehrenberg chronicled the Goliad campaign. He estimated the enemy number higher: "Santa Anna in person closed in around the Alamo with 7,000 men."[68]

Ehrenberg wrote that at one point Fannin decided to aid the defenders in the Alamo 100 miles away, but changed his mind. "In Goliad he held undisputedly the first position, which rank, however, he would have to resign if he combined with the main Army."[69]

When Fannin began to move his command, instead of taking all provisions and destroying artillery at the time of fleeing as Houston had ordered, Fannin did the opposite. He burned provisions, yet insisted on carrying nine brass cannon and 500 spare muskets — all of which the enemy captured. The oxen, nearly starved, were uncontrollable.

...said Attorney may see fit for the said ... Attorneys or substitutes, under ... to appoint, with like power and for the same purposes this power of Attorney, to be forever irrevocable, any law to the contrary notwithstanding.
And said ... acknowledge ... held and firmly bound unto ... in the just and full sum of ... Dollars, for the true payment of which ... heirs, Executors and Administrators, jointly, severally, firmly, by these presents, to be void on condition the said ... shall make to the said ... or assigns, good, lawful and sufficient Title for the aforesaid ... of Land, so soon as a Patent is issued for the same, and shall do and perform all things which may be necessary to be done, on ... part, to vest in the said ... heirs and assigns good and lawful Titles for the said Land.
In testimony of all which, the said ... hath hereunto set ... hand and affixed ... Seal, in presence of the undersigned, on the date first aforesaid.

Assignment of title to Louis Rose, through his attorney Frost Thorn, to one-third league of land. Rose placed his mark, an "x," on this land agreement. Courtesy Hazel Baimbridge

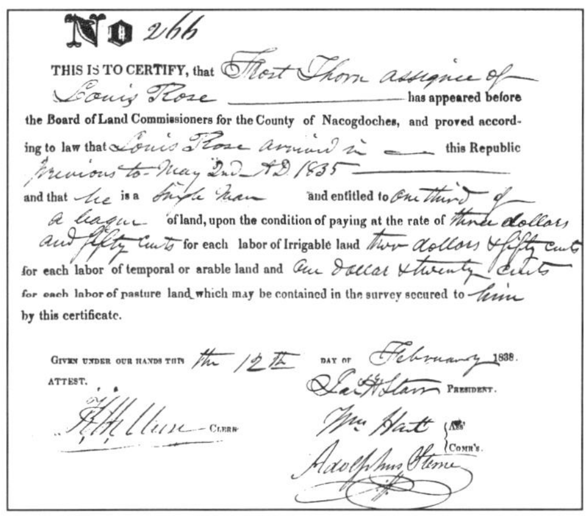
No 266
THIS IS TO CERTIFY, that Frost Thorn assignee of Louis Rose has appeared before the Board of Land Commissioners for the County of Nacogdoches, and proved according to law that Louis Rose arrived in this Republic previous to May 2d AD 1835 and that he is a single man and entitled to one third of a league of land, upon the condition of paying at the rate of three dollars and fifty cents for each labor of Irrigable land two dollars & fifty cents for each labor of temporal or arable land and one dollar & twenty cents for each labor of pasture land, which may be contained in the survey secured to him by this certificate.
Given under our hands this the 12th day of February 1838.
Attest. ... Clerk. ... President. Wm Hart, Adolphus Sterne, Comm's.

Rose document signed by Adolphus Sterne in 1838 states Rose was in Texas prior to May 2, 1835.

Courtesy Hazel Baimbridge.

EHRENBERG'S REPORT OF THE GOLIAD ARREST

Ehrenberg wrote:

"The number and size of the provisions and ammunition wagons that we took with us were too large and the power to move them was too small so that before we had gone half a mile, the way was strewn with objects of all kinds and here and there a wagon that was left standing or knocked to pieces." Not only were the oxen exhausted, but also the Mexicans were discovered advancing in the rear. Ehrenberg was with a group of scouts instructed to watch the forest to the left. After noticing "a long black streak on the plain... Hastily we mounted our horses and dashed off at full speed to our comrades to prepare them for the reception of the enemy." Not wanting to become embroiled in the battle, all the scouts galloped off "without even stopping to look at us, and under the strongest appliance of whip and spur." Only one, Ehrenberg, stopped to join the Texans. The Texans received the news of the enemy's approach with a "hurrah." Ehrenberg described the battle at Coleto Creek: "The effect of our fire was frightful. Herds of horses were running without rider while others were wallowing in blood and kicking furiously."[70]

Outnumbered three to one with no hope of reinforcements, and composed of inexperienced men facing seasoned veterans of Mexico's best general, Urrea, Fannin's euphoria turned to cold reality. More than fifty Texans were wounded, including Fannin, who had been shot in the thigh. His hope of getting help for the wounded Texan seemed to be foremost reason for surrender. The Texans gave up entirely to the enemy their 500 muskets and nine cannons before marching back to Goliad. They crowded into the church there under heavy guard. Ehrenberg remembered:

"The first night of our captivity passed away in discomfort. A burning thirst tormented us and although we asked repeatedly for water, we had to wait until eight o'clock in the morning before six of our men were allowed to go to the river and get water for themselves and the other prisoners. . . . The heat had become much greater, and was much more stifling than during the preceding night. Several of my comrades were so exhausted that they slept standing, for the crowded state of the prison prevented us from lying down. A few of our smaller companions who could sit down enjoyed greater repose than the others. But even they could not remain in their sitting position very long, for the atmosphere grew so close that squatting on the floor was bearable for a short time only."

The following day Ehrenberg suffered more:

"Now we had meat, but it was raw and we had no way of cooking it. We gathered pieces of wood . . . stripped the walls of their woodwork; and soon . . . had kindled two fires. But the fires had to be very small, as our heat and thirst were by that time almost unendurable and only a few of the men at a time could roast their meat; the night was over before we had finished our cooking. Those of us who stood farthest from the fire gave up the idea of cooking the meat and ate it raw since the fires merely added new misery to the horrors of our confinement."[71]

At the fort, the last act of the Goliad tragedy took place the week of March 20-27. The wounded lay groaning in the old church; several who had been struck by poisonous copper bullets were raving wildly in the delirium of a burning fever, which mercifully hid from them the horrors of their situation. The others who were less seriously hurt heard the musketry fire which destroyed their friends and guessed what had happened. Infuriated, they tried to tear off their bandages, with the hope perhaps of bleeding to death.

"Inwardly deeply humiliated, which showed itself on our faces, we walked up and down in our camp, casting angry looks at Fannin and the others." The violence of one of Ehrenberg's friends named Johnson, probably Edward Isaac Johnson, is described in detail: "Especially one American named Johnson made himself conspicuous because of his anger. Gnashing his teeth, he stamped on the ground." Later Ehrenberg wrote:

"Suddenly a light flashed through the misty morning, a dull report followed, and a terrible jarring of the air was combined with it. And then deathly stillness fell over the prairie, which was again covered with wounded men. Impenetrable suffocating smoke . . . rolled heavily over the dark green prairie. Wildly the horses of several of the enemy officers reared up and frantic with fear rushed out with their stupefied riders in uninterrupted speed with ruffled manes and flying tails into the safe distance. . . . Still half stunned, we went toward the place where the explosion seemed to have broken loose. The powder magazine had disappeared; only a part of the lower frame work remained. Around the place lay several men wounded . . . and a black body that barely looked like one of a human being. It was still alive but not able to speak. It was burnt coal black like the color of a negro, and it was impossible to tell who the unfortunate one was. Our glances wandered searching around; the roll was called and the missing man was Johnson. No one had noticed him before. Was it an accident or was it really his plan to kill himself and as many Mexicans as possible at the same time? At what he considered the favorable moment, he must have ignited the magazine. But as the lid was not locked, the main blast exploded upward, and thus his terrible plan missed its purpose."[72]

Besides sharing their wrath at the surrender, Johnson and Ehrenberg shared another bond in common — their youthful age. Johnson was only nineteen when he died, and Ehrenberg was the same age there at Goliad.[73]

EDWARD ISAAC JOHNSON

Edward Isaac Johnson was the son of a prominent Jewish family in Cincinnati.[74] The war for Texas independence won the imagination of many residents of that city, who sent both supplies and forces to Texas. After leaving Cincinnati, he volunteered for the Texas army at Maysville, Kentucky.

Johnson arrived in Texas in November of 1835 as a member of Captain Thomas K. Pearson's outfit. Johnson helped these men to transport a cannon salvaged from the wrecked schooner *San Felipe* from the Gulf of Mexico overland to San Antonio de Bexar to the army of General Edward Burleson. It is likely this cannon helped to account for the success of the Storming of Bexar in December. About February 5, 1836, he signed the memorial to the Washington Convention from the volunteers at Refugio. Johnson fought in the center of the hottest action in the Revolution. Midway between the Alamo and Goliad was another battle at Refugio (popularly pronounced "Ray-furio"; pronounced in Spanish "Ray-foo-he-o"). At this town twenty-five miles south of Goliad, 150 Texans were killed by Mexican cavalry.

March was a bloody month for the volunteers in Texas: the Alamo fell on March 6; the Battle of Refugio began on March 14; the Battle of Coleto, the final culmination of the Goliad Campaign, was fought near Coleto Creek on March 19 and 20; and the Goliad massacre of the men who had surrendered at Coleto took place on March 27. At Refugio, Johnson had served in a Captain King's company until King was killed. He then had marched with Dr. James Grant's forces to Goliad, where he joined a company under Captain Burr H. Duval, who also died at Goliad.

If the famished Texans had reached Coleto Creek and its nearby woods sooner, it is likely they could have survived the battle. Starving and fighting in an open plains, they were overtaken and marched as prisoners of war to Goliad.

After spending the three nightmare nights in the Goliad mission, crowded and miserable, the prisoners were released from the narrow walls of the church into the quadrangle of the fort, where they stayed several more days. On the morning of the seventh day, the Mexicans brought in another hundred prisoners, all volunteers from New York. After traveling several weeks, their joy at reaching the Texas coast was interrupted by their immediate capture by the Mexicans in a surprise attack.

On the morning of the eighth day, the men were ordered to leave the fort right away. They thought they were marching to a Texas port to embark there for New Qrleans. Then, according to Ehrenberg, "Our surprise was as deep as it was ghastly. The idea that they planned to shoot us seemed unthinkable."

Not until they heard screams did they realize what was taking place. At the place of execution, they were ordered to sit down with their backs to the guard. Two young men, flourishing their caps over their heads, shouted at the top of their voices, "Hurrah for Texas!"

Naturally, many tried to escape, but those who did were pursued by cavalry and, when located, shot. Only around seven made their escape.[75] Ehrenberg, Mordecai, and Moses numbered among these few. Three hundred and thirty suffered death — including the nineteen-year-old Johnson of Cincinnati. A Mexican officer who commanded one of the firing squads wrote in his diary:

"What spectator could view it without horror! They were all young, the oldest not more than thirty, and of fine florid complexions. When the unfortunate youths were brought to the place of death, their lamentations and appeals which they uttered to Heaven, in their own language, with extended arms, kneeling or prostrate on the earth, were such as might have caused the very stones to have cried out in compassion."

Ehrenberg described what happened to him and his friends when the moment of truth came:

"Our murderers yelled once more the command to kneel. A second volley of musketry . . . and a Wail of distress followed it, probably from those victims whose death had not been instantaneous. These sounds startled our friend . . . and with blazing eyes, he cried out boldly: 'Comrades, did you hear those shots? Did you hear those cries? The last hour of the Greys has come. Therefore, Comrades . . .' A fearful crash inter-

Drawing by Norman Price.

rupted him, then all was quiet; thick clouds of smoke rolled slowly towards the river. The blood of my lieutenant spurred on my clothes and around me the last convulsions of agony shook the bodies of my friends."[76]

EHRENBERG'S MIRACULOUS ESCAPE

The smoke from the Mexican muskets saved the life of Ehrenberg.

"Quickly making up my mind, I sprang up and took advantage of the thick smoke which hid me to rush along the hedge and make for the river . . . the murmur of the water alone guided my steps. A heavy blow on the head from a sword made me reel; the small form of a Mexican lieutenant emerged from the smoke in front of me and a second thrust of his sword hit my left arm. . . . I had nothing to lose, everything to gain. It was a matter of life and death. Behind me I had the bayonets of Mexican soldiers, in front of me the ineffective weapon of a coward who blocked my way to the river and safety. In a moment I was on him. I could not go back. He did not put up any fight, but fled. My path was clear and safety was in sight. Shouting 'The Republic of Texas forever!' I jumped into the waters of the stream and swam slowly and wearily to the other bank with bullets flying over my head. . . . It was then that I had the ill luck of losing the faithful dog of our company; he had been with us from the beginning of our campaign, and, following me in my dash for safety, had jumped with me into the river. The thought of retaining him as a companion during my flight through the prairie was already cheering my depressed spirits, when a bullet hit him and he sank under the water. As soon as I reached the other bank, I looked back at the place where my friends lay bleeding to death. The enemy was still shooting and yelling, and it was with a sorrowful heart that I listened to these shouts of triumph which in my fancy were mingled with the groans of pain of my dying friends.

". . . It was only when immediate danger was over that I began to feel shaken and deeply moved. I had read tales of horrible crimes, but none so horrible as the one which I had witnessed a few minutes before, and I could hardly believe that men who called themselves Christians could be guilty of such a dark and bloody deed."[77]

Ehrenberg also witnessed the dramatic execution of Fannin, writing, "Deeply he regretted that he had not hastened to the aid of the fallen garrison of the Alamo, or that he had not sooner followed Houston's orders to retreat behind the Guadalupe. Tears of deepest sorrow ran down his cheeks during the slaughter of his true and faithful comrades."

The citizens of Mexico were moved by the massacre and held Santa Anna to account. The general told his people that he ordered the men killed because there was not enough food for them. The United States was repelled and angered. Overnight United States neutrality changed to a fervent sympathy for the Texian cause.

To Southwesterners, the Alamo and Goliad rank alongside Lexington and Concord. "Remember the Alamo! Remember Goliad!" became the battle cry of the Texans.

Sam Houston heard the news about Alamo and Goliad on the night of March 13, 1836, when he arrived in Gonzales. The towns people were so full of grief, everyone spoke in a whisper, except for the wild shrieks of widows and the heart-rending cries of their fatherless children.

By the time Houston reached LaGrange, his force had increased to 600 men. "April" showers came early; the end of March found the volunteers already marching in a deluge of rain and mud. On March 31 they reached Groce's Plantation on the Brazos River and camped on an elevated area. Kokernot, now a captain, struggled at Groce's with Houston's retreating army. After the soldiers cleared out the dense brush, the river began to rise. Temporarily safe on their muddy island, the volunteers had twelve days to be shaped into an army.

THE TEXAS NAVY

Besides an army, the new government had begun to shape a navy. In 1836, Jews numbered among the warriors not only on horseback in cavalry with sabres and Bowie knives, but also as sailors in the Gulf of Mexico with the Texas Navy. In January 1836 the provisional government had authorized purchase of four schooners, and the Texas Navy included the *Independence*, the *Brutus*, the *Liberty*, and the *Invincible*.[78] The *Brutus* appeared in Texas waters early in February 1836. Dr. Albert Moses Levy, who had fought on land, joined the Texas Navy aboard the *Brutus*, a ship armed with "eight port guns and one pivot nine-pounder," or "nine short guns" and a long eighteen-pounder swivel. David G. Burnet, President of the Republic, signed Levy's appointment as a surgeon in the Navy of the Republic on March 20, 1836.

In March, the navy began intensive patrolling of the Texas Gulf Coast. On April 7, the Acting Secretary of War, David Thomas, sent Sam Houston a letter: "Dr. Levy has just arrived . . . from Galveston, brings intelligence of the arrival of the *Brutus*, Captain Hurd, and *Independence*, Captain Hawkins, in the Bay. The *Brutus* will proceed to New Orleans to be fitted out."[79]

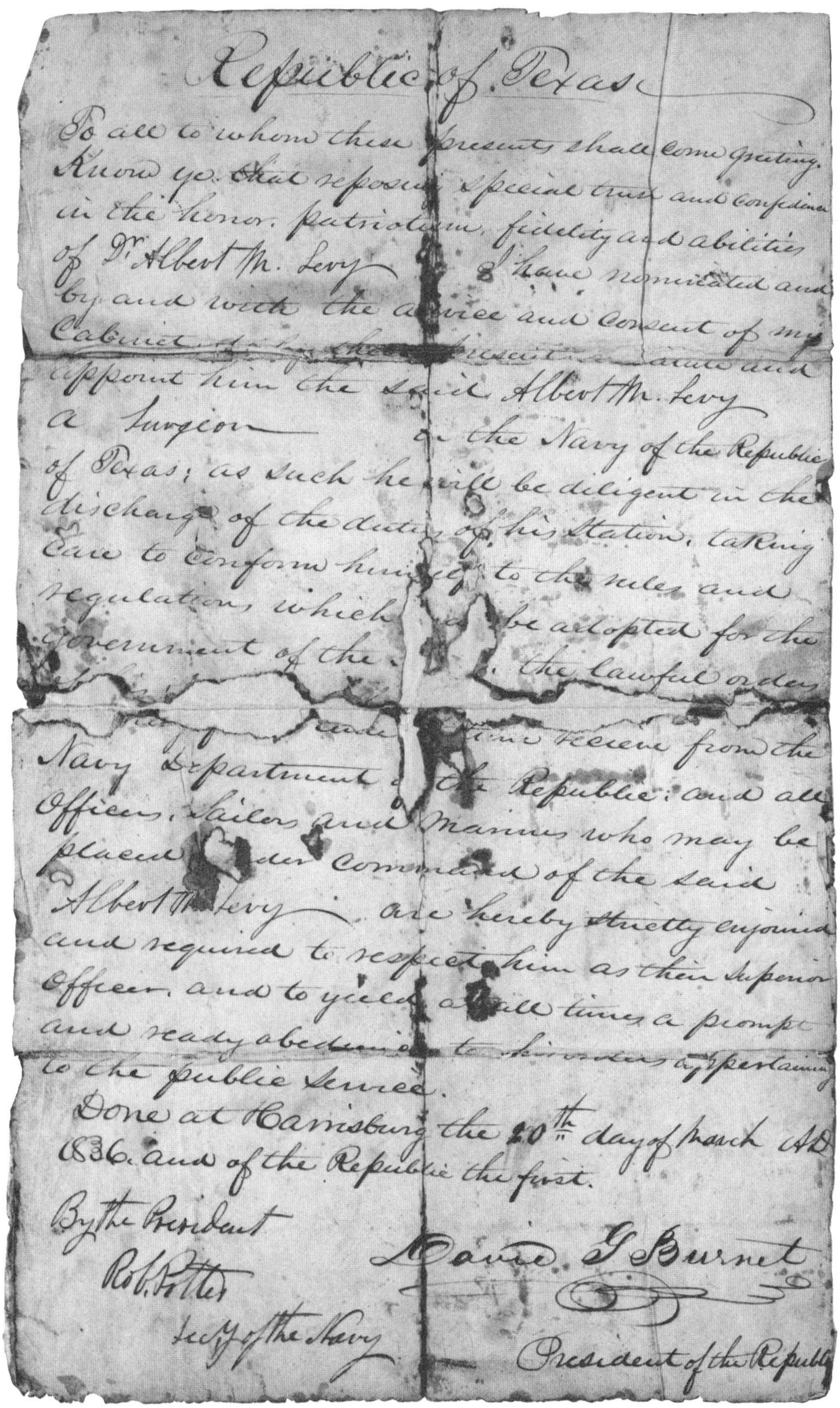
Republic of Texas
To all to whom these presents shall come greeting.
Know ye: that reposing special trust and confidence
in the honor, patriotism, fidelity and abilities
of Dr. Albert M. Levy I have nominated and
by and with the advice and consent of my
Cabinet [illegible] the present [illegible] and
appoint him the said Albert M. Levy
a Surgeon in the Navy of the Republic
of Texas; as such he will be diligent in the
discharge of the duties of his station, taking
care to conform himself to the rules and
regulations which may be adopted for the
Government of the [illegible] the lawful orders
[illegible] receive from the
Navy Department of the Republic: and all
Officers, Sailors and Marines who may be
placed under command of the said
Albert M. Levy are hereby strictly enjoined
and required to respect him as their superior
Officer, and to yield at all times a prompt
and ready obedience to his orders appertaining
to the public service.
Done at Harrisburg the 20th day of March AD
1836. and of the Republic the first.
By the President
Robt. Potter
Secy of the Navy
David G. Burnet
President of the Republic

Republic of Texas certificate signed by David G. Burnet, President, appointing Dr. Albert M. Levy "a Surgeon in the Navy of the Republic of Texas" on March 20, 1836.

The Brutus, *war vessel of the Texas Navy.*

Art copyright © by Port of Galveston

The letter about Dr. Levy to General Houston was written from Harrisburg, Texas, a town (near Houston on Buffalo Bayou) serving as the temporary capital. On the night of April 13, 1836, General Houston sent a confidential order to Captain Kokernot to go ahead of the army on a special mission to the town of Harrisburg, with dispatches for David G. Burnet, *ad interim* president of the Republic of Texas.[80]

General Santa Anna and about 700 to 800 men were riding hard to capture the *ad interim* government. On the night of April 15 they arrived at Harrisburg, only to discover their prey had escaped, likely due to Kokernot's warning which sent the Texans galloping off toward the Gulf coast. When Santa Anna found the president gone, he became enraged and set fire to the town and sent fifty dragoons in pursuit of the Texas government.

Because of Kokernot's warning, the president had a narrow escape. Kokernot's message was important because the safety of the entire cabinet was at stake. Besides the president, the fugitive government being driven into Galveston Bay by Santa Anna included Vice President Lorenzo de Zavala as well as the secretary of state, the attorney general, the secretary of the navy, their families, and hundreds of refugees. The well equipped Mexican army was only a few yards away, when a schooner, the *Flash,* came to the rescue, with the Texan officials barely making their escape to Galveston Island nearby.[81]

The president felt the government had a dimension of safety in Galveston because of the Texas Navy, which controlled the waters off the Texas coast. Besides patrolling the coast, the Texas Navy provided infinite service to the army in preventing the enemy from receiving supplies and ammunition.

From the Brazos River, the Texan army now journeyed east to Buffalo Bayou, north of Galveston. The five-week retreat now became an advance. The stage was set.

Commission of Leon Dyer as major in Texas Army signed by David G. Burnet and General Tom Green, May 18, 1836. *Courtesy Rosenberg Library.*

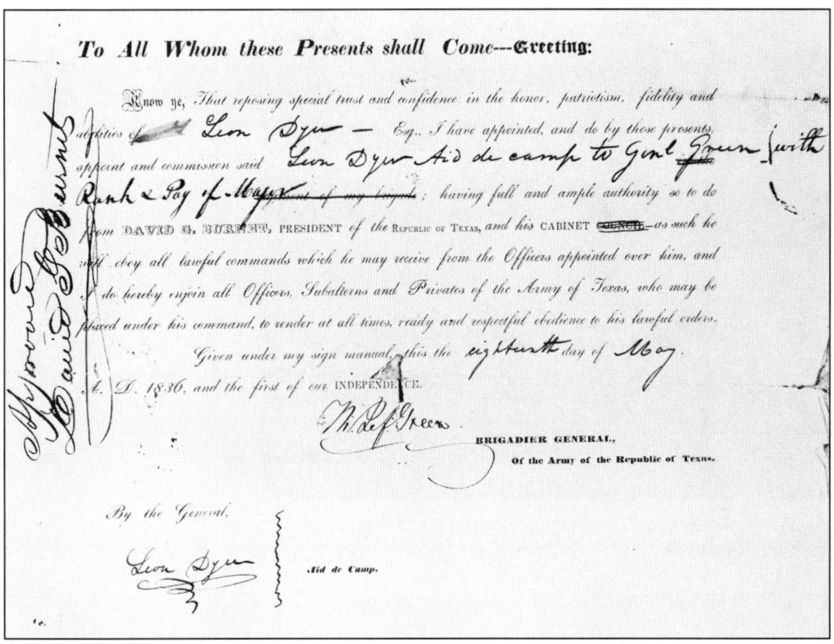

To All Whom these Presents shall Come---Greeting:

Know ye, That reposing special trust and confidence in the honor, patriotism, fidelity and abilities of Leon Dyer — Esq., I have appointed, and do by these presents, appoint and commission said Leon Dyer Aid de camp to Genl Green with Rank & Pay of Major ~~appointment of my brigade~~; having full and ample authority so to do from DAVID G. BURNET, PRESIDENT of the REPUBLIC OF TEXAS, and his CABINET ~~COUNCIL~~ as such he will obey all lawful commands which he may receive from the Officers appointed over him, and I do hereby enjoin all Officers, Subalterns and Privates of the Army of Texas, who may be placed under his command, to render at all times, ready and respectful obedience to his lawful orders.

Given under my sign manual, this the eighteenth day of May A. D. 1836, and the first of our INDEPENDENCE.

Th. Jef. Green
BRIGADIER GENERAL,
Of the Army of the Republic of Texas.

By the General,
Leon Dyer
Aid de Camp.

Approved David G. Burnet

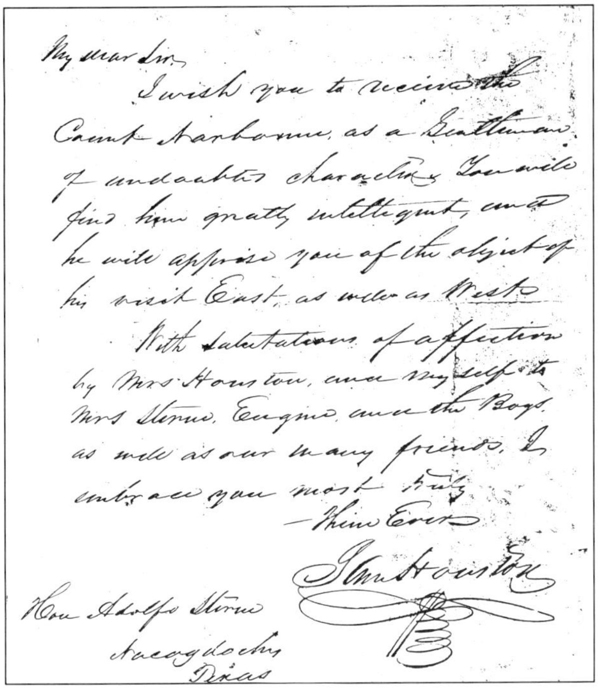

An 1842 letter with Sam Houston's distinctive signature, addressed to Sterne.

City of Houston
19th Mar 1842

My dear Sir,

I wish you to receive the Count Narbonne, as a Gentlemen of undoubted character. You will find him greatly intelligent, and he will apprise you of the object of his visit East as well as West.

With salutations of affection by Mrs. Houston, and myself to Mrs. Sterne, Eugenia, and the Boys, as well as our many friends. I embrace you most truly.

Thine ever,
Sam Houston

Hon. Adolfo Sterne
Nacogdoches
Texas

THE BATTLE OF SAN JACINTO

On April 20 the Texans reached the San Jacinto River. Santa Anna had preceded the Texans there, confident of victory. At the battleground, the Mexican infantry began an advance from the Southwest but was soon stopped.

A cavalry troop of eighty-five Texans sprang onto their saddles on a reconnaissance of the enemy position. The Texans succeeded in withdrawing with only two men wounded, some of the men riding double because their horses had been shot from under them.

The next day, April 21, a Thursday, 783 (Houston's count) Texans faced the best troops of Mexico, numbering about 1,500.The Jewish volunteers included Albert Emanuel (1808-1851) of Nacogdoches, who had volunteered in 1835, being a friend of General Thomas Jefferson Rusk of Nacogdoches and General Sam Houston.[82]

Texan scouts spotted a column of reinforcements headed across the prairie from Vince's Bridge toward the Mexican camp. Houston learned that Santa Anna had gone by the San Jacinto River, crossing by a bridge over Vince's Bayou, and would have to cross the same bridge to return. Houston sent Erastus "Deaf" Smith and a part of scouts to destroy the bridge. One of the several men Smith included in this mission was a soldier named Kohn.[83] This daring exploit successfully occurred almost in the presence of the foe. The wall of fire and the destruction of the bridge cut off the enemy's (and the Texans') only available avenue of escape and also prevented the advancement of new reinforcements.

The Texans now decided to attack Santa Anna in his entrenchments. Sam Houston strategically selected siesta time to begin the assault. The shout "Alamo!" and "Goliad!" rang along the entire line, as 800 Texans pushed forward. The army of the young Republic of Texas had received from citizens of Cincinnati, Ohio, two pieces of artillery, "The Twin Sisters," which belched forth a deadly rain of grape shot, canister, nails, and broken horseshoes. In eighteen minutes Santa Anna's legions were in retreat. Finding the bridge destroyed by Kohn and other Texans, a few Mexican soldiers plunged into the bayou like the Egyptians drowning in the Red Sea during the Exodus.

Seven hundred dead Mexicans atoned that day for the butchery of the Alamo and Goliad, and as many prisoners were in the hands of the victorious Texas army. Santa Anna tried to escape, but was discovered hiding.

General Santa Anna was taken to the quarters of General Houston. Said General Santa Anna, "You have conquered the Napoleon of the West."

The Texas soldiers requested Santa Anna be executed in revenge, but Sam Houston spared his life, recognizing his value in peace negotiations. A storm of popular indignation followed, and President Burnet ordered Santa Anna detained indefinitely as a prisoner of war. Santa Anna was at the lowest ebb of his popularity in Mexico, not only because he was a loser at last, but because his countrymen were feeling revulsion at his murders in a dozen cities in Mexico during his ascendency to power there, as well as his brutal orders for the massacre at Goliad.

He talked the Texans into sending him to Washington, D.C. Ostensibly, he was to visit President

Andrew Jackson to tell him that Mexico would make no further attempt to conquer Texas and had no objection to its independence. On November 25, 1836, seven months after his capture, Santa Anna, master negotiator, went to Washington, D.C., escorted by Major Leon Dyer of a pioneer Jewish family, as well as several other Texans appointed to the official escort.[84]

BATTLES AFTER 1836

The newly appointed Texas Minister to the United States, William H. Wharton, had left Texas for Washington two days before Santa Anna departed for Washington and spent months lobbying for a U.S. diplomatic agent to Texas. This was granted and Wharton headed back to Texas in 1837, boarding the ship on which Dr. Albert Moses Levy served in the Texas Navy. Dr. Levy had just transferred from the *Brutus* to the *Independence* early in 1837.

On April 17 the ship was met about thirty miles from Velasco by two Mexican brigs-of-war. After a severe fight the Mexicans overpowered the *Independence* and forced it into the Mexican port of Brazos Santiago. All passengers and crew were then transferred to Matamoros and confined. Only a year after surviving the violent storming of Bexar, Dr. Levy found himself in a Mexican prison.

How did they get out? First, the Minister to Washington's brother, Colonel John H. Wharton, tried to get his brother out of the prison. He obtained permission and a flag and proceeded with thirty Mexican prisoners to make an exchange. On landing in Matamoros, however, he also was made a prisoner and confined in a dungeon. After an imprisonment of six days, he made his escape and returned to Texas.

Levy and the minister were left to their own ingenuity. They remained in prison three months. Since help from the outside was unsuccessful, they looked to help from the inside. Thomas M. Thompson of English descent, who guarded them, had been in Mexican service many years and was a captain in the Mexican navy. The Texans won him over, and he aided their escape. After escaping prison in Mexico Dr. Levy swam the Rio Grande and traveled overland in Texas.[85]

After Levy left the *Brutus,* Captain Levi Charles Harby, age 44, became Commander of the *Brutus* in August of 1837. Born in South Carolina to a prominent Jewish family, he was uncle of Julian Harby. Levi was a professional naval officer. When the Mexican ship *Iturbide* attacked the Texas Navy's *Invincible*, Harby hastened to her aid. The *Brutus*, sole remaining effective Texas cruiser, was rendered helpless by loss of the rudder, and a few weeks later, in October of 1837, a terrific storm pounded her to pieces.[86]

Texas' military problems were not over following San Jacinto. Adolphus Sterne furnishes in his diary first-

In 1837 Dr. Levy served the Republic on the Independence, *was captured and imprisoned in Matamoros, finally escaping and swimming the Rio Grande to safety.*

Art copyright © by Port of Galveston.

hand accounts of the continuing struggle that lived on as a part of Texas life.[87] Six years following victory at San Jacinto, Sterne wrote:

"Saturday March 19 [1842] Finished planting corn today. Mr. Blake brought intelligence . . . that the Mexicans have taken San Antonio and Goliad, that 3000 men (Texians) are now in the field — 1200 were at Seguin (between Bexar and Austin) . . . with 350 was to join them on the 10th inst. and leave the Capital protected . . . Austin seems to be in danger of being attacked by the Mexicans, or Indians — Splendid Capital.

"Sunday the 20th . . . D. S. Kaufman arrived late this Evening, he reports that the Mexicans have evacuated San Antonio and that — that devoted City is again in possession of the Texians . . . Hurrah!

"Monday March the 21st 1842 . . . The war party from San Augustin have returned home. . . . Today we are without sugar, flour and nearly out of coffee, and no monay [*sic*] to purchase those articles. . . . If I had the money I expended in 1835 to recruit troops in New Orleans to bring me and my Family to the glorious state of Liberty? in which we are now, I would at least keep a *little* to purchase the necessaries of life."

In the Cherokee War — the only issue upon which he and Sam Houston disagreed — Sterne commanded a company of militia in the Battle of the Neches July 16, 1839.

AFTER THE BATTLES

Sterne remained active in the political life of Nacogdoches and Texas through the years of the Republic and during Texas' early years of statehood. He served as postmaster of Nacogdoches. His elected posts included deputy clerk and later associate justice of the county court (1841); justice of the peace; deputy clerk of the Board of Land Commissioners and Commissioner of Roads and Revenues; he served on a local board of health, and was an overseer of streets and roads in the Corporation of Nacogdoches. In 1844 Sam Houston wrote to Sterne and addressed him "Judge Sterne."[88]

In 1847 he was elected to represent Nacogdoches in the House of Representatives of the Second Legislature of the State of Texas, returned to the House of the Third Legislature in 1849 and advanced to the Senate for the Fourth Legislature in 1851.

Sterne became the first Mason in Texas, serving as Deputy Grand Master of the Grand Lodge of Texas (Scottish Rite and York bodies).[89] In his diary he mentioned the pleasure of attending balls and dances frequently. He became a substantial land owner, and estimates based on the Census of 1840 indicate that he owned or controlled at one time approximately 16,000 acres of Texas land. Sterne died in New Orleans March 27, 1852, and was re-buried in Oak Grove Cemetery in Nacogdoches.[90]

David Levi Kokernot left his mark on Texas through his name: Kokernot, Texas; Kokernot Ranch; Kokernot Spring, and Kokernot Spring State Park near Alpine, Texas.[91] After the battles for Texas independence, he went back to sea again, for three months, aboard the privateer schooner *Terrible*.[92] He engaged in farming and began his family's large cattle ranches in the Big Bend country of Texas. He and his French wife from Louisiana eventually had six daughters and two sons. Both sons became prominent stock raisers.[93] Pioneer David Levi Kokernot died December 10, 1892, in Gonzales County, Texas. Years later, his descendants held vast ranches near Alpine, Texas. By the 1980s, the Kokernot 0-6 Ranch had grown to approximately 60,000 acres.[94] None of the descendants is Jewish.[95]

Dr. Levy was cited for taking part in battles on both land and sea on two ships of the Texas navy and for taking care of the medical needs of the Texans during the Republic years. After his narrow escape from prison in the summer of 1837, he settled in Matagorda, Texas, and

Sword of Dr. A. M. Levy.

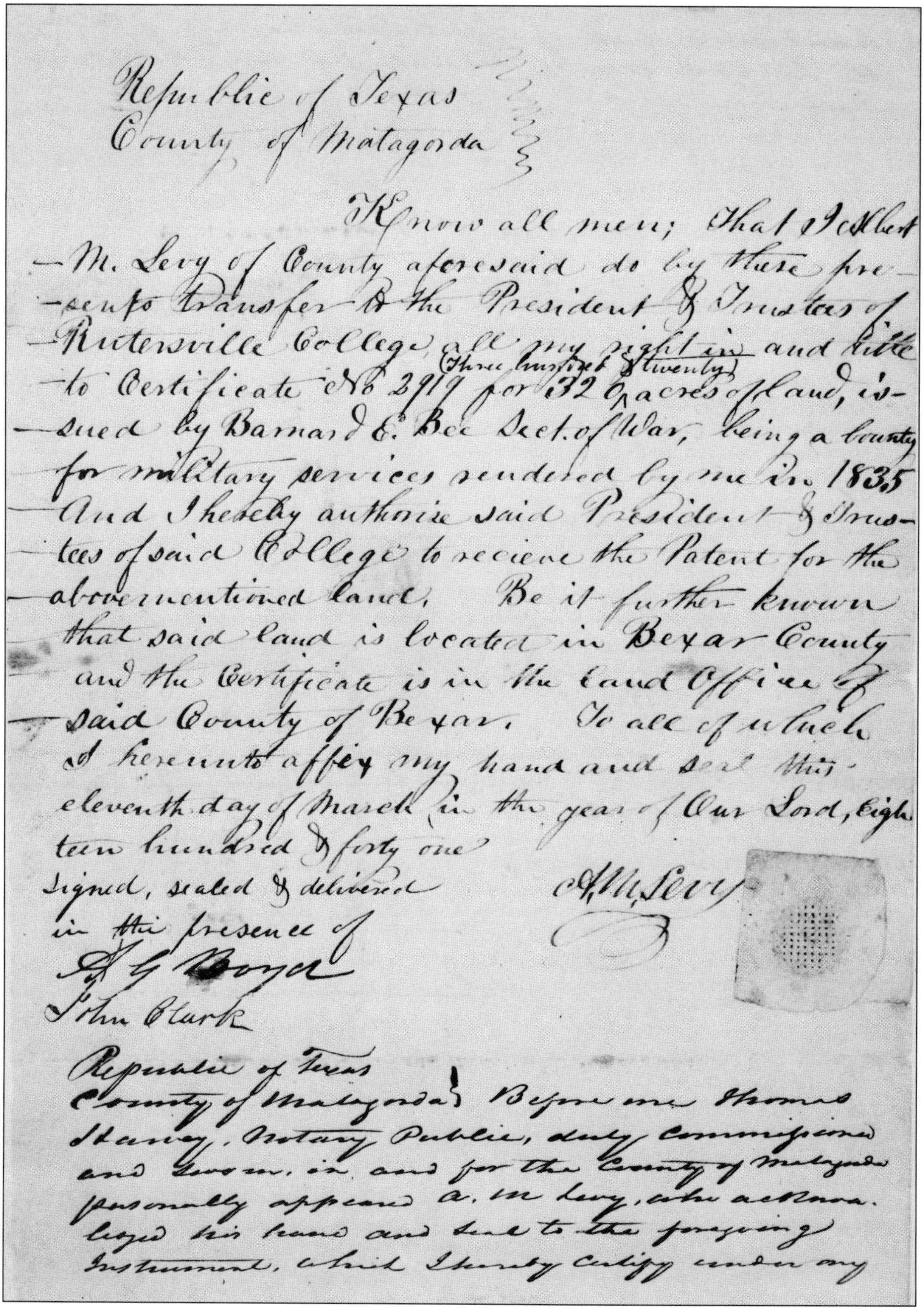

Republic of Texas
County of Matagorda

Know all men; That I Albert M. Levy of County aforesaid do by these presents transfer to the President & Trustees of Rutersville College, all my right in and title to Certificate No 2919 for 320 (Three hundred & twenty) acres of land, issued by Barnard E. Bee Secty. of War, being a bounty for military services rendered by me in 1835 And I hereby authorise said President & Trustees of said College to recieve the Patent for the abovementioned land. Be it further known that said land is located in Bexar County and the Certificate is in the Land Office of said County of Bexar. To all of which I hereunto affix my hand and seal this eleventh day of March in the year of Our Lord, Eighteen hundred & forty one

Signed, sealed & delivered in the presence of

A. G. Boyce
John Clark

A. M. Levy

Republic of Texas
County of Matagorda } Before me Thomas Harvey, Notary Public, duly Commissioned and sworn, in and for the County of Matagorda personally appeared A. M. Levy, who acknowledged his hand and seal to the foregoing Instrument, which I hereby certify under my

Historic marker at gravesite of Dr. A.M.Levy.

Courtesy Jessie Levy Foss.

served on a prestigious medical board.[96] His medical career is highlighted in chapter 13.

During the hostilities with Mexico after the official end of the war, he again enlisted in 1842. Although no history book mentions him, Dr. Levy served with much distinction and over a longer period of time than virtually any other Texan in the battles for Texas independence. He served seven years.[97]

An 1841 Texas land grant indicates Dr. A. M. Levy transferred to "the President & Trustees of Rutersville College" 320 acres. This college became Southwestern University at Georgetown, Texas. Levy's gift is likely the first major endowment by an individual to a Texas university.

Although he survived many battles and imprisonment, his life ended by suicide on May 23, 1848. The seeds of this tragedy had their roots in his first marriage in Richmond, Virginia, and the death of his wife when their daughter Rachel was only five or six months old. After his wife died, he had left to join his older brother Lewis A. Levy, then living in New Orleans, and while there, Albert Moses had joined the Greys and had come with them to Texas. Lewis also moved to Texas a few years later. He is profiled in the chapter on the merchant princes.

According to Dr. Levy's great-granddaughter, Jessie Levy Foss of Lafayette, La., when Albert Moses left Richmond, it created a break in his relationship with his family, particularly his father, Abraham Levy. Mrs. Foss said that his mother and sisters did try to maintain a relationship and gave him a sword that bore the inscription, "Presented to A.M. Levy by His Mother and Sisters. Richmond, Va., 1836."[98] Albert Moses's further break with his family came when he married out of the faith. His second wife belonged to the first Episcopal church in Texas, and although he never joined that denomination, they reared their five children as Episcopalians. After his second marriage he wrote pleading letters to his family begging them to correspond, to give him news of his daughter Rachel.[99] According to Mrs. Foss and Rosanne Leeson, another descendant, the family's refusal to communicate with him about Rachel triggered a depression that brought on his suicide.

Detail of sword engraved "Presented to A. M. Levy by His Mother and Sisters, Richmond, Va., 1836."

Photo copyright © by Natalie Ornish.

It is a sin to commit suicide under Jewish teachings, which declare that a person who commits suicide should not be commemorated with a eulogy service at burial. Consequently, the traditional Hebrew prayers of Kaddish never were recited at his funeral. He had no burial service of any kind, according to records in the Christ Episcopal Church in Matagorda of May 23, 1848. One hundred and thirty-six years later, in May of 1984, Mrs. Foss, a Catholic, arranged for a rabbi[100] to say kaddish in his memory, at Friday evening services near the anniversary of Dr. Levy's death.

On Sunday May 4, 1986, a Texas Historical Grave Marker was dedicated to Dr. Albert Moses Levy in the historic Matagorda Cemetery. Descendants from Louisiana, California, Chicago, and Florida attended, along with members of the Dr. Albert Moses Levy Post of the Jewish War Veterans of Houston.[101]

What happened to Edward Isaac Johnson?

Edward Isaac Johnson (see Appendix C), killed at the Goliad massacre, shared the fate of more than 300 young men: the partially charred remains of the executed men lay exposed to the elements for two months. On June 3 General Thomas Jefferson Rusk, secretary of war, passing through Goliad, buried them in a common grave just outside the walls of the presidio. In 1852 the burial site was marked, and in

Facing page:
Dr. A.M. Levy made the first major donation from the private sector to a university in Texas in 1841, 320 acres of land awarded him for military service, to Rutersville College, the first permanent institution of higher education in Texas. This document shows his signature.

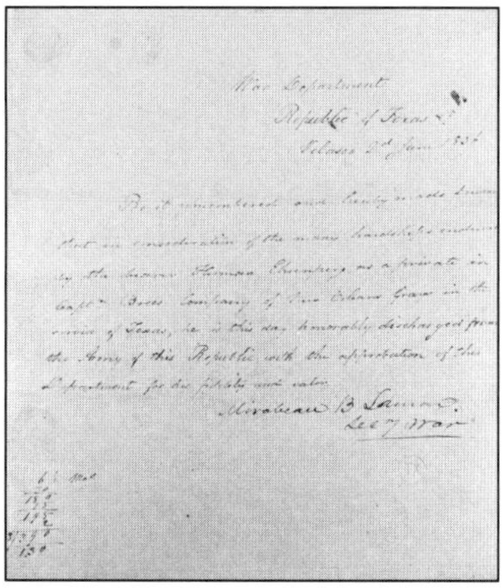

Document states:

War Department,
Republic of Texas, Velasco, 2d June 1836.
Be it remembered and hereby made known, that in consideration of the many hardships endured by the bearer Herman Ehrenberg as a private in Captn. Brees' Company of New Orleans Grays in the service of Texas, he is this day honorably discharged from the Army of this Republic with the approbation of this Department for his fidelity and valor

Mirabeau B. Lamar, Sec. of War.

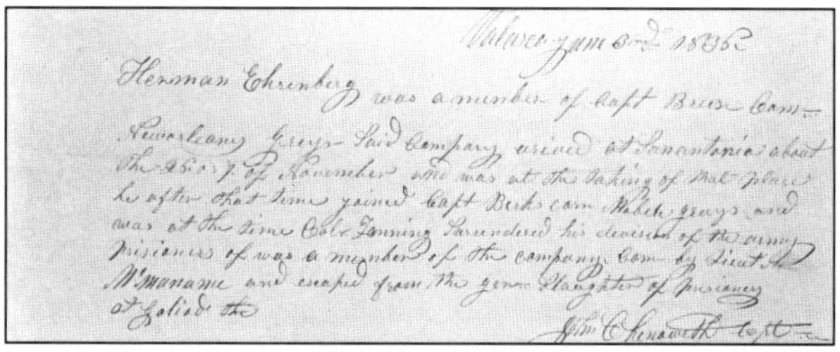

Document states:

Velasco, June 3rd, 1836. Herman Ehrenberg was a member of Capt. Breese Com., New Orleans Greys — Said company arrrived at San Antonio about the 26 or 7 of November and was at the taking of that place. He after that time joined Capt. Berks com. Mobile Grays and was at the time Col. Fanning surrendered his division of the army prisoners of war a member of the company com. by Lieut. M. and escaped from the slaughter of prisoners at Goliad.

John Chenoweth, Capt.

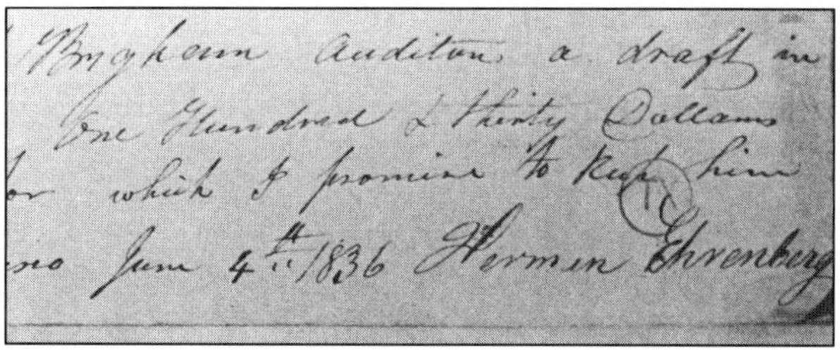

Brigham Auditor a draft in
One Hundred & thirty Dollars
or which I promise to keep him
June 4th 1836 Hermen Ehrenberg

Receipt with Ehrenberg's signature.

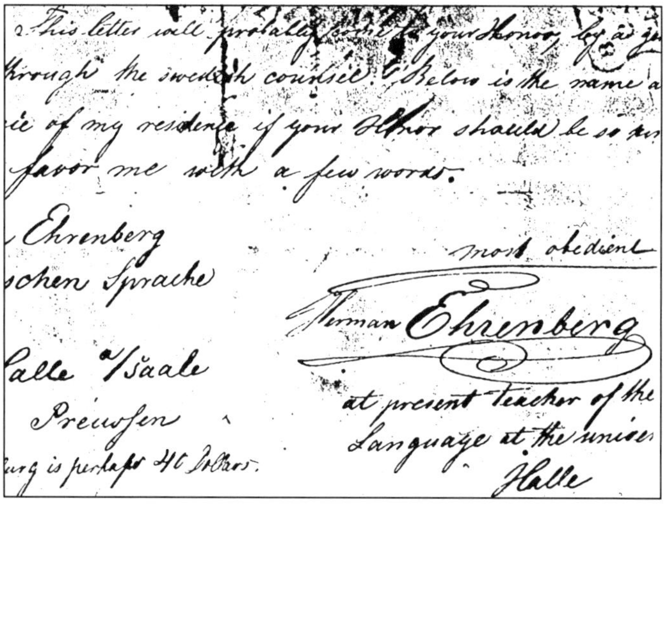

2 This letter will probably come to your Honor by a
through the swedish counsil. Below is the name a
of my residence if your Honor should be so
favor me with a few words.
Ehrenberg
schen Sprache
Halle a/Saale
Preussen
urg is perhaps 40 Dollars.
most obedient
Herman Ehrenberg
at present teacher of the
Language at the univer
Halle

Signature of Ehrenberg on a letter to Ashbel Smith, requesting that Smith loan him forty dollars to return to Texas.

1939 a memorial shaft was erected there.

The promise of free land to veterans had lured Johnson to Texas. The promise was kept, and the Johnson family received land in Erath County fifty miles southwest of Fort Worth on which it paid taxes but never saw. The land was sold in 1924.

Mordecai, who also fought at Goliad, fared better as one of three Jewish survivors, but shortly after that his luck ran out at the Battle of Plum Creek or Plum Creek Fight against the Comanches on August 9, 1840.[102] Although some historical reports of this battle give vivid accounts of the onslaught of the Indians on the colonists, in truth the colonists provoked the Indians into this retaliatory battle. In 1840, after more than a year of Indian raids and white counter attacks, President Mirabeau B. Lamar asked General Hugh McLeod to call a council of Indian chiefs in San Antonio.

Sixty-five Comanches traveled to San Antonio for the meeting on March 19, 1840. They had agreed to bring all their white captives, but when they arrived with only one, the angry Texans told them they would be held as hostages until the prisoners were brought in. A fight broke out and thirty-five Indians, including a woman and several children, were killed.

To retaliate, more than 1,000 warriors swept south down through the Guadalupe valley from the Hill Country to the Gulf Coast.[103] For eight days the Indians rampaged through Victoria, then to Linnville, where they broke into warehouses of merchandise and stole over 2,000 horses and mules. They spent the day in Linnville adorning themselves and their horses with colorful ribbons and decorative garments, then burned the town and rode back toward their home in the hills.

In the skirmishes with the Comanches up to Plum Creek, the Indians had killed twenty persons, among them Mr. Mordecai of Victoria, who had joined a group led by Capt. John J. Tumlinson.[104] By the time the Comanches reached Plum Creek, approximately 200 Texans gathered to fight the Indians. Approximately eighty-seven Indians died, as did their captive, Mrs. Crosby, granddaughter of Daniel Boone, and her infant daughter.

Herman Ehrenberg, who miraculously escaped the massacre at Goliad, wandered around South Texas, having several narrow escapes from Mexican scouts. Cold and hungry, he failed in a daring effort to steal a few coals from a Mexican campfire. Convinced he could not survive and make his way back to Houston's army without food, Ehrenberg decided to go boldly into a Mexican camp and pose as an American traveler who had lost his way. He told a long and ingenious tale to explain how he happened to be wandering about the prairie alone.

Ehrenberg remained with the Mexicans a whole month, until news came of Santa Anna's defeat and capture at San Jacinto on April 21. One night Ehrenberg and a Texan prisoner escaped and pushed on to Matagorda, occupied by Texan troops. On June 2, 1836, two months after escaping Goliad, Ehrenberg received an honorable discharge from the army of the Republic from Mirabeau B. Lamar, secretary of war, "with the approbation of this Department for fidelity and valor." For his service he was given a draft on the empty treasury for $130.[105]

He returned to Germany, studied mining at Freiburg University, and wrote a book giving a firsthand account of the Texas Revolution. In 1843 his memoirs were published in German; in 1925 Edgar William Bartholomae translated the 1845 (third) edition into English, and in 1935 Henry Smith edited a condensed edition for children.[106] Herman ended his book with a stirring description of the great future awaiting Texas, and in 1844 he wrote Ashbel Smith, *Charge d'Affaires*, Republic of Texas, who was then in Paris, requesting Smith loan him funds to return to Texas.[107] Likely someone else sponsored his trip, because when he returned to the U.S. in 1844, he joined the Fremont Expedition in California.

He helped rescue Americans held captive in lower California during the Mexican War. In April 1845 he sailed for the Hawaiian Islands, where the government employed him to survey the streets of Honolulu and draw the first map of the town. After the Mexican War he went to Sonora in Arizona, where he created the area's first reliable map and became a successful consultant and mining engineer. Herman was considered one of the greatest surveyors and map makers ever to visit Western United States.[108] The U.S. Board of Geographic Names honored him with "Ehrenberg Peak" in the Grand Canyon National Park.[109]

In 1854 Ehrenberg compiled a manuscript "Map of the Gadsden Purchase, Sonora, and portions of New Mexico, Chihuahua & California." He was responsible for the founding of the town of Yuma, Arizona. He never married. Ehrenberg died October 9, 1866, when murdered and robbed while asleep in a stage station at Dos Palmas, on California's Colorado desert, near present-day Palm Springs.[110]

In 1869, the town of Mineral City, Arizona, on the Arizona-California border, got a new name. "We learn today that the people of La Paz, Yuma county, have changed the name of their new location, Mineral City, to 'Ehrenberg,' in honor of the able mineralologist, daring pioneer and noble patriot of that name," wrote the *Weekly Arizona Miner,* August 14, 1869. Michel Goldwater, former Senator Barry Goldwater's grandfather, led the way to rename the town "Ehrenberg" in honor of his good friend Herman.[111]

Senator Goldwater said that his uncle Morris Goldwater always referred to Herman Ehrenberg as Jewish. "There has never been any question in my mind but what Ehrenberg was a Jew," he wrote.[112] "Herman Ehrenberg and my grandfather were the very best of friends. My grandfather and my uncle were the first to see the body of Herman Ehrenberg as he lay murdered in a small California stage station."[113]

"Personally I am inclined to believe he was a Jew," wrote Carlos E. Castañeda of the University of Texas department of history, in 1955.[114]

For Texans, Ehrenberg's greatest legacy is his account of the Goliad massacre, considered the best account ever written about any facet of the war for Texas' independence.

Second edition of Ehrenberg's book on his capture at Goliad in 1836, published in 1844.

Natalie Ornish Collection.

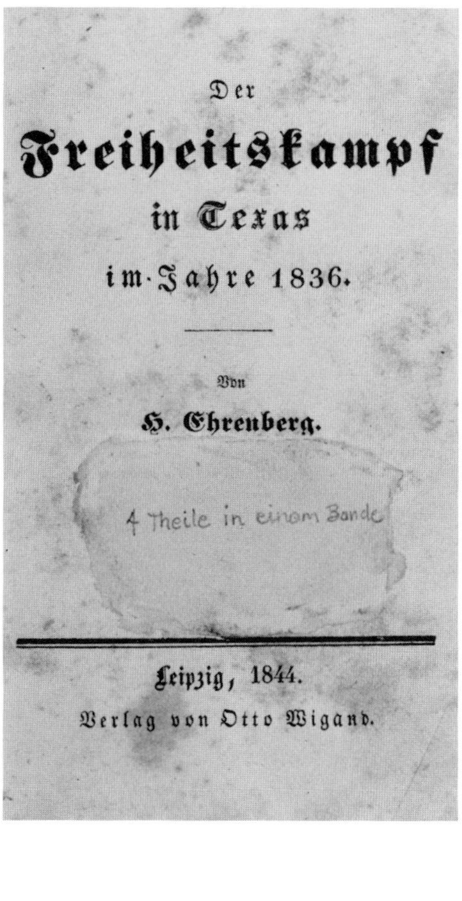
Der

Freiheitskampf

in Texas

im Jahre 1836.

Von

H. Ehrenberg.

4 Theile in einem Bande

Leipzig, 1844.

Verlag von Otto Wigand.

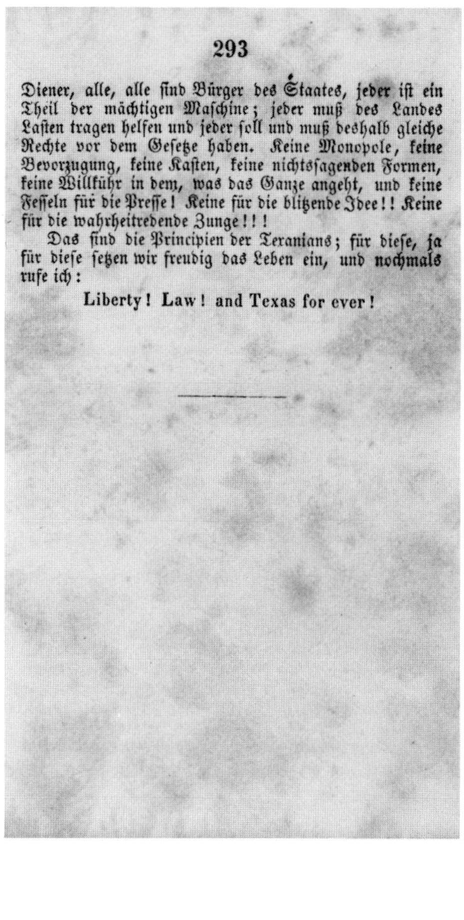
293

Diener, alle, alle sind Bürger des Staates, jeder ist ein Theil der mächtigen Maschine; jeder muß des Landes Lasten tragen helfen und jeder soll und muß deshalb gleiche Rechte vor dem Gesetze haben. Keine Monopole, keine Bevorzugung, keine Kasten, keine nichtssagenden Formen, keine Willkühr in dem, was das Ganze angeht, und keine Fesseln für die Presse! Keine für die blitzende Idee!! Keine für die wahrheitredende Zunge!!!

Das sind die Principien der Texanians; für diese, ja für diese setzen wir freudig das Leben ein, und nochmals rufe ich:

Liberty! Law! and Texas for ever!

In the 1500s, Jean de Castro, Viceroy of the Indies, founded cities for the glory of the Kings of Portugal. In the 19th Century, H. Castro, descendant in a direct line of the same Jean De Castro, founded cities in Texas for the glory of liberty. By strange coincidence, would one not be inclined to think that God's designs are revealed to certain families and become their heritage in the same manner as the heritage of nobility or of fortune.

Le Texas,
Henri Castro

Chapter 3

The Colonizers

Opening Texas' Lands West

Henri Castro of Paris, France, and Jacob De Cordova of Kingston, Jamaica — Texas empresarios of great importance — carried on colonizing in the manner of Stephen F. Austin following Austin's death in 1836.

Castro and De Cordova both were descended from great explorers of the sixteenth century. Joao De Castro (1500-1548), called *Castro Forte*, was viceroy of the Portuguese Indies and navigator in charge of a fleet of six ships. Francisco Fernandez De Cordova, a Spaniard, discovered the Yucatan on the Mexican coast in 1517.[1]

HENRI CASTRO
(1786-1865)

Henri Castro, a direct descendant of Portuguese royalty, was the person single handedly responsible for first civilizing the Texas land west of San Antonio, pushing the Texas frontier westward toward the Rio Grande.

Sam Houston appointed him "Consul General of the Republic of Texas for the Kingdom of France." Castro then wrote in French *Le Texas*, a booklet to lure French farmers to Texas[2]. In all, more than two thousand men and women heeded his call.[3] They came in twenty-seven ships from France to Galveston between 1842 and 1847.[4] They named their new Texas town Castroville.

Henri Castro, of Portuguese Jewish descent, was born in France in July 1786, three years before the French Revolution. His family, prominent and wealthy, was descended from one of the oldest Portuguese families, the Marrano clan of De Castro.

In 1804 Napoleon crowned himself emperor of the French, and the next year the provincial government chose Henri to welcome Emperor Napoleon when he visited Castro's region. Napoleon was impressed with the young man of nineteen, and a year later selected Castro to become one of his honor guards and accompany him on a visit to Spain.

Castro stands in sharp contrast to the Eastern European immigrants who left Europe to escape anti-Semitism in the late 1800s and early 1900s, with a bundle of clothes as their sole possession. In 1813 Castro had married Amelia Mathias, who brought to their marriage a dowry of fifty thousand francs comprised primarily of household goods.

Le Texas.
Apperçu
Historique & Statistique.

Julia Nott Waugh in her definitive work on Castro writes that this marriage seemed to define in a vague manner the remainder of Castro's life, "For it established some sort of Italian relationship, as to the nature of which we are not very clear. The two boys, Lorenzo and Orlando, usually spoken of as their sons, we believe to have been foster children."[5] Somehow through this Italian connection, Castro was appointed in 1827 Consul for the Kingdom of Naples at Providence, Rhode Island, and to the New England village he and his family set sail. He became an American citizen within a year.

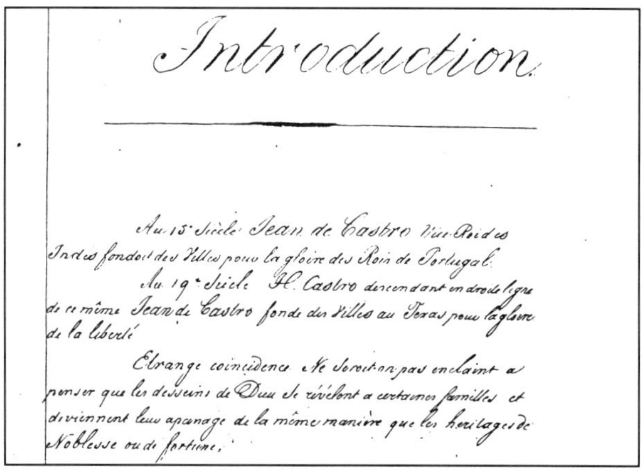
Introduction.

Au 15e Siècle Jean de Castro Vice-Roi des Indes fondoit des Villes pour la gloire des Rois de Portugal.

Au 19e Siècle H. Castro descendant en droite ligne de ce même Jean de Castro fonde des Villes au Texas pour la gloire de la liberté

Etrange coincidence Ne seroit-on pas enclaint a penser que les desseins de Dieu se révèlent a certaines familles et deviennent leur apanage de la même manière que les heritages de Noblesse ou de fortune.

For the next thirteen years, Castro tried to consummate commercial enterprises that swept from New York to Louisiana and also traveled often between America and France. He became a partner with M. Jacques Lafitte of Lafitte and Company of Paris, where he attempted to negotiate a seven million dollar loan for the Republic of Texas, then five years old.[6] During these negotiations, he traveled to Texas for the first time. He failed to secure the loan, but discovered personal opportunities available to him in the young Texas Republic.

On February 4, 1841, the Republic had passed a law that entitled the Texas President to write contracts for colonization of Texas land. Castro applied for such a contract and President Sam Houston granted it on February 15, 1842.[7] Castro was age fifty-five.

Castro was given a five year contract to settle a colony near San Antonio west of the Medina River.[8] In return, Castro was promised one-half of every parcel of land assigned to each member of the colony by the government. Land ownership offered the only form of financial profit he could expect to earn from his labors.

Sam Houston submitted to the Texas Senate in Austin on February 3, 1842, the nomination of Ashbel Smith as first charge´d' affaires for Texas to the Court of St. James in London and Henri Castro as consul general for Texas at Paris. The Senate unanimously confirmed these nominations.[9]

The secretary of state wrote to Castro, "The president of the Republic has been pleased in consideration of the services you have rendered to the cause of Texas as well as from your known zeal for her interests, and ability to protect and advance them, to appoint you Consul General of the Republic of Texas for the Kingdom of France."[10]

Both Smith and Castro were to assist other empresarios "to bring population and Money to Texas from the Storehouses of Europe."[11] Castro officially was empowered to solicit the French for suitable emigrants for his proposed colony.[12]

By May 15, 1842, Castro had set up an impressive office in Paris as headquarters for his emigration enterprise. "I was busily engaged in the execution of my contract by every means possible within my reach," he wrote President Houston.[13]

But, unfortunately, the timing was wrong. No sooner was the furniture moved into his office, than Mexico invaded Texas. "My early efforts were in some measure frustrated by rumors of the invasion . . which were wide and industriously circulated," he wrote from Paris. Later he wrote, "The war not only prevented the embarcation of emigrants from Europe, but also checked the settlement of the families previously introduced into the country, as well from the danger to be apprehended from the public enemy as from hostile bands of Indians."

Henri Castro as a young man.

Castro was hindered further by the French government, which was stepping up its campaign to encourage migration to its new colonies in Algeria. However, Castro continued to publish maps and books about Texas in French, German, and English. He traveled extensively. But he found few takers until he reached Alsace.

The Rhine Valley had always been a beautiful but troubled buffer between France and Germany. Wars have been waged over it. Castro found his people when he reached the valley checkered by tiny farms, populated by too many inhabitants. Victor Considerant, a French editor who also led a Texas colony, stated his thoughts in 1855 in a book called *European Colonization in Texas* that Castro quoted in his own book on Texas in 1855.[14] The French editor wrote: "Instead, then, of continuing to submit to silence, oppression, and crushing, in this antiquated Europe — inevitably doomed for a time to struggles between anarchy and despotism, to revolutions, to reactions, and to internal wars — it appeared to us certain that the best thing we could do . . . was to transport ourselves to America with our resources, our capital, our families, and our ideas, and by our example to show our brothers in Europe what can be accomplished under free and democratic institutions, by labor, by peace, and by the practice of sound economical and industrial principles. . . . We do not despair either of liberty or of the future of humanity. . . . But we comprehend the significance of that simple but sublime expression of Scripture, 'The field is the world.' We know that humanity is but one great family; we find our real country wherever we can most effectually serve the cause of universal good; and we recognize the fact that the American continent at this day is the land where every thing leads us to believe that the sovereign question of the destinies of collective humanity will obtain its solution."

Castro wrote, "This is an industrious population, among whom are found some of the best mechanics and agriculturists of France. For reasons unnecessary to state here, most of them are ready to emigrate." The way out for the hardy Alsatians was to pack up for Texas. To the immigrant, land was free — a full section, a square mile of 640 acres of territory for a man with a family — 320 acres for a bachelor colonist.[15]

Castro had very high standards which slowed the recruitment process considerably. He later wrote, "In selecting colonists I have uniformly required certain conditions. I have exacted first the necessary clothing, second, farming and instruments of labor, third, the means of paying their passage [which was $32] and fourth, means of subsistence during the first year."

On November 3, 1842, the first of twenty-seven ships he hired, the *Ebro*, left from Havre with 113 emigrants. The voyage lasted sixty-six days. Soon afterwards the *Lyons* left from Havre and the *Louis Phillippe* from Dunkirk. Aboard the *Louis Phillippe* was Abbe Menitrier, then priest at Versailles.

Six months later on May 4, 1843, the *Jeanette Marie* set sail for Texas with its human hopes high. On October 25 the *Jeane Key* left from Antwerp. These and Castro's other ships landed in Galveston. Colonists went overland to the Medina River.

Castro wrote to Sam Houston, "I continue my labors with the courageous perseverance belonging to my character and with incessant confidence in your Justice . . . identifying myself with the cause of Texas, and devoting to it my time, my fortune, and the future prospects of my family."[16]

Castro imported more than 2,000 persons to Texas, almost all from the Rhenish provinces, between 1842 and 1847.[17]

This empresario's greatest difficulty was not so much in procuring immigrants but in providing for them when they arrived in Galveston. Once they set foot on Texas soil, Castro had to have sheds built to house them until the journey to the interior could be made.

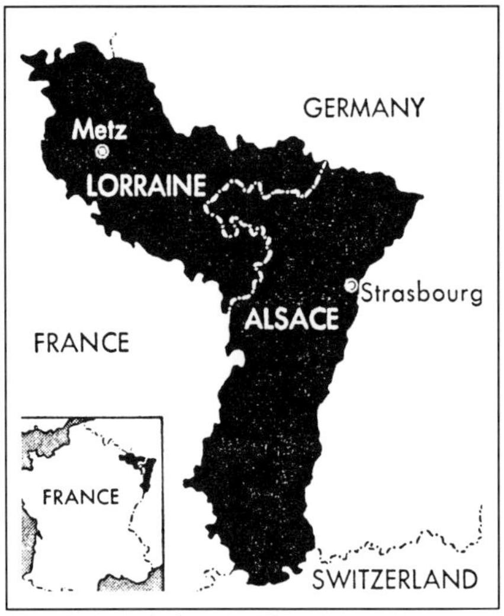

The regions of Alsace and Lorraine.

The Texas government advised the immigrants not to proceed west until a later time due to the threatening Indians. Although the first colonists were sent in November 1842, Castroville was not formally established until September 3, 1844. During these twenty-one months, Castro lost many colonists. Many did not wish to continue the arduous trip from the port city, Galveston, to San Antonio, and remained in Galveston or went to Houston. A few preferred the civilization of Mexico.

Ashbel Smith wrote at the time, "It appears to me that Mr. Castro's success in dispatching a respectable body of emigrants at this time when the idle threats of Mexico are so industriously circulated in Europe, is quite creditable to him. . . . So far as I am able to judge, Mr. Castro has labored to execute the terms of his contract with promptness, energy, and good faith."[18]

The Promised Land, their Utopia, did not materialize with their arrival in Texas. Castro's agents and Catholic Bishop Jean-Marie Odin were in Galveston to meet the ship and celebrate their safe arrival. However, the colonists did not realize that they must trek some 200 miles inland to their destination. After resting in Galveston a few weeks, the majority boarded another ship and sailed for Port Lavaca. Here they piled their equipment into ox carts, and the caravan of men, women, and children took the old Bexar trail. The chill of January and heavy rains plagued the pioneers as they slept outdoors. They trudged on to San Antonio, arriving in February, more than a year after the date of the signing of the contract.[19]

Not everyone was praising Castro, however. When Castro's colony was less than a year old, Sam Houston wrote a lengthy letter dated 21st July 1843 to Colonel Ashbel Smith, then in "London or Paris," repudiating Castro for his lack of an agent. "You may say to Mr. Castro that he has sent emigrants here without a guide, and he has no agent here. Do prevent his imposition upon the people of France, and you may assure him that my intention is to declare his contract forfeited, if he sends or attempts to send a family to Texas, until he has made some provisions and such as will insure their comforts on their arrival. It is calculated to injure the character of our country, and all this growing out of his cupidity, and baseness."[20]

Although some of the young men were affluent and even brought their tutors, many of the newcomers came ill prepared, despite Castro's desire for high standards, and others lost their household goods during the long trek from the Gulf to San Antonio. Castro paid the cost of this transportation, and when the town was finally formed, used his personal funds in Paris to supply food, medicine, and farm implements to the colonists. These expenditures eventually cost Castro his fortune.

By the spring of 1844, Castro concluded he must appear in Texas personally, put himself at the head of the 400 colonists, lead them into the wilderness, and help to make a thriving success out of his dream. In May he sailed to Galveston via Liverpool, Boston, and New Orleans.[21] He stopped at Washington-on-the-Brazos (the temporary capital) and met with Secretary of State Anson Jones, who received him cordially on his farm and assured him he had complied with the terms of his contract. Castro, while in Washington-on-the-Brazos, composed a lengthy letter to Sam Houston reviewing his accomplishments. He pointed out that not only had he fostered immigration, but also that his ships brought large amounts of cargo subject to tariff duties, thus enriching the Republic.

On August 25 Castro, a surveyor, seven of his men, and five rangers rode west from San Antonio to settle upon the site for a village.

"The first thing that I saw on my grant," he wrote, "was a bee tree full of honey."[22] He was pleased with the abundance of game and trout and the fertility and beauty of the country. It was not the arid waste which his enemies had tried to portray to potential settlers in France. In Texas, Prince Solms, his competitor, tried to lure to his colony Castro's settlers already in Texas. Castro tried harder. Now he promised his colonists "a home gratis . . . cows . . . rations until the first crop is gathered . . . salary for erecting buildings necessary for

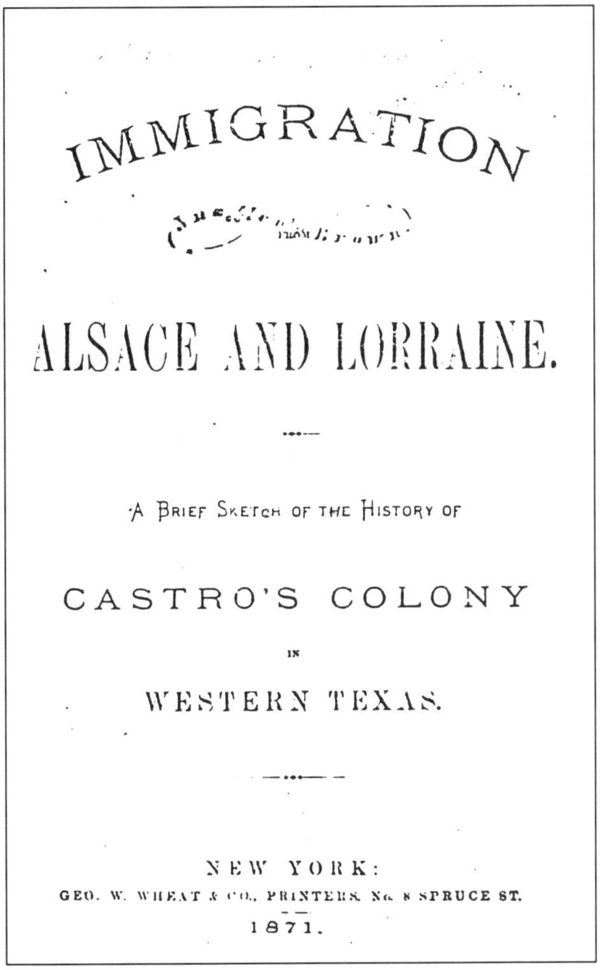
IMMIGRATION

[illegible]

ALSACE AND LORRAINE.

A BRIEF SKETCH OF THE HISTORY OF

CASTRO'S COLONY

IN

WESTERN TEXAS.

NEW YORK:
GEO. W. WHEAT & CO., PRINTERS, No. 8 SPRUCE ST.
1871.

the colony."[23] More expense was to come.

One of his wisest moves was the purchase of land adjacent to the running water of the river. When Castro arrived at his contracted land, he discovered that seventeen leagues of land lay between his grant and the Medina River. Castro wanted that waterway for his colony, so he purchased from an individual the land between the river and his contracted property.

After many delays, Castro formally inaugurated his colony on September 3, 1844. The town, twenty-five miles west of San Antonio on the west bank of the Medina River, was named Castroville by a unanimous vote of the colonists.

The river supplied the colonists with an abundance of fish. Wrote Castro in his diary, "My table placed under the leafy trees on the banks of the Medina. . . . I was able to offer to my guests, to the great astonishment of Monseigneur, vermicelli soup made with the bones of deer (nothing can be more delicate), fried trout, roasted turkey and partridges, filets of deer fricaseed. For dessert a cream made with eggs and milk produced in the colony, pecans gathered at the door of the dining-room, . . . and wild pomegranates. Red wines [are] made by a German of wild grapes. . . . At Paris one could find nothing more rare or more delicate, though he paid a great price. That is what is at the door of every colonist."[24]

Castro personally joined the other colonists in cultivating the land, growing vegetables in profusion. "It is quite certain that Castro had here the first experimental farm in Texas," wrote one biographer.[25]

The colonists' lots were either twenty- or forty-acre farms, which enabled them to settle together in towns and still have enough land to cultivate near their salt box homes. Location of lots for homes in the new Texas town were determined by a drawing to assure

Art by T. Gentilz, a resident of Castro's colony.

fairness. The drawing for the town lots was most important. The extensive but more distant land granted was not the big attraction to the colonists. More than ninety percent eventually sold their rights to large acreage to speculators for a mere trifle. Living on the frontier, they wanted to easily band together should they be attacked by Indians.[26]

Castro petitioned the "Texien government" for a detachment of the military at Castroville, "as it is now the extreme western frontier." The presence of the military, he said, "would produce an excellent impression in Europe, removing the fears of Indian excursions which have been suggested to emigrants by persons hostile to my undertaking."[27] The settling of this colony remained a bold venture, exposed as the location was to attack. Castro confronted dangers unknown to the first Texan colonists in 1821, for the Comanches now were accustomed to the use of firearms, and to the west the Mexicans were making inroads from the Rio Grande.[28]

Two years after establishing Castroville, Castro decided to return to France for a visit. Before he sailed, his colonists sent him a *bon voyage* message. On November 25, 1844, they wrote, "We take pleasure in acknowledging that you have treated us like a liberal and kind father. . . . Our best wishes accompany you on your voyage, and we take this occasion to express to you our ardent desire to see you return soon among us to continue to us your paternal protection." The heads of each of the families signed the letter.

Castroville circa 1850. *Art by T. Gentilz*

When he returned to Texas the following year, Castro settled the town of Quihi. In 1846 he brought immigrants to Vandenburg and in 1847 to D'Hanis.

Then came famine. Two years of drought in 1848 and 1849 forced the colonists to include in their diet soups of snake and lizards. In 1849 locusts blackened the sky, followed by a plague of cholera, and for six weeks a victim a day died.

Castro's exhuberance, resources, and a sense of destiny had given him momentum to launch and execute a colonization in Texas despite enemies in the form of Europeans, rival Texan colonizers, Comanches to the north, Mexican nationals to the west, and the forces of nature. Now he was old. His efforts to populate southwest Texas had exhausted his savings. He lived in a small two room cabin on the rugged frontier. It was a far cry from his house in Paris, with ornate mirrors, paintings, and chairs upholstered in red silk. He had spent more than $100,000 fulfilling his contract. He was age sixty-nine and wanted and needed his land to support his family.

In 1855 he sent to the Texas legislature a petition: "It is, I think, proper to mention that I have, in this arduous enterprise of colonization, employed thirteen years of my advanced life and over $100,000 capital. It is notorious, that with one-tenth part of this amount, and without any trouble, I might have acquired more lands than I am entitled to by my contract . . .

"I have periled my life and sacrificed my fortune to colonize with success for the State sixty miles of the country, without receiving any other compensation but sixty sections of 640 acres each as premium land. In

Comanches on the War Path near Castroville. Art by T. Gentilz.

conclusion, I have exhausted my physical strength and fortune in the enterprise."[29]

Castro petitioned his claim was "derived from the law of the 4th of January, 1841, authorising me to retain half of the land granted to the colonists, as recompense for their transportation, removal, and otherwise. . . . The State, in doing me justice, will, in any event, benefit half of the land unclaimed by individuals evidently introduced in the colony by me, having right to said lands but who do not claim them from cause of death, ignorance, neglect, or settlement in a distant part of the State."[30]

Castro's efforts were to no avail. The lawmakers did nothing.

When the Civil War broke out, Castro decided to visit France. Because the war blocked American ports, he planned to exit via Mexico. He traveled to Monterrey where his son Lorenzo lived, and became ill. He died in 1865 and is buried in Monterrey, at the foot of the Sierra Madre Mountains.[31] After Henri's death, Lorenzo carried on colonizing and writing in Mexico similar to that done by his father earlier in Texas. Lorenzo wrote a comprehensive book on the Republic of Mexico detailing its resources and history. In the introduction he wrote, he stated, "The writer, who assisted his father in his efforts to colonize Western Texas, has since the Confederate war, resided and travelled all over Mexico. He is well acquainted with the country, its language, laws, customs and the manners of its people. He has, since the War of Secession, devoted his entire time to make Mexico better known than it is by the generality of the American people; to develop its untold mining wealth, its agriculture and industry, and promote immigration."[32]

In 1876 the State of Texas honored Henri Castro's memory by giving his name to one of its new counties.[33] In 1931 the citizens of Castroville erected a statue in his honor.

Henri Castro

Castro was a friend of many faiths. Catholics, German Lutherans, and Methodists all had churches in his colony. Personally, he was a pious Jew. During his surveying tours, he would retire to the forest to *lay tephillin* — a traditional Jewish form of meditation.[34] Castro was to the end of his days a Jew born in France, whose children bore Italian names, doing the work of his life in America.[35]

When Henri Castro brought his first colonists to San Antonio, no settlement existed west of San Pedro Creek to the Rio Grande.[36] He succeeded in planting the first permanent settlement between San Antonio and the Rio Grande.[37] He was a man of courage who dared to bring civilization to a part of Texas where there was none before. In 1850 Sam Houston and other leaders signed a testimonial to Castro.[38]

Today, visitors driving west on U.S. Highway 90 along the hills leading out of San Antonio take a journey in time as well as in space. Wooden and rock homes that look like postcard photos of northeastern France appear among the mesquite, corn, and cactus. The inhabitants are the fourth and fifth generations of those who left their farms on the Rhine in Alsace-Lorraine to settle Castroville in the wilds of Texas. They represent the largest concentration of Alsatians outside of Europe.

Although there were no known Jewish settlers in Castroville except Henri's family, one hundred years later, in Spring 1969, students and their priest at St. Louis Church there named a historic building converted for their classes "Shalom House," getting the name from a song they liked. *Shalom* is the Hebrew word for peace. Although not intended as a memorial to Castro, the name was a fitting tribute to the city's founder.

Historian Amelia Williams wrote for the *Handbook of Texas*, "Henri Castro was a learned, wise, humane man. In the management of his colony he is more comparable to Stephen F. Austin than is any other Texas empresario."[39]

JACOB DE CORDOVA
(1808-1868)

> *We the undersigned Senators and Representatives from the State of Texas, . . . have no hesitation in saying that no map could surpass this in accuracy and fidelity. It has delineated upon it every county in the State, its towns, rivers, and streams; and we cordially recommend it to every person who desires correct geographical information of our State. To persons desirous of visiting Texas it will be invaluable.*[40]
>
> *[signed] Tho J. Rusk*
> *Sam Houston*
> *David S. Kaufman*
> *T. Pilsbury*

Jacob Raphael De Cordova literally put Texas on a map. He not only published the first official map of Texas, but also the first Texas encyclopedia, and two of the first newspapers in the Lone Star State.

Through maps, newspapers, pamphlets, and books, Jacob and his half-brother Phineas De Cordova played a prime role in selling Texas to the world in the era following the battles for Texas independence. He was called "Publicist of an Empire," and his writings and travels attracted thousands of Americans and Europeans to Texas in the period following the Revolution.

Texas bibliographer John H. Jenkins referred to the map De Cordova published as "his masterpiece" adding, "Sam Houston delivered a speech praising the map on the floor of the U.S. Senate and obtained a government purchase of five hundred copies." During the speech, Houston stated, "on account of the character of the individual who has been engaged in preparing it," it was "the most correct and authentic map of Texas."[41] Jacob, who called himself "The Wanderer," spent years traveling all over Texas, working on his map, and on it all future Texas cartography was based.

De Cordova literally sold Texas to the world.[42] He was also an engineer and land merchant and was one of the early promoters of Waco, then only a place where herds of longhorns crossed the Brazos.[43]

This pioneer became one of Texas' earliest state representatives. In 1847 Houston area voters elected Jacob De Cordova to represent Harris County in the Second Texas Legislature.[44] Previously in 1844, Houstonians had elected him an alderman and re-elected him in 1845.[45] The press heralded his election as ushering in a new era of religious toleration.[46]

But his main interest was in the buying and selling of Texas land. At his peak (around 1858) he controlled more than a million acres. His enthusiasm for Texas settlement and growth knew no bounds. From his home bases in Houston and later Austin, Seguin (near San Antonio), and Bosque County (in central Texas northwest of Waco), he built one of the most extensive land agencies in Texas. How did he do it?

Although briefly in the Texas House of Representatives, he made many good contacts.[47] His knowledge of languages became known, and officials called upon him to translate land grants from the Spanish. De Cordova could read and write English, Spanish, French, German, and Hebrew, and he learned to speak "enough Indian language and signs to enable him to make friends with the Indians."[48]

To translate earliest land grants for the Republic, he traveled on horseback, by horse and buggy, and by foot over large areas of Texas, learning the terrain. He became a living encyclopedia on Texas when it was in the Republic era and also after annexation to the United States.

Jacob first visited Texas with his father, a Jamaican

coffee grower and exporter. He served as interpreter for his father, and appeared a brilliant, well educated youth. The youngest of three sons of wealthy Jamaicans, Judith and Raphael De Cordova Jr., he had two half-brothers by his father's later wife, Leah.[49]

He was born on the island of Jamaica. Jacob's mother died in childbirth, bearing him on June 6, 1808. An aunt in England, who had no sons, reared him during his childhood and fostered his education. When he was old enough to realize his mother died giving him birth, he would not celebrate his birthdays in the usual way. Instead, he would always fast and keep the day sacred. His fasting was known only to his immediate family and close relatives.[50]

While Jacob was still a boy, the family moved from Kingston to Philadelphia. Here his father (in 1820) was president of Congregation Mikveh Israel.[51] His great uncle, Joshua Hezekiah De Cordova, had been the *Haham* (rabbi) in Amsterdam 1744-48, in Curacao 1748-55, and in Kingston from 1755 until his death in 1797.[52] Jacob's earlier ancestors had lived in England, Brazil, and Constantinople.[53] The De Cordovas were a titled family of Spanish Jews who had left Spain to escape the Inquisition.[54] Like his ancestors, Jacob learned to read and write Hebrew at an early age. He was scholarly in many fields, and married a well educated lady, Rebecca Sterling.

Jacob became ill from the Philadelphia winters, suffering from what he called "lung fever." Confined to his quarters for one year, he learned printing. For centuries his ancestors had made their living in the printing trade, publishing in Spain, Holland, and Dutch Brazil. The De Cordova interest in the printing craft goes back to 1555 when Fernandez De Cordova printed "the most important of all Texas books and the most sought."[55] It tells the personal narrative of Cabeza de Vaca, the first European explorer of Texas who was also the first historian of Texas. This book "may be considered the first contribution to Texas history."[56]

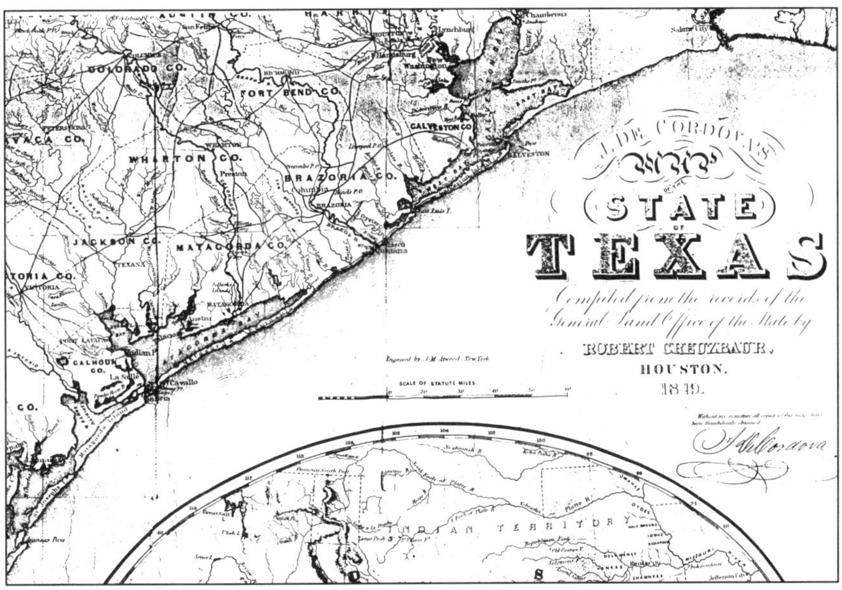

Lower right section of Jacob De Cordova's 1849 map, showing his signature at right.

Land handbill, 1858.

TEXAS LAND AGENCY

INSTITUTED IN THE YEAR 1845.

JACOB DE CORDOVA,

City of Austin,

WILL DEVOTE HIS ATTENTION EXCLUSIVELY TO THE

Location of Land-Script,
The Investigation of Land-Titles,
The Subdivision and Sale of Lands,
The Collection of Debts in Western Texas.

After his year of printing, Jacob was told by his physicians he should leave the cold climate. He had resided in Philadelphia approximately fourteen years — his late childhood, teens, and early manhood.

He returned to sunny Jamaica. He and his brother Joshua founded the *Kingston Daily Gleaner* September 1834. More than 150 years later, the *Gleaner* was still being published by members of the De Cordova family. It has been described as "the best known newspaper in the entire Caribbean area."[57]

In 1835 Jacob returned to Philadelphia briefly, and then sailed with his wife for New Orleans in 1836. It was an important trade center, especially because of all the shipping of supplies to the Texian forces, then battling for their independence from Mexico. During the Revolution he supplied the Texans with staples.

Jacob De Cordova.

Courtesy Helen and Gladys Kingsbury.

After the Battle of San Jacinto, Jacob was one of the earliest Louisianans to carry on extensive trading with the new Republic of Texas. In the immediate post war years, 1837 and 1838, he made intermittent trips to Galveston and Houston, bringing by boat from New Orleans merchandise to trade with the Indians and scattered settlers.

After the birth of a son in January 1839 in Louisiana and with the ending of his term as grand master of the Louisiana International Order of Odd Fellows in March 1839, he moved with his wife and two small sons and two daughters to Texas,[58] becoming a citizen of the new Republic of Texas, and a figure in the import-export business on Galveston island.[59] After less than a year, the family moved to Houston, where his cosmopolitan manners made him very popular.

In February 1846 Texas took down the flag of the Republic, after being annexed as the twenty-eighth star in the flag of the United States. With the barriers down, and after his short political career, De Cordova began in earnest to seek colonists to purchase the real estate he was beginning to manage. His health forced him to travel throughout Texas. When his doctor told him he should leave the low Gulf Coast where he had settled, he saddled his horse and explored far into West Texas, and up the Brazos and Trinity rivers, as well as in the more settled areas of South Texas, charting the country as he went.

In 1854 he owned scrip, which he had purchased or otherwise accumulated, for over a million acres of Texas land. At one time he was said to own land in at least forty-eight Texas counties.[60] He became known as the "Land Merchant of Texas" and as the "Publicity Agent for an Empire." He promoted Texas to benefit his land agency, which had the approval of Governor Peter H. Bell. It was a quasi-official immigration department of the Texas government and became the largest land agency that ever operated in the Southwest.

Galveston at the time Jacob De Cordova moved there, 1839.

One of his best known real estate projects was the city of Waco. As one of the three owners of the site, he laid out the town in 1848 and 1849, predicting it would become a major Texas city.[61] De Cordova served as land agent and George Bernard Erath as surveyor. Erath stated that the principals "gave De Cordova one third of the land, which was two leagues, and a half of 320 acres in the Northwest corner, which was to be laid off into a town."[62]

Town lots of an acre sold for five dollars while nearby Waco farm land brought two to three dollars per acre.

De Cordova supervised the layout of the city, reserving free locations for schools, churches, and commons. He persuaded a number of outstanding Texas citizens to move to Waco.

Jacob and his half-brother Phineas established a semi-weekly newspaper, the *Texas Herald* with a circulation of approximately one thousand. Other newspapers in the South and West freely reprinted its articles, which attracted many immigrants. Each issue, distributed free at country crossroads stores and post offices in the South, Southwest and Midwest, said, "Come to Texas. Come where your children can get a start on rich land that

Phineas De Cordova, Austin newspaperman during the Republic.

Courtesy Barker Texas History Center

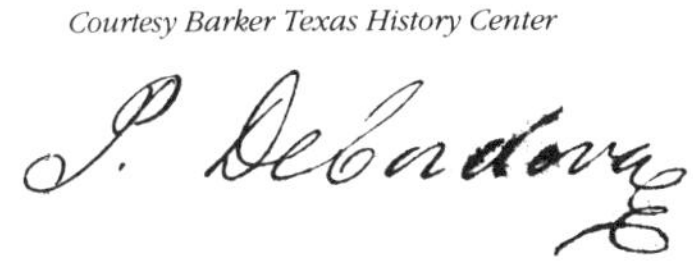

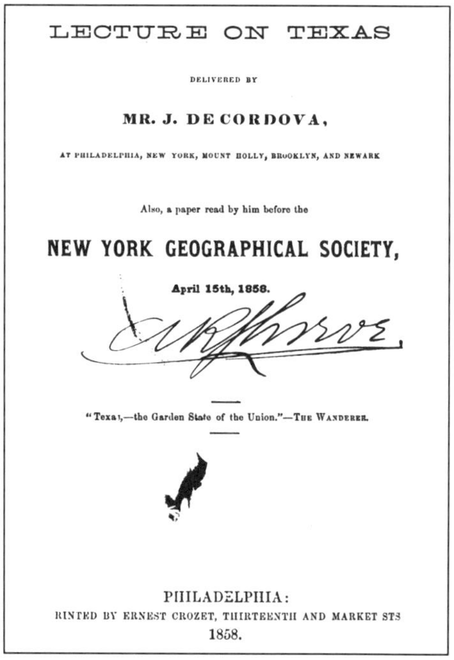

LECTURE ON TEXAS

DELIVERED BY

MR. J. DE CORDOVA,

AT PHILADELPHIA, NEW YORK, MOUNT HOLLY, BROOKLYN, AND NEWARK

Also, a paper read by him before the

NEW YORK GEOGRAPHICAL SOCIETY,

April 15th, 1858.

"Texas,—the Garden State of the Union."—THE WANDERER.

PHILADELPHIA:
PRINTED BY ERNEST CROZET, THIRTEENTH AND MARKET STS
1858.

Lecture on Texas published in 1858

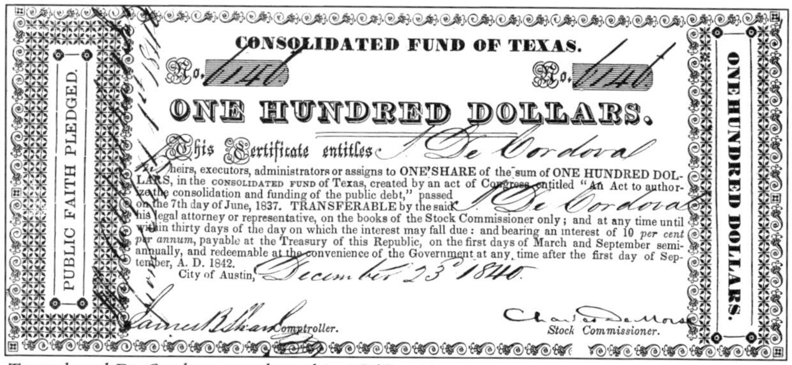

CONSOLIDATED FUND OF TEXAS.

No. 1140 No. 1140

ONE HUNDRED DOLLARS.

PUBLIC FAITH PLEDGED.

This Certificate entitles J. De Cordova

his heirs, executors, administrators or assigns to ONE SHARE of the sum of ONE HUNDRED DOLLARS, in the CONSOLIDATED FUND of Texas, created by an act of Congress, entitled "An Act to authorize the consolidation and funding of the public debt," passed on the 7th day of June, 1837. TRANSFERABLE by the said J. De Cordova his legal attorney or representative, on the books of the Stock Commissioner only; and at any time until within thirty days of the day on which the interest may fall due: and bearing an interest of 10 *per cent per annum*, payable at the Treasury of this Republic, on the first days of March and September semi-annually, and redeemable at the convenience of the Government at any time after the first day of September, A. D. 1842.

City of Austin, December 23 1840.

Comptroller. Stock Commissioner.

ONE HUNDRED DOLLARS.

Texas bond De Cordova purchased in 1840. © by Natalie Ornish

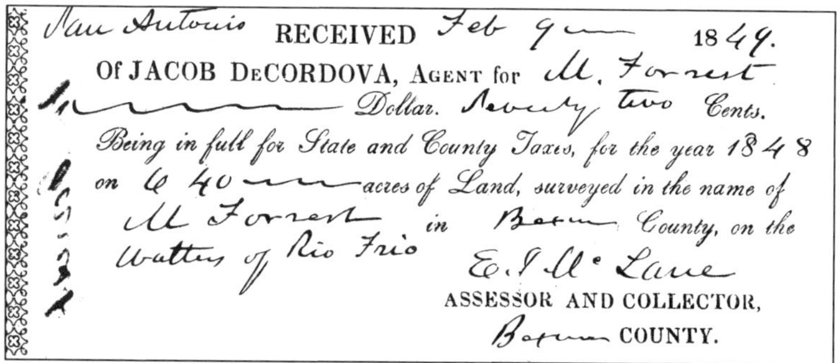

San Antonio RECEIVED Feb 9 1849.

Of JACOB DeCORDOVA, AGENT for M. Forrest

Dollar. Seventy two Cents.

Being in full for State and County Taxes, for the year 1848

on 640 acres of Land, surveyed in the name of

M Forrest in Bexar County, on the

Watters of Rio Frio

E. I. McLane

ASSESSOR AND COLLECTOR,

Bexar COUNTY.

Land receipt, San Antonio, 1848. © by Natalie Ornish

De Cordova served as attorney to present the claims of four Texans for service in the Vasquez Campaign in 1842, when Mexican commander Rafael Vasquez and more than 500 soldiers occupied San Antonio for two days — six years after San Jacinto. © by Natalie Ornish

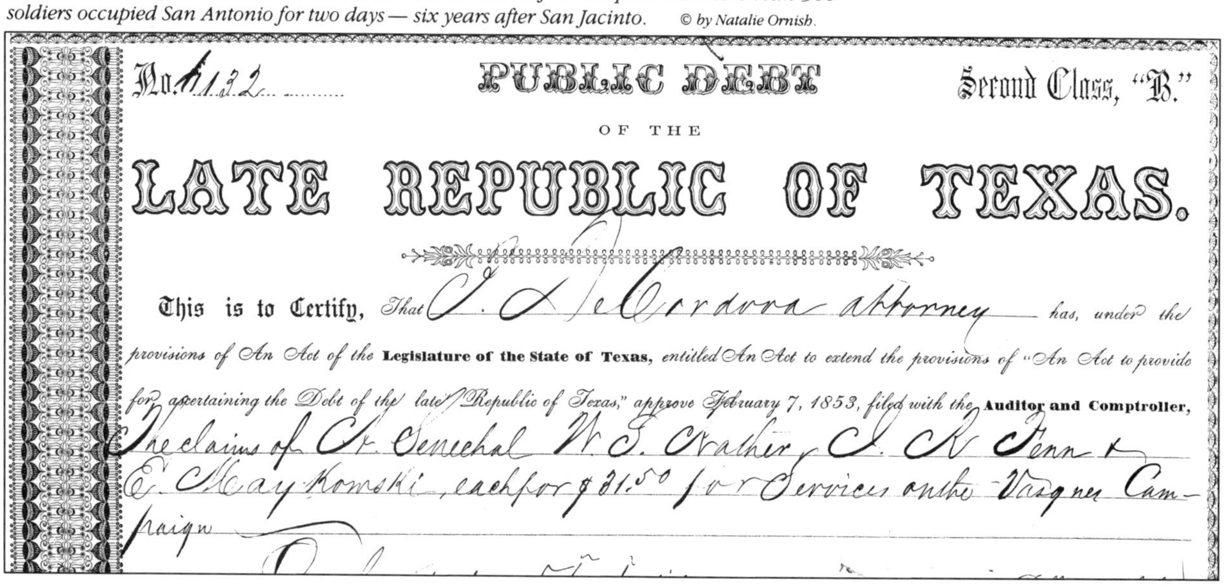

No. 1132

PUBLIC DEBT

Second Class, "B."

OF THE

LATE REPUBLIC OF TEXAS.

This is to Certify, That J. De Cordova attorney has, under the provisions of An Act of the **Legislature of the State of Texas,** entitled An Act to extend the provisions of "An Act to provide for ascertaining the Debt of the late Republic of Texas," approved February 7, 1853, filed with the **Auditor and Comptroller,** The claims of A. Senechal W. S. Prather, J. R. Fenn & E. Maykowski, each for $31.50 for Services on the Vasquez Campaign can be bought at a poor man's price."[63]

De Cordova went east and talked to absentee owners who had bought large tracts of Texas land as speculators, and induced them to cut it up into family-sized tracts to be sold at low prices to new settlers.

In 1850 Governor Bell successfully urged the De Cordovas to move their publishing and printing office to Austin. Jacob published and Phineas edited the *Southwestern American*, a newspaper that played a major role in bringing the railroads to Texas. Governor Bell and Texas' first congressman, David S. Kaufman, led Texas' claims that much land now New Mexico belonged to Texas, and the De Cordovas supported by lectures and in their print media Texas' claims to land beyond Sante Fe. A compromise was effected in 1850. The De Cordovas were among those instrumental in securing the payment by the U.S. government to Texas of ten million dollars to indemnify Texas for her claims to lost land.

After "The Compromise of 1850," Jacob moved from Austin to Seguin in Guadalupe County.[64] He built for his wife and five children a fine country home five miles from Seguin called "Wanderer's Retreat."[65] Although hidden in the woods on a farm/ranch north of San Antonio, De Cordova was very much in contact with the world at large. The popularity of his map had expanded outside state lines, and in 1856 New Yorkers and Philadelphians invited De Cordova to come and lecture on Texas, which he did.

"Wanderer's Retreat," residence of Jacob De Cordova near Seguin, around 1852.

Watercolor by Sarah Hardinge; courtesy Dorothy Sloan-Books.

In 1858 his most important work appeared, a 400-page book *Texas: Her Resources and Her Public Men, A Companion for J. De Cordova's New and Correct Map of the State of Texas.*[66] Bibliographer and author John H. Jenkins wrote, "The first attempt at an encyclopedia of Texas, this work contains a wealth of still-useful material. . . . De Cordova did some of the first genuine scholarly research ever done in Texas while compiling the book, interviewing leading men, researching newspaper files, searching county court records, and striving for pinpoint accuracy." De Cordova has been called "a walking encyclopedia of knowledge" about Texas and "a visionary Texan, only slightly ahead of his time."[67]

Title search indicates that De Cordova signed his name with a capital D. © by Natalie Ornish.

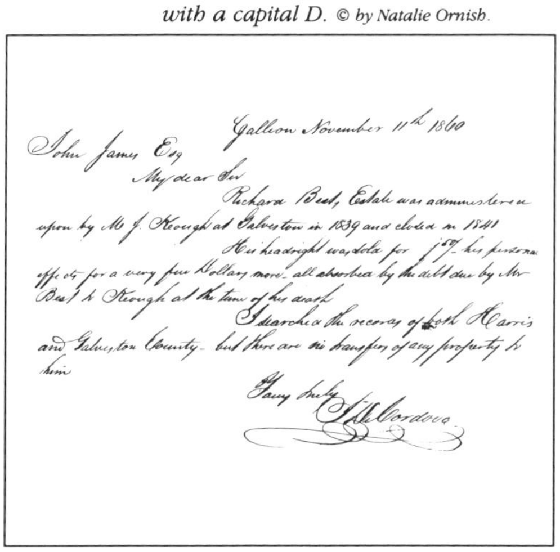

Gallion November 11th 1860
John James Esq
My dear Sir
Richard Best, Estate was administered upon by Mr J. Keough at Galveston in 1839 and closed in 1841
His headright was sold for $57- his personal effects for a very few Dollars more- all absorbed by the debt due by Mr Best to Keough at the time of his death
I searched the records of both Harris and Galveston County- but there are no transfers of any property to him
Very truly
J De Cordova

Texas: Her Resources grew out of two earlier works, *The State of Texas: Her Capabilities and Her Resources* (Galveston, c. 1858), and *The Texas Immigrant and Traveller's Guide Book* (Austin, 1856). De Cordova not only wrote the books himself from his wanderings on horseback or buggy, but also set the type for the books. About *Texas: Her Resources and Her Public Men*, the editor of a Galveston newspaper wrote, "This book contains more information about Texas than all the State papers issued by her Presidents, Governors, Comptrollers, and Treasurers combined."[68] Texas State Librarian E.W. Winkler a century later called it "a fine Texas encyclopedia."

The book is full of fatherly advice. In the chapter "A Word of Advice to Emigrants to Texas," De Cordova gave notice that Texas had sufficient doctors and lawyers but needed people knowledgable in agriculture and mechanical skills. He wrote,

"To the professional man we say that neither doctors nor lawyers are wanted. We have already a sufficient stock; and were it not that some of them have been wise enough to turn their attention to farming and stock-raising, a large number would starve. . . . To mechanics who . . . are of those trades that the wants of a new country require, we say come on; you will do well, for all who are willing to work are liberally remunerated.

"To teachers, both male and female who are competent, there are many openings. Texians are alive to the advantages of education, as is fully evidenced by her liberal appropriations of Public Lands for Common Schools, Universities and Colleges.

"The most suitable points . . . are the upper waters of the Brazos, Colorado, Guadalupe or Red River, where the country is rolling, the water pure, the lands rich, the atmosphere salubrious and invigorating, the hills affording a fine range for cattle, horses, sheep and hogs, with plenty of excellent building stone.

"Do not be deceived in supposing that you are coming to a country where there is an everlasting spring or summer; our winters are cold enough to require your warm clothing and comforters; and while packing these, do not forget to put up carefully a small but choice library, and above all your family Bible. . . Let a vegetable garden be the first thing. . . . Beware of the excessive use of meat in summer; fat and salted meat and strong coffee clog the system. Our advice to the Northern emigrant would be, always have vegetables and fruit in plenty. . . . A decrease in meat eating, especially in hot weather, and a more liberal use of nutritious vegetables and fruit, would end a large portion of sickness among the newly-arrived emigrants."[69]

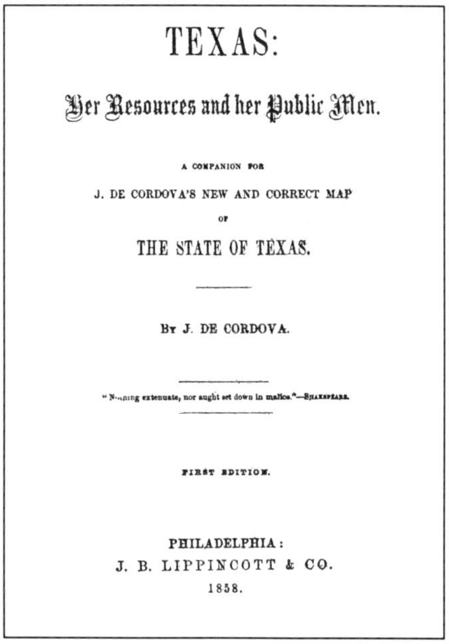
TEXAS:

Her Resources and her Public Men.

A COMPANION FOR

J. DE CORDOVA'S NEW AND CORRECT MAP

OF

THE STATE OF TEXAS.

BY J. DE CORDOVA.

"Nothing extenuate, nor aught set down in malice."—SHAKESPEARE.

FIRST EDITION.

PHILADELPHIA:

J. B. LIPPINCOTT & CO.

1858.

De Cordova suggested that immigrants arrive in early fall, when the yellow fever in Galveston no longer prevailed, and after the cool weather had set in. He also suggested they bring only essential items of furniture and farm equipment so as not to slow down the ox wagons.

Although De Cordova was realistic and gave practical advice, he sometimes tended to employ the notorious Texas brag to merchandise his product, Texas. "A cow can be raised in Tx. at less cost than a chicken in any other place in the United States. . . . The mortality among children is very light . . . our sugarlands have no equal out of the tropics . . . the cotton of Texas now commands a larger price than that of any other State in the Union."[70]

De Cordova went on a literary tour, promoting both his book and the Lone Star State. In 1858 he sailed again to Manhattan to describe Texas to the New York Geographical Society. He sailed to England to speak to the Cotton Supply Association in Manchester on Sep-

Guadalupe retreat near the residence of Jacob De Cordova. *Watercolor by Sarah Hardinge; courtesy Dorothy Sloan-Books.*

tember 28, 1858, on Texas and cotton cultivation. His speeches were published on both sides of the Atlantic and widely distributed.[71]

When De Cordova went to England in 1858 to promote his book and encourage immigration to Texas, he also had a third purpose. He tried to interest England's Cotton Supply Association into buying Texas cotton. English mills were looking for additional cotton-growing areas in the world for supplies to keep their plants running at full employment. De Cordova's (at the time) wild assertion that Texas had ten million acres (one-seventeenth of Texas' area) capable of growing a bale an acre later turned out to be remarkably accurate.

In those days, cotton was compressed and the bales sent to England for spinning. As a visionary, however, De Cordova dreamed of ginning the cotton and weaving it into cloth in Central Texas near the area where it was cultivated. He explored for a proper site for a cotton textile mill along the Brazos River, hoping to use the water's flow for energy. He developed a detailed plan for harnessing the Brazos and had solicited several wealthy Easterners to invest in the project, as well as investing heavily himself.

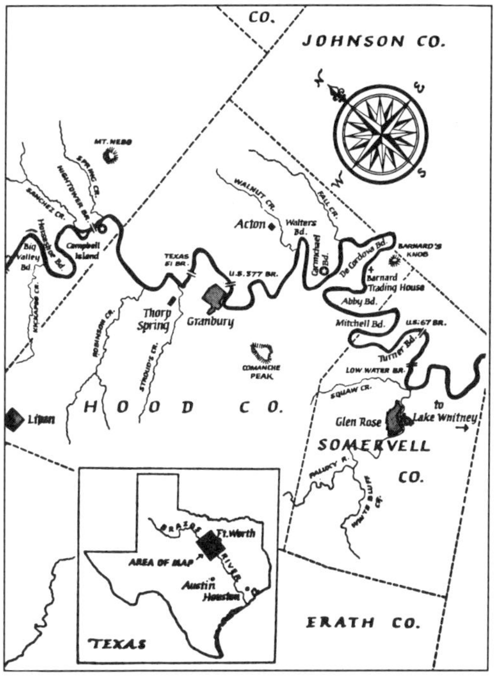

De Cordova Bend of the Upper Brazos River in Hood County.

De Cordova planned to cut a canal across the neck of the Brazos River at a point where the river makes a hairpin turn, just above Bee Mountain, to furnish water power for the mills to spin Texas cotton. He bought machinery in the East, had it shipped South by boat, and it was on its way to Bosque County by ox cart.[72] He was ready to begin construction on the mill when he got pneumonia and died January 26, 1868. Exposure to the cold while exploring the damp Brazos River bottoms of Bosque County caused his death. The Texas sun had saved him from death years before; a bitter Texas Norther cancelled his life.

De Cordova showed pride in his Jewish heritage. He knew Hebrew well. In Texas, he organized some of the state's first Jewish worship services. His razor-sharp memory permitted him to repeat the Sabbath and High Holiday services verbatim. He had an uncanny knack for imitation. He could imitate any rabbi's

Unique portrait of Jacob De Cordova.

Artist unknown. © by Natalie Ornish

inflections and mannerisms perfectly. During his long buggy rides over Texas, this talent provided a constant source of amusement to his listeners. He knew Hebrew calligraphy and several original Jewish marriage contracts (*ketubahs*) hand lettered by him were preserved in the American Jewish Archives in Cincinnati.[73] However, he married a gentile woman, Rebecca Sterling of a pioneer Philadelphia family.

Toward the end of his life, De Cordova suffered a series of financial reverses. His creditors were demanding immediate payment of him, although he had been generous during his lifetime. His integrity prevented him from foreclosing on the land he had sold when the settlers, who had come at his invitation, were unable to get their cotton through the federal blockade during the Civil War. He notified the settlers who owed him he would expect no more payments until peace had returned. He wrote to a friend, a Texas Ranger who had camped with him, "I lived well when my friends could pay me. If I shared good times with them, I have to share the hard times, too."[74] However, when he needed help after the Civil War, he struggled alone. The debacle of the war, debts from land purchases, the hard times of Reconstruction, and the cotton mill project cancelled much of his wealth. The Civil War brought such great financial reverses to De Cordova that when he died, January 26, 1868, less than three years after the War, he was a poor man, an ironic end for the man known as the "Land Merchant of Texas."

Twenty years after he died, the Grand Lodge of Texas, Independent Order of Odd Fellows (IOOF) in 1888 paid a proper tribute to his memory by authorizing a large portrait of him to be hung in the Grand Lodge Hall. At a later date the Lodge recognized him by having lithographed copies of his portrait distributed to all their other lodges, so that a wall in every lodge in Texas would carry a large portrait of Jacob De Cordova.[75] De Cordova had procured the first Odd Fellows charter in the jurisdiction of Texas in 1838 while on a visit to Texas and became its first deputy grand sire.[76]

More recognition came in 1935, when "The Wanderer" took his last trip. The bodies of Jacob and Rebecca De Cordova were removed from Kimball, Bosque County, and reinterred in the Texas State Cemetery in Austin. Jacob's brother Phineas was buried in the Jewish cemetery in Austin.[77]

The De Cordova Bend Reservoir is named for pioneer Jacob De Cordova. It lies south of Fort Worth, a part of the Brazos River's Lake Granbury, in scenic Hood and Parker counties. In 1987 a historical plaque was erected in his memory in Waco. These honors are but small tributes to the person who devoted all his adult life to the development of Texas. It is likely no one has done so much for Texas and in return received so little in the way of fortune or honors.

The first De Cordova reunion in history, held in Waco in 1987, included (from left): Vann De Cordova, Beaumont; Chester E. De Cordova, Dallas; the author; James De Cordova, Santa Monica, Ca.; Gladys Kingsbury, Dallas; and Mrs. M. De Cordova. Few if any of the De Cordovas have retained their Jewish faith, although they proudly acknowledge their Jewish heritage. Freddie De Cordova of the Johnny Carson "Tonight Show" on NBC-TV also is a member of this clan.

Oil painting of David S. Kaufman

Courtesy of Sam Houston Museum

Chapter 4

The Statesmen

Constructing a Republic and a Nation

DAVID SPANGLER KAUFMAN *(1813-1851)*

David Kaufman lived a short time, but he made monumental contributions to Texas history. He served as Texas' first representative to the United States Congress. One hundred and thirty-two years lapsed before another Jew served in an equal capacity.[1]

Kaufman used his extraordinary mind and oratory skills to persuade Texas to join the United States, then later to argue against the United States' taking vast territory that Kaufman stated rightfully belonged to the state of Texas. This land was equal in size to almost half of present-day Texas.

Kaufman's strong belief in integrity and what he repeatedly referred to as acting "in good faith" probably cost him his life when he lost the territorial debate and failed to persuade the United States to leave the whole of Texas intact. In December of 1850 the United States agreed to pay ten million dollars for land claimed by Texas that now comprises parts of New Mexico, Colorado, Kansas, Wyoming, and Oklahoma. The month after Kaufman lost the debate, he died of a heart attack at age thirty-seven.

Kaufman, whose family earlier had emigrated from Germany, was born in Boiling Springs, Cumberland County, Pennsylvania, on December 18, 1813.[2] He was thoroughly and classically educated, graduating from Princeton University[3] in 1830 at the age of sixteen and one-half. He made his way to Natchez, Mississippi, where he studied law and served an apprenticeship in the law office of John A. Quitman, who became a state legislator, a heavy contributor to Texas' independence, a Mexican War general, and eventually governor of Mississippi.[4] In Natchez, Kaufman was admitted to the bar. In 1835 he moved to Louisiana.

In 1837 at age twenty-four he moved to Nacogdoches, Texas.[5] Within months his intellect made him one of the foremost barristers of that Texas town. His growing law practice extended into Sabine, San Augustine, Shelby, and Jasper counties, all in East Texas near the Louisiana border.

Kaufman began his life of public service in the winter of 1838 when citizens of Nacogdoches County elected him to represent them in the Congress of the Republic of Texas, after being in the Lone Star State only a little more than a year. He was re-elected and twice served as Speaker of the House.[6]

In 1839 Major Kaufman fought in the Battle of the Neches that climaxed a tragic episode in Texas-Indian relations.[7] He served as an aide to General Kelsey H. Douglass and received a wound in the face. This battle, instigated by Mirabeau B. Lamar, president of Texas, and participated in by Gen. Edward Burleson, hero of San Jacinto, resulted in the death of Cherokee Chief Bowles, a close personal friend of Sam Houston. The battle had results second only to San Jacinto in securing the land for the white man, but it resulted in the expulsion of the civilized Cherokee tribe from Texas.

In 1840 Kaufman was elected again to the Texas Congress and was chosen Speaker of the House. Only twenty-seven years old, he already had a high profile in the Republic of Texas. "He was a pleasing and forcible speaker and was much in demand."[8] His oratory schedule included addresses at colleges, at Masonic gatherings, campaign speeches, and a graduation address at Princeton University.

But Kaufman directed his oratory chiefly to three targets: speeches for the annexation of Texas to the United States (1846), speeches explaining the causes of the Mexican War (1846-48), and speeches in defense of Texas retaining all of its claimed territory.

Kaufman was widely known throughout the State of Texas. Adolphus Sterne mentioned him twenty-seven times in his diary, calling him "Major Kaufman."

Kaufman developed a close friendship with Sam Houston, whom he first met in Nacogdoches. The Kaufman-Houston friendship is evidenced in much correspondence between them. Some letters reveal that for a time they courted the same woman, Miss Anna Raguet, the belle of Nacogdoches.[9] Kaufman married Jane B. Richardson of Sabinetown, where he moved his law practice.[10]

The following year, 1843, the citizenry of Sabine and two other counties elected him to the Texas Senate. He remained a senator until 1846, when the United States annexed Texas. Texas' last president, Anson Jones, who was pro-annexation, sent Kaufman as a diplomatic agent to Washington with the title of chargé d' affaires of Texas to the United States, but because that government had already adopted the bill for annexation, he was not received in his official capacity.[11]

During the fourteen months of President Jones' administration, Kaufman and James Reily each served as "Minister to the United States."[12] It was in these several capacities that Kaufman used his oratorical skills.

As chairman of Texas' Committee on Foreign Relations, a position in the Republic second only to the

David S. Kaufman, later portrait.

"Mr. Kaufman will be detrained [sic] on business." Letter signed by Sam Houston to Col. Henry Raguet, Nacogdoches.

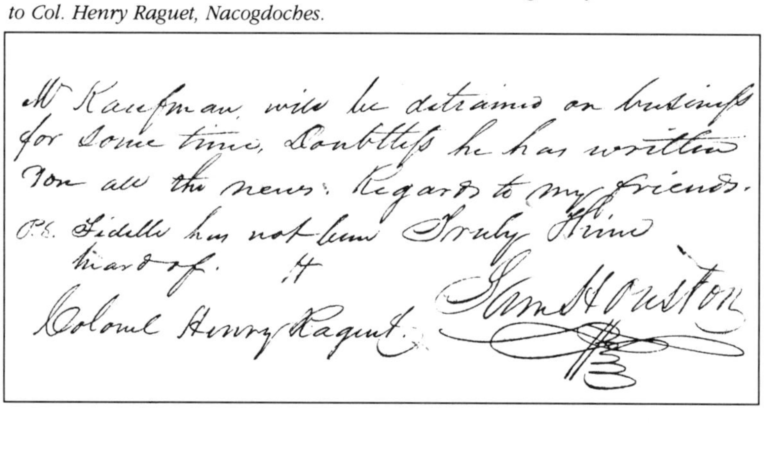

Mr Kaufman will be detraind on business
for some time, Doubtless he has written
You all the news. Regards to my friends.
P.S. Fidelle has not been Truly Thine
heard of.
Colonel Henry Raguet. Sam Houston

president, he argued before the Texas Senate, "It is generally admitted that there is no government on earth where rational liberty and the rights of man, combined with the protection that all men hold dear, are enjoyed to so great an extent as in the United States. Can it be possible that we would madly refuse to enjoy the privileges afforded by the most free and greatest nation of the earth?"[13]

After the United States annexed Texas on December 29, 1845, the people of Texas elected Kaufman one of its first two U.S. congressmen. He was the first man from Texas to be seated in the House of Representatives of the United States and was re-elected to the Thirtieth and Thirty-first Congresses. The territory he served encompassed all of Texas east of the Trinity River, where the majority of the population then resided.[14]

The biggest issue Texas faced in Congress dealt with a territorial dispute with the United States. In the U.S. House of Representatives, Kaufman eloquently argued Texas' claims for the land:

> As chairman of the Committee on Foreign Relations of the senate of Texas, it was my fortune to introduce and report to the favorable consideration of the senate the joint resolution which passed the Congress of Texas, giving the consent of the government of Texas to her annexation to the United States — a measure which I could not have supported but for this provision in regard to her territorial rights, now proposed to be disregarded and annulled.[15]

The northwest portion of the original state of Texas (until 1850) contained hundreds of thousands of square miles of disputed real estate. It was called New Mexico Territory, but Texas felt legally it was part of her territory by the 1848 Treaty of Guadalupe Hidalgo with Mexico as well as acts of the U.S. Congress.

The disputed territory consisted of lands that extended to present-day Sante Fe and included part of Oklahoma, the southwest corner of Kansas, most of lower Colorado, and a small chunk of Wyoming. The question was argued thus: Was the boundary of Texas all the way north hundreds of miles, to the source of the Rio Grande, or just the river's lower portion that flows into the Gulf of Mexico?

The map of Texas as we see it today in everything from ash trays to cookie cutters has a shape that is synonymous with the Texas mystique. But many persons do not realize that Texas did not always have that shape. For instance, the original Texas Panhandle did not look as it does today. The boundary formed by the upper Rio Grande created a thin panhandle to the northwest that reached into Wyoming. For so extensive a prize, Kaufman argued hard, pleading "that

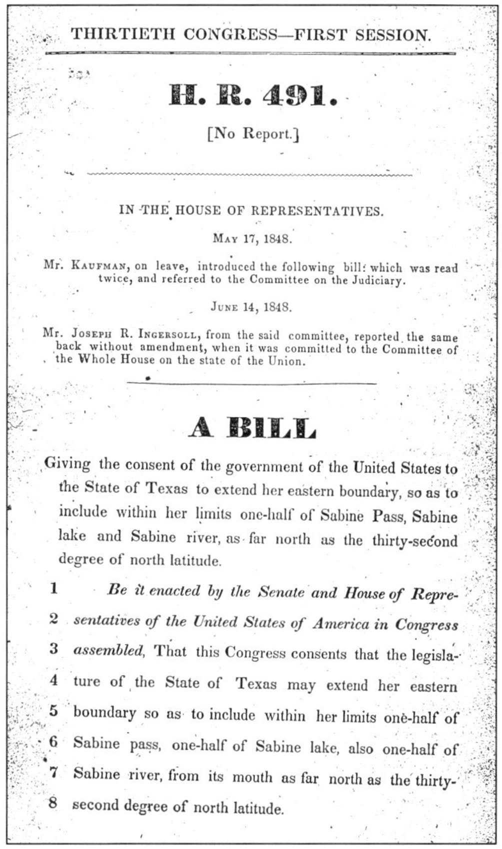

THIRTIETH CONGRESS—FIRST SESSION.

H. R. 491.

[No Report.]

IN THE HOUSE OF REPRESENTATIVES.

MAY 17, 1848.

Mr. KAUFMAN, on leave, introduced the following bill; which was read twice, and referred to the Committee on the Judiciary.

JUNE 14, 1848.

Mr. JOSEPH R. INGERSOLL, from the said committee, reported the same back without amendment, when it was committed to the Committee of the Whole House on the state of the Union.

A BILL

Giving the consent of the government of the United States to the State of Texas to extend her eastern boundary, so as to include within her limits one-half of Sabine Pass, Sabine lake and Sabine river, as far north as the thirty-second degree of north latitude.

Be it enacted by the Senate and House of Representatives of the United States of America in Congress assembled, That this Congress consents that the legislature of the State of Texas may extend her eastern boundary so as to include within her limits one-half of Sabine pass, one-half of Sabine lake, also one-half of Sabine river, from its mouth as far north as the thirty-second degree of north latitude.

This folio bill, unrecorded and hitherto unknown, introduced by Kaufman in 1848, acknowledges that the State of Texas rather than the U.S. owns the western half of the Sabine River. Later, when oil was discovered there, this bill proved of major value to Texas.

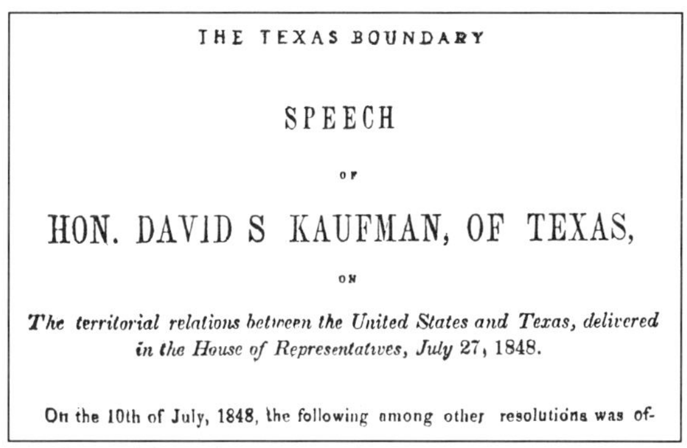

THE TEXAS BOUNDARY

SPEECH

OF

HON. DAVID S KAUFMAN, OF TEXAS,

ON

The territorial relations between the United States and Texas, delivered in the House of Representatives, July 27, 1848.

On the 10th of July, 1848, the following among other resolutions was of-

Kaufman delivered many speeches in the House of Representatives to preserve Texas territory.

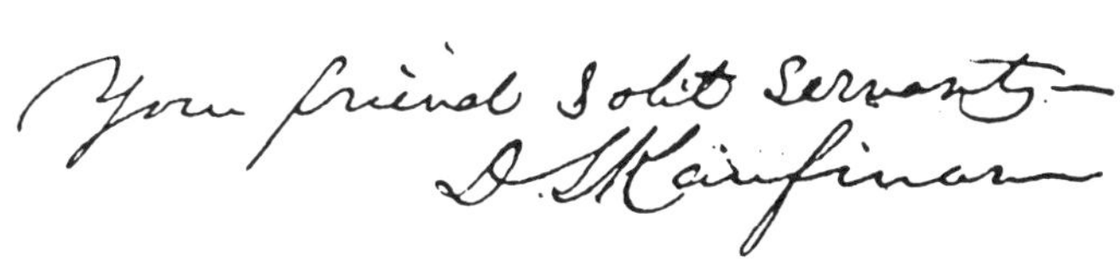

Texas extended to the Rio Grande, by the testimony of Mexicans, Texans, Democrats, Whigs, and impartial geographers."[16]

Kaufman researched Texas' rightful boundaries in law books, treaties, documents, even in Mexican laws and treaties, and statements made by Mexican officials. One of his primary strengths, he reported, came from an act passed by the Congress of the Republic of Texas that defined its boundaries.

> Beginning at the mouth of the Sabine river, and running west along the Gulf of Mexico three leagues . . . to the mouth of the Rio Grande, thence up the principal stream of said river to its source, thence due north to the forty-second degree of north latitude, thence along the boundary line as defined in the treaty between the United States and Spain, to the beginning. . . . Approved December 19, 1836.[17]
>
> There is in Texas, as her boundaries are defined by her act of Congress on December 19, 1836, an area of 325,520 square miles. . . . The area proposed to be left in Texas by the Compromise bill of the Committee of Thirteen is 203,986 square miles.[18]

The Panhandle of Texas prior to 1850 extended past Santa Fe and as far north as Wyoming.

Kaufman pleaded, "The character, the justice, the magnanimity of the nation repel the . . . mutilation of her boundaries."[19]

Kaufman had been noted for his quest for justice. Years before, he had argued in the Texas legislature to see that settlers were compensated for their improvements on the land, and his work became known as "Kaufman's Good Faith Law."[20] In Washington, he continued his theme of acting in "good faith," pleading "Mr. Speaker, the [boundary] limits claimed by Texas cannot be curtailed without an alarming and reckless violation of the faith of this nation."[21]

Texas suffered a vulnerability through its public debt because the state needed money to meet its obligations. When it became obvious that Texas had lost its argument to retain the disputed territory, Kaufman returned home to persuade his people that the U.S. government offered a fair fee and that they should accept the Compromise of 1850.[22] In consideration of the change in boundaries, Texas received ten million dollars in a "stock bearing five per cent interest, redeemable at the end of fourteen years."[23]

Congress ratified the Compromise of 1850 in December, and Kaufman died of a heart attack the next month on January 31, 1851. His funeral took place in Washington, D.C., on the third of February. The ceremonies — held in the House of Representatives — were attended by the president of the United States, both Houses of Congress, judges of the Supreme Court, General Winfield Scott, and members of the diplomatic corps.[24] His burial took place in the Congressional Cemetery in Washington, D.C.

His wife died eleven months later. The year 1851 also marked the death of their baby son, Sam Houston Kaufman. A daughter, Anna Kaufman, the eldest, a first grader when her parents died,

One of Kaufman's legacies is his name on numerous street signs, such as these in Rockwall, Texas.

Photos © by Natalie Ornish.

was reared with her two orphan brothers by an aunt and uncle, Eliza (Richardson) and Franklin Sexton. A descendant of the Sexton family, Harry F. Estill, who was not Jewish, became president of Sam Houston State University, and his daughter was Anna's biographer.[25] Anna's younger brother, Daniel Kaufman, changed his name to Richardson "so he could inherit from his grandfather, Daniel Long Richardson, according to his grandfather's will; name changed back to Kaufman in later years." Another son, David Spangler Kaufman, Jr., only lived to be a teenager.[26]

Kaufman's name has survived by means of the county and town near Dallas named for him at the pinnacle of his career when he was thirty-four.[27] He paid a high price for the honor. He died at age thirty-seven.

SIMON Y. WIESS
(1800-1868)

When President Sam Houston needed a Deputy Collector of Customs for the Republic of Texas, he appointed a world traveler who could fluently speak, read, and write in seven languages.[28] This expert linguist was Houston's close friend Simon Wiess who, at Houston's urging, permanently moved to Texas in 1836.

Wiess lived at various times in Turkey, Asia Minor, the Caribbean, South and Central America, and Mexico. He also traveled extensively through the United States and lived for a period in Louisiana before making his home in Texas.[29]

A successful merchant and cotton shipper largely responsible for the lucrative riverboat trade on the Sabine River, he fathered a family which played a significant role in founding Humble Oil and Refining Company, a forerunner of the Standard Oil Company of New Jersey.[30] His sons fought for the Confederacy before becoming even more successful than their father in the business world, establishing a true Texas dynasty. Besides oil, their influence extended to lumber, banking, cattle, and ranches.

Simon Wiess was born in Lublin, Poland, on New Year's Day, 1800.[31] He was raised in a traditional Jewish family.[32] At age sixteen he left home to roam the world seeking his fortune, which he finally found in Texas.

In the twenty years (1816 to 1836) between the time he left Poland and arrived in Texas, Wiess traveled on three continents. He joined the Masons and, like Adolphus Sterne, held prominent positions in Masonic circles. In 1825 he was a Royal Arch Mason at Constantinople, at the trade crossroads of Europe and Asia. He visited Boston in 1826 at age twenty-six, which is the first we hear of him in the United States. In 1828 he visited the islands of San Domingo (Haiti) in the Caribbean Sea and Barbados in the Atlantic Ocean.

His Masonic chart showed him in Ireland in 1829 and Galveston in 1840.[33] Wiess owned vessels plying the pirate-infested waters of the Spanish Main, owning several sailing vessels engaged in trade between New England and the West Indies.

During the war for Texas independence, the United States had four thousand troops stationed on the border between Louisiana and Texas. The U.S. anticipated that if General Sam Houston was forced into a disastrous retreat from Santa Anna, Houston might find help with these U.S. troops at Camp Sabine. Although this tactic proved unnecessary, the large number of military personnel created customs problems between the U.S. and the Republic of Texas. It was at Camp Sabine (later called Sabinetown) on the border that Wiess served as Deputy Collector of Customs for the Republic of 1836.[34]

Earlier that year he married Margaret Sturrock, a Scottish Presbyterian woman, whom he had met in Louisiana. They soon moved to Nacogdoches where, to support his bride, Wiess set up a merchandising business. She was twenty-two and he was thirty-six. Part of the time they lived in the town's historic stone fort, the place where Adolphus Sterne had been held captive during the Fredonian Rebellion. Wiess and Sterne had business relations together, and in his diary Sterne mentions he "translated a deed for Simon Wiess."[35]

Wiess made Texas business history when he used his trading and sailing expertise to make one of the first shipments of Texas cotton. He bought a keelboat in 1838, loaded his family and all his possessions on it, as well as a load of cotton, and set sail down the Neches and Sabine Rivers to Sabine Pass. It was the first time commercial cotton was shipped downstream from Nacogdoches to the Gulf. The bales of cotton went on to New Orleans after the Wiess family disembarked at Beaumont on the Texas Gulf coast. Here and at nearby Grigsby's Bluff he was interested in steamboating and merchandising cotton until 1840, when he moved to a village in Jasper County later named for him, Wiess' Bluff, then a well-established river port.[36] It became the site of a large lumber camp where logs were transported by floating them downstream.

Simon's twin sons, William and Mark, continued the family interest in boats and were owners and captains of river steamboats.[37] With another brother, Valentine (who at age sixteen had been "the youngest captain of the Southern armies"), they built the Reliance Lumber Company of Beaumont into one of the largest in Texas.[38] The Kirby Lumber Company in 1901 absorbed Reliance and its vast timber holdings.

The land which the Wiess family forested yielded more than yellow pine lumber. The Wiess estate was one of three owners of land upon which the famous Lucas Gusher came in four miles south of Beaumont. Captain Anthony F. Lucas supervised the drilling of the well on the Wiess, McFaddin, and Kyle Lease. It blew in on January 10, 1901, flowing 75,000 barrels of oil a day from a depth of 1,160 feet. The oil production that resulted made Beaumont a city and the Sabine District a major oil refining and exporting center of the world.[39]

Simon's grandson, Harry Carothers Wiess, an Episcopalian, entered the oil business in 1911 as vice-president of the Paraffine Oil Company, in which he and his family held interests. When Humble Oil and Refining Company was organized in 1917, Harry C. Wiess served as an officer. In 1919 Standard Oil of New Jersey purchased a leading interest in Humble.[40] Harry was the son of William Wiess who, like most of Simon's children, was born in Wiess' Bluff, Texas.

Simon remained in Wiess' Bluff until he died August 13, 1868.[41] When Simon Wiess came to Texas to seek his fortune, he surely did not realize how vast a business empire his descendants would build.

Simon Wiess. Courtesy Barker Texas History Center, University of Texas at Austin.

He ate with his hat on, for if he placed it on the ground, it was apt to be stepped on or some fellow puncher might spill beans or coffee or gravy on it. Besides, he was usually eating in the sun. When he ate in the rain, his hat was pushed back so that the water in the wide brim would not run into his plate.

The Cowman & His Code of Ethics *by* *Ramon F. Adams*

Chapter 5

The Ranchers

Giants of Texas' Great Cattle Herds

UP THE CHISHOLM TRAIL

The story of the Halff family captures the excitement, the muscle, and the riches of the cattle industry. At the height of its land acquisition, before the invention of barbed wire, the family's ranch lands sprawled across more than six million acres. Brothers Mayer and Solomon Halff were pioneers during the surging rise of the cattle kingdoms in the West. They are significant because their lives spanned the rise and fall of the open range. Long drives up the Chisholm Trail marked their early years, while their declining years paralleled the decline of the Longhorn as the cow for Texas ranges. Beginning in 1867, the Chisholm Trail was the cowhand's road to high adventure for more than a dozen turbulent years.

At first the Halffs sent their cattle to the New Orleans market, but later they took them north over the Chisholm and other trails.

Frontier Times magazine observed, "Those trails were far more hazardous to Halff brothers than had been the shorter and more clearly defined trails to the east. In the West, cattle herds had to beat out new trails, the outfits had to fight wild Plains Indians, cross rivers that sheltered deceptive beds of quick-sand, contend with stampedes, cattle thieves, blizzards, dry drives, and hope that they would not lose too many animals to these enemies of the trail. True, there was a big difference in cattle at three or four dollars a head in Texas and the same cattle at forty or fifty dollars a head in the northern markets, but

Mayer Halff.

Courtesy Alexander Halff.

between these two prices lay perilous months on the trail. Halff brothers as well as other cattlemen prospered, but it was not a business for the fainthearted."[1]

Halff ranches at one time or another included the Circle Dot Ranch (named for the design of their brand) near Marathon in Brewster County; the Quien Sabe Ranch in Midland County; the J.M. Ranch along the Pecos River in Crane, Upton, and Crockett counties; ranches in Bee and McMullen counties; the Mallet Ranch in Gaines County; and the Crouch Ranch in Frio County.[2] But this was not all. They also were part owners of a ranch in Wyoming, the Laramie Cattle Company, where cattle trailed up from Texas could rest and fatten. There also were various smaller ranches. It was more than a day's drive from the Circle Dot to the Quien Sabe or J.M. Ranch, and between these, Fort Stockton in West Texas was the stopping place.

Although his family lived in San Antonio, Mayer Halff spent most of his time on the ranches. He loved to ride horseback on the range and especially enjoyed a spirited horse. Home in San Antonio was 300 miles from most of his ranches, and for these longer trips he traveled in a buckboard, a four-wheeled open wagon with a springy platform carrying the seat. He rode the buckboard throughout his property, his ranch hands never knowing when or where he might appear. Once he came driving into camp — in North Dakota. In his youth, before the railroads reached Texas, he traveled thousands of miles annually on horsepower.

While Mayer rode the range, his brother Solomon minded the store, M. Halff & Bro., a wholesale dry goods company. Merchandising brought this Jewish family into the cattle business. When their customers did not have cash to pay for goods, they paid with cattle or produce. They bartered cows for coats, and sweet potatoes for pants.

The Halff brothers were born in Lauterbourg, Alsace-Lorraine, France.[3] The Republic of Texas had attracted wide attention in France, which maintained an embassy in Austin. Also, friends in Galveston wrote the Halffs of the opportunities in Texas. In the mid-1840s, when Texas was still a Republic, an older brother, Adolphe Halff, came to Galveston. He sold merchandise in the area from ox wagon or on horseback. He spoke French fluently and often was a guest in homes of other Frenchmen, who enjoyed conversing in their mother tongue with this charming peddler. After many years in Texas, Adolphe sent for his younger brother, Mayer, to join him.

Mayer was born in 1836, the year of the Alamo, and was fourteen years old when he sailed to Texas, arriving in Galveston in 1850. In May of 1856 the brothers opened a store in Liberty, Texas, forty miles northeast of Houston. Liberty, a port on the Trinity River, was at that time a leading trade center on the Old Spanish Trail, the road to Nacogdoches.

The Halffs opened their Liberty store one year earlier than the first Sanger Brothers store in Texas. They took out a large ad advertising "silks, satins, muslins, calicoes, Swiss collars" and clothing for men and boys. "The biggest market price paid for hides, deer skins, and beeswax."[4]

Three months after opening this store, Adolphe went on a buying trip for more goods, sailing from Galveston. The hurricane season was beginning its annual autumn visit to the Gulf, and three ships went down in a storm, including the *Nautilus*, which Halff was on.[5] His body was never found.

After the loss of his brother at sea, Mayer Halff for a few months tried to carry on the business alone. When the farmers came to town with their ox- or mule-drawn wagons, to buy his supplies, they brought along the products of their farms to be sold. He often accepted produce in lieu of cash. Then Mayer Halff began accepting cattle in payment of bills. Money was scarce but cattle were plentiful.[6] Soon the young merchant learned that it was not only expedient but also advantageous to accept payment in the form of Texas Longhorns, which were very profitably trailed to New Orleans. This started him on the path that would change his career from merchant to rancher.

In 1857 his nineteen-year-old brother Solomon joined him and the two formed a partnership, M. Halff & Bro. They began buying land on which to graze cattle. Mayer, who had been in Texas for seven years, managed the ranches. Solomon, the intellectual of the family, was given the job of taking care of the store.

With the duties so divided, the businesses began to grow. The brothers decided to leave Liberty for more open range, and in 1864 they moved to San Antonio where they began ranching and merchandising in a larger way. Their wholesale dry goods company became one of the largest of its type in the Southwest, with salesmen covering the state. Years later, in a speech to his employees, Mayer said success could come to any person in San Antonio who believed in "the gospel of Work" and "whose soul is in the struggle." He applied his energy to his cattle business also and began to divert his shipments from the eastern markets in New Orleans to the Chisholm Trail.

Solomon Halff.
Courtesy Institute of Texan Cultures.

The Chisholm Trail, which ran from the southern tip of Texas through San Antonio, Austin, Waco, and Fort Worth en route to its terminus in Abilene, Kansas, began in 1867.[7] For more than a dozen tempestuous years, thousands of cattle were driven up the trail, and many had the Halff brand.

Halff brands

Although J. Frank Dobie told the story of *The Longhorns*, it is historian Wayne Gard's *The Chisholm Trail* that succinctly describes the adventure: "It held the excitement of sudden stampedes, hazardous river crossings, and brushes with Indian marauders. It promised, at the end of the drive, hilarious celebrations in the saloons, gambling parlors, and dance halls of frontier Kansas. . . . For others, the Chisholm Trail meant more than rousing experiences. . . . This pathway, which took the imprints of several million Longhorns, helped Texas dig herself out of the poverty that followed the Civil War."[8] It was an economic safety valve; it released for sale millions of head of cattle in Texas.

The Chisholm Trail beginning in 1867.

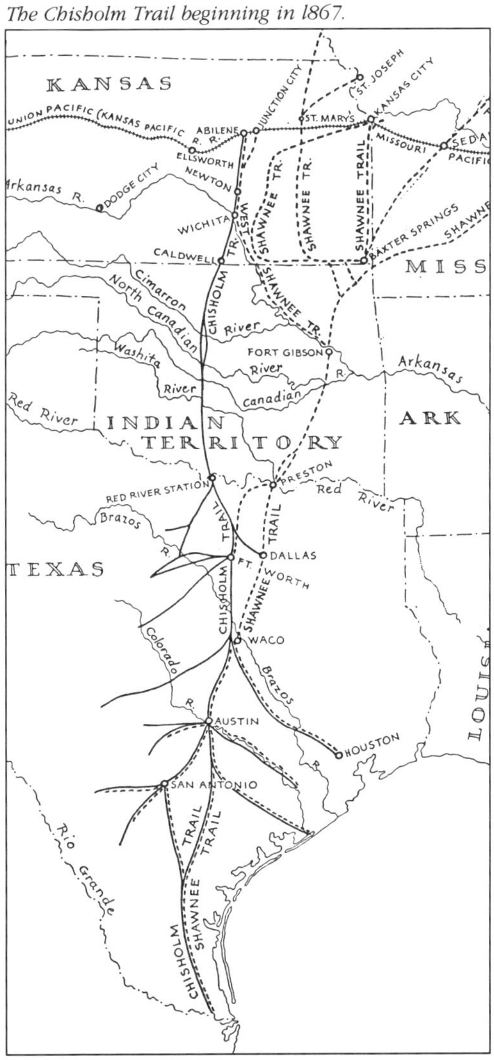

At the end of the war, five million Longhorns roamed the ranges, grazing and multiplying. Many were unclaimed and unbranded. It was the period of the Longhorn and the trail driver, but into the picture also went grass, water, trails, cowboys, Indians, droughts and blizzards, horses and stampedes, and the Texas cowman. Foremost in the picture was "that fierce composite of horns and hide, the Longhorn, equally Texan, equally important to the Texas tradition."[9]

In 1874, much to the disgust of the cattleman, successful barbed wire fencing was developed and within a few years began encroaching on the free range and water. Men now had to pay for the right to graze their herds, or else fence off their own ranges. It was to put an end to the open range.

Although the Chisholm Trail was abandoned around 1884, Halff cowboys continued to drive cattle, often to Colorado. On one such trip, the Halff cowboys encountered a new hardship, as one of them, Bob Beverly, recalled: "In 1893, Mr. Halff had sold a lot of two year old steers, to be delivered in Colorado overland by trail; they went up the Pecos River into New Mexico, . . . following pretty much the old route laid off by Charles Goodnight. Just north of Fort

Henry M. Halff residence, Midland.
© Betty Halff Llewellyn.

Sumner, N.M., there came up an awful hailstorm, one of the worst . . . in the west. There was several herds by different other ranchers, along in that section, scattered from ten to fifty miles apart, all headed for northern states. But it so happened that the hail only hit Mr. Halff's herd, and it killed some five or six hundred steers and several saddle horses, but only rained on the other herds. . . . The nearest railroad was Pecos, Texas, and this herd had to stop on the trail until they could get word to Mr. Halff, to come and get them started again. Mr. Halff was in Toyah, Texas, when the rider found him. . . . Mr. Halff questioned the rider very closely, and at last Mr. Halff said, I guess I will have to go up there, (about 250 miles overland by buckboard) but you tell me that the storm never killed any of the Gentile steers? The man said no, there was none killed in their herds. Well, Mr. Halff said, I do not understand just what God is up to now, killing a poor Jew's steers and not bothering the Gentile herds."[10]

Rancher Henry M. Halff during Spanish-American War, 1898.

© Betty Halff Llewellyn.

Although barbed wire fencing meant the doom of the open range, fencing made it easier to improve the herds. Economics demanded cattle have marbled meat, rather than be tough on the hoof and have the horn needed to survive the drives and the frontier. The Halffs were among the first ranchers in Texas to bring Hereford cattle to the state. Mayer's son, Henry Mayer Halff, went to Iowa, purchased prize Hereford bulls at $250 each, and brought them to the Halff ranches. He put the pure-blooded Hereford strain into the veins of thousands of Texas cattle. For a time, the 200,000-acre Halff ranch near Midland, Texas, held the largest number of Herefords in the Southwest. Henry's older brother, Alexander Halff, also ran the cattle ranches, and one year the Halffs and their cowboys branded 35,000 calves from all their ranches and ranked third in the nation for cattle production.

When the golden era of the cattle kingdom ended, the Halffs changed with the times. Mayer was a founder of City National Bank of San Antonio, and he and Solomon founded Alamo National Bank. Both were founding members of Temple Beth El in San Antonio. Both brothers died in 1905. The Mayer Halff home was restored and stands on San Antonio's HemisFair grounds at the entrance.

Mayer Halff always affectionately called his cowboys "my boys." Bob Beverly, one of his "boys," wrote: "I know more of the Quien Sabe ranch operation than any of the other ranches. . . . Henry, when quite a lad, would come to the ranch and ask me to let him ride my horse, many times at night to stand my guard and let me sleep, and of course I never objected, if the herd was broke in and the weather was good. Henry wanted to be an active cowboy, and in after years was a great polo player, and when the Spanish [-American] war broke out in 1898, Henry, like a lot of us ranchhands, volunteered and wanted to go with the Rough Riders, but Mr. Halff finally got him out. . . . He [Mayer] was a pioneer and built always for the future. . . . He not only taught his men to save and accumulate, but he practiced what he preached, and made a fortune in the land that Charles Goodnight called the Graveyard of the Cowman's hopes, along the Rio Pecos and Rio Grande. . . . Mr. Halff gave me good advice, and I still love him for it."[11]

Rosa Wechsler, daughter of the manufacturer of Manhattan Shirts of New York, married Henry M. Halff and moved to West Texas.

© Betty Halff Llewellyn

Henry organized a Midland polo team, using Halff cowboys. He took his polo team all over the United States and Europe and also organized a women's polo team.

Henry's parents, Mayer and Rachel Hart Halff, had four children, two of whom married into the Oppenheimer banking family of San Antonio which financed many of the early cattle drives.[12]

Other members of the Halff family also combined business with ventures in land. Felix Halff, a first cousin of Mayer and Sol, at one time owned extensive orange groves in California, as well as ranches in Texas. Born around 1822, Felix served as mayor of Galveston.[13] An early member of Congregation B'nai Israel, he became its president in 1879, a decade before Henry Cohen arrived.[14] Later Halff moved to Houston and opened a dry goods store (on Fannin at Franklin), covering 30,000 square feet, the largest concern of its kind in Houston and one of the largest in the state. The firm, Halff & Newbouer Bros., had a New York buying office and salesmen covering Texas and Louisiana. It also factored cotton.[15] But his lands were not so expansive and vast as those in Texas belonging to his cousins, Mayer and Solomon Halff.[16]

Solomon married Fannie Levi of a banking family of Victoria, Texas. Their five children, all born in Texas, included Minnie Halff, who married Edward S. Levy, founder of E.S. Levy & Co., Galveston's leading department store for a century; and Godcheaux A.C. Halff (1879-1950). Godcheaux made substantial contributions to the nonsectarian National Jewish Hospital in Denver, where his portrait hung for many decades.

Godcheaux began his business career in 1903 with A.B. Frank Co., wholesale dry goods, and eventually

Felix Halff. © by Betty Stagg.

Henry M. Halff, Rosa W. Halff, and children, Mayer, Ernestine, Betty, and Albert. Young Studio, Mineral Wells, Texas.

© by Betty Halff Llewellyn.

G.A.C. Halff (1877-1950). In 1922 he founded WOAI radio station, one of the first in Texas.

became its president. He became one of the first auto dealers in Texas, selling Pierce-Arrow and other cars in San Antonio, Houston, Dallas, and Austin. In 1911 he founded the first wholesale outlet for auto supplies, soon adding radios to his lines.

Godcheaux perceived that entertaining broadcasts would attract more radio purchasers, so in 1922 he founded radio station WOAI, San Antonio, which began broadcasting September 25, 1922, one of the first broadcasting stations in the country. Godcheaux was not a radio fan, however. "I do not listen to the Lone Ranger or, for that matter, many things on the radio," he wrote a cousin Jane Mayer of Corpus Christi, in a letter preserved in the Barker Texas History Center in Austin. In 1949 his Southland Industries and WOAI-TV inaugurated television broadcasting in Southwest Texas.[17] His business interests included real estate and extensive ranches in Brewster County in the Big Bend area.

The Halffs covered a broad expanse of Texas history — from frontier days of the cattle drives to the era of radio.

THE WEIL RANCHES, CORPUS CHRISTI

The Cross Six for years meant Weil cattle and Weil kinfolks in South Texas.

When the Weil family had its reunion every five years in the 1970s and 1980s, a Corpus Christi *Caller Times* photographer came to take pictures of the "delegates" wearing sun hats with wide brims to protect them from the South Texas heat. Their hats were monogrammed with the brand of the ranch, +6, the Cross Six. They drank from cups custom-made by a Texas potter, each souvenir cup adorned with a Cross Six brand.

Charles Weil, who originated the brand and acted as the patriarch for five generations of Texans, built a ranch in South Texas that bounded on the famous King Ranch. It comprised 40,000 acres. "In that part of the country, that was a very small operation. Very small," observed a granddaughter, Sarah Weil Kahn of Cincinnati, Ohio.[18]

The younger children who attended these reunions were fifth-generation native-born Texans. Others came from as far as Boston, Cincinnati, Newark, and Norman, Oklahoma, to talk about the days on the ranch near Hebbronville, Texas. Like the time in 1891 when Charles' son, Jonas Weil, was part of a group that tried to break a Texas drought utilizing a cannon hauled from the King Ranch headquarters to a site in Duval County. They soaked cloth bags in nitroglycerine then fired them and exploded iron shavings they had gathered from a blacksmith shop while a meterologist watched from a balloon. It rained.[19]

At the Cross Six reunions, they told stories like these: "My mother's uncle was on a cattle drive up in Dodge City in 1878, and after driving the herd of cattle there, was shot and killed in a saloon over a twenty-five cents bet."[20]

They learned of despair and suffering: "We've come a long way from the time when my great-grandfather deserted my great-grandmother. She died young and left small children, who were put in the Jewish orphanage in New Orleans," said one Weil descendant.[21]

They heard of friendships extended to the Jews: "When the Jews of Corpus Christi needed a cemetery, Captain King of the King Ranch donated the land."

Of power: "Captain King and Charles Weil's brother-in-law, David Hirsch, founded the first bank in Corpus Christi, the Corpus Christi National Bank."[22]

Of whimsey: "My father's father was a drummer boy during the Civil War. We still have the drum. It's with a relative in Beaumont."[23]

But the central figure is always Charles Weil, patriarch of the clan. Born in Surbourg, Alsace, France, in 1847, he came to the United States in 1867 and to Corpus Christi in 1869.[24] He opened a general store, Frank and Weil, in partnership with a brother-in-law. Weil's business sold the ranchers of northern Mexico their needed supplies such as leaf tobacco, jeans (then made of a twilled wool fabric), and kerosene in five-gallon cans. Goods were brought into Corpus Christi by ships in the Gulf and overland to Mexico by wagon trains, lumbering Spanish carts that traveled in heavily-guarded groups. The Mexican dollar was the medium of exchange and was brought to town in nail kegs. With the completion of the Texas-Mexican Railroad to Laredo, direct Mexican trade with Corpus Christi virtually ceased, and the Weil mercantile firm in 1888 became a ranching business.

Originally the Weil cattle grazed near the town of Bishop, Texas, outside Corpus Christi, but later the ranch was located further west near Hebbronville. In 1940 the County Agricultural Agent for Hebbronville, G.W. Brown, wrote, "The main Weil ranch is known as La Palangana, comprising about 25,000 acres, and in addition there are some 15,000 acres leased. The ranch is stocked primarily with white-faced cows, and the raising of horses and mules is just a side line."[25]

Patriarch Charles Weil eventually turned over the ranch to his son Jonas. Charles' daughter recalled, "Eight or ten years after Papa went into the ranching business, Jonas joined in the management of it. Previously he had worked in Del Rio in the store of our uncle, Joseph Hymans."[26] Of patriarch Charles Weil's eleven children, ten spent their lives in the Corpus

Sara and Charles Weil shortly after their marriage January 1, 1874.

Rancher Jonas Weil on the porch of the Weil ranch house in Hebbronville, circa 1930.

Christi area and one in Waco.

The Weil ranch that attracted writers was the Jonas Weil ranch of 40,000 acres near Hebbronville, fifty miles from the Rio Grande. Writer Fred Gipson often used tales of the Weil clan in his columns. He told how a son-in-law from New York, on his first trip to the Weil ranch, saw his first cow slaughtered and became a vegetarian and never went to the ranch again. Jonas and his ranch were good "copy" because of the colorful happenings. After dinner on the Weil Ranch, Gipson, who was a frequent visitor and author of *Old Yeller, Hound Dog Man,* and other novels, often joined the vaqueros and others in swapping yarns. Weil tells about a fishing trip up Devil's River where they found a panther in a cave. As a young cowboy tried to smoke out the panther with a flaming coal-oil-soaked rag on the end of a long stick, the panther reached out and peeled part of the young cowboy's scalp forward over his eyebrows. They got the panther and sewed up the boy's scalp.

© *by Betty Halff Llewellyn.*

In another column Gipson wrote: "In the capacity of official gate-opener, I prowl with Jonas Weil again on his Hebbronville ranch. His men are cutting out and

Plaque states Mayer M. Halff and Brother were among the first noted ranchers in the "cradle of West Texas cattle industry."

Kokernot Ranch, Alpine.

making up a herd of cows and calves to move to his lower ranch and he has to be on hand to direct them — he says.

"Just between us, Weil's foreman is plenty capable of cutting that herd. He's been doing it for thirty years. And the real reason that his boss is going down to the ranch is the same reason I've got — an insatiable longing to be out in the open, among good cattle and horses and the wild things of the woods. Let a kid roam the game and cattle trails of the range for a few years and he can't live long enough to get it out of his system."[27]

Except for Jonas, and Charles' grandson, Alex Weil, Jr., most Weil descendants preferred the mercantile business to living on ranches.[28] Jonas' daughter, Carrie Weil, married S. J. Lichtenstein, Corpus Christi merchant prince and owner of Lichtenstein's Department Store. Hattie Weil married pioneer merchant Julius Schwarz of Hempstead, Texas, of the same clan that includes former U.S. Trade Ambassador Robert Strauss.

Each generation returns to the Weil ranches to savor the game and the cattle trails of the range, just as Charles did in the 1860s.[29]

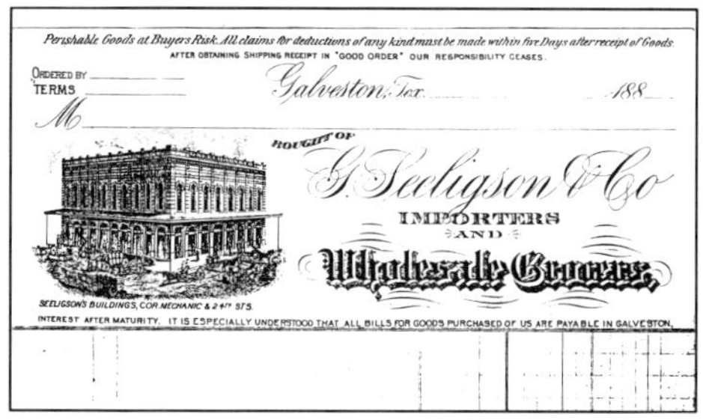
Perishable Goods at Buyers Risk. All claims for deductions of any kind must be made within five Days after receipt of Goods.
AFTER OBTAINING SHIPPING RECEIPT IN "GOOD ORDER" OUR RESPONSIBILITY CEASES.
ORDERED BY
TERMS
Galveston, Tex. 188
M
BOUGHT OF
G. Seeligson & Co
IMPORTERS
AND
Wholesale Grocers,
SEELIGSON'S BUILDINGS, COR. MECHANIC & 24TH STS.
INTEREST AFTER MATURITY. IT IS ESPECIALLY UNDERSTOOD THAT ALL BILLS FOR GOODS PURCHASED OF US ARE PAYABLE IN GALVESTON.

Michael Seeligson, Galveston mayor in 1853.

Courtesy Rosenberg Library.

Weil family reunion at wedding anniversary celebration of Charles and Sara Weil, shown with their eleven children and their grandchildren. © *by Minna Susser*

THE SEELIGSONS

Another early Texas pioneer rancher, Michael Seeligson, originally lived in Philadelphia, Pennsylvania, where he participated in activities of Congregation Rodeph Shalom (1823-24). He married Adelaide Gottschalk, aunt of the first major American pianist and the first national composer.[30]

Michael and Adelaide found their way to Galveston in 1838, shortly after independence, and became civic leaders. Seeligson was elected mayor of Galveston in 1853. However, after serving a few years as mayor, he bought 4,442 acres near Goliad, Texas. Here he lived the remainder of his life on a ranch raising cattle.[31]

Michael Seeligson's son's Galveston home, shown in 1897, has been torn down.

THE T-HALF CIRCLE, SAN ANGELO

Frederick Mayer, a German immigrant, like most other Jewish ranchmen, began as a merchant. He came through New York and settled in Philadelphia. After hearing about Texas, he went to San Antonio in 1856. He established a successful business in San Antonio, but he quickly decided the future lay in livestock. In 1879 he moved his family 140 miles northwest of San Antonio to Ft. McKavett, Texas, where he engaged in mercantile and livestock interests. Then he moved his family to Sonora.[32] In 1888 he organized F. Mayer & Sons, a livestock company. One of his two sons, Solomon, developed a remarkable aptitude in dealing with livestock.

When fifteen years old, Solomon Mayer became a cowboy. He had discovered he had an eye problem and was afraid he could not become academically oriented, so he decided upon a career on the Texas range. As an adult, he earned the title, "Dean of West Texas ranchmen."[33]

At the age of twenty-six Solomon Mayer became general manager of a major livestock concern that "in 1893 handled $120,000 worth of cattle and 9,000 sheep."[34] In 1894 he pastured "10,000 head of cattle and an equal number of sheep" on 85,000 acres of leased land.[35]

Solomon became a director and president of San Angelo National Bank.[36] He built San Angelo's first long-distance telephone service, and served as president of the National Wool Marketing Corporation.

Solomon was mayor of San Angelo, according to his daughter Gladys.[37] He lived on the T-Half Circle Ranch until he died on February 18, 1957.

THE HENRY LEVY RANCH

Although Sol Mayer started out as a cowboy when just a teen-ager, Henry Levy and A. Levytansky did not become career cowboys until nearly age fifty. At age fifteen Henry Levy became an orphan and began to apprentice as a cobbler in Alsace, France, where he had been born on February 22, 1825. At age eighteen he moved to Paris. He later served for several years in the French Marines under Napoleon III before coming to Texas.

With his cousin, Abraham Levi, who later became a Texas financier, Henry started a wholesale grocery business in Victoria. Shortly before the Civil War, he went into business on his own in Refugio, Texas. In 1862 Henry was conscripted, but his experience as a cobbler in France came to his rescue, and he was ordered to stay in Victoria and make boots for the army. After the war he joined Levi again and spent more than a decade building up this pioneer firm. In 1879 Henry sold his interest to two of Abraham's sons and invested $16,000 of his profits, a considerable sum at the time, in cattle and bought a 2,140-acre ranch near Victoria. He was a rancher for more than twenty years.[38]

THE LEVYTANSKY RANCH

A. Levytansky lived in eight towns and cities in Texas before trading his jewelry stock for 3,300 acres and becoming a full time rancher and stockman, possessing what has been called "one of the most attractive and modernly improved ranches in all Texas."[39]

Southwest Texas was the location for this wanderer, who came to Texas in 1882, settling at Luling. He was born in 1865 in Suwalki, Lithuania. With eight dollars worth of jeweler's tools he entered business in Luling as a teen-ager, later moving to Hallettsville (Lavaca County), Yoakum, Flatonia, Lockhart, Victoria, Laredo, and San Antonio. The Levytansky store in Yoakum was the first business there.

Levytansky took up farming and ranching full time in 1914 at age forty-nine. His ranch sprawled over parts of LaSalle and Dimmitt Counties. He had nine buildings just for his employees, which included a graduate agriculturist as superintendent of the ranch. He also had a farm on the Nueces River, where he planted 1,000 trees, experimenting with the olive tree with the intention of raising olives commercially in Texas. He raised cotton and also tried to introduce silk-worm culture through the mulberry tree.[40]

A HALF CENTURY OF RADIO-RANCHING

"The Farm and Ranch News has wired together the livestock breeders of Southwest Texas with the cotton growers of the Rio Grande Valley and all the men and women in between who trace their roots to the land." So writer Bob Boyd in 1972 described a long-running Texas radio show begun in 1935, saluting its host, Perry Kallison, then seventy years old.[41] Perry felt his show was a public service to the rural areas of Texas, so after the article was published, he continued his thirty-six-year-old show nine additional years for a total of forty-five years of broadcasting. He retired as he approached age seventy-nine. His "Farm and Ranch News" became the longest running radio program of its kind in the nation.

Long before the advent of videotape and audiotape, Perry was up at five a.m., when his listeners, the South-Central Texas farmers and ranchers, got up. The cattlemen, sheep ranchers, and citrus farmers were all his "neighbors," men and women who loved the land and livestock of Texas. He "provided a fine service to people in rural areas who did not receive daily newspapers."[42]

In 1899 Perry's father Nathan had opened in San Antonio a supermarket of a general store that provided almost anything a farmer or rancher needed.[43] In 1910 the elder Kallison added raising Durum wheat to his enterprises. The Diamond K Ranch began in 1932 with a polled Hereford herd.[44] Later the Diamond K was known for its prize-winning show herds, which took awards in Kansas City and Denver expositions as well as Texas shows, according to Perry's wife, Frances Rosenthal Kallison.

Perry started his radio show in 1935, and after being on the air for more than thirty years, the show was syndicated and appeared in scattered cities so that it could be heard all the way to the Rio Grande.[45]

THE FREEMAN BROTHERS

A member of the board of the San Antonio Livestock Exposition, Joseph Freeman persevered in his efforts to make a new Bexar County coliseum a reality. He and his brothers, Harold M. and Clarence S. Freeman, raised fine stock on their Hays County Ranch.[46] When the coliseum opened, the directors named it the Joe and Harry Freeman Coliseum. The Freemans have willed their showplace ranch near San Marcos to Southwest Texas University, San Marcos.[47]

CATTLE AS STEAK

Isaac Dahlman of Fort Worth thought of cattle as steak, not on the hoof. While cattlemen were driving herds to railroad sidings, loading them into cars, and shipping them to packing plants in Omaha, St. Louis or Chicago, Dahlman opened in Fort Worth in 1889 the Dahlman Dressed Beef Company, which marked the beginning of a new era in the Texas livestock industry.

Dahlman was undercapitalized, his supply of beef erratic, and his refrigerated boxcars limited, when he began his project in 1885, buying out a Chicago firm's Texas branch that had failed. Finally, in 1889 he contracted with an English syndicate to ship refrigerated beef through Galveston and New Orleans to Liverpool, England, and this too failed because much of the meat spoiled during the long journey, and the losses caused him to go bankrupt.

His example, however, was a bellwether for others who succeeded, and a few decades later Fort Worth became a major world cattle market.[48]

Fanny Dahlman became a U.S. citizen in 1861 in New York before becoming a Fort Worth pioneer.
© by Helen (Mrs. Nathan) Dahlman.

UNITED STATES OF AMERICA.
STATE OF NEW-YORK.
BE IT REMEMBERED, ... Ninth ...
Fanny Dahlman
SUPERIOR COURT OF THE CITY OF NEW-YORK
CITIZEN OF THE UNITED STATES OF AMERICA.
Robert D. Livingston

Rancher Perry Kallison hosted "Farm and Ranch News," a South Texas radio show, for nearly half a century.

Courtesy Frances Kallison.

Abraham Levi

Chapter 6

THE FINANCIERS

New Frontiers in Banking

DOUBLOONS AND BURIED TREASURE

Merchants performed the first banking services in Texas, banking usually being an adjunct to other business pursuits. The financial history of Texas follows the demographic patterns, with the embryo of banking beginning with the buccaneers on Galveston Island. In all probability, the de la Porta brothers became the first Texas bankers when Morin de la Porta financed the first buccaneer camp on Galveston Island in 1816 and his brother, Jao de la Porta, exchanged captured Spanish goods for Karankawa Indian produce and crafts or American money.[1]

Street scene in Victoria, 1873. Third building from left is A. Levi & Co. Bank.

In 1833 a few small businesses began along the Galveston bay front, combining exchange of money with trading and selling merchandise, catering to sailors and mariners.

Joseph Osterman was one of Galveston's first financiers, often helping the infant city of Galveston meet its debts.[2] He built the first strongbox or vault in Texas to safeguard customers' valuables and papers and was one of three early Southern bankers to make loans on cotton and growing crops.[3]

A. Levi & Co. Bank

THE VICTORIOUS LEVIS

Abraham Levi (1822-1902)

Godcheaux Levi (1852-1914)

Many stores on the Texas frontier had two standard fixtures. One was a barrel of whisky with a tin cup for thirsty customers. The other was a big iron safe in which cattlemen could place their cash in shot bags branded with their names. This practice led some merchants into lending money and discounting notes, thus edging themselves into the banking business.

Certainly the story of Abraham Levi, who worked his way up from a peddler to become the first banker in the Texas town of Victoria, illustrates the origin of frontier Texas banks.

Abraham Levi was born in the village of Hatte, Alsace, France, on June 24, 1822, to Getchell and Rachel Levi.[4] His father died when Abraham was eight, and at age thirteen Abraham peddled ribbons and notions.

At age twenty-four Abraham boarded a boat for New Orleans, arriving in America in 1846. Knowing no one, he became a menial laborer, working his way up the Mississippi River to Natchez.

After working for a butcher, he became a foot peddler. He had a melodious voice, and, playing up his French accent, he prospered. He then took a job with A. Schwartz, a merchant in Liberty, Mississippi.

The year 1848 became a turning point for both Levi and Texas. With the Mexican War ending in 1848, Texas' southern border was defined. That year Levi's employer arranged for him to open a business in Texas. A. Schwartz had a brother-in-law in New Orleans, Jacob Halfin, who advanced $3,000 for the business in Texas.[5] Jacob and his younger brother Henry hired Abraham to investigate Victoria, one of the first three Texas towns granted a charter of incorporation. Levi reached Victoria with the goods in 1849, selling "dry goods, groceries, liquors, and pecans in the west wing of the Globe House, a hotel at 116 West Forest Street."[6]

That same year, Abraham married Henry's sister, Mina Halfin. The union produced seven children.[7]

By 1861, shortly before the Civil War began, the business had become the largest dry goods establishment in southwest Texas.

At the business' height, a fire totally destroyed Halfin, Levi & Co. The two men dissolved the partnership, and Abraham spent the Civil War years in France.

In 1865 Abraham set up a business in Matamoros, Mexico.[8] When losses mounted, he returned to Victoria. There he found his stately prairie house occupied by federal troops. Eventually he regained possession of his home.

In 1866 he opened another store, A. Levi & Co., a wholesale grocery business with his cousin, Henry Levy, as a partner.[9]

Abraham developed a reputation as a friend of the farmer and cattleman, carrying them through droughts and other hard times. He began to sell bank notes. Soon the banking business grew bigger than the grocery. Abraham and Henry decided to formally organize a private banking business and set aside part of their two-story structure for the bank.

That was the beginning of a financial institution which was to grow with Texas and the Gulf Coast area and eventually become, under the name of the Victoria Bank & Trust Company, the biggest state-chartered bank in Texas.[10] The banking house of A. Levi & Co. opened its doors in March 1875 with a capital of $50,000, which by 1894 had increased to $365,000.

The bank's prosperity led it to build a new building on a grand scale. Galveston's Nicholas J. Clayton, nationally prominent architect, designed the building, erected in 1891. It contained the most modern equipment of its day. People marveled over the Diebold vault surrounded by three and one-half inches of chrome steel and the self-acting, automatic lock. It offered one of the safest depositories for the funds of customers in the Southwest.

CANNED SWEET POTATOES AND KRAUT

You can find these articles on sale at any grocery store... Did you ever look to see where they were put up then think where they were grown? Do we pay the freight two ways on them? Why not avoid the possibility of doing this by canning our own potatoes and putting up our own kraut?

It is not so much what we make as what we save that enables us to build up a good credit balance with the Bank.

THE LEVI BANK & TRUST COMPANY

VICTORIA, TEXAS

FOUR PER CENT INTEREST PAID ON TIME DEPOSITS

Ad in Victoria Advocate.

Beides banking, the Levi Company at one time owned 25,000 acres of land in six Texas counties and had large cattle interests. The Levi wholesale grocery in 1894 formed the largest business house in Victoria. The family sold the wholesale grocery to Groce-Parrish in 1908. In 1910 the bank was incorporated under the name of Levi Bank & Trust Company, and Victoria's prominent citizens were named as directors.

When the bank was sold, two of Abraham's sons, Charles G. and Godcheaux Levi, went to Dallas to open a bank there. Abraham's son-in-law, J.K. Hexter (who had married Melanie Levi), stayed in Victoria a year to teach the new owners how to manage the bank.[11]

Abraham's community work[12] included his service as president of Victoria's Jewish congregation for a quarter of a century, two terms on the town's Board of Aldermen (1856 and 1867), chairing charity meetings for relief when hurricanes ripped through Lavaca Bay, and financing the area's first electrical generator at ice plants.

Abraham sent Godcheaux A. Levi, his oldest son, to Columbia College in New York. Entering college at age fifteen, he completed two years there and returned to Victoria in 1869 when he joined his father in business.[13] He later served as president of the bank and also the Victoria Light, Power & Ice Company. In 1882 he was elected treasurer of the New York, Texas & Mexican Railroad connecting Victoria and Houston.

The Godcheaux A. Levi Scholarship established in 1908 was the first privately funded scholarship granted for a male student at the University of Texas.[14]

The Levi Bank continued to serve as a memorial to the Texas pioneer who started it. "They are still very respectful of its beginning," said a descendent of Abraham. "They have an Abraham Levi Room with a piece of furniture from his home. It was too tall for the room, so they cut a hole in the ceiling and raised a small area. The room is used for committee meetings. They still use the logo of his cattle brand on the bank stationery. The bank's letterhead shows an oil derrick, a head of cattle, and the cattle brand. The brand was a plain *u* up and *u* down. Abraham would say, 'Sometimes you're up and sometimes you're down.'"[15]

Jules K. Hexter, A. Levi's son-in-law.

Godcheaux A. Levi

Grandson Marcus and his wife Delano Hirsch Levi.

Courtesy Marie Levi Bitterman.

The Levi home, Victoria, a historic Texas landmark.

Four generations of Delano Levi.

Courtesy Marie Levi Bitterman.

Reunion of the family of Abraham Levi, who is shown in center with white beard. Beginning at top row: Charles G. Levi, G.A. Levi, Leo N. Levi, Henry L. Halff, S. Halff, Moses Haas, Julius K. Hexter, Regina Levi, Theresa Levi, Ray C. Levi, Abraham Levi, Fannie Halff, Rosa Haas, Melanie Hexter, Godcheaux C. Levi, Chas. A. Levi, Cecile F. Haas, Florence G. Levi, Alice Haas, Leo S. Levi, Minnie R. Levi, Mina E. Levi, Rosa Levi, Minnie Levi Haas, M.L. Halff, Cecile Halff, M.C. Levi, G.A.C. Halff, Minnie Halff, Minnie Levi 1886.

A PRIVATE MATTER OF PRIME INTEREST
The Oppenheimers

Anyone who has made a loan application knows the stress of dealing with a savings and loan or bank: the demands for complete financial records, including the most recent years' returns to the Internal Revenue Service, high fees for processing even if the loan is denied, multiple applications necessary to different loan institutions, and torturing delays. Private persons feel queasy about strangers scrutinizing their most personal business, and many are shy about having their lives become an open book. They may fantasize about a bank where they could walk in, be greeted by their first name, eyeball a long-time friend across the desk, state the request for the loan, and get an immediate commitment.

Such places did exist in a bygone era, and the D.&A. Oppenheimer Bank of San Antonio stood as one of the last vestiges of these historic institutions, rapidly becoming extinct. The species is called "The Private Bank." This is how banking was done in Texas when bankers financed early trail drives from Texas to Kansas, up the Chisholm and other trails. For more than one hundred years the D.&A. Oppenheimer firm wore the banner "oldest private bank west of the Mississippi." It became a living museum of how banking once was conducted.

"Swift personal service distinguishes D.&A. Oppenheimer Bankers (Unincorporated) . . . probably the only bank in the nation that never publishes a statement of condition," reported the *Wall Street Journal* in a page-one story in 1968.[16] It is a bank where the executives seldom take longer than five minutes to decide about a loan. They don't inspect collateral ("Our loans are all character loans"), don't have an outside audit ("Only one defalcation in 110 years") and don't advertise ("It would only bring in a lot of little accounts, and we don't want the business."). D.&A. does not offer safe deposit boxes, savings accounts, drive-in windows, and other modern conveniences.

Daniel and his younger brother, Anton Oppenheimer, founded the bank in 1858 as a general store in the small East Texas town of Rusk.

"Grandfather already had an uncle over here in Palestine, Texas, and went to work as a small merchant, a peddler, going from town to town," related Dan Oppenheimer II. "Banking developed as a sideline. My grandfather Kempner also went into various businesses before he evolved as a banker."[17] Dan's parents were Hattie Kempner, sister of I.H. Kempner, Sr., of Galveston, and Henry Oppenheimer, a former co-owner of the bank and son of the founder Daniel.

"In 1854 my grandfather, whose name was also Daniel Oppenheimer, came to this country from Burgkunstadt, Bavaria, Germany.[18] He came first to New York, sailed to Galveston, and then moved on to Palestine, Texas, where an uncle named Leopold Veith lived. Dan was seventeen years old at that time. He then worked for his uncle as a peddler for a couple of years in Palestine. This job would correspond to being his uncle's traveling salesman. Peddling was very common, particularly among the Jewish immigrants, as opposed to other immigrants, because the Jewish forebears and they themselves had been merchants of one type or another. The German government restricted Jews from practicing medicine or law, and most became merchants, thus they practiced that trade in Texas.[19]

"Dan then moved on his own to Rusk, Texas,[20] about thirty miles east of Palestine. . . . In 1856 he set up more of a peddling operation than what you would call a real store. He just traveled in the country selling goods.

"In 1858 he sent for his brother, Anton Oppenheimer, and they formed a fifty-fifty partnership called D.&A. Oppenheimer. From 1858 to 1861 they operated as very small merchants in Rusk and in the surrounding country. They handled . . . dry goods, groceries, and other odds and ends. . . . In rural areas merchandise was sold by a man with a horse and buggy, or by a man in a cart. In 1861 they closed their little store, left the remaining merchandise with their uncle, and joined the Confederate Army."[21]

At the war's end, Dan found himself in Franklin (near Nashville), Tennessee, and walked all the way back to Texas. He was penniless. He met his brother in Rusk, picked up some merchandise from his uncle, and moved to faster growing San Antonio, then the largest city in Texas. The brothers reopened their firm and became more and more interested in land and cattle.

"They became significant land and cattle owners along with their merchandising efforts," said Dan. "I think that very often they would trade merchandise that was needed by ranchers for cattle. They operated some big ranches. I was told (but I think that it may be an exaggeration) that they ran as many as 15,000 head at one time, until they sold their largest ranch in 1908.

"Land in those days was acquired very cheaply. Acquisition was principally done by surveying the land and by putting in a patent application at Austin. Dan's principal associate in this venture, the man with the surveying knowledge, was William Cassin. They acquired the land for twenty-five cents an acre, blocked it up, put it together, and fenced it as time went on. That is the way that large ranches were acquired. You could go back to Captain King's famous King Ranch. . . . The application fees were very small. . . . There were open ranges and you could get them for little or nothing.[22]

"I remember when I was very young that my grandfather told me that he could have bought all of the land from San Antonio down to the Rio Grande for ten cents an acre, immediately after the Civil War. And I was pretty outraged that he had not bought it. I said, 'Grandpa, why didn't you buy the land for ten cents an acre?' He replied, 'I did not have the ten cents.'"[23]

Dan, only seven when his grandfather Daniel died, remembered riding on the range with him. "They owned a big ranch. One was 110,000 acres in several counties, McMullen and Atascosa. He had other smaller ranches closer to San Antonio, 5,000 to 8,000 acres. "One was really a sheep and goat ranch, called the Hord Ranch. My grandfather imported from South Africa the first fine goats into Texas. Cattle, goats, and sheep are all important to the Texas economy: wool from sheep, mohair from goats. The big ranch had cattle. I still have a cattle brand: D-A for horses and D-A-O for cattle.[24]

"My grandfather visited the range very often. Often you'd drive a horse and buggy a couple of days to get from San Antonio to the ranch, traveling through dangerous Indian areas around there, but he never carried a gun. He was a very peaceful, very popular man. . . . The Halffs were active in the cattle drives up the Chisholm, but the Oppenheimers were active in financing but not driving them.[25]

"As merchants, they turned into bankers because

D.&A. Oppenheimer Bank, San Antonio, circa 1900. Courtesy Dan Oppenheimer.

they gave credit to ranchers who were buying hats and shoes and goods. Then when the cattle were sold and driven up to the Midwest, the ranchers came back with lots of money and they not only paid their accounts but they left their surplus money with D.&A. Oppenheimer, which was the beginning of a bank; they just left it on deposit because the merchants were the only people who had safes to keep money in. It just sort of evolved from peddling to merchandising to factoring and banking.[26]

Daniel Oppenheimer

"They had many years of bad times, like the Panic of 1907, which was a money panic and period of collapses in wool or cattle prices. There were periods when they had to carry their customers for years, much beyond the time that they had expected. They earned a great deal of personal loyalty by the way they treated people and by the way they operated their business."[27]

Since banking was a natural corollary of merchandising, and the Texas constitutions forbade chartering banks, merchants became, in effect, the only bankers.[28]

After the turn of the century, the Oppenheimer Ranch lost its identity. In 1908 Midwesterners bought Dan and Anton's large ranch South of San Antonio, which extended into McMullen and Atascosa counties, and consisted of considerably more than 100,000 acres. The purchaser brought to Texas people from the St. Louis and Chicago areas in this early land promotion. "They colonized it and split it into small tracts."[29]

"I think they sold the ranch . . . for $4.50 an acre. . . . There are now three or four oil fields of some significance located on what was once the Oppenheimer ranch. However, it was still not a bad sale. It produced over half a million dollars in cash, and it was only then that the banking function came of age."[30]

Dan Oppenheimer II, grandson of the San Antonio bank's founder, with portrait of his grandfather.

Anton, who was a partner from the business' inception in 1858, was not as prominent in the firm as his brother Dan. "Anton and his family disappeared from the San Antonio scene before 1907. He died and his wife, Adelaide, and her children moved back to New York. She came from a very cultured family and felt there weren't enough cultural aspects to Texas in those days."[31]

However, Dan's wife, Louisa, also a New Yorker, came to Texas as a bride and remained until she died at age seventy-eight. Dan and Louisa had seven children, four of whom married into prominent Texas Jewish families. Besides Henry, who married a Kempner, another son, Dr. Frederick G., married Lucille Joske of the department store family.[32] Alma married Alex Hart Halff, and Jesse married Lillie Halff, daughter of Mayer Halff.[33]

When Daniel died in 1915, his eldest son, Jesse D. Oppenheimer, then forty-five, became executive head of the bank and held this position for fifty years.[34] Both Dan II and his uncle Jesse attended Yale.

The story is told that when Jesse rejected a loan applicant, the would-be borrower begged him to reconsider and take it up with the bank's loan committee. Mr. Oppenheimer rose from behind his rolltop desk and faced the wall for a moment, then turned around:

"The loan committee has decided. The answer's still no."[35]

"I was one of his great admirers," said his nephew Dan. "He was a very great man in all respects. His only failing, if it is a failing, would be that he was unambitious and did not change with the times and that he did not take out a state or national charter to enlarge this bank.

"He was the founder of one of the original associations for charity here [San Antonio] — the forerunner of the Community Chest which later became the United Fund. He was quite philanthropic and his interest in religious affairs was intense. He was treasurer of Temple Beth El here for more than fifty years." Later Jesse's son Herbert took an active role in the bank.

The D.&A. Oppenheimer Bank observed its one-hundred-twenty-fifth anniversary in 1983.[36] "They are adept but eccentric," said Tom Frost, Jr., director of a San Antonio banking empire, on the anniversary occasion.

Anton Oppenheimer

In Dan's office, where employees worked at rolltop desks behind wooden railings with swing gates, an ancient Moser "screw door" from the bank's original vault was displayed as a decoration. One of the portraits shows the bearded patriarch Daniel holding his grandson Dan, then only a few months old.

"My grandfather Daniel was a remarkable person. So was my grandfather Kempner, the same way. The rest of us have just been inheritors, if you want to call it that. We inherited our jobs and our land and our money, whatever you inherit.

"My grandfather Daniel held the fam-

San Antonio's active downtown business district, circa 1870, at Commerce and Main showing D.&A. Oppenheimer's.

ily together, and long after he died his widow had all the family over every Friday night to dinner. When his wife, Louisa, would say, when he came home, 'You have to give Jesse and Henry a spanking because they were very bad boys today,' he would say, 'I will not spank anybody for anything not done in my presence.' But they set some very good examples. It was not by coercion, but by requiring certain behavior. They were not good disciplinarians; they set more by example," he recalled in an interview with the author in 1984.

With the death of Dan Oppenheimer II at age seventy-nine on October 17, 1987, the family quietly began closing the bank, with it finalized December 1, 1988, terminating an enterprise that emanated from the pioneer cattle drives in 1858.

Morris Lasker.

Courtesy Lasker Library, Temple B'nai Israel, Galveston.

LASKERS AT HIGH TIDE

Morris Lasker (1840-1916)

Morris Lasker was always his own person, even while growing up in Jarocin, then Prussia-Poland, where his brother Eduard Lasker became a celebrated German politician and author.[37] Morris hopped a schooner at age sixteen for the United States to seek his own fortune. By the time he died at age seventy-six, he owned four mills, real estate, and served as president of three banks, (a national bank, a state savings bank, and a trust company), all of Galveston.

Morris was born February 19, 1840. His mother died when he was only eighteen months old. His father, a moderately well off merchant, died when Morris was twelve.[38] Then a wave of anti-Semitism started to make life difficult for German Jews and intellectuals. In 1856 Morris set sail on a clipper ship that got carried off its course by winds and stayed at sea thirteen weeks before it landed at Norfolk, Virginia. Morris, who knew almost no English, arrived penniless and got a job as a clerk in a store in Portsmouth, Virginia.

Nettie Lasker

He learned fast and saved some money. He decided to better his fortune and took off for New York City, but he failed to find what he sought there and took a steamer for Savannah, Georgia, where he stayed a short period of time. Next, Florida caught his attention because of its fast developing commercial importance. Again he depleted his small savings in railway fares going from city to city. He returned to Savannah.

Here in 1857 he met Philip Sanger, who worked for the wholesaler who supplied Morris with goods he peddled on foot in Georgia. Morris Lasker was age seventeen and Philip Sanger age sixteen when they met. Lehman Sanger, Philip's brother, also came to Savannah for a year but returned to Texas. In 1860 Lasker followed him to Weatherford, a small village on the frontier west of Fort Worth founded only four years prior to his arrival. He worked for the Sangers, then opened his own store in Weatherford.[39]

Home of the Heidenheimers, whose niece married Morris Lasker.

When the Civil War broke out and business became slow, he joined a company of rangers and served under John S. Ford. This regiment of cavalry first entered into state service for frontier protection, but was soon mustered into the Confederate army. After four years of service in the army, Morris walked from San Antonio to a friend's home in Waco.[40]

He joined Lehman and Philip Sanger again, this time in Millikin and then Bryan. Lasker then moved to Galveston, where he associated with M. Schram in the jobbing business. In 1872 he became a partner in the firm of Marx and Kempner, and later was a partner in the LeGierse Co., wholesale grocers.[41]

Albert D. Lasker at the age of three.

By 1875 Morris had established his ability to succeed. In that year he met Nettie Davis, a young woman from New York state visiting Galveston. On the island, her uncle was a member of the prominent Heidenheimer family. Nettie was seventeen; Morris was thirty-five. The Davises, from German-Jewish stock, lived near Rochester and derived their name from Nettie's father's idea that Davis sounded more like a real American name than his actual name of Schmul Schmulian. He picked his new American name from the janitor of the rooming house where he lived.[42]

Albert D. Lasker as a young man.

Nettie had large luminous brown eyes. Her spoiled, and not particularly affectionate or intelligent personality contrasted enormously with the ferocious Morris.

Morris and Nettie had eight children, two of whom were boys who died at birth.[43] The second oldest surviving son, Albert David, proved to be not only famous but also wealthy, and his impact on society became a lasting and influential part of the American way of life. Albert and his wife Mary made great contributions to medical research, to the American Cancer Society, the Planned Parenthood Association, and the Lasker Foundation, which has continued to be a major national force in philanthropy. Next to the Nobel Prize, the Lasker Awards in Medical Research are the most prestigious and coveted awards in medical and clinical research. Lasker award winners often have won the Nobel Prize.

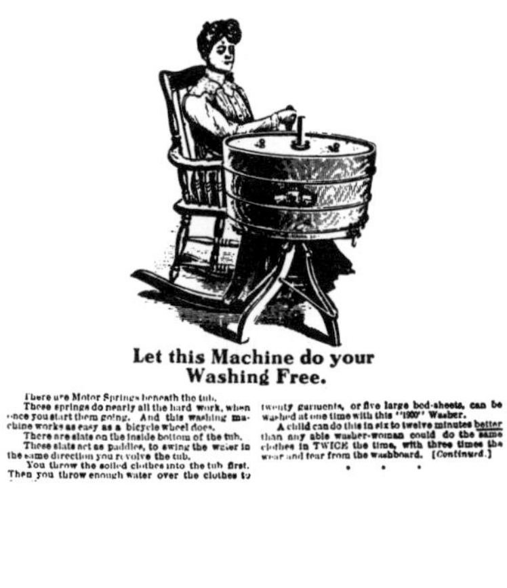

Early Lasker ads.

Albert Lasker became internationally known with the tag of "The Father of Modern Advertising." Morris, who feared Albert might never make money as a reporter,[44] the career to which he aspired, had persuaded him to go into advertising. Morris called on a business acquaintance in Chicago and asked the man to hire Albert into the advertising firm of Lord and Thomas in Chicago. Forty-four years later, Albert served as president and owner of the firm.

Albert's prodigious contributions included the popularization and the spawning of trademarks for such firms as Lucky Strike, Pepsodent, Kleenex, Palmolive, Studebaker, Sunkist, RCA, and Frigidaire. Albert innovated the merchandising of canned foodstuffs and evaporated milk and helped make citrus fruits something to drink as well as to eat, encouraged women to smoke, and introduced them to Kotex. He became one of the first to see the power of radio advertising. He produced radio's first soap operas. He is credited with inventing the singing commercial and helped make broadcasting a national force.

By the time Albert was ten his father Morris had sold his interest in the Le Gierse Co. and established the Lasker Real Estate Company.[45] Then came the panic of 1893 and Morris lost everything. When the market collapsed, his tenants could not pay their rent, and he could not pay his loans to the banks and mortgage companies. According to John Gunther, Morris owed a British syndicate more than a million dollars.

Morris packed his wife and several of his children off to Germany for a year, an action he would follow again after the great Galveston storm in 1900, with the excuse that living would be cheaper in Germany. He kept only Albert, thirteen at the time, with him. He shut the house down except for his bedroom and had Albert sleep on a cot beside his bed, telling the boy that he was lonesome. Night after night Albert awoke to the sound of his father scratching the rug on the floor, a subconscious reaction to his anxieties about failure. Eventually, Morris settled his affairs to his satisfaction and continued his climb to security and wealth.[46]

Morris acquired interests in different banking firms and became president of the Citizens Loan Company, a bank he founded. He then established the Island City Savings Bank, where he served as president for thirteen years. For eighteen years he carried the title of vice-president and chairman of the finance committee of the First National Bank.[47]

Around 1906 he purchased the Texas Star Flour Mill and as president worked as active head of that firm the rest of his life. He expanded his milling business to include properties in Wichita Falls and Waco, and in the process developed into an extremely shrewd grain buyer. He spent a lot of time in the Amarillo area, to the point that he became known as the "Grandfather of the Panhandle."[48]

As Morris developed his business acumen, his physical appearance refined itself, and he became a distinguished-looking man who some said resembled Dr. Albert Schweitzer. John Gunther described him as having "piercing blue eyes and two swords of pure white moustache. When he smiled, his face took on a subtle, complacent air, and he looked like a stout cat full of cream, licking its chops. His manner was commanding, and his temper bad. When he laid down the law, he expected instant obedience.

"He was also an extremely good citizen, far in advance of his time. He went into the banking business partly because the existing banks in the city were untrustworthy. His mill was the second in the United States to install an eight-hour day for labor, something almost unheard of in that period. He said, 'I don't deserve a decent living if the people who work for me don't have a decent living.'"[49]

Texas Star Flour and Rice Mills, Galveston.

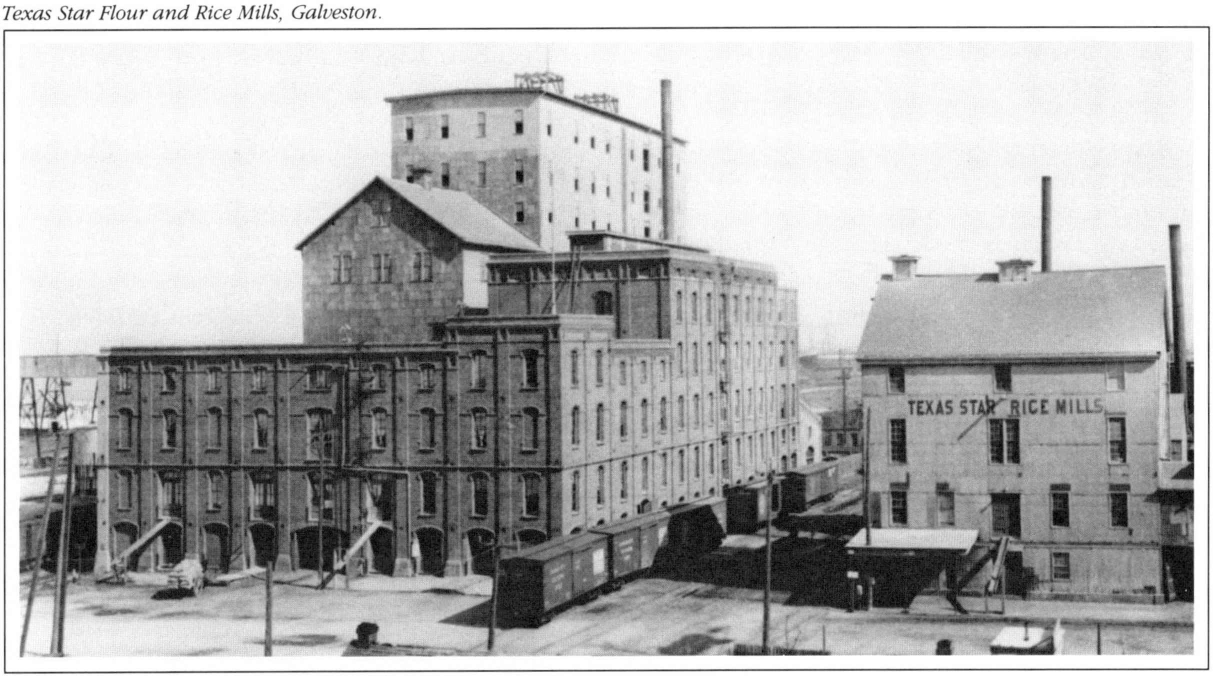

Morris Lasker home, 1728 Broadway, later demolished.

He became interested in the cotton business and at one point was president of the Galveston Cotton Exchange. He also made a trip to Egypt to investigate the cotton business there.

He actively worked to build the Gulf, Colorado & Santa Fe Railroad and acted as one of the principal leaders in the construction of that line between Galveston and Belton. He developed a lively interest in politics and served in the Texas State Senate when elected in 1895, but refused to run for any political office thereafter. He introduced and pushed through bills that regulated the fishing and oyster industries in Texas waters. He became one of the chief supporters of Governor Culberson in an extra session to suppress prizefighting. After the disastrous 1900 hurricane, he served on the building committee of the Central Relief Committee and actively led the rebuilding of Galveston.

He took a keen interest in Galveston's educational problems and served for many years as a member of the Board of School Trustees.[50] He particularly concerned himself with homeless children, and though he donated parts of his fortune in anonymous ways, it is known that he gave assistance to the Adoue Seamen's Bethel, Osterman Widows and Orphans Fund, the Johanna Runge Free Kindergarten, the Galveston Orphans Home, and the Letitia Rosenberg Home for Women. He was a generous contributor to the Protestant and Israelitish Orphans Home, which was renamed the Lasker Home for Homeless Children.

Morris Lasker died February 28, 1916, a venerated figure in his community. He left a substantial fortune and named his son Albert as the executor of his estate. In 1917 the Morris Lasker Educational Loan Fund was established in his honor at the University of Texas.

A son, Edward Lasker, placed a marble slab in the center of the Morris Lasker playground in Galveston with the legend "Dedicated in memory of Morris Lasker to the children of Galveston whom he loved so well." It characterized in a single sentence Lasker's altruism.

When Morris was in his seventy-fifth year, he had become interested in a proposed "farm school" for indigent boys. Morris died the next year, and Albert presently gave $50,000 to the National Farm School and Junior College in Bucks County, Pennsylvania, to encourage the interest of Jewish students in agriculture and as a salute to the memory of his father.

"His methods were constructive, and he aimed to make people independent," Rabbi Henry Cohen of Galveston said of Morris at the dedication of the Morris Lasker Hall, a building called the heart of the college. "Children to him were but the promise of larger possibilities, and for the good of future civilization these potentialities were to be intensely cultivated. This expresses but a part of Morris Lasker's attitude to humankind."[51]

Albert, who throughout his life had a warm and close relationship with his father, never forgot the trauma of his father's digging up the carpet in his anxiety over real estate losses, and promptly sold Morris' real estate. The Lasker properties included what later became some of the richest oil land in the world near Galveston, and about a quarter of downtown Houston, properties that eventually would be valued at more than a billion dollars. Nettie Lasker lived another fourteen years and died in 1930 at age seventy-two in her suite at the Hotel Chatham in New York City.

SWEET INVESTMENTS

Harris Kempner (1837-1894)

Isaac Herbert Kempner (1873-1967)

"Father came to Texas," I.H. Kempner said, "and opened a small store after settling at Cold Spring — why, we never knew." But I.H. did know that his father Harris Kempner left Poland in 1853 to avoid forced service in the Russian army because "a private was made a virtual serf."[52] Yet, Harris Kempner enlisted in the Confederate Army after four and a half years at Cold Spring.[53] "He seems to have been impelled by his gratitude for the manner of his neighbors in accepting him, a foreigner and an advocate of a different religious belief."[54]

When sixteen-year-old Harris had arrived in New York, he found a job as a hod carrier, bringing brick and mortar for bricklayers. A short time later he opened his own small business as a subcontractor and also attended night school to learn English. His beginning work in America is in contrast to later multimillion dollar Kempner enterprises that included Texas banking, cotton, real estate, insurance, sugar refining, rice plantations, and hotels.

Kempner was the prototype of the nineteenth-century entrepreneur. The family became a dynasty, acting as a major factor in the economic development of the Texas Gulf Coast. Harris Kempner was a director of eleven national banks scattered throughout the state: at Galveston, Giddings, Cameron, Mexia, Ballinger, Athens, Groesbeck, Marble Falls, Gatesville, Velasco, and Hamilton. His son I.H. Kempner conceived the idea and was "Father of the Commission Form of City Government," which he implemented for the first time after Galveston's 1900 storm. For half a century the Commission Form was the primary structure for U.S. city government.

From the beginning, Harris Kempner focused on personal and financial success. After four years in New York City, he had managed to save between four and five thousand dollars. After ten years in Cold Spring (now Coldspring), he had acquired a fortune of about $45,000, according to his son, I.H.[55] He started San Jacinto County Bank. Although Cold Spring was the county seat of San Jacinto County, Kempner felt it was too small and moved to nearby prospering Galveston in 1870. There he met Marx Marx of Salt Lake City and the two formed the wholesale grocery firm of Marx & Kempner.[56]

In 1872 Harris Kempner married Eliza (Lydia) Seinsheimer of Cincinnati, Ohio, and fathered eleven children.[57] Harris was all business, even with members of his family. It was a trait that stayed with him all his life. He awoke before daybreak and was in his wagon on his way to work as morning's first rays of sunlight reflected in the waters of the Gulf of Mexico. He would return home for breakfast at nine-thirty to eat with his

Harris Kempner.

Courtesy Tim Thompson.

Eliza Seinsheimer Kempner.

Courtesy Tim Thompson.

family, then go back to his store, sometimes arriving home after seven p.m. If the family ate at its customary hour of five p.m., Harris returned to the store after dinner. He revered work and education.

Harris doted on his eldest son's education. In a letter to Professor W. R. Abbott of Washington and Lee University in Virginia, he wrote, "I am in receipt of report of my son for the month of December 1886 and note that his course of instruction includes only the following, viz: Latin, German, mathematics, orthography, and Bible Lessons. Does he not study Geography, History, Rhetoric or Composition etc.? Please let me know everything he studies even to the books he is using. I want to know what my boy is doing."

Eight years later he wrote to his son I.H. (Isaac Herbert), whom he affectionately called Ikey, "It is my wish and desire that you should after finishing at Lexington go to Germany and remain there until you have learned to speak the German fluently and from there proceed to France and learn the French." I.H. recalled that "father envied the complete education enjoyed by many of his business associates, but which had been denied him."

H. Kempner's Merchants and Planters Compress Co., west yard .

After the wholesale grocery firm became one of the largest in the Southwest, Harris turned his attention to cotton, becoming one of the largest cotton factors in the Southwest. His firm advanced credit against the cotton crop just budding. When it was picked, he received it at a predetermined price and sold it overseas or to New England cotton mills. Kempner's cotton firm, founded in the 1880s, was still active in the 1980s, with offices in all major European capitals.

From cotton he expanded to land investments, particularly timber and agricultural lands. Harris Kempner early felt a need to preserve Texas' water resources. He invested in corporations to erect and maintain dams on the Comal River at New Braunfels and on the Colorado River at Marble Falls near Austin.

I. H. Kempner

Besides long hours of work, his formula for success included paying attention to detail. For example, when he was informed that a large quantity of railroad cross-ties were unlawfully cut from his acreage near the San Jacinto River and sold to a railway company, he wrote, " . . . in justice to myself I shall require of you to account to me for said ties now delivered on your road and about to be used and appropriated by you."[58]

In a similar vein, Kempner wrote to the foreman of one of his ranches and asked to be given full details: "How is the grass? — have you plenty of it — are the cattle in a good condition — . . . how many calves have you branded this fall? . . . How much cotton has been ginned at our gin? What has been done with the cotton seed?"[59]

The 1906 I.H. Kempner house, 1502 Broadway, is on tours of historic Galveston homes.

Courtesy Galveston Historical Society.

Residence of Mr. J. Seinsheimer. Mrs. H. Kempner, Sr., was a Seinsheimer.

But his attention to detail did not guarantee that he won at every enterprise he pursued. During the Depression of 1884, he expressed anger at a $5,000 stock loss. It was not the money loss that bothered him as much as his belief that a great wrong had been practiced on the stockholders.[60]

This strong sense of justice came from Harris' grandfather, a rabbi in Russian-Poland whose parents had thoroughly, but often secretly, schooled him in Old Testament, Talmud, and synagogue ritual. The rabbi quoted repeatedly that in the Talmud, *charity* was synonymous with, and could be translated only as, *justice*, according to I.H. Kempner.

Harris' sense of justice directly tied to his strong belief that every able-bodied person should work and carry the responsibility for himself. He gave generously to persons who could not care for themselves and helped his family by offering jobs to relatives and investing their funds, but he could not tolerate any form of laziness. His philosophy is possibly best recorded in a letter he wrote to his nephew, Ike Markowitz, whom Kempner had employed as a salesman:

> I note your remarks i.e. you can make no money on borrowed capital, and Julius [another nephew] is in your way etc. etc. also that California is worse than Texas — Now Ike if you are not insane your [*sic*] doubtless a complete crank — the ideas which you advance show absolute signs of insanity on your part. If California is 1000% worse than Texas it is still good enough for a rational working saving man to make several fortunes. Yet you have reasons to lay round and do nothing and furnish lame unreasonable excuses such as no one but a finished crank would furnish — Your actions are disgraceful — the idea that a young man of your age should lay round, do nothing in a country like this is positively unexcusable — such a thing had never been heard of before only from a crank or a lunatic — this country is large, full of wealth and resources in endless quantities — no country in the world like this — and yet you who claim to be sound minded, young, and experienced cannot make a living for yourself . . . you can start as most men have started say Blum, Weis, Heidenheimer & others with an apple stand or a bundle on your shoulder. You are no better than other people who now stand on the top of the ladder, but you are seeking an easy position . . . your style and ideas are not in accordance with my style and ideas.[61]

Kempner also believed in fiscal responsibility and not deficit spending. He advised his nephew, "You wrote me explaining why your personal expenses were so much and you stated that if you had lived in Cold Spring your expenses would be less — allow me to state that the principal of a man living within his income is good regardless wherever he may live, even at Paris or London. No man can sustain himself by spending more than he makes. Now is your time to work and accumulate, and spend your money liberally *after* you make it and when you are older."[62]

This save and work ethic propelled Harris to serve on the board of directors of eleven Texas banks, including the United States National Bank of Galveston. When patriarch Harris died unexpectedly in 1894 at age fifty-seven, I.H., his eldest son, had to drop out of college at age twenty-one to take over his father's enterprises. I.H., who became the most widely known of Harris' sons, noted that his brother Dan, who joined the firm in 1898, was Harris' only child who finished college with a degree and brought "valuable economic improvements" to the Kempner empire.

Dan expanded the Kempner cotton warehouse operations and real estate holdings. In 1907, with W. T. Eldridge, Jr., the Kempners acquired a 12,000-acre sugar mill plantation and refinery, a venture the families managed jointly for twenty-five years.[63] When Eldridge died in 1932, I. H.'s son, Herbert (I.H., Jr.), managed the company. It is in Sugar Land, Texas, west of Houston. The Kempners later diversified into building homes on land they developed in Sugar Land.

The Kempners expanded into life insurance when I.H.'s youngest brother, Stanley, who worked his way up from office boy, took over the Texas Prudential Insurance Company.[64] I.H.'s brother Lee was chief executive officer of the U.S. National Bank for almost fifty years following World War I.

I.H. served as a Galveston mayor. Galveston's 1900 storm, a hurricane that killed 6,000, was followed by chaos and martial law which convinced him that a new form of municipal government was needed.[65] He was a guiding force in evolving the Commission Form of Government in Galveston, first in the nation to implement it. Kempner was a member of Galveston's first city commission and for many years was finance commissioner. With this form of government, a commissioner heads each of four departments: finance and revenue, waterworks and sewage, streets and public properties, and police and fire protection. A fifth commissioner who acted as mayor-president coordinated the work of the other four. The Commission Form of Government spread rapidly in the United States, with more than 400 cities adopting it.

In 1902 I. H. married Henrietta Blum, granddaughter of Leon Blum, often referred to as the Merchant Prince of Texas.[66] Their eldest son, Harris Leon Kempner, married Ruth Levy (1917 -   ), daughter of former mayor Adrian F. Levy. Ruth led a movement to restructure the Galveston City Charter along the council-manager form and in 1961 became the first woman to serve on the Galveston City Council.

Ruth and Harris Kempner's son, Sandy Kempner, was killed in 1966 fighting with the Marines in Viet Nam.[67]

Sandy's father, Harris, was a third generation participant in the affairs of the firm.By 1958 the name "H. Kempner" became known in many foreign lands. "We have expanded operations and have agents in all cotton consuming countries in Europe. We have our own salaried representatives in Italy, Germany, Belgium, France, and Japan."[68]

I.H. Kempner's pragmatic approach derived from his family. I.H. recalled that after his parents died, the estate was not divided among the surviving heirs, but kept intact. The surviving eight children all jointly owned and administered as a unit the estate that their parents had built up over a sixty-year period.

I.H. recalled, "Our mother's efforts to keep the family intact, united, respectful of each other's rights, have proved a marvelous contribution to our financial progress and intrafamily adherence."[69] "To keep our family relations free from strife and the family fortune intact has been our goal."[70]

A WELL OILED BANKING MACHINE
Fred Farrel Florence (1891-1960)

Most persons familiar with Texas history know that Fred Farrel Florence was one of the first to lend money on oil in the ground. "Through his bank, he played an important role in financing the development of the giant East Texas oil field, at that time the biggest oil field in the world, which brought riches to many landowners, wildcatters, and petroleum and gas companies," Western historian Wayne Gard observed.[71] But his real significance was the fact that he played a key role in providing loans at critical times to businesses and industries, a feat that impacted the economic growth of Texas. Some of the better known of these are Texas Instruments, Neiman-Marcus, and Temple Industries, which converted East Texas pine trees to paper for *Time* magazine.

"He had a great knowledge of people's potential," recalled his widow, Helen. "Erik Jonsson, Cecil Green — who started T.I. — they will tell you they are where they are because of Fred Florence. Whenever either makes a talk, he mentions Fred Florence. Fred gave them their start for their business, which evolved into Texas Instruments. There are so many things overwhelming with the man."[72]

Neiman-Marcus had been established for a dozen years before Florence came to Republic Bank, but "Republic was the bank of Neiman-Marcus from the time that Fred Florence came in [1920] . . . because of Fred and because my father was on the board of the bank," said Stanley Marcus. "Dad had a tremendous respect for Fred. . . . Fred was doing an aggressive job of merchandising money, which was the only way to come into this town that was sewed up by the First National Bank.[73] Fred eventually came on the Neiman-Marcus board.

"He knew how to do things with a beau geste. . . He saw how the big bankers acted, and how they entertained. . . . Fred had meticulously good taste . . . and he was very interested in everything that Helen bought. He sat in while she fitted clothes and helped select them — I don't think she ever bought a thing that he didn't personally approve of. . . . He'd come in on Saturday afternoon, and I guess he spent a good portion of his Saturday afternoons in the fitting rooms at the store. . . . He always appreciated beauty," said Stanley Marcus.[74]

Florence's obsession with keeping up his image as a successful banker dictated that he get a haircut every day. When he met important clients in his work, he was always prepared. *Time* magazine published an article about Florence in 1958 that gave another side of his character. Fred's picture accompanied the article, with the caption: "Dallas' Florence — From the Texas league to the majors." *Time* said, "The man who best combines such Texas talents is taut, wiry, fiercely competitive Fred F. Florence, 67, head of Dallas' Republic National Bank, who for years has been locked in an epic duel with Dallas' First National Bank. The prize: the title of No. 1 bank in Texas. Last week Banker Florence . . . moved Republic out of the Texas League into national banking . . . Fred Florence aims to make Republic far more than a bustling regional institution. Hanging in his sumptuous third floor office is a painting of cowboys rounding up wild horses, entitled *Bringing Them In.* 'When it came to business,' says he, 'that's my motto.'"[75]

It was no coincidence that the vice-chairman of the board of Time, Inc., became one of Republic's clients. But he was no ordinary client. Arthur Temple served as an officer of Time, Inc., which published *Time, Sports Illustrated, Fortune, Money, People*, and *Life* magazines. This company also owned the Book-of-the-Month Club, Inland Container Corporation,

Fred F. Florence in front of Florence Hall, SMU.

and cable television networks. Temple and his family became the largest stockholders of the company, and he commuted weekly from his home in southeast Texas to Time, Inc. headquarters in New York.

Arthur Temple tells this story of his relationship to Fred Florence: "Our company, which was then Southern Pine Lumber Company . . . in East Texas, went through a period of borrowing and growth. . . . I'm going back to the '26-'28 period, which was before my time . . . my grandfather was founder of the business . . . They borrowed two or three million dollars . . . a lot then. . . . When the Depression hit, we had several hundred thousand acres of timber land . . . but you couldn't sell it. We found ourselves with what my father thought was a tremendous debt — we'll say it was three million. The loan was held by a group of banks which included the Republic [as well as banks in Houston, Texarkana, and New Orleans]. We would have gone straight into bankruptcy and couldn't have kept out of it, if it hadn't been for Mr. Fred Florence. . . . My dad didn't sleep at all during the night because he just worried. . . . So as the day for the creditors' meeting approached, well, Dad, of course was just terribly restless. . . . And they had the meeting at the old Texarkana National Bank . . . and Dad went through the whole story and told them about all the land we owned . . . and the retail lumber yards we had throughout Texas . . . and Mr. Wagonfeuer [of New Orleans] was insistent on putting us into bankruptcy. And Mr. Florence and Mr. Gosset [of Houston] calmed him down and said, 'Now let me tell you something, we don't know a damn thing about running a lumber company. . . . We know Arthur' — that was my father — 'we know he's honest . . . and if anybody can do it he will, and we're a lot better off to just ride with Arthur and Southern Pine . . .' and they gave him the time it took, and within two years Dad had paid them off."[76]

Arthur Temple, Jr., was a child when Florence helped save his family's lumber business. He met Florence twenty years later at a party in Austin. He decided to bank with Republic. A few years later, he approached Republic bank officials for a six-million-dollar loan when he decided his firm should cease being just a sawmill and diversify. "Bear in mind, I was thirty-four years old. . . . I started this presentation and I'd been going about forty minutes . . . [when] he turned to Oran [Kite, Fred's right-hand man who did his investigative work], and he says, 'Oran, let this boy have the money at the prime rate. . . Seven years okay.' And then he got up and started out and smiled and he says, 'Hell, Oran, this boy is going to be real important to this bank.' Those were his words. . . . Other bankers would always sit down and tell how they were worried but they were going to stick their neck out for you, young fellow! I'd borrowed a good bit of money from other banks before that, and they always made you listen to that speech. . . . What did Florence do? He turned to his chief lieutenant and said, 'Oran, this boy's going to be important to this bank.' Now, I was smart enough to know what he was doing. I knew he was pumping me up. But at the same time, think how flattered a young fellow from East Texas was, that Fred Florence would take the trouble, and to think that I was important enough to be pumped up, you see? That was the greatness. . . . And what do you think I've done the rest of my life, and I'm now fifty-nine? I've worked my *tail* off to prove that Fred Florence was right!"[77]

"He had a quick mind," said Helen, years later. "He made immediate decisions. He kept his desk out front so he could greet the customers. His philosophy was, 'What can we do to make your business grow?'"[78]

Florence was exuberant in his civic work as well as in business. When he saw a need for more trained physicians for the state of Texas, he, in conjunction with Karl S. Hoblitzelle and Dr. Edward H. Carey, Sr., acted as one of the three principal founders of Southwestern Medical Foundation, which established and operated Southwestern Medical Center. The original institution later became the University of Texas Southwestern Medical Center at Dallas. Florence served as vice-president and treasurer of Southwestern Medical Foundation from its beginning in 1939 until his death in 1960. The Fred Florence Bioinformation Center stands as his memorial.

Florence believed in all peoples, a true ecumenical man. He and Hoblitzelle also were instrumental in getting Southwestern to provide land for St. Paul Hospital, a large Catholic medical center in Dallas, and headed its building campaign. Pope John XXIII awarded Florence the Benemerenti Medal, the highest honor that can be bestowed on a non-Catholic. "A rabbi's son-in-law got a medal from the Pope. We had a beautiful audience," recalled Helen.[79]

Fred was the fourth of six children born to Moses and Celia Freedman Fromowitz. His parents had lived in Lithuania. They left there in 1883 and lived in New York almost nine years before moving to Texas in the Spring of 1892. Fred missed being born a Texan by around four months; he was born in New York City November 5, 1891. The family's move to New Birmingham in the piney woods of East Texas followed the boom of iron ore development there.[80] Fred would spend almost half his life in East Texas.

In 1894 the family moved to Rusk, also in Cherokee County, where the Oppenheimer brothers had settled thirty years before. Moses worked as a merchant in a grocery store next door to a bank. Fred's career began in Rusk, where at age fifteen in 1907 after

graduating Rusk High School, he did odd jobs and swept floors at the First National Bank. In 1911, at age nineteen, the president promoted him to assistant cashier.[81]

The previous year, his older brother M.E. ("Mike"), then twenty-seven years old, had the children's last name changed from Fromowitz to Florence. Fred added a middle name, Farrel, taking the name from a favorite baseball player. Fred's father never changed his name from Fromowitz. The parents moved to Dallas in 1915, and after the father's death in 1926, Fred's mother used the name Florence.[82]

Fred lived in East Texas the first twenty-eight years of his life. (At age nineteen he moved to Dallas to attend a business school, then returned to Rusk.) He briefly worked at a bank in Ratcliff, Texas, leaving to accept the vice-presidency of the Alto State Bank in nearby Alto, Cherokee County.[83] A year later he became its president in 1915.

Fred resigned his Alto State Bank position to enlist in the Signal Corps Aviation School of the U.S. Army with the rank of corporal in 1918, stationed at Love Field, Dallas, the field that began during World War I to train aviators. He later served in New York and Georgia, assembling planes, and was commissioned Second Lieutenant. At the close of the World War I, Fred returned to Alto and resumed his banking post. He became an alderman and in 1919 was elected mayor. In 1920 he moved to Dallas after being recruited by the Guaranty Bank and Trust Company. Historian and columnist Frank Tolbert wrote in the *Dallas Morning News* that "Banker [W. O.] Connor knew what he was after: Fred Florence."

Guaranty Bank and Trust Company (later Republic) officers elected Fred first-vice-president in 1920, the same year the bank became a member of the Federal Reserve System. In 1922 officials applied for a national bank charter with a new name for the bank, Republic National Bank of Dallas. As a national bank, it could increase the size of its loans.

Florence served as vice-president until January 8, 1928, when he was elected president. The next month (February 21, 1928) he married Helen Lefkowitz, daughter of David Lefkowitz, then rabbi of Temple Emanu-El of Dallas. They became parents of two adopted children, David Lewis and Cecile Ann.

"We met at Temple," recalled Helen years later. "He was an observant Jew. He attended Temple pretty regularly, and he became devoted to and attentive to my father, even before we were married. Father helped to guide him in his public service. Father saw a great potential in Fred's interest in people. He got him interested in philanthropy and public service. They developed a beautiful relationship of working together for many causes for the benefit of all [Texans]."[84]

Although public spirited, he was devoted to his immediate family, and telephoned his mother every day except when he traveled out of town. He was tender and sentimental, shedding tears when filled with emotion.[85] But to the outside observer, he was the impeccable dresser, always wearing a dark suit and white shirt with French cuffs. He usually did not drive a car because his mind wandered on so many other things. Helen assigned herself as his chauffeur.

Under Florence's guidance Republic became the first bank in the Southwest to make foreign loans on a broad scale. Florence renamed the "Commodities" or "Foreign" Department the "International Department," which pioneered in hiring personnel of Mexican descent. Republic also pioneered in the Southwest two services which patrons take for granted today, traveler's checks and the lockbox.

Florence insisted on diversification, a balance of oil, cotton, and industrial loans, as well as loans to corporations and individuals. Cotton loans became big business for the bank. But the biggest was oil.

Nathan Adams and the First National Bank of Dallas can lay claim to making the very first oil production loan, but Florence and Republic Bank gave it new significance. Florence, Adams, and R.L. Thornton, Sr., of Mercantile were largely responsible for Dallas becoming the banking center of the Southwest.[86] David Nevin wrote in *The Texans,* "These were the men with the financial foresight, the resources and, most of all, the downright courage to take the next step in oil: they began lending against the reserves. They were lending on an asset that no one had ever seen."[87]

The demands for loans escalated when the oil boom hit with the 200-square-mile East Texas Oil Field. At the time, banks could make only short term six month loans safely, loans based on the amount of oil to be produced in that time. Therefore, drillers began pumping frantically. When Columbus (Dad) Joiner, a wildcatter who brought in the first well in the East Texas Oil Field in 1930, announced his strike, five thousand persons swarmed into Kilgore in one day. In 1931 at the height of the boom, wells were brought in at the rate of one an hour, even in the front yards of residences.

In 1932 the Texas Legislature passed an act giving the Railroad Commission power to regulate oil production so that supply would not exceed anticipated demand. The proration stabilized prices and conserved oil supply. This regulated production, and the impact was that oil reserves still in the ground became a bankable commodity. It was possible to make excellent estimates as to how much oil could be expected, and banks could know with fair accuracy how a loan would be amortized. Republic established a Petroleum Department. It was an innovation for a bank to employ geologists and engineers, but through Fred's guidance, by the late 1940s the department had four vice-presidents and four geologists assigned to making oil and gas loans.[88]

Fred's neighbor who lived across the street, the late Algur H. Meadows, a founder of General American Oil Company, benefited from Fred's financing of proven reserves and his lending money on interest bearing oil payments. General American officials publicly credited Republic Bank for contributing to their success.[89] (The Meadows Foundation has contributed internationally to the fine arts.)

The Texas Bankers Association elected Florence its president in 1935.[90] The next year found Fred preserving Texas history, not making it. In 1936 Texas celebrated its centennial. A group of civic leaders worked to enable Dallas to be the site of the celebration, an important milestone in establishing Dallas as a major American city. Florence at age forty-five was named president of the Texas Centennial Exposition. Helen, only thirty years old at the time, served as chairman of the Women's Division of the Centennial, as well as head of the Visiting Nurses, an association brought to Texas by her mother to treat the ill at home.

In 1951 Fred's friend Karl Hoblitzelle contributed funds for the remodeling of a building used by the Law School of Southern Methodist University and requested it be named "Florence Hall." At the dedication, Hoblitzelle said, "He justly deserved this honor because of his manifold contributions to . . . the great Southwest, and for his unselfish and enthusiastic support of every worthwhile educational, constructive and charitable enterprise [in Texas] during the last thirty years."

Their offices were next door. "Karl and Fred would discuss all of their civic situations and work them out," recalled Helen Florence years later. "They were a team in both civic and business projects — largely civic."

In 1955 he was elected president of the American Bankers Association — the first Jew to be elected and the only Jew to receive this honor as of this writing.

In 1960 Helen and Fred Florence took a round-the-world tour with Peggy and Joe C. (Jodie) Thompson, president of Southland Corporation, operators of the 7-Eleven chain of retail food stores. Less than a year later, both men had died. When Florence died December 25, 1960, Helen's nephew asked another intern to take his place at the hospital where he worked as a medical resident, so he could attend Fred's funeral. The other young doctor said he too would like to attend Fred Florence's funeral, because Fred had paid for his medical education, as he had done for many deserving students. The funeral took place at Temple Emanu-El, where Fred had learned the Jewish teaching that charity and justice meant the same thing.

Like the *Old Man and the Sea,* Fred fantasized about bringing in a bigger fish until the very end. A week before he died, he told an associate, "I've figured out a way we can double the bank in half the time I had planned."[91]

Fred symbolized a civic climate that emanated from Dallas during the middle of the twentieth century. It had a spirit, a soul, a creative mind. Patrick Haggerty, the Texas Instruments chairman of the board who succeeded Erik Jonsson when he became mayor of Dallas, expressed it this way:

"There was a climate in Texas, an attitude that made things possible. . . . This is even more true of Fred Florence. The fact that he would accept our plans when he couldn't possibly understand the technicalities of what we were doing, and that he would lend us what then was for us a truly huge sum of money at a time when our cash position was low and our book value relatively poor, meant that he was betting on people and on performance instead of sticking to banking standards. I don't think there were many places where that could have happened."

Regarding Texas Instruments' move into transistors, Haggerty said, "I think that if Erik Jonsson had hesitated and Fred Florence had been conservative, we can speculate that the whole thrust of electronic technology might have been delayed in this country and that would have had consequences beyond imagining."[92]

A RAILROAD PERKS UP

Moritz Kopperl (1828-1883)

Moritz Kopperl as a young man.

Courtesy Rosenberg Library.

Significant bankers like Oppenheimer, Levi, Lasker, Kempner, and Florence created new banking practices in Texas, but other Jewish financiers made important contributions to banking, although they did not instigate major innovations. Moritz Kopperl and Hyman Pearlstone were such Jewish Texas bankers.

Moritz Kopperl is best remembered for having saved the Gulf, Colorado & Santa Fe Railway from bankruptcy. He made Galveston one of the largest coffee importing ports in the world. In 1876 Texans elected him to the House of the Fifteenth Texas Legislature, where he was chairman of the Committee on Finance and Revenue. He played a significant role in refinancing the government of Texas. Kopperl arranged for municipal bonds to be sold in New York, a sale based on his personal recommendation and guarantee, without his asking or receiving any part of the commission authorized by law.

Born October 26, 1828, Moritz was well educated, having studied in his native Moravia as well as in Vienna, Austria.[93] On the invitation of his uncle, Major Charles Kopperl of Carroll County, Mississippi, he migrated to the United States in 1848. For nine years the young Moritz lived with his uncle, learning the ways of the new country, especially, the deep South.

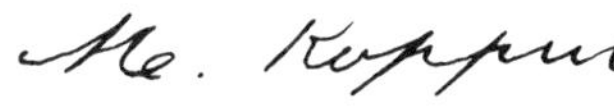

Courtesy Rosenberg Library.

In 1857 Moritz and A. Lipman, a business partner in Mississippi, set out for Texas. They settled in Galveston and started the dry goods firm of Lipman and Kopperl, which flourished until 1861 when the federal blockade of merchandise caused many businesses to cease. During the Civil War their business house was burned. When the war ended, Kopperl went into the cotton commission business.[94]

He diversified from exporting cotton to importing coffee, bringing into the United States through Galveston the finest quality coffee from Brazil.

In 1866 Moritz married Isabella Dyer of the Dyer family from Baltimore.[95] Her uncle, Major Leon Dyer, had escorted the captured General Santa Anna to Washington after the Battle of San Jacinto. Her aunt, Rosanna Dyer Osterman, nursed the wounded of both sides during the Civil War and became a Texas philanthropist who left millions in bequests throughout the United States. Isabella composed music which Dr. J.O. Dyer copyrighted.[96] She specialized in trying to bring culture to Texas.

Kopperl specialized in breathing life back into failing businesses. He first moved into the Texas National Bank and became its president in 1868. The bank verged on failure. His management placed it on sound financial footing, and eventually it became one of the most prosperous in the Gulf Coast area.[97]

His greatest coup came with putting the Gulf, Colorado & Santa Fe railroad back on the track. He was offered the presidency of the railroad in 1877, when it stood on the brink of insolvency. At first he declined, but the challenge won out. He was president from 1877 to 1879, carrying the railroad over a critical period until its success was assured.[98]

This railroad was born out of rivalry of two cities. When Galveston became the richest city in the state, her rival, Houston, diverted trade from her. Cotton exporting had made Galveston a trade center, and after the Civil War nearly all Texas cotton moved south to Galveston by rail or wagon. Galveston served as the distribution hub. However, Houston used the yellow fever epidemics, that every few years hit the Gulf Coast, to quarantine people and goods in and out of Galveston. The Galveston, Houston & Henderson (G. H. & H. Railway) to Houston offered the only feasible way for Galveston to distribute bagging and other supplies needed by cotton planters. It occurred to Houston merchants that if, at the strategic moment, they ordered a quarantine against Galveston, Houstonians would have no competition. Galvestonians decided in Spring 1873 to build their own rail line to bypass Houston. Among the civic leaders who volunteered to buy shares was Kopperl's relative Isadore Dyer, president of the Union Fire & Marine Insurance Company.[99]

Moritz Kopperl saved the Gulf, Colorado & Santa Fe Railroad from bankruptcy.

Courtesy DeGolyer Library, SMU.

Although named the Gulf, Colorado & Santa Fe, the line had no connection with the original Atcheson, Topeka & Santa Fe. The Texans borrowed the image of the established name. (It later became part of the Santa Fe system.) By 1875 the line was ready to begin. In 1877, however, the road was "down and almost out."

Hyman Pearlstone. © L. H. Budner.

When Kopperl moved into the president's chair, the company was without means or credit and was harrassed by tax collectors. Competitors in Houston fought vigorously to terminate the effort. Kopperl put both his reputation and financial fortune on the line. He contracted for the construction of the new road and personally paid U.S. back taxes to save the railroad's charter until he could organize a consortium to bail out the line.

Despite business posts in importing, with the railroad, and as president of an insurance company, he found time for civic work. In 1871 and 1872 he was elected to Galveston's City Council and worked to develop the harbor's shipping facilities. He served as chairman of the city's finance committee and devised the means to meet Galveston's indebtedness and protect its credit rating.

Kopperl became a delegate to the presidential

national convention in Baltimore in 1872 which nominated Horace Greely. In 1876 he was elected a state legislator.

He was connected with many charities and for many years was president of the Protestant Orphans Home.

In 1883 his health began to fail. He sailed to Europe to improve his health, but died in Bayreuth, Bavaria, on July 3, 1883.

Moritz Kopperl is buried in Galveston in the old Hebrew Benevolent Cemetery No. 1 on Broadway. His magnificent towering granite tombstone is an obelisk with the words, "I pray thee, then, write me as one who loved his fellow man."[100]

During a trip to Redlands, California, in 1902, his widow Isabella was thrown from a horse-drawn carriage (a tallyho) and died from injuries. The *Confederate Veteran* magazine wrote: "She was a consistent member of the Jewish congregation of Galveston." Services were held at the family mansion on 24th and Broadway, officiated by her rabbi, Dr. Henry Cohen.[101]

The town of Kopperl, Texas, on the Santa Fe Railroad in Bosque County is named for this pioneer.[102] This is ironic, because Kopperl never lived there; whereas Jacob de Cordova, who lived the last years of his life in Bosque County, platted Waco, wrote books on Texas, and published her first official map — had no town named for him anywhere in Texas.

Besides Kopperl, other Jewish Texans who served as directors of the Gulf, Colorado & Santa Fe also had towns named for them, including Heidenheimer, Texas; Blum, Texas; and Kempner, Texas.

Isaac M. Pearlstone of Buffalo, Texas, grandfather of Hyman Pearlstone.

BIG LEAGUE BUSINESS
Hyman Pearlstone (1878-1966)

In 1899 when Hyman Pearlstone, cashier of the First National Bank of Buffalo, Texas, married Mabel Roxanna Ash, daughter of Henry Ash, "one of Palestine, Texas' most influential bankers,"[103] banking momentum was launched that for decades made waves in the Texas business community.

Like most of the high profile Jewish bankers who preceded him in Texas, Hyman specialized in bailing out companies in trouble. He was the first of this early group to be a native born Texan.

Even Hyman's father, Barney, was a native American, born in Syracuse, New York. "Hyman's grandfather, Isaac, was to invest in a small business with the Sanger family in Waco, and that was the real reason they moved to Texas," according to Hyman and Mabel's daughter, Helen Pearlstone Loeb, who said her father had told her that story.[104]

The Pearlstones came to Texas circa 1869, according to Hyman's grandson, Dallas banker Lawrence H. Budner.[105] They emigrated on a boat from — not Europe — but Ithaca, New York, traveling to Galveston. From there the family went to Jewett, Texas, where Odd Fellows certificates show I.M. served as president of the lodge there in 1875.

The family then moved to Buffalo, Texas, in Leon County, a town established in 1872 when a railroad set up a station there. The town took its name from the herds of buffalo which had formerly roamed the area. Barney married Lena Hart of Summit, Mississippi, and Hyman was born in Buffalo in 1878.[106]

When Hyman was fifteen, his father lost his entire fortune in the Panic of 1893, speculating in cotton and land. "In the cotton business you're rich one day and broke the next," said his daughter.

Two years later Hyman began his banking career as a bookkeeper and teller with the Farmers and Merchants National Bank at Waco and a year later was made manager of the Waco Clearing House Association. On a visit to the bicycle races in Palestine he met his future wife, Mabel. He resigned from his Waco job to move to the hometown of his bride, Palestine, where he established the Pearlstone Grocery Company in 1899, his first venture in business. He also established a connection with the First National Bank of Palestine for more than twenty years, serving as vice-president and director. "He liked being a big fish in a small pond," recalled a grandson.[107]

"In 1921 Mr. R.W. Higginbotham of Dallas asked

Hyman to move to Dallas and take over his business, the Boren-Stewart Co. [wholesale grocery also], as it was in bad shape financially. Daddy not only came here but in no time at all had the company making money," his daughter said. They phased out of groceries and bought a hardware company, and Hyman served as president of Higginbotham-Pearlstone Hardware Company.

In 1924 Hyman Pearlstone became a director of the First National Bank in Dallas, (later InterFirst), a post he held for thirty-eight years.[108]

On August 11, 1936, Tucker Royall, chairman of the board, and Nathan Adams, president of the First National Bank, announced the election of Hyman Pearlstone to the office of chairman of the executive committee. The announcement said "he brings to his office a thorough comprehension of the business life of the community, a sustained and dynamic energy."[109]

At that time Hyman directed the operations of many companies: president, Higginbotham-Pearlstone Hardware Company, Dallas; vice-president, Pearlstone Mill and Elevator Company, Dallas; director, Higginbotham-Bailey-Logan Co., Dallas; chairman of the board, Pearlstone-Joyce Company, Palestine; chairman of the board, Pearlstone-Ash Grocery Company, Longview; chairman of the board, Pearlstone-Bolton Company, Denton; chairman of the board, Lasswell Grocery Supply, Waxahachie; vice-president, Enid [Oklahoma] Terminal Elevator; director, St. Louis-San Francisco Railway Co.; Director, Burlington-Rock Island Railroad. During World War II he was also chairman of the Dallas N.R.A. Board.

Hyman's younger brother Julius became prominent in banking and business, too, owning Pearlstone Mill and Elevator Company. For generations, Dallasites driving along what is now Interstate 30 could see a tall grain elevator with the name Pearlstone crowning the tallest tower. Julius served as a director of the Republic National Bank of Dallas and became a friend of Fred Florence.

Hyman early developed a friendship with Connie Mack, owner and manager of the Philadelphia Athletics baseball team. In 1909 the *New York World* called Hyman Pearlstone "America's Number One Baseball Fan" said his daughter Helen. "Among our father's many personal effects were fifty years' memorabilia of famous baseball players — his friends. Upon Hyman's death [in 1966] we sent most of this to the Baseball Hall of Fame in Cooperstown, New York." [110]

Barney Pearlstone, left, and his son Hyman Pearlstone, above.

© L.H. Budner.

Haymon Krupp (1874-1949) drilled the Santa Rita No. 1, which gave the University of Texas System a magnificent fund.

Photo copyright © by Mrs. Maxine Krupp

Chapter 7

THE WILDCATTERS

From Pipes to Oil Leases

University students continue to benefit from one of Texas' Jewish pioneers, a wildcatter who gave the University of Texas system the largest endowment in the state's history. Haymon Krupp, who went from merchant to wildcatter, and Texas Jews who worked in the oil fields, pulling pipe and reselling it, had all started as impoverished immigrants. They used the profits from their oil ventures to leave lasting benefits, from education to health, for Texans who followed generations later.

Haymon Krupp knew what it meant to be poor. In 1890 he emigrated from Lithuania to El Paso to join his brother Harris who had preceded him. The boys were from a family of thirteen children. When he arrived in El Paso, Haymon worked as a clerk in a dry goods store.[1] He saved his money, opened his own retail clothing store and in 1910 established a wholesale dry goods house, pioneering in the southwest outdoor clothing industry.

Probably because he had felt the pinch of poverty himself, he became liberal in charitable donations even before he began to prosper and become an unlikely Jewish wildcat oil developer. When Krupp began his first oil well, a well so significant it changed the course of Texas history, he already was giving tons of coal to the poor in El Paso.

Every winter for years, El Paso newspapers carried an advertisement signed "H. Krupp" which read "Free Coal for the Poor" and instructions telling how the coal could be obtained. He also left standing orders with coal companies to supply fuel for the needy. His goal was to lessen suffering.

His humanitarian behavior generated so much interest that in 1925 Owen P. White, a Texan on assignment for the *New York Times*, wrote a story that would later appear in the Sunday *Times Magazine*.[2]

"When Krupp started this charity, which is a purely personal one and has cost him many thousands of dollars, he was far from a rich man," White wrote. "If there is any truth in the saying that 'he who giveth to the poor lendeth to the Lord and is repaid an hundred fold,' then Haymon Krupp is a striking example of its operations, except that he has been reimbursed many thousand times in place of a mere paltry hundred. In addition to having recently become excessively prosperous himself, Mr. Krupp, apparently guided by Providence, has opened up a way whereby the University of Texas bids fair to become one of the richest institutions of learning in America."

White painted a poignant panorama of the campus in 1925."In place of looking like a college of the first class," White wrote, "the University of Texas, when viewed by a stranger, looks like a second-rate dairy farm. The campus is enormous; in the middle rises a somewhat pretentious building (put there thirty-five years ago); around this are clustered two or three modest brick structures, and then, scattered over the place and resembling the wooden shacks that were used in the war cantonments, are a great number of long, low, one-story frame buildings of the very cheapest possible construction. In these clapboarded hovels absorbing knowledge, much as Abraham Lincoln absorbed it in a log cabin, are 5,500 students." It was said that Krupp "unshacked the campus."

Haymon Krupp and his oil lease partner, Frank Pickrell, changed all that when they brought in Santa Rita No. 1, the first producing oil well on university-owned land. Krupp certainly did not fit the mold of a Texas wildcatter, and the story of how he and Pickrell came to be oil men is the stuff of legend.

When Krupp was elected to the El Paso Hall of Fame in 1970, Chris P. Fox of the El Paso County Historical Society wanted to remember the man rather than the wildcatter whose perseverance brought the University of Texas System income of

The Permian Basin, a vast area in West Texas near the Pecos River, was explored for minerals by adventurer Castaño in 1590 and by Krupp more than three hundred years later. Map shows Reagan, Upton, Irion, and Crockett counties.

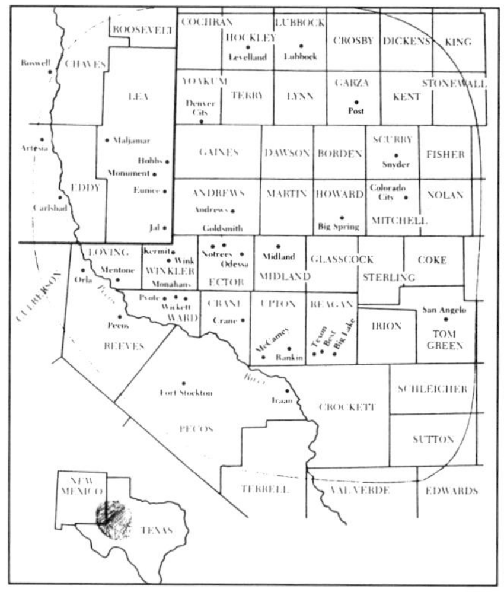

Two decades after his death, Haymon Krupp was elected in 1969 to the Petroleum Hall of Fame, where this portrait of him as a young man was dedicated.
Courtesy Mrs. Maxine Krupp.

more than one billion dollars.[3]

Chris Fox spoke of his business experience with Krupp. "Back in the late 20s, Mr. and Mrs. Krupp had generously donated funds with which to build the B'nai Zion Temple on North Mesa. Robert E. McKee was the general contractor, and we had the subcontract to erect the steel. It was a *hot summertime*, well ahead of air conditioning, the kind of summertimes when the coffee in your lunch bucket never cooled, it was just as hot at noontime as it was when your bride filled it from the early morning coffeepot. Things were not going too well on the job that day when Mr. Krupp made one of his rounds.

Santa Rita. *Courtesy Mrs. Maxine Krupp.*

"But on this day he wasn't pleased with the way the job was going. . . . I told him things should level off in a day or two. He asked me why they couldn't 'level off *before that*' and walked away. . . . About five-thirty he came by again, and said that we had been doing a good job, and that he was sure we would be on schedule soon. He didn't need to come back and cheer me up."[4]

It is a long jump from a dry goods distributing company and a work clothes factory to an oil field. Krupp was looking to diversify even further and to invest in oil exploration when, in 1916, a geological report was issued by a Swedish immigrant scientist who was on the faculty of the University of Texas. In his report to the University Board of Regents, Dr. Johan Augustus Udden suggested the possibility of minerals in the Permian Basin and Reagan County area. Udden said, "there are natural chances for finding accumulations of gas as well as oil."[5]

Three workmen are shown with Haymon Krupp (far right) and his wife, Leah Silverman Krupp, inside the Santa Rita derrick.

The geological report by Dr. Udden involved lands owned by the University of Texas. The origins of the lands go back to March 1836, at the Convention assembled to declare Texas' Independence. One of the indictments brought against Mexico stated: "It has failed to establish any public system of education, although possessed of almost boundless resources (the public domain), and although it is an axiom in political science, that unless a people are educated and enlightened, it is idle to expect the continuance of civil liberty, or the capacity of self-government."

When Texas won the Battle of San Jacinto that same year and became a Republic, the Texans provided for the education of their young when they wrote into the Constitution of the Republic of Texas to set apart "for the endowment, maintenance, and support of said University and its branches" one million acres of land. In 1876 the Constitution took away the farm lands granted to the University under an Act of 1858 and gave in lieu one million acres of grazing lands farther west. To the lands previously set apart and appropriated for the endowment, the Legislature in 1883 added one million acres.

In 1906 a boy, Rupert T. Ricker, and his father left North Central Texas to search in West Texas for land on which to establish a ranch, and which they eventually found in Reagan County. Here the boy grew up. He entered the University of Texas in 1912, earned a law degree in 1915, and served in World War I, before returning to the family ranch.

A severe drought had crippled the family cattle business, so Rupert decided to search for oil after he learned of successful strikes in other parts of the state and following the Udden report. However, many previous efforts had been made to find oil in West Texas, and the region — from Amarillo to the Rio Grande — became known as the "Petroleum Graveyard of Texas" because drillers continued to come up with dry holes.[6]

To increase his chances in finding oil, Rupert decided to lease or "block up" a large amount of acreage. Instead of contacting innumerable small land owners, he decided to lease land owned by the University of Texas, the largest land owner in Reagan County. He finally leased 674 sections totaling 431,360 acres — all of the University's land in Reagan, Irion, Upton, and Crockett Counties. He hoped to sell permits to drill on the property to enough wildcatters so that he could drill his own well. However, he was unable to raise the $43,136 rental fee (ten cents per acre) needed to pay the state. With only a few days left on his option, Rupert Ricker sold his lease option to Haymon Krupp and another El Pasoan, Frank T. Pickrell, for five hundred dollars.[7]

These men paid the rental fee and turned their efforts toward raising the money to drill their own well. According to the lease they signed, Krupp and Pickrell had to begin to drill within a certain specified time or lose their leases in forfeiture. If they struck oil, the University was to receive as its royalty one-eighth of the gross production.

Krupp and Pickrell set off for New York to sell drilling permits on their leased land. They came back empty-handed. New Yorkers remained skeptical of investing with two men who had no drilling or oil business experience. In order to develop their leases, in 1919 Krupp and Pickrell organized the Texon Oil and Land Company with Krupp as president and Pickrell vice-president.[8] They capitalized Texon at two million shares valued at one dollar each, then executed an agreement with New York brokers authorizing Texon to geologize and select two hundred thousand acres in payment for the total capital stock.

But even this imaginative financial approach failed. Eastern brokers found it impossible to sell stock in a wildcat well to be drilled by a company that had no oil production. Krupp and his partner tidied up this problem by purchasing three producing wells in Burkburnett, Texas,[9] almost 300 miles from the drilling site. "Haymon Krupp personally furnished the money, approximately $25,000, for the purchase, taking credit on the Texon books for the advance."[10] The idea worked. Texon became a producing company. Ultimately some 685 Certificates of Interest were sold in New York for as much as $200 each.

By the time Krupp and Pickrell raised enough money to start drilling and had bought their equipment, time was running out on their drilling deadline. Stories vary about what happened next. Writer White gives this account: "With only a few days to go, he [Krupp] took to the road with three trucks loaded with drilling equipment and started for his location, which was far distant from a railroad. When Krupp was still several miles away from the precious stake, which had cost him several thousand dollars to have driven in the ground, one of his trucks broke down completely and — there he was!

"He had only two days left. What should he do? There was no possibility of his being able to reach his desired destination with his outfit. The breakdown had occurred on land covered by the lease and so, with no high-salaried geologist at hand to advise him but merely because the ox was in the ditch and he had to

Photo by L. Lawrence, Ranger, Texas; Courtesy Mrs. Ivy Rabinowitz

act at once to prevent forfeiture, Krupp set up his rig at the scene of the disaster and went to work."[11]

Actually, Krupp and Pickrell both acknowledged that Dr. Hugh H. Tucker, geologist for the Texon Oil and Land Company, drove the stake at the site of the Santa Rita and it was upon his recommendation the well was drilled.[12]

The book *Santa Rita* by Martin Schwettmann focuses on Frank Pickrell and had him arriving in San Angelo, Texas, on January 6, 1921, two days before forfeiture. Pickrell decided to solve two drilling problems with one solution: the drilling of a legitimate hole by the deadline established by law and the securing of a supply of water required for the actual oil well drilling operation. He acquired a "rattle trap" water well drilling outfit in San Angelo and moved it to the drilling site via the Orient Railroad. He hired Walter Brown, a water well driller, and W.C. (Uncle Bill) Latham, an Old Spanish Trail teamster, to assist on the job.

The train reached Best at seven o'clock on the last

Rig of the old Santa Rita, a monument on the campus of the University of Texas at Austin.

day of grace, January 8. If no legitimate hole was drilled by midnight, the permit acquired from the state would expire. They had five hours. Pickrell and his associates won the race against time by beginning the hole just before midnight. The work on the water well continued for three months. The original water well 'dried up,' and W.P. Holt was employed to extend the original shallow well down to a depth of 425 feet. In June, Pickrell employed R.S. McDonald to build the wooden derrick with which the oil well was to be drilled. The material was shipped in from Ranger, Texas for this eighty-four-foot structure. Carl G. Cromwell was then employed as the driller of the oil well.

Somewhere between January and June, Krupp and Pickrell named their well Santa Rita. On one of their trips to New York seeking financing for their well, they had solicited funds from a Catholic group. Because the potential investors realized that such speculative investments involved serious risk, they sought the counsel of their priest, who advised them to invoke the aid of Saint Rita, Saint of the Impossible. Two Catholic women investors gave Frank a red rose, requesting that he sprinkle the petals over the derrick. When he returned to Texas, Pickrell climbed to the top of the derrick, crushed the petals, and sprinkled them over the derrick's top — the crown block — christening the well "Santa Rita." The New York name was changed slightly due to Texas' Hispanic influence.[13]

The drilling dragged on through 1921 and 1922. Ranchers in the area felt sorry for Carl Cromwell, his helpers and family. A University of Texas publication, *Santa Rita No. 1*, recorded: "The ranchers were touched, in their bluff way, by the pathos of two men, a woman, and a little girl set in desert country beside a rusty railroad pecking a hole in the rocks in search of oil."

On Sunday afternoon, May 27, 1923, Carl Cromwell and his tool dresser, Dee Locklin, cleaned out the hole with a bailer. After two years of drilling, they had reached the depth of 3,055 feet. The material they brought to the surface in the bailer showed some oil, so they lowered the bailer to the bottom of the well again and this time it was filled with oil when they got it to the surface. They decided to tell no one, build a trap door to close the hole and to board up the bottom of the derrick.

The next morning while Mrs. Cromwell prepared breakfast for her husband and their small daughter, Carlene, she heard a hissing noise. It sounded like a rattlesnake at the doorstep of their driller's shack, she remembered. As they reached the door, the members of the family saw a thin column of gas and oil vapor rising above the top of the derrick. In great astonishment, Cromwell said, "Well, I'll be damned!" This flowing well stood in the center of the sixty-four square miles of leases.[14]

Santa Rita No. 1, the discovery well of the University Lands, blew in May 28, 1923, in Reagan County.

The Santa Rita No. 1 flowed three times that first day, May 28, 1923, two times the next, and once each day for the following thirty-five to forty days. Because there were no storage tanks, oil flowed on the ground until earthen reservoirs could be dug. When these filled, oil again flowed on the ground for weeks. At first, it flowed about 100 barrels a day. But when pumping operations began, it produced 200 barrels a day which, by industry standards, is not a large producing well but it foreshadowed the future.

A town came to life around the Santa Rita No. 1, a town named Texon. The Reagan County field spread north from Texon and took its name from Big Lake, an area east of Texon. Peak production came to 10,937,000 barrels in 1926, and in 1928 wells of the Big Lake Pool reached nearly 9,000 feet, at that time among the deepest in the country. After this success, wildcatting spread far and wide in West Texas, opening up several large producing areas. The University's grazing lands which formerly had produced an income of $1,000 a year, saw millions per annum begin to flow into its treasury, with increases annually.[15]

The original rig worked at the site for nineteen years until Dr. Walter Prescott Webb, a director of the Texas State Historical Association and editor-in-chief of the original *Handbook of Texas*, award-winning author, and distinguished professor of history at the University of Texas at Austin, recommended in 1939 that the rig be moved to the University campus. The rig was dismantled in 1940, but it remained in storage until 1958, when it finally found a home on the campus at Austin, where it stands as a reminder of many events and people, among them Haymon Krupp. Now a campus monument, it is recognized every May 28, the anniversary of the original gusher.

Haymon Krupp died on February 21, 1949, and on February 28, the Texas State Legislature's *Journal of the House of Representatives* carried the following H. Krupp memorial:

"Whereas, Haymon Krupp, a respected citizen of El Paso, seventy-four years of age, a pioneer in that section of the state, a successful merchant, manufacturer, oil developer and philanthropist, died on Monday afternoon, February 21, 1949, at a Rochester, Minnesota, hospital; and

"Whereas, The departed Haymon Krupp was instrumental in developing the fabulous wealth of the University of Texas lands in West Texas by being the first man of means to take the risk of investing a part of his accumulated wealth in drilling a wildcat well and developing same into a great producer of crude oil, the first well to be drilled with success in the Big Lake Field which was the beginning of the development of oil production on lands belonging to the University of Texas which have resulted in an increase of many millions of dollars in the permanent fund of the University and the revenue derived from such permanent fund has assisted materially many of our younger people in procuring higher education; and

"Whereas, Mr. Krupp prior to and after bringing in the great gusher at Big Lake continued his residence in El Paso and was one of the great merchants and manufacturers of West Texas, and in the use of his wealth he became noted as a philanthropist. Even before the beginning of his oil developments and before natural gas came into El Paso as a fuel, Mr. Krupp paid out thousands of dollars for tons and tons of coal to be delivered to the poor people of El Paso to warm their homes and cook their food and otherwise spent huge sums in caring for the poor people of West Texas; now, therefore be it

"Resolved by the House of Representatives of the State of Texas of the Fifty-first Legislature, That we the Members thereof recognize and appreciate the great services rendered not only to the State of Texas but to hundreds of needy persons, and appreciate him as a public spirited citizen; and, be it further

"Resolved, That an enrolled copy of this resolution be forwarded to his widow, Mrs. Rebecca Krupp, to his son, M. Bernard Krupp, both of El Paso, and to his two daughters, Mrs. Leland H. Hewitt, Seattle, and Mrs. H. James Stone of Brockton, Massachusetts."[16]

"All of the money in the world won't create a great university," University of Texas Vice-President William Livingston told *Time* magazine in April, 1982. "But you can't create a great university without it."[17]

The endowment at the University of Texas System, which includes Texas A&M and other state universities, was surpassed only by Harvard's; it generated $128 million in income from oil and gas leases in 1982 alone. And the university system then was trying to endow one hundred more chairs to recruit more first-class scholars. The University was indeed carrying out the intent of the fathers of the Constitution of the Republic of Texas — with the assistance of Haymon Krupp.

OTHER WILDCATTERS

Krupp proved to be an exception in many ways. Certainly as a Jew who speculated in oil, who bought and sold leases and hired geologists and drillers, he remained a rarity in the business. Irvin Beren, president of Spandsco (a contraction of Standard Pipe and Supply Co.) observed, "Frankly, it was unusual [to find Jews in the oil business]. There were not too many in the business, particularly not as operators. There was a Jewish law firm in Henderson that was the best law firm in town. We used them on contracts, title work, things like that."[18]

The attorney Beren referred to was Judge Charles Brachfield, who in 1931 was elected first president of the East Texas Lease, Royalty Owners and Producers Association. This organization fought the battles for the independent oil producers, taking on such targets as the Texas Rangers and the U. S. Supreme Court. The issue: handling over-production in the face of legislated controls. Eventually, there was legislation to prevent waste and conserve natural resources.

The Danciger family, for whom the Jewish community center of Fort Worth is named, began litigation. Danciger Oil and Refining Company of North Texas was one of the first companies to file suit seeking an injunction that would allow unlimited production. The price of oil plunged to fifty cents a barrel. On February 13, 1931, the same judge who had temporarily favored Danciger Oil denied its request for a permanent injunction, affirming the authority of the Texas Railroad Commission to prorate production.[19]

Many major production companies did not hire Jews. For many years, Jews were not hired in several departments of the Humble Oil and Refining Co., according to Max A. Morchower of Baytown, Texas, a long time chemical engineer with that company.[20]

Most of the Jews who got into the oil business in Texas did so by starting out as scrap metal salvage dealers, purchasing second hand pipe from the oil fields and selling it to oil producers. The pipe their companies sold came from used pipe the men bought from oil and gas companies, from pipe that did not meet government standards, and pipe they pulled from abandoned oil wells, according to Irvin Jaffe of Dallas.

Jaffe's father, Max, started this way. Because many of the speculators had no money either, Max and his partners traded pipe and oil materials for oil leases. Columbus M. (Dad) Joiner, the wildcatter who discovered the East Texas Oil Field — one of the largest oil fields in the world — was one of their customers.

For three years, Max and his partners traded pipe and supplies to Dad Joiner in return for Joiner's leases, which he originally had made with farmers and ranchers who owned land in East Texas. Joiner had no cash and bartered leases for materials. When Joiner came into Dallas to buy pipe and to conduct other business, he had Sunday dinner regularly at the home of his pipe supplier, Max Jaffe. "He loved my mother's kosher cooking," said Irvin Jaffe. "He enjoyed her veal chops, lamb chops, and also Jewish delicacies such as carrot *tsimmes*, matzo balls, and noodle kugel."

It was a question of the poor feeding the poor. Irvin Jaffe remembered how most families struggled. "They were struggling to make a living — struggling very hard. The seven children in our family shared everything. We used to pass our shoes down," Jaffe said. "My sister Louise was younger than me and when I got through wearing my shoes, my sister Louise wore them.

"One night Mother said to Daddy, 'Morris wants to go to Harvard Law School.' My brother Morris had just graduated from the University of Texas in Austin, where it cost only twenty-five dollars a semester or a year, whatever it was in those days. This was before the [oil] fields came in, and Daddy said, 'He'll go to

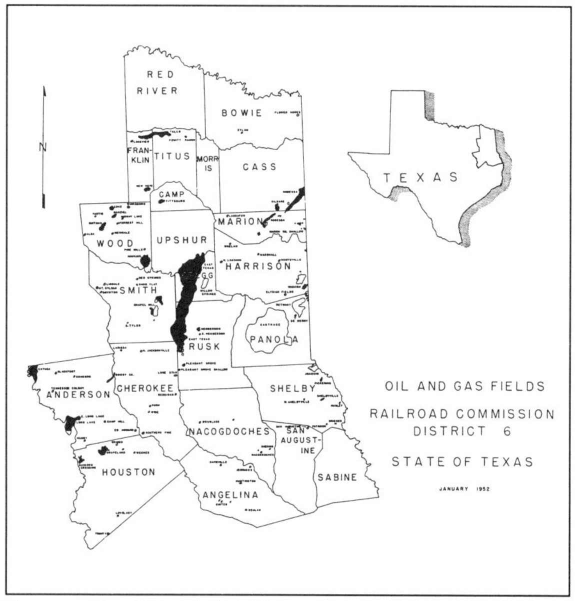

The great East Texas Oil Field.
Courtesy Texas Petroleum Research Committee.

Max Jaffe (1883-1951)
sold Dad Joiner the pipe that went into the discovery well that opened up the great East Texas Oil Field, biggest of them all, during the Great Depression. Courtesy Irvin Jaffe.

Harvard.' Mother said, 'How?' He said, 'I don't know how but we'll arrange it.' And he did go to Harvard. The fields came in about the time he was to go to Harvard. I remember the Harvard graduation: Einstein was on the program."[21] Morris eventually became one of the partners of what was during his lifetime one of the largest law firms in Dallas.[22]

The Spandsco partnership included Max Jaffe, his brother-in-law David Caplan, Jacob Beren, and Beren's son, Irvin Beren. Jaffe and Caplan knew the pipe business but knew nothing about oil production, according to both Irv Jaffe and Irv Beren. It was the Berens who traveled to East Texas and contracted for the oil drilling and production.

Jacob Beren's father, Elias Beren, had emigrated from Riga, Russia, in the 1890s and bought a farm in Ohio. He later sent for the rest of his family. Max Jaffe immigrated to the U. S. when he was nineteen. At that time there were oil fields in Ohio and West Virginia, and Jacob and Max would ride horseback into the oil fields, where they bought and sold pipe. Soon they started an oil-pipe yard. From this, Jacob got into oil production and found his way to Tulsa, in order to develop oil leases someone had sold him. In 1923 Jacob moved his family to Dallas.

Max Jaffe arrived in Texas in 1922 from West Virginia with his young bride, Esther, and had already set up a pipe business with his brother-in-law, David Caplan. When Jacob arrived, he became part of the business.

The Jaffe family's struggle was typical of how the depression years affected many families not only in Texas but throughout the United States. The Jaffes were a microcosm of the entire state of Texas. However, their plight was relieved when the East Texas Oil Field began production. Department stores that were suffering from too many accounts receivable and little traffic began selling furs and jewels. Neiman-Marcus had a field day. It was the era of H.L. Hunt and other luminaries. When the East Texas Field was discovered in Rusk County by Joiner in October 1930, it was the "biggest of them all."[23]

The success of this well, drilled on land condemned many times by geologists of the major companies, was followed by the biggest leasing campaign in history. The field soon was extended to Kilgore, Longview, and northward. The pipe suppliers — having been given some oil leases in return for product — now began to drill on property they held leases on.

The Standard Pipe and Supply Company furnished the string of pipe that went into Dad Joiner's discovery well. "When the East Texas field came in," said Irvin Beren, "Dad and I went to East Texas. We contracted for a drilling rig and drilled on property we held leases on, which were not far from Dad Joiner's well. We hit our first well a few months later."[24]

Oil became their ticket to a better life, just as it did for other Jewish families. Fort Worth oil man Sol Brachman arrived in Texas from Ohio by much the same route taken by the Berens. He graduated from Marietta College in Marietta, Ohio, and married an Ohio girl, Ella Beren. They moved to Fort Worth in 1919. He founded Producers Supply & Tool Company. In 1950 Texas Christian University appointed him a trustee.

Even while Brachman was out in the Texas oil fields drilling, he still managed to work for the betterment of his fellow Texans through serving on the boards of the Harris Memorial Hospital, the United Fund, the Red Cross, and the National Conference of Christians and Jews. At a testimonial dinner in his honor, a NCCJ citation stated that he was "a symbol to all who wish to safeguard the blessings of the Judeo-Christian tradition which is the basis of our democratic society."

Sol Brachman's son Malcolm noted, "My father always sold new pipe and drilling equipment." Malcolm earned degrees from Yale and Harvard and a research fellowship from the Atomic Energy Commission in the late 1940s. After working in the Argonne National Laboratory in Chicago, he returned to Texas to join his father as an independent oil producer and became an international bridge champion.[25]

David Flesh, a geologist, discovered his first well in 1910 on Caddo Lake near the Louisiana border. In 1937 he hit in the Rodessa (Texas) Fault. In 1938 he brought in his first of a series of wells in Jefferson, Texas, the Flesh & Hootkins No. 1.

As a child, Fay Stein observed her father's oil pipe business in Ranger and other Texas towns. Years later (as Mrs. David Giller of Dallas) she recalled, "When an oil well was abandoned, and they decided not to drill or pump anymore, or if it was a dry hole, they had sunk a lot of pipe into the ground. The pipe could be pulled out of the ground, retrieved, and resold. The junk and pipe businesses were periphery to the oil business and important to it. When I went out in the junkyard in Overton, there was a lot of seedy-looking pipe, a lot of different fittings and parts of equipment connected with the oil business. As a child, I knew of other Jewish families in that business in Kilgore and in Longview and other areas. Everywhere in Texas where there was oil, there were pipe and supply companies, and Jews were among those earliest pipe suppliers."[26]

Born in 1909, M.B. (Mayer Billy) Rudman and his father also sold oil field supplies and later entered the drilling business. When M.B. became a wealthy independent oil producer, he began to wear high-fashion attire and was referred to as "The Duke." He founded the Anti-Smoking League of America long before it became a popular cause and later turned his ranch near Dallas into an exercise activities center to encourage fellow Texans back to health. He explained his motivation: "When I was a little boy, I was very frail and sickly. The kids around me tormented me. They called me 'Jew Baby.' I was miserable. That's how I got interested in physical fitness. I wanted to be strong enough to confront them."[27]

Rudman was born in Bonham, Texas, of a mother born in St. Louis and a Russian immigrant father. Early in life he sold newspapers and shined shoes. As a teenager, he worked in the oil fields and as a bell hop. "I was a bell hop in Oklahoma City and I saw all these oil men throwing their money away. I figured I was as smart as they were," he said. Rudman drilled twenty-nine dry holes before he hit oil. Once he did, he was hooked. "The oil business is exciting. When you're drilling a well and it comes in, it's like running through tacklers on a football field."

"The main thing about Billy is he is a wildcatter," said his wife Josephine, "which means one who drills in unexplored areas, before an area is opened. The first well drilled in an area is a wildcat well. A wildcatter is a certain breed of man or woman, and has more guts than other oil producers. It is fascinating.

"Billy's parents, Ike and Rose Rudman, lived in Henryetta and Okmulgee, Oklahoma, where they had general stores. Later they moved to Wewoka and went in the secondhand oil well supply business, better known as junk. Then they moved to Tulsa and Oklahoma City before moving to East Texas in 1931 at the time of the East Texas oil boom. A guy with no money could take a string of pipes, and as collateral could take an interest in a well. That's how those junk men got in the oil business. A string of pipe would lead to a lease. Then people would bring leases and hire a drilling contractor.

"All the oil he [Billy] found in the beginning was from a small interest of ownership in a well. He didn't have the money or the credit to drill a well himself. People brought him deals all the time. He started his own business by taking 'farm-out deals.' He would hear of wells abandoned and get geological information and take a farm-out lease. He started with one in East Texas and one in Wewoka. We had no money; picture shows were a quarter but we seldom went. I learned to knit and play bridge," Mrs. Rudman recalled in her saga of how one becomes a Texas millionaire.

"Billy learned all he could about everything by personal research. His big break came in 1950 when he promoted drilling for oil in North Dakota. It took him five years. A lot of people knew about it but were not interested. He finally got the Amerada oil company of New York to drill. It became our first big strike."[28]

Jo Rudman's father also followed the oil field discoveries in Texas, and eventually bought leases. In the beginning, Ephraim Henry Davis and his wife, Rose, Jo's parents, came to America from Russia and settled in Joplin, Missouri, where Jo was born in 1913. He peddled in Shreveport, Louisiana, two years before coming to Texas. "They opened a little store in Ranger, Texas, about as big as my kitchen. We had an outdoor toilet and no bath. You could hardly go down the street without getting stuck in the mud. Yet a lot of Jewish people lived in that area, all the way to Abilene and Sweetwater, and in the summer they held a picnic near Abilene so they could meet each other.

"When the Navarro County Oil field came in, my parents opened a store in Corsicana, where I grew up until I graduated from the University in Texas in 1933. I taught school in Gladewater one year; Bill was working in his dad's secondhand pipe business when we met. We married June 23, 1935, in Tyler. When the Navarro County oil field died and East Texas opened, we moved to Tyler. That's where our pipe business led to drilling.

"When we moved to Dallas in 1942, Billy couldn't afford an office. He just had papers in all his pockets," recalled Josephine.[29] At that time their son Wolfe was a baby and son Michael, who became a famous theatre director in London, was age three.

In 1968 Rudman led a group of oil men who met in New York to form a national organization of persons in oil exploration. Originally called Explorers, the group later changed its name to the All American Wildcatters.

As Duke Rudman succeeded as a wildcatter, he became an activist for preventive medicine. In the 1960s and 1970s Rudman successfully lobbied the Dallas City Council to establish city ordinances to prevent smoking in elevators, nursing homes, and hospitals.[30] He gave to research on respiratory diseases and cancer. "He gives to the needy and not the greedy," said Josephine. He sponsored many humanitarian causes, among them the St. Paul's Industrial School in Malakoff, Texas, which cared for abandoned black children and was supported by private and public funds.[31] His compassion for the poor is the trait he shared with Krupp, the wildcatter who preceded him by half a century.

Chapter 8

The Humanitarian

Galveston and the Gateway Immigration Movement

One characteristic of most Texas Jewish leaders has been their sense of community responsibility — feeling the need and the impulse to give back something to the people with whom they live and work. In no man's life was this truer than in that of a small, wiry Texan, Rabbi Henry Cohen of Galveston, who influenced his fellow Texans, directed a gateway immigration movement that brought thousands to America, and whose efforts reached across the globe.

In the White House, President William Howard Taft listened patiently as Cohen pleaded for a boilermaker who, because of illegal entry, was about to be deported to his country of origin. "He'll face a firing squad," said Cohen. "In Texas I can find him a job."

The president said there was no alternative to deportation but added, "I certainly admire the way you have gone to so much trouble and expense for a member of your faith."

"Member of my faith!" exclaimed Cohen. "This man is a Greek Catholic. A human life is at stake."

Impressed by the range of Cohen's sympathy, President Taft rang for his secretary. "Say: Release Demchuk to the custody of Dr. Cohen."[1]

Rabbi Cohen did not have the looks or speech of a typical Texan. Born April 7, 1863, in London and educated in England, he later lived in South Africa, Jamaica, and Mississippi. When he came to Texas in 1888, he brought along a British accent and humanitarianism that reached beyond his Galveston congregation and sometimes beyond the boundaries of the state.

He had charisma before the word was popularly known, this man who wore a black tuxedo-type suit with white starched formal bow tie. He made his way around Galveston on a bicycle until he turned fifty, then rode in a chauffeured limousine with a list of his daily missions pencilled on his white left cuff. Once he lifted his left coat sleeve to show the words written on his rigid starched cuff, saying, "There's a lot of sorrow but a lot of happiness, too, on my cuff."[2]

Cohen as a young rabbi in Kingston, Jamaica, 1884.

Courtesy Rosenberg Library.

President Woodrow Wilson called him "The First Citizen of Texas."[3] There are Henry Cohen incidents with President Wilson, President Taft, the Texas Prison Board, a Catholic cardinal, a young girl held prisoner by a madam in Galveston's old red-light district, and writer O. Henry.

Perhaps the reason why thousands of Jews live today in the South, Southwest and the Midwest of America rather than in New York City and the East can be traced a few generations back to Henry Cohen. He was a driving force behind "The Galveston Movement" when approximately 10,000 immigrants embarked at Bremen, Germany, to Texas. In 1939 *Reader's Digest* found him to be an "unforgettable person."[4] Another writer praised him as "The Man Who Stayed in Texas."[5]

A writer for *Rotarian* magazine observed: "You can pick up innumerable tales about Rabbi Cohen all through the Southwest. Some are true, some may be true and some, if they aren't, ought to be."[6]

Rabbi Henry Cohen, D.D., D.H.L., LL.D. 1863-1952

A tale about Rabbi Cohen that showed one of his many dimensions concerned a prostitute. Once Cohen received word of a girl being held against her will in the red-light district of Galveston, then on west Post Office Street. He promptly mounted his bicycle, which he usually rode during his early years in Galveston. In the brothel he forced his way past the number one madam of the town, marched upstairs, and found the semi-nude girl, her clothes having been taken from her so she would not run away. He pulled blankets from the bed and wrapped them around her and trudged through the main street of Galveston, guiding the bicycle with one hand and gripping the girl wrapped in blankets with the other. Into a clothing store they charged. "Fit her out from head to foot!" he commanded. After outfitting her with new clothes, he took the girl to her home. Later he got the young woman a job.

News of the rabbi traveled through the back streets of Galveston. Later when the madam of another bordello asked the rabbi to say the burial service over a girl who, while dying, had requested a "decent Christian funeral," the rabbi did not inquire whether she had been refused by any other minister. He went to the cemetery and, in the presence of a large part of the population of Galveston's red-light district, performed the last rites with prayers from the New Testament.[7]

The people of Galveston became well acquainted with the humanitarian side of his personality when the hurricane of 1900 hit Galveston, killing six thousand people. It stands as the nation's greatest natural disaster. When the wind and flooding died, he made sure his family was safe, then immediately set out on foot for the hospital to see if he could help. He got a horse-drawn cart and delivered medicine throughout the city for days, working side by side with many civic leaders, especially his close friend Father Kirwin.[8]

Little Henry Cohen worked well with men of all faiths. Front row: rabbis Hyman Judah Schachtel, Henry Cohen, Henry Barnston, Alfred Barnston. Second row: Dr. Charles R. King, Dr. Harry Knowles, Dr. Paul Quillian, Leopold L. Meyer, and Bishop Clinton Quin.

For communities unable to afford a rabbi, Cohen traveled throughout Texas, from Nacogdoches on the east to Brownsville on the southern border, burying, marrying, teaching, and preaching the words of the fiery Old Testament prophets. While traveling through the Texas prairies, the rabbi had an opportunity to visit many far-flung places where history had been made. He was impressed by the roles Jews had played in the settlement of the state and wrote a booklet on Henri Castro, published by the American Jewish Historical Society, which as early as 1894 had published other Cohen works on early Jewish Texans.[9] He was the first to begin to record the history of the pioneer Jewish Texans, some of whom he knew personally.

But Cohen's greatest achievement came with the Galveston Movement, a remarkable event at the turn of the century, when ten thousand immigrants began a new life in the South, Southwest, and Midwest, rather than in the crowded ghettos of New York City and the Eastern seaboard.

The millions of Jews who came to America during the twenty years before the turn of the century and the twenty years after changed American culture. And America changed their culture. Whole families changed both geographical and religious roots with the hope for a new life in America. They clung together in the New World, many of them passing from the Ellis Island examination station to Hester Street on the lower East side of New York City, where they lived in congested quarters, impoverished beyond description, fearful of going beyond the boundaries of their language and culture. Some immigrants slept in hallways. Often a family of six lived in one room with no running water, parents and children crowded together in one sleeping space. These conditions began to breed child labor and crime.

American Jewish philanthropists took note of this, not only out of humanitarian reasons. Frankly, they were embarrassed. Many of these Jews in New York were descended from pioneer Americans who had long made their homes in the new country and had risen to economic success. These earliest Jews from England, Holland, France, Spain, and Germany were embarrassed at the sight of their coreligionists who had recently escaped the pogrom of Kishineff and other towns in Eastern Europe. The ragged, Yiddish-speaking Jews from Russia's outposts, ghettos, and *shtetls* appeared in marked contrast to the "Our Crowd" Jewish families of New York: the Seligman, Guggenheim, Loeb, and Schiff families. The great J.P. Morgan had admitted Jacob Schiff as his only equal.[10]

Schiff took such a personal interest in the immigrants that he has become identified with the Texas movement that diverted new European arrivals away from New York, with one professor referring to the plan as "Jacob H. Schiff's Galveston Movement: An Experiment in Immigration Deflection, 1907-1914."[11]

Clarence Darrow, Dr. Henry Cohen, and Dr. Clarence True Wilson, Methodist Episcopal temperance leader and author.

With U.S. government approval, Schiff contracted with a European group, the Jewish Territorial Organization (JTO), to screen Russian and Eastern European immigrants in terms of health and useful occupations. If they met the criteria, JTO provided the immigrant a ticket on a boat out of Bremen, Germany, sailing directly to Galveston, thus diverting the immigrants from the New York City port. Schiff selected Galveston because the Lloyd-German steamship line had direct service with this Gulf port. It also was sufficiently small so that it would not likely attract immigrants to settle there permanently in preference to locations arranged for them.

Rabbi Cohen pointed out also that in 1907 Galveston was "contiguous to and in direct railroad communication with the large country West of the Mississippi," with connections to Denver, Kansas City, St. Louis, and points farther north, whereby newcomers could be distributed throughout the areas.[12]

Schiff dispatched Morris D. Waldman, a young social worker, from New York City to Galveston with letters of introduction from Schiff to Rabbi Henry Cohen to "organize an immigration office in connection with the movement which we are endeavoring to inaugurate for diverting a part of the Russian Jewish immigration through the Gulf ports." In January 1907 the new Jewish Immigrants' Information Bureau (JIIB) rented a building, ordered stationery, and began negotiating for

Jacob H. Schiff, New York financier, philanthropist, and protagonist of the Galveston Movement

Galveston immigration ship. *Courtesy Rosenberg Library.*

a half-rate on the railroads to ship immigrants into the interior.[13] Schiff was a friend of railroad management, and his firm Kuhn, Loeb & Company dominated the field of railroad financing in an era when railroads dominated the American financial scene. His railroad clients included Missouri Pacific, the Southern Pacific, and the Texas & Pacific.[14]

Schiff donated $500,000 for the specific purpose of redirecting Jewish immigration.

The JIIB dispatched the immigrants to (in numerical order) Texas, Iowa, Missouri, Minnesota, Nebraska, Louisiana, Colorado, Illinois, Oklahoma, Kansas, Tennessee, Arkansas, Wisconsin, North Dakota, and Mississippi.[15] Iowa received 1,225 immigrants, second only to Texas. Of the first thousand immigrants, one hundred went directly to Kansas City, Missouri. During the seven years of the Galveston Movement, 1,099 went to Missouri. Immigrants received railroad tickets and money. Cohen wrote letters to New York, notifying what occupations were needed in these areas mostly west of the Mississippi. Often prominent citizens in each town would write directly to the New York office, stating their needs. El Paso requested trunk, harness and saddle makers. Corsicana requested "Weavers, spinners and doffers" for an emerging textile industry. Waco wanted cobblers, adding that they did not need any more hatmakers.[16] Most prevalent occupations requested were tailors, clerks, shoemakers, and carpenters.

The Galveston Movement's first arrival was the SS *Cassel*, which docked on July 1, 1907, with fifty-four Russo-Jewish immigrants. The mayor met the ship and addressed the group in a few well chosen words, which Rabbi Cohen translated. The chief magistrate shook hands with each one of the individuals. Cohen continued to meet most of the ships as they arrived in the Galveston port. Here officials examined, questioned, and tagged, as at Ellis Island, detaining some

Henry Cohen, left, met immigrants at the dock. *Courtesy B'nai Israel Archives and Institute of Texan Cultures*

immigrants for medical reasons, but admitting most.

However, in 1913 a change of policy became evident. More than five percent of all arriving aliens were found ineligible for entry. After days on board, many Jews arrived in Texas only to board another ship back to Europe after being refused entry. Jews were found to be especially rejected in the categories of hernia and defective vision. While the leaders of the Galveston Movement did not question the fact that the doctor was a "thoroughly conscientious official," he was "unduly severe in his examinations," magnifying "minor ailments to the point of unfairness," with the result that the "percentage of exclusions at Galveston" became "the highest from any port in the U.S." The Galveston route lost its popularity among immigrants from Russia.[17]

Some of the first Jewish immigrants to arrive during the Galveston Movement, 1907-1914.

Another factor that helped terminate the Movement was the unwillingness or inability of Jewish organizations in Europe to surmount jealousies and rivalries for autonomy that divided them, plus the unwillingness of European financiers such as the Rothschilds to support the European side of the Movement. Moreover, a severe economic depression in the United States made employment difficult for the newcomers.

Although the Galveston plan did not bring the millions anticipated, the routing of ten thousand persons into the interior of the United States between 1907 and 1914 was significant. Of Schiff's original $500,000, some $235,000 was spent.

From 1914 to 1915, Rabbi Cohen administered a relief fund of $75,000 to aid six hundred refugees from Mexico, at the request of William Jennings Bryan, then secretary of state.[18] During World War I he played a key role in establishing legislation to provide Jewish chaplains in the U.S. Navy. President Woodrow Wilson sent him the pen he used to sign the Naval Jewish Chaplain Bill.

After World War I ended, Cohen directed his energies to prison reform. Cohen was at his best making winners out of losers, giving them the confidence and support many never had known. He often visited the Texas State Prisons, traveling all over Texas at his own expense. It was said he felt equally at home in Huntsville, Austin, or the Galveston County jail, as on his own pulpit.

One of the legends concerns his aiding O. Henry to get out of an Austin, Texas, jail on parole, when he felt that writer was wrongfully convicted. When asked about this incident, Dr. Cohen refused to discuss it. "There always are living descendants of a man who could be offended by the publicity, even if the man were innocent," he said.[19]

A series of letters in the archives of the temple in Galveston show how Rabbi Cohen helped a young gentile man who was in the Galveston jail in 1926 on a charge of tampering with the mail. Cohen wrote the judge saying that he had obtained a job for the repentant youth in case he were paroled.

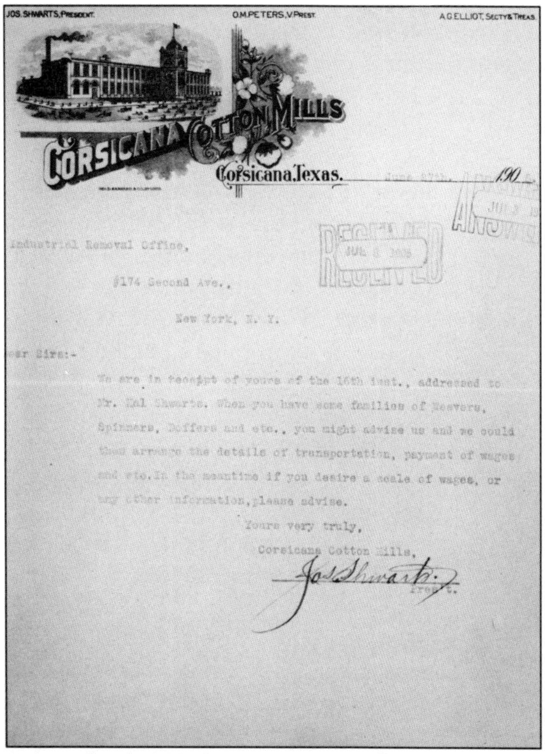

JOS. SHWARTS, PRESIDENT. O.M. PETERS, V.PREST. A.G. ELLIOT, SECTY & TREAS.

CORSICANA COTTON MILLS

Corsicana, Texas. June 27th. 1905

RECEIVED JUL 3 1905

ANSWERED

Industrial Removal Office,

#174 Second Ave.,

New York, N. Y.

Dear Sirs:-

We are in receipt of yours of the 16th inst., addressed to Mr. Hal Shwarts. When you have some families of Weavers, Spinners, Doffers and etc., you might advise us and we could then arrange the details of transportation, payment of wages and etc. In the meantime if you desire a scale of wages, or any other information, please advise.

Yours very truly,

Corsicana Cotton Mills,

Jos. Shwarts

Pres't.

In letter dated 1905, Corsicana Cotton Mills wrote New York, "When you have some families of Weavers, Spinners, Doffers and etc., you might advise us."

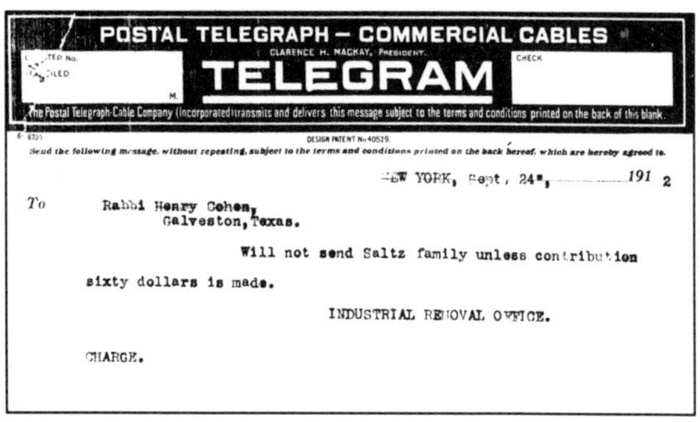

POSTAL TELEGRAPH — COMMERCIAL CABLES

CLARENCE H. MACKAY, PRESIDENT.

TELEGRAM

The Postal Telegraph-Cable Company (Incorporated) transmits and delivers this message subject to the terms and conditions printed on the back of this blank.

DESIGN PATENT No. 40529.

Send the following message, without repeating, subject to the terms and conditions printed on the back hereof, which are hereby agreed to.

NEW YORK, Sept. 24th, 1912

To Rabbi Henry Cohen,
Galveston, Texas.

Will not send Saltz family unless contribution sixty dollars is made.

INDUSTRIAL REMOVAL OFFICE.

CHARGE.

The rabbi then offered to lend the young man $175 to use to replace what he had stolen. With the judge's permission, the young man took a job in a dry goods store. Soon afterward he wrote Rabbi Cohen that he had saved enough money to buy a needed suit of clothes and planned to take Spanish lessons and business courses at night school. He thanked the rabbi for his help, expressing the hope that he would "become the man you want me to be."[20]

Each Cohen parolee received his wages from the business firm that hired him. Old time Galveston pioneers believed that wages for parolees came from a fund raised by anonymous friends of the rabbi. After the parolee proved his worth, gained experience, and earned the employer's confidence, the firm assumed responsibility for payment of its new employee.

Rabbi Cohen pressured the Texas Legislature month after month, year after year, to change the age of consent in Texas from ten years old to eighteen; he started his campaign when a man who had raped a girl of twelve was allowed to go free. Then Cohen launched campaigns to separate first offenders from hardened criminals. This led him to become a nationally recognized pioneer in parole. He served on the Texas prison board and worked for legislative reforms under Governor Dan Moody. When he resigned, he told Governor Moody he felt he could do better work off the board on an individual basis.[21]

Cohen's agenda on his cuff took him to hospitals, where he would go from bed to bed, never questioning the religion of the patient. He was widely known for his statement: "There is no such thing as Episcopalian scarlet fever, Catholic arthritis or Jewish mumps." One Galveston family remembered Cohen at the hospital at five o'clock in the morning when their four-year-old son was hospitalized for surgery. In the early morning's darkness Henry Cohen appeared in the doorway, his presence like a high-energy cosmic ray.

"How is the BOY?" It was unmistakably Dr. Cohen. "I couldn't sleep, and my wife Mollie said if I was worried, I should go see for myself and get it off my mind."[22]

Although he visited the boy as an act of compassion, others might have seen it as a small drama because he conducted his life with a sense of drama. Early in Cohen's ministry, Roman Catholic Cardinal Satolli visited Galveston. At a public dinner in the Cardinal's honor, he asked Dr. Cohen to say grace, and the rabbi said it in Latin — after which the Cardinal responded with a blessing in Hebrew.[23]

Henry Cohen spoke many languages — eleven well: English, Hebrew, Latin, Greek, Spanish, French, German, Yiddish, Arabic, Chinese, and the so-called "Click" language of the Kaffir tribe of Africa. Cohen had

Mollie and Henry Cohen.

reached age seventy-five when this author was a child attending his Sunday school. He was my rabbi. I well remember sitting next to him in his car one day when he gave me a ride home from Sunday School. He amused me with tales of his life in South Africa, when he had been hit over the head with the butt of a gun during a revolt of the Zulus; then he started talking to me in the "Click" language.

In another trip in his car he told me of a harrowing experience in the Kimberley diamond fields of Africa, when the elevator came crashing down the mine shaft. Then he signaled the fun was over. "You'll be all right in life," he prophesized in his British accent, "You're cut from good cloth. Remember that." I got ready to leave, but a booming voice held me back "Now kiss me," he ordered. And I planted a kiss on the cheek of Dr. Cohen as I left considering events in South Africa.

He had gone to South Africa with a brother at the age of eighteen, spending a couple of years there working at various jobs.[24] He continued studying to be a rabbi while he worked as an interpreter and in a dry goods store. He returned to England where he completed his studies for the ministry at Jews' College in London, and then served as a rabbi a year in Kingston, Jamaica, and three years in Woodville, Mississippi. He arrived in Texas at age twenty-five and stayed until almost age ninety, from 1888 to 1952.[25]

During the sixty-four years in Galveston he assembled a personal library that reflected his many interests. Besides books on rabbinica, Hebraica, Judaica, and comparative religion, the collection included volumes on travel, sociology, psychology, literature, history, and criminology. Four years before his death, Dr. Cohen donated approximately 5,000 books from his personal library to The University of Texas at Austin. Henry Cohen had a love affair with the colleges and universities in Texas and was a visitor on the campuses annually, often giving baccalaureate and commencement speeches. When he chose Texas as recipient of his books, papers, and memorabilia, understandably, this alienated the great depositories of Jewish learning in Cincinnati, New York, and Boston. Although he was synonymous with charity in Texas, his name was almost unmentionable among some Jewish archivists, who felt slighted that Cohen felt more Texan than Jewish.[26]

But Texans knew his universal value. His book collection will be used for generations. "It will unquestionably be a treasure to future generations of Texas scholars," wrote Alexander Moffit, University librarian, upon accepting the collection.[27] Under terms of the gift, the University Library was permitted to distribute the volumes in such a manner that they were shelved with similar works.

Dr. Henry Cohen visited persons of all faiths in keeping with his saying, "To me there is no such thing as Episcopalian scarlet fever, Catholic arthritis, or Jewish mumps." He is shown at John Sealy Hospital, Galveston, in 1938.

Many prominent Texans visited Mollie and Henry Cohen at "The Rabbinage" at 1920 Broadway, since torn down.

Dr. Henry Cohen reading a Megillah, one of several antique parchment scrolls he owned.

Courtesy Rosella H. Werlin and Institute of Texan Cultures.

Dr. Henry Cohen and Temple B'nai Israel, second Jewish congregation established in Texas

Dr. Henry Cohen at his desk in the Cohen Community House, a Sunday school.

Photo by Felder, Austin.
Courtesy Charlotte Royal Moskowitz.

Ernest Winkler, bibliographer and librarian at The University of Texas who packed the library, wrote, "Doctor Cohen appealed to me as a teacher. He would have filled the chair of a professor perfectly, had he been cast in that role. He invited inquiry on the part of others and was always ready to answer questions, having a rich store of knowledge and experience to draw on."[28]

Harry Ransom, former UT Chancellor, wrote, "No Texan standing between Ashbel Smith and our future appeals to me more than Rabbi Cohen, of whom I have many unforgettable impressions and to whom the University owes a great debt."[29]

In addition to his books, Cohen donated his papers to The University of Texas at Austin. The 300 folders of correspondence reside in the Barker Texas History Center. Dr. Cohen died in Houston June 12, 1952, ten months prior to his ninetieth birthday.[30]

The year he died, his last biography in *Who's Who in America 1952-53* sprawls down the page in small type for seven inches, recording his activities on international levels in Zurich and China, as well as Texas.

Three years after his death, a sixty-minute television special about Cohen premiered on the NBC network.[31] The show opened with a ballad singer strumming a guitar and singing a song more country-Western than Jewish:

Decades later, his memory was kept alive through the Henry Cohen Humanitarian Award Contest, films, and theatre. After viewing a film written, directed, and produced in 1976 by the author covering the history of the pioneer Jewish Texans, which included a segment on Rabbi Henry Cohen and the Galveston Immigration Movement, other filmmakers began to produce a feature motion picture on Cohen's work in the Galveston Immigration Movement, which premiered in Dallas in 1983. A few years later, Mark Harelik, descendant of immigrants who came through the port of Galveston before settling in the towns of Hamilton and Waco, wrote a play recalling his roots and his grandfather Haskell Harelik. The Denver Center Theatre Company, which commissioned Harelik to write *The Immigrant — A Hamilton County Album*, premiered it, and, following its successful Colorado debut, the play was produced by the Alley Theatre in Houston (March 5-April 5, 1987) to standing ovations, and went on national tour.

Along with such memorable Texans as Sam Houston, David Crockett, Ashbel Smith, and Gail Borden goes Rabbi Henry Cohen, who helped to write a unique era of Texas history. If there were Jewish saints, the name of Dr. Henry Cohen would surely go down as one. Meanwhile, because there are not, he goes down in history as a great Texan — which is probably what Henry Cohen would have preferred, anyway.

In all the State of Texas,
From Fort Worth to San Anton'
There's not a man who hasn't heard
Of Rabbi Henry Cohen.

He was born in England
Across the wide, wide sea.
From there he went to Africa,
Cape Town and Kimberley.

In Woodville, Mississippi
His reputation was begun,
And soon he was invited
To dear old Galveston.

Now, the Alamo is famous
In historic San Anton'
But in Galveston the tourist
Was shown Rabbi Henry Cohen.

Max Maas

Chapter 9

The Great Merchants

Some Called Them Princes

They may have lived as conquistadors, buccaneers, ranchers, seamen, or oil men — but they were all merchants.

They traded with the Indians on the frontier. They sold them booty from the Spanish Main. They brought cargo from Charleston and returned with Texas cotton. They bartered calico, cattle, and oil field pipe.

Merchandising often served as a springboard for other careers. Jewish colonizers like De Cordova had general stores before they began to sell real estate. Financier Morris Lasker peddled along the Georgia countryside before he came to Texas.

From Jewish carpenters for Cortés, to Jewish Texans who left to pan gold in California, as postmasters and *alcaldes*, with few exceptions, they were all merchants.

Jewish merchants chronicled as great merchant families impacted the merchandising business as never before or since in Texas. Their businesses mostly dealt with merchandise of the general store type, usually the dry goods company — and in their growing success many became household names, so that today, in Texas, to say "Jewish merchant" brings visions of high fashion, costly, dazzling apparel, and glamorous careers.

It is incredible that it took just fifty years for Texas to progress from Samuel Isaacks and his ox wagon to Neiman-Marcus.

ELIJAH AND SAMUEL ISAACKS

Elijah Isaacks, born in North Carolina in 1775, came to Texas January 10, 1820, two years before Stephen F. Austin and his first colonists arrived in December 1821. He and his wife settled in East Texas near the Neches River and at age 57 he was elected a delegate from that area to the historic Convention of 1832 presided over by Austin, in which the colonists asked Mexico for government reforms. He died in Jasper County in 1859.

Their son Samuel Isaacks, born in Tennessee in 1804, came to Texas with a friend around 1819, preceding his parents. One of ten children, he was age fifteen when he arrived. He joined Austin's first Colony of Three Hundred. As a colonist he received in 1824 a Spanish grant of one league and one labor of land (4,605 acres) in a bend of the Brazos River near the present site of Rosenberg. Two bounty warrants were issued to him for military services from June 9, 1836 to January 1, 1837. After living in Angelina County, where his children were born, Isaacks moved in 1855 to Harris County and built wharves. He freighted supplies from Galveston by ox wagon, opening a road north to Coldspring. He later lived on Taylor's Bayou near Seabrook, where he died in 1878. His grandson, Judge S.J. Isaacks, who was reared Methodist, served as first mayor of Midland.[1]

SAMUEL MAAS

Samuel Maas was not the typical Jewish immigrant who came to America to escape the Czar on a fifteen-dollar steerage voyage across the Atlantic. Maas sailed the Atlantic many times, always in a luxury cabin. He spoke English perfectly before he emigrated from Germany. He corresponded with such Texas luminaries as Henri Castro, French colonizer of the frontier, occasionally giving Castro unasked-for advice. When Maas went back to Europe to carry on trade for Texas, he held a letter of recommendation from no less a person than Sam Houston. When he went looking for a wife, he made another trip to Europe to win the hand of the daughter of a rabbi. She was Isabella Offenbach, an opera singer and sister of Jacques Offenbach, a composer whose light operas inspired the French can can, at the time a very scandalous dance.

Excerpt from Maas Journal.

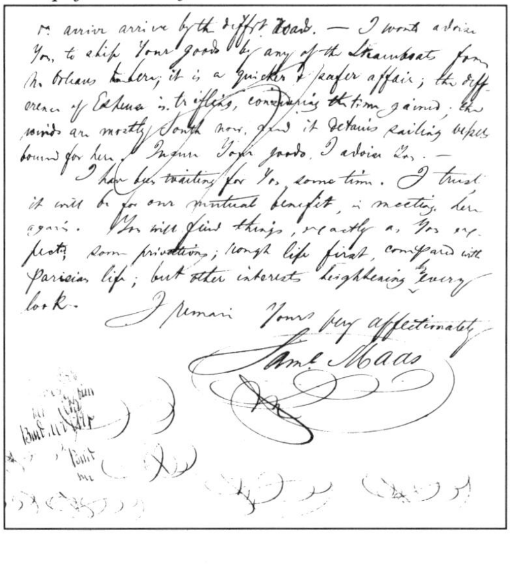
to arrive arrive by the diff't road. — I would advise You, to ship Your goods by any of the Steamboats from N. Orleans [illegible]; it is a quicker & safer affair; the difference of Expense is trifling, considering the time gained; the winds are mostly South now, and it detains sailing vessels bound for here. Insure Your goods, I advise You. —
I have been waiting for You, some time. I trust it will be for our mutual benefit, in meeting here again. You will find things, exactly as You expected; some privations; rough life first, compared with Parisian life; but other interests heightening every look.
I remain Yours very affectionately
Sam'l Maas

Sam Houston wrote to Ashbel Smith on behalf of Samuel Maas July 21, 1843, when Dr. Smith was Charge d'affaires to England and France:[2]

> Dear Sir:
>
> Captain Sam'l Maas, a citizen of Houston, intends to visit Europe, and will be pleased to present himself to you. I think you have known him at Galveston. For several years I have known him favorably. He has sustained an irreproachable character. . . . He is a gentleman of business habits, close attention, sober, and in short, he is one of the few gentlemen in Texas against whom I have never heard an imputation of any kind. If you can with propriety advance the views and interests of Captain Maas, I will be gratified to know that you have done so. And his amiable character assures me that your civilities will be esteemed, and valued by him.
>
> Sam Houston[3]

Maas immigrated to the United States in the 1830s, first living in Pittsburgh and then South Carolina where he had relatives. But he had his heart set on Texas and at age twenty-six boarded a schooner headed there. The boat was loaded with lumber to

Maas house where Isabella Offenbach had an auditorium for concerts.

build a home in Galveston.[4] A violent tropical storm sank the ship off the Florida keys, and Samuel swam to shore. He made his way to Texas, arriving in Nacogdoches county in 1836, just after the battles of the Alamo and San Jacinto.

Maas, who already spoke German, French, and English, became fluent in Spanish and found work translating Spanish land titles into English. After it became the capital, he frequently traveled to Austin for this purpose and gained a knowledge of title of land. In 1839 he set up a mercantile business in Galveston where, except for a brief stay in Houston during the Civil War, he lived until his death.[5]

He made frequent trips overseas to visit his homeland.[6] One evening in Cologne he went to the Cathedral to hear songs of the Old Masters sung by Isabella Offenbach. He found her strikingly beautiful, and as her voice permeated the cathedral, Maas fell in love. Talented and beautiful, courted by dukes and barons and other members of nobility, she seemed out of reach to the young man without a title.[7] Through perseverance, the enterprising young Texan worked to earn her love. In the spring of 1844 they married in Cologne, and she moved from one of the world's most cultured cities to the raw village of Galveston as his bride. (Isabella's dedicated effort to bring music to the frontier appears in chapter 12.)

When Maas returned to Texas a married man, he started a ship chandlery business which became quite successful. He began investing in real estate and became one of Galveston's most prominent citizens. He constantly kept abreast of world affairs, and for fifty years he subscribed to *The Courier*, a French newspaper, and became one of the first subscribers to the *Galveston Daily News*, out of which grew the *Dallas Morning News*. One of his favorite expressions was, "What is there stirring?"

Samuel Maas kept a journal in the 1840s in which he recorded his transatlantic courtship of Isabella, correspondence with Henri Castro, and other unpublished Texana.[8] Maas in a sense served as an intelligence officer or reporter for Castro. In his letters, he kept Castro — who was in Paris — up to date on the events in Texas including the drive for annexation and the latest report on Castroville.[9] Some entries are more personal. For example, the respectable but lonely Galveston businessman traveling in Europe confided to his diary a night of comfort with a streetwalker of Paris.[10]

Samuel Maas made drafts of letters sent, and his journal with these copies reveals how he felt about merchandising. In 1835 he wrote to a cousin (in Charleston): "I hated that common retailing business. Went up the Mississippi with the most dreaming plans — did not care much about clerking either — tried a diversion of instructing in French and German. . . . As to the advantage of instructing, I feel that I gain every day in knowledge of correct ideas through local and foreign literature . . . have acquired a pretty good knowledge of the Spanish tongue [official language of Texas before 1836] and during my hours of diversion I have scientifically pursued music, for which I now have a grand passion."[11]

Maas lived torn between day-to-day life and his love of languages, translating, teaching, and music. His inner struggle between his desire to be a man of letters and pursue his interest in music conflicted with the hard realities of having to earn a living. As a linguist by profession, he could have eked out an existence as a teacher and translator, but that would not support a family. Although he proved successful in business, neither money nor power overly motivated him. He never sought public office because he did not want it. He spent much of his later years almost hermitlike; he felt at home reading the French newspaper he had subscribed to for fifty years. There was much music in the home because of his wife's interest in music.

Like many members of minority groups in America's melting pot, Maas felt that prejudice against his people existed, although often subtle and not overt. His constant yearnings, his lost dreams, his difficulty at having to adjust to a community in which he belonged to a minority, the demands of business, and sensitivity to prejudice, in their total effect, summed up the lives of many of the Jews who settled in Texas. His story can be repeated in Dallas, Houston, and small towns where artistically gifted persons live but find those qualities unmarketable.

He died at his home January 10, 1897, at age eighty-seven. By that time he had seventeen grandchildren. His obituary read, "Death of a Pioneer."[12] Isabella had died six years earlier.

Maxwell Maas became the couple's most prominent son. After the Civil War, he joined his father in the family's ship chandlery business, later working for the well-known Heidenheimer brothers, Sampson, Abraham and Isaac, pioneer Jewish merchants, who had stores in far West Texas as well as in Galveston. Max Maas then joined the prestigious George Seeligson and Co. Maas served as tax collector of Galveston County following the 1900 storm that devastated the island, and his work in helping to raise tremendous amounts of bond funds to finance the Galveston seawall is his legacy to Texas.

Max Maas married Sarah Davis, sister of Mrs. Morris Lasker.[13] They had nine children.

Max and Sarah occupied what has remained known as the Maas house, a historic structure at 1802

Sealy (Avenue I), shortly after they married.[14] In Maas' day, Sealy was one of the nicest residential streets in the city. The Sonnenthiel family had built their classic gingerbread-trimmed home on the same block. Morris Lasker built an outstanding residence one block south, and the Heidenheimer Castle at 1604 Sealy was one block west. Temple B'nai Israel, to which they all belonged, fronted on 22nd near Sealy, a walk of four blocks from the Maas home.

The house had two stories and a large attic. Max Maas loved oleanders and surrounded his house with them. The 1900 storm badly damaged the home. Maas' daughter remembered "the water rose to the piano keys. We could see that by the white water mark on the piano."[15] When Max died, his widow, Sarah Davis Maas, and children lived in the home until they sold it in 1911. It later fell into such disrepair the city condemned it. The Island City Development Corporation, a nonprofit corporation managed through Kempner family interests, paid the back taxes and purchased it to save it from the wrecking ball. They held it until a preservationist appeared. On July 24, 1972, Percella (Pat) Berntsen bought it and began to restore the house.[16] The Texas Historical Commission designated the Max Maas home a Texas historic landmark, and it wears a medallion. It also merited the National Register of Historic Homes. A visitor to the home can imagine Isabella playing the piano and singing to entertain her children as she once performed before European royalty.

The Samuel Maas family is one of the oldest in Texas. He was one of the first Jewish Texans, and the Offenbach-Maas-Levy family is significant because it is the oldest Jewish family in Texas in continuous residence. Most of its members settled permanently, did not return to the North, get killed in battle, nor disappear from the Texas scene.

HARRY AND E. S. LEVY

One of the daughters of Sarah and Max Maas, Nettie Maas (named for her aunt, Nettie Davis Lasker), married another of Texas merchant princes, Henry (Harry) Levy, Sr., who, together with his older brother Edward S. Levy, was partner of E.S. Levy & Co. in Galveston.

The store had been founded by Abraham Levy and L. Weis in 1877. Shortly thereafter, Weis died. When Abraham died June 23, 1879, at age fifty-three, his son E.S. Levy took over and changed the name from Levy & Weis to E.S. Levy & Co. In 1892 E.S. erected the five-story building at Tremont and Market streets. After the 1900 storm, E.S. Levy sold his interest and moved to New York City. Although E.S. never returned to Texas,

Abraham Levy married Esther Halff, daughter of Felix Halff, early Galveston mayor.

Nettie Maas, granddaughter of Isabella and Sam Maas, married Harry Levy, Sr.

Harry Levy, Sr., head of E.S. Levy 1901-1956.

Edward S. Levy headed E.S. Levy for 22 of its 100 years, until 1901.

New Advertisements.

LEVY & WEIS,

115 Market St., News Building,

BEG LEAVE TO INFORM their friends and the public generally that they have opened their

NEW STOCK OF CLOTHING,

Gent's Furnishing Goods, HATS, CAPS, TRUNKS, Valises, Rubber and Oil Clothing,

and all the latest novelties in their line. Their Stock is NEW and FRESH, and has been very carefully selected especially for this market and trade. They propose to sell at prices that can not fail to command a liberal patronage from all classes. N. B.—CHILDREN'S, BOYS' and YOUTHS' CLOTHING made a specialty.

au2 3m

the store kept his name.

For nearly half a century, Harry Levy, Jr. managed the store. He served as president from 1956 to 1974. His Galveston County civic work included president of the Chamber of Commerce in 1948, campaign chairman of the United Fund in 1961, and chairman of the board of trustees of Galveston Wharves in 1969. In 1974 he sold the store to his son Harry Levy III, who retired in 1977. The store, whose motto was Reliability Since 1877, lasted a hundred years. It was one of the few Texas department stores that remained a family-owned business that spanned four generations.[17]

Harry Levy, Jr., merchant prince.

Ad in Galveston City Directory, 1911.

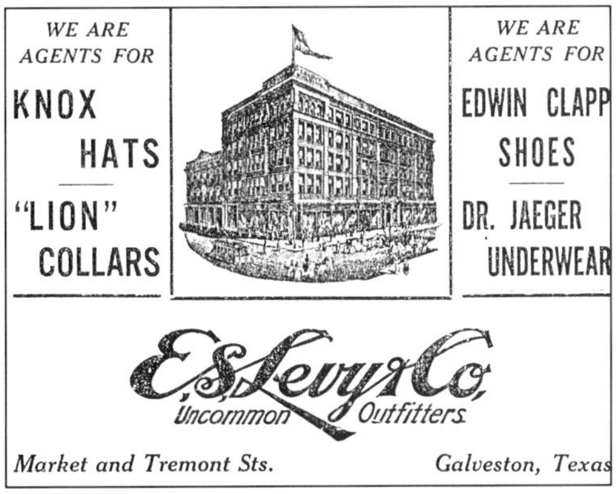

E.S. Levy & Co. served Galvestonians for 100 years, 1877-1977. Medallion recognizes building as historic landmark.

E.S. Levy department store and office building, circa 1900.

Lewis A. Levy came to Texas in 1841.

Mary L. Levy. Courtesy Rosanne D. and Daniel N. Leeson.

LEWIS A. LEVY

Levy was born in Amsterdam, The Netherlands, in 1799 and his wife, Mary, was a native of England. He lived in Philadelphia, Pensylvania; Richmond, Virginia; and New Orleans, Louisiana, before arriving in Texas at age forty-five. He came six years following his younger fighting brother, Dr. Albert Moses Levy, who organized the battle force after Ben Milam was killed at the Storming of Bexar at the Alamo in 1835.

At the beginning of his residence in Houston, around 1841 or 1842, Lewis A. Levy trafficked in a small way in land certificates.[18] The exact date of his arrival in Texas is not known, but it has been ascertained he was in Texas prior to January 1, 1842, the deadline for receiving a headright certificate for 640 acres.

In 1842 the Harris County "chief justice," or judge, appointed Levy one of three trustees, or assignees, in the bankruptcy of Jacob De Cordova in that colonizer's embryonic years in Texas.[19] Levy was well acquainted with De Cordova, who listed him in his 1858 book, *Texas: Her Resources and Her Public Men.*[20]

In 1843 Levy purchased from President Sam Houston a tract of land a mile and a half southwest of town known as the Houston Ranch.[21] The following year Levy purchased half an acre southeast of the courthouse and built his permanent home there, later acquiring fifteen acres adjoining it.

Although history looks at Levy as "Father of Houston Hebrew Charities," both the 1850 and 1860 census records list him as a merchant. His store occupied a frame building on the west side of Main Street, and the site eventually became home of the Continental Bank and Trust Co., in the heart of the downtown business district.[22]

Like De Cordova, but on a much smaller scale, Levy publicized Texas. Levy wrote a letter published in New York in the first major Jewish weekly in the United States, recommending the United States as a haven for the persecuted of Europe.

"In our own State, thousands of acres can be bought, within the settled portions of the State, for the small sum of from 25 cents to $1 per acre; good arable, fertile land, where a man can make his living to his liking, and [be] more independent than the Autocrat of Russia or the Emperor of Austria themselves. Indeed I would not exchange my fifteen-acre lot, with the house on it, and the garden around it, which I possess near the city of Houston, for all the thrones and hereditary dominion of both those noted persons."[23]

Lewis died in 1861 and was buried in the cemetery founded by the benevolent association he pioneered.

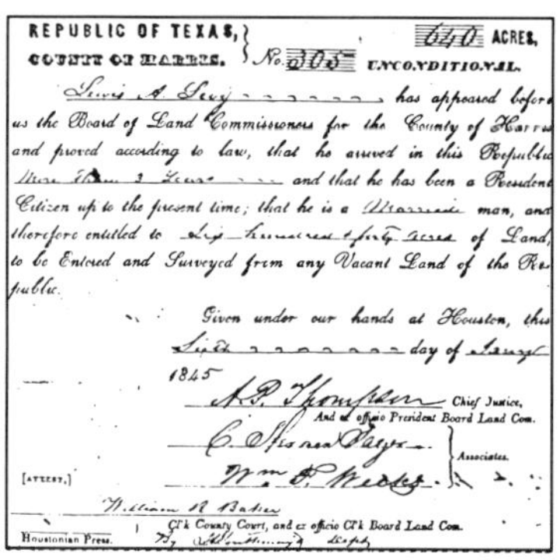
REPUBLIC OF TEXAS, COUNTY OF HARRIS. No. 305 640 ACRES, UNCONDITIONAL.

Lewis A. Levy has appeared before us the Board of Land Commissioners for the County of Harris and proved according to law, that he arrived in this Republic ... and that he has been a Resident Citizen up to the present time; that he is a ... man, and therefore entitled to Six hundred & forty acres of Land, to be Entered and Surveyed from any Vacant Land of the Republic.

Given under our hands at Houston, this Sixth day of ... 1845

A. P. Thompson Chief Justice, And ex officio President Board Land Com.

Associates.

[ATTEST,]

William R. Baker

Cl'k County Court, and ex officio Cl'k Board Land Com.

Houstonian Press.

Republic of Texas land grant to Lewis A. Levy, 1845.

ANOTHER LEVY CLAN

The name Levy is a common one, but this Levy family developed into an uncommon one.

Joseph and Bernard (Ben) Levy started in the livery stable business in Galveston, calling their firm J. Levy & Bro. The firm became a pioneer Texas institution. They expanded their business and established one of Texas' first funeral homes in 1868.

Ben Levy's daughter Edith married Abe Kaufman, whose father, Hirsch Kaufman, had founded Kaufman-Meyers Furniture Co., "the oldest furniture store in Texas," established in 1876.[24]

Around 1919 Ben's oldest son, Jack Levy, joined Gus Kahn and established Kahn and Levy, for decades one of Galveston's finest furniture stores.

Ben's son Adrian F. Levy, a native Galvestonian born in 1895, graduated from the University of Texas School of Law. Adrian Levy served as mayor of Galveston from 1932 to 1936. Adrian's brother, Marion J. Levy, Sr., also became an attorney, whose son, Marion J. Levy, Jr., held an important chair in American education, serving as Professor of Sociology and International Affairs at the Woodrow Wilson School of International Affairs of Princeton University.[25]

Besides Adrian Levy, Jews have served as mayors of other Texas cities, mostly small towns. These include Alto, Austin, Brownsville, Corpus Christi, Dallas, Dublin, Eagle Pass, El Paso, Fort Worth, Hearne, Jefferson, Joseyville (now named Luling), La Grange, Laredo, Lockhart, Marshall, McCamey, Nacogdoches, Plano, San Saba, Schulenberg, Sherman, South Padre Island, Tyler, Waco, and Ysleta (a suburb of El Paso).

A generation after Adrian Levy's mayoral term, Edward Schreiber, a furniture merchant, served several terms as mayor of Galveston.

Joseph Levy (1844-1922).

Bernard (Ben) Levy (1849-1908).

Courtesy Helene Levy.

Ambulance of J. Levy & Bro. Funeral Directors, 1926.

Mayor and Mrs. Adrian F. Levy in New York with aviator "Wrong-Way" Corrigan, a native Galvestonian, 1938.

Adrian F. Levy, mayor of Galveston in the 1930s, son of a pioneer family.

Photo: Gittings

THE SONNENTHEILS

The Sonnentheil home in Galveston is a historically important and restored treasure in Galveston's east end.

The home at 1826 Sealy was built in 1887 for Jacob Sonnentheil. The picturesque architecture stems from Gothic revival, and it appears that a carpenter spent years on the intricate lattice work.

Jacob Sonnentheil and his brother Julius were Galveston merchants who joined Congregation B'nai Israel on September 11, 1869. Early Galveston city directories (1878-1884) reveal they were partners with Sylvan Lion in Sonnentheil and Lion, a dry goods store on Tremont street. In 1884 they joined Louis Block and Leopold Oppenheimer in forming Block, Oppenheimer and Co., wholesale dry goods.

Mr. and Mrs. J. Sonnentheil occupied the house from 1887 until he died in 1908 at age sixty-seven. His widow, Sallie, lived in the house until 1910, when she moved into New York's Hotel Ansonia.[26]

The Sonnentheil House.

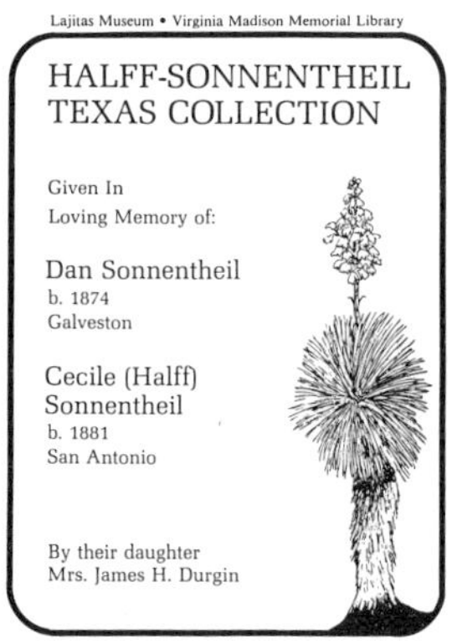

Bookplate from Lajitas Museum, Big Bend area of Texas.

Courtesy Jane S. Durgin.

LEON AND H. BLUM

Buildings built by Jewish merchants shaped the face of Texas cities from the earliest days of immigration. One of the most significant still stands in Galveston. Built by Leon Blum to house his wholesale dry goods business, the Blum Building is in the Strand historical district. The ornate brick structure built in 1879 had

Leon & H. Blum's building.

Leon Blum of Galveston.

reached 105 years of age when restored by Houston preservationists Cynthia and George Mitchell. Mitchell, a geology graduate of Texas A&M University, became chairman and president of Mitchell Energy, one of the nation's largest independent gas and oil producers.[27] The renovation took two years and cost 12 million.

The block-long building is of the neo-Renaissance style and features an arcade of open bays and stately masonry piers. An ornamental cornice decorates the new mansard roof. The building housed the *Galveston Tribune,* among other businesses, after the family-owned Blum business closed in the early 1900s. Converted in 1984 to a four-story hotel with 111 luxurious rooms and renamed the Tremont House, the historic building returned to the grandeur it knew in earlier years.[28]

As early as 1855 Leon Blum, twenty-two, had sailed from France to Texas. Before moving to Galveston he was a partner in Blum and Mayblum, the largest store in Richmond, a small town near Houston.[29] With his brothers Hyman and Sylvan, Leon later established in Galveston the first major wholesale dry goods business in the state. The firm, called Leon & H. Blum, did an annual business of five million dollars before the turn of the century and employed a staff of 125.[30]

The June 21, 1870, issue of Galveston's newspaper, *Flake's Bulletin,* reported that H. Blum sold wholesale dry goods: "fabric, hats, boots, shoes, and cutlery." The Galveston City Directory for 1886-87 showed Leon & H. Blum wholesale dealers in dry goods. The Blums added staples to the goods at a later date. The business, begun in 1866, the year after the end of the Civil War, continued until 1908.

The brothers also headed the Leon & H. Blum Land Company, then one of the largest land and livestock companies in Texas. The land company, incorporated in 1882,[31] controlled land said to include property in every Texas county at that time.

The historic 1879 Leon and H. Blum Building came alive again as the Tremont House, a 111-room hotel of rare character and style.

Leon & H. Blum Land Company advertised real estate in 150 Counties in Texas.

A. C. LABATT

Abraham Cohen Labatt is significant as the first Jewish trader of record to come regularly to Texas and Mexico and because his long and various life reflects the typical Jewish pioneers who brought goods to settlements across the country. He serves as a model of the enterprise they displayed and the adventure they sought. The period spanned by his date of birth, in 1802, and his death at the age of ninety-seven, in 1899, covers the time which saw major Jewish accomplishments in U.S. merchandising.[32]

Born in Charleston, South Carolina, Labatt's ancestry descended from the Dutch and German. His father emigrated from Amsterdam, Holland, and his mother was a citizen of Hamburg. Abraham lived in Charleston until a young man, learning the trade of general merchandising. In later years Labatt remembered the primitive nature of his family's life in Charleston: They "did not know what it was to have a match," he said, "and the only way to light the fire was with a tinder box."[33]

Labatt's name appeared as a subscriber to the constitution of the Reformed Society of Israelites of Charleston, the first reform synagogue in the New World.[34] The constitution is dated February 15, 1825. The next day he married Caroline Hyams, from an internationally prominent family, of Charleston.[35] They later moved to Charlotte, North Carolina, and in 1831 to New Orleans. In every place he settled, Abraham worked actively in all Jewish communal affairs. In New

Orleans, Labatt also became an important Masonic figure.[36] He earned his living there as a merchant and trader.

In the early 1830s, New Orleans served as almost sole purveyor to Texas trade, but by 1837 ships from distant ports began to make their way to Galveston, and merchants there found Atlantic coast cities eager to cultivate their commerce. A heavy immigration swept into Texas during 1837, bringing about considerable increase in means. Crops were good, the cotton alone worth about two million dollars; the harbor of Galveston kept busy with shipping, and four steamboats plying the Buffalo Bayou testified to the rapid growth of Houston.[37] This year Abraham made his first trading visit to Texas. The *Galveston News* in 1899 published Labatt's recollections of the event:

"I came here on the first steamer that ever touched Galveston Island. It was in 1837. The trip was made to see about establishing trade between Charleston and Texas and Mexico. The steamship was the *Columbia* and was captained by 'Bully' Wright. We landed just below where the John Sealy Hospital now stands. I remember well when we landed here. We arrived outside at four o'clock in the afternoon and the captain had a gun fired for a pilot. None came that night, and early the next morning we fired another gun. Still no pilot came. Then the captain, who did not wish to take the risk of running in alone, left it to a vote as to what he should do. We had every confidence in him and decided to run in without a pilot. He gave us all cork jackets [life preservers] to put on and we started. We drew twelve or fourteen feet, but we got over [the bar] all right, although we plowed up lots of mud.

"There was not a house on the island, and at the time [1837] the brig *Elba* was used as a customs house and prison, and the *Alliance* lay 100 yards from her, and we used her as a kind of hotel. I was in especial charge of Mrs. Barnard E. Bee.[38] [General Barnard E. Bee founded the Texas Army and served then as secretary of war.] . . . Her husband was at that time in charge of Santa Anna at Quintana [farther south on the Texas coast]. I remained here long enough to take her to Houston, where I obtained a conveyance and sent her overland to her husband. We took back with us to Charleston a load of freight for the interior. This was the first steamship that ever came into Galveston harbor."[39]

Abraham Cohen Labatt (1802-1899).

Photo: Morris, Galveston. Copyright © Richard Torbert.

In 1849 Labatt joined other "forty-niners" in the Gold Rush, continuing in California mercantile pursuits as well as those relating to the Masonic Lodge. Freemasonry attracted Jewish merchants because it offered, at modest costs of initiation and annual dues, social associations with prominent men, a highly regarded badge of respectability, and a pastime. For travelers, the ability to visit other Masonic lodges throughout the world had many advantages.[40] Labatt made full use of the opportunities offered by the lodge. He also served it in important capacities. In San Francisco he established and became first Master of one of the first lodges in the West, which he named the Davy Crockett Lodge.[41] At the time of his death he was the second-oldest living Mason. In 1850 he helped found and served as the first full term president of San Francisco's downtown Congregation Emanuel.[42]

In the 1860s the Labatt family moved back to Louisiana. They lived there for the near decade which included the Civil War. Labatt's son Henry J. Labatt had become a lawyer of some reputation during the California years. (Henry's pioneering work in law appears in chapter 14.)

In 1869 Abraham Labatt moved again, this time to Waco, Texas, where his wife of fifty-seven years, Caroline Hyams Labatt, died in 1878.[43] He then moved to Galveston.

Abraham Labatt lived to age ninety-seven and was survived by sixteen children, including Judge David C. Labatt, New Orleans; Henry J. Labatt, the attorney; and Joseph Isaac Labatt, who married Emily Dyer, niece of Major Leon Dyer and Rosanna Dyer Osterman.[44]

Although Abraham Labatt engaged in trade for most of his long life, he is not known for the establishment of a mercantile empire like the Sanger Bros., or the Marcuses. His presence as a respected member of the cities in which he lived, however, makes him impossible to overlook in any historical account of Jewish traders. Like others in the early days of the country, he sought his fortune on the road west, going from the Atlantic to the Pacific. He was a wanderer who covered the country on horseback, sailing vessels, steamships, and railroad.

JOSKE

When Lucille Joske and her husband, Dr. Frederick G. Oppenheimer, donated their extensive art collection to three leading museums in San Antonio, they followed a tradition of visual acuity set by Mrs. Oppenheimer's grandfather, pioneer Julius Joske. Joske's department stores had been sensitive to the display of merchandise since their inception as a frontier trading post. The main Joske's store on San Antonio's Alamo Plaza became a landmark.[45]

In 1867 when Julius Joske emigrated from Germany, he selected San Antonio as destination because it contained an important supply depot, serving military installations in Texas, the Indian Territory to the north, and Mexico to the south.

In the last half of the nineteenth century, most San Antonio businesses clustered around Main Plaza and Military Plaza. Joske's first venture was a small store on Main Plaza.[46] It took six years to accumulate sufficient funds to return to Germany to get his wife and three children. He sold the San Antonio store and returned to Germany to close up the home there. In 1873 Joske immigrated a second time and opened J. Joske & Sons in a small adobe house near the U.S. Army corral.

After two years, he moved to Alamo Plaza near the Grand Opera House located across the Plaza. The William and Mary Menger boardinghouse, which later became the Menger Hotel (famous for its beautiful old patio garden), faced the Joske's site. Here cattle barons stayed during the era of the great cattle drives, and here Teddy Roosevelt recruited his regiment of "Rough Riders" for the Spanish-American War.[47] Trade in the area thrived.

Later J. Joske & Sons moved to a larger location on Alamo Plaza. Here began a shift from Joske to his sons. In 1883 Julius Joske, his wife, and one son returned permanently to Germany. They, like some immigrants, did not entirely acclimate to Texas, preferring the civilized country they had left behind to the rougher frontier.

Julius Joske's other sons, Alexander and Albert, changed the name of the store to Joske Brothers. Like other second-generation retailers, the brothers recognized competitiveness of the market and became innovators. They promoted the First International

Joske Brothers store, northeast corner of Alamo and Commerce Streets. Built in 1889, its shell was incorporated in later expansion.

Courtesy Estate of Robert M. Ayres and Institute of Texan Cultures.

Mrs. Alexander Joske with her grandsons, Frederick Oppenheimer, Jr. and Alexander Joske Oppenheimer, and her son-in-law, Dr.Frederick Oppenheimer. She was dressed in mourning clothes following the death of her husband. Taken at dedication of Joske Boy Scout Center, 1926.

Trade Fair, an ambitious project opened in November of 1889 by telegram from President Porfirio Diaz of Mexico.[48]

In 1903 Alexander Joske purchased the interests of his father and brother and became the aggressive force behind the continued expansion of Joske Brothers.[49] He sent key employees east to study the operations of other larger stores. He created a customer service department to handle complaints and promote goodwill. He launched the first fleet of delivery wagons in San Antonio and led in promotional devices, such as setting a 3,000-candlepower searchlight atop the store to draw attention to the building.[50]

Joske's had the distinction of becoming the first fully air-conditioned store in Texas, in 1936. Although by then the store had passed from family hands, the first use of air-conditioning continued the practice of innovation started by the Joske family.

Before Alexander Joske's death in 1925, Dr. Frederic Goldstein Oppenheimer, Alexander's son-in-law, operated the store. Dr. Oppenheimer, a member of the Oppenheimer banking family of San Antonio, had left his medical practice in New York to manage the San Antonio store.[51] In 1929 Hahn Department Stores purchased Joske's, and in 1932 the store became part of the Allied Store Corporation.

Frederic and Lucille Joske Oppenheimer became internationally famous art collectors. For many years they had a private seven-room museum of art in an addition to their home. The Joskes built the house in 1920 and added the wing around 1930 or 1931, according to a son, Frederick Joske Oppenheimer.[52] They donated numerous paintings of the Early American Hudson River School to the San Antonio Art League and the Witte Museum and donated their main collection to the McNay Institute of Art, where it was housed in a wing bearing their name. The Joske collection included Flemish, Impressionists, Medieval, and Renaissance paintings, as well as sculpture and room paneling.

Although the name Joske is symbolic with art and beauty, few realize the personal tragedies and despair the family has known. When Lucille's brother Harold drowned in the Guadalupe River at the New Braunfels rapids in a swimming accident at age twenty-two, their father Alexander Joske became so depressed he killed himself.[53] Lucille became the only child and the name died out locally, since Alexander Joske's brother had returned to Europe with his parents. Libby (Mrs. Alexander) Oppenheimer recalled, "My mother-in-law [Lucille] would say, 'The woods are full of Oppenheimers, but there are so few Joskes.' Alexander Joske wanted his only daughter back in Texas. That is why Lucille and Dr. Frederic G. Oppenheimer moved back from New York."[54]

Though their son, Frederick Joske Oppenheimer, lived in a house with an art museum attached, the unusual arrangement didn't make him feel different. "I went to public school; I led an ordinary life," he said.[55]

His brother Alexander Oppenheimer and his family donated funds for a Boy Scout Home and "Home for Wayward Girls." Alexander recalled that for many years the San Antonio store's motto was The biggest store in the biggest state.[56]

Although the Joske stores had been owned by the Allied chain since 1932, the stores still carried the Joske name half a century after being sold. So respected was this name that Allied, which also owned the Titche-Goettinger stores of Dallas, eventually changed all of the Dallas store names to Joske's. Twenty-seven stores carried the name Joske's. However, in late 1986 Campeau Corp. of Toronto, Canada, acquired Allied Stores Corp., and in April 1987 Dillard Department Stores of Little Rock, Arkansas, bought from Campeau the Joske chain, putting the name Dillard's on all twenty-seven Joske stores.[57]

LEVY BROTHERS DRY GOODS COMPANY

A pioneer Houston merchant from Glenfern, Ireland, William L. Foley, provided the training ground not only for his nephew Patrick, who founded Foley Bros., but also for a Jew named Abraham M. Levy, who founded Levy Brothers Dry Goods Company.

Begun in 1887, Levy's mercantile establishment at one time employed four hundred people and was "the largest in the South."[58]

Levy's parents, Adeline and M.H. Levy, were pioneers who had come to Texas in the 1850s. Abraham was a native Texan, born in Houston in 1859. His father died in 1876, and the widow Adeline continued the business of "dry goods, boots, shoes, and c. [etc.]" on Preston between Main and Travis. Abraham worked as a clerk for William Foley, before founding his own business with his brother Leo.[59] Other brothers who joined the firm included Hyman, Haskell, Joe and Isaac Levy, and a brother-in-law, Joseph Goldman. A dress-making department and later women's fashions and millinery became the store's specialties.

Levy Brothers was one of the first retail stores in the nation to take employees into the firm on a cooperative basis. Abe Levy, president, developed a reputation for his good communications with his employees, and he insisted on his office not having a door so he could be always accessible.

Just as Foley's had been Levy's merchandising school, so the Levy store served as the training ground for many of Texas' leading merchants.

When Abe Levy died in 1924, his family donated funds in his memory to old historic Congregation Beth Israel to cover "the entire cost of the grounds for building the new Temple."[60]

Abe M. Levy, born in Houston in 1859, founded Levy Brothers Dry Goods Company. He is shown in 1912

SAKOWITZ

Tobias Sakowitz, a founder of a pioneer department store chain, began as Tevye Kallman Shaikevitch, born in the town of Korosteschev, Kiev state, Russia, in 1882. His father Leebe (1851-1921) emigrated to America via New York port before the turn of the century and peddled bananas. He left Tevye in Russia with his brothers Shama (Sam) and Shimsum (Simon), his sister, Rebecca, and his mother, Leah.

Simon and Tobias Sakowitz (left to right). *Photo: Gittings*

Tevye soon moved in with his grandfather, who hoped Tevye would become a rabbi and taught him Hebrew. However, after three or four years, when Tevye reached the age of eight, his grandfather died at age seventy. Tevye's grandmother "treated him badly after the death of his grandfather,"[61] so, at age nine Tevye left his grandmother's house and became apprenticed to a bookbinder. He made himself independent and moved to nearby Jetooma, where he learned stencil painting and paperhanging. He combined these trades with bookbinding because employment was seasonal, available mostly in fall and winter.

Despite the father's lack of great success in America, he sent funds for his wife, Leah, and three of their four children, leaving Tevye behind. When Leah arrived, she brought some money with her to America, around $6,000 of her husband's father's estate. The Shaikevitch family at one time had been wealthy in Russia.[62]

With this money, they went to Texas and, learning of the cotton mills in Galveston, they moved there. Father, mother, and oldest son went to work in the mills. Leah soon became a foreman, "but Leebe, her husband, had difficulty with his hands which seemed very soft. He gave up the job finally and started to peddle again. Leah took in boarders."[63]

Leebe wanted to settle on the land in a community of Jews. The Shaikevitch family savings went into purchasing property in Dickinson, Texas (near Galveston), where they moved with some other Jewish families. But the small commune did not last long. Finances ran so low that at one time, the families ate nothing except sweet potatoes. Leah took her beloved candlesticks into a pawn shop in Galveston, and with this money the family returned to Galveston, where they again took in boarders.

The Shaikevitch family opened a small dry goods store in Galveston and simplified their name to Sakowitz. Shama became Samuel, Shimsun became Simon. When Tevye finally arrived after his father sent for him around 1895 or 1897, he became Tobias, or Toby. Their sister, Rebecca, kept her biblical Hebrew name.

Samuel, the eldest, worked with his father, Leebe (Louis), in a store they opened in Galveston in 1902, while the two younger brothers, ages nineteen and seventeen, worked in other Galveston firms, such as Hauser and Klein Wholesale Dry Goods Co. "Both my father Tobias and his brother Simon, when they were working, lived with their parents and they paid their mother for their room and board. She put it aside. When they were ready to go into business, she gave them that money," Tobias' son Alex recalled[64]

After Tobias and Simon worked together in their Galveston store several years, Simon started a second store, in Houston.[65] Tobias left Galveston in 1917 as a result of the violent storm of 1915, more turbulent than the notorious 1900 storm, but one that caused few casualties due to the seawall.

In Texas, Tobias had two sons, Alexander and Bernard. Alexander, who changed his surname to Sackton, was a Ph.D. graduate of Cambridge and became a professor in the English Department at the University of Texas at Austin. Tobias' son Bernard and his wife, Ann, became parents of Lynn Sakowitz, who married Oscar Wyatt, Jr,; and Robert Tobias Sakowitz, who continued the family mercantile business. Lynn became an international socialite, intimate friend of such luminaries as Princess Grace of Monaco, and was annually voted one of the best dressed women in the world. "She is, quite simply, the Queen of Texas Society," wrote one journalist.[66]

Debrett's Peerage and Baronetage, for 214 years the register of Britain's titled lords and ladies, included the Sakowitz family in *Debrett's Texas Peerage*, calling Robert Sakowitz and his sister, Lynn, Mrs. Oscar Wyatt, Jr., "beautiful people superstars" and "the only sister and brother to make the Best-Dressed List," the International Best-Dressed Hall of Fame. After graduating *cum laude* from Harvard, Robert worked for a bank in Europe, and in Paris he joined Galleries Lafayette, largest department store chain in France. *Texas Peerage* called him "the crown prince of panache."[67]

Samuel Sakowitz, Tobias' brother and the eldest son of the original Sakowitz family, remained in Galveston and never participated in what became Sakowitz Bros. Samuel died in 1923 at age forty-eight.

Rebecca Sakowitz, who had come to America with her brothers at age two, spent approximately fifteen years in Galveston where she married Max Henry Nathan. They moved to Houston in 1910. Nathan founded one of Houston's oldest menswear specialty stores. As a young matron of twenty-three, Rebecca

(Left to right) Tobias Sakowitz, Dr. Hyman Judah Schachtel, Leopold L. Meyer, and Simon Sakowitz, 1963

called a meeting of like-minded women to see what could be done to make wagon drivers take better care of their horses and mules. She went on to become a founder of the Houston Humane Society and helped start classes of English in Houston public schools for women of foreign birth.[68] Mr. and Mrs. Nathan helped found the Houston Round Table of Christians and Jews, which became a section of the National Conference of Christians and Jews.[69] For her work in interfaith projects, the YWCA honored her as one of Houston's four top women civic leaders. She died in 1974 at the age of eighty-seven.

Rebecca Nathan's husband had a younger brother, Dave Nathan, who opened Nathan's in Galveston, which for decades served as the island city's premiere specialty shop. Dave's daughter married Morton H. Meyerson, president of E.D.S. of Dallas, where the symphony hall is named for him.

Robert I. Cohen.

Rebecca Nathan's daughter Leah remembered her mother and uncles. "Brothers Tobias and Simon, founders of Sakowitz, were different from each other, but a good combination," she said. "Tobe was a financial person, the businessman, cold and forbidding. Simon had a warmer personality and was active in the city, starting the 'Council House,' a social service house, and served on the symphony board. Civic wise, Rebecca was the most important."[70]

Sakowitz, never a public corporation, was the last of the major family-owned department stores in Texas. Leah stated, "They didn't try to be all over the world." Although Sakowitz expanded to Dallas, Phoenix, and Midland, the firm began to consolidate into fewer stores in mid-1985 due to the soft petroleum market, which cooled the economy of many Texas cities.[71]

ROBERT I. COHEN AND GEORGE (FOLEY BROS.) COHEN

In 1917 the Foley brothers sold their Houston store to Robert I. Cohen, Sr., owner of Robert I. Cohen, a pioneer Galveston department store. Cohen kept his Galveston store and left the Foley name on the Houston enterprise, which he bought for his son George, 32.

In response to the biblical commandment to honor parents, George Cohen built a tribute to his parents while they lived, the Cohen House, Rice University's faculty club.

1928 photo courtesy Rice University.

George immortalized his parents when in 1927 he gave the money for the Robert and Agnes Cohen House on the campus of Rice University. Faculty and ex-students occupied the mansion for meetings and events.

George Cohen's enthusiasm for Houston and its growth knew no bounds. He chartered and brought to Houston its first passenger liner from Europe in 1925.[72] He had a hand in the city's first airlines in an era when commercial planes flew only by day and Texans rode trains all night to make it to New York in thirty-eight hours.

But most of all, Cohen devoted his money and facile mind to the people of Houston from all walks of life. He was a philanthropist as well as patron of the fine arts.

George Cohen was born in Galveston on a night in 1885 when a fire destroyed his parents' home and forced his mother to go to the home of a midwife to give birth. While growing up, he developed a love for the sea and liked to go with the fishing boats from Galveston to the coast of Mexico.

Cohen kept his store until he sold it to Federated Department Stores in 1945.[73] Cohen, then sixty, continued performing civic work for Houston until his death at age eighty-six.[74] His obituary in December of 1971, entitled "The flair of George Cohen," reported that "He did not conform to the public conception of a merchant. He was imaginative and with a feel for adventure. . . . Cohen was a good man for this city to have had."[75]

George Cohen who with his father, Robert I. Cohen, bought Foley Bros. in 1917.

Mrs. George S. Cohen was the former Esther Regina Meyer, sister of Leopold Meyer, medical benefactor.

Hebrew lettering on plaque in Cohen House means "Honor Thy Father and Mother."

Courtesy Rice University.

E. M. Kahn store at Elm and Lamar, Dallas, 1918.

E. M. KAHN

When the Texas & Pacific Railroad extended its terminus to Dallas, the small town attracted many, among them young Emanuel Meyer Kahn (pronounced Can) who in 1872 founded E.M. Kahn & Co., which continued for ninety-two years as a family-owned business.

For fifty years E.M. Kahn served as the president; his son Laurence followed as president for nearly twenty-five years; and his grandson Eugene Sanger served as president for seventeen years until the sale of the firm to a national organization, Eagle Clothes, in 1969. The new owners kept the name E.M. Kahn & Co. and made another grandson, Alex F. Weisberg, Jr., president. In the 1970s, after ninety-two years, the stores closed.

"E.M. Kahn, besides being the oldest [retail] store in Dallas, had the distinction of being the first air-conditioned store in town. It was the first store west of the Mississippi to have fixed prices. One didn't bargain," said Eugene Kahn Sanger. Until the late 1930s E.M. Kahn operated as a men's clothing store; then in 1936 Laurence Kahn added women's and children's departments. In the 1950s, Kahn's branched into the suburbs.

E.M. Kahn literally presided over his store. "He did not sit in an office, but sat on a raised dais in the center of the store to see if everyone was getting service. The chair was upholstered in a green hard woolen fabric with gold-colored rings around the skirt. In those days, customers got waited on," said Sanger. "The policy was The Public be Pleased. His son Laurence sat in the same chair for many years. Morton Sanger [a cousin of Eugene, who became comptroller of the company] moved the chair to the side. When Laurence died in 1947, I sat for seventeen years in that chair. Laurence Kahn, my mother's brother, was more dominant in my life than the Sanger family, so I went to work for E.M. Kahn rather than Sanger Bros.," Eugene Sanger explained. "But I was born in grandmother Sanger's house."[76]

E.M. Kahn was born in Alsace-Lorraine, that beautiful countryside which constantly drove France and Germany to war. At age fourteen, when his parents died, his relatives enrolled him in rabbinical school, and he accepted a position as a cantor and schoolteacher before coming to America.

He landed by packet boat in Georgia, where he worked as a merchant before moving to Mississippi. He moved to Dallas in 1871 because he felt those Texans "walked with a purpose, thought faster and spoke faster," according to Eugene Kahn Sanger.

E.M. Kahn and his wife, Lily Belle (Hurst), had six children, five of whom lived to maturity. The third child, Felice Kahn, at age fifteen, became a violinist with the first Dallas Symphony Orchestra. However, in those days home and career did not combine, and she gave up her music when she married Alex Sanger of Waco and moved away from Dallas. Alex's father Sam was one of the original Sanger brothers. Alex and Felice lived in Waco forty years or more, until 1938. In Waco she was a founder of the free-lunch program at the schools.

"Mother was never happy in Waco," her son Eugene pointed out. "There was little opportunity for music there and few cultural influences, just agriculture and the Katy train running through Waco. She felt stultified. She told me, 'If you can talk your daddy into moving to Dallas, I'll buy you a car.' So I worked at it, and my mother was in her sixties when she returned to Dallas, and my father came to live here for the first time. I got a Packard convertible."

E.M. Kahn was one of the founders of Temple

E.M. KAHN G. DREYFUSS A.K. HURST

N.Y. OFFICE 565 & 567 Broadway Dallas, Texas

Bought of E.M. Kahn & Co

The Leading One Price Clothiers,

GENTS' FURNISHERS & FASHIONABLE HATTERS,

SOLE AGENTS FOR

THE CELEBRATED DUNLAP HAT

Emanu-El of Dallas; the State Fair of Texas; the Phoenix Club, which later became the Columbian Club; an original founding stockholder of the American National Bank, which later became InterFirst, and of Southwestern Life Insurance Co.

He built his first store on the courthouse square in 1872, a few weeks before the Sanger brothers arrived. Kahn had arrived in Dallas in 1871 and for a short time worked in partnership with his cousin Moise Kahn. That same year he associated in business with Gerard Dreyfuss, his wife's brother-in-law, under the name Kahn and Dreyfuss. After a severe dispute between the men, Gerard Dreyfuss moved to a location at Main and Ervay, where Dreyfuss & Son sold fine men's wear for many years.

Gerard's son Sol Dreyfuss at one time owned the Dallas Baseball Team. Gerard's daughter, Hortense Dreyfuss, married Lawrence Pollock, Sr., founder of Pollock Paper Co. The Pollock Gallery of art at Southern Methodist University is named for this family, which donated their home on South Boulevard to the Visiting Nurses Association.

For all his accomplishments in business, E.M. Kahn was not a businessman: "He loved art and music and played the violin. He was an esthete. As he walked to the streetcar line each morning, he had three props: a fresh flower from his garden in his buttonhole, an umbrella, and his Masonic book," according to his daughter-in-law Ruth Hexter Kahn. In Masonry, E.M. reached the thirty-third degree, the pinnacle. His wife's brothers, Max, Melvin, Sr., and Edgar, followed her to Dallas. After working in the Kahn store, they established Hurst Brothers, a men's clothing store, shortly after the turn of the century.

When E.M. Kahn died in 1923, his son Laurence took over. Laurence, born in 1887, graduated from Sachs Preparatory School in New York. He went directly to work in the store, chiefly to support his father in his father's profound grief over the death of his son Ernest, and later to assume most of the responsibilities of the operation of store. "Like his father, he was self-effasive, gentle of manner, but rigidly demanding of himself," recalled Ruth Hexter Kahn years later. "He devoted himself to his parents, his business, and his community to the extent he remained a bachelor until his forty-seventh year. He never accepted leadership positions, but preferred to operate behind the scenes. Many leaders sought his advice, from the director of the Community Chest to the president of the art museum.

"Laurence Kahn became an expert in the selection of fabrics. He could quickly ruffle a batch of swatches and select just the right fabrics for the manufacturer to use. He had just completed buying for the seventy-fifth anniversary celebration of the store's founding when he died suddenly in his sleep at the age of fifty-nine."[77]

E. M. Kahn

Ruth (Mrs. Laurence S.) Kahn, daughter-in-law of pioneer E. M. Kahn. *Photo copyright © by Natalie Ornish.*

TITCHE

"Every institution, like every individual, to be successful must be useful," said Edward Titche, early Dallas merchant and department store founder.[78] And Titche lived by those words. Only a few months before his death in 1944 he purchased a Dallas mansion and presented it to the Dallas chapter of the Red Cross. Titche became a charter member of the Dallas chapter when it was organized in 1905. At that time he was a partner in Titche-Goettinger Company, then a widely known dry goods and fashion establishment, which merged with Joske's and later Dillard's.

Titche, born in Louisiana, had early experience in merchandising. His father owned a store, and as a boy, Edward worked for him as janitor and clerk. At nineteen he and his older brother moved to Birmingham, Alabama, and opened a fancy grocery store there. Tiring of lettuce and tomatoes, the brothers dissolved the business and Edward migrated to New Orleans where he clerked in a department store.[79]

In 1894 his uncle Aaron Titche of Dallas died, leaving no heir. Edward was chosen to run the store his uncle had owned. He renamed the store The Edward Titche Company, but six years later he met Max Goettinger and the two formed a partnership and called the store Titche-Goettinger. Under this name the store achieved its greatest success.

After being married for less than two years, Edward Titche lost both his wife and their small child. Although he never remarried, he acted as guardian of his nephew, Henry Titche Levy of Mississippi, whose father and mother both died before the child reached thirteen months old. Titche brought the child and Rose Titche Spencer, his sister, to Dallas and the two raised the child. In later years Levy became general manager of the store his uncle owned.[80]

In 1922 Titche served as a charter trustee of the Dallas Historical Society. After his retirement in 1929, he served as a director of the State Fair of Texas, became a thirty-third degree Scottish Rite Mason, a vice-president of the Dallas Scottish Rite Hospital for Crippled Children, and adviser to Baylor Medical Center of Dallas.

The downtown store in the 1950s mushroomed into branch stores opened in Dallas suburban shopping centers, and the name gradually shortened to "Titche's." Some years after the Allied chain bought Titche's the name was changed to Joske's, another of their holdings. Thus Joske's entered the Dallas market with nine Titche's stores already well-known to the public. When in 1987 Dillard's purchased Joske's, the names Joske's and Titche's became only a memory.

SANGER

Many great merchants became philanthropists, but the Sanger brothers became the only ones whose philanthropy grew so extensive that they put themselves out of business. During the years when their firm reigned as the greatest dry goods company west of the Mississippi, the family seemed invincible. In Dallas they were the "epitome of royalty."[81]

They left a trail of stores in many Texas villages in their progress, in an era when chains were virtually unheard of. After beginning in 1857 at the edge of the Indian frontier at McKinney, thirty-five miles north of Dallas, the brothers started stores in Decatur and in Weatherford (near Fort Worth). After the Civil War, the brothers in 1866 advanced with the Houston & Texas Central Railroad as it built north from Millican (near Houston), opening stores in Bryan, Hearne, Calvert, Bremond, Kosse, Groesbeck, and Corsicana (though not all at the same time). Following the railroad, in 1872 the Sanger brothers reached Dallas and made it their central location. Later they branched off south to Waco, north to Sherman, west to Forth Worth, and even built a store in Clarendon up in the Texas panhandle. Thus, Sanger Bros. stores had covered the state from Oklahoma to the Gulf of Mexico at one time or another.[82]

The Sangers lived like Texas royalty and laid the foundation of Dallas being a city of fashion and good taste. They set the stage for the merchant princes. The founder of Neiman-Marcus got his start as a Sanger's salesperson.

The coming of the railroad made the Sangers boom. Most Texas towns depended entirely on rail service for their prosperity. Dallas, which until 1872 was a four-week ox-wagon ride from the port of Houston, managed to secure a connection to the Houston & Texas Central line. Without this railroad connection Dallas would have remained an obscure landlocked hamlet and the vast empire of the Sanger brothers would have had another location.

The Sanger brothers, seven of ten siblings of a Jewish family in Obernbreit am Main in Germany, spent their early years doing everything from weaving to winemaking, and selling their products at neighboring fairs. Isaac, the eldest son, entered retailing as an apprentice at a dry goods house in Germany. In 1851 he arrived in New Haven, Connecticut, to clerk with cousins, and two years later, Lehman, one of his brothers, joined him, and three years later, brother Philip arrived.

After six years of working for the New England clothier, Isaac headed for Texas in 1857. After stop-

Longhorn cattle and oxen sit in the street in front of store owned by Lehman and Philip Sanger in Bryan, Texas, 1860s.

Sanger Bros., Corsicana, 1871.

overs in New Orleans and Houston, he took a stagecoach to McKinney, north of Dallas, where he and a Mr. Baum opened Baum & Sanger at the edge of the wilderness. Lehman Sanger joined Isaac after the Panic of 1857. The brothers and Mr. Baum moved to Weatherford, closing the McKinney operation, and there encountered religious prejudice. In an attempt to become part of the community and help their store, the brothers made substantial contributions to various Weatherford churches.

Their fortunes somewhat in decline, brothers Isaac, Philip, and Lehman joined the Confederate cause when the Civil War broke out. At the end of the war they were almost destitute, and Philip had been slightly wounded. Lehman, too poor to buy a horse, walked back to Weatherford where he found that a friend, to whom he had entrusted $300 in gold bullion, still had the gold. He bought a ticket on a stagecoach to Houston and on the journey passed through Millican, Texas, a railhead. It seemed like an ideal place to start a store. For five dollars a month, Lehman and Isaac rented half of a store from a cobbler. Wrote Lehman, "My entire inventory could be contained in one small Saratoga trunk. I paid cash. Could have bought goods on credit, but things looked rather 'squally' and it was against my policy to involve myself until things looked more settled."[83] It took only twenty-four hours for the initial stock to sell out completely.

About this time the Sanger brothers took in a former competitor as partner who was not a brother. He was Morris Lasker, who years later moved to Galveston and eventually became a famous financier. "In those days, we all slept in the store by making pallets on the floor. Beds were a luxury, the limited space of the room did not permit beds and we preferred to sleep in the store as a matter of precaution," Lehman recalled.[84]

In 1867 railroad management announced its new terminus would be Bryan, Texas. Brothers David and Jacob, who had been living in Cincinnati, joined the Millican store, but almost immediately an epidemic of yellow fever killed them as well as Baum. The Millican stores closed, and they moved the business to Bryan, where the brothers first used the name Sanger Bros.

The five Sanger brothers.

Elm Street, Dallas, 1890.

Elm Street, Dallas, 1895.

November, 1890.] MONTHLY MAGAZINE. 127

Fall Styles

Latest Arrivals

Misses' Cloaks.

No. 3. No. 14. No. 15. No. 7. No. 5.

Children's Cloaks.

No. 1. Gretchen, made of striped wool material with sailor collar, revers and large pocket laps, 4, $5; 6, $5.50; 8, $6; 10, $6.50; 12, $7.

No. 2. We have almost any grade of goods desired, in either short or long cloaks, from $2 each to $25.

No. 3. Gretchen, made of all-wool imported material with revers and belt, 4, $6.25; 6, $6.85; 8, $7.45, 10, $8; 12, $8.65.

No. 5. Handsome Gretchen made of all-wool plaid cloth, velvet cuffs and yoke, pleated cape with girdle 4, $67.50; 6, $25; 7, $8; 10, $8.50; 12, $9.25

No. 7. Misses box jacket of scotch plaid melton, ages 12, 14, and 16, at $3.95.

No. 9. Same style in all-wool chevron, colors black blue, green, brown and slate, at $5 for all sizes.

No. 11. Child's Gretchen of imported plaid cloaking, cloth yoke and cuffs 4 yrs. $8.95; 6, $9.05; 8, $10.85 12, $11.50.

No. 13. Gretchen of fancy all wool material with velvet yoke, collar, revers and cuffs, a decided novelty, 4, $10.95; 6, $11.85; 8, $12.75; 10, $14.50; 12, $14.25.

No. 14 and 15. Loose front, box newmarket of striped and checked cloaking medium weights, 12, $8.75; 14, $9.25; 16, $10.

No. 17. Same style in all wool chevron, all colors, 12, $9.25; 14, $10.20; 16, $11.

In plush, flannel, cloth, etc., we are showing some very nobby things in Infants' and Children's short coats from $1.50 to $12.50 each.

Misses Loose Jackets.

With Vests made of imported tailor material; outside vest lined with satin. Hansome girdle to match, $12.50. Sizes 12 to 16 yrs.

No. 3. No. 11. No. 13.

In addition to the illustrated garments we have an immense and very handsome assortment of Misses and Children's Jackets, New Markets Connmaras, Gretchens etc., at low figures. We closed out several lines of light and medium, spring weight garments at less than one-half value. Our customers will find these goods on our counters, and as they will be quickly sold we do not illustrate them, as no more can be had at present prices when these are sold out. Prices range from $3 up to $10.50 for Newmarkets, Connemaras, Gretchees, etc. Misses Jackets at $2.50 to $8. These are best values ever offered.

A page in Sanger Bros. Monthly Magazine, *November 1890.*

By the time the railroad reached Dallas in 1872, the Sanger brothers were respected throughout the state. By the turn of the century Sanger Bros. had become the greatest dry goods company west of the Mississippi. Not only did it have retail stores, but also a wholesale business second in importance only to that of Marshall Field's in Chicago. Sanger Bros. sold saddlery and crockery, harnesses and plows, as well as clothing, "ribbons, perfumery, occasionally a fiddle or accordian."[85]

As Dallas grew, so did the Sanger brothers' fortune. It was their job to outfit both the home and the person of the city's civic elite. And the families of the brothers, including Alexander, who had joined the operation, lived as well or better than any of their customers. The first posh section of Dallas was called "The Cedars" and both Philip and Alex owned residences there. Philip's home, nicknamed "The Mansion," became a showcase, copied after a summer mansion he had seen on the New Jersey coast. Built in 1885, the home caused writer Edna Ferber to exclaim, half a century later, "It's worth a trip to Texas just to see it."[86]

Alex, not to be outdone, built a three-story house complete with chandeliers handmade by Louis Comfort Tiffany. The house had a butler's pantry with a sink just to wash fine crystal and a special dining room for poor relations. Joseph Sanger Linz, a grandson of Philip Sanger, one of the original brothers, remembered his weekly Saturday visits to his grandparent's "mansion," which he described as "wood with gingerbread trim." When asked what he remembered best about his uncle Alexander's home, Joseph replied, "Alex's grandchildren: Frances Sanger Mossiker [highlighted in chapter 12] and her brother Everett [who moved to California] had a marvelous electric train set in the attic. This was around 1922," Joseph recalled more than sixty years later.[87]

Alex Sanger served as president of the Texas State Fair in 1894. He was the first Jew to be appointed a regent of the University of Texas. In the halcyon days of their success, Alex, a civic leader, promoted the store's image through his many philanthropies. When disaster hit the Sangers with the unexpected death of Philip in 1902, the store moved forward under its own momentum for about five years. But Alex — who had established the city's first library, organized what became the United Fund, brought the first professional city planner to Dallas, and helped secure the Texas State Fair for the city — proved unable to take the stringent business tactics necessary to maintain the success of the store. He allowed the store to become more and more extended to its creditors, permitted its customers more credit than they could afford, and

In 1906, a year before Neiman-Marcus opened, Sanger Bros. advertised as *The Largest House West of the Mississippi*.

Alex Sanger.

The Alex Sanger home, circa 1895. It stood near downtown Dallas.

pursued ambitious expansion plans during the days of shrinking sales.

In 1926, after years of decline caused by Alex's charities and Philip's son-in-law Clarence Linz's inability to realize that a bloated payroll and an open checkbook were not sound business practices, Sanger Bros. was sold to Stifel, Nicholas & Co., a St. Louis merchandising concern. For the first time since 1857, someone other than the Sanger family held responsibility for the empire. "It was a stupid sale," said Hortense and Morton Sanger, descendants, years later. "It didn't have to be sold."[88] The store changed hands again in 1951, when Federated Department Stores purchased the company. Ten years later Federated bought A. Harris & Company and merged the two former competitors under the name Sanger-Harris. In 1965 Sanger-Harris opened a new store covering almost an entire city block in downtown Dallas, and Dallas Community College occupied the original Sanger's store nearby.

Alex Sanger's son, Elihu (Eli), father of Frances Sanger Mossiker.

Sanger Bros. proudly displayed their many delivery wagons in 1915.

In 1987 Federated, which also owned the Foley's stores in Houston, renamed all Sanger-Harris stores "Foley's," and the names Sanger and Harris disappeared from Texas retailing. With the luck of the Irish, Pat Foley's name was one of the few that remained of the original merchant princes — even though Foley had sold out to Robert I. Cohen in 1917.

Sanger Bros. goes down in history because it initiated a series of firsts: The first Texas store to open a buying office in New York (headed by Isaac); the first Texas business to institute sales training; the first to offer free home delivery (which they publicized highly with photos of their many horse-drawn wagons, and later motor vehicles), and to set up gaslights in Dallas. In 1881 they bought the first Dallas telephone, which linked the store with the palatial home of Phillip Sanger at Ervay and St. Louis streets. It was the first telephone in the entire state of Texas. In 1883 they installed electric lights. They installed elevators in 1889, and an escalator in 1911 — other Texas firsts.

The Sanger brothers created the first dry goods empire in Texas. Their innovations, their charitable contributions, and their civic authority provided a model for later department store magnates to emulate.

Sanger Bros. delivery truck.

A. Harris

A. HARRIS

In 1859 Adolph Harris arrived in Galveston from Prussia at the age of seventeen. He had worked in Prussia in the ship chandlery business just long enough to earn enough money to marry a rabbi's daughter. They moved to Houston, where he ran a dry goods business and served as alderman for several years.[89] The Houston City Directory for 1877-78 shows Adolph Harris and his brother Jacob Harris operating A. Harris & Brother. Adolph later moved to Galveston.

A. Harris' grandson Arthur Kramer, Jr. told his account of why Harris left Galveston, then a most important city, for Dallas, then a relatively unknown town: "Adolph Harris was a partner with his father-in-law, Grumbach, in Fellman, Grumbach & Harris in Galveston. George B. Dealey also lived there, a trusted young employee of the *Galveston News*, and Harris and Dealey were very good friends. Dealey urged Harris to leave Galveston and come to Dallas with him, and two years after the *Dallas Morning News* emerged in 1885, Harris moved to Dallas also."[90]

In 1887 he headed Fellman, Grumbach & Harris' Dallas store. He then established A. Harris & Company in the center of downtown Dallas.

In 1910 A. Harris' daughter Camille married attorney Arthur L. Kramer, and in 1912 Kramer joined his father-in-law's company. Only one year later, when Adolph died, Kramer became president of A. Harris & Company.

Arthur L. Kramer, Sr. determined, to a large degree, the way Dallas citizens looked during his thirty-seven years as president of A. Harris & Company department store.

Looking south at the intersection of Akard and Main, Dallas. At far right, Fellman, Grumbach & Harris, 1887.

ARTHUR L. KRAMER

Of German-Jewish descent, Arthur L. Kramer was born December 17, 1880 in Louisville, Kentucky to Maurice and Julia Weil Kramer, youngest of seven children. The family moved to Dallas when he was age nine. He received a law degree from the University of Texas and practiced law in the firm Hexter and Kramer from 1902 to 1912. He served as president of A. Harris & Co. from 1913 until his death in 1950.

Arthur took on not only running the business, but also promoting it. As part of his promotional efforts, he immersed himself in the arts. Kramer served as president of three arts organizations: the Dallas Symphony Society (1925-1939); Dallas Art Association (1929-1941), and Dallas Grand Opera Association (1939-1950). He also served on the Dallas School Board, which named the Arthur Kramer Elementary School for him in 1955.

Arthur Lee Kramer.

Portrait by Janet Faunce.

Over a period of eight years, Kramer pursued without success the idea of bringing to Dallas the Metropolitan Opera of New York. On one of these visits in January of 1939, he learned that the company planned to play in New Orleans the coming April and needed a city with which to split the week. Met officials asked Kramer if Dallas would put up a guarantee of $65,000 for four performances.

Kramer telephoned the Dallas Chamber of Commerce immediately, but they hesitated to put up so large a guarantee. Kramer asked his Met friends for a few days "to work out details" and caught the first train back to Texas. As soon as he arrived in his office, he began to call individuals and firms he thought would be interested and raised the money in a matter of hours. So successful became the annual Met tours that, during his years as president of the Grand Opera Association, he did not call on guarantors to contribute funds.

Whether these men and women of the merchant families acted from a love for the arts, from a recognition that Texas would never equal other markets until it could compete culturally, from a desire for social status, or whether those artists who wished to perform in a wider market persuaded them to raise funds for them, hardly matters in the end. There can be no doubt that these merchants were primarily the ones who put their own money into the arts and persuaded others to do so. A top salesman at A. Harris & Co., Abraham Lincoln (Al) Neiman, married the top saleswoman at A. Harris & Co., Carrie Marcus, aunt of Stanley Marcus.

HERBERT, MINNIE, CARRIE, AND STANLEY MARCUS

When Stanley Marcus graduated from Harvard and decided to enter the Neiman-Marcus firm, he told his father, Herbert Marcus, that he thought Neiman's should have a fine stationery department, and got the green light to set it up. Stanley did not place an ad in the local help-wanted columns for someone to head that department, nor did he look among the store's personnel. He called on the head of Crane papers, finest in the world, and asked, "Who sells more fine paper than anyone in the country?" He was told, "A young woman at B. Altman in New York." Stanley said, "Get her for me."

The Crane executive in New York learned that Charlotte Kramer Hafter was out of town, in Portland, Oregon, visiting her family. He sent her a telegram, asking her if she would like to head the stationery department at Neiman-Marcus in Dallas, Texas. "Where is Dallas?" she asked her mother, getting down an atlas. When she returned to New York, Al Neiman, in town on a buying trip, interviewed her and gave her a ticket to Dallas on the train

THE DALLAS MORNING NEWS, SUNDAY, SEPTEMBER 8, 1907.

Outer-Garment Shop"

Neiman-Marcus Co.

Elm and Murphy Streets, Dallas

"The Outer-Garment Shop"

Cordially Invite You to Attend the Formal Opening of the New and Exclusive Shopping Place for Fashionable Women, Devoted to the Selling of Ready-to-Wear Apparel

Opening Day, Tuesday, September Tenth, from 10 A. M. to 10 P. M. A Fashion Show Pre-eminent—Artistic Souvenirs

Tuesday, September Tenth, marks the advent of a new shopping place in Dallas—a store of Quality, a Specialty store—the only store in the City whose stocks are strictly confined to Ladies' Outer-Garments and Millinery, and presenting wider varieties and more exclusive styles in these lines than any other store in the South.

All are cordially invited to attend the Opening, to view the initial presentment of the most advanced and authoritative styles in Ready-to-Wear Apparel for Fall and Winter, to accept one of the handsome Souvenirs which will be distributed in honor of the occasion.

Our Store

In extending you an invitation to be present at the opening of the new store on Tuesday, September Tenth, we present herewith some of our claims to your valuable patronage.

Our decision to conduct a store in Dallas was not reached on impulse. We studied the field thoroughly and saw that there was a real necessity for such a shopping place as ours.

Our preparations have not been hasty. We have spent months in planning the interior, which is without an equal in the South.

We Will Improve Ready-to-Wear Merchandising

A store can be bettered by specialized attention.

Knowledge applied to one thing insures best results.

We began our intended innovation at the very foundation; that is to say, with the builders of Women's Garments.

We have secured exclusive lines which have never been shown in Texas before, garments that stand in a class alone as to character and fit.

Buying Facilities

Backed by the best sort of buying connections in every market, stocked by a corps of skilled buyers, managed by an experienced and expert store management, we are confident of our value-giving supremacy, and no store in the country where qualities and styles equal to ours are sold can offer lower prices.

Our Styles

All the pages of all the fashion journals, American and Foreign, can suggest no more than the open book of realism now here, composed of Suits, Dresses and Wraps of every favored style.

For the most important occasion of Formal Dress.

For the Informal afternoon call.

For Shopping or Business wear.

The selection will meet every taste, every occasion and every price.

Our Qualities and Values

As well as the Store of Fashions we will be known as the Store of Quality and Superior Values.

We shall be hypercritical in our selections. Only the finest productions of the best garment makers are good enough for us. Every article of apparel shown will bear evidence, in its touches of exclusiveness, in its chic and grace and splendid finish, to the cleverest designing and the most skillful and thorough workmanship.

Opening Souvenirs

As a memento of the occasion we will present a handsome Souvenir to visitors on opening day. These Souvenirs will be worthy of the offerings of the new store.

Announcement of Neiman-Marcus' opening, September 10, 1907.

Carrie Neiman, 1948.

Photo: Langley.

The original Neiman-Marcus specialty store.

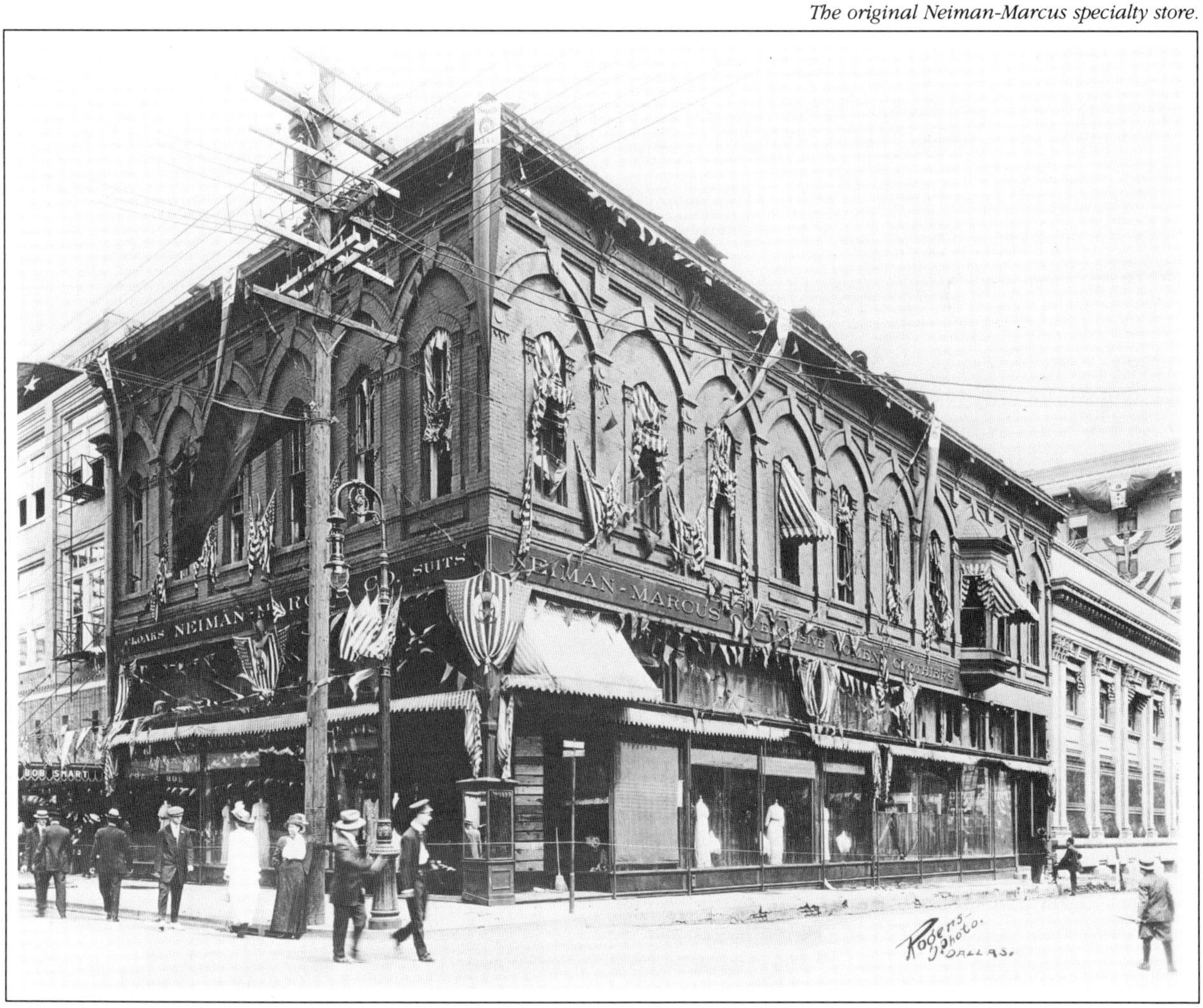

and fifty dollars. "Be seein' ya, honey," he said in his Atlanta drawl.[91] And so began Stanley Marcus' search for the finest talent to locate the finest merchandise to build what became one of the world's finest stores. It was only natural, then, that when Stanley wrote about his personal preferences, he titled it *Quest for the Best.*[92]

But the real story of the store called "The Best Known Landmark in Texas since the Alamo" is not only the quality of the merchandise but also the service that accompanied it. Here are a few examples of that service:

One spring, a young woman shopped in Neiman-Marcus trying on hats. She removed her coat and hung it on the back of a chair facing a dressing table. She purchased a hat and drove home, where she remembered she had left her coat downtown in the store. She called the hat department and was assured her coat remained where she left it. "We'll send it to you tomorrow on our next truck," the salesperson said, happy to deliver free a coat that carried the label of a competing store.

Herbert Marcus, Sr.

A bride-to-be, her mother, and sister made a trip to Dallas to purchase her wedding gown at Neiman's. After shopping in the bridal salon, the mother asked the salesperson to make them a luncheon reservation in the tearoom. After the trio finished their luncheon and asked for a check, the waitress told them they were guests of the bridal salon.

A secretary of modest means came to Dallas to buy fall clothes at Neiman's. As she stood before the mirror in a fitting room, a saleslady from millinery brought in armsful of hats, another staff person brought in shoes her size, and a third from the lingerie department even brought a girdle. She did not have to leave the spacious fitting room all afternoon and completed her fall shopping in a few hours before taking the five o'clock train back to her home town.

The store has serviced its customers in many ways. When *South Pacific* was the hottest show on Broadway, the New York buying office procured 783 tickets for Texas customers. The Paris office has been known to find babysitters for American customers who want to shop at the Place de la Concorde.

For more than sixty years, before being sold to a national chain, Neiman-Marcus exuded an intensity of service that made its clients feel they luxuriated in the arms of a loving Jewish mother. "Eat, eat. Enjoy, enjoy," the store seemed to sing. It was an aura, a radiance, a love. "You don't like it? We'll be delighted to exchange it for something you like, or even take it back." Every client was made to feel special and spoiled.

Exclusivity followed service in importance. "Only at Neiman-Marcus in the world," boasted ads on items from vicuna coats to perfumes. Once a saleslady at the

Carrie Marcus Neiman, 1903, age twenty.

store with a sense of humor confided to a friend that she had told a visiting client from out of state that Neiman-Marcus had its own special silkworms in air-conditioned cocoons spinning silk for their dresses, and the client believed her.[93]

Minnie Lichtenstein Marcus.

Within this fantasy a substantial reality existed to merit the image the store flaunted. Stanley Marcus did travel throughout the world to bring to Texas enough merchandise that he became a trade ambassador for Texas to the world. The store worked hard to give an image of quality, appealing with masterful strategy to all five human senses. For decades, callers to the store heard a voice with a spendid British accent, not a Texas twang. They smelled fragrances from Paris and New York. They tasted the cuisine of author Helen Corbitt. They felt the softest cashmere from South America and the smoothest silks from the Orient. And everywhere they beheld flowers and greenery; the store became an opulent greenhouse.

Behind this facade of elegance worked a *real* loving Jewish mother, Minnie Lichtenstein Marcus, wife of Herbert and mother of Stanley and three other sons. When not attending board meetings of the Dallas Jewish Welfare Federation, Temple Emanu-El, or the Dallas Home for Jewish Aged, she worked at the store potting and pruning. Ferns, begonias, and caladium cooled the store in the summers, making it an oasis in the Texas heat that often soared to three digits. Decades before ecology became a popular cause, she worked to beautify Dallas parks and founded the Dallas Garden Center. Civic leaders called her "Dallas' Grand Dame."

Minnie, a native of Dallas, was born in 1883. Her husband, Herbert, born in Louisville, Kentucky, in 1878, left home at fifteen to join his older brother Theo Marcus, a cotton broker in Hillsboro, an agricultural center sixty-three miles south of Dallas.[94] Herbert read encyclopedias and harbored enormous ambition. After the turn of the century, he worked in Dallas for Philip Sanger as salesman and later buyer of boys' clothing.

At this time Herbert married Minnie. "We hadn't a penny," recalled Minnie. "Papa said, 'You have to save $500 the first year of marriage,' so every day Herbert went to work carrying his lunch in a brown bag. He was always so elegantly dressed, even then, and that brown bag just didn't fit."

Ervay Street entrance to Neiman Marcus.

Stanley Marcus.

Then Minnie became pregnant. Herbert wanted to move his family to a place of his own and asked for a raise. When Alex Sanger offered only an additional $1.87 more per month, Herbert quit.[95]

That "no" made Texas merchandising history. Herbert persuaded his doe-eyed sister Carrie Marcus, top saleswoman at A. Harris & Company, and her husband, Abraham Lincoln Neiman, to start their first business venture. Carrie and Al Neiman, together with Minnie and Herbert Marcus and their six-week-old son, Stanley, moved to Atlanta. For two years the family held distress sales for merchants throughout Georgia.

Al's business embraced "putting on sales." He would take other people's "markdowns" and create a circus atmosphere so merchants could sell their close-outs. The often outrageous Neiman would string banners across Atlanta's Main Street announcing give-away bargains or hire a local brass band to blare music through downtown to awaken interest in his sales. Wrote Leon Harris in *Merchant Princes*, "Neiman was a wonder at whipping up excitement and helping less imaginative merchants to move their mistakes."

After two years in Atlanta, Carrie wanted to move back to Dallas. The family received two bids for their Atlanta enterprise, one for $25,000 in cash and another for a franchise in the state of Missouri for Coca-Cola. They took the cash.

In 1907 Neiman-Marcus became a reality. Herbert's and Carrie's brother Theo gave additional financial backing. Herbert was twenty-nine; Al, twenty-seven; and Carrie, twenty-four. From the day they first opened their store, they stuck to their winning formula of creating an aura of being the most elite store in Dallas. They surprised Sanger Bros. and other stores: they sold only ready-to-wear clothing. In those days, the affluent of Dallas bought fabric, or "piece goods," and had the various stores' seamstresses custommake the gown or suit. Neiman-Marcus had no piece goods department.

The store's ideas worked. Although seven railroads declared bankruptcy in 1907 and thirteen New York banks failed, Neiman-Marcus succeeded. Al Neiman provided promotional flair and bargains. Herbert and Carrie scouted the country, buying the best quality and the most fashionable clothes. Often they paid a manufacturer to create goods exclusively for Neiman's. The three family members also roamed the floors and fitting rooms, catering to customers.

In the early days, Herbert's and Carrie's father, Jacob, stood or sat by the front door of the store, personally greeting customers and welcoming them in.[96]

A fire in 1914 forced the young store to move from its first location at Elm and Murphy to Main and Ervay. That store's lease was believed to be the first ninety-nine-year lease in Texas history.

When in 1926 Sanger Bros. was sold, this spurred the success of Neiman-Marcus. When Sanger's new owners fired top employees, Neiman-Marcus quickly hired them. Recalled Stanley Marcus, "One salesperson alone sold over $200,000 her first year at the store."[97]

When the stock market crashed in 1929, so did Al Neiman's future at the store. He and Carrie divorced, and Herbert bought out his shares. The void left by Al's departure was filled by Herbert's and Minnie's sons, Stanley, Herbert, Jr., Edward, and Lawrence, each just coming of age. The eldest, Stanley, was then in his twenties.

Stanley, from the time he could walk, lived in the store. Some of his earliest recollections are of playing on the floor where dresses were altered, where he made toy carts from empty thread boxes and spools. "While the store was growing up, so was I," he wrote.

Stanley had an unhappy freshman experience at Amherst College, where he was scorned and rebuffed because he was Jewish. He later entered Harvard Business School. Here he became president of a Jewish fraternity. In 1926 he returned home to the number one passion in his life: the store. "The store — it was almost like a religion," he later recalled.[98] Selling was supreme in his being. In 1946, after World War II, Stanley met General Dwight D. Eisenhower. There was talk Eisenhower might run for the presidency. Even before the election Stanley convinced the ex-Texan to buy his wife's inaugural gown from him. When the general was elected president of the United States, his wife came to Dallas to live up to the promise.

Stanley had a genius for public relations. He used national media such as *Vogue* and *Harper's Bazaar*. Suddenly America began reading about a store in the Southwest named Neiman-Marcus. The image of the Southwest itself began to change.

Splendid gift wraps helped to sell Neiman-Marcus merchandise. At the beginning, for thirty-five cents, a gift wrap that enhanced the gift greatly could be added to any purchase. The idea started with a young woman in their gift wrap department, Beverly Morgan, who began to replace ribbons with small items of adornment. So successful was this merchandising innovation that it launched the gift wrap war of 1947 and 1948.

The idea of syndicating these ideas and materials developed, and Harold Cole of Dallas, with the backing of Ralph Schnitzer of Magnolia Paper of Houston, teamed to form Modern Packaging, stealing Beverly Morgan from Neiman-Marcus. Then in his early twenties Theodore (Ted) Strauss, who later became a banker, apprenticed under Cole, learning about ribbons and foils and how to structure a gift packaging business. He approached Stanley Marcus on the idea of starting a new gift packaging business with him, and Susan Crane Packaging resulted. The circle was complete. Stanley again had control, but he could not lure back Morgan, who had married an independent oil operator and retired. However, using the Neiman-Marcus name as reference, the business grew and soon department stores across America offered elegant gift wraps in the Neiman-Marcus manner.[99]

The store's most sensational publicity came from tales of Texas millionaires who, in both fact and fiction, came to Dallas to purchase outrageous, opulent gifts.

Stanley Marcus left the store a few years after selling it in 1968 to Broadway-Hale of California (Carter Hawley Hale), a national retail chain. He became a consultant and his son Richard became president of Neiman-Marcus. The new owners built Neiman-Marcus clones throughout the United States, from Bal Harbour, Florida, to San Francisco, California.

At age seventy-six Stanley Marcus launched a new career as a lecturer on a nationally syndicated radio program.[100]

THE DALLAS MORNING NEWS. FRIDAY, OCTOBER 20, 1899

"The Finest Jewelry Establishment in the World"

Grand Opening

TO-MORROW.

A CORDIAL INVITATION is extended to the Citizens of Dallas, the Students and ex-Students of the University of Texas and all Visitors to the Great Texas State Fair to participate in the Grand Opening of "The Finest Jewelry Establishment in the World" To-morrow (Saturday), October 21, from 10 a. m. to 10 p. m. This event will be made memorable by the Most Gorgeous and Dazzling Collection of Diamonds, Watches, Jewels and Fine Art Goods ever shown in the south.

PROGRAMME

Music by Carrico's Orchestra

Souvenirs for Ladies and Gentlemen

AMERICAN BEAUTIES for each lady and CARNATIONS for each gentleman ...During reception hours

We Desire Especially to have all our friends and customers participate in this opening. The like of it has never been attempted in Texas before and the occasion will be long remembered. Plenty of electric fans will keep our store cool and no pains will be spared to make your visit pleasant.

COME ALL—YOU WILL BE WELCOME.

JOS. LINZ & BRO.

JEWELERS.

ESTABLISHED 1877 ESTABLISHED 1877

LINZ BUILDING

The above advertisement appeared Friday, October 20, 1899 to announce the formal opening of the Linz Building. This 7 story structure was the tallest fireproof building in the South at the time.

Announcement of opening of the seven-story Linz Building, considered in 1899 a "skyscraper."

LINZ BROTHERS

An aura of graciousness and opulence pervaded the establishment called Linz Bros., Jewelists, when actress Lillian Russell bought her turquoise-studded necklace there. When Natacha Rambova bought her specially-designed jeweled slave bracelet, the store was the talk of Dallas. When Rambova brought her husband, Rudolph Valentino, to buy rare black pearl evening studs, the store reported four salesladies fainted to the floor.[101]

Simon Linz changed the Dallas skyline when he erected one of the first modern office buildings there.

However, Texas had an entirely different aura when Joseph Linz opened his first store in Denison, Texas, in 1877. So quickly did Linz succeed in bringing the appreciation of fine jewelry to Texas, that the transition from rough frontier to fashion-conscious state was soon effected.

An orchestra opened the Dallas store in 1899. The new Linz Building, considered Dallas' first "skyscraper," rose to a seven-story structure with a roof garden. Flowers were handed to customers, and the reception — the first to open a Texas retail establishment — became a society item in the newspapers. The event marked the success with which the Linz brothers, first Joseph, later Elias, Simon, Ben, and Albert, adapted their selling techniques to Texas.[102] They did not just sit back in their store waiting for customers to arrive. Their salesmen took to the road in slack times of the year. They took their jewels to customers all over the state.

These long-term employees used cloak-and-dagger techniques to protect their goods and themselves. They only called on businessmen and families they knew; they treasured anonymity, often using assumed names at hotels and disguising their telegraphed reports back to the store. The Linz brothers nurtured loyalty from their salesmen by instituting pension and profit-sharing plans.

Even in the Depression days of the thirties, Linz salesmen continued to do good business, and money from East Texas oil fields went into Linz diamonds. Many cattlemen, oil barons, and wheat farmers amassed sizable fortunes in the early days of Texas' prosperity. Some ranchers in the Panhandle dine nightly on antique silver because their grandfathers bought silver from a Linz traveling salesman.

In the family-owned business, each Linz brother contributed his specialty. Joe and Simon directed operations. Elias died shortly after coming to Texas from St. Louis where the brothers were born. Ben managed the wholesale department, and Albert began the traveling salesman staff. He made long, cross-state drives in a rented surrey and horse.[103] When he sold to people in one town, he would get a letter of recommendation to their friends in the next. Many old Texas families remained loyal customers of Linz Bros.

The Linz brothers considered diamonds their "bread and butter" item. In order to become expert in the diamond trade, Clifton Linz, son of Simon, went to Amsterdam to learn to appraise diamonds. Linz staff said their store treasured its record that it never had to apologize to a customer for the grading of a gem.[104]

Joseph Sanger Linz, a vice-president with Linz Bros. for twenty years, pointed out that a minor rivalry between the Linz and A. Harris families existed for decades. Many persons are aware of the consciousness of identity of the German Jews over the Russian Jews, but few realize a similar attitude existed between the French and German Jews. "My dad was a bad boy, even as a kid," Linz said. "He got into a fight with Leon Harris, Sr. Mrs. Harris dressed Leon in splendid clothes and dad thought he looked like little Lord Fauntleroy, so he proceeded to tear Leon's clothes off. Leon resented this fight, of course, and took pokes at Linz. Mrs. Harris was furious and told off Mrs. Linz. The Harris and Linz families took verbal pokes at each other for generations. In his book *Merchant Princes* Leon Harris, Jr. repeated a risque story about my father that was told in confidence. The Harrises were great Frenchmen and spoke French. The Linzes were German."[105]

Clarence E. Linz, son of Joseph, married Bettina Lois Sanger, daughter of Philip Sanger.

Harry B. Gordon, left, and Aron S. Gordon.

Gordon's began with a general store in Houston in 1905 and did not enter the jewelry business until 1916. At the end of their 1982 fiscal year, the Gordon chain operated 681 units in forty-four states and Puerto Rico.[106] The publicly held corporation became the second largest retail jewelry chain in the nation. Only the Zale Corporation, another Texas organization, became larger in number of stores and volume sold.

The publicly held Gordon's corporation operated through four divisions: contemporary jewelry, traditional jewelry, catalog, and leased fine jewelry. The company acquired fine jewelry stores, including Linz Bros. and Sweeney's.

Gordon's founder, M.M. Gordon (1882-1957), right, with his wife Ida and her brother Louis Sampson, circa 1910.

Like many Jewish pioneers the Gordons settled in small towns at first. Around 1894 Meyer Morris Gordon, age sixteen, and his sister Annie Gordon, age thirteen, left Lithuania and immigrated through Galveston. Their father had settled in East Columbia, Texas, sixty miles southwest of Houston near Wharton, Texas. (Annie later married S.P. Finger of Finger Furniture industries.) In 1897 the Gordons moved to Galveston. M.M. worked in Galveston three years, leaving just before the 1900 storm.

In Houston with $400 capital, M.M. Gordon opened a general store with groceries, shoes, and hardware. In 1916 he launched his first jewelry as a partnership — McGaughon and Gordon at 808 Preston in Houston. After World War I, the stores became Gordon's. M.M. Gordon and his wife, Ida, passed the business leadership onto their sons, Harry B. and Aron S., their daughter, Bertha, and her husband I.L. Miller. Aron's sons, Daniel and James, later joined the board of directors.[107]

Even in their seventies, the brothers Harry and Aron poured unlimited energy into their dedication to business. Both worked about twelve hours daily Monday through Friday, and on Saturdays they spent most of the day "visiting" stores.[108]

Gordon's left a legacy, the Meyer and Ida Sampson Gordon Camp, twenty-two miles southwest of Houston. The 150 acres served both old and young people. Temple Beth Israel in Houston is site of the Gordon Chapel.

Although Gordon's second jewelry store, below, was founded in 1929 ten days before the Depression, the firm grew to become the second largest jewelry chain in the nation.

Mayer Morris Gordon, 1955.

ZALES

In 1985 Morris Bernard Zale, founder and chairman of the board emeritus of the Zale Corporation, largest retail jewelry chain in the world, summed up his formula for success: "Go to work earlier and stay later. That's what it takes."[109]

Arriving ready to work before 6:00 A.M. was a daily habit of M.B., his brother William, and M.B.'s brother-in-law, Ben Lipshy, who also merited the title chairman of the board emeritus. Lipshy, during his presidency, established an organizational structure that launched massive expansion. In the decade between 1958, Lipshy's first full year as president, and 1968, Zale's increased its number of stores by more than ten times, growing from 86 stores to 907.[110]

But another person is also responsible for there being a Zale's in the first place. He is Morris' uncle, Sam Kruger. Sam was the brother of Libby Kruger Zalefsky, M.B.'s mother.[111] Born in 1882 in Russia, son of a poor shinglemaker, Sam as a teen-ager went to Odessa, Russia, on the Black Sea and worked as a watchmaker. At eighteen he and a brother moved to a nearby town and launched a small jewelry business.[112] Little did he realize that eighty-five years later that nucleus would grow to a business whose credit division mailed monthly statements to more than six-hundred thousand charge customers.[113] Herein lies one of the secrets of Zale's success: It was one of the first jewelers to extend credit to the average American consumer.

"My father [Sam Kruger] started the Zales in Wichita Falls. Morris Zale [Sam Kruger's nephew] had the idea for credit jewelry," recalled Bert Kruger Smith. Morris Zale's genius is what made the Zale stores great. He was twenty-six and had been working for my father. It took a Morris Zale to bring it to fruition.[114]

"Dad brought all these people over and trained them. They worked for a ticket for a relative, who would come, and then saved for a ticket for another member of the family. The saddest thing happened: My father was working and making a fine living in America, but could not bring his mother out of Russia. She died of starvation. They were from Shereshov, near Poland, in the Soviet Union.[115]

"My father, Sam Kruger, escaped from Russia in 1904, coming to New York. He arrived in Fort Worth around 1907," Smith continued.[116]

Libby Kruger Zalefsky with her children William (left) and Morris B. Zale. Courtesy Edna Zale.

Sam Kruger.
Courtesy Rotary Spokesman.

Kruger afforded a new life for his relatives left behind in Czarist Russia at the turn of the century. They followed Sam to New York and in 1908 joined him in Fort Worth, where he had a jewelry business.

Young Morris began his career working in his uncle Sam's jewelry store. He spent two years under the tutelage of his uncle in Kruger's Jewelry Store. After working for his mentor in his uncle's stores in Wichita Falls, Texas, and Burkburnett, Texas, Morris moved to Graham, Texas, where he put showcases in a drugstore and opened his own business. "In those days, jewelry wouldn't have been enough to keep me alive," he recalled, "so I got the Victrola [phonographs] agency. In the drugstore I had the Victrolas set up, and we played 'Turkey in the Straw' and things like that to attract a few customers. There were not too many people coming in to buy a piece of jewelry."

This act of creative merchandising was typical of Morris' use of new ideas. When he moved back to Wichita Falls in 1924 to take over a store that belonged to his uncle, Zale Corporation was formed.[117] "My uncle took two-thirds interest and I took one-third," said Zale. "I took over the lease, and that was the beginning of the store. We made a corporation out of it."[118]

For many years it was a family-held corporation. M.B. married Ben Lipshy's sister Edna in 1926. Ben, barely in his teens, had an after-school job cleaning the store and repairing Victrolas.

"We had a phonograph department. And that's where I really spent most of my time," Ben recalled. "We sold records and radios, . . . and I'd go around to people's homes and fix their phonographs. All of them were the crank kind. I'd always get down pretty early and then go on to school at nine-thirty. I'd get off at three, miss my study period, so I could put in the hour working."

Although Sam Kruger had focused his energy on attracting an elitist carriage trade, M.B. and Ben focused on the local oil field workers and cotton farmers. When M.B. opened the first Zale's, he offered practically anything in the store for as low as one cent down, one dollar a week. Installment buying not only brought people into Zale's store who might never have come otherwise, it also kept them coming back week after week to pay off their purchases and, hopefully, make new ones. M.B. Zale, called "the most famous apostle of installment buying in retail jewelry history," has often boasted that he himself never bought any personal item on credit.[119]

Sam Kruger in Fort Worth store.

M.B. turned to advertising merchandise. He celebrated his first year in business with a special eight-page section of the *Wichita Daily Times*, a record then for the number of pages used at one time by any Texas retailer in a newspaper.

During the 1920s Zale's began to expand to multiple stores, opening Zale's in Tulsa and Oklahoma City, newcomers to the oil boom scene. Only a few months after their third store opened, disaster came in October 1929 in the form of the Great Depression. Not until 1934 did the fourth store open; this time M.B. chose Amarillo, Texas, another oil town.

Ben Lipshy managed the Amarillo store, and he introduced numerous innovations: mail-order catalogs and door-to-door selling. His success was awarded with a commission equal to five percent of the store's profits. Profit-sharing became one of the cornerstones of the Zale Corporation.

After World War II, when Zale's annual sales surpassed eleven million dollars, Leo Fields, the corporation's former Guild Division chief, recalled that there were congratulations all around. However, Fields remembered that M.B. remarked, "We must gear up the company to do fifty million."[120] Between 1945 and 1954 it opened fifty new stores. When M.B. was in Anchorage, Alaska, during a stopover from Japan, he decided he had to open a store there. Zale stores abound all over the world.[121] Barbara Gutow, wife of Zale's real estate executive, William R. Gutow, recalled a trip they took to London. After finishing with business, they decided to spend a relaxing Saturday afternoon driving along the English countryside. "I was in Stratford-on-Avon, and I looked up and there was a Zale store facing me," Barbara recalled.[122]

M.B.'s two sons, Marvin and Donald, learned the Zale business at an early age, and Donald became president when Ben Lipshy became chairman of the board. Later Donald Zale rose to chairman of the board, and Ben's son, Bruce A. Lipshy, moved to president and chief operating officer. Marvin Zale was elected vice-chairman of the board.

Despite their power positions, not only in Texas but the world, the Zale and Lipshy families remained low-profile. Their hobbies were the stores. They participated minimally in the fine arts and did not aspire to the social scene. M.B. said in an interview with the author, "Just take advantage of the opportunities as they come along. Whenever opportunities came along that we thought we could handle, we'd do them. If we couldn't handle it, we'd pass it. Never tried to be fancy,

William Zale, Morris B. Zale and Ben A. Lipshy. Courtesy Joy L. Burk.

never aspired socially or banking-wise."

The Zale world headquarters is a modern, rambling building where swing sets and slides stand on a playground visible near the entrance. The Zales established a day-care center and nursery for employees' children. Here, employees could visit their children during lunch hour and work with peace of mind. It became a model for the nation.

The family-owned empire ended just as many other great Jewish businesses founded by earlier generations. In 1986, in a hostile takeover, Peoples Jewellers, Ltd. of Canada bought Zales.[123] The buyout signaled the end of the Zale family relationship of a multimillion dollar corporation that started with one store in Wichita Falls.

However, the Zale Foundation continued, benefitting the disadvantaged and minorities and making significant gifts for medical projects.

The Zale-Lipshy University Hospital came closer to reality in 1987 with groundbreaking ceremonies for the nine-story, 160-bed hospital. Ben Lipshy was the initiator for a new hospital to serve the faculty of the University of Texas Southwestern Medical Center, Dallas, and he worked hard for four years as chairman of University Medical Center, Inc. until his death in November 1985, when philanthropist Ralph B. Rogers, and later Donald Zale, served as chairman. The Zale Foundation pledged almost nine million dollars to this teaching, research and referral hospital, scheduled for completion in 1990.[124]

SAM R. BLOOM

Zale Corporation gave Sam Bloom, one of the giants in Texas' advertising trade, the foundation for Bloom Advertising Agency that opened its doors November 22, 1952.

His father, a merchant, had emigrated from Germany to Texas where he met his future wife, Fannie Solomon, a native of Fort Worth. Sam was born in Clarksville, a town of less than 5,000 in Red River County, Texas, near the Oklahoma border, shortly after the turn of the century, and he grew up there before his family moved to Fort Worth, "He went directly to work from high school at age seventeen," said his son Robert."In fact, there is some question as to whether he even finished high school. He had no real formal education. He was a salesman."[125]

Sam worked as a traveling salesman for Marshall Field & Company, Montgomery Ward, and for several wholesale companies. He entered the newspaper business as an advertising solicitor for the old *Fort Worth Record* and worked for several Scripps-Howard and Hearst newspapers in El Paso and San Antonio before he started at the *Dallas Times Herald* in the early 1920s. At first he sold suburban advertising, then he rose to assistant advertising manager in 1929 before being promoted to advertising director in 1941.[126]

Sam "raised himself up to a vice-presidency. He had been in charge of all advertising sales. He had led the paper into a period of booming profits. He had been the greatest salesman of his day, the Paul Bunyan of advertising lineage. Bloom had done so well, had become such a dominant force on the paper, that the presidency was all but inevitable. He would surely become the boss. That in itself would have been unusual." Bloom was Jewish; the family that owned the newspaper was not. When newspaper executives passed over Sam for the presidency, he quit to form his own agency.[127]

Members of the Zale family bought stock in Sam's company to help give him working capital, then served as the agency's largest account for several years. But other retailers—Affiliated Food Stores, Skillern's Drug, Tom Thumb grocery, and car dealers — who formed the backbone of the *Times Herald* advertising lineage, joined as Sam's clients. David Ritz, who worked for Bloom in those beginning days as a copywriter, described what separated the Bloom agency from other agencies. "Normally, large retailers do their own advertising because of the daily changes and the absence of creative requirements. They just don't need an agent or a middle man. But Bloom quickly built up a large art department to handle such traditionally nonagency accounts. Mr. Bloom himself was a master of the Old

Top: *Ben Lipshy*

School of Advertising. He *loved* the bold, black headlines, the screaming *10% OFF, BUY NOW!* For the founder, advertising was no laughing matter." He sought any form of advertising that represented volume. And he succeeded.[128]

He possessed an intuitive sense about what sold, not only in retail goods, but in his community. Other establishment busenessmen looked to him to solve their business and community problems and images. The president of the United States even turned to him. How did Sam do it? Again, David Ritz provided part of the answer. "Do what works. And be smart enough to figure out what works. Couple that with intrinsic good business sense and an intuitive feel for political moderation. Put that in a body whose frame more befits a Comanche chieftain than a local businessman. Let that pragmatism and business sense and political moderation be articulated in the most eloquent and stunning language. Give it a voice which is mellow, deep, confident, and lilting and you have a man capable of dealing with ease in both the sensitive world of civic public relations-diplomacy and the tough world of large retail newspaper advertising."[129]

Below: Morris B. Zale, founder of the Zale Corporation.

In the early 1960s, Sam received a phone call from President John Kennedy asking that Sam come to Washington to meet in the president's office. Evelyn, Sam's wife, remembered that the president said that he'd "asked around different cities for a civic-minded man. When they met, Kennedy told him, 'Sam, I'm going to put the civil rights movement in your lap. I want Dallas to be the first city to be completely integrated.' So Sam came home and called Stanley [Marcus] and told him that he had been to Washington and this was the president's wish, 'and I thought if you could give me a hand, I'd like to start with your store'"[130]

Sam suggested that Stanley invite a group of black women to have lunch in the store's tearoom and that Sam and Stanley watch to see if anyone made a fuss. "Not an eyebrow lifted," Evelyn said. Sam called and wrote other store owners, theater and restaurant owners. He produced a film, *Dallas at the Crossroads*, and showed it throughout Dallas.[131] No violent incidents erupted when integration came that fall, and many credited Sam..[132]

Evelyn said that Sam's commitment to the welfare of all persons began as a boy when he observed his mother's work. "One time she went down to the jail, wanted to see what it looked like. There was a woman there for pickpocketing. She was an artist and had beautiful art work she had done. And mother Bloom went back and put curtains in her cell, so she wouldn't have to look at the iron bars. Whenever she could help anybody who was having hard times, she was always there; they would call on her."

Sam followed her example. Evelyn told of Sam's action during the polio scare in the 1950s. "When they decided to give the polio vaccine, and people needed to have vaccinations, at his own expense he stationed people to give these shots at premises every few miles apart. He was never too busy or too rushed if he saw a purpose in doing something that would help the population of Dallas. He had foresight. He loved Dallas."

Dallas' business establishment called on Sam again when President Kennedy planned to visit Dallas, figuring that "he could get our liberal president in and out of town without an incident. He worked out a nonpartisan invitation list for the Market Hall luncheon.

"He met Mr. Kennedy and told him that he didn't approve of him riding in an open car, he should ride in a limousine. Kennedy said, 'I want to see the people who put me in office.' So Sam said, 'Well, please put a bubble on.' Kennedy said, 'No.'"[133] When the Ruby trial began, the business establishment offered Sam as the public relations counsel for the presiding judge.

Sam P. Bloom

Sam worked within the Jewish faith, too, commanding respect and offering his skills. "He was elected president twice of Temple Emanu-El," said Robert Bloom, his son. "That has not been duplicated to date." He had first served as president in 1949 and, in 1973, when an internal dispute broke out, they called on him to take over again and calm things down. "He remained a towering and sobering influence."[134]

When he died in 1983, Bloom Advertising had billings of $150 million, employed 350 people, and had such national accounts as Colgate-Palmolive and Maybelline cosmetics.[135]

Chapter 10

SIGNIFICANT MERCHANT FAMILIES

Laying the Economic Foundation for Texas' Future

Few persons, even Jews, know the role of the significant merchants who brought needed goods to the settlers who populated frontier Texas in the early days of the Republic and later of the state. These merchants contrasted greatly from the merchant princes, with their great department stores in Texas and their aura of glamour generated by proficient public relations counsel, a story well told by Leon A. Harris, Jr., in *The Merchant Princes.* Facts show that more Texans shopped at chain stores in small towns, such as Weiner's Stores, K. Wolens, and The Fair, than they did at Neiman-Marcus or Sakowitz. More Texans wore the boots, men's hats, and clothing designed and manufactured by Jewish Texans, than those of the most celebrated *haute couture* designers. In sheer volume it is likely many merchant dukes outdid the merchant princes.

Yet, the hardships the significant merchants endured, the ways they sought to practice and retain their religious beliefs, how they depended on relatives to build their businesses, their efforts to contribute to their communities to show gratitude for opportunities, and their sense of isolation, set them apart from others.

THE MEAT BISCUIT,

A new and useful preparation of concentrated EXTRACT OF BEEF, baked in flour,

INVENTED AND MANUFACTURED BY

GAIL BORDEN, Jun.

GALVESTON, TEXAS.

Patent secured in the United States, Feb. 5, 1850. Patent secured in England, Sept. 5, 1851.

DIRECTIONS FOR COOKING.

This article is highly concentrated, and is intended as a stock for Soup, and to be combined with other articles of food, to improve the nutrition and taste. It requires attention in cooking, principally in taking right proportions, and for soup, be sure not to scorch it. It should be properly diffused in water, fruit, or other substances, to bring it to its original state in taste or flavor.

TO MAKE A SOUP.—The BISCUIT being ground or made fine, stir it into sufficient cold water to form a thin batter; then pour it into boiling water, and boil it until it is thoroughly macerated or decomposed, requiring 20 to 30 minutes; stirring frequently, until it boils, to prevent burning or scorching.

Add salt and pepper to suit the taste. Such condiments may also be added as are used in other soups. The addition of a little sweet milk or good fresh butter makes an improvement, as in oyster soup. The plain soup is improved by the addition of a little sugar, say a tea-spoonful to the pint.

The BISCUIT batter as above, put into the liquid of well-boiled vegetables, strained through a cullender, or with the whole substance, as may be preferred, makes a soup unsurpassed.

The Ostermans worked with Gail Borden in developing a dried, portable food that enabled travelers to open the frontier.

JOSEPH OSTERMAN

Joseph Osterman, who came to Galveston in 1839, became a wealthy philanthropist, though certainly not all pioneer merchants shared that kind of bountiful reward. He was born in Amsterdam, Holland, in 1810 and at age nineteen had

Galveston's Strand grew from a few tents and shops in Osterman's time to a significant mercantile center in a later era, as shown above.

Courtesy Rosenberg Library.

immigrated to the United States.

At first he located in Philadelphia. He then moved to Baltimore and became a charter member of the Baltimore Hebrew Congregation. In 1830 he married Rosanna Dyer, a woman of high standing (profiled in chapter 13). She was the sister of Major Leon Dyer, who escorted the captured Santa Anna to Washington, D.C. Leon's son Dr. J.O. Dyer was a physician, historian, and journalist. Osterman kept a diary, and years later, Dr. Dyer transcribed his uncle's notes.[1] Dr. Dyer's transcriptions vividly describe life during these pioneer days in Galveston.

Major Dyer had visited Galveston and was impressed with Texas, so he advised his brother-in-law Joseph Osterman to try his luck in the new Republic. Joseph left his wife and her parents in Baltimore and took a steamer to New Orleans, where he "received a short course of instruction in American business methods, especially of the newer states and territories. . . . Major Dyer stocked a little schooner, a cargo of what was then known as general merchandise which included everything: from horseshoes, to a coffin, to a bag of coffee. It took the schooner a week to make the trip from New Orleans."

At that time Galveston consisted of two cities: Saccarap, a business district that derived its name from a small port in Maine and extended from about Eleventh Street to First Street, some ten blocks; and Galveston, which extended westward from Eleventh Street, and where a few merchants had erected frame shops on the Strand. These shops extended over the water so skiffs could approach at the back doors.

"Finally Joe got his entire stock on shore, and having wisely brought a large tent along, opened for business on a vacant lot. . . . There were strangers coming into the port every day and the state bought nearly everything in Galveston in 1839.

"When Osterman had safely gotten his goods on shore, he remembered he had failed to pay duties. The collector of the port was the genial Gail Borden, Jr., who later became world famous as the manufacturer of condensed milk. The two men became fast friends. . . . Mr. Osterman at first slept in his tent and store building using a hammock suspended from a wood frame, as the rattlesnakes were so plentiful. Early Galvestonians liked molasses, and all the stores had barrels stacked up on a little platform so that the syrup could run down from the bunghold along a wooden gutter into the gallon measure. There always was some waste of the sticky syrup, and the rattlers, attracted by the pungent odor, often nestled below the molasses barrel. Merchants in the morning could exercise by killing snakes with a long flail."

Joseph brought the first ready-made coffin to Galveston: "a box of pine wood with a lid, both covered inside and outside by a cheap black velveteen fastened down by rows of brass tacks. When yellow fever broke out the year after Mr. Osterman's arrival. . . . Every mercantile establishment had its stack of coffins on the sidewalk."

He imported from Holland a cargo of wines. "He specialized in the famous three M's — Moselle, Muscat, and Madeira, all family drinks formerly, for these fine wines were served at the meals of all the wealthy Southern planters. In his quaint Dutch-English, Mr. Osterman often observed how 'many more frents have the three M's made me than the old pine coffins; and when I added Malaga wine to my collection, nopoddy thought of death.'"[2]

He brought lime juice in barrels from the Caribbean islands. His schooner made trips to Jamaica to bring rum and sugar, and he brought in tubs the first palms and oleanders to the island in 1842. He imported the first lucifer matches and brought to Texas the first percussion caps and revolvers, which he sold to officers of the Texas Navy.

Joseph eventually built the first two-story house in Galveston. He fitted the lower floor as the store and used the second floor for his residence. Probably no other house in early Galveston figured so prominently in social events as the Ostermans' home. Mrs. Osterman gave Gail Borden, Jr., a constant visitor, her recipe for meat biscuits, a historically important food item that permitted travelers to carry portable food and helped open up the frontier west. The biscuit consisted of dried powdered buffalo meat, beans, and cornmeal. Joseph's money financed Borden's experiments to perfect the preserved product, which in turn inspired the idea of condensing milk. Osterman's money rented Borden's brick store and built the ovens. Borden's other partner, Dr. Ashbel Smith, promoted the biscuit in London at the 1851 World's Fair where it won a gold medal and attracted world attention.[3]

Osterman's money rented the press from Samuel Bangs, who printed an early newspaper, and Osterman's ads filled a good share of its pages. That newspaper served as the forerunner of the *Galveston News*, one of the oldest newspapers in Texas.

The Ostermans entertained in their home early presidents of the Republic, including David G. Burnett, M.B. Lamar, Sam Houston, and Anson Jones.[4] Joseph became so successful that by 1842 he sold out to his wife's brother, Isadore Dyer, and retired. Isadore Dyer, Sr., (1815-1888) was president of Union Marine Insurance Company. He had several namesakes.

Joseph Osterman was one of only two men Jacob De Cordova listed in his section on "the Jewish Denomination" in his book, *Texas: Her Resources and Her Public Men*, noting he donated the oldest Jewish burial ground in Texas in 1852, the Hebrew Benevolent Cemetery in Galveston.

Joseph and Rosanna died during the Civil War years. Joseph was accidently shot August 19, 1861, and died a few days later. The Osterman house at Twenty-fourth and Broadway became the home for the YWCA in 1921.[5]

JOSEPH AND HELENA LANDA

Joseph Landa came to Texas in 1845. He was born in Prussia near Kempen in 1810. Joseph lived in Mississippi and Louisiana before arriving in San Antonio, then a frontier town of very few stores. He opened a store and developed a trade that brought customers from miles around. He opened a second store in New Braunfels. From earnings, he began to buy land across Texas, accumulating over thirty thousand acres.

In 1851 Landa married Helena Friedlander, who was born in Kempen, too, and they had seven children.

After President Lincoln's 1863 Emancipation Proclamation, Joseph freed their slaves, only to be tried by local Confederates. He fled to Mexico to avoid being hanged, and Helena took over their businesses, operating the general stores, sawmills, and the cotton gin. She preserved Jewish traditions by reciting Friday night prayers, lighting candles, and observing Passover. After the Civil War, Joseph returned home and continued building his many enterprises.

A large tract of the land they owned lay along the Comal and the Guadalupe Rivers, with two miles fronting the Comal River and two miles fronting the Guadalupe. Here in 1875 he built a five-story flour mill.

Joseph Landa of New Braunfels.

Helena Landa (1835-1912)

Photo by Cones, courtesy Mrs. Robt. Murray and Institute of Texan Cultures.

He operated the mill until he decided to retire and turn over his interests to their son, Harry. Joseph died on August 19, 1896, at age eighty-six.[6] He left his estate to his wife who acted as an adviser to their son, Harry.

Harry and Helena managed the Landa Roller Mills, the Cotton Oil Factory, the Electric Light and Power Plant, an ice manufacturing plant, a stock farm, and acres of irrigated gardens. They built a cold-storage warehouse next to the ice plant and a pumping system that supplied water for the ice plant. Harry stocked about five thousand acres of land with thoroughbred cattle and became a renowned authority on cattle breeding. He used the hulls from the cotton seed to make the best fodder for his cattle.

"He advised a lot of young fellows coming up," remembered Beulah Keller, Harry's first and only secretary for twenty-five years. "They would come up from A&M College. The phone rang constantly for information, and he had a wealth of information. It wasn't college education, it was what he'd learned. They wanted to know about cattle and breeding." He specialized in Aberdeen and Hereford cattle, Mrs. Keller said.[7]

Harry eventually sold the mills in New Braunfels and moved to San Antonio in 1929. Morris Wise, who officed next to Harry, said that Harry owned a bank in San Antonio. "Harry wrote a biography of his father, and established the Hannah Landa Memorial Library, named for his wife," said Wise. "It is a branch library near Trinity University. He left his home in his will to the people of San Antonio, for a library."[8]

Mrs. Keller believed that the Landas, particularly Harry, left a legacy of knowledge, gathered through his parents' experiences and his self-taught programs in cattle breeding and feeding.

HENRY LESINSKY

Henry Lesinsky lived in Poland, England, and Australia before coming to the American Southwest, where he mined copper in Arizona and built a large jobbing business in El Paso. He carried the mail by stagecoach from El Paso west into the Indian territory.

In 1891 at the age of fifty-seven Henry wrote a series of letters to his son that described his bitter childhood in Poland. "[M]y dear Albert, . . . up to the age of seven I remember nothing. . . . Perhaps you will think the statement overdrawn if I say that I do not remember a single happy day between my seventh and my fourteenth year." Henry's family had lived in grinding poverty and his father, a poet and writer, never earning enough. Yet, Henry attended school, learning Hebrew and German. Henry's father died when Henry reached fourteen. "No gift was ever placed in my hands, no book suited to a child. Nothing but dry dust — nothing but bitterness, poverty and tears! . . . I was sent to London where the brother whom I described as a student had by this time settled. I was to learn a trade in London and began with the wood and stone carving business. One long year I worked at this."

When Henry heard a woman lecturing on a new land of gold in Australia, Henry decided, "I must find gold enough to relieve my poor mother and my brother the discharged soldier." He learned of an emigrant aid society, applied, and boarded a ship for Australia at age twenty. "That first night out I sat alone in an obscure corner and wept bitter tears of anguish all through the long night."[9]

Henry labored in the mines with his bare hands. He struggled, but failed. When Henry found no gold in Australia, he moved to California in 1858. When he found no gold there, he followed the rumors of gold in New

The Lesinsky-Weisl family of Texas and New Mexico, 1880. A member of this family, after struggling in poverty on several continents, discovered a copper mine in Arizona. Front row: Bertha W. (Mrs. Charles) Lesinsky, Mathias and Emma W. Recht, Sigmund Weisl, Charles Lesinsky. Top row: Simon and Rosa W. Hood, Bernard, Frances, and Anna (Mrs. S.) Weisl.

Mexico, where an uncle lived. He arrived in Albuquerque in 1859 and found the rumor to be false. At age twenty-five, he was the government agent for the supply of grain for the troops. In time, he sent for his brothers Charles and Morris to join him in business.

The years rapidly passed, and Henry began to entertain hope of returning to his home and seeing his mother. "I had been away about fifteen years now. My great dream was about to be realized. To go home and see them relieved from want was always the great desire of my soul. Early in 1866 we began the trip [his uncle and family, and his brother Charles]. The great joy to which I was looking forward, the happiness that was to reward me for long and bitter years of toil failed to become a fact. The town, the streets, the people — all had somehow dwarfed into wretched insignificance. My schoolfellows were toiling fathers and careworn husbands. I wished myself millions of miles away. Added to all my bitter reflections was the painful consciousness that I could no longer harmonize with those most dear to me. They had remained in the restricted groove of their narrow surroundings. Their religion, orthodox and unforgiving, was hateful to me. I had learned to seek God in the solitude of the mountain, or in the privacy of my heart. Here I had to go back to the old outward ceremonies. . . . I sickened at the thought. I longed to be back again even among the ignorant Mexicans. They at least had been friendly to me — I was at home amongst them."[10]

Henry went to New York in 1867 where he met his future wife. The lack of a suitable marriage partner became one of the hazards for Jews living in the Southwest. Many traveled to the East Coast to go wife hunting, or returned to their native European countries to bring back a childhood love. Prosperous merchants, after achieving their fortunes, moved to the East Coast to encourage their children to marry within the faith and to give them a proper education. Henry followed this pattern.

After Henry and his wife spent seven years in the West, he built a home in Brooklyn, and his wife and three children moved East while Henry remained in Las Cruces, New Mexico to manage his business. "We ran passenger coaches for a distance of six hundred miles through the worst Indian country West of the Rocky Mountains. It was profitable, but replete with danger. Then I furnished the government with flour and grain for the troops. My native restlessness was the true cause of my success. I left nothing untried or undone. Neither the fear of Indians or other attendant danger kept me from my business. In the following seven years it [his capital] grew to three hundred thousand dollars."[11] Not long after that, one of his employees brought him a sack of copper ore located from a site in the San Francisco Mountains about 220 miles from Las Cruces.

Samuel J. Freudenthal

El Paso's Freudenthal family, early 1900s.

"Not long thereafter I was in my saddle and started for the copper mines. . . . We were six days in finding the place again. Rivers had to be crossed, mountains ascended, and a careful watch for Indians maintained." Indians did steal their horses and provisions, but nothing could detour Henry from his mine. With $10,000, he bought controlling interest in the mine. He invested $20,000 more in a Baltimore Copper Works crew to set up a smelter because the nearest railroad was twelve hundred miles away. Production soared but the price of copper dropped from twenty-five to fifteen cents a pound in 1878, and the mine remained in debt. Henry asked the miners to accept a pay cut, he sold his house in New York, brought his family back to Las Cruces, and after two years the mine made a profit.

In 1882 a group of English and Scotch investors bought the enterprise for $1.2 million. Henry wrote his son, "The ten years of agony were forgotten. My craving after mines that had inspired my work for seventeen years turned out to be the true lodestone that led the wanderer in the right direction. Forgotten the despair, the unspeakable sufferings, the mental torture. My heart went out and embraced all things, animate and inanimate. So it is when peace and contentment enter your heart."

He moved with his family back to New York. But he never adjusted to the New York environment. "I felt stranded on a foreign land. The very language was strange to me. I found no sympathy among my new associates. It was rush and toil, care and competition, and fraud and cheating, such as I had never dreamed of. I felt like one dropped from the moon."[12]

He looked to the family group he trusted and had done business with for years. His nephew, Samuel J. Freudenthal, owned a wholesale grocery in El Paso that went bankrupt in the late 1890s during that depression. Henry Lesinsky intervened, pumped in the needed cash, and formed the H. Lesinsky Company with Henry, president and Samuel, general manager. Every year the private company held its board of directors meeting. And every year Henry Lesinsky caught a train from New York with his wife and sons for the meeting. Samuel wrote, "He continued this custom, even when well past the four score year mark. He was indeed our 'grand old man' and his judgment remained keen, as his mind was active to the day of his death in 1924."[13]

Henry died at the age of eighty-nine, having opened the first mining operation in Arizona and built a successful jobbing company in El Paso. He shipped the first pound of copper from Arizona from mines eventually owned by Phelps-Dodge.[14]

Nephew Freudenthal started a chamber of commerce in El Paso and was elected its first president. He led the fight for securing the construction by the United States of the Elephant Butte Dam in New Mexico on the Rio Grande, a project that afforded the valley above and below the city an ample supply of water for irrigation purposes. He served as a county commissioner for ten years.[15]

Ad in an early Houston City Directory.
Courtesy Houston Public Library.

MICHAEL L. WESTHEIMER

Houston still bares witness to M.L. Westheimer, a pioneer from Baden, Germany, who came to Houston in 1852 and built a road that has become one of the city's major thoroughfares. M.L. had bought the land to graze his horses.

Originally, Houstonians considered Westheimer's location west of the town undesirable. Wagon drivers going into town in the morning had the sun in their faces, and drivers going home in the evening had to squint their eyes in the setting sun. Generations later, Westheimer Road was an elitist address and included

The five Westheimer brothers, nephews of M. L. Westheimer, played a significant role in Houston's business development. Seated: Max and Sidney. Standing: Adolph, Sigmund J. and David.

Houston's most lavish shopping center, The Galleria, and finest hotels. Was M.L. a visionary or lucky?

His daughter, Mrs. Hettie Westheimer Ray, said her father had been a miller in Germany and owned a flour mill in Houston, too. But in the 1850s and 1860s he made a name for himself as a hay merchant. He bought his land almost by accident, she said.

One day as he walked by the courthouse, he heard a farm being put up for auction, obviously by a man who needed the money. A bidder had offered twenty-five cents an acre for the 640 acres, and no one else was bidding, so M.L. entered the contest and finally bought the land for $2.50 an acre. The farm made a wonderful place for children, Mrs. Ray said. Her mother and father reared sixteen children, including eight of their own, three orphans, and five children of relatives.

There were no free schools in Houston at that time, so her father built one on his farm, with a fenced-in acre where the children could leave their ponies. He hired a teacher, and let all the community children come free. Her father, an educated man, had many advantages in the young Houston because he spoke seven languages and was often called on as an interpreter, particularly at the bank and post office.[16]

M.L. built a crude trail from his front door to town, a distance of about five miles in the mid-1870s. To help friends and acquaintances find his place, he attached the family name to the trail. In 1895 he deeded part of the trail to the city for a right-of-way, and Westheimer Road began.[17]

David Westheimer

M.L. opened the Houston Livery stable around 1880, then sent for his nephews Sidney and Sigmund J., who still lived in Germany. Together, the nephews established the Westheimer Transfer and Storage and a funeral home. M.L. built the city's first streetcar rails, too. A third nephew, Adolph, joined the family in Houston about twenty-five or thirty years later. Adolph's son David became a successful author.

David grew up in Houston and attended Rice Institute where he majored in chemistry. "But," he said, "I was always interested in writing." When he graduated in 1937, he worked at the *Houston Post* as a television critic.

David served in World War II in the U.S. Air Force in Europe, was captured and made a prisoner of war. This experience inspired him to write a book, *Von Ryan's Express*, which became a motion picture. He wrote thirteen novels. "The only award I have ever won," he said, "is the Texas Institute of Letters award" for *Summer on the Water* in 1948.[18]

David decided to return to the newspaper business in 1984 and began a newspaper column, published three times a week, for the *Houston Post*. The column weaves the past with the present, spanning Europe to Japan, and drawing on his experiences as a boy growing up in Houston and now living in Los Angeles.

Sigmund, Adolph's older brother, left his own legacy when he donated the Attwater collection of natural history to the city of Houston. Sigmund had purchased the collection from Professor H.P. Attwater, considered one of the best natural historians in Texas. The collection, made up of relics and curios peculiar to Texas, represented the life work of Professor Attwater.

One observer commented that "this collection will be like an open wonderbook that unfolds our state page by page, and leaf after leaf until we know its hills and its valleys. Mr. Westheimer has given his community a truly noble gift and every following generation will grow to thank him."[19]

HARRIS AND JOSEPH WEINGARTEN

Indirectly, Harris and Joe Weingarten gave Houston and the world a noble gift — the modern supermarket. They revolutionized how customers bought their food in stores.

Harris was born in the small village of Lanout, Galicia, later a part of Poland, in June of 1854. Around 1880 he left his wife, Belle, and son, Joseph, and set out for New York. He suffered hardships his first years in America, selling matches on the streets of New York. He borrowed money and took a boat to Galveston, then journeyed to Houston.[20]

With financial assistance from friends, he purchased a small amount of merchandise and peddled around the city. He later opened a commissary near what is now Sugar Land and earned enough income to move to Richmond and open a store. His earnings permitted him to bring his wife and six-year old son to America in 1890.

He came back to Houston where he opened a general dry goods store. Known as "The Cent Store" (all items were priced in odd cents), it proved to be an innovation and prospered.

When a fire in 1901 destroyed the small store, Belle Weingarten put up her household money, $300 she had saved over the years, and launched the family's first grocery store. The family lived over that store, and the entire family worked in it, including the four children, Joseph, Solomon, Abraham, and Ann.

Harris would rise at 4:30 A.M. to make the rounds of the produce markets and buy the day's supply for his store. Joe had the store ready to open by 6:00 A.M. During the slack hours of the day, Joe and later Abe knocked on doors to solicit grocery orders, and then delivered the grocery orders by horse and buggy. The family worked until the store closed at 9:00 P.M.[21]

As the store prospered, Harris moved to larger and larger stores until finally in 1920, Harris and Joe changed the business to cash-and-carry and self-service. A newspaper noted that the system brought something entirely new to Texas and the South, and that competitors made jesting remarks about customers serving themselves, but that such remarks did not deter Harris and his sons.

Joe Weingarten, who became known as the Bread Basket Prince, credits another Houston man, Franklin P. Davis, of originating the self-service idea in 1917. "He had the idea before Piggly Wiggly, myself, or any of the big national chains," Joe said.

Joe, though, pioneered the idea of a store with groceries, produce, meat department, delicatessen, bakery, drugs, cigars, and candy, all under one roof. A former A&P executive said of Joe, "Back in the early thirties we and Kroger's were thinking of a 4-5,000-square-foot store, Weingarten was thinking in terms of 30-40,000 square feet. That's how far out front he was in his thinking."[22]

The Weingartens developed their own poultry processing plants, special coffee blends, their own bakery and sold these products under their own label to provide their customers with the finest quality foods.

Harris died in 1935. He had taught his sons well. In 1938 when Joe testified before President Franklin D. Roosevelt's conference on small business, only Joe pleaded for regulating wages and hours. He argued that a wage-hour law with a minimum wage of forty dollars per week was "the only democratic way under our form of government to increase purchasing power. See that they earn more money," he said, "and you can't keep them from spending it with a shotgun." His father had always told them that they should live in harmony, love one another and do what they could to help their fellow man.[23]

Joe Weingarten founded and headed a peace foundation for many years. He served on the board of the Jewish Theological Seminary.[24]

In 1949 the Weingarten chain was selected by the information branch of the U.S. State Department as its model to illustrate to Europeans what an American supermarket looked like. Over five hundred photographs of the Weingartens and information translated into fifty-five languages told their story to the world.

In 1980 Weingarten's sold the company to Grand Union owned by Sir James Goldsmith of England. The approximately 110 stores were in Texas, Louisiana, and Arkansas. Grand Union kept the Weingarten name on the stores until 1984, when they sold them, and the Weingarten name vanished from Texas retailing, after having a high profile for almost one hundred years.

BATTELSTEIN

Philip Battelstein turned his fine tailoring expertise into a store that was enlarged to ten floors in downtown Houston, plus several satellites. Supervised over by Philip and later his sons Abe, Harry, and Ben for more than eighty-three years–1897 to 1980–the stores were sold to Manhattan Industries.

Harris Weingarten

THE SCHWARTZ FAMILY

Historian Floyd S. Fierman called the Schwartz family of El Paso "a socio-economic institution." The Schwartzes followed a pattern typical of the Jewish settlement of the Southwest. Once one Jew transferred from migrant to resident, once he had an economic foundation, he encouraged members of his family in the Old World to migrate, making promises of work opportunites and assuming some responsibility for the newcomer's welfare. The Schwartzes never forgot who they were and from where they had come. "Once they gained momentum, they became prominent in the general community and dominant in the Jewish community."[25]

They, like the Weingartens, innovated selling techniques. For example, they gave away cantaloupes. In 1914 *El Paso Times* advertisements announced: "Everybody's policy is to encourage home industry. To prove the superiority of the El Paso Valley Cantaloupes, we will give everyone who visits the store Wednesday and Thursday a Choice Valley Cantaloupe, FREE." The farmers prospered, the customers stayed happy, and the store benefitted. The Schwartzes called their store the Popular Dry Goods Company.

Adolph Schwartz was born in 1866 in what is now Czechoslovakia. He left his native country at age sixteen and arrived in the United States in 1883. Compulsory military service, oppressive and demeaning to Jews, acted to drive him from his home. Too, Jews could not enter either the government or private schools. It took him thirty days to cross the Atlantic, and he landed in New York with fifteen cents in his pocket. He lived in Cincinnati and San Francisco before coming to Juarez, Mexico.

Adolph Schwartz, wife Fanny Amstater, and children Manuel, Ervin, and Ruth.

Courtesy Ann S. Goodman

Adolph worked on the railroad between Juarez and Mexico City. He saved nine hundred pesos and joined an acquaintance, Simon Picard, in partnership in Juarez. They opened a store, calling it the "Three Bs" (*Buena, Bonita, Barata* — Good, Pretty, Cheap). He met Fanny Amstater of Hungary who was visiting her sister in Juarez, and they married and moved to El Paso. After Adolph began bringing relatives to America in 1890, Fanny daily served dinner at noon, to five to ten persons, six days a week in their home.

Adolph named his first store on the American side of the Rio Grande The Fair. Then he and Bernard Blumenthal operated the Golden Eagle clothing company. In 1902 he sold The Fair and formed the A. Schwartz Company and operated it in partnership with I. Weiss, J. Zelman, and J.C. Zozaya. The partners then organized the Popular Dry Goods Store.

Schwartz "understood Hispanic people and spoke their language."[26] When Adolph celebrated his sixty-ninth birthday, he advised others how to succeed. "I started working when I was twelve and have been working ever since," he said. "I now come to the store early and remain late. I know that if I had not worked I probably would have been under the sod before this, or not able to get around. Loafing is the hardest job there is. It will kill anybody. If people want to be successful, happy, and contented, they had just as well make up their minds they will have to work."[27]

That same year, Adolph married Jeane Berg, a widow. He also had the pleasure of seeing his daughter marry into the Zork family of Germany.

His family left a legacy of rescuing countless boys and girls in Czechoslovakia and Hungary from the Nazis.

Nathan J. Klein Courtesy Joe Samuels

Joseph H. Goodman

JOSEPH H. GOODMAN

Another El Paso Jew, Joseph H. Goodman, acquired the nickname as "a one-man immigration service" for his aid in helping fifty-seven family members in Lithuania, who faced increased religious and economic persecution, come to El Paso. The relatives worked in the family fuel and grain business that Goodman started.

NATHAN J. KLEIN

Nathan J. Klein of Houston rescued over one hundred Jews from the Holocaust, signing affidavits of responsibility for them and caring for these refugees during World War II. Klein was a major founder of Temple Emanu-El of Houston and served as its first president in 1944, according to the temple's founding rabbi, Robert Kahn, who actively served at Emanu-El from 1944 to 1978 and then as rabbi emeritus. Klein contributed generously to the Salvation Army, gave numerous scholarships, and supported medical and other humanitarian causes.[28]

SADIE LEVENE UTAY

Jewish women left their stamp of good taste on early Texas mercantile establishments. Like Carrie Marcus Neiman, Sadie Levene Utay was typical of countless Jewish women who laid the foundation for early Texas businesses.

Sadie, born around the turn of the century in Dallas of parents from Lithuania, became head of one of America's first discount jewelry companies. Typical of the mores of that era, the company was named after her husband and her brother. The Ben Morris Jewelry Company, discount jewelers since 1927, flourished across the street from Dallas' historic Majestic Theatre and, at its height, sponsored a leading radio show, the Ben Morris Hit Parade. Sadie's sense of style and good taste, together with her intense energy, helped build the company to high volume, despite its small downtown space, especially compared to decades later discount houses such as Frances and Ervin Donsky's Sterling Wholesale Jewelry of Dallas, which covered acres of showrooms for household goods.[29] Like Sadie and Ben, both Frances and Ervin worked. The Donskys reached the pinnacle of leadership in the Dallas Jewish community, which called Ervin "Mr. Federation."

Sadie had married a football player and they entertained his athletic friends and teams in a stately

Moshe (Moses) Levitansky (1825-1905) immigrated to Texas in 1863, at the height of the Civil War. He is a patriarch of the Levine family that gave America many prominent physicians.

Courtesy Annie Lee Brachfeld.

Dr. A.L. Levin (1881-1940), eminent scientist who originated the famous "Levin Stomach Tube."

Courtesy Rosa Toubin.

Ittie (Mrs. Avremel) Levitansky (1834-1906) of Lithuania. Her daughter and son-in-law went to Waxahachie in 1875 to seek better health; however both Channa L. and Fyvel Pizer died in their 30s and are interred at Waxahachie.

Great-grandchildren of Moshe—the Mayer Shapiro family of Galveston, 1916. Top row: Bessie, Nettie, Frank. Front: Annie Lee, David and Maurice. (Not shown: baby I.J.) The family grew up on 14th and Strand, one block from the remains of Laffite's home.

Courtesy Annie Lee Brachfeld.

University Park home on Windsor Parkway.

Sadie had descended from sturdy stock. Her great-grandfather, Moshe (Moses) Levitansky, had come to the United States at the height of the Civil War in 1863 with his younger brother Yonkel, a wanderer nicknamed "Yonkel the Mahzik" (Johnny the Mischief), who had first come to America in 1843. Yonkel was born in 1827. After his first crossing of the Atlantic at the age of sixteen as a stowaway, he was sent back to Lithuania. Subsequently, he crossed ten or eleven times. He was in business in Marshall, Jefferson, and Brenham, Texas, and in Shreveport, Louisiana. He covered territory from Fort Worth and Denton to Galveston in a horse-drawn and ox-drawn covered wagon, a regular traveling store with shelves and showcases.[30]

Mayer Yossel Levitansky (1826-1910), brother of Moshe, Yonkel, and Meta

Dr. Samuel Albert Levine (1891-1966), Harvard Medical professor, became one of the nation's most distinguished cardiologists

Genealogist Etta Levine, Mrs. Jacob Levin, sister of Max, 1929.

Dr. Max Levine (1889-1963), "Father of America's Water Purification," receiving an honorary Doctor of Science degree in 1960. Photo: Honolulu Star-Bulletin.

Yonkel came to America many times before the Civil War. He landed in New York and learned there was a bounty of $300 for entering the Army. He decided to enter the Army for somebody else, a common practice in those days for both sides. Genealogist Etta Levin of Los Angeles wrote, "A few years later, on one of his visits to relatives in Chicago, he announced he was going to Texas. Naturally, this was cause for amazement. But he did go there and went into business in various cities in Texas. Members of the Levitan family recall some of the visits he made to the home of their parents in Chicago and the fact that he always came dressed as a cowboy although he actually never worked as one.

"On one of his trips to this country he landed at Ellis Island, dressed in the long coat worn at the time by Jews in Eastern Europe; had long sideburns — and cowboy boots. One of the immigration officials jostled him and our ancestor, being a strong-willed individual, hauled off and hit the official, meanwhile pouring forth

"Yonkel the Mischief" (1827-1919), who first came to the U.S. in 1843 and made eleven crossings before settling here in 1863 with his brother Moshe.

Yonkel's son Schlaime Isaac (1854-1938) with his wife Channa at the time of their marriage in Dallas in 1878. Yonkel and son opened stores in Shreveport, La., and later in Jefferson, Marshall, Brenham, and Dallas, beginning in the 1860s.

Ox cart such as the one driven by Yonkel Levitansky from Galveston to Denton with shelves for dry goods.
Courtesy De Golyer Library, Dallas Morning News Collection.

a string of cuss words in the most curious Russian-Texas drawl. They then decided to deport him forthwith. However, when they found out he was a citizen of the United States and showed evidence that he had fought in the Civil War, he was admitted."[31]

But Yonkel's brother Moshe did not remain in this country very long. He had been educated for the rabbinate and found things in America not traditonal and kosher enough, so he returned to Lithuania in northern Poland, across the Baltic from Sweden. Their younger sister Meta lived in Sweden.[32] Moshe did not return to America, but his son, Avrum Schlaime Levene, did come around 1902 with his wife, Leah, and settled in Brenham, Texas, where his descendants six generations later owned department stores more than a hundred years after Moshe's arrival.[33]

Before they became merchants, they worked as peddlers, journeying between Houston and Austin from their homes in Brenham, La Grange, and Sealy. Some covered the small towns along the Brazos River,

Meta Levitansky (1837-1915), younger sister of Moshe, Mayer and Yonkel. Although her seven brothers had lived in Lithuania, Meta lived in Sweden before coming to Texas, having a store in Marshall in 1877 and Dallas in 1878.

Meta's husband, Jacob Laib Barkovsky took the name Levine and became a pioneer Texas merchant. Eventually he and Meta rejoined family in Boston.

Their grandson Abraham Levine, right, had two stores in San Antonio from 1913 until his death in 1920.

such as Somerville, Lyons, and Caldwell. Here Avrum's daughter, Minnie, and her husband, Mayer Shapiro, lived, with Mayer peddling calico from a horse and wagon along the Brazos countryside.

The lifestyle of these pioneers shows that the early Jewish settlers in Texas cannot be stereotyped. Not everyone lived like the Sanger brothers in their mansions, or Stanley Marcus and his family. In Lyons, the Shapiro family was so poor they lived in a house with a dirt floor. "When I was twelve I went from Dallas on the train to visit my cousins in Lyons," recalled Fannie Levene Ornish, older sister of Sadie Levene Utay. "When I arrived, there was not even a depot, just a barn with Lyons written on it. I was afraid to get off the train. There were no paved roads. The town did not even have lights, and that night we walked to the ice cream parlor, and it was so dark I fell over a cow sitting in the road. I never will forget that dirt floor. It was deplorable."[34]

Not all Jews lived like the Sangers. When the Levine family came to Brenham, they lived in a house with a dirt floor, similar to the one shown above with Avrum Schlaime Levine in front with his horse. Courtesy Rosa L. Toubin.

When the Shapiros came to America, they had traveled fourth class. Years later Bess Shapiro Moskowitz, who remembered vividly the horrors of the trip she endured at age four, made a joke of it. "Do you know why we came fourth class?" she would ask. "Because there was not a fifth."[35]

One of the family's few possessions was a small bible, which Mayer read when he was not peddling, while his wife grated potatoes for the potato pancakes they ate daily, usually with sardines, or small portions of herring.

Despite their poverty the children of these early merchants strove to improve their lot. Mayer's daughter Bess studied English literature at Brenham's Blinn College before her family moved to Galveston. Her brother I.J. received a law degree from the University of Texas at Austin, and her brother David became a physician. Education was paramount, and many Levines rose high in their professions (spelling their name various ways: Levene, Levine, Levin, Levitan).[36]

Bess Shapiro Moskowitz of Brenham and Galveston, circa 1919.

Sadie's baby brother, Gus Levene (profiled in chapter 12), was born in Dallas and at age eighteen composed a ballet suite, "Exodus," which the Dallas Symphony Orchestra performed.

Within this one family can be seen the great diversity in styles of Jewish merchants. While Sadie Levene Utay's great-grandfather's brother Yonkel the Mischief never stopped traveling, Sadie devoted her life till the end merchandising in the store named for her husband, Ben, and her brother Morris. At the age of 52 she suffered a brain hemorrhage and died.

Sadie's granddaughter, Marcia Plumb of Houston, became the first Texas woman, and the first woman in the Southwest, to become a rabbi. She was ordained in New York in 1988.[37]

George I. Moskowitz (1892-1977) circa 1920, and as he appeared at age 75. George was President of Texas Produce and Commission Co. on the northwest corner of 21st and Strand in the 1920s.

Esther Goldberg Moskowitz, mother of George. During the 1900 Storm the family survived by seeking refuge at the old Alamo School nearby. When she died, her youngest children went to the Jewish Orphans Home in New Orleans.

The children of George and Bessie Moskowitz included Natalie, Ronald, Esther, and Charlotte. The eldest, Herschel, died as a child.

JULIUS SCHEPPS

The hardships that Julius Schepps and his parents suffered as immigrants altered Julius' life. It determined his mission in life — to help the unfortunate. His own son called him the Jewish Abraham Lincoln.[38]

His parents, Russian Jews, immigrated to the United States in 1890, living first in New York for a year before they moved to St. Louis where Julius was born in 1895. His parents moved to Dallas in 1901, and the family, which included Julius' sister and an uncle, lived in two rooms that fronted on an alley. The father started a bakery which prospered and, by the time the father died in 1922, it baked eighty percent of the bread eaten in Dallas.

"I never was a boy," Julius said. "I never had time to be."

During those early years, he helped deliver bread and in 1912 became a carrier for the *Dallas Morning News*. In 1914 he left a circulation department position on the *News* to attend Texas A&M on a basketball scholarship.

"They asked me two questions on the entrance exam," he said. "Who is the head coach at A&M? What is your roommate's name? That qualified me for a two-year agricultural course."[39]

Seventeen days into campus life they discovered that Julius had no high school diploma. He departed, but he never forgot the camaraderie of young men who stood together as equals. The lack of discrimination impressed him. Twelve years later he became the Aggie president of the former students association.

After his brief stay at A&M, Julius headed west on the train bound for California, hoping to find a newspaper circulation job. He carried a letter of reference from G.B. Dealey, owner of the *Dallas Morning News*. Julius stopped off in El Paso and decided to apply for a job there. The nineteen-year-old Julius handed the *El Paso Times* official his application, on which he had inflated his age to thirty-one, and the letter from G.B. Dealey. The official asked Julius to return the next day for an answer and then wired Dealey to ask Julius' age.

"Mr. Schepps is whatever age he says he is," Dealey replied. Julius got the job.[40] Seven months later he married Phyllis Eickman of El Paso and stayed in El Paso for two years. He returned to Dallas in 1922 when his father died, and helped the family run the bakery.

The family sold the bakery in 1928, providing the family with enough money to buy stock. "We bought stocks alphabetically," Julius said. "We didn't even know what they were." Julius came out of the 1929 stock market crash with debt totalling $540,000. He vowed to pay off the debt if he had to live to be ninety-one. Times got so hard that Julius broke open the piggy banks of his three children to buy groceries.

The crash did leave him with $2,800 worth of stocks. Julius opened an insurance office. In 1934 he organized the Schepps Brewing Company and sold it the following year.

Financier John T. Higginbotham put up the money for him to go into the wholesale liquor business in 1935. He developed other business interests as well, which included the Golman Baking Company, Oak Cliff Baking Company, radio station KIXL, a directorship on Mercantile National Bank board, and he and his brother George bought an interest in the Dallas Baseball Club.[41]

At the beginning of World War II, Julius vowed, "I am too old for the armed forces, but there is going to be a lot of money made in this war. I am going to make my share of it and give it away." After World War II he borrowed $200,000 to buy Higginbotham's share of the wholesale liquor business.The liquor business would act as Julius' launching pad to fulfill his mission.

In a letter to his son Phil, who served as a corporal in the army engineers in Europe, Julius wrote: "Dear Boy: Regarding the home for the Community Chest, in which I have today purchased the property and gave it to them, giving it in the name of the Schepps children and grandchildren as a memorial to Joe and Jennie [Julius' parents]. I bought the property for $32,000." Another letter followed: "Dear Boy: I shall slow down on the giving for a while, as I had to give the Community Chest $12,500 more to be able to put the building in proper shape."

Julius' letters to his son reveal his profound philosophy of giving rooted in his Jewish faith that guided his life. In 1945, during World War II, he wrote Phil, then overseas, "Quite naturally, . . . the only difference over there is life and death. Over here it is a constant struggle against abuses and disconcerting animosities.

"You are fighting for what we would like to call Democracy. I have not yet reached an age when I can become a qualified judge to say just what Democracy is, but I have concluded definitely there will be a Jewish question as long as one Jew remains alive in this world, and I shall continue, whenever I have honest knowledge, going straight to those who oppose us — because I can't use the dogma of letting a sleeping dog lie,' because I definitely don't think the dog is lying for the purpose of sleeping, but for the purpose of lying."

Later, Julius wrote: "The more he [Mr. Schepps' father] accumulated, the greater believer he was that poverty was created by selfishness and not by God. I don't think that poverty should ever return again if the good people of this world would just think of it was a challenge and not an ideology."

Robert Cullum, who owned the Tom Thumb grocery stores in Dallas and served with Julius on the Dallas Citizens Council that, in that era, handpicked the city's mayors and council members, said, "Julius borrowed to give, and he was a great influence on others to give to charity.

"He was an intensely proud Jew. He would kid about his long nose and joke about his Jewishness. But he wouldn't lower his voice when he spoke about what he called the Jewish question.

"There used to be the Big Three on the Citizens Council — Julius Schepps, R.L. Thornton, Sr., and Fred Florence," Cullum said. "They would eyeball each other and cuss it out. It's a different group now, and things are not done with the same flair. Now it takes six men to do what Julius could have done with one phone call. The extent to which Julius touched so many private lives was his particular genius. There is no reckoning as to how many Julius Schepps helped through his wisdom, spirit, time and money."[42]

In 1945 he anonymously gave $120,000 to a lagging Salvation Army drive to push it over the top. On a Sunday in the 1950s when a young minister stood before his congregation in the First Presbyterian Church and told of the needs for remodeling and expansion of facilities, he asked members to rise and show their commitments. In a middle pew two men rose. One was Julius Schepps, and the other was Fred Florence who had come to help their Presbyterian friends rebuild their house of worship. Both pledged $5,000.[43]

Julius ignored religious affiliations in his community work. "I don't ask a man what his nationality or religion or political inclination is," he said. "I've never recognized the difference in any religious sect. I feel I'm just as good a Baptist as a Baptist is, just as good a Protestant as a Protestant is, just as good a Catholic as a Catholic is."[44]

When a Dallas newspaper publisher invited him to an event held at the Dallas Petroleum Club that excluded Jews from membership, Julius wrote: "Dear Jim and Betty: Your invitation to Cocktail-Buffet to be held at the Petroleum Club on October 6th received, and it is with sincere regrets that we are compelled to decline the invitation. I wish to remain honest with both of you because of our sincere affection for you makes it rather hard for me to give our reason. We just do not attend functions at Northwood, Dallas Country Club, Brook Hollow or the Petroleum Club owing to the fact that our Faith does not qualify for membership."[45]

Dallas mayor R.L. Thornton, Sr., said, "Julius is not a brass-band type. Besides possessing all the qualities of a fine business man, he recognizes his obligations to society and civic progress and gives them time and thought equal to his business interest. His complete integrity, his simple, plain manner plus the fact that he enjoys everything he does, inspire implicit confidence. His appeal reaches across all groups in this city, rich or poor, high or low, irrespective of race, color, or faith."

Julius had his own way of describing his philosophy. He once told a reporter, "I don't own an airplane or a yacht, or even a rowboat. I don't own a country home, or have a foundation or trust for my children or grandchildren. I live in a mortgaged home. I've never had enough money ahead to pay my pledges, but I've always had faith in God."[46]

Rabbi Gerald Klein captured the essence of Julius when he called him a "walking brotherhood movement."[47] When Dallas needed an individual who held the trust of the white power structure as well as the black community, both groups looked to Julius to head the committee to work for a peaceful integration in the 1960s. A. Maceo Smith, a leader in the black community at that time, said, "He was genuinely dedicated."

Many groups and organizations recognized Julius' healing gifts. In 1965 he received the B'nai B'rith Humanitarianism Award, the first such award presented in the Southwest. He received the Linz Award as Dallas' outstanding citizen; and the press recognized

Raymond Holbrook, president of the Press Club of Dallas, presented the "Headliner of the Year" award to Julius Schepps in 1962. Courtesy Raymond and Helen Holbrook.

him with the "Headliner of the Year" award from the Dallas Press Club; the Texas Welfare Federation named him as the person contributing most to the welfare of his community; and the Jewish Welfare Federation named its newly constructed, million-dollar development the Julius Schepps Community Center.[48]

Because Julius devoted his life to building a brotherhood in Dallas, groups and writers focused almost totally on that dimension of his community work. Yet, he used those same talents in his business, which provided him the money he gave to others, and in his relationship with his employees. Jeanette O. Levey, Julius' private secretary for two and a half years, from 1941 to 1943, said, "He used to say that he spoiled his employees so that they couldn't work for anyone else. Nobody left there unless they got married and left town, or went into military service. Every now and then, every three months, he would go to the payroll fellow, Mr. Mac, and tell him to give all employees a bonus. He would say, 'Give everybody two weeks salary instead of one.' He would give Christmas bonuses a month ahead of time, so you could go out and buy things.

"At least once a week, he would say to a group of his employees: 'You're going to lunch with me today.' He took every girl — at least twenty — to lunch at Vick's downtown. During World War II he would save U.S. Savings Stamps for each employee. When I got married, he presented me with books of these savings stamps. If you had to leave, he would give them to you as a bonus. When an employee got called into the service, he cried. It was like one of his children was leaving. I saw him cry."[49]

Mrs. Levey remembered that Julius brought many relatives to the United States to save them from the Holocaust. Through the marriage of Julius' sister, Rebecca, to Carl Metzger, the family formed a bond with the pioneer family of dairymen.

When Julius died in 1971, Congressman Jim Collins read a dedication to him into the *Congressional Record*, and the Sixty-second Texas State Legislature offered a resolution honoring Julius Schepps, referring to him as "Mr. Dallas."

The Dallas City Council honored him after his death by naming the Julius Schepps Freeway as his memorial.

Julius Schepps at dedication of Julius Schepps Community Center, May 1962.

ISADORE AND MEREDITH R. CARB

Although a few scattered Jews had arrived in Fort Worth before Isadore Carb, he became its first significant Jewish merchant. A native American, he was born in Mississippi Nov. 6, 1853, and grew up in New Orleans.

His parents were David Carb of Alsace-Lorraine and Babette Rosenbaum Carb of Germany and France. They met in New Orleans, (where Babette was living in the 1850s), married, and moved to his Mississippi farm. "It wasn't lofty enough to be called a plantation," said a great-granddaughter.[50] They had six children, including a son, Isadore. During the Civil War they moved to New Orleans.

In 1871 Isadore came to Texas to peddle sewing machines for a New Orleans company. He settled in Fort Worth and became a successful merchant. "His enterprise and public spirit helped the city grow in the critical years of the [eighteen] seventies."[51]

After being a merchant several years, he entered the real estate brokerage business. A son, Meredith R. Carb, entered the business at age twenty-one and in 1909 made his first sale, a five-room house for $800.[52] Meredith constructed one of Fort Worth's first housing developments in 1923, ten clapboard houses in Arlington Heights. He built hundreds of Fort Worth homes and was also known as an appraiser from the 1920s through the 1950s. Meredith Carb, born in 1888, lived to be one hundred years old.

Meredith's older brother, David Carb, also born in Fort Worth, was graduated cum laude from Harvard University in 1909 and taught English at M.I.T. He later moved to New York to become drama critic of *Vogue* magazine for eleven years. David became a playwright and novelist. During World War I he volunteered with the American ambulance corps and joined the French Foreign Legion.[53]

Meredith Carb, Jr., while stationed in England in World War II, completed eighty bombing missions as a Liberator co-pilot. His many decorations include the Distinguished Flying Cross.[54]

Babette Carb

Meredith Carb as a young man.

WASHER BROTHERS

By 1882 Fort Worth had grown to a population of 6,000, and Jacob and his brother Nathan Moses (Nat) Washer arrived from Tennessee.

Washer Bros. Clothiers prospered, selling such frontier items as boots and bandanas. In 1889 Nat moved to San Antonio to open a Washer Bros. store there. In 1893 he laid the cornerstone of Fort Worth's County Court House while serving as grand master of the Masonic order's Grand Lodge of Texas. In San Antonio he served as president of Temple Beth El where the rabbi, Ephraim Frisch, was married to Rabbi Henry Cohen's daughter.

In 1895 the brothers sold their Fort Worth store to Leon Gross, a partner. The Washers continued active in community affairs. Nat helped found the Masonic Home for Widows and Orphans near Fort Worth in early 1899. He was an orator, singer, and writer. In 1932, exactly fifty years after he arrived in Texas, Nat served as president of the State Board of Education.

Gross, also a native of Tennessee, continued as president of Washer Bros. for half a century. One of his early customers was Theodore Roosevelt, who came in on April 8, 1905, and purchased a Stetson hat and two blue army shirts. Gross married Edith Mayer, and when Gross died in 1945 their nephew, Raymond Mayer, who had been managing the store, became president. Mayer owned Washer Bros. until 1966, when he sold it to Hart, Schaffner & Marx of Chicago. The Chicago firm added suburban stores and combined them with James K. Wilson. In the late 1980s the name Washer Bros. was dropped.[55]

ABRAHAM ROSENTHAL

Abraham Rosenthal, born in Russia, attended a *yeshiva* (Hebrew school) in Konigsberg, Germany, where he met two students from Rochester, Minnesota. They invited him to meet their sister Rachel (Rae) Myers, age fifteen. Rosenthal came to America and married Rachel in l880. Her uncle was a partner in the original Hart, Schaffner & Marx Co., manufacturers of men's suits. Rachel's family, of German descent, looked down on Abraham as a poor Russian refugee.

Both Abraham's and Rachel's voyages to America were unusual. Rachel was born on the high seas on an English ship. At the end of Abraham's trip, in the New York port, Abraham — whose last name was Schultz in Russia — went up to an immigration officer to ask him a question. The officer had just called out the name Rosenthal when he saw the young immigrant standing there, thought his name was Rosenthal, and tagged him with that name.

In Rochester, Abraham began training to be a *hazzan* (cantor) and *schochet* (ritual meat slaughterer). The young couple moved to St. Paul, Minnesota. While he made a living as a cantor, he learned kosher slaughtering in the packing houses in the area. Rosenthal brought his family to America. The entire family then moved to Chicago where Abraham's father, Rabbi Beryl (Bernard) Rosenthal, became the rabbi of Sons of Jacob Synagogue.

In 1900 Abraham and Rachel Rosenthal moved to Dallas, where he had been hired as cantor of Congregation Shearith Israel. In addition to performing for the synagogue, Abraham opened a kosher meat market.[56]

Jews who keep kosher do not eat the hindquarter of meat, so Abraham started a second market to dispose of the *trafe* (unkosher) part of the animal.

Abraham became one of the early buyers of cattle at the Fort Worth stockyards. His son Harry would drive the cattle to Dallas on horseback. One day he received a traffic fine on Lamar Street in front of Sanger Bros. department store for exceeding the cattle limit. Though it was legal to drive cattle through the streets of Dallas, the law set a limit on the number of cattle that could be herded through town at one time. On one of the cattle-herding expeditions, when Harry and his brother Ike had been sent to bring cattle from a farm to Dallas, Ike fell from his horse crossing the flooded Trinity River and died.

In 1908 Abe gave up being a *hazzan*, moved his family to Fort Worth, and started the Packing House Market at the corner of Houston and Twelfth Streets where he employed ten butchers. Gradually, other members of the family began to go into various aspects of the meat business, such as wholesale meat jobbing, simple meat packing, and with advancing technology, meat processing. They serviced boardinghouses, cafes, trains and train stations.

Six of Abe and Rachel's twelve children continued in the meat business, Max Sam, Louis, Sol, Harry, Ben, and Dave. Ben (uncle of the Dallas builder of the same name) went into the wholesale meat business, supplying hotels and restaurants. In 1926 he formed the Western Dressed Beef and Provision Company and nine years later Standard Meat Company. Ben's son E.M. (Manny) Rosenthal became its president in 1946. In 1982 Manny sold out to Sara Lee Co. of Chicago, a division of Consolidated Foods.

A building on the campus of Texas A&M University was named in 1987 for the Rosenthal family.[57]

HENRY GERNSBACHER

Henry Gernsbacher was a civic leader in Weatherford, Texas, for decades before moving to Fort Worth, where he began Fort Worth's first Reform Jewish congregation.

His parents, Loeb and Caroline Grabenheimer (later changed to Gernsbacher), had emigrated from Germany to New Orleans, where Henry was born in 1858. He received his education in New Orleans schools. In 1876 he arrived in Texas, first in Lovelace and then in Weatherford. Here he helped organize the Weatherford fire department, acted as its president for seven years, and served as Weatherford's mayor pro tem. He married Julia Falk in 1880 and completed his family of six children.

He moved to Fort Worth in 1900, operating wholesale and retail hardware stores. Soon he became known as the dean of Texas china merchants, selling china, glass, and home-furnishing goods. A descendant recalled that they had a system of making change by dropping money into a copper metal tube and hooking it onto a cable and pulling it by hand, like a clothesline.

Henry's business became "one of the high-class mercantile establishments of the metropolitan district of Fort Worth . . . and widely known."[58] The Texas Retail Merchants Association elected him as president.

"In the early fall of 1902, after earnest efforts on the part of Mr. Gernsbacher and constant agitation, it was determined to formally organize a Reform congregation, and to that end, Beth-El Congregation became incorporated, Mr. Gernsbacher being selected as its first president."[59] In 1907 the Council of Jewish Women, which had paid the choir, helped purchase a lot for a temple. Henry also served as first president of the Elias Sanger Lodge of B'nai B'rith in 1902, which helped with the Galveston immigration movement and maintained

H. Gernsbacher

Gernsbacher's, 1922. The seven automobiles comprised a "stage line" that carried passengers between Fort Worth and Weatherford.

a branch of the Industrial Removal Office of New York.

Henry died in 1936, and four of his sons — Meyer, Jake, Aaron, and Roy — branched into related fields. His youngest son, Laurence, attended law school. Henry's grandson Larry became an architect, founder of The Institute of Professional Suicidology in Albuquerque, New Mexico, and author of *The Suicide Syndrome*.[60]

SAM ROSEN

Sam Rosen came to Texas in 1882 and established his pioneering real estate merchandising in 1902.

At the age of twelve he had left Russia to escape abuse from teachers who resented his Jewish heritage.

"The teacher would find a way each day; there would always be a reason," he said, "that I deserved punishment." Then he would be shamed and beaten. He worked his way on a boat bound for the United States. His older brother, Isaac, had already established himself as a farmer on land in southwest Dallas now known as Oak Cliff. Sam, too, worked on a farm.

In 1884 he moved to Fort Worth to work as a peddler. Later he sold novelties as far west as El Paso. He amassed enough capital to open a dry goods store in downtown Fort Worth that stocked a variety of notions, clothing, and crockery.

Sam Rosen home.

After Swift and Armour meat-packing companies came to Fort Worth at the turn of the century, Sam felt that people who worked at the packing plants would want to live nearby, thus avoiding the trip from the southside. Because there was only raw land, without streets, north of the river, he bought a large tract of land on the heights west of the stockyards and subdivided it into lots. His tract of land became known as Rosen Heights.[61]

Residents then needed transportation across town since few had an automobile or a horse and buggy. He started construction on a streetcar line that he originated at his property and extended to existing tracks. He then went to the owners of the competing line and proposed that he provide free passes to passengers who wanted to transfer from theirs onto his line to Rosen Heights. The other company turned him down. He persevered and got a permit and laid tracks all the way into the city.[62]

To encourage the use of his streetcar system and to stimulate growth of Rosen Heights, Sam built an amusement park, White City, containing a baseball diamond, theater, carnival, artificial lake, and dance pavilion. Rosen's concern for the families who lived on his real estate was evident. He provided free land for a church. During the Depression, he never foreclosed on a house, and even paid the utility bills for needy families.

Rosen Heights developed into one of the most densely settled parts of Fort Worth. Sam Rosen became one of the largest real estate developers in Fort Worth. He died December 20, 1932, at age fifty.[63]

Sam Rosen

SEYMOUR DRESCHER

Fifteen-year-old Seymour Drescher arrived in Galveston in 1910, with ten dollars in his pocket. He made his way to Gainesville where he worked for five years as a tailor's helper, earning ten dollars a week, regularly sending a portion to his parents in Brody, Poland.[64]

By 1915 he moved to Fort Worth. He worked for Kean and Levine clothiers, first as a tailor, then salesman, and finally owned the business. He transformed the clothing store into Seymour's White Front Store, the largest dealer in western wear at that time, and the store stayed in continuous operation at the same location for fifty years despite serious setbacks.

His first major challenge came in the 1920s with the resurgence of the Ku Klux Klan that preyed on Jews, lighting burning crosses in front of their homes and businesses. Klan members, riding horseback, swooped down on Jews and their customers. Fearful non-Jews avoided Seymour's store, even his side of the street.

In 1942 Seymour survived a flood that inundated his store, later drying money from the safe on a clothesline in front of his daughter's oven. Over the years his store was also the target of several robberies.

In time, he became a major business force, selling merchandise throughout America, Canada, and Hawaii. The Shriners honored him for his business and charity before he retired in 1966 and his White Front Store passed into history.[65]

AUGUST LORCH

August Lorch became the first of several Jewish pioneers who started as merchandisers and evolved into manufacturers. Their goods, while originally designed for Texans, would generate national demand, with customers including presidents of the United States.

When August Lorch came to Dallas in the late 1880s from Germany, he took the name of a small German town, Lorch, located thirty miles from where he had been raised in Mainz. During that era, Jews commonly would take the name of the town nearby. The family had been in the winery business, and August had a wealthy cousin in the brewery business in New York. Later, in Dallas, August first worked for the local YMCA as a physical education instructor. The work did not require that he speak much English, and he had been a champion swimmer, gymnast, and oarsman in Germany, winning medals for his rowing and swimming speeds in the Rhine River. He then went to work as a clerk in Rose Dry Goods Company in Wills Point, Texas, owned by a distant relative.

In 1892 he returned to Dallas and obtained a license from the City Hall for a one-horse peddler. He peddled in and around Dallas for several years, selling calico and piece goods, sleeping with his horse since he had no place to live. But before long, he graduated to a two-horse wagon. "He moved to Greenville, where I was born and all the rest of the children," said his son Lester, "and he peddled there, selling notions, thread, needles, fabrics, not apparel." Sometime during this period, he moved to Bowie and opened a dry goods store with a brother-in-law, Robert Weil, calling the store Weil-Lorch Dry Goods Company. When he opened his store in Greenville, he named it Lorch Dry Goods Company.

He returned to Dallas in 1909 where he started a wholesale house, featuring exclusively ladies wear, and named this business Lorch Manufacturing Company. "Lorch Manufacturing Company was not a manufacturer, but jobbers, wholesalers," said Lester. "They went to New York and bought merchandise from manufacturers and bought it several months in advance, put it into stock, and sold it to retailers all over the Southwest, mostly Texas." August used the word *manufacturing* in the company's name "to fool the retailers that he dealt with, who were second- and third-class retailers," said Lester. "They were not big stores like Sanger Bros. or A. Harris, or Titche-Goettinger. I went into the business in 1920, went to New York, and bought from this or that manufacturer — coats, dresses — and bought a dozen or twenty-five or fifty of a style, and always marked on an order 'confined in Dallas' among jobbers or wholesalers. But they never kept their word.

"In 1924 I had been after my father to open up a factory so we could have exclusive merchandise of our own. Once, after coming back from a buying trip, he met me at the depot, and he says, well, we're a manufacturing company. He bought out a company that had been manufacturing house dresses. We made wash dresses that retailed from $1.95 to $5.98. We got out of the wash-dress field; we couldn't make it selling them for $1.98." The Depression years made business difficult; Lorch went to Washington to represent the Texas manufacturers and persuaded Sam Rayburn to give them a forty percent discount off the minimum wage. "If we had not received this ruling," Lester said, "there would not be a manufacturing industry in Texas."[66]

Lester assumed responsibilities of operating the company when August died in 1939. In 1945 the Lorch family formed Westway of Dallas, Inc., which manufactured high-quality little girls' dresses and sportswear. This succeeded from the beginning. In 1948 the two companies of Lorch and Westway built a modern dress factory, which became the first completely air-conditioned plant of its kind in the United States. The building housed the two companies, plus Kohen-Ligon-Folz, with whom the Lorch family had been associated since 1935. (It was named for August's brother-in-law, a salesman for August, and August's son-in-law.) In 1964 the three companies merged into one entitled Lorch-Westway Corporation.[67]

LOUIS W. KREDITOR

In 1950 Lorch's production manager since 1935, Louis W. Kreditor, Russian-born and New York-bred, left Lorch to start his own manufacturing business. He ultimately opened twenty factories in various Texas towns, plus two in Louisiana and two in Orlando, Florida.

"Lorch brought me down here," he remembered.

Kreditor launched his first factory in Hubbard, Texas. Here the townspeople renamed the street in front of his plant Kreditor Avenue. He located other of his plants in towns from West Texas to Louisiana to the Oklahoma border. He opened virtually a plant a year in such Texas towns as Frost, Waxahachie, San Antonio, New Braunfels, Mount Pleasant, McKinney, Muenster, Gainesville, Myra, Colorado City, Big Spring, Mount Vernon, Troup, Edgewood, Mineral Wells, Mexia, and Waco.

In San Antonio two factories covered approximately twenty- and thirty-thousand square feet of space each. He maintained his headquarters in Dallas, under the name of Jerell, Inc.

Kreditor enjoys telling a story of how a natural disaster missed his plant, the antithesis of Mayer Halff's story about how a storm damaged only his cattle on a cattle drive.

"I put a *mezuzah* on the door of my factory in Hubbard. [A *mezuzah* is a small parchment scroll inscribed with Deuteronomy 6:4-9 and 11:13-21 placed in a case fixed to the doorpost by some Jewish families as a sign of their faith.] I told my employees, 'This is a religious thing. If you have that on the door, nothing can happen to the building.' I told it in jest. Then in 1970 Hubbard had a terrible tornado. Almost the entire town was wiped out. I just suffered two little windows broken. The government came and offered help to all the people. When they came to me, I told them my damage amounted to only $1.75. All my employees said, 'It was on account of that little religious thing you have on the door, that's why your bulding stayed intact.' I said, 'That's right.' So my employees asked me if I could get them some of those little 'electronic' things to put on their doors. I had brought some back from Israel and I gave them out. Now many Christian people in Hubbard have *mezuzahs* on their doorposts."[68]

ERNEST G. WADEL

Though August Lorch pioneered as the first Jew to have turned a business jobbing clothing into a clothing manufacturer, Ernest G. Wadel became the first Jewish manufacturer of apparel in Texas who did not begin as a jobber. Ernest and his partner, Lester Lief, took over the Marcy Lee label, a line started in 1927 by a family named Mermer. The close proximity in origin of the Lorch and Wadel manufacturing operations caused one descendant to suggest that determining who came first resembled an attempt to split hairs.

Ernest had a brother Felix and a sister Helen and was a native of Tyler, Texas. He trained as a chemical engineer at Columbia University and worked in New York as a chemical engineer where he owned his own company. When he returned to Texas to manufacture the Marcy Lee line, he developed the company into one of the oldest and most respected names in the southwest apparel industry. His first wife, Reba Mallinson Wadel, served on the national United Jewish Appeal board and was killed in a plane crash while returning from a UJA meeting. For nearly half a century Ernest operated Marcy Lee, Inc., making misses and half-sized dresses for a thousand retail accounts.

At first they sold their dresses in Mexico, offering wash dresses and "good ole button-down-the-front dresses," Irene Wadel, his second wife, said. But when Lester Lief contracted cancer, Ernest did not want to continue in the business alone. In December of 1966 he sold the company to Howard B. Wolf, Inc., a Texas corporation.[69]

At its peak in 1969, after the merger, the Wolf company did business with more than three thousand retail stores nationally. Production facilities for Howard B. Wolf Inc. included two plants in Dallas totaling 94,000 square feet, plus plants in Bowie, Houston, Mesquite, and Greenville, Texas. The Howard Wolf label was well established in the better-priced market. The company bought Marcy Lee intending to operate this acquired division in the lower mass-merchandising market. Although Ernest Wadel was no longer associated in the industry, he continued to office at the Howard Wolf Company until his death.[70]

ABRAHAM LUSKEY

A cobbler, Abraham Luskey, stepped out of a boat in New York in 1908 from Pinsk, a Russian-Polish town where Jews bore the brunt of misery.

But Abraham found himself just as miserable on

New York's Lower East Side. He worried about his son whom he'd left in Russia, fearful that the Czar's army might conscript the boy, a practice the military had of taking Jewish boys as young as ten years of age. His anxiety forced him back to Russia.

In Pinsk he returned to his cobbler's bench. But his brief taste of freedom became an obsession to return to America. In 1911 he heard the Hebrew Immigrant Aid Society (HIAS) offered to relocate Eastern European Jews directly to Texas. Galveston had become the Lone Star State's Ellis Island.

Abraham immigrated again to the United States, this time arriving in Texas, where he prospered. In 1913 he sent for his wife, Molly, his three daughters, and son, Jacob, who had just celebrated his bar mitzvah. Jake helped his father in their Fort Worth boot shop that Abraham had started. Jake repaired shoes and shined the boots of the cattle barons and cowboys in town on business. The shop became so successful that Abraham put the profits back into the business and expanded the line of goods to include clothing. By 1919, A. Luskey & Son had become a going concern.

Then Luskey's Western Stores, Inc. expanded again to sell cowboy chic in Dallas, Lubbock, Amarillo, Abilene, Odessa, and Fort Worth, its headquarters. When Abraham died in 1933, Jake took over the stores.

Jacob, following his parents' example, involved himself in the Jewish community and traditions. At age thirty-six in 1936 he served as president of Fort Worth's oldest Hebrew congregation. "At the time," he said, "I was the youngest president of Congregation Ahavath Sholom, actually the youngest president of any Hebrew congregation of over four hundred members in the entire United States."[71]

Jacob and Rose Frauman Luskey, who had married in 1920, lived to celebrate their sixtieth wedding anniversary. Their grandson, Kenneth Luskey, M.D. participated as a major member of the research team (at the University of Texas Southwestern Medical Center at Dallas) headed by Joseph Goldstein, M.D. and Michael S. Brown, M.D., who won the Nobel Prize in medicine in 1985.

Luskey's Western Wear's Jake Luskey, seated, with sons David, left, and Louis. The pioneer store was founded by Jake's father the year Jake was bar mitzvaed.

Courtesy Mike McLean, Dallas Times Herald.

EDWARD R. BYER AND HARRY ROLNICK

Harry Rolnick's family started in Dallas a men's hat manufacturing business that Harry eventually would take to international celebrity.

Harry had grown up in a Jewish neighborhood in Brooklyn, and in the early 1900s his family moved to Dallas and opened a hat renovating shop in 1917. In 1925, Harry observed that tastes in dress hats had begun to change toward narrower, turned-up brims. He took some overstocked homburgs, built new hat blocks, and began experimenting. He found an investor in Nathan Florence, who liked Harry's designs. In 1926 the Florence Hat Company came to life.

When Nathan Florence died in two years, it left Rolnick without capital. Nathan's younger brother, banker Fred Florence, suggested that Edward R. Byer buy the Florence Hat Company.[72]

Ed Byer was born in Des Moines, Iowa, and his wife, Mabel, in Omaha, Nebraska. They came from similar backgrounds, their families having immigrated before the turn of the century, settling in Cleveland, Ohio. Ed had begun his entrepreneurial success with the American Gear Company in Jackson, Michigan. The business grew to twenty-seven stores across the country and, on a visit to his San Francisco store, he met and married Mabel, who was living in California with her sister but previously had met Ed's brother, Carl Byoir (later Byer), who had pioneered in public relations and built one of the country's top public relations corporations.[73]

"He [Byer] and Rolnick complemented each other," said Henri Bromberg, attorney for the Mabel and Ed Byer estate. "Harry Rolnick knew the hat manufacturing process from the bottom up and had a great sense of style and promotion. Byer had none of these but had remarkable foresight and financial ability, and they were a great team. He [Ed] ultimately disposed of most of the people working for Florence, but kept Harry on. Mabel, Ed's wife, had a son Arthur by prior marriage, and he moved to Dallas as an adult and changed his name to Byer."

The company created its first branded line, the Resistol hat, in 1930-31 with one of Harry Rolnick's inventions. Harry hit on the idea of making his hats sweat-proof. He began introducing patented interior leather headbands constructed to allow for expansion — and to "resist" confining contact with the head. The idea was to create a hat that would rest on top of a

Mabel Byer shown in 1974 with President Ephraim Katzir of Israel. Courtesy Ronald Weiss

head with a maximum of cool and comfort. Their next innovation came in 1935 with the excitement of the approaching Texas Centennial when Byer-Rolnick began manufacturing its line of Western hats. At first Western hats accounted for only ten to fifteen percent of their business. Then they decided to go head-to-head against the most famous Western hat company in the world — Stetson in Missouri.

"Mr. Byer realized early that the U.S. would be involved in World War II, and there would be scarcities of materials. He caused Harry Rolnick to buy fur, from which hat bodies are made, tremendous quantities, much to Mr. Rolnick's concern, and also machinery and equipment, with the result that Byer-Rolnick Company was one of the few hat companies in America that could produce men's hats during the war, that could establish accounts with retailers, notably Neiman-Marcus Company with whom they had been able to sell previously."[74]

People who knew Harry Rolnick said he could sell anything. He made a point of calling on Hollywood figures and seeing that both Western and dress-style Resistols appeared on legendary heads. Clark Gable, William Holden, Humphrey Bogart, Alan Ladd, John Wayne, and Henry Ford wore them. Presidents Harry Truman, Dwight D. Eisenhower, Lyndon Johnson, and Ronald Reagan made a point of being seen wearing them.[75]

Byer-Rolnick made another first: the company's main plant in Garland became the first hat finishing plant to establish "straight line" production; the Longview plant was the first fur felting plant ever successfully established outside of the East Coast. In 1965 the company expanded their quality-clothing division and purchased the Weinberg Corporation of Chicago, makers of Oxxford Clothes for men, the premier tailors of men's suits in the country. Every Oxxford suit was hand cut and hand tailored by the largest assemblage of expert tailors under one roof anywhere in the world.

Byer-Rolnick developed a chain division that manufactured hats under private labels for major retail chain-store operations. The Chain Division sold to all three of the major national chains: Sears Roebuck, Montgomery Ward, and J.C. Penney. An investment banking firm estimated that Byer-Rolnick supplied well over half of the middle and more than ninety percent of the hats in the upper price range sold through these merchandisers.[76]

In 1968 clothing manufacturer Koret of California bought Byer-Rolnick. In 1979 Levi Strauss and Company bought Koret. In 1985 Irving Joel from Richmond, Virginia, bought Resistol under the name RHE Inc. His stable of hats included Resistol, Dobbs, Churchill, Adam and London Fog.

Ed Byer left in his will the largest single gift ever made to date to the United Jewish Appeal. In Israel, the Edward and Mabel Byer Absorption Center stood as a living memorial to the oppressed from all over the world who gather in the Center, looking for a hopeful future. Byer Square Activities Center at the Dallas Home for the Jewish Aged included apartments, a library, lounge, cafeteria, and other amenities.

THE FRANKFURT SISTERS

When Elsie Frankfurt, a student of design and mathematics at Southern Methodist University, observed that her older sister's pregnant appearance looked so horrible that "I had to do something," her design inspiration revolutionized maternity clothes for women.[77]

Elsie created a window skirt for her sister Edna by simply cutting out a U in the front of a sheath skirt, so that it fit well over the hips, and did not rise in front. Its success led to the beginning of the Page Boy business.

The sisters' father, Ben Frankfurt, had emigrated from Russia, and their mother, Jennie Bergman, had come from St. Louis. Their father worked at first for his uncle before moving to Cushing, Texas. "Father opened a dry goods store selling material and men's suits," said Louise Frankfurt Gartner, the youngest of the sisters. "He didn't have enough money to fill the shelves, so he put curtains in front of them so they didn't look empty." From there he moved to Dallas and went into the used-car business and bought real estate.

"Edna started a little shop in the Medical Arts Building," Louise remembered. "I was in high school and after school I'd go down and help her. She bought from all local manufacturers, and she would take me with her to decide what to buy. Elsie was in college, and Edna pregnant, and the two came up with this idea of the hole in the skirt with the little boxy jacket. This friend of Elsie's [Miriam Zesmer] took this dress to New York to sell. Best and Company were the first to buy. Then they [Edna and Elsie] opened a factory. First they had dressmakers working, and they would go to dressmakers' homes. Then they opened a small room in the Medical Arts Building with women sewing there. When I graduated from college, I won a scholarship to Traphagen School of Design. Edna had gone to California and opened a shop there, and she kept writing me she needed me out there to help her.

"When I got out of college, I went to California, and we had a workshop out there. I remember Alice Faye — if she liked something, she bought it in various colors. I remember her because her pictures were in all the movie magazines with our dresses on her."[78]

By now the sisters had given their maternity dress manufacturing company a name — Page Boy, a name inspired by the page boy of olden times who heralded the coming of a son and heir. The film colony rushed to their door and included Shirley Temple, Deborah Kerr, Betty Hutton, Mrs. Alan Ladd, Loretta Young, Mrs. Ronald Coleman, Mrs. Hal Roach, Mitzi Green and Margaret Sullivan. The most popularly priced dresses had a price tag of $30, and their couture styles up to $80. In ten years their $500 investment in 1938 had grown to a million-dollar business.[79]

With Edna and her husband Abe Ravkind working the California operation, and Elsie running the Dallas business, Louise did the designing. Their biggest boost came with a style show at the Stork Club in New York. "That really started getting publicity. That was when we got the Lord & Taylor account," Louise said. "They did more maternity clothes business than anyone in the country. Their maternity buyer became one of my dearest friends; she was a fabulous promoter. Then we started getting national publicity."

Elsie Frankfurt, right, became the first woman member of the Young Presidents Organization made up of heads of million dollar corporations under age forty. Sisters Edna Ravkind and Louise Gartner directed production and design for Page Boy, Inc.

A story in *Time* magazine highlighted their one hundred employees in Dallas, Los Angeles, Indianapolis, and San Francisco.[80] *Life* magazine featured the company's unusual yoga breaks. "She [Elsie] believes that it relaxes her employees, helps their morale and gives them new energy that lasts even after they get home at night," *Life* wrote. "It accomplishes in five minutes relaxation what would take several hours," Elsie told a writer.[81] *Life* magazine pictured Louise and Edna standing on their heads, with Elsie looking on.

Louise explained how they had come to use the exercise and postures. "We had been out in Mexico at Rancho La Puerta, when we met Indra Devi, who was opening a place to teach yoga. When she got a permit, we were her first ones she taught. She said she had the dream of a business where they had a yoga break. When we got back to Texas, we had these breaks in the afternoon." By then the Frankfurt sisters manufactured all apparel sold in their shops. "We had wholesale; we had retail," Louise said.

"Go into business with *women*?" Bunny Feldman Mayers said her father, Max Feldman, exclaimed when the sisters offered him a partnership to work with them. He sold them piece goods, and his company, Leighton Manufacturing, laid the first patterns for them. Later he exclaimed, "My God, look what it turned into!"[82]

In 1951 Elsie became the first woman member of the Young Presidents Club, an organization composed of presidents of million-dollar corporations under the age of forty. Elsie was thirty-three. In 1952 she won *Mademoiselle's* Merit Award. By 1958 Page Boy, Inc. had grown to an enterprise worth more than two million dollars with shops all over the country.[83] The sisters worked together for twenty-six years.

THE BADT FAMILY

The Badt family serves as an example of how pioneer Jews living in small country towns retained their Jewish identity. Joseph Moses Badt established a hardware store in 1870 in Tyler and later in Mount Pleasant.

"We stayed away from school on Jewish holidays and closed the store," said Augusta Badt Brin, who in her eighties recalled life in an East Texas town. "But we had no formal training in religion. Young Jewish men selling goods traveled to Mount Pleasant and looked up my father. Dad took them home to have dinner. All the girls married at age eighteen to Jewish men." Because there was no rabbi in Mount Pleasant, Dr. Faber of Tyler came by train to marry couples.[84]

Augusta's father, Joseph, had come to Texas around 1870 at the age of thirteen from Krakow, Poland, through the port of New Orleans. In 1882 he married Augusta Spiro of New Orleans and brought her to Texas.[85] Joseph and Augusta had ten children, four daughters and six boys. "My folks sent all ten to college, though Father couldn't speak English," Augusta recalled.

One of the brothers, Clarence Badt, attended Rice and served as an officer of Linz Brothers for almost fifty years. One brother went to West Point and another to Annapolis. Harry Asher Badt of Texas attained rank of commodore, a flag rank between captain and admiral. "He was one of the few Jewish captains in the United States Navy," Augusta said. He earned public acclaim when, as a decorated commodore, Badt, aboard the *Tuscaloosa* in 1939, ordered his men to rescue 579 German seamen who clung to wreckage of the S.S. *Columbus*, a German battleship scuttled in the Atlantic after being pursued by a British destroyer. U.S. newspapers and later books applauded the Jewish commodore for his act of humanity in saving the lives of Germans at the beginning of Hitler's reign.[86]

Son of a pioneer Mt. Pleasant merchant, Commodore Harry A. Badt, U.S. Navy, rescued hundreds of German sailors at the beginning of World War II in an incredible submarine episode. Photo shows Badt in 1944. *Official U.S. Navy Photo.*

SAM TOUBIN

The New York stores had a big name, but they served small towns and communities in Texas. Sam Toubin, who bought the original New York store in 1923 from Cather and Buster who had founded the firm in 1888, expanded throughout South Texas.

Sam's father, Louis Leon Tabakin, had come to America in the 1890s and survived the 1900 storm in Galveston. He returned to Lithuania to his family, but decided to send his son Sam, born in 1892 in Lithuania, to America when Louis feared Sam would have to serve the Czar's army. The family made arrangements for him to stay with friends of the family living in Des Moines, Iowa. After a year or two of selling hot dogs in Iowa, Sam moved to Austin, Texas, to live with two uncles, Israel and Leopold Cohen, who owned a dry goods store there. Sam worked for Cohen Brothers before moving to New Braunfels, where he sold iron, barrels, and other junk and scrap metal. He then moved to Smithville, Texas, where he opened his first store with his brother Haskell.

"He didn't like Smithville," said his widow, Rosa Toubin. "They were not nice to Jewish people and he felt anti-Semitism." He heard that a store in Brenham was for sale, so he purchased the store and the inventory he needed and began his Brenham operation in partnership for a year or two with his uncles who remained in Austin.[87]

Sam purchased his store in 1923, and in 1925 he married Rosa Levene, a native of Brenham born there in 1897. Her parents, had come to Texas in 1890 through the port of New York from Krasnapoli, Poland, and then married in Brenham. Although the Fink and Toubin families remained visible in Brenham, records show that Jews came to Washington County as early as the early 1860's when B. Levinson and the Alex Simon family arrived and became prominent in the community.[88]

By 1970 Sam Toubin's success with the New York stores could be seen with stores in Brenham, La Grange, Halletsville, El Campo, Port Lavaca, Bellville, Needville, and near Columbus, Texas.

K. WOLENS

Kalman Wolens came to the United States from Poland in 1895. He lived in Chicago before moving to the Lone Star State.

In Texas the family lived in Palestine and later in Corsicana, then an oil boom town. Kalman eventually expanded to sixty-five stores. The late Raymond Holbrook, an editor with the Associated Press, noted, "Almost every little town in Texas had a K. Wolens store. More Texans shopped at K Wolens than at Neiman-Marcus." In 1976 the Chromalloy American Corporation purchased the many K Wolens.[89]

Kalman Wolens' great-grandson, Steve Wolens, in the 1980s became a state representative in the Texas Legislature.

ISAAC A. GOLDSTEIN AND LOUEY MIGEL

Since 1886, Texans in Waco have enjoyed the dry goods brought to them by Isaac Goldstein, a native Texan, and Louey Migel of Russia.

Isaac A. Goldstein was born in Hays County, Texas, near San Marcos, in 1860, the son of Moses and Amanda Goldstein. The 1880 census lists Moses as a "Jewish Rabbi." The family moved to Waco in 1886, and Isaac graduated from Baylor University.[90]

Louey Migel was born in 1859 in Courland, Russia, and came at age thirteen to Galveston, where he remained until 1880, when he moved to Waco. In 1885 he married Rebecca Goldstein,[91] younger sister of Isaac.

The next year Isaac and Louey organized the Goldstein-Migel Company. In 1892 Isaac began publication of the *Gossip*, a weekly society paper, but changed its name the next year to the *Artesia*, which it continued under for the next ten years. Both men participated heavily in Waco civic activities, with Isaac pursuing his interest in the public library, while Louey served his interest in religion.

The Waco Public Library Association first elected Isaac president in 1904, and he served on the board of directors for twenty years. Through his efforts, he interested Andrew Carnegie in Waco's public library, and Carnegie provided the funds — a grant of $30,000 from the Carnegie Foundation — to build the first Waco library. [92]

Louey Migel, pioneer merchant of Waco.

I. WEINER

Born in Lithuania in 1894, I. Weiner came to the United States at age twenty-two. After four years in Brooklyn, he found his way to Houston after a brief detour in Rosenberg. In Houston he peddled ladies silk hosiery, until he found employment in a general store.

In 1925 he opened the first I. Weiner, a small dry goods store. The Great Depression of 1929 hit hard, and in 1932 he was forced into bankruptcy. After he reopened, he voluntarily repaid (over several years) all creditors in full, even though the debts were discharged by the bankruptcy court.

He opened the second I. Weiner store in 1937 and additional stores thereafter. At the time of his death in 1978, he and two of his sons, Leon and Sol, operated sixty-two retail stores in Texas as Weiner's. Leon and Sol continued operation and expansion of the company. In 1988 there were 125 Weiner's stores throughout the Lone Star State and one in Louisiana. They

I. Weiner

extended from South Padre Island to Louisiana, with most stores in the Gulf Coast area.[93]

A pioneer in equal rights during his lifetime, I. Weiner served on a committee to abolish the poll tax in the late 1930s and was one of the first employers of blacks in retail sales positions in Houston.

He served as president of Congregation Beth El, which later became Beth Yeshurun, and organized other Conservative synagogues in Houston, San Antonio, and New Orleans. He was elected a trustee of the Jewish Theological Seminary of America. His numerous awards include the Max H. Nathan Brotherhood Award, and he was honored by the National Conference of Christians and Jews.

I. Weiner left his legacy in the I. Weiner Jewish Secondary School, created in 1983, which provided Jewish students of high school age with both a Jewish and a secular education in a unified environment.

"When I think of I. Weiner," said his son Sol, "I think of his thirst for Jewish education, his love for Israel, and his ardent support of Conservative Judaism."[94]

THE FAIR, INC.

Spindletop launched The Fair in East Texas. The chain grew to twenty-four stores throughout East Texas and along the Gulf Coast, from Beaumont, Port Arthur, Lake Charles, and Orange near the Louisiana border, to Lufkin in the piney woods of East Texas. Fair stores sprang up in Houston, Galveston, Texas City, Baytown, and Conroe, as well as across the border in Shreveport, Alexandria, Lafayette, and Lake Charles, Louisiana.

When Benjamin and Jennie (Ben and Jen) Greenberg lived in Chicago, they admired The Fair department store there. When they moved to Beaumont following the Spindletop oil boom, they copied the name of the Chicago store. Ben started with one store in Beaumont, later expanding to multiple stores in other cities. Ben was the son of Sprincie and Frank Greenberg, who had given their children such old-fashioned names as Ben, Dave, Jake, Annie, Sadie, Rose, Dorothy, and Gertie.

Rose's husband, Maurice Moskowitz, headed the large Fair Store in Port Arthur for forty years (1925-1965).

Ben and Jen's two sons, Sigmund and Sheldon, continued to operate the stores with Albert Klein, husband of their daughter Martha. Years later Ben's and Jen's grandson Jerald Klein served as operations manager.[95]

MARTIN WEISS

Martin Weiss founded one of the first department stores in Beaumont. He, like others, became attracted to the area because of the Spindletop oil field.

He was born in Hungary and immigrated to the United States in 1887, coming to Texas in 1893. He opened his first general store in San Marcos. After he opened his Beaumont store, he formed the Alamo Oil Company in the same town. He later moved to Dallas, then Texas' headquarters for the greatest number of independent oil operators, and became one of the founders of Methodist Hospital where he served on the board of governors. He supported hospital improvements through the Martin and Charlotte Weiss Foundation.

He served on the Dallas Park Board at the time it planned the permanent buildings for the Texas Centennial. Many civic leaders praised him for his work, including John W. Carpenter, Woodall Rogers, and George B. Dealey. In 1931 the City of Dallas dedicated a new park in his honor, the Martin Weiss Park.[96]

SIMON GUGENHEIM

Simon Gugenheim's home in Corpus Christi was eventually moved to a public park/civic center, receiving a state of Texas historic plaque and providing a charming glimpse into the past.

Simon Gugenheim was born in Yorktown, Texas, and at nineteen went to work for A&S Levy Co., a Victoria dry goods store. Two years later he arrived in Corpus Christi, looking for work, with forty dollars in his pockets. He established in 1891, with partner Herman Cohn, the Gugenheim-Cohn dry goods business.

At the turn of the century, Simon and his wife, Lila Belle, built the house on Chaparral which became a historic treasure. The Gugenheims were active in the Jewish community life of Corpus Christi and in its civic affairs. They donated four lots to the YMCA for a new clubhouse. When the YMCA opened, a portrait of Simon was unveiled.[97]

Gugenheim house, Corpus Christi.

BEN GOLD

Ben Gold was a New York native who contributed to the growth of the Dallas fashion industry.

Jewish Texans worked closely with blacks in helping them set up their own businesses, especially the apparel business. Clyde Crockett of Dallas, who is black, told how Ben Gold and he served as liaison between Jewish and black businessmen.

"They have racial pride. They want to pull themselves up by their bootstraps; you gotta give them the bootstraps. I introduced them to the right people, who had patience and talent, like Ben Gold. He shared his information; he ought to be remembered.

"He taught them to crawl before you walk. He taught them how to buy. They grew and grew. Now some have several stores, all over Texas. Ben Gold didn't need the money. I can tell a shyster, a hyper, a con artist, out for his own interest. Then there's the tolerant philanthropist. Ben Gold was not a hustler.

"I traveled with the salesmen, and we did trunk shows. I set up sample rooms. I loved the rag business. I traveled with Jack Goldman." Clyde dropped names like Herman Marcus and lesser-known manufacturers. Now semiretired, he remembered details about his long gone era, recalling suitcases one salesman had with "patches over patches," yet the salesman showed generosity in other ways. Clyde's business travels covered Louisiana, Mississippi, and Tennessee. "I loved Louisiana Jews," he recalled. "Turn your back [and listen] and you couldn't tell if they were white or black. It was a long way from Brooklyn and Queens." Born in Kansas City, Clyde had lived in New York.

"Once when I was traveling with Bernie [Bernard] Kahn, he flew home for Yom Kippur, and I was driving the van alone with the sample racks. I was going from Jackson, Mississippi, to Memphis, Tennessee, and the town of Grenada was between. Dr. Martin Luther King was having a march and rally in that town, and the Ku Klux Klan came out on the opposite side of the street. Damn! I didn't know it. But I made it, and set up a sample room in the Peabody Hotel in Memphis. This was around 1968."[98]

Tremont Street, Galveston, 1881. Sign on building at right says: Isaac Bernstein & Co., Manufacturers of Clothing and Dealers in Gent's Furnishing Goods.

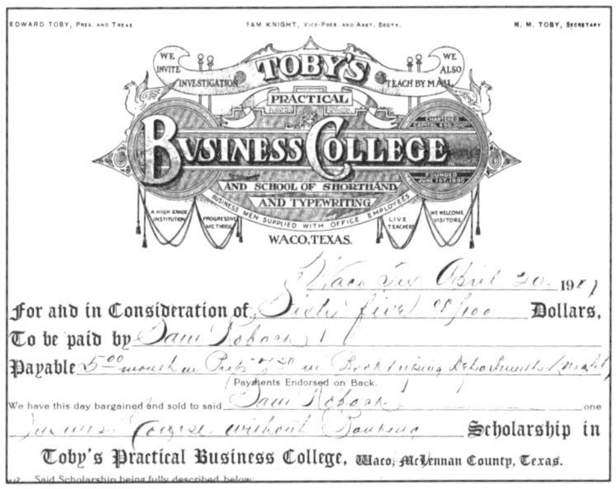

EDWARD TOBY, PRES. AND TREAS. SAM KNIGHT, VICE-PRES. AND ASST. SECTY. N. M. TOBY, SECRETARY

WE INVITE INVESTIGATION — TOBY'S — WE ALSO TEACH BY MAIL

PRACTICAL BUSINESS COLLEGE AND SCHOOL OF SHORTHAND AND TYPEWRITING

BUSINESS MEN SUPPLIED WITH OFFICE EMPLOYEES

A HIGH GRADE INSTITUTION — PROGRESSIVE METHODS — LIVE TEACHERS — WE WELCOME VISITORS

WACO, TEXAS.

Waco Tex April 20 1907

For and in Consideration of Sixty five 00/100 Dollars,

To be paid by Sam Roback

Payable 5.00 month ...

Payments Endorsed on Back.

We have this day bargained and sold to said Sam Roback one ... Course without ... Scholarship in

Toby's Practical Business College, Waco, McLennan County, Texas.

Said Scholarship being fully described below:

Newly immigrated in 1907, Sam Roback paid five dollars a month to attend business college in Waco, where he worked as a laborer unloading bales of cotton. Later he settled in Dallas, where he became a very successful businessman.

License to foot peddle, 1882.
Courtesy American Jewish Archives.

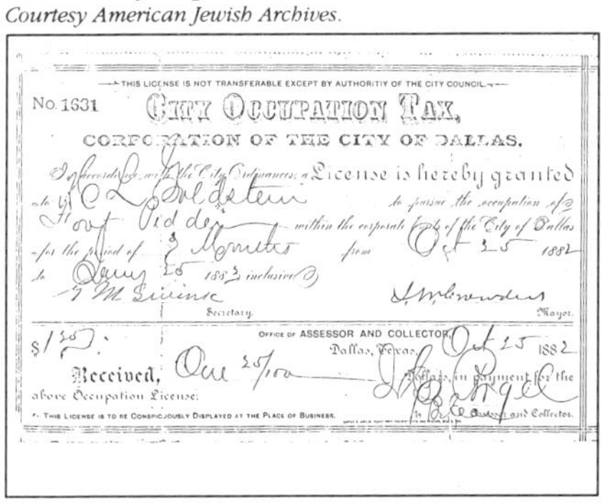

THIS LICENSE IS NOT TRANSFERABLE EXCEPT BY AUTHORITIY OF THE CITY COUNCIL.

No. 1631 CITY OCCUPATION TAX,

CORPORATION OF THE CITY OF DALLAS.

In accordance with the City Ordinances, a License is hereby granted to ... to pursue the occupation of Foot Pedler within the corporate limits of the City of Dallas for the period of 3 Months from Oct 25 1882 to Jany 25 1883 inclusive.

Secretary. Mayor.

$1.25 OFFICE OF ASSESSOR AND COLLECTOR, Dallas, Texas, Oct 25 1882

Received, One 25/100 Dollars, in payment for the above Occupation License.

THIS LICENSE IS TO BE CONSPICUOUSLY DISPLAYED AT THE PLACE OF BUSINESS. Assessor and Collector.

Jennie Wolfe Blumenthal held by her grandfather Mattathias Garonzik. At right is Harry Garonzik. Dallas, circa 1903.
Courtesy Jennie Blumenthal.

Joe Ablon, center, who migrated to Texas from Krasnapole, Poland, in 1882, became one of the founders of Dallas' orthodox synagogue Tiferet Israel. The Joe and Anna Ablon family, 1908, appear on the gallery of their home at 212 Caroline. Left to right: son-in-law Louis Barzune, baby grandson Benjamin Barzune (later an M.D.), daughter Fannie Ablon Barzune, daughter Mary Ablon, and son Esir Ablon. *Copyright © Ben M. Ablon*

Ben Ablon delivery wagon. © Ben M. Ablon

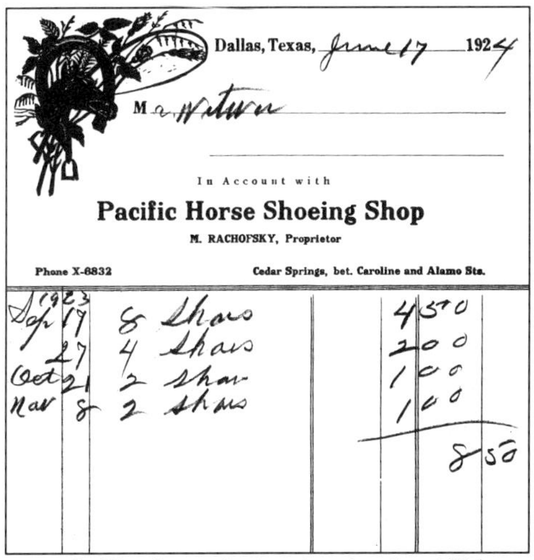

Dallas, Texas, June 17 1924

M r. Watson

In Account with

Pacific Horse Shoeing Shop

M. RACHOFSKY, Proprietor

Phone X-6832 Cedar Springs, bet. Caroline and Alamo Sts.

1923 Sep 17	8 Shoes	4	50
27	4 Shoes	2	00
Oct 21	2 Shoes	1	00
Nov 8	2 Shoes	1	00
		8	50

M. Rachofsky's horse shoeing shop invoice, 1924.

Ablon family and friends in South Dallas.

Store in Dublin, 1914. W.H. Novit and his brother-in-law Morris Hoffman, who became Mayor of Dublin.

In the Jewish teachings, love in the home outweighs prayer in a temple. Above: Steven and Hannah Hoffman Ornish (1894-1964).

Louis Ornish store at 1812 Elm at St. Paul, Dallas, circa 1918. The building eventually was incorporated into Volk Bros.

During the pogroms at the turn of the century, brothers Louis and Abe Ornish, top row, fled Odessa on the Black Sea in Russia, hid under hay in a wagon to cross the border, and sailed from Bremen, Germany. Sisters included Becky Wilensky, Fagie Kimmell and Dorothy Barnett, all deceased.

After Wolf Novit came to Texas in 1907 through Galveston, he peddled with a banana wagon for four years, before moving up to a grocery and then clothing store. Courtesy Stella and Morris Novit.

Grandmother Baile Harelik with her grandchildren. Hamilton, Texas, 1924.

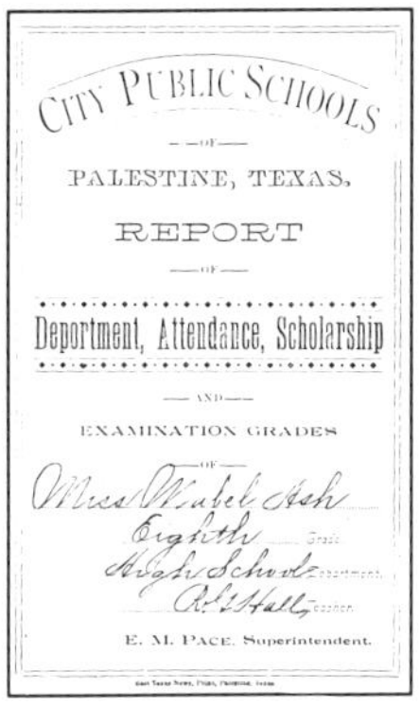
City Public Schools
of
Palestine, Texas.
Report
of
Deportment, Attendance, Scholarship
and
Examination Grades
of
Miss Mabel Ash
Eighth Grade
High School Department
R. L. Hall Teacher
E. M. Pace, Superintendent.

Chapter 11

The Educators

The Paul Reveres of Education

The best charity, suggested Maimonides, a twelfth-century Jewish philosopher and major theologian of Judaism, is to help a fellowman to educate himself to become self-supporting. Centuries later, Jewish Texans who lived by this principle laid the foundations for Texas educational systems and imbued their descendants, who continued to pioneer in education, with this belief. Their contributions ranged from donations to educational institutions, individual talents in teaching and research, to global politics; they also changed Texas.

EMANUEL M. TILLMAN

Born in 1841, Emanuel M. Tillman, after receiving his master's and doctorate from the University of Heidelberg, came

to Natchez, Mississippi. Here he became known as a scholar and was appointed assistant state geologist. In 1871 he came to Texas and started a wholesale grocery business with Moses Ullman.

Dr. Tillman became an ardent worker for the intellectual advancement of early Dallas, was a founder of Congregation Emanu-El, and was elected to the Dallas City Council November 15, 1879. He was reelected in 1880 and 1882, and in April 1883 he was elected mayor pro tem under Mayor W.L. Cabell.[1]

HYAM SCHWARZ AND THE STRAUSS DESCENDANTS

When Hyam Schwarz arrived in Hempstead, Texas, at age fifty-one, he had already established himself as a renowned Hebrew scholar and rabbi in Poland and Germany. He immigrated to the United States at the urging of his sons to live in voluntary retirement.[2] When he arrived in 1875, his sons and a brother had lived in Texas a number of years.

Actually, Rabbi Schwarz picked up the threads of his life and transferred them to Texas, where he continued a legacy in education established by his father, a tradition the rabbi would leave to generations of his descendants.

Hyam (a.k.a. Chaim, Heinrich, Henry, Herman) Schwarz had been born in Kempen, Prussia (located in southwestern Poland), in 1824, the oldest son of a great Hebrew scholar and Talmudist from whom he received his early training in Hebrew. He pursued his secular studies at the Catholic seminary in Posen where he graduated. He then worked as a private tutor to earn the money to continue his studies at the University of Berlin, where he earned his Ph.D.

At the age of twenty-five he married one of his pupils and began his family, eventually having eleven children, seven sons and four daughters. He began his life's work in education as he filled several rabbinical positions, contributed regularly to the *Hamagid*, a Hebrew paper, and wrote for several other publications. He published several Talmudic tracts and a book of songs in German for the use of his congregation.[3]

By the time that Hyam Schwarz decided to take "early retirement," he had established an international reputation as a writer on the Jewish religion. "Rabbi Schwarz was one of the widely known and venerated exponents of the Jewish faith, in both this and the old country. He was master of the Latin, Greek, German, French, and Spanish languages. He was a prolific writer on all subjects pertaining to Jewish religion and kindred topics for the American and German press, and was also author of several books. . . . From his nineteenth to his thirtieth year, he was professor at colleges in Germany."[4]

It was from this background that he arrived in Texas, where he would plant the Jewish tradition of education that his descendants continued. When he arrived in Hempstead, his younger brother Sam already had established himself as one of the leading

Although many early Jewish pioneers married non-Jewish women, the son of the learned Rabbi H. Schwarz of Hempstead, Texas, went back to Breslau, Germany, to select his bride, a rabbi's daughter. She was Selma Weinbaum and her father is the tall man next to her. Rabbi Schwarz is the little man with the white hair standing next to the groom, Leo Schwarz, around 1881.

merchants. Hyam settled into Hempstead and picked up the life he had left in Europe.

When the first Jewish temple in North Texas, Temple Emanu-El of Dallas, was dedicated May 28, 1876, Rabbi H. Schwarz officiated at its impressive dedicatory services with the temple's first minister, Rabbi Aaron Suhler, who had arrived when the congregation was founded the previous autumn (1875).

Rabbi Schwarz pursued his literary works and Talmudical writings. A journalist visiting Texas in 1878 called him "the learned Rev. Schwarz." He established himself as "one of the most learned men in Jewish literature within the United States."[5] His home became the center for religious services that drew travelers and residents from across central Texas. A resident in 1891

A descendant of Rabbi H. Schwarz and the mother of Robert Strauss, Edith Schwarz Strauss is shown as a child with her sister, Flora, and also as an adult.

Both photos courtesy Flora's granddaughter, © Ms. Sydney J. Levine, Los Angeles.

Robert Strauss

described the ambience in his home.

"Every Pesach [Passover] his well kept house is thrown wide open to all Jehudim living here. This custom he has kept up ever since he came to Texas. The ritual used by Rabbi Schwarz is the most impressive, the old style, which reminds one of the happy days of childhood and of the parental roof."[6]

Rabbi Schwarz's impact still lives in Texas. Out of Hyam Schwarz's family came descendants Robert Strauss, former head of the National Democratic Party and U.S. Trade Ambassador, and Ted Strauss, a Texas financier. Annette Strauss, Ted's wife, became the first Jewish person, and the first woman, to be elected mayor of Dallas.[7]

Robert S. Strauss first came into national prominence when he took over the chairmanship of the Democractic National Committee, a position he served in from 1973 to 1976. He had been born in Lockhart, south of Austin, and reared in Stamford. He graduated from the University of Texas at Austin, and though he became a prominent attorney, he made his impact felt through his work in national and global politics. After his success in establishing the Trade Act of 1979, he served as a representative to the Middle East Peace Negotiations.

Mayor Strauss' husband, Ted, and his brother, Robert Strauss, are great-grandsons of Rabbi Schwarz.[8] Other members of the family continued the Jewish tradition of reverence for education.

Rabbi Schwarz's great-nephew, Lawrence Gale, (grandson of the rabbi's brother Sam), Gale's wife, and son established in the 1970s the Gale Professorship in

The sweetest part of Jewish tradition is the celebration of family occasions around the table, with young and old in attendance. Young Lawrence Gale, right, on the occasion of his grandfather Sam Schwarz's 70th birthday in 1910. Gale became a prominent Beaumont businessman and patron of Texas education. Photo © by Edwin Gale.

Judaic Studies, later upgraded to the Gale Chair at the University of Texas at Austin. "We established," said Lawrence Gale's son, Edwin, "a Professorship in Small Business and Entrepreneurship in the College of Business at U.T. Austin, and these were made into Chairs at the time of my mother's death by additonal contributions. I later established a Regents Professorship in Business in honor of my wife, Rebecca, and the Regents matched this with a professorship in geography. My mother endowed two professorships at UTMB [University of Texas Medical Branch] - Galveston. One professorship is in psychiatry and one is in internal medicine. Both are named for my mother, Marie Gale."[9]

That the Gale educational endowments did not become media events and that few Texans know of the Gales' belief in education as the traditional Jewish philosophy offers an insight into the Jewish pioneer families. Ruth Kahn, for more than eighty years an observer of pioneer Jewish Texans, said, "Jewish people have not been flamboyant in their giving." Among the many Jewish families Ruth Kahn cited as making major contributions in a quiet way was the Lawrence Pollock family who founded the Pollock Paper Company and in the 1960s gave money to the Meadows School of the Arts at Southern Methodist University.[10]

So quietly did Edmund J. Kahn give that the Dallas Public Library, which he gave, had no file on him and no reference librarian had heard of him.

EDMUND J. AND LOUISE W. KAHN

The unassuming nature of Jewish giving to education to improve the human condition is told by Professor Luís Martín of Southern Methodist University who became in 1973 the original holder of the Edmund J. and Louise W. Kahn Chair in History.

Edmund J. Kahn (1904-1984) gave $13 million for a new Dallas Public Library, named for his friend Erik Jonsson.

Photo copyright © by Andy Hanson.

Professor Martín, a native of Seville, Spain, had been teaching in the SMU history department since 1968 and, as part of his work, taught an adult education class through SMU's School of Continuing Education. Martín remembered Edmund Kahn as just another face in class when Edmund asked the professor to go to lunch. As they talked about the University and liberal arts, Edmund told Martín that he and his wife wanted to do something for SMU. "We've been thinking about endowing a Chair," Martín remembered Edmund saying. "How much do you think that would cost us?"

Martín replied, breaking the news as quietly as possible, "Well, that's a lot of money."

"He said, 'How much?' and I said, 'Well, a half a million, ideally a million dollars.' "

"That's about what we thought," Edmund replied.

"I dropped my knife, my fork," Martín said. "I couldn't believe it."[11]

Possibly Professor Martín had no way of knowing the history of the Kahn family or of their philosophy of education in Maimonides' tradition of helping people to help themselves through jobs. Certainly the professor's definition of history suits that philosophy. Martín taught that "the study of history is the study of how to be human. All of us are born at a particular time and place and these elements condition the kinds of persons we become."[12]

Edmund's father, Jacob, had come to Dallas from New York when A.L. Wolf & Company of New York, whom Jacob represented buying and selling cotton, opened a branch in Dallas. Edmund went into business with his father, eventually took office as president of the Dallas Cotton Exchange, and then became an independent oil producer. For many years he served as chairman of the Dallas City Planning Commission. Kahn led the committee that created the Dallas County Community College District in 1965.[13]

"He was the conscience of the junior college system in getting it done right," said former Mayor Erik Jonsson, who worked with Kahn on large civic projects. "He was one who helped select sites for the community colleges and made sure they were suitable." He also was on the site selection committee for the Dallas City Hall.

Kahn gave $13 million for a new Dallas Public Library, which was named for his friend Erik Jonsson. Kahn assured through contributions and advice that it would be a library of the future, Jonsson said.

In 1976 Kahn and his wife, Louise, donated more than $1 million to Kahn's alma mater, the University of Pennsylvania, and $1 million to Louise's alma mater, Smith College in Northampton, Massachusetts. They contributed to the Dallas Museum of Art. Because of Louise's love for music, they donated funds for the Louise W. and Edmund J. Kahn Music Library and Archives Room in the Morton H. Meyerson Symphony Center. Besides giving to education and fine arts, they gave to medicine. Kahn served as an orginal trustee of Presbyterian Hospital of Dallas.

When Kahn died in 1984 at age eighty, his family requested memorials be sent to the Dallas Public Library or SMU. Hal Williams, dean of Dedman College at SMU, said, "He was just a wonderful man with a wonderful commitment to education. He was among a handful of extraordinary people I've known."

"He was a simple man, in the best sense of the word, as well as a humble man," said Mayor Jonsson. A columnist reflected, "He was also an extremely moral man in an oftimes amoral society."

On December 10, 1987, Louise donated a gift in seven figures to help build the Edmund J. Kahn Job Training Center, contained in the Bill J. Priest Job Training Complex, according to announcement by the Dallas County Community College District.

Louise explained, "The reason for picking out the job training center as something I cared to do stemmed from my knowledge of his [Edmund's] interest in helping people who could not do what they might be able to do. In the sense of helping people, he had a great interest in education."[14]

ISADORE LOVENBERG

Jews traditionally have given their time to build educational systems in their communities, and one of Texas' earliest, Isadore Lovenberg, joined the Galveston Board of School Trustees more than a hundred years ago and served on this Galveston school board more than thirty years.

Born in Paris, France, in 1844, he came to the United States at age fourteen and settled in Alabama, then moved to New Orleans, before coming to Galveston in 1867.

In 1875 he married Jennie Samuels, half-sister of Mollie Cohen, wife of Rabbi Henry Cohen.[15] Lovenberg was one of the organizers of Congregation B'nai Israel and served as its vice-president many years. He served as president of the Hebrew Benevolent Society for fourteen years.

Jennie also came from an educated family. A year after she married, a relative of hers, Meyer Cohen, enrolled in Texas A&M University in 1876, the year it opened its doors to become Texas' first publicly supported institution of higher education.[16]

Lovenberg was an original member of the board of directors of The Rosenberg Library, a treasure of the historic island city. He served as president of the Board of Managers of the Galveston Orphans Home for twenty-one years, as well as a trustee of the Osterman Widow's and Orphan's Fund, and on the board of the Lasker Home for Homeless Children. Lovenberg also served as president of the District Grand Lodge of B'nai B'rith.

Isadore and Jennie Lovenberg were remembered decades later as unusual dressers. Isadore often wore a top hat as he visited fellow Galvestonians along the Strand. Jennie wore big, black taffeta hoop skirts long after they had declined in fashion.[17]

Lovenberg owned an insurance business, and at

Isadore Lovenberg, for whom Lovenberg Junior High School was named, stands second from left. Other members of the Galveston School Board of 1893 are (standing) Geo. Doherty, Superintendent Oscar C. Cooper, Mayor Roger L. Fulton, County Judge S.S. Hanscom, and (seated) T.J. Ballinger, Forster Rose, R.B. Hawley, H.M. Trueheart, and Henry A. Landes.

the time of his death he served as president of both the Galveston Board of Underwriters and the Board of School Trustees. The last thirteen years of his life he acted as president of the school board and even in the last week of his life in October 1917 he presided.[18]

Fourteen years after his death the school board decided to name a new school (at Thirty-ninth and Seawall Boulevard) the Lovenberg Junior High School in appreciation of his thirty years of service. In appreciation of the gesture, his widow gave $50,000 to the board to set up a pension fund for teachers. At that time Texas law prohibited either collecting or spending tax money for pensions; the Texas legislature enacted a new law to make the Lovenberg gift feasible, which had long-term benefits for Texas teachers.[19]

OLGA B. KOHLBERG

Olga Bernstein Kohlberg arrived in El Paso to forever alter the educational systems in Texas. As Mrs. Charles A. Goetting said of Olga Kohlberg years later, when the El Paso Historical Society bestowed upon Mrs. Kohlberg the Hall of Honor Award, "There are phases of city building when the work of courageous, well-educated women overshadows that of their husbands, fathers, brothers."[20] Olga Kohlberg proved to be such a person.

In 1884 Olga, bride of Ernst Kohlberg, businessman in El Paso since 1875, arrived from the green Rhineland country of Germany to the barren village of El Paso, population 761. She stepped off the train into a territory in which the first train had made its way to town only three years before. Olga, a university student, had been reared in the finest traditions of European culture and gracious living.

To visualize the environment in which Olga found herself, it is necessary to read the letters written by her husband, Ernst Kohlberg, and published by the University of Texas Press, El Paso. Though Ernst established the first cigar factory in the Southwest, helped found the El Paso Electric Railway Company, and owned a hotel, he made his place in history through his letters home to Germany. They became the basis for the fictional character of Ludwig Sterner in *The Wonderful Country* by Tom Lea.

Olga Bernstein Kohlberg of El Paso started Texas' first free public kindergarten and brought civilizing influences to early West Texas.

In 1875, when the eighteen-year-old Ernst arrived in El Paso, it was known as Franklin, while Juarez, Mexico, had the name of Paso del Norte. Ernst had left Westphalia, Germany, to escape the draft and agreed to work without salary for Solomon Schutz, an early Jewish settler in Franklin, in exchange for partial payment of his passage.[21]

Ernst arrived in Franklin in a stagecoach drawn by four mules, and the sight of the adobe village made him write of Franklin as being "nearly the end of the world and the last creation." Later, he wrote, "If I had known what I know now I would not have come here." With good reason. The area had acquired a reputation as the Texas Bad Lands, and writer George Sessions Perry described it as "where Texas travels farthest West and then dies of thirst. . . . It is said of this country, that everything either stings, sticks, or stinks."

That description could have served as Ernst's opinion of enchiladas. "Enchiladas," he wrote to his family, "are thin slabs of dough that have been fried and covered with red chili on both sides. At first, chili and everything connected with it was a hellish kind of food for me, but one becomes accustomed to anything and now I can swallow it like a Mexican, and I miss it if it is not served."[22]

Olga lost no time in seeking companions with whom she could share a semblance of what she had

The mixture of Texas and Mexican cultures in El Paso is reflected in the clothing worn by Ernst Kohlberg, who came to Texas in 1875.

Courtesy Institute of Texan Cultures.

left in Germany. She helped start a "study circle" with friends. In 1889 they decided to advance and promote the idea and interest in education for very young children. The women bought equipment, employed a teacher from St. Louis, Missouri, and brought her to El Paso. Following their successful effort, they offered to donate their materials and teacher to the El Paso schools if its Board of Education would make the kindergarten part of the public school system. In 1892 El Paso became the first city in Texas to have a free public kindergarten.[23]

That same year Olga happened onto a sick man left to die on the platform of their town depot. She led a group of women under the name of The Ladies' Benevolent Association and opened the town's first hospital. As the women's group, with whom Olga worked, changed its name numerous times, Olga focused on her mission to civilize West Texas. When Mary I. Stanton started the first free public library in El Paso, Olga's group ran and financed it until it became tax-supported. Then she served on the first board and as president for more than a quarter of a century, helping to build the library into one of excellence.

One of her unique projects carried the name of the Cloudcroft Baby Sanitorium. Babies, dying from the intense heat of El Paso, were taken on a small mountain-climbing train to the cool pines of Cloudcroft, New Mexico. Olga's son-in-law served as the physician-director. Olga died in 1935.

For more than fifty years Olga Kohlberg worked, shaped, and molded the harsh Texas environment.

In Dallas, Temple Emanu-El also took a lead in early education, offering boys and girls of all faiths day school at the Temple. At the time the first temple was built in 1876, school facilities in Texas were meager, so the congregation hired a competent corps of teachers and organized its own school system, which became one of the best in the city.[24]

Olga and Ernst Kohlberg, right, and their children.

LEONORA DE LYON HARBY RANDALL

Leonora Harby is best remembered because in 1862 she organized and taught the first Jewish Sunday School in Texas.[25]

She was born January 24, 1824, in Savannah.

She was a Hebrew scholar from a well-known Jewish family in Georgia. Her father was Levi S. De Lyon, judge of the County Court of Chatham County, which includes Savannah. One of her brothers had graduated from Yale University at age sixteen, and another had graduated from West Point.

When the beautiful Leonora was only eighteen she eloped to marry a man best described as a warrior, Levi Charles Harby (1793-1870) of a prominent American family, a bachelor age forty-nine. They had three children.

Zacharias Emmich was the first formally ordained rabbi of Houston's Congregation Beth Israel, first temple in Texas, organized in 1854. He is shown around 1862, the year Leonora Harby started the first Jewish Sunday school in Texas.

Harby, of Georgetown, South Carolina, as a teenager had joined the United States Navy as a midshipman. During the War of 1812 he was captured and spent eighteen months imprisoned in England. He resigned his U.S. commission when the war for Texas independence broke out and served in the Texas Navy. Later he fought in the Mexican War. He also fought in Tripoli and Bolivia.

Leonora and Captain Harby arrived in Texas in 1859. Leonora helped organize the Ladies Hebrew Benevolent Society of Galveston. She pioneered a Sunday School for Temple B'nai Israel in 1862.

When the Civil War began Harby joined the Confederate Navy. He served as captain of the port of Galveston when, on New Year's day 1863, the steamboat *Neptune*, clad with bales of cotton, rammed into the USS *Harriet Lane*, an important Confederate victory known as The Battle of Galveston. He was age seventy at the time, having served more than fifty years as a naval officer. Later he commanded a fleet of gunboats on the Sabine River.[26]

Captain Harby died December 3, 1870. Leonora had his tombstone inscribed, "And with my last breath on the threshhold of death, I proclaim my faith in Israel's God."

In 1879, at age 55 Leonora married a prominent physician of Galveston, Dr. Edward Randall. When she died November 2, 1888 in Galveston, lengthy newspaper editorials memorialized her.

Melanie (Mella) Weil (1876-1971) continued in Galveston decades later the teaching started by Leonora Harby.

Courtesy Esther M. and Harry Rosenthal.

JACOB JOSEPH TAUBENHAUS

Dr. Jacob Joseph Taubenhaus, one of the great plant pathologists in the twentieth century, came to Texas A&M in 1914 with his father's blessing and sense of mission. His father was the foremost writer of Galilee and Samaria who wrote for all the renowned Hebrew newspapers of Palestine and Europe. By no accident did Jacob feel an affinity for plant life and the soil. He subsequently identified a plant disease that before 1920 had cost farmers in the United States more than $10 million a year.[27]

Here are the genealogical roots from which emanated the great scientist Jacob J. Taubenhaus, who made some of the most significant strides ever taken in the control of plant diseases.

Meir Taubenhaus, Jacob's father, had been born in Jerusalem, the fourth generation of Rabbi Meir'l Promishlan. Meir studied under the best teachers of the Cheder, Talmud-Torah, and in the High Theological College of Jerusalem. Before the age of seventeen his family proposed a match to a girl of Safed. For more than seven days he rode a mule, saddled highly, in the Arabian style, without bridle or halter, until he reached the high hills of Safed. In 1881 he married the girl, Bat-Sheba, his same age and from a family of great rabbis, one who descended from David, King of Israel, and a minister of Poland elected King of Poland for one day.[28]

As a young couple, Jacob's parents settled in the arid northern Palestinian town of Safed where they raised five sons and four daughters. Meir devoted himself to his family and to educating members of his community in practical and spiritual matters. With his own money, he purchased tools and equipment for tradesmen and distributed them without charge to shoemakers, carpenters, tailors and, using himself as their example, ordered knitting machines for his own house. He and his wife opened a small cottage industry, knitting sweaters, veils, stockings, as he continued to work with other tradesmen, teaching them to work. On his door he tacked a sign that read, "Hate Idle and Love Work."

The writer I. Karniel best described Meir's daily life, and the one that shaped Jacob.

"His house was open to scholars of every class, his living room was furnished with a big library, containing old and new literature, and on his table the *Berliner Tageblatt* was to be found.

"When passing by his store, I used to see Mr. Meir leaning over his books, his pen serving at the same time two purposes: marking his accounts, and corresponding to the Hebrew papers different articles. Between internals of one customer to another, he translated into Hebrew hygiene books which were written by the best German physicians.

"In his store I often met great scholars, as the late David Schub — the founder of Rosh Pinah, and Walkomitch the Chief of Education Department at the Upper Galilee, and teachers of the colonies who found it their duty to visit Mr. Meir, for short intercourse, and regular discussions as between scholars of religion.

"He endeavoured to educate his sons to the love of nature and kind feelings to the animal, vegetable and mineral kingdoms —this love of nature it seems was inherited by his three elder sons."[29]

Rabbi Meir sent these three sons (Jacob and two brothers) to study in Europe and the United States when he found that Palestine could not offer the teachers or intellectual pursuits to which his sons aspired. The youngest of the three, Moshe, became a specialist in poultry and fowl diseases and eventually settled in New York to work in the American Museum of New York.[30]

Haim, two and a half years younger than Jacob, after finishing school in Israel, headed for Constantinople to study law and finally made his way to Breslau University in Germany to study geology. He graduated *cum laude* with a doctorate in philosophy, and founded a Hebrew library. With further work, he became the first paleontologist and geologist of the Yishub and opened a new area of study for Jews in Palestine. He eventually moved to England and taught in a London Hebrew School before becoming teacher and headmaster of the Hebrew school at Belfast, Ireland.[31]

Jacob had gone to the Agricultural School in Israel before journeying to the United States to complete his studies at the National Farm School at Doylestown, Pennsylvania. After he graduated in 1903, he entered Cornell University and graduated with bachelor and master degrees in science, specializing in plant pathology and physiology. He left for the University of Pennsylvania and graduated in 1913 with a doctor of philosophy degree.

By 1916 Jacob had become chief of the Division of Plant Pathology and Physiology at Texas Agricultural Experiment Station. His work focused on identifying root-rot diseases, particulatly cotton root-rot which had been especially destructive to an agricultural society in his new homeland. After years of laboratory and field research, he found that a fungus that lived in the roots of cotton and other wild plants caused the disease. It spread more rapidly in wet years but could be controlled and destroyed by plowing adjacent fields, since the fungus could not live in the sun's rays. Dr. Taubenhaus applied his research to the diseases of other plants: sweet potatoes, onions, melons, and tomatoes.

Jacob J. Taubenhaus, eminent scientist who researched in College Station from 1916 to 1937.

Courtesy Texas A&M University.

He wrote and published more than one hundred articles and four books explaining and describing his research. He developed such a reputation that in 1926, when he served as the principal speaker and guest of honor at the banquet to honor the National Farm School, one thousand guests paid $1,000 each to attend. He died in 1937 in College Station.[32] On his death a *Dallas Morning News* editorial noted, "His discovery of the cause of root rot in cotton and the means by which it can be successfully overcome . . . constituted an epoch in cotton production."

HYMAN J. ETTLINGER

Hyman J. Ettlinger, a former All-American football player with a Ph.D. from Harvard, took so seriously Russia's lead over the U.S. in science even before Russian scientists launched the first true space traveler, a satellite called *Sputnick I*, on October 4, 1957, he traveled all over recruiting young students for science, earning the name "The Paul Revere of Education."[33]

Hyman, born September 1, 1889, in St. Louis, later had a four-year scholarship to Washington University there, but graduated in three years. A Phi Beta Kappa, he attended the University of Chicago and then Harvard, where he earned a doctorate in mathematics.

In 1913 he moved to the University of Texas at Austin, where he met married a Texan. The Board of Regents appointed him UT director of athletics for two years, and he arranged the only gridiron game between Harvard and UT.

In 1925 Dr. Ettlinger coauthored a calculus textbook which Professor Pierpont of Yale University predicted would "mark a new era in math because it surpassed previous calculus books by showing the student the foundation upon which the subject is built, rather than plunging him immediately into a maze of mathematical vagaries." Dr. Ettlinger's articles on mathematics appeared in scholarly journals in countries throughout the world, including Japan, Great Britain, and Poland.[34]

Right: Hyman Ettlinger, All-American football player, math professor, author, and lecturer, shown with his distinguished colleague, professor Robert Lee Moore.

Courtesy Hyman Ettlinger. © by Natalie Ornish.

He served a triple role at the university — math, sports, and human relations. "Many times," he told students, "difficult as problems in a laboratory are, they are not nearly so complicated or important as learning to deal with the everyday problems of human beings."[35]

His sense of fair play and his devotion to students brought him into conflict with Huey P. Long, governor of Louisiana. In 1931 Hyman agreed to referee a game between the Arkansas Razorbacks and the LSU (Louisiana State University) Tigers at the Louisiana State Fair. After the kickoff, a squatty man left the stands and began leading LSU fans in yells. He passed out dollar bills to band members and shouted encouragement to the LSU football players.

Dr. Ettlinger, refereeing in the position as head linesman, stopped the game and walked over to the man, who turned out to be Huey Long. Hyman, who stood more than six feet tall, looked down at the Kingfish and told him to take his seat. Governor Long stood silent in front of Dr. Ettlinger, who then pointed his finger to an empty seat and said, "Governor, I mean it!" Huey Long took his seat, and the two men became friends for the remainder of Long's life.[36]

Hyman spent thirty-seven years officiating. "Sports give me an entree into a community," he said. "Who's going to listen to some mossback Ph.D. on a stage if he hasn't done something to interest young people in the first place?" But the youth of Texas did listen. He reached approximately 40,000 students around 1955 with his call to young Texans to interest them in careers in math and science. He traveled to more than thirty cities in Texas with the message that America and the free world must recruit the scientific manpower essential to our way of life or forfeit technological supremacy to the communist nations.

"There is greater evidence than ever before that Russia and China hope for victory over the free world by outrunning us in time in trained scientific manpower," he said in 1955. He based this on a world tour he had made. He noted that the communist countries, by dictating courses of study for their young people, were building up a strong manpower potential, and that China was benefitting from the return of U.S. trained technicians to the Bamboo Curtain. He was a prophet, as only two years later the Russians launched *Sputnick*.

When the National Conference of Christians and Jews honored Ettlinger in 1953, columnist Lynn Landrum wrote, "You could hold several such dinners and not overdo the honors due. Or, if you want to swing away over into another area of his eminence, you could recall the long years in which his giant frame has dominated the gridiron as a football official. He is so fair, and so big, that it just doesn't seem natural to question his decisions." Landrum called him "a scholar who for forty years has been an outstanding servant of the University of Texas."[37]

In presenting the award, Nobel Prize physicist Dr. Arthur H. Compton, then chancellor of Washington University, called the honoree "a brilliant mathematician, a great humanitarian, and a valiant champion of fair play and team work."

When Dr. Ettlinger semi-retired in 1962, he had served as chairman of the department of pure mathematics for more than twenty-five years and had taught in Texas for forty-nine. The University appointed him Professor Emeritus, and he served more than sixty years on the faculty.[38]

DANIEL STERNBERG

Daniel Sternberg — conductor, composer, pianist — came to build one of the most respected music schools in Texas.

Daniel's flight from death had come in September 1938 with the dreaded middle-of-the-night knock on the door in Vienna. Hitler's henchmen ordered Daniel to Gestapo headquarters in the morning, and when he left, he never expected to see his wife or parents again. Instead, after hours of interrogation, he received a stay of forty-eight hours to get out of the country rather than being sent immediately to a concentration camp. For two days he frantically tried to get out of Austria. With a few hours left, he learned that Memel, Lithuania, still accepted German passports. From there he and his wife went to Latvia. But the quota to the U.S. remained full for a year, and the Sternbergs escaped a few hours before the border closed. They arrived in New York on one of the last passenger boats to cross the Atlantic during the war.

To his dismay Daniel, age 26, found that a glut of musical giants, such as Igor Stravinsky, Sergei Rachmaninoff, Arnold Schoenberg, and Bela Bartok, had passed through Ellis Island before him and now filled the important music posts. Daniel and his wife boarded a bus, stopping in Virginia, North Carolina, Georgia, and New Orleans before finding themselves in Dallas. He talked to John Rosenfield, arts critic for the *Dallas Morning News*, who put Daniel in touch with the Hockaday School, a private girls school, where in the fall of 1940, he began directing opera productions and teaching piano.

After a year in Dallas, Daniel began making inquiries, sending his resume and recommendations from conductor Fritz Stiedry and pianist Arthur Schnabel. Roxy Grove, chairman of the School of Music and Fine Arts at Baylor University in Waco read Daniel's letters and knew that Schnabel seldom gave recommendations. She took young Sternberg to Pat Neff, president of Baylor, where the two, in some ways, symbolized a meeting of two worlds: a Jewish musician from the great Central European tradition in education who had led the Leningrad Philharmonic and survived Nazism and Stalinism, and a seventy-year-old son of Reconstruction-era Texas who had earned his place in Texas history as a Klan-fighting, Prohibition-preaching, strike-breaking governor in the 1920's.

Within a few months Grove decided to return to teaching, a position she preferred over administering, and Neff turned the department over to Daniel. A Baptist university embraced a European Jew and gave him the materials to create. He remained loyal to

Baylor and Waco for the remainder of his professional life.

He gave to Waco what he had intended to teach in Europe. He wife, Felicitas, a dancer, served as his dramatic director and set designer for Baylor opera productions. Daniel translated Italian, German, French and Russian librettos, and together they produced operas for more than twenty-four years. Daniel began Baylor's orchestral program in 1944. In 1962 he founded the Waco Symphony.

"There is a certain vigor," he said, "a certain zest, a certain desire to accomplish in this still very young country. This is a country that has reached its frontier physically but not spiritually."[39]

Daniel Sternberg, music educator, Waco.

PAUL AND LEAH ALPER LEWIS

Paul Lewis determined to act as a builder and educator of this country's spirituality.

Lewis, born in Lodz, Poland, December 20, 1900, lived in Berlin, Germany, as a teenager and immigrated to America in his twenties.

Leah Alper was born in Seltz, Russian Poland, December 25, 1907. Her family immigrated to New York, where she attended college, as few women did in those days. In 1922 Paul came to New York where he met and married Leah. By the time Hitler came to power, he was 39 and had been in the United States for seventeen years.

In 1943 they decided to join Leah's uncle, James Alper, a merchant who owned general stores and a hotel in Marfa, a West Texas town with a large air force base during World War II. Lewis opened his own general stores in Presidio and Marfa. Lewis conducted religious services for transient Jews and servicemen. His home in Marfa served as the synagogue.

After seven years in West Texas, they moved to Dallas, where Lewis became a prominent builder. They left West Texas so their children could get a Jewish education and marry within the faith. Paul and Leah suffered the loss of a son, attorney Morton Lewis, who died August 19, 1966, at age thirty-three, of a rare blood disease at the peak of his career. Years later, they suffered again from the sudden death of Morton's son, Scott Lewis, handsome and affectionate, who died at age twenty-seven from a rare heart ailment. Scott was also the grandson of Udys and Ben A. Lipshy, because Morton had married Barbara Lipshy.

In Dallas, Lewis became interested in martyrology.

One of the many memorials throughout the U.S., in memory of the six million Jews, donated by Paul and Leah Lewis.

Bas relief commissioned by Paul and Leah Lewis.

He had lost a brother and a sister and the sister's seven children in concentration camps, and he wanted to teach a lesson in history by keeping alive the memory of the six million Jews who died during the Holocaust and also the righteous Christians who saved Jews from the Nazis.

Paul and Leah Lewis. Photo © by Dean Ornish.

"History is written from a distance," his daughter, Mimi Barnett, said, "but he was impatient. He did not want to wait for someone else to memorialize these people killed in his own generation. Many people didn't want to admit that we permitted this to happen."

Lewis worked with the Jewish Theological Seminary. He gave funds so new prayer books for Passover, which had not been changed for generations, could be rewritten to include the martyrs of the twentieth century. He and Leah erected large marble monuments in synagogues throughout the United States. These memorials, financed with their own funds, were erected in Dallas, San Antonio, Brooklyn, Washington, Houston, Chicago, Memphis, Long Beach, Denver, and other cities across the United States. The Jewish Theological Seminary awarded Leah and Paul Lewis the Louis Marshall Medal for a lifetime of service.

"Those lost were illustrious people," Lewis said. "The dead are ours, but the loss is to all mankind. If we forget, nobody is safe. Only if we remember can we prevent it from happening again."[40]

JACOB AND SARA BEREN FELDMAN

Jacob Feldman was born in Sevastopol, Russia, on August 24, 1906.

He received the B.S. degree from Southern Methodist University in Dallas. Jacob served as president of Commercial Metals, Inc., since 1930. In 1934 he married Sara Beren and they had three sons, Daniel, Moses, and Robert.

When Israel received its independence, he helped restore the city of Jerusalem. He also gave a park in the Arab section.

Jacob, in memory of his parents, donated the Moses and Annie Feldman Educational Wing of Congregation Shearith Israel, Dallas. He also was active in educational institutions nationally and internationally, including SMU, the Jewish Theological Seminary, and American Friends of Hebrew University.[41]

Jake and Sara Feldman Photo © by Natalie Ornish.

HYMAN JUDAH SCHACHTEL

Hyman Judah Schachtel, an emigrant from London, England, devoted his life to interfaith relations and delivered the inaugural prayer for Lyndon Baines Johnson, thirty-sixth president of the United States.

He was born May 24, 1907, in London, where he lived until he was seven years old. Schachtel received a bachelor's degree from the University of Cincinnati and was ordained at Hebrew Union College, Cincinnati, in 1931.

While serving a Manhattan congregation for twelve years, he wrote extensively and spoke on the "Message of Israel" radio program.

"I became," said Rabbi Schachtel, "a physician of souls. It is the greatest privilege a man can have."[42] He began his mission of combating hate as a young rabbi in New York. Among his friends he counted composer Richard Rodgers. One evening he went to a special performance of Verdi's *La Traviata* with Dick and Dorothy Rodgers. At one point Rodgers turned to the rabbi and said, "Rab, if I could have composed that opera, I would throw away all the junk I have written." Rabbi Schachtel replied, "Your music has a special eloquence that's very spiritual. You never write better than when you're dealing with your song 'You've Gotta Be Taught to Hate.'"[43]

On Richard Rodgers' advice and his observation that no one would notice him in New York, Rabbi Schachtel accepted the call to Houston. In 1943 he became chief rabbi of the oldest established Jewish

Dr. Henry Barnston, rabbi of Beth Israel for nearly half a century.

At right, Dr. Schachtel, 1954, and Dr. Maurice Eisendrath, then president of the Union of American Hebrew Congregations who spoke at Beth Israel's Centennial. Founded in 1854, it was the first Jewish congregation in Texas.

Martin Zielonka, ordained at Hebrew Union College in 1899, served Temple Mt. Sinai, El Paso, for 38 years. Courtesy El Paso Public Library.

house of worship in Texas, Beth Israel, founded in 1854. He followed Dr. Henry Barnston, a great intellect at Beth Israel since 1900. He soon became a builder of bridges between peoples and faiths.

In 1949 he began a series of book-review lectures that had impact on the entire Houston community. His weekly radio program "The Humanitarian Hour" reached a wide audience. In 1953 he began a weekly *Houston Post* column, "Enjoyment of Life." While reaching out to the general community he continued to serve as pastor to his flock at Beth Israel, with hospital calls, study groups on family relations, and Bible institutes.

He taught philosophy at the University of Houston from 1950 to 1955, and he also lectured on theology, history, and philosophy at St. Mary's Catholic Seminary, Houston.

"He loves to teach," observed his wife, Dr. Barbara Levin Schachtel, "and he is a fine orator, but the most important part is the pastoral part. He goes to hospitals to call on people. He writes books and is a learned man, but the key is going to the people, not just remain in academia.

"He loves playing the piano. Once, at Hebrew Union College in Cincinnati, he showed Gershwin around the campus. When they got to a room with a piano, Gershwin played 'Someone to Watch Over Me.'

"On his radio programs, he included interpersonal relationships, marriage, bereavement, holy days, retirement."

Although Dr. Hyman Schachtel reached his eightieth birthday in 1987, he continued to actively build bridges between Jews and members of other faiths with a weekly column, Sunday morning radio program, and teaching at his temple and churches.

"He is an intellectual and a marvelous preacher, but mainly he is a lover of people," said Barbara.

He wrote five books: *The Life You Want to Live, The Real Enjoyment of Living, The Shadowed Valley, Aspects of Jewish Homiletics*, and *How to Meet the Challenge of Life and Death*.

Dr. Schachtel's educational mission climaxed when he was invited by a president of the United States to deliver the inaugural prayer, reaching a whole nation. On January 20, 1965, Rabbi Schachtel prayed before a national television audience, "We ask for no miracles beyond the miracle [of] . . . the power of love to transform foes into friends, slaves into free men, the curse of war and poverty into the benediction of concord and plenty."

One of Schachtel's latest projects was working on a national team to encourage judges to sentence first offenders guilty of non-violent crimes to time spent working for charity organizations and to encourage them to learn skills and repay victims.

At left, the president of the Kallah of Texas Rabbis, Abraham Brachman, is shown with leaders of the Dallas Jewish community, Julius Schepps, Judge Irving Goldberg, Sam Bloom, and Louis Tobian, during the dedication in 1957 of Temple Emanu-El. Decades later Ruth (Mrs. Milton P.) Levy, Sr., gave the Levy Building for educational and fellowship purposes.

The historic synagogue in Jefferson, Texas, founded in 1872. Other early temples: Brownsville 1870, Dallas 1872, Calvert 1873, San Antonio 1874, Austin 1876, Waco 1879, Victoria 1880, Gainesville 1882, Tyler 1882, Marshall 1884, and Texarkana 1888.

Fort Worth's Ahavoth Sholom, 1906, described then as one of the most handsome Orthodox synagogues in Texas.

Rabbi Raphael Gold and Shearith Israel confirmation class, Dallas, 1939.

Nineteenth Century opera singer.

Chapter 12

THE ARTISTS

Vanguards in the Arts

While the Texas frontier meant opportunity to the peddler, trader, land dealer, and merchant, many of the musicians, writers, and painters saw it as a form of banishment.

ISABELLA OFFENBACH

Isabella Offenbach was born in Cologne, Germany, March 11, 1817. She was the daughter of the rabbi of Cologne and was the talented older sister of Offenbach, the famous composer. She toured Europe with young Jakob (Jacques) and another brother Julius. Isabella Offenbach was an important European opera singer, and royalty competed for her hand. At age twenty- seven she met a pioneer Texan, Samuel Maas, and that was the turning point of her life.

Maas, then thirty-four, while in Europe for his import-export business, attended an opera performance in a cathedral and heard Isabella singing. After an exciting courtship, he won her hand and her father's approval, and in the spring of 1844 they married in Cologne, after which Isabella left the salons of Europe for the saloons of early Texas.

Isabella had a violent attack of yellow fever eight days after she and Samuel arrived in Galveston on their wedding trip. "Out of a population of about 2,500, already 200 have died," Maas wrote in a letter to his cousin Henri Hart of Charleston, South Carolina, on August 13, 1844. "Things here leave you cold or filled with disgust when in comparison with Europe."

In the Republic of Texas, Isabella dedicated herself to bringing music to the pioneer Texans. She continued her singing, mostly among family and friends, and appeared in occasional operatic concerts for charity. Isabella and Samuel arranged for opera to be performed in a growing Galveston and Sam wrote reviews of music events for the early newspapers. They made Texans aware of the fine arts and encouraged citizens to participate in them. Sam kept a journal (1835-1850) in which he revealed how he needed the arts and loved music "with a grand passion."

Isabella and Sam had four children.[1] But life was not easy on the island. After a violent hurricane, the water rose to the keys of the family's grand piano.

The Maas house at 18th and Sealy housed a small stage, where Isabella performed.[2] But Isabella lived a profoundly unhappy life and in her later years kept her own house diagonally across the street from Samuel's, according to Harry Levy, Jr., great-grandson of Samuel and Isabella.[3] She kept active to the end and served as vice president of the German Ladies Benevolent Society. At her death she left sixteen grandchildren. She died February 19, 1891.[4]

ADAH ISAACS MENKEN

Adah Isaacs Menken (1835-1868), who died at age 33.

Adah Isaacs Menken, an actress, dealt with frontier reality by creating a fantasy life. In Texas she became known as the Naked Lady from Nacogdoches,[5] and her significance hinges on her having helped emancipate the American theater from its European heritage when, "in an age of hoop skirts and pantalettes, she offered the female figure unadorned."[6] Adah appeared on the New York stage in a flesh-colored body stocking in 1860, when she played the role of Mazeppa.

Life hadn't always been so exciting for Adah. Most research points to her birth in Memphis, Tennessee, on June 15, 1835. Her maiden name was probably Adah Bertha Theodore. Her father died when she was two, and her mother then married a man by the name of Josephs, who moved the family to New Orleans and later to Nacogdoches. Some historians state Adah attended Nacogdoches University and met Alexander Isaacs Menken, a member of a traveling opera troupe, when he came through Nacogdoches. Others state they met in Galveston. After a whirlwind courtship Adah married Menken in Livingston, Texas, on April 3, 1856, according to historian Llerena Friend.[7]

Adah enjoyed leaving a trail of mystery about herself. A biographer wrote, "Both the name and nationality of her mysterious parents were soon to change as often as, with far less reason than, the style of her hat."[8]

Adah began to write poetry. She and Menken lived with his parents in Cincinnati, Ohio, where she met Isaac Mayer Wise and began to contribute regularly to the *Israelite,* an important Jewish publication edited by him. Some writers state he was her teacher. She wrote for the *Israelite* from 1857 to 1859. In her poems and essays, Adah showed a devotion to the Jewish past and the Jewish people. She showed a knowledge of Hebrew and of the bible.

Menken made possible Adah's stage debut in New Orleans, followed by her success in New York. Though she divorced Menken and subsequently married three more times, she retained his name as her stage name. Adah became one of the most popular actresses of her time.

She appeared in New Orleans, then Havana, and back to Texas, where she played in several theaters. She toured the country in her famous role of Mazeppa. When she appeared on the London stage, the *Court Journal* of London said, "Menken is the fashion of the Metropolis. She is the most talked of actress in London, and in society, at the clubs, in the streets, the name of Menken reigns supreme."[9]

After London she played the Gaiete Theatre in Paris, appearing in *Les Pirages de la Savanna,* which became a hit and ran for one hundred nights. She appeared in Vienna but with less success. Among her friends she counted such celebrities as Walt Whitman, Charles Dickens, and Alexandre Dumas. Writers called her the most photographed woman of her time.

In June 1868 she died after collapsing on stage while rehearsing in Paris. Her collection of poems, titled *Infelicia,* was published the year of her death. She was buried in Cemeterie Pere la Chaise in Paris, but a friend had her remains moved to Montparnasse. In her book *Infelicia,* which means unhappiness, Adah spoke of the person she kept hidden from the world.

Adah Isaacs Menken, extraordinary actress and poet.

Poster of Menken's appearance at Theatre Royal.

Autograph on her book.

THE OPERA HOUSES

Actors and entertainment troupes moved across Texas, appearing in theatres many called opera houses. One of the earliest of these was the Simon Opera House.

Alexander Simon was born in Poland December 11, 1825 and came to Texas, where he settled in Houston. He married Julia Levy, daughter of Lewis Levy, early Houston land merchant whose brother fought in the battles for Texas independence. In 1863 Simon went to Brenham, where he owned and operated the Simon Grand Opera House above his general store. It was described as "the prettiest and best conducted small theatre in Texas, and many really great artists appeared there each season, among them Adelaide Prince."[10]

Alex and his wife Julia had thirteen children, and one of them, Rosa, married Sam Rubenstein whose sister, Adelaide Rubenstein Prince, starred in theatrical circles. Adelaide's descendant, Harold Prince, became a Broadway theatre and film director.

When the days of vaudeville waned, the Simon family converted the opera house for motion picture use in 1926. A newspaper reported, "The opening

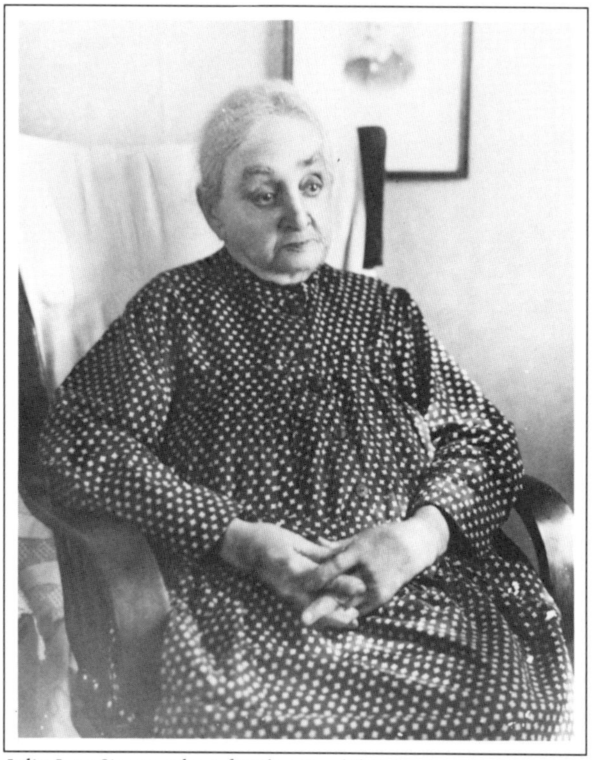

Julia Levy Simon, whose family owned the old opera house in Brenham. Portrait was taken in 1930 on her 90th birthday. She was niece of Dr. A.M. Levy. Courtesy Rosanne Leeson.

photo-play was *The Merry Widow.*"

After Alex Simon died October 4, 1906, his widow Julia continued to operate the opera house. Julia lived to be ninety-one (born in Philadelphia on July 2, 1840; died in Brenham February 25, 1931.) She was joined in the business by sons Alex Jr. and James H. Simon. Three generations of Simons ran their opera house.[11]

The Brin Opera House came into existence in much the same way that other art forms found a home in Texas: a Jewish merchant saw an opportunity to attract potential customers. Philip Brin, a Polish Jew who immigrated to the United States in 1868, and his brother Harris came to Terrell in 1873 and made their living as peddlers throughout Kaufman County. The brothers prospered and soon established a store in Terrell. Brin Street in Terrell was named for Harris Brin.

In 1895 Philip Brin built the Brin Opera House, a structure with the ground floor housing the Brin Store and the upper floor housing the Opera House. The Opera House featured a plaster dome with cherubs, highlighted with chandeliers in the dome on the third floor.[12]

Here audiences saw such luminaries as Lillian Russell and Eddie Foy, Jr. and — while on one of his campaign swings through Texas — William Jennings Bryan delivered a speech there. Local theater groups and amateurs, among them Colonel E.H.R. (Ned) Green, who owned the Texas Midland Railroad and whose mother bore the unflattering tag "Witch of Wall Street," regularly used the Opera House to stage plays.

Many opera houses during this time burned, and that fear caused Philip Brin to close his in 1903. The building was remodeled in 1922 and converted to offices, while maintaining many of the original features. Over sixty years later, after the opera house was sold, it was restored again, and on April 27, 1985, U.S. Congressman Ralph Hall delivered the dedicatory address.[13]

Former Harris Brin home on Brin Avenue, Terrell, Texas.

A new sign for the old Brin Opera House, Terrell.

Ad in old Galveston City and Business Directory.

E. G. SHIELDS. F. S. MENDENHALL.

Levy Opera House,

SHIELDS & MENDENHALL,
Lessees and Managers.

Capacity, 800; Stage, 36x50 Feet. Lighted by Electricity.

ALBERT CULBERSON, Stage Carpenter.

HILLSBORO, - TEXAS.

ANNA HERTZBERG

Born in New York, Anna Hertzberg, a talented pianist, studied at the New York Conservatory of Music. After she graduated, she married Eli Hertzberg, a jeweler, and they set off for Texas, arriving in San Antonio in 1882.

In 1901 she organized the Tuesday Musical Club with seven charter members. The club sponsored performances by nationally known artists and developed an audience for fine music in the San Antonio area. Under her direction and leadership, the club established a scholarship fund to aid talented students in their studies at the New York Conservatory of Music. The Tuesday Musical Club continued at this writing, almost ninety years later, and had its own building.

Hertzberg also became a founder of the San Antonio Woman's Club which started San Antonio's first public library. She was president of the Texas Federation of Women's Clubs (1911-13), working for laws to protect married women's property rights. But Anna's most lasting legacy is the fact that she organized and served as president of an association which launched the first San Antonio Symphony Orchestra.[14]

Before World War I, Anna Hertzberg founded and served as President of the original San Antonio Symphony Orchestra.

Courtesy of Judge Walter Loughridge & Institute of Texan Cultures.

PAULINE AND MAX REITER

Hertzberg's original San Antonio Symphony Orchestra had its last conductor in 1919. Two decades later Jews took a leadership role in re-establishing a symphony in San Antonio.

Max Reiter was born in 1905 in Trieste. As a musician, he conducted in Berlin, Munich, Milan, and Rome. Yet, when the Fascists came to power, he had to flee the anti-Semitism of his home in Italy. In January of 1939 he arrived in New York, where the Steinway piano family advised him to go to Texas.

He stopped in Waco and at Baylor University founded the Waco Symphony Orchestra (which he conducted for ten years.) The Novich sisters in Waco helped Reiter organize it.

A few months later Reiter met San Antonio wholesale produce executive Nat Goldsmith, who decided to give Reiter financial assistance. Goldsmith also introduced Reiter to his ex-wife, Pauline Washer Goldsmith, an extraordinary force who soon founded the Symphony Society of San Antonio. Reiter conducted both orchestras from San Antonio. Pauline married Reiter seven years later and remained the Society's chief fund raiser until her death, seeing the San Antonio Symphony become one of the top ten orchestras in the country.[15]

Reiter died in San Antonio, December 13, 1950.

Joseph Finger

History best remembers Joseph Finger as the architect who designed Houston's City Hall and the Harris County Courthouse. In 1937 the Houston City Council strongly disagreed with Finger over his proposed ultra-modern plan for a new city hall. The mayor favored Spanish-Renaissance style.

Finger countered, "Here in America we are rapidly developing our own type of architecture, which is far above that of foreign countries." He won the contract, and the Houston City Hall won architectural awards. His art deco designs included the James M. West, Sr. ranch home in Clear Lake valued at $600,000 in 1929, Battelstein's, and the Texas State Hotel. Joseph Finger died in 1953.[16]

JOSEPH FINGER

As Texas began to embrace the arts, a young architect added another dimension. Joseph Finger became one of the first architects in Houston to design in the Moderne manner.

Joseph, born in 1887 in Austria, received his training at the Royal Institute of Technology in Vienna. He immigrated to the United States in 1905, and in 1908 with ten dollars and a canceled railway ticket in his pocket, he came to Houston. He worked for fifty dollars a month with a firm of architects, and later he formed his own business. He worked most often alone, but at various times associated with other Houston architects, including Lewis Sterling Green, James Ruskin Bailey, and Lamar Q. Cato. The Plaza Apartment Hotel became one of the larger projects of his early period, and after its success he turned to the Moderne styles popular throughout the country in the late 1920s and 1930s. Finger's most notably successful interpretation of the Zigzag Moderne is found in the Houston Turn-Verein Clubhouse built in 1929 and now listed in the National Register of Historic Places.

Left, Gus Levene in1955, with his closest friend Joe Lilley (who wrote "Don't Fence Me In"), at Paramount Studios.

GERSHUN (GUS) LEVENE

As merchants brought the arts to Texas cities to promote business, the children of Jewish merchants manifested the arts most profound effects. They became artists.

As a small boy, Gershun Levene spent all his first savings to buy himself a banjo because he was too small to play a guitar.[17] His family lived in Dallas, where for two years he attended Southern Methodist University, majoring in music. He played guitar, violin, and viola. He became chief arranger for the pit orchestra at the Palace Theater in days of vaudeville, and he played in the WFAA radio station orchestra. Levene composed for string quartets performing in Dallas.

But his greatest Texas triumph came on September 4, 1932, when the Dallas Symphony Orchestra performed his "Ballet Suite Exodus" before a capacity crowd. Gershun had written this symphony at eighteen and was only age twenty-one at its world premiere. In his review, *Dallas Morning News* arts critic John Rosenfield said that the symphony established Levene "as one of the most promising musical intelligences discovered hereabouts. There is no doubt that his suite. . . attracted and pleased the audience. . .The audience signified its approval with loud applause, and members of the orchestra, to whom Gershun is Gus, pushed him forward to take four bows."[18]

The next year he married, and Gus and his wife, Julia, went to New York, where he studied music while working as an arranger and guitarist for Andre Kostelanetz and Ray Bloch. In the late 1930s, he joined CBS radio. He decided to try Hollywood.

Gus and his family remained in Hollywood, where his creativity flourished. He became arranger for Metro-Goldwyn-Mayer, Twentieth-Century Fox, Paramount, and every other major motion-picture studio, according to his widow Julia. He arranged all the music for the motion picture *The King and I* with Yul Brynner. At the time of his death, he was working as arranger and recording consultant for Dean Martin. Gus died in 1979 at the peak of his career.

Gershun (Gus) Levene © *Julia Levene.*

Summer Symphony Series Ends

Premiere of Levene Work, Concerto Played by Frank Renard and 300-Voice Choir, Heard Sunday Night.

Personalities of last "Bowl" Concert: Frank Renard, piano soloist; David Guion, Dallas composer who was represented by three works; Gershun Levene, Dallas composer, whose "Ballet Suite: Exodus" had its world premiere; Alexander Keese, conductor of the finale program of the season.

BY JOHN ROSENFIELD JR.

The Bowl concerts ended Sunday night in a downpour just as they began ten weeks ago. For the second successive Sunday the stadium was abandoned and the Fair Park Auditorium used instead. And when you recall how hard it was raining between 7:30 and 8:30 you will understand the amazement of the Bowl managers to find the lower floor of the hall filled even to extra chairs. The official attendance count was 2,211. What other show in Dallas did as well?

Premiere of Levene Work.

The first performance anywhere of Gershun Levene's "Ballet Suite: Exodus" was hardly of secondary importance. In discussing this work it is difficult to dissociate the composition from the Levene saga. We are naturally disposed to like "Exodus" when we remember that the composer is a 21-year-old Dallasite who escaped the parental grocery store by teaching himself to play the banjo, escaped jazz bands by tutoring himself on the viola, and is about to hoist himself out of the back chair in the orchestra by allowing the late Nicholas Rimsky-Korsakov to teach him orchestration through the medium of a monumental monograph on the subject. Young Mr. Levene dove into the work and came out eighteen months ago a full-fledged composer. He then wrote "Exodus," not to astound the world, but to exercise his newly-won knowledge. He entered the composition in the NBC Composers' Contest and was not surprised when it bounced back without reaching the finals. He worked on it again, this time in the light of some recently heard Wagner, and then asked Mr. Keese to play it.

We offer this story, not in extenuation of "Exodus" but to explain its strength and its weakness. Young and provincial, Mr. Levene conceives the Scriptures as Hollywood's Mr. De Mille did "The Ten Commandments." In the second book of the Bible, the composer, himself a Jew, found little of racial frustration, social oppression, steadfast faith or spiritual profundity. He saw, instead, vivid drama and sensuous Oriental pageantry. The third movement, obviously set down in duty, employs (perhaps anachronistically) a Hebrew chant which sounds its thanks in a curious clarinet-oboe duet. This is, by long odds, the most fumbling, groping idea of the score and is made to sound worse by the extraordinary brilliance of the second and fourth movements that surround it.

The second is a depiction of the Red Sea Crossing, for which Mr. Levene introduces a gallop of winning melody and infectious rhythm. Equally good is the last movement, a bacchanale representing the worship of the Golden Calf. For this there is another apt, brightly inventive tune which is treated, like the second movement, to full, richly-colored development throughout the orchestra. The first movement, telling of the Egyptian bondage, is, perhaps, too literal in its efforts to follow a scenario.

Composer Wins Respect.

In retrospect the second and fourth movements establish Mr. Levene as one of the most promising musical intelligences discovered hereabouts. There is no doubt that his suite, during these movements, attracted and pleased the audience beyond merely sympathetic interest. Mr. Levene manifestly has the flair. His head teems with musical ideas and if he uses somebody else's idioms to express them, he does so with a sure instinct for what is right and proper. His suite may be a little sketchy but certainly it is neither crude nor gauche. This maiden effort was not at all hard to hear and Mr. Levene deserves the encouragement, nay, the explicit commission of our orchestras for further evocation of his gifts.

Following the presentation, the audience signified its approval with loud applause and members of the orchestra, to whom Gershun is Gus, pushed him forward to take four bows.

Gus Levene symphony reviewed by John Rosenfield, 1932.

Right, Levene with singer Dean Martin, left, at a recording session at ABC-TV.

© Julia Levene

FANIA KRUGER

Fania Feldman was born March 8, 1893, in Sevastopol, the Crimea, Russia, and attended the gymnasium, a preparatory school. She became involved in revolutionary politics to oppose the brutality Jews experienced there.

"I remember," Fania told an Austin reporter, "my father telling me, 'Fania, you don't look Jewish. Walk away straight and slow and go home. They will not suspect you.' And I remember him hiding behind the counter — so straight and clean. I remember when he came home, his well-kept beard was dirty and bloody. I would often awake at night drenched with icy perspiration to imagine that Cossacks stood above me ready to kill me."[19] Her poetry arose from these experiences.

In 1906, while in high school, she became a partisan and worked underground. "My parents," she said, "realized the danger of my being sent to Siberia or being put to death," she recalled. In 1908 her family left for America and arrived in Fort Worth.

In 1912 Fania married Sam Kruger, and they moved to Wichita Falls. Sam Kruger was a founder of what became Zale Jewelry.

A daughter, Bert Kruger Smith, remembered when her mother began to write poetry. "The clicking of the typewriter down the hall was often the first sound I heard in the morning. Tiptoeing to my parents' room, I stood in the doorway, a chubby five-year-old, staring at my mother, who was bent over a sheet of paper. The braids around her head moved slightly with the rhythm of her typing. I patted my own Dutch bob and listened as Mother mouthed the words to the poem she was composing.

"Those are my early memories — not nursery rhymes, not fairy stories — but poems, deep with meaning, serious, portraying sad events in the far-off world of Russia, from which she had come. I ingested the rhymes with my breakfast cereal. Mother was able, to my wonder, to create, out of her head, a whole world on paper, to make people see sights far away, to make them feel emotions they might never have considered. In the small, dusty north Texas town of Wichita Falls, she was a celebrity. Her poetry made her special.

"I too wanted to write. And I began as soon as I could put down words. By the age of nine, I had completed a book of poems. Mother was my mentor throughout my writing years. She and my father read every word of *A Teaspoon of Honey* [a novel based on their lives] and advised me about it.

"While she was encouraging me, she was moving on in her own career, winning national awards, having stories and articles published in *Southwest Review*, *Redbook*, and other magazines, and authoring three books of poetry."

In 1946 the American Poetry Society named her poem, "Passover Eve," the best poem of the year. The next year the Society gave her "Blessing the New Moon" the Lola Ridge award, and she became the first Texan to win this national award. The *Saturday Review of Literature* reviewed her most famous work, *The Tenth Jew*, and described her poems as "simple, eloquent, and rich in the poetric tradition of the Jew."

Another reviewer felt, "There is fear here, and terror, yet the predominant feeling I receive from the poems is admiration for a people whose inner life burned with a zeal for God, even in the worst of times."[20]

After her husband died in 1952, Fania attended Brandeis University for a year before moving down to Austin, where her children lived. She died July 16, 1977.[21]

Texas poet Fania Kruger.

FRANCES SANGER MOSSIKER

Frances Mossiker's family history in the arts started two generations before her birth. Her grandfather, Alexander Sanger, one of the founders of Sanger Bros., was an active civic leader. Her parents were Elihu and Evelyn (Beekman) Sanger. By the time Frances was born April 9, 1906, her family knew few hardships. This privileged little girl, whose parents' prairie mansion stood on the site where the Dallas City Hall was built decades later, seemed an unlikely candidate to be a celebrated author.

Writer A.C. Greene in his eulogy for Frances at her funeral in 1985 told one of his favorite stories she had shared with him. It described her at age ten, arriving for a dance recital in a park in a chauffeur-driven limousine.

Miss Fanny grew up speaking three languages — English, German, and French. In the summers she visited her mother's relatives near Strasbourg, France. At one point she tried to join the circus as a dancer, but the circus owner knew her grandfather Alex. She attended the Hockaday School, a Dallas private girls' school, and Forest Avenue High School before enrolling in Smith College in Northampton, Massachusetts.

While attending Smith, she did manage to slip away to New York where she secretly met her love, Frank Beaston, an actor she had met when his Broadway cast was introduced during tea at Smith. After they eloped, she transferred to Barnard, where she graduated Phi Beta Kappa in 1927 and then did graduate work at the Sorbonne, University of Paris. She then moved to Detroit and Hollywood with her husband. The marriage floundered and they divorced.

Frances returned to Dallas around 1929 where, with the encouragement of Stanley Marcus, a childhood friend, she began reviewing books for WFAA radio. She then had her own radio program in Fort Worth and discussed books, arts, and current events. Then she met Jacob Mossiker, who owned a retail shoe and bag company. They married in 1934. They had no children. Frances returned to travel, bridge, and reading. "I was sort of asleep. I can't tell you what I did all day. I just frittered away the time," she remembered. That life ended when in her early fifties she experienced a major trauma — a radical mastectomy. She escaped into writing books.

She went to France to research in archives there the mysterious disappearance of Marie Antoinette's million-dollar diamond necklace. The result was the non-fiction mystery, *The Queen's Necklace*, published in 1961. The *New York Times Book Review* called her first work "a narrative as exciting as a novel, swift-moving, suspenseful, hardly to be put down; yet more important than any novel, a turning point in history explored in depth." In 1961 *The Queen's Necklace* won the Carr P. Collins award of the Texas Institute of Letters — the first for a woman and for a book not about the Southwest.

Frances Sanger Mossiker, prize-winning author.
Le Roux portrait, courtesy Institute of Texan Cultures.

She followed with *Napoleon and Josephine: The Biography of a Marriage*, a 1964 Literary Guild selection; *The Affair of the Poisons* (1969) on the loves of Louis XIV; *More than a Queen: The Story of Josephine Bonaparte* (1971); *Pocahontas: The Life and Legend* (1976); and *Madame de Sevigne: A Life and Letters* (1984).

Frances Sanger Mossiker received an honorary doctorate in 1972 from Southern Methodist University. She donated her papers to the Harry Ransom Research Center at the University of Texas at Austin, Boston University, and Smith College. She died on May 12, 1985 of a heart ailment.[22]

LEON A. HARRIS, SR. AND JR.

When Leon Harris, Sr., died, arts critic John Rosenfield wrote in the *Dallas Morning News*, "The late Leon Harris was of vast importance to the things that pass for art, music, and drama in Dallas. . . . He was so sound and secure in his good taste that he felt free to enjoy what should be enjoyed whether it wore the local or imported label. . . .A fine standard of Dallas taste was formulated in the Harris drawing room on Lakeside Drive. . . . His presence at exhibitions and concerts was the cue the thing might be good. His absence — when he was not out of town — meant the contrary; although he was the last man in town to realize that by staying away he was damning the event."[23]

Leon Harris, Jr., grew up in this deparment-store family, as the grandson of one of the merchant princes, A. Harris. Leon played in the family store or traveled on buying trips with his father and his mother, Lucille Herzfeld Harris. Leon Senior died when his son and namesake was only eight years old.

The younger Leon became a talented writer. His books included *The Fine Art of Political Wit* (1964), *Only to God* (1967), *Upton Sinclair (1975)*; and his well researched *Merchant Princes: An Intimate History of Jewish Families Who Built Great Department Stores* (1979). Leon Harris contributed articles to numerous magazines, including *Town and Country*. He was made a DeGolyer Fellow of Southern Methodist University.[24]

LEAH COHEN HARBY

Leah Cohen Harby, one of Texas' earliest women journalists, was the daughter-in-law of Levi Harby, early American naval officer and captain of the port of Galveston during the Battle of Galveston. Leah, who wrote under the name of Lee C. Harby, was born in Charleston, South Carolina, September 7, 1849, descended from Revolutionary ancestors on both sides of her family.[25] She was the fifth of six children of Marx E. and Armida (Harby) Cohen. In 1869 she married a cousin, John De La Motta Harby.

She served as a contributing editor for *Jewish South* in New Orleans. The Harbys came to Texas in the mid-1870s, first living in Galveston, where her essay "Christmas Before the War" appeared in a local newspaper in 1873. The Harbys lived in Texas more than twenty years, mostly in Houston. She wrote the lyrics to the "Flag Song of Texas," which won a hundred dollar award from the Daughters of the Republic of Texas and became the official state flag song.

In 1880 she read one of her poems at the Texas Press Association's annual meeting, and in 1888 her article in the *Magazine of American History* titled "City of a Prince," attracted favorable press in Russia, England, and Germany and won her recognition from the Historical Association of New York. The article was on New Braunfels, Texas. In 1883 she published an essay, "On Women and Their Possibilities," advising Jewish women to become educated and self-reliant.

She began to write extensively on early Texas history, and her works included "The Stone Fort of Nacogdoches" in *The American Magazine* and "The Earliest Texas" presented at the 1891 annual meeting of the American Historical Association. Her writings also appeared in *Harper's* and *Ladies Home Journal*.[26]

Mrs. Lee C. Harby *Courtesy © Marianne L. Swan*

JOHN ROSENFIELD

Max John Rosenfield, Jr., served as catalyst to spark the growth of the arts in Texas as arts critic for the *Dallas Morning News*. In this position he emerged as the leading cultural voice in the Southwest for decades. Twice *Newsweek* profiled him, and he became the subject of articles in *Look*, *Life*, *Harper's*, and other national magazines.

John was born in Dallas in 1900 and attended the University of Texas at Austin. World War I interrupted his education, and he finished at Columbia University in New York. His father said, "I sent John to Columbia University, but he went to the Metropolitan Opera instead."[27]

While in New York, John met and married Claire Burger. He began work as a motion-picture reviewer for the *New York Evening Mail*, and soon joined Paramount Picures in their publicity department. Paramount transferred John to Dallas. "John Rosenfield was in his lifetime the nation's top film critic," said G. William Jones, who founded the USA Film Festival.[28] Dr. Jones later was Professor of Cinema at SMU.

During an interview, Claire Rosenfield told why she and John left the East to come to Texas. "He saw an opportunity to make, as he thought, Dallas a fit place to live in because there was nothing here. There was the Dallas Little Theater. We had no museum, we had no orchestra, we had nothing."[29] He took a position as head of the amusements department for the *Dallas Morning News.*

John encouraged Texas communities to fund the arts. He met with businessmen and persuaded them to donate money to revive the Dallas Symphony Orchestra in the mid-1920s. He helped select several of its conductors. He encouraged Margo Jones establish her professional theatre. He was a vanguard in the movement that resulted in the building of the Dallas Theater Center designed by Frank Lloyd Wright and built on land donated by Sylvan T. Baer.

He had a compassion for the creative individual and lectured extensively on the arts.[30]

John received many forms of recognition and treasured the letters he received from celebrities, such as Barbara Stanwyck and Mary Martin, with whom he shared friendships. He received the Southwest Theatre Conference award twice, the Critics Award from Screen Directors Guild, and an honorary doctorate of literature from Southwestern University in Georgetown.

Time magazine once wrote that the "fact is that culture in Dallas has blossomed like a rose on the dry plains of the Southwest, thanks largely to Rosenfield." In its obituary on John in 1966, the *New York Times* wrote, "It can be argued that John Rosenfield did more for the arts in Dallas than any other person during a long reign as 'cultural pontiff of the Southwest.'"

EVELYN OPPENHEIMER

Many Texans attribute their interest in reading to Evelyn Oppenheimer, who traveled about Texas reviewing books and brought thousands of books to life in her weekly radio broadcasts.

Evelyn's grandparents immigrated to the United States from Alsace-Lorraine and Germany before the turn of the century.

After living in Chicago and other midwestern cities, her parents moved to Texas. After Evelyn graduated from high school in Dallas, she attended the University of Chicago, then worked on Chicago newspapers as a book reviewer and feature writer. When she returned to Dallas, she saw a great potential in the new profession of oral book reviewing. "But such programs were limited to private clubs," she said, "and I wanted to reach the general public.

"E.P. Simmons, then president of Sanger Bros., engaged me to begin such a series of review programs in the store auditorium. Then Milton Pandres, advertising manager of Titche-Goettinger Company, offered a larger auditorium, and in the war years of the 1940s we went from a monthly to a weekly series of programs to accommodate the audiences. In order to reach the largest public possible, I began broadcasting book reviews on radio. Since 1948, this continues to be the longest-running book program on the air in the U.S. and has always been sponsored."

Evelyn's success brought offers from universities to train others. She began teaching the techniques of oral reviewing at Texas Tech University, Southern Methodist University, University of Texas at Austin, University of Dallas, and University of California at Los Angeles.

Later Evelyn became a literary agent and author. Her published works include *Book Reviewing for an Audience, The Articulate Woman, Red River Dust, Texas in Color,* and *Frank Tolbert of Texas.* She coedited with Bill Porterfield *The Book of Dallas.*[31]

Patsy Nasher's mother, Ivy Topletz Rabinowitz, shown in 1924 before marriage in the music room of the home of her parents, Rebecca and Sol Topletz, Atlanta and Forest, Dallas.
Copyright © Ivy Rabinowitz.

PATSY RABINOWITZ NASHER AND
RAYMOND D. NASHER

When Patsy and Ray Nasher started collecting art, they didn't envision themselves as creating one of the finest private art collections in the world. Over time, they helped lift Dallas' reputation in art and architecture and shared their art collection with an international audience.

Patsy Rabinowitz was born in Dallas and graduated from Highland Park High School. She attended the Hockaday School's junior college and then Southern Methodist University and Smith College in Massachusetts, where she graduated *magna cum laude* in 1949. That same year, she married Ray Nasher, a Boston-reared real estate developer who held degrees from Duke and Boston University.

In 1950 they moved to Dallas, where their family grew to include three daughters: Andrea, Joan, and Nancy. Ray became involved in the development of industrial sites, planned residential communities, office parks, and shopping centers. Ray's innovative shopping mall, NorthPark, was one of the first enclosed air-conditioned shopping centers in the nation.

As Ray earned a reputation in building and architecture, Patsy began collecting art objects that held special meaning for her. At first, she gathered driftwood on the beaches in Massachusetts. In Dallas she started buying pre-Columbian artifacts and moved on to paintings by Texas artists, Guatemalan textiles, and Indonesian gold.

Over a period of thirty years Patsy and Ray built an extensive art collection. Patsy helped to build her community as well. She was instrumental in founding the Martin Luther King, Jr. Community Center in Dallas. Three weeks before she died, she asked a friend to take

MRS. ANNIE M. RABINOWITZ

Dec 26 1948

Funeral Rites Set Sunday for Mrs. Rabinowitz

Funeral services for Mrs. Annie M. Rabinowitz, 73, a Dallas resident for fifty years, will be held at 11 a.m. Sunday at Weiland's Funeral Church, 2909 Live Oak.

Mrs. Rabinowitz died Friday at the home of her son, Myer Rabinowitz, 4324 Beverly Drive, after a long illness.

Dr. David Lefkowitz, Rabbi Pierce Annes and Rabbi Rubin Kaplan will officiate at the services. Burial will be in Shearith Israel Cemetery.

her to see the Community Center, and she was pleased with how the Center looked and how it was maintained. She also served as a board member of the Dallas Musuem of Art and the Fort Worth Art Musuem.[32]

The Nasher Company received the Business in the Arts Award for sponsoring ballet, symphony, and theater performances in company-owned business developments, and the American Institute of Architects award, "Design of the Decade — 1960," for NorthPark. Ray coauthored the National Science Foundation book *Land* and in 1967 served as a U.S. delegate to the General Assembly of the United Nations. An honorary doctorate was conferred upon him by Southern Methodist University. Patsy received an honorary doctorate of humanities from Northwood Institute.[33] While Ray lectured nationally on art, architecture, and land use, Patsy traveled throughout the world collecting.

On April 5, 1987, "A Century of Modern Sculpture: The Patsy and Raymond Nasher Collection" opened at the Dallas Museum of Art and then went to Washington, D.C. for exhibition during the last half of 1987 at the National Gallery of Art. The collection then moved to Madrid, Spain; Florence, Italy; and other cities. Although Patsy was in great pain, she traveled to attend the exhibit's openings in Washington and Madrid. After battling cancer for thirteen years, Patsy died July 1, 1988, shortly after the collection began its European tour.

After her death, Ray reminded viewers at the Forte di Belvedere in Florence, "I hope you all feel the spirit of my wife, who was the true curator and developer of this exhibit. She's here with us in spirit." An editorial in a Dallas newspaper called Patsy "a civilizing force in Dallas . . . Patsy and Ray Nasher have meant a lot to this city."[34]

The City of Dallas named Raymond D. Nasher its first ambassador of cultural affairs.

Raymond and Patsy Nasher during construction of NorthPark shopping center, 1965.

Chapter 13

The Doctors and Other Healers

From the Alamo to the Nobel Prize

Dr. A.M. Levy served Texas with both the scalpel and the sword.

Art by J.F. Schwarting.

The practice of medicine and dentistry in Texas — from livery stable surgeons to Nobel Prize-winning medical scientists — evolved in a short one hundred and fifty years. Along the way, Jewish physicians and dentists played pivotal roles in pulling Texas from a territory that provided no medical and dental training to a state boasting renowned research institutions that graduated some of the world's top men and women in their fields.

The Jewish pioneers who opened new frontiers in scientific research and treatment and the Jewish men and women who provided the funds to make medical research possible, lived Hippocrates' belief that "wherever the art of medicine is loved, there also is love of humanity."

ALBERT MOSES LEVY

An early Jewish physician before the Republic of Texas era, Dr. Albert Moses Levy served as surgeon in chief of the volunteer army from October 22, 1835, to February 10, 1836.[1] He then served in the Texas Navy aboard the *Brutus* and *Independence*, at one moment healing wounded bodies of his comrades in arms, and at another inflicting wounds on his enemies with his trusted sword. After two powerful Mexican vessels captured the *Independence*, Dr. Levy spent three months in a Mexican prison, before escaping in the summer of 1837.[2]

Lewis Fisher Levy, son of Dr. Albert Moses Levy.

He settled in Matagorda to practice medicine, and that winter he received an appointment to a prestigious medical board created by both houses of the Congress of the new Republic of Texas. The formation of this first medical board is a medical milestone in Texas history.

Anson Jones, M.D., before he became President of Texas, had petitioned Congress for legislation to regulate medical practice in the Republic, but his lobby did not bring immediate results. Then the *Telegraph and Texas Register* took up the cause, writing on June 24, 1837: "These pseudo M.D. or Drs. are . . . more dangerous than the hostile Indians, and not considerably less numerous. Certainly more brave men have fallen under their hands than the rifles of the Caddos, Wacos, Towaccaines [*sic*] and Comanches ever reached. We had rather at any time see a company of armed Mexicans in battle array, than a squad of these grave gentry, parading with their Pandora boxes in the shape of pill bags . . . with medical knowledge acquired in a livery stable, cook shop, or tan vat . . . [A doctor] in one of the villages of the Brazos, a few months previous, was a shoemaker in Tennessee!"

On December 18, 1837, the Second Congress elected "eleven medical gentlemen to regularize the practice of the healing arts in Texas." Albert M. Levy of "Matagorda, Jackson, and Victoria" was named along with R.A. Irion of Nacogdoches, then Sam Houston's secretary of state; Ashbel Smith, medical scholar; Isaac Jones; Asa Hoxey; George W. Hill; J.M. Stewart; Thomas Anderson; Joel Jackson; J.B.P. January; and H. Bissell.

The Board of Medical Censors outlined the qualifications necessary for physicians to be licensed to practice in the Republic of Texas and to examine a candidate for a license.[3] The Second Congress also considered the incorporation of the University of Texas but voted to postpone action because the Republic had not yet provided an elementary school.[4]

After Dr. Levy received his medical board appointment in 1837, he continued to practice medicine in Matagorda, and around 1840 he and four other doctors in Matagorda published a schedule of charges for their community. They set day visits at five dollars, night visits, ten dollars; consultations, fifteen dollars; bleeding, two dollars; labor cases, thirty dollars.[5]

Some historians state that Dr. Levy served on the medical board after he retired from military service. However, after the medical appointment in 1837, the fighting Dr. Levy served in the Texas Navy again, when he reenlisted in 1842.

JOSEPH HERTZ

In 1832, several years before Texas' independence, Dr. Joseph Hertz and his brother, Hyman Hertz, arrived in Nacogdoches from their home in Germany. Dr. Hertz practiced medicine in the 1830s in and around Nacogdoches, where he often traveled fifty to sixty miles to treat patients at distant points. At times, when he treated the Indians, he traded his work for pelts and hides.

Hyman Hertz, a merchant, lost his life in 1833 when the steamer *Pioneer* burned and sank on a trip to New Orleans.

Dr. Joseph Hertz continued practicing medicine in East Texas until the strenuous work affected his health, and in 1835 he move to Natchez, Mississippi. Several years later he returned to Europe, where he remained the rest of his life.[6]

ISAAC LYONS

Dr. Isaac Lyons, a native of Charleston, South Carolina, filled the position of Surgeon General of the Volunteer Army of Texas for three months, from October 10, 1836, to January 16, 1837; in all, he served in the Texan army from May 18, 1836, to January 16, 1837, under General Tom Green.

In January of 1837 Dr. Lyons went to New Orleans and died shortly thereafter at the age of twenty-six at the home of A. C. Labatt, a trader who later moved to Galveston.[7]

ARTHUR S. WOLFF AND OTHER EARLY PHYSICIANS

Dr. Arthur S. Wolff was born in Lyons, France, in 1819. His father, Dr. Simeon Wolff, had been a noted physician in Paris.

In 1867 Dr. Arthur Wolff arrived in Galveston, then went to Brownsville, where he became a quarantine officer for the State of Texas.

He later went into private practice. He remained in Brownsville, healing residents of South Texas until he died in 1904 at age eighty-five.

Dr. Arthur Fishell Sampson, born in 1855, graduated in 1878 from the department of medicine of the University of Virginia at Charlottesville. He went to the then booming port of Galveston, where he performed pioneer work in the treatment of dysentery. Dr. Sampson later moved to San Francisco.

During this same early period, Dr. Daniel M. Appel became post surgeon at Fort Elliot, Texas, and in1883 he served as post surgeon at Fort Bliss, Texas.[8]

ROSANNA DYER OSTERMAN, JOSEPH OSTERMAN DYER, AND ISADORE DYER

One of Texas' earliest and most generous benefactors was Rosanna Dyer Osterman. She was born February 26, 1809 in Germany, and married Joseph

Osterman in Baltimore on February 23, 1825 at age sixteen. Her older brother, Major Leon Dyer, had escorted the captured Santa Anna to Washington late in 1836.

At Leon's urging, her Dutch-born husband traveled from Baltimore to Galveston to establish a business in the new Republic, and the next year, 1838, Rosanna traveled to the Gulf port to join him. In Galveston she helped her husband in his business, as she had done in Baltimore.

When the Civil War broke out, military forces blockaded Galveston, and business came to a standstill. During battle, many Galvestonians evacuated to the mainland. Rosanna stayed to nurse the sick and wounded on both sides. After Galveston fell to Union forces, she acted as a courier of military information to Confederate officials in Houston. Her information helped the Confederates retake Galveston on New Year's Day in 1863. Three years later Rosanna drowned following the explosion of a steamboat on the Mississippi River near Vicksburg.

In her will she left a fortune to medical facilities throughout the United States. She bequeathed several gifts of three-thousand-dollars each. These went to Jewish hospitals in New York, New Orleans, and Cincinnati. Her funds formed the Hebrew Benevolent Society in Galveston that fed, clothed, and sheltered the impoverished, nursed the sick, and performed merciful deeds for all faiths. The gift was timely, because fifteen months later a yellow fever epidemic's large toll included forty members of the Jewish community.

Her will also left funds for the founding of a nondenominational Widow's and Orphan's Home in Galveston, funds to a Jewish Foster Home in Philadelphia, $5,000 to build a brick synagogue in Galveston, $2,500 to build a synagogue in Houston, $1,000 to the first "Jewish Benevolent Society" in Houston, and funds to similar charities in New Orleans and Philadelphia. Her gifts also included $1,000 to the Galveston Sailors Home.[9]

At the time of her death in 1866, the *Galveston News* paid her this tribute: "The history of Rosanna Osterman is more eloquently written in the untold charities that have been dispensed by her liberal hands than any eulogy man can bestow." It said her work made her distinguished for "unselfish devotion to the suffering and the sick."[10]

Dr. Joseph Osterman Dyer (1856-1925) was Rosanna's nephew, being the son of Major Leon Dyer, her brother.

Dr. Dyer was born in Mayence Dessau or Alzey, Germany, and at age twenty came to Galveston. He soon went to Louisville for his medical course. He told of his struggle for a medical education, citing instances of how he would sweep out the dissecting room for the privilege of attending lectures.

He returned to Galveston in 1881 and started his medical practice. He also served his community in connection with raising of the city's grade following the 1900 storm. When it faced opposition, he went to the Texas legislature and pushed through a bill granting tax remission for another period of years.[11]

Dr. Dyer wrote for the *Galveston News,* and his

Rosanna Dyer Osterman

Dr. Joseph Osterman Dyer, Galveston physician and historian.

Photo: Pach Bros. N.Y.; copyright © by Richard Torbert.

columns were widely read throughout the Southwest. He loved Texana and his home contained a museum. Dyer traveled to New Orleans to interview Gershom Kursheedt regarding early members of Laffite's commune.

He continued his writing and his practice of medicine until he developed a heart illness. When he died at the home of his brother, Alex A. Dyer, D.D.S., at age sixty-nine, Rabbi Henry Cohen officiated at his funeral. Rabbi Cohen said, "Joseph Dyer was a giant in the intellectual and medical world, for he never was satisfied with what he knew, but strove always to improve himself by medical research."[12]

Isadore Dyer of Galveston, whose son became Dean of Tulane School of Medicine.
Photo: P.H. Rose; copyright © by Richard Torbert

Rosanna and Leon had a brother Isadore Dyer (1815-1888), a native of Baltimore who also came to Texas. He developed his own insurance company (Union Marine) in Galveston. In 1841 Isadore married Amelia Lewis, an Episcopalian whose family had come to Galveston in 1835. When their six-year-old son died Aug. 13, 1852, they decided to give him a Jewish burial. As there was no Jewish cemetery in Galveston at the time, Isadore had a burial ground consecrated a few weeks later as the Hebrew Cemetery, with the Rev. M.N. Nathan, minister of the New Orleans Portuguese Hebrew Congregation, delivering the address on August 29, 1852. The *Galveston Daily News* reported, "We presume that the services of Sunday morning were the first ever performed publicly by a Hebrew minister in Texas. But, we anticipate the organization of a Jewish congregation and the addition of a synagogue to the number of our places of public worship at no very distant date."[13]

GALVESTON 1903–1904 DIRECTORY.

DYER ALEXANDER A., dentist, office 310 Levy bldg, phone 26, bds 801 22d. 2. See front cover.
Dyer Amelia (wid Isidore), r. 2419 I. Phone 887.
Dyer Benjamin F., carrier Galv. Tribune, h. 1313 M.
Dyer Ellen (wid James), r. 2124 Winnie.
Dyer Isabella Miss, h. Dr. J. O. Dyer.
Dyer Joel (c), lab Galv. Whf Co., r. 1005 B'dway. 3.
Dyer Joseph O., attorney, h. 2419 I.
Dyer Joseph O., physician, surgeon, office 1427 Market, phone 312, r. 406 15th cor Market.
Dyer Lizzie E. Miss, slslady GARBADE, EIBAND & CO., h. 2124 Winnie.
Dykes Thomas J. (c), screwmn, bds 3223 L.

Dyer family listings in early Galveston City Directory.

The first Jewish services in Galveston were held in the home of Isadore Dyer, and he is credited with helping to bring Rabbi Cohen to Galveston.

Isadore and Amelia had another son, Isadore Dyer, Jr., (1865-1920), an 1887 graduate of Yale who became Dean of Tulane University School of Medicine. Although a modest man, Dr. Dyer, a dermatologist, received international recognition for founding the leprosy asylum in Louisiana. His daughter, Emily, married Joseph Labatt, son of A.C. Labatt. Emily and Joseph

Historic old home in Galveston, then the Dr. J.O. Dyer residence, with oleanders in front.

had one child, Amelia Rosanna.[14]

Isadore Dyer, M.D., of New Orleans, the third Isadore and grandson of the original Galvestonian, was reared a Catholic. He continued the family's medical tradition by becoming professor of obstetrics at Tulane University School of Medicine.[15]

RAY KARCHMER DAILY

Dr. Ray Karchmer Daily was born in Vilna, Lithuania in 1891 and arrived in the United States at age fourteen with her parents, Anna and Kalman Karchmer, who took the family to Denison, Texas. From high school in Denison, she went directly to the University of Texas Medical Branch in Galveston, where she became the first Jewish woman to graduate from a Texas medical school.

"It was difficult enough, when I was young, for a woman to get a medical education," she said, "and when I was graduated from medical school in 1913, it was not easy to get an internship and impossible to get a residency."[16]

She interned at Women's Hospital in Philadelphia because it was the only hospital with a dormitory for women.[17] Years later, she continued to work on the housing problem for women, as shown in a letter to her from Homer P. Rainey, president of the University of Texas. "I have your telegram," Rainey wrote, "of August 29 relative to the housing problems of the women medical students at Galveston. . . . I assure you and the women doctors of Texas that we are going to do everything that we can to take care of this situtation."[18]

In 1914 Ray returned to Houston to marry Dr. Louis Daily, whom she had met in medical school. They also joined in an office practice. When World War I ended, doctors Ray and Louis Daily took turns maintaining their office practice while the spouse participated in European studies. In 1923 and 1924 Dr. Ray Daily remained in Vienna, Austria to specialize in ophthalmology.

Dr RAY K. DAILY, F. A. C. S.

We, the Senior Class of 1932, dedicate our Year Book to Dr. Ray K. Daily, the first woman president of the Staff of Physicians and Surgeons of Memorial Hospital.

Dr. Daily has won our sincere love and admiration and has been a loyal friend to our institution. She is well known throughout Houston, being a leader in all worthwhile activities. She has recently been reelected a member of the School Board of Houston.

Tribute to Dr. Ray K. Daily at age forty.

Their son, Dr. Louis Daily, Jr., in an interview, remembered traveling to Europe with her in the summers. "She would hire a young man to chaperone me," he said, "then she would go to clinics. My mother spoke five languages. To her, her work wasn't a way to make a living. She was devoted to it. She loved it and made me love it."[19]

She then began working as a clinician, refining her surgical techniques that enabled her to become an eminent surgeon specializing in cataract removal.

She also ran for the school board in 1928. When she won, she became the voice for those who needed special care, for the impoverished, and for those shut out because of discrimination. She promoted the first classes for children suffering reading defects now known as dyslexia.[20]

She was instrumental in founding the University of Houston. According to minutes of the Board of Education of the Houston ISD, on April 30, 1934, she made the motion "authorizing expanding Houston Junior College into four-year college." The resolution was adopted, and the small two-year college in time became the University of Houston. "I turned the first spade of dirt for the initial building on the University of Houston campus," she later recalled.[21]

The denouncement of Dr. Daily by anonymous sources in 1943 as a "Russian born Red Jewess under FBI surveillance for Communist activities" foreshadowed the climate of hate that came in the 1950s to Texas. There were public forums about "reds" in the schools and about an alleged danger of UNESCO.[22] However, she won reelection to the Houston School Board in 1943.

Dr. Daily became first woman president of the medical staff at Houston's Memorial Hospital, and in the 1950s served as president of the medical staff at the large Jefferson Davis Hospital. Her poor attendance at school board meetings contributed to her 1952 defeat, after serving on the school board twenty-four years.

She continued her educational work in the medical field, producing 16 mm films on surgical procedures, which Harvard and other medical schools used.[23] She authored nine books, some in collaboration with her husband or their son, who joined his parents' practice.

She translated to English articles in ophthalmology journals published in foreign languages, abstracting the articles for the *American Journal of Ophthalmology.* She became widely known in the United States because she signed her pieces.

A national honor came to her when the American Academy of Ophthalmology and Otolaryngology elected her vice president.

On June 10, 1970, she received from her alma mater the coveted Ashbel Smith Distinguished Alumni Award.[24] She continued the legacy of Dr. Albert Moses Levy who served with Dr. Ashbel Smith on Texas' first medical board.

Above and below: The ten-story Ben Taub Research Center at Baylor College of Medicine in Houston opened in 1986 with a ribbon-cutting-by-laser ceremony symbolizing its state-of-the-art laboratories.

BEN TAUB

Ben Taub's father, Jacob Nathan Taub, came to Texas in 1882, an almost penniless Hungarian immigrant who sold newspapers and notions to eke out a living. He opened a cigar store in downtown Houston and became a tobacco wholesaler. By the time his fourth child, Ben, was born in 1889, the Taubs had become comfortable.

Ben grew up in Houston, where he attended Welch Preparatory School. During World War I he served in France, then returned to Texas to work in the family business. He expanded beyond the family enterprise and created his own real estate development firm. At one time he served on the boards of directors of twenty-three corporations, including an investment firm, two banks, an insurance company, and four universities.

In 1936 he donated thirty-five acres toward establishing the University of Houston. He then persuaded the heirs of the J.J. Settegast estate to donate approximately seventy-five acres to enlarge the campus.[25]

He is credited with persuading Baylor University in 1943 to place its medical school in Houston's Texas Medical Center. He then guided the county hospital to the highest quality of research, teaching, and patient care through affiliation with Baylor College of Medicine, which in 1949 joined the city and county in providing care for indigent patients. The idea was born in a meeting between Dr. Michael E. DeBakey, Chancellor, Baylor College of Medicine, and Taub, then chairman of the board of Jefferson Davis Hospital.[26]

Dr. DeBakey, the renowned heart surgeon, said of Taub, "He was greatly interested in developing the highest quality of medical care for the medically indigent. He was deeply interested in this. I recall as an example how every Sunday morning I would meet him at the hospital," said DeBakey, "and he'd make rounds and see the patients himself."[27] Taub never married, and his hobby was visiting patients in the hospital. Phy-

Mr. Ben Taub

sicians and patients all called him "Mr. Ben."

For years he helped run the DePelchin Faith Home for homeless children. He worked with the Pauline Sterne Wolf Foundation. He was a director of the Texas Medical Center, headed the United Way, gave scholarships, and sponsored visiting medical professors. Although a list of his civic offices filled pages, his longest civic job was serving as chairman of the Jefferson Davis Hospital from 1935 to 1964, almost thirty years.[28]

When a new charity hospital was being built, Taub recommended that it be named to honor his friend Jesse Jones; however, the hospital board overruled him. In recognition of his service, Ben Taub General Hospital was given his name when it opened in 1963. Its features of excellence include being one of the nation's top trauma centers.[29]

"Not only was he committed to the teaching hospital concept but also he was an early supporter of clinical research. The Ben Taub Hospital stands as a testimonial to this remarkable man's concern for humanity," said Dr. DeBakey. The heart surgeon revealed that it had been Taub who persuaded DeBakey not to leave Houston.[30]

"Ben Taub could have looked across Houston and realized that he had shaped, changed and guided the growth of his city to make it a far better and kinder place for the poor, the orphaned, the foreign, the ill, the old," said the *Houston Post* in an editorial when Ben Taub died at age ninety-three.[31]

LEOPOLD MEYER

"My love of charity was not a happening of chance," Leopold Meyer wrote in his memoirs. "It was learned in my home as a child." He clearly remembered his mother, although of modest means, performing acts of charity.[32]

Leopold Meyer lived as a messenger of good men. He thought of his life's mission as a fund raiser, and members of Houston's medical community and those who gave their money and time thought of him as "The Fund Raiser." They credited him with the vision to organize the building of the Texas Children's Hospital, which he headed for decades.

His mother, Malline Kahn, was born in New Orleans and his father, Achille Meyer, was a native of Alsace-Lorraine.[33] Leopold was born in 1892 in Galveston and later worked for E.S. Levy and Co. In 1918, when the Cohens bought Foley Bros., he joined Foley's, working his way up to executive vice-president and credit manager. Leopold's sister, Esther, married Foley's owner George Cohen.[34]

Leopold Meyer invested in other businesses and, as he said, "I made and lost millions of dollars, the loss factor more often attributable to my unbelievably boundless confidence in the men with whom I dealt."[35]

After his marriage in 1930 to Adelena Levy Goldman, member of a pioneer Houston family, he became aware of the need for specialized medical care for children.[36] Mrs. Meyer's daughter from a previous marriage, Meyer's step-daughter, Fan Harriet, died in October 1939 at the age of sixteen, and this tragedy brought home to Leopold the medical needs of youth.

For the rest of his life he devoted time to building and maintaining Texas Children's Hospital and served as president from its beginning. He worked for decades on medical causes and helped to establish Houston's St. Luke's Episcopal Hospital.

He presided over the raising of millions of dollars for the Texas Children's charity fund through horse shows, rodeos, and livestock shows and helped start the Muscular Dystrophy Telethon. Meyer was cited for outstanding contributions to the Child Guidance Center, the Houston Pediatric Society, and the Texas Association for Retarded Children.

He endowed the Chair for Developmental Pediatrics at Baylor College of Medicine. Dr. William T. Butler, President of Baylor College of Medicine, said, "Not only Houston but the world will long benefit from his immense foresight, his tireless effort, and his personal generosity. His legacy of good works will live on for generations to come."[37] The Leopold Meyer Center for Developmental Pediatrics annually evaluates hundreds of children for disabilities.

At age eighty-three, when Leopold Meyer looked back on his life, he wrote, "Although I stayed with Foley Bros. for twenty-seven years, I despised the dry goods business from the first day in Galveston with E.S. Levy & Co. and could never have become a merchant. I considered it the lowest form of livelihood conceivable — a slight degree above street peddling, but perhaps not as respectable."[38]

In reference to Leopold's life, one of his friends observed, "A man's dreams may be splintered many times, yet he never gives up. Instead, he gathers the fragments of a fallen scheme and creates again yet another enduring reality."[39] He died in 1982 at age ninety.

Leopold L. Meyer (1892-1982). *Photo: Karsh, Ottawa.*

MEYER BODANSKY

Dr. Meyer Bodansky, a pathologist whose research and textbooks received world recognition, suffered enormously when he could not persuade others to bring Jewish scientists and physicians out of Nazi Germany.

Bob Hope sells Leopold L. Meyer a $100 milkshake for the benefit of Texas Children's Hospital in Houston, May 1958.

Meyer was born in Elizabetgrad, Russia, on August 30, 1896, one of seven children of Phineas and Eva Bodansky, who brought him to the United States in 1907. He received his B.A. from Cornell University in 1918, his M.A. from the University of Texas in 1922, his Ph.D. degree from Cornell in 1923, and his M.D. degree from the University of Chicago in 1935.

From 1919 to 1925 he taught biological chemistry at the University of Texas Medical Branch, Galveston. He left Galveston in 1925 to teach for a year at Stanford University in California, and returned to direct the research laboratories at the John Sealy Hospital and teach.

Dr. Meyer Bodansky

For the school year 1932-33 Meyer, his wife and daughters moved to the eastern shores of the Mediterranean, where Bodansky served as visiting professor of physiological chemistry at the American University at Beirut.[40]

Dr. Meyer Bodansky revolutionized the view of biochemistry in disease and rescued great scientists from the Nazis.

During this productive period he wrote two biochemistry textbooks used in medical schools nationally, *Introduction to Physiological Chemistry* and *Laboratory Manual of Physiological Chemistry.* With his brother Dr. Oscar Bodansky, who served as chief of biochemistry at Sloan-Kettering Institute for Cancer Research, he wrote *Biochemistry of Disease*, which was translated into several languages and used worldwide in medical schools.[41]

A third brother, Aaron Bodansky, Ph.D., the eldest, also became an eminent scientist.[42]

In 1937 the Texas Pathological Society presented Dr. Meyer Bodansky its award for outstanding medical research, calling his thesis "The Chemistry of Heart Action" the "greatest contribution to medical science by a Texan during the preceding year."[43] He pioneered in researching the chemical factors that affect calcium absorption, vitamin deficiencies, kidney diseases, and endocrinology.

At the height of his research and writing that revolutionized the view of body chemistry in disease, Dr. Bodansky reached out to save European physicians from extinction by the Nazis. In the late 1930s he began to work with New York's Central Committee for the Resettlement of Foreign Physicians and the Boston Committee on Medical Emigres. The committees sought to bring these refugee physicians to the United States, then place them in small rural communites that had no physician or in research laboratories. Bodansky did not anticipate the resistance from doctors who felt their economic well-being threatened by what they perceived as a flood of doctors into the United States.

Dr. Oscar Bodansky served in the late 1920s as professor of pharmacology UTMB, Galveston, where he researched coronary flow and embolism and wrote The Biochemistry of Cancer.

Meyer Bodansky, on the advice of the committees, sought to find a non-Jewish physician to head the committee in Texas. He wrote hundreds of letters, spoke to groups, met in private sessions with Jewish and non-Jewish physicians, and met with refusal after refusal. He despaired over his lack of success. His daughter Samona, who later married a Waco physician, said, "He suffered personally. I can remember how upset he was. It was more than empathy; it distressed him terribly."[44]

Dr. Bodansky did meet with one distinct success when Dr. Irving Graef of the New York University College of Medicine sought his help in placing Dr. Ludwik Anigstein of Poland.[45]

Within a year after Dr. Anigstein arrived in Texas, Dr. Bodansky died, on June 14, 1941, of a pulmonary infection and acute hemorrhagic nephritis following an operation for mastoiditis. This was shortly before the discovery of antibiotics. His death at age forty-four came at the peak of his brilliant scientific career.[46]

Dr. William Levin, president, UTMB Galveston, said Bodansky "established the principle that biochemistry is the basis for many, many diseases. He was the first one to organize the information in a textbook form, and among the first, if not the first, to write a textbook on this. His impact was very significant."[47]

A Seventy-five Year History by the faculty and staff of the UTMB cited Dr. Bodansky's brilliant text, *Introduction to Physiological Chemistry*, as one of "the three epoch-making books in the history of teaching physiological chemistry in this country."[48]

In 1952 Jewish and medical organizations sponsored the first of a series of annual lectures in memory of Dr. Meyer Bodansky.[49]

LUDWIK ANIGSTEIN

When Ludwik Anigstein fled the Nazis in 1939, he intended to return to Europe after he managed to secretly move his family out through Switzerland.[50] Instead, after a year in California, he settled in Texas, where his research discovered the cause and cure of diseases that infected men as well as those that infected cattle and caused heavy losses to cattlemen along the Texas coast.[51]

As an international authority on typhus fever and malaria eradication, he demonstrated the use of DDT in anti-mosquito campaigns and introduced drugs such as chloroquine and laludrine.[52]

Ludwik had been born in Warsaw, Poland, on February 2, 1891, to Isidore and Helen Anigstein. He attended universities in Europe and received the Ph.D. degree and two separate M.D. degrees.[53]

In 1939, while attending a National Research Council meeting in Washington, D.C., at the invitation of the United States, Ludwik made his decision not to return to Poland. In 1940 he came to the University of Texas Medical Branch at Galveston. He brought his wife, Dr. Luba Anigstein, a pediatrician, and their two children, Alice and Robert. Luba, a public-school physician, lived only three years in Texas before she died of heart disease.[54]

Ludwik married again, this time to Dorothy Whitney, a scientist who worked with Ludwik in his laboratory and with whom he coauthored numerous research papers on rickettsial diseases. He wrote nearly two thousand articles for scientific journals, and coauthored a textbook.[55]

In the United States, one of his greatest contributions came with his work in rickettsial diseases carried by ticks. During World War II, the disease caused sickness in hundreds of American soldiers, and it became so severe in Camp Bullis, Texas, that the disease took on the name Bullis Fever.[56]

"His work on Bullis fever is one of his legacies," said Dr. Donald Vincent Moore, director of parasitology at the University of Texas Southwestern Medical Center at Dallas. "It was a problem, a febrile illness that could not be diagnosed. We didn't know what made these soldiers sick. I was director of the division of parasitology of the Texas State Health Department in Austin. Dr. Anigstein found the organism and was able to prove it was the cause.

"He was a pioneer in antibiotic use. When antibiotics first came into play, we needed to find out what they would do other than attack bacteria."[57]

In 1950 Dr. Anigstein acted as a consultant for the U.S. Atomic Energy Commission at the Oak Ridge Institute for Nuclear Studies Medical Division.[58] That same year, his discovery of a blood-derived antibiotic,

Dr. Ludwik Anigstein, eminent research scientist.

Courtesy Galveston Daily News.

previously extracted only from molds or bacteria, made news on two continents and appeared in the "Proceedings of the Society for Experimental Biology and Medicine." His work represented the first official report on the use of blood as a source of antibiotics.[59]

"I was never satisfied with the way of living and politics of Europe," he said. "It didn't agree with my philosophy of life. In Europe there was too great a difference between the student and the professor. Here we can influence our students much more because we place ourselves on the same status. Our American students have as much voice in the classroom as the instructor."[60]

Ludwik was a strikingly handsome man with tremendous vitality and great personal charm.[61]

BERNHARD GOTTLIEB

In 1941, the year after Ludwik Anigstein found a home at the medical school in Galveston, Bernhard Gottlieb arrived at Baylor College of Dentistry in Dallas on his way out of Nazi-infested Europe. Here he continued his work that would alter forever the research and practice of dentistry in the United States and the world.

Bernhard Gottlieb was born in 1886 in Kuty, Austria, the country where he continued his schooling, receiving his Doctor of Medicine degree from the University of Vienna. He attained the degree of Doctor of Medical Dentistry from the University of Bonn in Germany.[62]

Dr. Bernhard Gottlieb *1946 Photo: Chas. Arnold; © by Harold Younger*

His life in Vienna was best described by Dr. William C. Hurt of Dallas in a lecture to the American Academy of the History of Dentistry. Dr. Gottlieb had belonged to a group of Vienna scientists who built the scientific foundations for the clinical sciences of periodontics, orthodontics, pedodontics, endodontics, and oral surgery.

"One of the things that was unique at the University of Vienna was that every patient that died at the hospital was autopsied. All the tissues were studied and the cause of death determined. This was peer review back in the 1920s.

"The Herr Professor of Dentistry, Doctor Bernhard Gottlieb, saw to it that specimens of jaws were examined along with other parts of the body. In doing so he acquired histologic material from about the head and neck that was, and is, unique," Dr. Hurt told members of the Academy.[63]

"Meanwhile, in 1938 in Vienna, Nazi storm clouds were gathering. When the Nazis had first taken over Austria, research and teaching continued. But one day the inevitable happened. Gottlieb and others walked into the lecture hall and over here was a good friend in a Nazi uniform — over here another and over here another.

"Gottlieb was very distraught at the sight of all this. He had been a very cosmopolitan individual who had no religious inclinations. But it is said that from the moment that he saw his friends in a Nazi uniform, he became a militant Jew." Gottlieb left Vienna and went to Palestine, where he worked feverishly to build up the dental profession. He came to America in 1940.

"Gottlieb was never happy after he left Vienna," Dr. Hurt said. "No longer was he the great professor with disciples at his feet. No longer was he the leader of a team of world renown scientists. His students were all settled and successful, but he was not. He was not welcomed anywhere with the respect and honor he felt he was due. Even students had the audacity to challenge him and his concepts. His former associates had little time for him."

He was associated briefly with Columbia University and the University of Michigan, then came to Baylor College of Dentistry in Dallas, "where he assumed the position of professor and head of the department of pathology and research. He held this position until he died a broken man on March 15, 1950."

Dr. Gottlieb left a legacy to the world in the form of his former students who became great professors and authors, four textbooks he wrote, hundreds of scientific articles, and his oral histology slides. He pioneered in new fields. Because he is acknowledged to be the first dentist to truly integrate basic science information with clinical treatment, he is called the Father of Oral Histology.

In 1985 two researchers wrote, "Fortunately, even after his passing, his legacy continues, serving to link the past with the future. It manifests itself in the form of his incomparable collections of oral histology slide sections. Technically, there are no other slides like these in the world. The information preserved on these fifty and sixty-year-old sections can be successfully incorporated into our contemporary teaching and research programs as well as serving as a foundation for the realization and development of new ideas and concepts. Each slide chronicles the evolution of our current instructional rationale regarding oral histology and will apparently serve in this capacity for many years to come."[64]

ROSE G. SCHNEIDER

Rose Grundfest Schneider, world renowned scientist in hemoglobin research, was born in Minsk, Russia, in 1908. She arrived with her parents in the United States through New York when she was five years old. The family settled in Kearny, New Jersey, where her father worked as a merchant and her mother as a midwife whose interest in medicine would influence Rose and her three brothers to pursue medicine.[65]

She attended Barnard College while living at home and went on to earn her master's degree at Radcliffe (Harvard).

Rose married a professor of medicine at the University of Chicago and continued her schooling at Cornell Medical School in Ithaca, New York, where she earned a Ph.D. degree. She married a second time, in 1939, this time to Dr. Martin Schneider, a radiologist, and with him moved to Texas in 1941 and to Galveston in 1942. An anti-nepotism law precluded her employment at the UTMB, where her husband was professor of radiology, until a friendly professor of hematology offered her a position on his grant, not considered part of the university budget. The position allowed for some research, and she worked on sickle cell anemia.

"This was 1948, before the existence of abnormal hemoglobins was known, so I entered the field when it was almost bare. . . . During the next four decades I saw the growth of a scientific skyscraper, into which I was even able to insert a few small bricks."[66]

Dr. Rose Schneider's research, in which she always insisted she had many collaborators, dealt with many aspects of abnormal hemoglobins. She surveyed thousands of persons — adults and newborns — and was among the first to prove that sickle cell anemia and other hemoglobinopathies can be accurately diagnosed at birth. The improved medical care that such diagnoses made possible not only greatly improved the quality of life of the affected children but also prolonged their lives.

To facilitate hemoglobin screening, she developed new or improved methods, which became widely adopted throughout the world. She was appointed to the Expert Panel on Abnormal Hemoglobins and Thalassemia of the World Health Organization (1975-1978). Dr. Schneider has detected many rare or new abnormal hemoglobins in her laboratory.[67]

In an interview, she said, "Hemoglobins are very important in that they have many ramifications, not only for medicine, but for anthropology, for history, and a great many areas." One of the new hemoglobins "we found in the Alabama Coushatta Tribe in Texas. And it was subsequently found in parts of Asia, and it probably represents a time when there was a land bridge between Asia and the North American continent.

"I've been working in the field of abnormal hemoglobins for many years, and I've discovered several dozen new ones and described their properties and pathological effect. And I've discovered several different methods for identifying hemoglobins and also for studying their pathogenesis, their reason for causing disease."[68]

Dr. Rose Schneider, research professor of pediatrics and professor of human biological chemistry and genetics at the University of Texas Medical Branch in Galveston, has had published more than one hundred scientific articles. In 1975 she received the Sigma Xi John Sinclair Award for "excellence in pursuit of scientific knowledge." In 1985 she received the Texas Genetics Society Award for "outstanding contributions to genetics."[69]

A colleague said, "I know from my association with investigators in the field of hemoglobin research that Dr. Schneider is internationally known as a leading scholar."[70]

Dr. Schneider sees another of her legacies as having proven that "women can work and receive some recognition in science as well as raising a family. I have three children and both my daughters graduated from Barnard. My oldest daughter is a professor at the University of Massauchusetts, and the second is a lawyer married to a physician. My son is director of a blood bank, specializing in encouraging people who will need transfusions to store their own blood before surgery," she said with as much pride in her children as her medical research.[71]

Dr. Rose Schneider

WILLIAM C. LEVIN

Dr. William C. Levin became the first Jew in Texas to head a medical school.

Bill's grandparents had emigrated from Europe, his father's parents coming through New York and his mother's family through New Orleans. His parents were native born. His mother, Jeanette, married Samuel P. Levin of Waco, where the couple first lived and where Bill was born in 1915.

"Bill's father was with Sanger Bros. of Waco at the time," Mrs. Jeanette Lipson, Bill's mother, remembered. "He was doing the wholesale buying in the notions deparment." When Bill was a year-and-a-half old, the family moved to New York, where an influenza epidemic took Samuel Levin's life.

"I couldn't see raising my baby in New York," Jeanette said, "so we came back to Lockhart, and that's where I raised him." She remarried and sent her son to the University of Texas at Austin, where he graduated before going to the Medical Branch in Galveston in 1937.[72]

Bill completed graduate medical training at Michael Reese Hospital in Chicago, University of Texas Medical Branch, and Washington University in St. Louis. Dr. Levin chose to spend the rest of his medical career at the Medical Branch in Galveston. He served on the faculty beginning in 1944, rose to a full professor in 1965, and received appointment as Warmoth Professor in Hematology.

He became President of the University of Texas Medical Branch at Galveston in 1974. At his retirement in 1987, he held the Ashbel Smith Professorship.

He was recognized for developing the Clinical Research Center and the Cancer Center and wrote more than one hundred scientific papers. He served on national committees concerned with cancer. The French government made him, among the many honors he has received, a Commander of the Palms, its highest honor for academicians.[73]

JOSEPH L. MELNICK

Joseph L. Melnick, who was born Oct. 9, 1914, in Boston, Massachusetts, arrived in Texas to pioneer in new frontiers in virology, climaxed with his being elected to the Polio Hall of Fame for his contributions leading to the vaccine against poliomyelitis.

Joseph graduated from Wesleyan University in Connecticut. He then earned his doctorate in 1939 at Yale University and began his teaching career there, remaining on the Yale faculty for fifteen years. Later he took over as chief of virus laboratories of the division of biologic standards at the National Institutes of Health.[74]

In 1958 he was asked to set up a department of virology at Baylor University College of Medicine in Houston, the first virology department in any medical school in the entire country.[75] He eventually received the title Chairman and Distinguished Service Professor and Dean of Graduate Sciences.

In Houston, Dr. Melnick began his life's work to find a way to eradicate polio throughout the world. He developed a way to prevent heat from destroying vaccines, which permitted their use in underdeveloped nations without freezers in which to store fragile vaccines.[76] His work prevented a polio epidemic in Israel, and the Israeli government showed its gratitude by presenting Dr. Melnick the Maimonides Award. The Maimonides quotation that appeared with Dr. Melnick's photograph on the program when he received a tribute from the Houston Maimonides Award committee had served as his guiding force: "The heart's intention is the measure of all things."[77]

For more than forty years he tracked the elusive viruses: in studies that found herpes viruses are present in atherosclerotic deposits; in studies on congenital malformations caused by rubella virus; in studies of mechanisms by which viruses cause cancer; in microscopic studies of developmental forms of herpes viruses. Dr. Melnick pioneered and became the first to obtain a human virus in crystalline form.[78]

His research isolated a number of viruses from the cerebrospinal fluids of patients suffering from multiple sclerosis. He developed methods to identify carriers of hepatitis virus, to reduce getting hepatitis from transfusions.

Dr. Melnick developed a more accurate, cheaper, and faster test for detecting common urinary infections, a test that can be done in a minute for less than a dollar. The previous method took an entire day and cost eighteen dollars or more.[79]

His research has taken him into the battle to unlock the secret to the Auto-Immune Deficiency Syndrome (AIDS) virus, the most deadly virus the world has ever known. His pioneering research can be seen in an article published in 1977 in *Science*, in which he wrote, "There is now no question that the AIDS virus is harbored in the brain. What we see in our tiny samples of tissue probably represents what takes place in thousands of places in the brain of an AIDS patient."

He described the Baylor group's efforts to find areas of brain cells that contained virus particles as extremely laborious. He said he thought their ability to examine fresh, not post-mortem, tissue was a key factor in making electron micrographs that show both intact virus and viral budding from brain glial cells.[80]

Dr. Melnick wrote several medical textbooks and more than a thousand research papers in virology. His textbook, *Medical Microbiology*, sold more than a million copies and was translated into sixteen languages. He served as director of the World Health Organization's International Center for Enteroviruses and chairman of an International Conference on Viruses in Water in Mexico City. He served as professor of microbiology at universities in Buenos Aires and

Dr. Joseph L. Melnick at the time he headed the Department of Virology and Epidemiology, Baylor College of Medicine, Houston. He helped eradicate polio throughout the world.

Santiago and held visiting professorships in Beijing, Shanghai, and at Hebrew University.[81]

Besides electing him to the Polio Hall of Fame in 1958, his colleagues recognized him by awarding him the International Gold Medal for Research in Poliomyelitits, the Eleanor Roosevelt Humanities Award, and the Modern Medicine Distinguished Achievement Award. He is listed in *Who's Who in Frontiers of Science*.

From his first wife, Sarah Chasnoff Melnick, there was a daughter, Nancy. His wife of many years, Dr. Matilda Benyesh Melnick, held a full-time faculty position in virology at Baylor and later became a psychiatrist.

Dr. Melnick saw his legacy as his students. He trained over one hundred virologists who later held important posts throughout the world.

"The first Joseph L. Melnick Professor of Virology has been named at Baylor College of Medicine," he said in 1987, the year he retired, "and it turns out to be a very distinguished young virologist, Janet S. Butel, the first woman ever to have an endowed chair at Baylor College. So I think that's my legacy."[82]

Dr. Michael E. DeBakey, chancellor of Baylor College of Medicine, said of Dr. Melnick, "His scientific contributions have extended to humanitarian applications, which is the goal of all medical scientists and practitioners."[83]

Joseph Melnick summed up his own philosophy toward humanity when he addressed a crowd of Wesleyan University students, "You have a debt to society which in its long history laid the foundation and paid for your education — an education that doesn't belong to you alone; it also belongs to the society that paid for it. To repay your debt to society, you have to continue to learn forever, for the rest of your lives. You will enrich your own enjoyment of life and will improve the society of which you are a member. This is the payback you owe, that I hope you will repay."[84]

Dr. Melnick paid back his debt to society throughout his life, following the teachings of Judaism. Of these teachings he said, "They provided me with the background and foundation for my feelings and standards regarding ethics, morality, justice, fairness, love, compassion, curiosity, dedication — all of which are expressed in my scientific and personal life."[85]

DONALD W. SELDIN

Dr. Donald Seldin dreamed of building one of the finest medical schools in the world, calling it his "New Jerusalem." Although Moses could not enter the promised land, Seldin reached his goal. After Seldin spent thirty-four years as chairman of internal medicine at the University of Texas Southwestern Medical Center at Dallas, his achievement was properly confirmed when one of his former students received the Nobel Prize.

Dr. Donald W. Seldin

Donald Wayne Seldin was born October 24, 1920, in New York City and received the B.A. degree from New York University in 1940. In 1943 he received the M.D. degree from Yale University School of Medicine and married Muriel Goldberg.[86] After internship and residency at Yale University School of Medicine, he remained on their staff until he began active duty in the Army. He served at the 98th General Hospital in Munich, where he provided expert medical testimony at the trial of a Nazi physician at Dachau.

He returned to Yale to teach in the department of internal medicine another three years. In 1951 he arrived in Dallas to become Associate Professor, Department of Internal Medicine, University of Texas Southwestern Medical Center.

"The medical school turned out to be in shacks," Seldin remembered. "We were in abandoned Army barracks erected during World War II. If the weather got cold, the pipes froze and the school would close." After a time, all the school's top professors left, and Dr. Seldin planned to go back to Yale Medical. However, a new dean, Dr. George Aagaard, arrived in Dallas and persuaded Seldin to stay on as William Buchanan

Professor and chairman of the department.

While teaching, Dr. Seldin also found time for advisory committees and learned societies. He served as member and chairman, Scientific Advisory Committee, Massachusetts General Hospital, Harvard Medical School, from 1978 to 1982. He served as consulting editor to seven medical journals and became president of the International Society of Nephrology.[87] In 1988 he retired as dean of Southwestern, after helping to build it into one of the finest medical schools in the world.

President Ronald Reagan awarded the National Medal of Science to doctors Goldstein and Brown, Nobel Prize winners and holders of the Lasker Award. From left: President Reagan, Dr. Brown, U.S. Secretary of Commerce William Verity, and Dr. Goldstein, at the ceremony at the White House.

Photo: The White House.

One of Dr. Seldin's top accomplishments was the quality of his students. "Some of the students worked with me. Then I sent them away for further training and brought them back to the school," Seldin explained. "Some of them became the best in the world."

"His genius is seeing something in people. He chose out small-town Texas boys — rough people, not cultured in any way — and he made us into something," said Dr. John Fordtran, chief of internal medicine, Baylor Medical Center at Dallas.

"He inspired us to be better than we thought we could be," said Dr. Jean Wilson, professor of medicine at Southwestern.

Although many of his students became equal in stature, very few called him Don. "I just can't do it," said Dr. Dan Foster, also a professor. "I call the president 'Charlie,' but I call him Dr. Seldin."

"I would guess he contributed more to the academic environment than anyone in the school," said Dr. Charles Sprague, president of the University of Texas Southwestern Medical Center at Dallas, "and that is the strength of this institution."[88]

JOSEPH L. GOLDSTEIN AND MICHAEL S. BROWN

As Dr. Donald Seldin's protégé, Dr. Joseph Goldstein carried research to new heights when he and his colleague Dr. Michael Brown received the 1985 Nobel Prize in Physiology or Medicine for research in cholesterol metabolism that could lead to new treatments for coronary artery disease.

Born April 18, 1940 in Sumter, South Carolina, Joseph graduated from Washington and Lee University in Virginia. He obtained his M.D. degree at Southwestern Medical in 1966. Joe's brilliance was recognized during his student days and prompted Dr. Seldin to offer him a future faculty job even before his graduation from medical school.[89]

"I came to Dallas as a medical student in 1962," Goldstein said. "He saw something in me that clicked, and he worked closely with me and that had a great influence on my career. I wanted to be in internal medicine, and he said, 'Why don't you consider genetics?' I went off for six years to study, and I came back. It's unlikely I would have stayed in Dallas if it hadn't been for

Dr. Seldin."

He continued his education at Massachusetts General Hospital in Boston. Here he met Dr. Michael S. Brown, who was born in New York City April 13, 1941, and had graduated from the University of Pennsylvania and its school of medicine. At Massachusetts General Hospital they served for two years on the medical house staff.

They both then went to the National Institutes of Health in Bethesda, Md., as clinical associates — Goldstein in the National Heart Institute and Brown in the Institute of Arthritis and Metabolic Diseases. Brown married and had two children, while Goldstein remained single.

Brown joined the faculty of the University of Texas Southwestern Medical Center at Dallas in 1971, while Goldstein went there in 1972 after his two-year fellowship in Seattle in medical genetics. Their collaboration started immediately and led to the various discoveries.

Their research discovered special molecules called receptors on the surface of cells. These receptors remove cholesterol from the blood and carry it into cells. If the receptors are not functioning properly, cholesterol deposits can build up in coronary arteries, leading to heart attacks.

Between them, Goldstein and Brown have authored a textbook, eighteen textbook chapters, and (with others) three hundred scientific papers. Among their long list of awards is the Albert D. Lasker Award in Basic Medical Research.[90]

Top: Baylor's Jewish Institute for Medical Research is a nine-story building for research in cancer, hepatitis, water pollution, multiple sclerosis, atherosclerosis, sleep, and pain control. The 1984 board of trustees included Dr. Joseph Melnick, far right in lab coat.

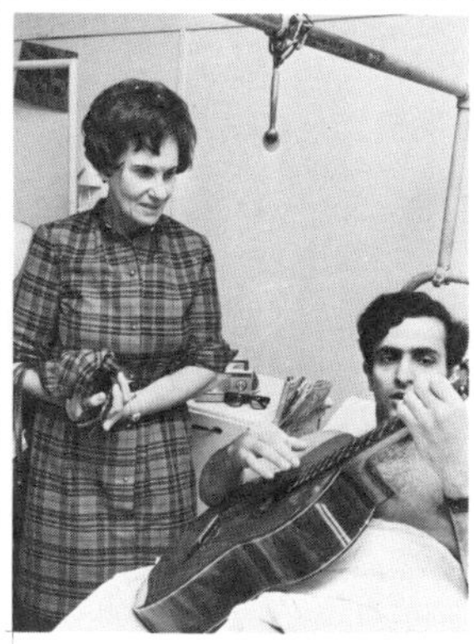

Fannie Schaenen of Dallas visits a young Israeli patient.

Nancy Goodman Brinker, fourth from left, shown with Mrs. Gerald Ford, Mrs. Ronald Reagan, and Mrs. Lyndon Johnson, pioneered in prevention and early detection of breast cancer, raising millions of dollars for education and medical research.

Nancy Brinker, seated, at a fund-raising event October 27, 1988.

Simon Mussina

SIMON MUSSINA

Simon Mussina never intended to become an attorney, but a judge dealt him an injustice so great that he became one of the most astute lawyers in nineteenth-century Texas. He specialized in Texas lands and land titles.

Though some historians have questioned the Jewish ancestry of the Mussinas, others provide substantial documentation of German or Polish descent of Simon's father, Zachariah Mussina, who identified himself as a Dutch Jew.[1] Henry Cohen of Galveston identified Simon as a Jewish settler who arrived in Galveston in 1836 with his brother Jacob.[2]

Simon was born on July 8, 1805, in Philadelphia, Pennsylvania, where he received a good education.[3]

In 1821 Simon set up a mercantile business in Mobile, Alabama, where he developed one of the largest mercantile businesses in the South. Despite a large fire, he continued his business there until he decided to move to New Orleans.

In 1837, Mussina moved his family to Matagorda, Texas, at the mouth of the Colorado river, where he bought the *Matagorda Bulletin*, a weekly four-page newspaper, editing it until 1839. He then moved to Houston, where he edited the *National Banner* in order to advertise his West Texas lands.

He then went to Matamoros, Mexico, near present day South Padre Island, and in 1848 he bought a newspaper, the

American Flag of Matamoros, and developed it into one of the most popular newspapers of the time, the only American newspaper published in that part of Mexico. He was one of the surveyors who laid out the town of Brownsville and moved his press there.

During this time, Simon became a close friend of Sam Houston, who encouraged Simon as the chief plaintiff against Judge John C. Watrous charged with corrupt decisions concerning land claims in and about Brownsville. This notorious case had a great effect on Simon's life because it drew him into extended land litigations from which he never seemed to escape for the rest of his life.

On August 6, 1859, Sam Houston wrote Simon: "My Dear Mussina, I could not tell what had become of you, so I was rejoiced to hear from you. I had seen your late expose — Beautiful! The jig is up with Watrous. . . . Do write me often. Ferret out those rascals. I told you of my suspicions."[4]

In 1868 Simon moved to Austin and began proceedings for the La Vega land grant, an eleven-league grant that embraced a part of eastern Waco. This case stayed in litigation for years. Simon, now in his sixies, became established as one of the most astute land attorneys in Texas. From 1870 to 1873 he served as president of the board of trustees for the State Blind and Insane Asylums, and in 1871 he served as alderman of the city of Austin. Simon never married, but he almost solely reared his father's family. When he died at age eighty-four, his sister, who had married a Presbyterian minister of Galveston, buried him in Galveston.

Brownsville, the city Mussina founded, grew to have an organized Jewish community and in 1870 had the third Jewish congregation chartered in Texas, following Houston and Galveston.

DAVID ALBERT AND SAMUEL COHEN ELDRIDGE

Two of Texas' earliest Jewish attorneys emerged from Jefferson. Their father, Philip Eldridge, was born in Prussia in 1833, leaving at age fourteen. He established a successful mercantile business in Jefferson. Philip Eldridge served on the committee that charted Congregation Mount Sinai in Jefferson in 1872, the fourth Jewish congregation in Texas.

He believed his best legacy could be the education of his six children, and he saw to it that each attended college. David and Samuel Eldridge attended Cumberland University in Tennessee and both became prominent lawyers.

David began his practice in the firm of Todd and Eldridge in Jefferson, then moved in 1886 to Dallas, where he became a prominent Dallas County judge.[5] He practiced in Dallas until his death at age seventy-nine. "He had a deep feeling for people and love for the law," said his grandson.[6]

Samuel Eldridge opened his law office in San Antonio in 1893 and practiced for fifty years. He served as an assistant city attorney and Bexar County judge.

THEODORE MACK

The youngest of nine children, Theodore, born in Cincinnati in 1864, graduated from the University of Cincinnati Law School in 1886. In 1888 Tay, as he came to be called, moved to the drier climate of Texas to relieve an asthmatic condition. He was twenty-four. He first lived in Albany, Texas, where he was elected county attorney of Shackelford County. He argued the first case on the docket of the Second Court of Civil Appeals when it was established in Fort Worth in 1892. He moved to Fort Worth in 1894, becoming the first Jew to establish a law practice in the city. He served as special associate justice of the Court of Civil Appeals.

On a trip back to visit his parents in Cincinnati, Tay met Pauline Sachs; they married and soon began to work actively in Jewish and other causes in Texas. In 1907 she led a committee, anchored by the Council of Jewish Women, that raised the first funds to create Temple Beth El of Fort Worth.

When the Ku Klux Klan controlled Tarrant County juries, Tay refused to try any case in Tarrant County from 1918 to 1924. "He did not feel that a client represented by a Jewish lawyer could receive a fair hearing," said Ellen Mack, family archivist, Fort Worth civic leader, and wife of Tay's grandson, Theodore Mack II. "While referring these cases to others, he developed his appellate practice," Ellen explained. "By the end of his long career, Mack had argued over 1,000 cases in the appellate court."

Tay served as one of the first delegates to the American Law Institute at its founding. In 1925 he and his son Henry formed the law firm of Mack and Mack. Years after Tay's death, the dynasty continued when his grandson, Theodore Mack II, became a partner.[7]

HENRY J. LABATT

Henry J. Labatt distinguished himself as a lawyer, journalist, author of books on law, and defender of Jewish rights before the mid-1800s. Like his father Abraham Labatt, one of the early Texas merchants, Henry became known as a civic and religious figure in California and Texas.

He was born in 1832 in New Orleans, where he grew up. He attended the University of Louisiana and received his degree in law, before going on to Yale

Henry J. Labatt

University to receive a master's degree in law. He then went to California, filled with Gold Rush fever.

Even in his early twenties, Henry began to distinguish himself. Daniel Levy of San Francisco, a French-born social critic, in 1856 referred to Henry as one who enjoyed "an honorable position" among colleagues. This paid a high compliment to Henry because Levy had no great love for lawyers. "In California, the law is a career that is open to anyone, so that these gentlemen multiply in a distressing fashion and become a real social plague."[8]

Henry built up a law practice, and at twenty-three he won the election for clerk of the Superior Court. He began writing books that condensed decisions by California courts in order "to lessen the difficulty experienced in the preparation and trial of causes, from a want of knowledge of our code of civil practice, by attorneys assembled here from various States of the Union."[9] Six books emerged.

Labatt edited the San Francisco City Directory starting in 1856, and his interest in journalism continued when Labatt (and his friend Rabbi Herman M. Bien) founded the *Voice of Israel* in September 1856, printing 2,000 copies every Friday.

Labatt employed all of his skills to combat one of the nastiest of the few anti-Semitic events in early California. William W. Stow of the California State Assembly in 1855 used the Sunday closing bill as an opportunity to propose a Jewish exclusion act for California, to expel Jews from the state. Stow felt that Jews and Catholics threatened Anglo-Protestant power. Henry took up his pen to express astonishment. In numerous articles Henry fenced with Stow, and when Stow became a candidate for governor he was defeated at the convention.[10]

Eventually Henry moved his law practice to Texas. He served as Galveston's city treasurer in 1869 and in June 1870, eighteen years before Rabbi Cohen came to Texas, he gave the principal address at the dedication of the cornerstone of Galveston's Temple B'nai Israel. He served in the Texas House of Representatives in the Seventeenth and Eighteenth Legislatures from January 1881 to April 1883. In 1883 he became a founding member of the Texas Bar Association.

A Texas town bore his name, possibly because of legal work he performed for the railroad. Walter Prescott Webb wrote in the 1952 Handbook of Texas, "Labatt, in western Wilson County on a mail route from Floresville, is a one-store community on the former ranch property of Francisco Flores de Abreyo. In 1886 Labatt became a flag stop and switch on the San Antonio and Aransas Pass Railroad and was named for Henry J. Labatt, a Galveston attorney."

Henry's life ended when he and members of his household died in the great storm of September 8, 1900, that swept Galveston Island.

LEO N. LEVI

Leo Napoleon Levi became one of the first Texas-born Jews to achieve national recognition.

He was born in Victoria September 15, 1856, one of six children of Mina and Abraham Levi. After graduating high school in Victoria, he entered the University of Virginia in Charlottesville at age sixteen. He was graduated in law. His college experiences may have influenced the direction of his career, climaxed in defending persecuted Jews.

His granddaughter, Margaret Levi Strauss of Larchmont, New York, remembered being told of those experiences. "He was one of the only Jewish students there and the butt of anti-Semitism. The other students picked on him terribly. One of his fellow

Leo N. Levi

Leo N. Levi

Nineteenth-century residence of Leo N. Levi, Galveston.

students was Thomas Nelson Page who became an author and based a character, Wolfert, in one of his books on Leo. Leo was a strong person and stood up for his rights.[11]

He gained, among other university distinctions, the medal for being the best university debater. By the time he graduated, he had finally won admiration and respect on campus.

He married a Virginian, Ray Bachrach, and they had six children. After college, Leo settled in Galveston, where he joined prominent law firms.[12] In Galveston he continued to use his talent as a speaker. "Even when he was a little boy eight or nine years old," Margaret Strauss said, "men would stand him on a box and enjoy listening to him talk." He became a well-known orator, and even though he had attended the University of Virginia, officials at the University of Texas at Austin invited him to give the commencement address in June of 1899. The Independent Order of B'nai B'rith published this and other speeches by Levi in a book in 1905, a year after his death, in which the editor called him "an orator unexcelled in his generation."[13]

Leo established himself as a prominent lawyer and civic leader in Galveston, and when Benjamin Harrison, president of the United States, visited Galveston, city officials asked Leo to be one of three persons to escort the president. "I heard stories that women in Galveston placed flowers throughout the president's train," Margaret said.[14]

In 1887 Leo was elected president of Temple B'nai Israel, and the next year he brought Rabbi Henry Cohen to Texas. He retained the presidency twelve years. He joined B'nai B'rith, a Jewish fraternal organization, and was elected president of District 7 covering seven Southern states. In 1900 in Chicago, Leo was elected national president of IOBB, and after living in Galveston for twenty-three years (1876-1899), he moved in 1900 to New York City to work with B'nai B'rith.

In this capacity Leo N. Levi penned a petition on July 4, 1903, demanding of Czar Nicholas II, after the massacre at Kishineff, that Russians stop abusing Jews. Leo N. Levi had several personal interviews with President Theodore Roosevelt. Secretary of State John Hay signed the Kishineff Petition and sent the cable of it to the U.S. Ambassador at St. Petersburg. Secretary of State Hay said, "You are a diplomat, Mr. Levi, and would make a great ambassador." President Roosevelt called him "a great man."[15] Less than six months later, Leo N. Levi died of a heart attack on January 13, 1904, at age forty-eight.

In Hot Springs, Arkansas, the Leo N. Levi National Arthritis Hospital stands as his memorial.

JULIUS KANN HEXTER, VICTOR HEXTER, LOUIS J. HEXTER

The Hexters, who became related by marriage to Leo N. Levi's family, pioneered and forever changed the abstract and title business in Texas. The brothers and their descendants could have become wealthy through their enterprising businesses, but instead chose to counsel owners with growing real estate businesses and to pursue their own creative hobbies.

The oldest brother, J. K. Hexter, born Aug. 13, 1860, in Baltimore, Maryland, arrived in Texas in 1883 and settled in Victoria.[16] There he joined the pioneer banking firm of A. Levi and Company and served as vice-president of the Levi Bank and Trust Company. He married Melanie Levi, sister of Leo N. Levi. Hexter served on the Victoria city council.

In December 1909 the Hexters moved to Dallas, which was becoming the financial center of the state. J.K. became president of Provident Loan Society and vice-president of the Morris Plan Bank. He located his office in the old Linz Building. He died Nov. 19, 1936.[17]

J.K.'s brother, Victor H. Hexter, was born March 21, 1864, in Baltimore. Their mother, Amanda Kann Hexter, was part of a family that had come to Baltimore in 1826.

"Mr. Victor Hexter was dean of the people in the abstract world," recalled Ruth Brown Hexter Kahn, former wife of Victor's son Louis. "In his legal work as an attorney, he examined a lot of titles and did business with a lot of real estate dealers. Victor was so versed in the history of Dallas real estate that he knew an abstract from its origin. He didn't have to examine a title from its beginning. He knew the whole area."[18]

Victor H. Hexter

His grandson, Victor Hexter II, explained: "My father [Louis Hexter] was working for a title company in Dallas, and it went into receivership. My father and grandfather bought the company from the trustee in bankruptcy. It was out of New Orleans, Union Title and Trust Company, and they renamed it Hexter Title Company. My grandfather, because he already had been doing that kind of work, then did all the examinations of the titles and gave the opinions."[19]

"Arthur Kramer, Sr., worked for Victor when Arthur first came out of college," said Ruth Kahn. Both Victor Hexter and Arthur Kramer served on the Dallas school board, and both have elementary schools named for them. Victor served on the 1931-1933 Dallas City Council.[20] "He could have been a wealthy man," Ruth said, "but he was not a good businessman. He spent much of his time in the library. Every day he went to the library, came home for lunch at noon and read. He read a book a day. He made a bequest to the library in his will, in a day when few people thought of giving to the library." Victor Hexter died in Dallas in 1951 at the age of eighty-seven.

Victor's son, Louis, followed his father's interest in law. After graduating from the University of Texas, he attended law school at the University of Chicago. Here he met a soft-spoken undergraduate student, Ruth Brown, who came from a pioneer Jewish family from Muskogee, Oklahoma. They married in 1923.[21]

Louis Hexter, like his father, mingled the arts with finance. However, theater — chiefly Broadway — rather than books, attracted Louis. He became an actor, playwright, and director. He helped found the Dallas Little Theatre in 1920 and in 1929 established the Dallas Negro Players, the first all-black company to perform in the Southwest. He enjoyed anonymously pouring substantial sums into productions for theatre on Broadway, motion pictures, and in its embryonic years, educational televison.

But his greatest impact on Texas history came in business. Hexter became one of the most influential men ever to participate in the growth of Dallas. He developed Dallas' Preston Center, where he leased land to Neiman-Marcus for its first suburban store. He helped change Dallas from an average Texas town to "Big D." He helped launch, or move along, the careers of scores of widely known developers, including Raymond D. Nasher, brothers Frederic and Martin Tycher, John F. Eulich, and I.C. Deal.[22]

Frederic Tycher said, "He was considered to be in sort of a dean's position. He had effervescence. He had a beautiful grasp of Dallas' potential growth and his judgment proved to be quite correct. He helped many people and assisted in the development of Dallas."[23]

I.C. Deal recalled that Louis "would say, 'What the mind can conceive, it can achieve.' That was the brand that he left. It was a very exciting time for Dallas. At that time it had three or four hundred thousand people. There wasn't a Richardson to speak of, nor a mid-cities to speak of, but he kept thinking in those terms.

"He was extremely influential, and when you're starting a business and you're an entrepreneur and you're undercapitalized, he would offer solace, good logical thinking, that kind of expertise."

Deal summed up his impressions of Louis Hexter: "I think he was a very unusual person. He was extremely broad-gauged and very unselfish. He took sort of a Socriatic approach to those he counseled."[24]

Louis J. Hexter

Raymond Nasher, an innovator in shopping centers when he built NorthPark, said that he met Louis Hexter through a tennis-playing friend. Nasher called Louis "the guru of real estate in Dallas at that time," and Nasher began an intensive apprenticeship in the world of development.[25]

John F. Eulich, founder of Vantage Companies, remembered three things most about Louis: "He was extremely intelligent. He knew real estate business backwards and forwards. He was quite accessible."[26]

Victor Hexter II felt his father was "a complex kind of person with a multifaceted personality. I think he always sort of regretted that he hadn't done more theatrical work. I don't think he wanted to make the sacrifices; he didn't want to be a starving artist."[27]

Both Louis and his brother George (born Jan. 30, 1896) had the middle name Jules.

Living in the shadow of his father, Louis said he believed his business success resulted from the life-long compensation for "my feelings of worthlessness." His philosophy was, "Losing is only a temporary condition between trying and winning."[28] Louis Hexter died April 2, 1977.

Louis J. Hexter in roles as an actor.

CHARLES LOUIS BRACHFIELD

Louis Hexter's philosophy on losing applied to Charles L. Brachfield, the first Jew to seek a statewide office in Texas — that of attorney general.[29] Though he lost the election, in part because too many candidates entered, he served as a state senator, judge, head of his own successful law firm, and two banks in Henderson. He became known as the respected Judge Brachfield.

His mother Yetta Baruch, born in Telset, Prussia, was a distant relative of Bernard Baruch who served as adviser to several presidents of the U.S. His father, Benjamin Brachfield, born in Cracow, Poland, had a brother, Charles Louis, who lived in Vienna, Austria, and served as court jeweler in the Court of Hohenzollern. Charles Louis became namesake for Judge Brachfield and his two nephews, both of whom became partners in the judge's law firm.[30]

Benjamin arrived in the U.S. in 1862. His wife came in 1866 sponsored by a cousin, Simon Baruch. The couple settled in Vicksburg, Mississippi, where Charles was born on January 10, 1871, eldest of seven children. In 1877 Charles and his family moved to Henderson, Texas, where his father worked as a merchant.[31]

Charles later attended Henderson College. He became a student of law in the office of Judge J.H. Wood in Waco and was licensed to practice law by the District Court of Rusk County, Texas, in 1890, at the age of nineteen. He set up his law practice in Henderson and held his first public office, county judge, in 1897 and was reelected in 1898 and 1902.[32]

Judge Brachfield had the distinction of having a

Brachfield, a judge at age 26, was provincial.

photo © Shirley Marwil Sanger.

Hirsch was urbane. Shown is symphony program cover.

road and town named for him. A pioneer in Henderson, Lee Maxwell, told this version of the naming:

"Judge Brachfield was running for county judge. He came to a store down there on the Brachfield Road, intersects with 840 out of Henderson. He was making a political speech, and that crossroad place there didn't have a name. So some suggested, 'Why don't we called it Brachfield?' My daddy suggested it to Newt Orr, who was always a spokesman. The judge was the most illustrious-looking person I ever did know. He was all head. And he was a very brilliant man. I was just a kid when all this took place."[33]

Newton Orr, who operated a sawmill, is credited with officially suggesting the name. The story was told that Charlie L. Brachfield stood on a stump at this community and made one of his first political speeches.[34]

For eight years Judge Brachfield served in the Texas Senate, from January 1903 through September 1910.[35] Judge Brachfield won the office of district judge, which he served from 1921 to 1928.

When the First National Bank went under during the Depression, around 1929, they reorganized the bank with the judge's help, his former secretary, Florence Rettig, said. "The reason they wanted him down there was that everybody in Rusk County respected him and knew he would pull everyone together to pull it out."[36]

Judge Brachfield's law practice brought diverse clients, including the independent oil producers, the Methodist Church in Old London, Texas, the Norfolk Baptist Church in Old London, Gulf Oil, Magnolia Oil, and many landowners, most of whom needed settlements on land titles and boundaries.

The judge never married, but when he died June 6, 1947, a Methodist minister and a rabbi conducted services attended by friends from throughout the nation.

MAURICE HIRSCH

Maurice Hirsch's father, Jules, came to Houston from Alsace-Lorraine in 1870. Jules married Theresa Meyer of Mobile, Alabama, and their only son of three children, Maurice, was born in 1890 in Houston.

Just as Leo N. Levi before him, Maurice attended the University of Virginia, where he received his B.A. and M.A. degrees. He attended Harvard School of Law, where he received his law degree. From the University of Texas School of Law he obtained a master of laws degree.

He founded his own law firm, Hirsch, Westheimer, Block & Wilk, in Houston, where he practiced for the remainder of his life with the exception of his work in the U.S. government, for which he received the Distinguished Service Medal.[37]

When World War II erupted, Maurice called a former Harvard classmate, Under Secretary of War Robert Patterson, and told him he wanted to assist in any possible way. Patterson said he critically needed someone who had an understanding of business and law for a completely new organization — the War Department Renegotiation Board.

"We were to renegotiate contracts with one purpose in mind — to avoid excessive profits from the war," Maurice said. "The object was to eliminate excessive profits from the war effort without destroying incentive, which was a definite criteria.

"I am happy to say that although we collected back $13 billion, fewer than twenty corporations objected to our act."[38] Maurice, who had started as a colonel in the judge advocate general's office, became chairman of the Renegotiations Board, and was promoted to the rank of brigadier general. From that moment on, Maurice became known as General Hirsch.

He returned to Houston to continue his law practice, but this time he returned with a wife, Winifred, who had been working in Washington. They had married in Washington, with Secretary of War Patterson serving as their best man.

In Houston, General Hirsch set about continuing what his mother, a singer, had started — building Houston's orchestra into a world-class organization. She had been one of the founders of the Houston Orchestra and had trained her children to love music. Maurice's sister Rosetta, a violinist, had been the first instrumental artist to perform as a soloist with the Houston Symphony Orchestra. His sister Josie became a concert pianist.

General Hirsch served the Houston Symphony Society as president for fourteen years, which included the years when famed conductors Leopold Stokowski and Andre Previn held the baton in Houston. Maurice had his own ideas about qualities necessary to preside over the Houston Symphony, which he expressed when the Society refused to renew Previn's contract.

"A lot of people criticized me severely for not holding him," Maurice said. "He was not loyal to his wife, Dory, whom he later divorced to marry actress Mia Farrow. He'd been denied admission to clubs because he dressed like a hippie. He just wasn't a proper example for young people of the community. And he was not loyal to us."[39] At the same time he conducted Houston's Symphony, Previn conducted the London Symphony.

General Hirsch led in the development of Houston's parks, camps for children, hospitals for crippled children, Rice University, the Houston Museum of Fine Arts, Houston Grand Opera and the Society for the Performing Arts, as well as the International Council of the Museum of Modern Art in New York.

In 1976 the Houston Museum of Fine Arts appointed him a lifetime trustee, and in 1979 the third wing of the museum was named the Winifred and Maurice Hirsch Gallery. In 1980 he and his wife gave a $500,000 library endowment to the museum.

At age ninety-three he died in Hong Kong while on another of his world adventures.[40]

IRVING L. GOLDBERG

Irving Goldberg came to play a critical role in the federal government, just as Maurice Hirsch had. Irving became the first Jew appointed to a federal judgeship in the South.

Irving was born in 1906 in Port Arthur, Texas, where his father, Abraham, a native of Lithuania, and his mother, Elsa, operated a dry goods store. His father was recognized there as a civic leader for his work with the Boy Scouts of America. Irving graduated from the University of Texas in 1926 and received his law degree from Harvard.

After Goldberg served in the navy during World War II, he practiced law in Dallas. He worked actively in the Jewish community, serving as president of Dallas Home for Jewish Aged and as a board member of the National Conference of Christians and Jews.

In 1966 President Lyndon Johnson appointed him to the Fifth Circuit Court of Appeals in New Orleans.[41]

HERMINE DALKOWITZ TOBOLOWSKY

Hermine Tobolowsky traveled thousands of miles within Texas, crisscrossing the state, giving as many as five speeches a day and spending $80,000 of her own money to right a wrong. Her efforts changed the laws of Texas, altering a state that had the most repressive laws against women, and earned for her the title Mother of the Equal Rights Amendment in Texas.

Hermine was born in San Antonio on January 13, 1921.[42] Her father, Maurice, a merchant in San Antonio, had emigrated from Lithuania when he was a teenager. He encouraged her, even as a six-year-old child, to attend law school because, "He thought that if a woman didn't know how to take care of herself, somebody would take advantage of her," Hermine said. "He felt that a girl, even more than a boy, needed a good education because he felt that men had an easier time. He was certainly far ahead of his time."[43]

Her mother, Nora Brown Dalkowitz, set an example by working in a San Antonio store at a time when it was considered a disgrace for a woman to be in business. Hermine attended Incarnate Word College and Trinity College in San Antonio, taking more than twenty hours each semester and attending summer school. She completed her bachelor's degree work in only two years (1938-40). When she entered the University of Texas School of Law in 1940, she became one of 11 women in a class of 350.

She received the bachelor of laws degree in 1943,

completing undergraduate and law school in five years, though several of her professors tried to block her success. "One of them sent a notice out to all the girls," she said, "asking them to come to his office, individually. When we got there, he told us he would give us a list of eligible bachelors in the school so we wouldn't have to take up space in the law school. I assured him that I would be there on graduation day."[44]

Hermine served on the editorial board of Texas Law Review, did research for several professors, and became a quiz master, an honor reserved for the top ten students. When she graduated, one of the largest law firms in Houston offered her a position, but she turned them down. "The man interviewing informed me that if they hired me, I would never see a client, that they would only permit women to brief," she said. When the job offer came, she informed them that she wouldn't be interested in working for them because of their attitude toward women.

Instead, she accepted a position with a law firm in San Antonio with a promise of $200 and the opportunity to present a brief on a case before the Texas Supreme Court. "You don't get out of law school and start with a brief to the Supreme Court," she said. The going rate for lawyers at that time was $75 a month. She discovered that no one in the firm wanted the brief, knowing that the case would be lost. It had been an early civil rights case that Hermine believed would have been won in the courts in another twenty years.

Attorney Hermine Tobolowsky, Mother of the ERA in Texas.

Photo © by Natalie Ornish

She stayed with the firm four years before opening her own corporate law practice. Shortly thereafter, she met her future husband, Hyman, an executive with a Dallas retail store. They married in 1951 and settled in Dallas. Hyman died in 1968. The couple had no children.

Almost from her earliest experiences, Hermine Tobolowsky seemed destined to champion the rights of women under the law. The events that set her clearly on such a course happened in 1957, when she journeyed to Austin to testify before a legislative committee on one of many laws that discriminated against women. This particular law prohibited a woman from selling property that she either owned before marriage or had acquired afterward by gift or inheritance, without her husband's consent.

The lawmakers politely listened to her as she stood before them wearing gloves and a large hat, her dark hair pulled back in a knot. One of the senators said, "There's no woman who has sense enough to sign a deed or convey her stocks without the advice and consent of her husband." Another said, "If you don't like my attitude, why don't you go down to my district and tell the stupid, little women down there about it and see if they'll listen to you?" Still another wanted to know what problems she had with her husband.

"When I'd had enough," she said, "I just put my brief down and gave them a little lecture on good government and reminded them that they were employees of the people of Texas, including women, who represented more than one half of the population.

"One of the senators on the committee passed a cigar down to me and said, 'Here. You want to be a man, smoke it.'"[45]

That became a turning point for Hermine. She took the senators' advice and traveled to their districts and gave voters their message to women. She traveled to other districts, quoting the senators, and, in time, those senators on the committee lost their elections.

At the same time, she spent two years researching the legal dimensions of sexual discrimination. Her research became the basis of the Texas Equal Legal Rights Amendment, first introduced in the Texas Legislature in 1959 and reintroduced in every session until it became law in 1972.

Time and the recognition of her significance and wisdom have brought her many awards. The University of Texas Law School named an award for her, and she was named to the Texas Women's Hall of Fame.

Oscar Mauzy, a Texas supreme court judge, said he considered her a lawyer's lawyer, a description she shares with other Texas Jewish pioneers in law who pulled their fellow citizens up from oppression and discrimination. The Texas pioneers educated themselves and made their skills available to serve all persons, whether in Texas, the United States, or the many countries of the world.

Acknowledgments

This book resulted from the cooperation of many persons who helped, some as individuals and others as part of scholarly institutions. Persons who gave oral history interviews are referred to in the notes. Those who loaned photographs are credited near the illustrations. Others who helped are the following:

Katherine J. Adams
Sara Alpern
Donald Altschiller
William Austin
Paula Barber
Dr. Inci Bowman
Donaly E. Brice
Betty Brown
Arlen Bryant
Carolyn Buckner
Donald E. Carleton
Martin A. Cohen
Jack M. Corbin
Susan Cramer
Geraldine Cristol
Thomas W. Cutrer
Dan Dailey
John De Troye III
Joan Dobson
Travis Dudley
Cathy Dummer
Ralph L. Elder
Lucille Enix
Tracy Epstein
Carolyn Ericson
David W. Farmer
Edwin Gale
Wayne Gard
Doris Glasser
Alan Glazener
William H. Goetzmann
A. C. Greene
Casey Edward Greene
Dr. Salomon Grimberg
Uli Haller
W. Phil Hewitt
Glendora Hill
Joanne Hill
Betsy Hudon
Jean Hudon
Susan Dyer Johnson
Nathan M. Kaganoff
Jane A. Kenamore
Chester V. Kielman
Larry Landis
Herbert Lang
Wilhelmina Lawley
Edwin Lax
Dawn Letson
Helene Levy
Seymour B. Liebman
James W. Long
Joann Long
Lloyd Lyman
Mavis Harby Malarek
Jacob Rader Marcus
Stanley Marcus
Kathryn A. McBride
Tom McBride
Lt. Gen. John R. McGiffert
Gayle McNutt
James C. McNutt
E. Kelly Merritt
Howard Miller
John Molleston
Irene Moran
Dr. Charles Morrissey
Charlotte Royal Moskowitz
Ronald D. Moskowitz
Judith Murphy
Patrick Murphy
Patrick O'Brien
Dr. Dean Ornish
Dr. Edwin P. Ornish
Kathy Ornish
Laurel Ornish
Dr. Steven Ornish
Lyman D. Platt
Ruth Rafael
Becky and Andy Reisberg
Maureen Reister
Alan D. Rosenthal
Esther M. Rosenthal
Marilyn and Tom Ross
Susan P. Schoelwer
Albert H. Schroeder
G. L. Seligmann, Jr.
Tom Shelton
Cindy Smolovik
Jon Stedman
Brigitte Steinig
Malcolm H. Stern
Norton B. Stern
Marvin Stone
Bernice Strong
Richard C. Torbert
Richard A. Valente
Saul Viener
Bart A. Walker
Bernard Wax
David J. Weber
John Edward Weems
Seth Werner
John Wheat
Edwin Wolf II
Larry J. Wygant

In the Jewish teachings, we are admonished not to glorify, nor put our trust in man, only God. When Jews read the story of the Exodus at the Passover seder, the booklet they read from does not even mention Moses, their deliverer from Egypt.

With this in mind, the author wishes to emphasize that the purpose of this book was not to glorify any individuals or families, but rather to show that there was a Jewish presence in Texas from the very beginning, even before the days of the Republic.

The main accomplishment of this book is that information of the pioneer Jews of Texas, always fragmented, has now been collected for the first time. When Henry Cohen began to write about certain pioneers he knew or knew of in 1894, it was a significant beginning. However, the minimal articles after that were generally merely re-writes of the first articles. To date, no substantive research was done covering this vast and diverse subject, until this volume.

It is important that pioneer Jewish Texans not be stereotyped. Physically, they ranged from small Rabbi Cohen to the tall football player, professor Ettlinger. Some lived in mansions, while others lived in homes with dirt floors. Although we have singled out those who accomplished much, many of these pioneers became land poor or in serious economic straits. Everything in life is cyclical, and of those who amassed vast resources, few descendants of these pioneers can live today in the same lifestyle as their ancestors.

Pioneers were selected to become biographees on the merit of whether their lives had impact on the state. Jewish Texans have a double heritage of which to be proud, that of Texans and of Jews. Hopefully, with this book, the reader could experience how the pioneers lived, to connect with them as human beings and to have the power to experience life as it was then, to sense the pioneers' assertive commitment to achieve, even when hopes were dashed and dreams deferred. When success came, most tried to return part of their resources to their communities.

"The whole earth is full of His glory," is another Hebrew saying in which these pioneers maintained a strong belief. The conquistadors wandered thousands of miles seeking minerals. Colonizers predicted Texas lands would grow cotton in quantities then unbelievable. A West Texan bottled and sold the pure mineral water on his ranches. A plant pathologist learned the secret of better Texas crops. Financiers lent money on cotton still to be grown, and in a later day, on oil still in the ground. These pioneers were all cut from the same cloth.

The first commandment is a reminder of freedom. In every generation we must go out of the house of bondage. In the early days of Texas, under Spain, the long arm of the Inquisition made its terror felt. We have tried to present the Jewish attitude toward glorification of freedom and reverence for life. The sages said, "I have given you life and death; choose life." It is a universal story. It is the struggle to survive with human dignity, and to then make contributions to the human race.

This is not a roster of heroes. The purpose is to show a people, not to focus on individuals. It was intended to be a history told through the people who made that history. It is to mirror, often in the pioneer's own words, his struggle, which is the struggle of the human spirit to survive.

Appendix A

Laffite a Jew?

There is some indication Laffite was a Jew, and if this is true, his hatred of the Inquisition could explain his acts of violence in attacking ships sailing under the flag of Spain. According to Stanley Clisby Arthur in *Jean Laffite, Gentleman Rover*, on a flyleaf of Laffite's family Bible, Laffite wrote (translated from the French), "I owe all my ingenuity to the great intuition of my grandmother, a Spanish Jewess, who was a witness at the time of the Inquisition."

This grandmother was responsible for rearing one-year-old Jean and the other children when their mother died in 1783 in Port au Prince, Haiti, leaving eight children (three daughters and five sons). Jean was the youngest. Various birthplaces have been assigned as those of Laffite, including Bordeaux, St. Malo, and Marseilles, France.

When he was eighteen, Laffite married Christina Levine, of Jewish descent, a native of St. Croix, Virgin Islands. Besides his grandmother, Zora Nadrimal, his maternal grandfather allegedly also became a victim of the Inquisition, which persecuted, jailed, and tortured him before he died in prison at Zaragoza, Spain, September 9, 1760.

To authenticate Mr. Arthur, the author of this material, I interviewed several persons:

Maurice Ries of Sarasota, Florida, who was with the Middle American Research Institute of Tulane University, New Orleans, for eleven years (1931-1941) while writing for the *Times-Picayune, New Orleans States*, and *New Orleans Item*, said, "Arthur was a newspaper man in New Orleans in the 1930s and so was I." Ries also was with the U.S. Department of State (1941-43) and coordinator of Inter-American Affairs (1944-46). From 1946 to 1948 he was director of the Laboratory of Anthropology in Santa Fe, New Mexico. Ries stated that Arthur was a man of education, did accurate research, and had integrity as a historian. (Int., Ries, 1984)

Winston de Ville of Mobile, Alabama, a reliable researcher who has written on the Spanish period in New Orleans, took this viewpoint: "Arthur was absolutely sold on the authenticity of it. I don't know where to document it. None of us in historical circles gave any credence to it. The New Orleans Historical Society did not ask to see the Bible. There is no record of the president then [1954] inquiring about it." (Int., de Ville, 1984)

Stanton Frazar, Director of The Historic New Orleans Collection, and F. M. Jumonville, head librarian of the Collection, referred to pages 121-129 of *Great Forgers and Famous Fakes* by Charles Hamilton, which states that John Andrechyne Laffite (born John Laflin) manufactured his ancestral relationship to Jean Laffite with forgeries. Hamilton quoted Charles van Ravenswaay, former director of the Missouri Historical Society, who called Laflin's materials "his obvious fabrication" and said Arthur used some of these materials. (Int., Frazar, 1984)

The 1984 president of the Louisiana Historical Society, Raymond Samuel, whose field of expertise is the Battle of New Orleans, questioned whether Laffite wrote the paragraphs in French about his Jewish ancestry during the Spanish Inquisition that are reproduced in Arthur's book. Said Samuel, "Experts have tried for years but have not been able to corroborate his ancestry." (Int., Samuel, 1984. Other source: Parsons Collection, Harry Ransom Humanities Research Center, The University of Texas at Austin, for Laffite handwriting comparisons.)

Dr. J.O. Dyer's information on the de la Portas and Laffite is derived partly from primary source material from Dyer's father's business associate, a Colonel Graham of New Orleans, who actually had visited Laffite in Galveston in 1818. (J.O. Dyer, *Galveston News*, September 19, 1923)

Bertram W. Korn discusses the possibility of Laffite being a Jew in his book *The Early Jews of New Orleans*, pp. 98-100, 296.

Appendix B

Goliad's Edward Isaac Johnson
An International Family

Lawrence P. Johnson, who in 1981 was age seventy-five, recalled in an interview with this author that Edward Isaac Johnson, who died at Goliad, was his grandfather's brother and that the family name originally was Disraeli of the famous family that included Lord Beaconsfield. The name was changed under unusual circumstances. The Goliad martyr's grandfather, a Britisher, saved the life of the Prince of Wales, later George IV. While in the red-light district of London he saw the prince attacked by thugs. With his cane he helped the prince fight off the thugs and knock them to the ground.

According to the story, the grateful prince told Disraeli he would like to repay the favor, whereupon Disraeli told his mentor he would like a commission in the British army. He got it, but had to change his name.

Later, he had two sons, Phineas Israel Johnson and David Israel Johnson (born in Portsmouth, England, in 1795), father of Edward Isaac Johnson. David married Elizabeth David of England, and she bore him eight children, Edward being the oldest, born in Portsmouth in 1816. He was age twenty at Goliad. When he was only a year old, Edward had been brought to America by his father, mother, and uncle Phineas. Edward's family settled in Cincinnati while "Phineas Israel Johnson was the first Hebrew to settle at St. Louis." (Isaac Martens, *The Hebrews in America*, p. 107) Phineas, uncle of the Goliad martyr, married Clarissa Clark, grand-niece of a signer of the U.S. Declaration of Independence.

Edward came to Texas to acquire land to help support the large family. When he left Cincinnati in 1835, the children ranged from age four to nineteen, with another born the year Edward was killed. All had exciting lives. Edward's brother Henry, born in 1819 in Brookville, Indiana, became a "forty-niner" and went to San Francisco for the gold rush. When not panning for gold, he was a professional gambler and at age thirty was poisoned by his mistress in 1849 in California. The third brother Frederick (1821-1893), who his descendant said was the first Jew born in Cincinnati, served in the Ohio House of Representatives. Sister Selina, born in 1823, was the first Jewish female born west of the Alleghenies. Well educated, she became principal of a school. The martyr's brother Samuel was born in 1825 and started the family archives. Three other brothers included David Isaac, born 1828; James W., born 1831; and Edgar M., born 1836, the year after the oldest brother went to Texas. Edgar served Ohio as a prosecuting attorney from 1857 to 1861.

The next generations of Johnsons included noted businessmen, professionals, and soldiers. Selina's grandson was the late Lou Rosenstein, head of Schenley Distillery, whose two children died at an early age and left no descendants. Samuel's son Simeon headed Cincinnati's Democratic party. Simeon, who collected the data of the Johnson family, died in the 1940s nearly one hundred years old. Samuel's great-grandson, a major, came with the first Allies who landed on Omaha beach, Normandy, France, June 1944 in World War II.

Edgar Johnson's grandson, also an attorney, became a partner in the law firm that included a former governor of Ohio and Jacqueline Onassis' grandfather, John V. Bouvier, Jr. (The firm was Hoadley, Lauterbach and Johnson.) Edgar Johnson II had been admitted to New York's Columbia University at age thirteen and graduated at seventeen. Lawrence Johnson said Edgar was too young to join his father's law firm at that time, so he went on a world tour with a noted gambler, Harry Rosenfield, who took the lad to Monte Carlo, where they tried to break the bank. Edgar II then joined the law firm of his father and later founded his own firm with Sidney Streicker. A Republican, Johnson was majority leader in the Ohio State Senate (1908-1912). He married Celia Pollak of the Pollak Steel family, and their son, Lawrence P. Johnson, leaves no descendants.

Edgar Johnson III, a surgeon, served on the Board of Governors of Yale University. He died at age fifty-five, leaving no descendants. (Lawrence P. Johnson, interviews and correspondence with author, 1981; *Cincinnati Enquirer*, April 29, 1937; *Cincinnati Times-Star* [now *Post*], April 29, 1937; John N. Davis, *The Bouviers*, pp. 184-185.)

Appendix C

Ehrenberg's Jewish Origin
Documenting Ehrenberg Sources

In Ehrenberg's case, it was necesssary to establish through research his Jewish origin because, although only one person ever challenged his Jewish origin, her persistence raised questions for scholars.

Miss Maria Augusta Ehrenberg of Rome, Italy, filed a claim in 1930, sixty-four years after Ehrenberg's death in 1866, although it had been clearly established that he was murdered then near Palm Springs, California, by an unknown person. She sought to establish her relationship to lay claim to his worldly goods. The State of Texas did not act on her claim.

Professor Carlos E. Castañeda of The University of Texas at Austin's History Department listed Ehrenberg as a Jew in volume 6 of his series *Our Catholic Heritage in Texas 1519-1936.* Castañeda wrote, "The brave messenger who chose to share the fate of his companions was Herman Ehrenberg, a volunteer German-Jew" (vol. 6, p. 297). "Herman Ehrenberg, the German Jew who chose to remain with Fannin at Coleto when his two companions galloped away, lived many years after the massacre. He wrote one of the best accounts of the Goliad tragedy" (vol. 6, pp. 299-300). Dr. Benjamin Sacks, an Arizona physician who spent many years researching the identity of Herman Ehrenberg, sent a query to Professor Castañeda. In answer to Sack's query, here is what Castañeda wrote him on January 21, 1955:

"As far as I know, the first to make a public statement about Ehrenberg being a Jew was Clarence Wharton. Wharton was a prominent lawyer and historian of Texas, who gathered a respectable library of Texana and wrote extensively on various topics connected with the Texas Revolution."

Wharton wrote in his book *Remember Goliad*, "Herman Ehrenberg, a young German Jew, halted and dismounted and took his place with his comrades" (p. 43). "One of the most interesting of these refugees was a young German Jew named Herman Ehrenberg" (p. 52); "the restless wandering Jew" (p. 55).

Castañeda continued in his letter, "Ehrenberg was befriended by Adolphus Sterne of Texas, who was a liberal and a Jew prominent in early Texas history. Mr. Cohen and Friends' book probably was the source of Mr. Wharton. Personally I am inclined to believe he was a Jew unless more definite and concrete evidence is found to the contrary.

"As you know, he left Germany in 1835, came to New York first and then went on to New Orleans, where he joined the New Orleans Greys, took an active part in the Texas Revolution, miraculously escaped the Fannin Massacre, returned to Germany, studied at Freiburg University, studied mining, returned to U. S. in 1844, joined the Fremont expedition in California, and after the Mexican War went to Sonora and Arizona, of which he made the first reliable map."

In 1869 the town of Mineral City, Arizona, got a new name. "We learn that the people of La Paz, Yuma county, have changed the name of their new location, Mineral City, to 'Ehrenburg,' in honor of the able mineralologist, daring pioneer and noble patriot of that name, who was so foully murdered some time ago. . . The new name suits us." (*Weekly Arizona Miner*, August 14, 1869, 2:3).

"Michael Goldwater led the way in the establishment of a new port. He found a suitable location at a site known as Mineral City, some seven miles below La Paz. Goldwater renamed the town Ehrenberg in honor of his friend and pioneer Arizona mining engineer, Herman Ehrenberg, who had been murdered at Dos Palmas on California's Colorado Desert in 1866." (Dissertation by B.P. Lamb, "Jewish Pioneers in Arizona 1850-1920," Arizona State University, 1982, p. 46)

Frank C. Brophy asserted in his *Arizona Sketch Book*, "Some of the best and earliest cartography, after the Guadalupe-Hidalgo Treaty in 1848, was done by that scholarly Jew, Herman Ehrenberg."

In correspondence with Dr. Sacks, Barry M. Goldwater said about his own family, "My uncle [Morris Goldwater] always referred to . . . [Herman Ehrenberg] as Jewish [and] there has never been any question in my mind but that. . . he was a Jew."

In another letter dated September 26, 1940, to Dr. H. Fuchs of Berlin, Barry Goldwater stated, "Herman Ehrenberg and my grandfather were the very best of friends. My grandfather and my uncle were the first to see the body of Herman Ehrenberg as he lay murdered in a small California stage station. My grandfather, prior to Mr. Ehrenberg's death, had founded a new town on the Colorado River, and after the passing of his good friend he named the town Ehrenberg in his honor.

"Herman Ehrenberg was responsible for the founding of the town of Yuma, Arizona, and if Frederick

Ehrenberg does not know the details of this story, I will be glad to send the information to him

"Herman was and is still considered one of the greatest surveyors and map makers ever to visit the western United States. His abilities as a mining engineer were also thoroughly recognized by experts in that field."

In another letter to Dr. Sacks, Barry Goldwater said, "I have a book in my library in German, the title of which slips my mind at the present time, which lists the outstanding Jews in America and was written, as I recall, sometime in the 1880s. This work includes the life of Herman Ehrenberg.

"There has never been any question in my mind but what Ehrenberg was a Jew, and should you care to avail yourself of letters and books in my library that would tend to substantiate this, I would be very happy to allow you to use them, should you ever come to Phoenix," said Goldwater.

In the 1880s, the State of Texas granted Herman Ehrenberg's worldly goods, which amounted to 1600 acres of land near Liberty, Texas, to Emil Ehrenberg, who the State determined to be Herman's brother. Emil, a resident of Teplitz, Bohemia, drew up an agreement with a Bohemian merchant, Heinrich Cohn. If Cohn would pay Emil Ehrenberg's expenses for a trip to America, he would receive half of Herman's estate, 800 of the 1600 acres. (These figures are from the Sacks Collection. T.L. Miller's reference book on bounty land grants, *Bounty and Donation Land Grants of Texas 1835-1888*, pp. 247, 248, and 763, states the heirs of Herman Ehrenberg received on 13 May 1880, 960 acres under Bounty Warrant 93, and 640 acres under Donation Certificate 36.)

In 1884 both Emil and his backer came to Houston via New York City, where Emil transferred the entire 1600 acres to Heinrich Cohn for $800 in cash and a promissory note for $615 (averaging 88 cents per acre). In 1885, Cohn and his wife in Teplitz conveyed 400 of the 1600 acres to one Stanley Epstein of the County of Bexar, Texas, for an undisclosed sum. Cohn gave the Steiner Brothers of New York, merchants, a mortgage on his 1200 acres to secure payment of a balance of $3500 owed them. The Steiners, on March 19, 1912, sold the 1200 acres to W.H.H. Miller of Harris County, Texas, who in two weeks sold the land to the Old River Rice and Irrigation Co. of Jefferson, Texas. This company eventually sold it, including mineral rights, to the Kirby Lumber Company of Houston.

For some unlikely reason, Maria did not file her claim until 1930, a claim that was never recognized by the State of Texas.

Appendix D
Sterne's Family Background

Adolphus Sterne's parents, according to Bertram W. Korn in *Early Jews of New Orleans*, were Emanuel Sterne and his first wife. Later Emanuel married Jeanette Hunt Sterne. Korn wrote, "nor is there any suggestion of how Jeanette Hunt Sterne may have been related to Solomon Hunt. But in view of the dealings Mrs. Kokernot had with Mrs. Hunt, it is possible that all these people constituted one vast clan through natural and marriage relationships." Sterne had two sons, Adolphus, by his first wife, and a younger son Isaac, by his second. The elder Sterne had gone bankrupt in New Orleans in 1824. On June 2, 1828, Adolphus married Eva Rosine Ruff in a civil ceremony in Natchitoches, La. Both his father and stepmother died in July, 1828, three days apart.

Sterne's Diary, published in the *Southwestern Historical Quarterly* over a period of years and later in book form edited by professor Archie P. McDonald, reveals Sterne had a knowledge of Jewish ritual and some rudimentary ability to write Hebrew and Yiddish. On October 6, 1840, Sterne wrote "to night is *erev Yom Kippur*" [eve of the Day of Atonement]. On July 15, 1841, he reported that a neighbor, Michael De Young, ("a German Jew of the old reverend class") of San Augustine had sent him "A Book containing the Service of *Yom Kippur* in the Portuguese ritual." On October 4, 1843 he wrote "to day is *Yom Kippur* Mr. Flatau [a Jewish partner of De Young] is doing Penance, nonsense, to keep up a Religion only one day in the year." On December 22, 1843 Sterne wrote in his Diary about "a Paper to be called the *San Augustin Literary intelligencer*, Edited or Fathered by ...T.M. Flatau, the Paper is to be a Methodist Paper — (oh! dear) — & to be under the management of a *Son of Abraham*." (See McDonald, pp. 4, 50, 175, and 186. Sterne consistently spelled the name Flatau, but Korn spells it Flateau.)

Korn says, "All this speaks too clearly of Adolphus' rearing as a Jew. Emanuel had obviously remained a Jew. Besides the half-brother Isaac, Adolphus also had a sister named Nancy who kept in touch with Isaac and "a stepbrother in New Orleans named Bernard Cohen." Korn writes, "It is impossible to explain how Adolphus could have had a stepbrother named Bernard Cohen unless the first Mrs. Emanuel Sterne was divorced and married a Mr. Cohen," or the second wife had a first husband named Cohen. Korn concludes, "I am inclined to believe that, while Adolphus was in no way an observant Jew, if he was anything at all, he was one of those secularized Jews who make Masonry their religion."

Appendix E

Relatives

The more one researches, the more evidence one discovers that the families of Adolphus Sterne, David Levi Kokernot, and Avram Wolf cross over.

When Sterne's half-brother became an orphan, he went to live with his aunt, Mrs. Van Ostern. Benjamin Van Ostern, a Hollander like the Kokernots, was a brother-in-law of Louis Kokernot, brother of David Levi Kokernot, Texas pioneer who settled in Gonzales. David's mother, Betsy Levy Kokernot, and his brother Louis were in New Orleans by 1820 at the latest. After the death of the father, Levi Moses Kokernot, his widow and son Louis operated a retail store at the corner of St. Louis and Levee streets in New Orleans. When Betsy married Alexander Hart, Hart and his son Isaac joined her business in 1836, and her son Louis became a partner of his brother-in-law, Benjamin Van Ostern. Louis was married to Nancy Van Ostern. They were divorced in 1839, probably the first divorce in New Orleans in which both husband and wife were Jews, according to B.W. Korn in *Early Jews of New Orleans*. Korn stated that Alexander Hart was born in Portsmouth, England. When he married Betsy Kokernot on July 26, 1836 (in New York) he gave his Hebrew name as "Alexander the son of Master Yehudah who is called Hart" and Betsy as "Billah the daughter of Master Nachman."

The Dyer family of Baltimore and Galveston had been called Nachman. (This was the Germanized form of Nahmani, a clan going back to the third son of Aaron in the bible. The Nahmanis became famous in the holy land, Greece, Algiers during the Inquisition, and later Germany, according to historian Dr. J.O. Dyer, descendant of the Nachmans.)

Alexander Hart may or may not have been related to Jacob Hart. Born in Philadelphia in 1781, Jacob was in New Orleans before 1805, when he shipped a cargo to the West Indies, with his vessel captured and ending up in the Mexican port of Campeche. In 1809 he was a member of the New Orleans Chamber of Commerce. That same year Mexican officials heard rumors that Jacob Hart's schooner was one of the vessels being fitted out for an invasion of Mexico. Upon arrival at the Yucatan peninsula in Mexico, the ship was confiscated. In 1810 the schooner was returned to New Orleans, and the captain became a partner with Hart in his business. In a few months the partnership was dissolved, and it was learned that the captain was charged by a grand jury with piracy. Although Hart's captain had become involved with Laffite, Jacob Hart's name never appeared in the records which concern Laffite's exploits.

Jacob Hart's younger brother David Hart of New Orleans may have been an ancestor of David Hart of New Orleans, the father of Regina Pierce, who said she was a descendant of A. Wolf who died at the fall of the Alamo in 1836. Four years younger than his brother Jacob, David Hart resided in New Orleans by 1810, for the brothers were living together on Royal Street when the federal census was taken that year. David is listed in *Whitney's New Orleans Directory* for 1811. In the 1820 census David, 35, and his brother Jacob lived on Chartres Street. (Their sister Ella or Ellen Hart in 1809 had married Haym M. Solomon, son of Haym Solomon who loaned funds to Congress during the American Revolution.)

In an interview on July 23, 1987, with Regina Pierce in Dallas regarding her great-great uncle, A. Wolf who was killed at the Alamo, she told this author, "He had been with Laffite in his encampment and went from New Orleans to Galveston. He was the black sheep of the family, and nobody wanted to talk much about it. As a child growing up I heard about him on my mother's side. She was Flora Wolf, who married David Hart. My mother was born in New Orleans [circa 1870]. My father came to America at age thirteen to work for his uncle in Athens, Alabama, who had a great big old-fashioned general store and sold cotton material, and later on my father became a cotton buyer in Bryan, Texas. As long as I knew him he was a cotton buyer in Bryan. My mother was raised there in Bryan and I was born there in Bryan. I have a marriage contract of my mother's mother and father dated 1865, the time of the Civil War. My grandfather, Mr. Wolf, in New Orleans had a shoe factory there. And he was with a commission that went to England to try to get money for the Confederacy. Also, at the end of the war, he lost everything he had. Some of the information I received from my mother's brother, David Wolf of Galveston, but he died at least fifty years ago and they had no children. All I heard about A. Wolf was that he had been the black sheep of the family, that he had been a pirate with Jean Laffite, and that he was killed at the Alamo. When New Orleans chased Laffite and his troops out of New Orleans, they went to Isle of Galveston. And when the call came to go to the Alamo, that's where he went."

Laffite's encampment left Galveston in 1820.

Archives in the Texas State Library show an A. Wolf was in Texas as early as 1822, accompanying Don

Antonio Mexia, the Baron de Bastrop, Francisco de Castañeda, and others, and serving as interpreter on a scouting mission to the Cherokee Nation, in the neighborhood of Nacogdoches. ("Agreement between the Captain of the Cherokee Nation and the Governor of Texas," Nov. 8, 1822, Nacogdoches Archives, vol. 23, pp. 52-54.) In a later document, Juan Seguin refers to him as "Constable Anthony Wolfe." (Nacogdoches Archives, June 23, 1823 to May 29, 1824, transcript vol. XXIV, p. 149, January 17, 1824.)

Following Wolf's death, David S. Kaufman inquired about Wolf's land. He may have acted only as attorney, or he may have known Wolf personally.

Appendix F

Jacob De Cordova's Publishing Background

Some sources say he learned printing from his wife's cousins. However, there were printers in the De Cordova family for many centuries, going back to a printer named Fernandez De Cordova in Valladolid in 1555. Fernandez De Cordova printed "the most important of all Texas books and the most sought" (according to Eberstadt's *Catalog of Texana*, pp. 43-44). It tells the personal narrative of Cabeza de Vaca, the first European explorer of Texas who was also the first historian of Texas. This book "may be considered the first contribution to Texas history" (C.W. Raines, *Bibliography of Texas*, pp. ix, xiv).

Rabbi Bertram W. Korn of Philadelphia ends his fourteen-page article on the *Haham* in the November 1966 issue of *American Jewish Archives* with the conclusion that many De Cordovas made their livelihood in the printing trade. Jacob's ancestor Moses Raphael De Cordova was a printer. He went from Constantinople to Holland before 1641.

His son Jacob Hayim De Cordova was active in the printing trade in Amsterdam and "spent some time in Dutch Brazil and may have been the first Jewish compositor, known to us by name, in America."

Jacob Hayim's sons, Abraham and Isaac De Cordova, also were printers. Bibliographers have located twenty books with Isaac's name, more than for any other member of the De Cordova family. He lived in Amsterdam, publishing from 1688 to 1726. Abraham De Cordova of the printing house of M. Mendez is believed to have been the father of the Haham of Jamaica (B. W. Korn, "Haham De Cordova," *American Jewish Archives*, November, 1966, pp. 154-155).

Appendix G

Museum Quality Articles in Private Collections

Sabre used by Dr. Albert Moses Levy in the Texas Revolution. Lewis Levy, Pass Christian, Mississippi, is the owner. Sword bears the engraving, "Presented to A. M. Levy by His Mother and Sisters, Richmond, Va., 1836."

Republic of Texas document, declaring Dr. Albert Moses Levy's appointment "A Surgeon in the Navy of the Republic of Texas" on March 20, 1836, signed "David G. Burnet, President of the Republic." Owned by Mrs. Mildred Levy George, New Orleans.

Embroidered alphabet sampler made by Sara Levy, niece of Dr. Albert Moses Levy, in 1840. Owned by Miss Helen Kursheedt, New Orleans.

Sterling kiddush cup given to the Reverend H. Schwarz by his congregation in Germany upon his departure for Texas. Engraved with names of congregants, roses, and "dem Precliger Herrn. H. Schwarz, L. Anderken, v. seiner Gemeinde i Reichenbach, 1859." Owned by Bernice R. Davis, Dallas.

Branding irons formerly owned by Dan Oppenheimer II, San Antonio. Two brands, D A O for cattle and D A for horses, were in his home when the author interviewed him, a year before he died.

The author asked Dan Oppenheimer whether the family name were pronounced "Op-penheimer" (as in *opera*) or "Ope-enheimer" (as in *open*). "Up-penheimer," Dan replied.

Appendix H

Land Grants

Thomas Lloyd Miller's *Bounty and Donation Land Grants of Texas 1835-1888* includes the following entries:

DYER, LEON

Received Bty Wnt 57 for 640 acres from AG on 16 May 1846 for service from 18 May to 18 Nov 1836. 640 acres in Hays Cty were ptd to Isaac M. Lyons, asgn, on 20 Apr 1847. Pat 97 Vol 4 Abst 154 GLO File Travis Bty 48.

EHRENBERG, HERMAN (HEIRS)

Received Bty Wnt 93 for 960 acres from CC on 15 Oct 1859. "320 acres for service and 640 acres in consideration of said Ehrenberg having fallen with Fannin in 1836." 960 acres in Lib Cty were ptd to his heirs on 13 May 1880. Pat 133 Vol 16 Abst 440 GLO File Lib Bty 214.

Received Don Cert 36 for 640 acres from CC on 15 Oct 1859 for his having fallen with Fannin. 640 acres in Lib Cty were ptd to his heirs on 13 May 1880. Pat 192 Vol 4 Abst 439 GLO File Lib Don 215.

HARBY, JULIAN

Received Bty Wnt 3824 for 320 acres from S War on 12 June 1838 for service from 22 Oct 1835 to 1 Feb 1836. 320 acres in Archer Cty were ptd to H.P. Levy, asgn, on 4 Oct 1858. Pat 98 Vol 9 Abst 185 GLO File Fan Bty 600.

ISAACS, SAMUEL

Received Bty Wnt 3638 for 320 acres from S War on 31 May 1838 for service from 9 June to 9 Sept 1836. Dup Wnt 834 was issued by AG on 31 May 1851 and upon the Dup 320 acres in Jasper Cty were ptd to Elisha Powell, asgn, on 24 May 1853. Pat 590 Vol 6 Abst 318 GLO File Jas Bty 59.

Received Bty Wnt 1374 for 320 acres from AG on 21 Sept 1853 for service from 1 Oct 1836 to 1 Jan 1837. 320 acres in Polk Cty were ptd to D.D. Moore, asgn, on 8 Dec 1857. Pat 188 Vol 7 Abst 333 GLO File Lib Bty 150.

JOHNSON, EDWARD J.

Received Don Cert 1242 for 640 acres from S War on 14 Feb 1846 for being in the battle of Coleto, 19 March 1836. 640 acres in Erath were ptd in his name on 20 May 1846. Pat 3 Vol 1 Abst 449 GLO File Mil Don 313. [Author's note: grant was made to heirs of Edward I. (not J.) Johnson.]

KOKERNOT, D.L.

Received Bty Wnt 3815 for 960 acres from S War on 11 June 1838 for service from 29 June 1836 to 28 Apr 1837. 960 acres in Cherokee Cty were ptd to Mason W. Cope, asgn, on 30 Jan 1850. Pat 490 Vol 5 Abst 498 GLO File Nac Bty 190.

Also received Bty Wnt 4109 for 320 acres from SW on 27 July 1838 for the same service. 220 acres in Angelina Cty and 100 acress in Cherokee Cty were ptd to WIlliam F. Gray on 28 Aug 1860 and on 31 Aug 1860. Pats 256 and 261 Vol 12 Abst A-401 C-502 GLO File Nac Bty 537.

LEVY, ALBERT M.

Received Bty Wnt 664 for 1280 acres from S War on 2 Dec 1837 for service from 22 Oct 1835 to 8 Aug 1837. 1280 acres in Llano Cty were ptd to him on 31 Dec 1845. Pat 133 Vol 3 Abst 454 GLO File Mil Bty 260.

Received Bty Wnt 2919 for 320 acres from S War on 17 Apr 1838 for service from 27 Oct 1835 to 10 Feb 1836. 195 acres in Lee Cty were ptd to the Presdt and Trustees of Rutersville College on 3 Apr 1856. Pat 109 Vol 7 Abst 206 GLO File Mil Bty 1117.

Received Don Cert 151 for 640 acres from S War on 20 May 1838 for being in the Siege of Bexar. A survey intended for 640 acres but actually containing 723.8 acres was ptd to him on 3 Mar 1847. Pat 24 Vol 2 Abst 637 GLO File Bexar Don 344.

LYONS, ISAAC M. (HEIRS)

Received Bty Wnt 6057 for 1920 acres from S War on 2 Jan 1839 for his service from 18 May 1836 to 16 Jan 1837 when he died in the Service. Two surveys, 640 acres and 1280 acres in Uvalde Cty were ptd to the heirs on 27 Aug 1847. Pats 378-9 Vol 2 Absts 317-18 GLO File Bexar Bty 458.

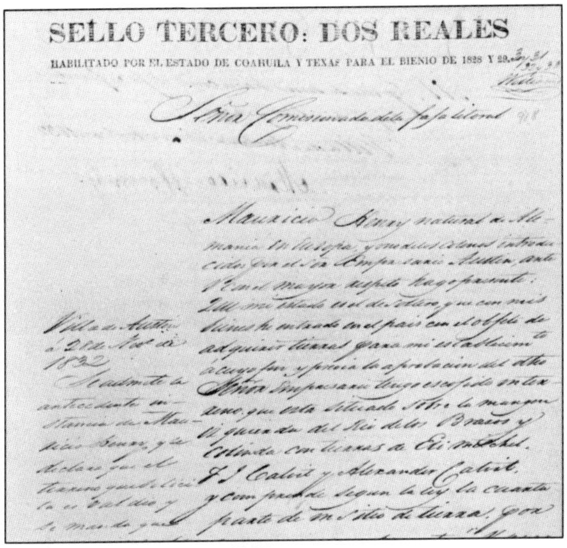

SELLO TERCERO: DOS REALES

HABILITADO POR EL ESTADO DE COAHUILA Y TEXAS PARA EL BIENIO DE 1828 Y 29.

Deed to Maurice Henry, 1832

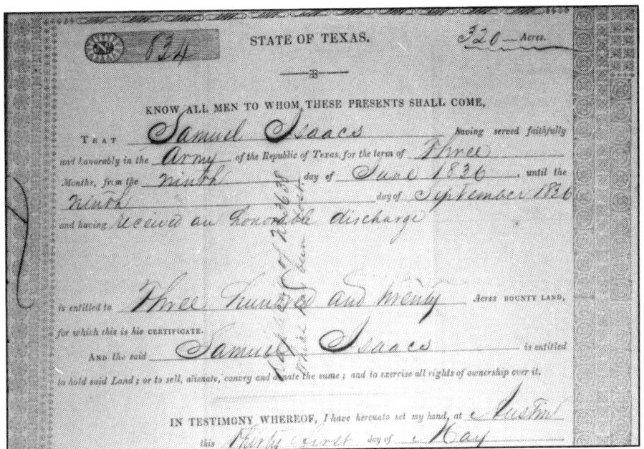

No. 834 STATE OF TEXAS. 320 Acres.

KNOW ALL MEN TO WHOM THESE PRESENTS SHALL COME,

THAT Samuel Isaacs having served faithfully and honorably in the Army of the Republic of Texas for the term of Three Months, from the ninth day of June 1836 until the ninth day of September 1836 and having received an honorable discharge is entitled to Three hundred and twenty Acres BOUNTY LAND, for which this is his CERTIFICATE.

AND the said Samuel Isaacs is entitled to hold said Land; or to sell, alienate, convey and donate the same; and to exercise all rights of ownership over it.

IN TESTIMONY WHEREOF, I have hereunto set my hand, at Austin this thirty first day of May

Honorable discharge and certificate for 320 acres bounty land to Samuel Isaacks.

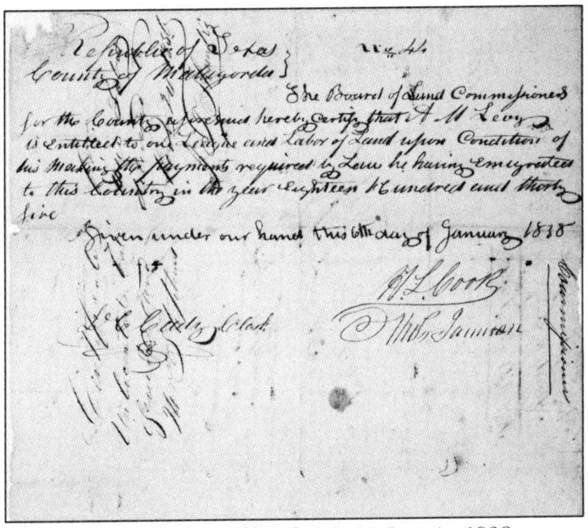

Republic of Texas, County of Matagorda } No. 44.

The Board of Land Commissioners for the County aforesaid hereby certify that A. M. Levy is entitled to one League and Labor of Land upon Condition of his making the payments required by Law he having Emigrated to this Country in the year Eighteen Hundred and thirty five

Given under our hand this 6th day of January 1838

W. L. Cook

Clerk

Thos. Jamison

One league and labor of land to A. M. Levy in 1838, "he having emigrated to this country in the year eighteen hundred and thirty-five."

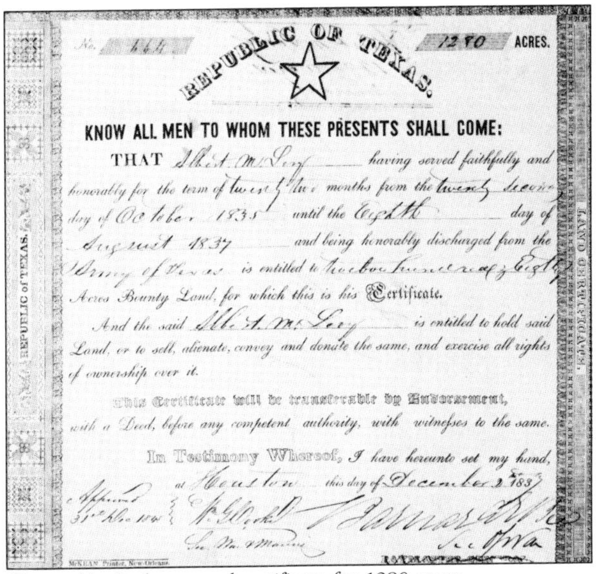

No. 644 1280 ACRES.

REPUBLIC OF TEXAS.

KNOW ALL MEN TO WHOM THESE PRESENTS SHALL COME:

THAT Albert M. Levy having served faithfully and honorably for the term of twenty two months from the twenty second day of October 1835 until the Eighth day of August 1837 and being honorably discharged from the Army of Texas is entitled to Twelve hundred & Eighty Acres Bounty Land, for which this is his Certificate.

And the said Albert M. Levy is entitled to hold said Land, or to sell, alienate, convey and donate the same, and exercise all rights of ownership over it.

This Certificate will be transferable by Endorsement, with a Deed, before any competent authority, with witnesses to the same.

In Testimony Whereof, I have hereunto set my hand, at Houston this day of December 2 1837

Honorable discharge and certificate for 1280 acres bounty land to Albert M. Levy for service October 22, 1835, until August 8, 1837.
Signed by Barnard Bee, Secretary of War.

Abbreviations used in notes and bibliography

AJA	*American Jewish Archives*
AJH	*American Jewish History*
AJHQ	*American Jewish Historical Quarterly*
AJHS	American Jewish Historical Society
Int.	Indicates interview by author
PAJHS	*Publication of American Jewish Historical Society* (predecessor of *AJHQ* and *AJH*)
SWHQ	*Southwestern Historical Quarterly*
TSHA	Texas State Historical Association
TSHAQ	*Quarterly of the Texas State Historical Association* (predecessor of *SWHQ*)
UTMB	University of Texas Medical Branch
WSJH	*Western States Jewish History*
WSJHQ	*Western States Jewish Historical Quarterly*

Notes

Introduction to a People

1. Martin A. Cohen, *Martyr*, pp. 69, 70, 305; Vito Alessio Robles, *Coahuila y Texas en la época Colonial*, pp. 89-90; idem, *Monterrey en la historia y en la leyenda*, p. 97; Alonso (de León), "Historia de Nuevo León" in G. Garcia (ed.), *Documentos Muy Raros*, vol. 25, pp. 90-95.
2. Bertram W. Korn, "The Haham De Cordova of Jamaica," *AJA*, November 1966, p. 145n.
3. "It would be stretching coincidence too far to imagine that there was no connection between the 85 years — 1641 to 1726 — during which the De Cordovas had supported themselves as printers, and the day when Jacob De Cordova and his brother Joshua established the *Daily Gleaner* newspaper and printing business which has played so significant a role in the cultural, political, and economic life of . . . Jamaica." Ibid., p. 155.
4. De Cordova's *Texas: Her Capabilities and Resources* encouraged England to import Texas cotton. The publication includes two lectures given by De Cordova in Manchester, England, in 1858.
5. Harold Preece, "He Brought Families to Texas," *Congress Weekly* (a publication of the American Jewish Congress, New York), vol. 23, no. 2 (Aug. 20, 1956), pp. 11-13. A quarter of a century later, at age seventy-eight, Preece said he wrote about Jews because in his childhood in Austin a Jewish teacher, Moselle Litman, had encouraged him. "We were just Texas farm folks and no one in my family had gone past the sixth grade. But this very fine teacher and friend encouraged my creativity and I was grateful the rest of my life." Int. Preece, 1985.
6. Fred F. Florence raised financing for the East Texas Oil Field through the Republic National Bank of Dallas.
7. David M. Bressler, "Results and Significance of the Galveston Movement," *Jewish Herald*, Aug. 6, 1914; Henry Cohen, "Galveston Immigration Movement," *Federation Review*, March 1908, pp. 1-8; Gary Dean Best, "Jacob H. Schiff's Galveston Movement," *AJA*, vol. 30, no. 1 (April 1978), p. 55; Ronald A. Axelrod, "Rabbi Cohen and the Galveston Immigration Movement," *East Texas Historical Association Journal*, vol. 15, no. 1 (1977), p. 29.

Chapter 1
The Adventurers

1. Jewish soldiers went with Pánfilo de Narváez in 1519 to capture Cortes in Mexico. When Cortes defeated Narváez, his troops joined Cortes, who completed the conquest of the Aztecs in 1521, thereby beginning the Spanish colonization in the new hemisphere. S.B. Liebman, *New World Jewry 1493-1825*, p. 15.
2. The first Mexico *auto da fe*, in October 1528, included four Jews. Hernando Alonso, a conquistador with Cortes, and Gonzalo de Morales went to the stake. Gonzalo's brother, Diego de Morales, and Diego de Ocaña were reconciled and ordered exiled to Spain. Only de Ocaña returned to Spain. Ibid., p. 39.
3. Hammond Innes, *The Conquistadors*, pp. 12-21.
4. After first coming to Mexico with conquistadors in 1519, Jews continued to come between 1521 and 1580. Because the Inquisition was worse in Spain, the colony continued to grow through the sixteenth century. Francisco Fernandez del Castillo, an authority on the Inquisition and director of the Mexican National Archives, wrote that in the 1550s Mexico City had a Grand Rabbi and more Jews than Catholics lived in the village. Liebman, *New World Jewry*, p. 22; F. Fernandez, *Libros y libreros del siglo XVI*, p. 584.
5. "Its first mayor was Gaspar Castaño, alleged to be a son of Jewish *conversos*, who came to New Spain with Don Luis." S.B. Liebman, *Jews in New Spain*, p. 149. "Castaño . . . was also a 'New Christian.'" Carl L. Duaine, *Caverns of Oblivion*, p. 58.
6. Mormon archives reveal Castaño may have carried on trade from the Phillipines after his exile. Scholarly research by Lyman D. Platt, American Fort, Utah. Int. Lyman D. Platt, 1984. Although it has been reported that Castaño was killed while on a ship in the Philippines, another theory suggests he died aboard a ship off the coast of Mexico, not the Chinese seas. At the time of his death, Texas had two names: "La Provincia de los Tejas" because of the East Texas Tejas Indians, and "New Philippines" honoring the king of Spain, Philip II (1527-1598). Both the Philippine Islands and New Philippines (Texas) were possessions of Spain. There was direct trading between Mexico and the Philippines by way of the Manila Galleon, which had a regular sailing schedule from Acapulco to Manila. It is possible that earlier writers could have confused the two similar names. The word

"exile" in those days usually meant to be exiled from Mexico City. Therefore, Castaño may have been exiled to northern Mexico, carrying on trade with the Philippines, or living in Texas. Int. John Wheat, Bexar Archives Translator, Barker Texas History Center, University of Texas at Austin. However, he may have exiled himself or been exiled to the Philippines. During the Inquisition trials, sentences often included "consignment to serve as an oarsman on the galleys between . . . Acapulco and the Philippines." Liebman, *New World Jewry*, pp. 27, 53. "The fact is that we have no information on him after he left for China, and neither does Genaro Garcia." Letter, George P. Hammond to author, 1984.

7. A. Schroeder and D. Matson, *Colony on the Move*, p. 6.
8. Vito Alessio Robles, *Coahuila y Texas en la epoca Colonial*; M. Cohen, *Martyr*, p. 70.
9. N. De Lafora, *Presidios Internos*, pp. 79, 173, 178, 245 in notes by Alessio Robles. Monterrey, near Texas, is more than 500 miles north of Mexico City. When the trials of the Inquisition in Mexico City began to accelerate, Castaño moved from Monterrey approximately 100 miles farther north to Monclova (Almadén), where he began his expedition to Texas and New Mexico.
10. Cohen, *Martyr*, p. 180; Inquisition trial record of Governor Luis de Carvajal, Feb. 26, 1590, Archives, AJHS.
11. Translation, Castaño journal, typescript, archives, Bancroft Library.
12. Schroeder and Matson, *Colony on the Move*, pp. 34, 180.
13. The West Texas future towns of Iraan and Sheffield, on Castaño's path, later became part of an oil field. "Marathon Oil, the primary producer in the area, hasn't slowed from pumping 125,000 barrels a day in the oil-rich Yates Field," by Laura Stone for AP in *Odessa American*, May 5, 1984.
14. Schroeder and Matson, *Colony on the Move*, pp. 6, 101.
15. Ibid., p. 160; D. Hull, *Old Santa Fe*, p. 329. "He was fair minded," said anthropologist and author Schroeder. Int. A. Schroeder, 1980.
16. Schroeder and Matson, *Colony on the Move*, p. 102.
17. Ibid., p. 5; Paul Horgan, *Great River*, p. 158.
18. Translation, Castaño journal, typescript, archives, Bancroft Library.
19. Schroeder and Matson, *Colony on the Move*, p. 9.
20. Laws of Settlement of 1573, Ordinance 1; Hull, *Old Santa Fe*, p. 332; Pacheco y Cardenas, *Col. Doc. Ined.*, vol. 16, p. 143.
21. Cohen, *Martyr*, p. 312, n. 40.
22. Archives, Bancroft Library; Schroeder and Matson, *Colony on the Move*, p. 172.
23. Hull, *Old Santa Fe*, pp. 332, 332n; Schroeder and Matson, *Colony on the Move*, p. 160.
24. Archives, Bancroft Library.
25. Hull, *Old Santa Fe*, p. 332.
26. Archives, Bancroft Library; Schroeder and Matson, *Colony on the Move*, p. 173.
27. Horgan, *Great River*, p. 160.
28. Int. A. Schroeder, Santa Fe, N.M.
29. Fernando Benítez, *Los Primeros Mexicanos*.
30. Luis reported in his memoirs the operation was painful and clumsily executed, but that he became joyous once he had fulfilled the divine precept and thereafter believed that the circumcision provided a powerful restraint to his lust. Cohen, *Martyr*, p. 102.
31. Ibid., p. 39.
32. Guiomar de Ribera used her mother's maiden name. She was the daughter of Miguel Nuñez of Lisbon and later Seville, who held slaving contracts granted by the kings of both Portugal and Spain, until his death around 1577. Ibid., p. 38.
33. Cohen, *Martyr*, p. 65.
34. Seymour B. Liebman, "Mestizo Jews," *AJA*, November 1967, p. 153.
35. Cohen, *Martyr*, pp. 73-76.
36. Ibid., p. 104.
37. The Carvajal charter described land as extending "from the port of Tampico on the Panuco River and the mines of Mazapil to the borders of New Galicia and New Biscay (*Nueva Vizcaya*), and thence northward, whatever can be discovered from sea to sea, provided that the territory does not exceed two hundred leagues in latitude and two hundred leagues in longitude." The territory embraced almost all of Coahuila, all of the contemporary Mexican states of Nuevo Leon and Tamaulipas and part of San Luis Potosi. Because the boundaries of New Galicia and New Biscay were not firmly fixed, the deed led to controversies around the town of Saltillo. Cohen, *Martyr*, pp. 69, 305; S. Roel, *Nuevo León*, pp. 155, 158.
38. "Inquisition in Mexico: Trial of Luis de Carabajal, 1590" Inquisition Vol. 1487, Mexico. Archives, AJHS.
39. Cohen, *Martyr*, pp. 69, 103, 110.
40. Ibid., p. 238.
41. Archives, AJHS, Inquisitorial papers, 1595 and 1596.
42. Cohen, *Martyr*, p. 259.
43. Liebman, *New World Jewry*, p. 52.
44. The Inquisition's men arrested Ana in 1596, but judged her "reconciled" in 1601. She married Cristobal Miguel and named a son Gaspar de Sosa. After being arrested again in 1643 as a "relapsed Judaizer," she spent six years in a jail cell until she died in 1649. Cohen, *Martyr*, p. 333.
45. Int., Malcolm Stern.
46. Some Carvajals became Baptists. Letter, J.M.D. Carbajal to his mother, Lexington [Kentucky], July 2d, 1826, Stephen F. Austin Papers; H. Bancroft, *North Mexican States and Texas*; *Handbook of Texas*, p. 294. The Lexington letter is signed "Joseph M.D. Carbajal" (not M.J.).
47. Int., Irving (Pancho) Greenblum, 1985. A similar story appears in "Chicano Jews in South Texas." "In personal interviews in South Texas, I have been informed that many Chicano families who have resided there for over 200 years are descendants of Jews. Today most of them are Catholic. The conversions took place during the past 150 years. A few have converted back to Judaism. Others have Jewish family relics going back to previous years. Beyond that there is solely oral tradition." C.M. Larralde, pp. 6, 58. Californian Larralde interviewed in South Texas with a Ford Foundation grant.
48. Liebman, *New World Jewry*, p. 45.
49. "Spain herself was the loser, for [Jews] represented the most cultured, industrious and knowledgeable section of the community." Innes, *Conquistadors*, p. 21.
50. Archives, Institute of Texan Cultures; F.R. Kallison, "One Hundred Years of Jewry in San Antonio," p. 3; F. Chabot, *San Antonio*, pp. 23, 128.
51. Proceedings of the cabildo June 28, 1745, *Libro de Cavildo 1742-1749*, Nacogdoches Archives; Mattie Alice Austin, "Municipal Government of San Fernando de Bexar 1730-1800," *TSHAQ*, vol. 8, no. 4, pp. 291-92; Chabot, *San Antonio*, pp. 23, 128.
52. "The Inquisition records of the 17th century indicate that close connection existed between the Conversos in the Canaries and those in England and northwestern Europe. Among those announced were Antonio Fernandez Carvajal, a founder of the London Jewish community." *Encyclopedia Judaica*, p.117; Int. S.B. Liebman, 1984.
53. M. A. Austin, "Municipal Government of Bexar," *TSHAQ*, vol. 8, no. 4, pp. 293-94.

54. I. J. Cox, "Early Settlers of San Fernando," *TSHAQ*, vol. 5, no. 2, pp. 147, 151. Cox also noted: "In the presidial records are to be found among the names of soldiers and *vecinos agregados* those of Carabajal." Ibid., p. 148.
55. *Handbook of Texas*, vol. 2, p. 551; E. McMillan, *San Antonio in the 18th Century*, p. 59.
56. Noah graduated Dec. 9, 1807. G.W. Cullum, *Biographical Sketches, U.S. Military Academy*; S. Wolf, *American Jew as Patriot, Soldier*, pp. 34-37; Max J. Kohler, "American Jewish Patriotism," *PAJHS*, vol. 4, 1896, pp. 90-93.
57. *The Jewish Encyclopedia* (1905), vol. 9, p. 323.
58. Cohen, *Martyr*, p. 272.
59. H. Yoakum, *History of Texas*, vol. 1, pp. 150-51.
60. Ibid., p. 153.
61. This was the origin of the league head-rights later granted in Texas.
62. Yoakum, *History of Texas*, vol. 1, p. 162.
63. Ibid., p. 166; H. S. Thrall, *A Pictorial History of Texas*, p. 117.
64. Yoakum, *History of Texas*, vol. 1, p. 168.
65. Account of Col. J.A. Navarro in Thrall, *Pictorial History of Texas*, pp. 118-19; Yoakum, *History of Texas*, vol. 1, p. 169.
66. L. Huhner, "Jews in the War of 1812," *AJHQ*, vol. 26, 1918, p. 180. Mordecai Manuel Noah was "the most conspicious figure in the American Jewish community between the War of 1812 and the Mexican War." R. Learsi, *Jews in America*, p. 61.The eminent historian Jacob Rader Marcus, director of the American Jewish Archives, called M.M. Noah "the best-known Jewish layman in the country in the decades before the civil War" in his *Memoirs of American Jews*, p. 117. A letter from M.M. Noah's mother implies she had three sons, M.M., Uriah, and Samuel. "Mrs. Noah speaks of Uriah and of 'my dear Sammy' as she might her own children." I. Goldberg, *Major Noah*, p. 16n.
67. National Archives and Records Service, G.S.A., Washington, D.C., Bounty-land file of Samuel Noah, BL Wt 16349-150-55.
68. S. Wolf, *American Jew as Patriot*, p. 37; M. Kohler, "American Jewish Patriotism," *PAJHS*, vol. 4, 1896, pp. 92-93.
69. "Winter of 1813 found Texas devastated, its population diminished, herds destroyed, and food in short supply." David J. Weber, *The Mexican Frontier 1821-1846*, p. 10.
70. Letter, Luis Aury to his sister, Jan. 14, 1817, Galveston, typescript translation in Barker Texas History Center, University of Texas; Yoakum, *History of Texas*, vol. 1, pp. 181, 184; Harris G. Warren (trans. and ed.), "Documents Relating to the Establishment of Privateers at Galveston 1816-1817," *Louisiana Historical Quarterly*, vol. 21 (October 1938), pp. 1104, 1106; *Dyer Scrap Book*, p. 84.
71. *Dyer Scrap Book*, p. 18.
72. Dr. Joseph Osterman Dyer, *Galveston News*, Dec. 17, 1921.
73. See Appendix A, "Laffite a Jew?"
74. Dyer, *Galveston News*, Jan. 12, 1924.
75. It has not been established whether Jose Manuel de Herrera was related to Manuel de Herrera, a relative of Castaño de Sosa, or Simón de Herrera, Governor of Nuevo León in 1813.
76. "Laffite stayed on Galveston Island exactly three years and gave his settlement the name of Galvez-town in 1819. . . . Laffite during the period of his residence on the island, never left it. . . . In three years the thirteen cruisers of the Commune defied the largest naval power in Europe. . .
When he left Galveston Island in May, 1820, he became a trader in Yucatan, where he died in 1826." *Dyer Scrap Book*, p. 90. Although other sources state Laffite left Galveston in 1821, Dyer had contact with near-primary sources. Laffite's death is as mysterious as his birthplace. "'Wednesday, July 12 (1827) Laffite died at Las bocas 59 leagues from Campeche on the North Coast of Yucatan . . . and was buried at Salam, two leagues from Las bocas.' This I had from an old Mexican, half Indian named Gregorio who stated he had been prisoner with him, and had been at Galveston Island. He died of fever." Letter, S.R. Fisher, Sec., Texas Navy, Matagorda, May 1, 1838, to Gen. M.B. Lamar. *Papers of M.B. Lamar*, vol. 2, p. 152.
77. Information used in the de la Porta section was obtained chiefly from the *Dyer Scrap Book*, press clippings of articles on Galveston and Texas history, mostly from *Galveston News*, Dec. 14, 1919 to Sept. 19, 1926, by J.O. Dyer, M.D.
78. Gershom Kursheedt's father was Rabbi Israel Baer Kursheedt of colonial New York whose grandfather was Gershom Mendes Seixas, who had been rabbi in New York until 1776, when the British captured the town, and he moved to Philadelphia. Gershom Kursheedt's son married the niece of Dr. Albert Moses Levy. Learsi, *Jews in America*, pp. 32, 36, 82. The Kursheedt family also appears in Bertram W. Korn, *Early Jews of New Orleans*.
79. Dyer, *Galveston News*, Dec. 1, 1923.

Chapter 2
The Soldiers

1. Little more than 30,000 persons populated the entire state in 1836; Gifford White, *1840 Citizens of Texas*, vol. 2, preface. Earliest Jewish settlers in Texas during the fifteen years between Austin's colony in 1821 and the revolution in 1836 are not all included in this text.
2. Grievances leading to war included closing of immigration to Texas, no appellate court in Texas, no trial by jury, and prohibition of any other than the Roman Catholic religion. Eugene C. Barker, ed., *Austin Papers*, vol. 2, pp. 934-40; Stephen F. Austin, "Texas Grievances," in Eugene C. Barker, ed., *History of Texas*, pp. 194-208; David J. Weber, *The Mexican Frontier 1821-1846*, pp. 7, 38-40.
3. Archie P. McDonald, ed., *Diary of Adolphus Sterne*, p. xii.
4. James Carter, ed., *First Century of Scottish Rite Masonry in Texas 1867-1967*, p. 19.
5. H. Yoakum, *History of Texas*, vol. 1, pp. 247-49; Clarence R. Wharton, *History of Texas*, pp. 89-92; Eugene C. Barker, *Life of Stephen F. Austin*, pp. 192-99; David M. Vigness, *Revolutionary Decades*, pp. 79-83.
6. Carter, *Scottish Rite Masonry in Texas*, pp. 18-21, 56-61, 421-22.
7. Ibid., p. 18.
8. His mother Betsy Kokernot and older brother Louis came to New Orleans in 1820. In 1836 his mother married a second time, to Alexander Hart of New York. Malcolm Stern, *First American Jewish Families*; B. Korn, *Early Jews of New Orleans*, p. 138. See Appendix E.
9. The 1831 Texas hurricane was Kokernot's second shipwreck. On September 24, 1824, he had been shipwrecked near Haiti, barely escaping by clinging to a rock all night. Gonzales *Inquirer*, June 22, 1878; Gonzales *Weekly Inquirer*, July 19, 1923, p. 4-C.
10. Gonzales *Weekly Inquirer*, July 19, 1923.
11. David Weber, *Mexican Frontier*, p. 155; Eugene C. Barker, *Mexico and Texas*, p. 108.
12. The Anahuac disturbances of 1832 and 1835 were the first skirmishes on the path to the revolution; the first shot is officially credited to the Battle at Gonzales on Oct. 2,

1835; the first battle of sizeable importance was the Grass Fight, Nov. 26, 1835.

13. Jim Dan Hill, *The Texas Navy*, pp. 12-14; John Henry Brown, *History of Texas*, vol. 1, p. 181. Kokernot called this skirmish "The Anahuac Scrape." D.L. Kokernot, "The Battle of Anahuac," Gonzales *Inquirer*, May 4, 1878, reprinted in Gonzales *Weekly Inquirer*, July 19, 1923. F.W. Johnson, *Texas and Texans*, vol. 1, p. 68ff., 77, quoting Commodore Kokernot. Edna Rowe, "Disturbances at Anahuac in 1832," *TSHAQ*, vol. 6 (1902-1903); H.S. Thrall, *A Pictorial History of Texas*, p. 506; Barker, *Mexico and Texas*, pp. 104-7, 112-13, 136, 152.
14. D. Kokernot, "Early Reminiscences in Texas," Gonzales *Inquirer*, Aug. 17, 1878, reprinted in Gonzales *Weekly Inquirer*, July 19, 1923, p. 5-C.
15. M. K. Wisehart, *Sam Houston*, p. 111.
16. The friendship of Sterne and Houston continued for years. In a letter from Sam Houston from Washington-on-the Brazos July 28, 1844, to Sterne, Houston wrote, "I intend to be with you at Nacogdoches by the 10th of August." Williams and Barker, eds., *Writings of Sam Houston* , vol. 4, p. 342.
17. H. Cohen, "Settlement of the Jews in Texas," *Publication, PAJHS*, vol. 2, 1894, p. 143; idem., "Early Jewish Settlements in Texas," 1936, pp. 6-7.
18. McDonald, ed., *Hurrah for Texas*, p. x.
19. Ibid.
20. McDonald, ed., *Hurrah for Texas*, p. 19; J. H. Jenkins, *Basic Texas Books*, p. 522.
21. Wisehart, *Sam Houston*, p. 125.
22. Presiding was William Christy, chairman of a New Orleans committee to aid Texas.
23. Carter, *Scottish Rite Masonry in Texas*, p. 19; Yoakum, *History of Texas*, vol. 2, p. 23.
24. T. C. Richardson, *East Texas*, vol. 3, p. 1406.
25. Eugene C. Barker, *The Father of Texas*, p. 198.
26. "Battle of Conception, 94 Texans, 400 Mexicans;" *Papers of M. B. Lamar*, p. 509.
27. Cohen, "Settlement of the Jews in Texas," *PAJHS*, p. 151.
28. Yoakum, *History of Texas*, vol. 2, p. 22.
29. Kokernot, Gonzales *Weekly Inquirer*, July 19, 1923.
30. Saul Viener, "Surgeon Moses Albert Levy," *AJHQ*, (December 1956), pp. 101-113.
31. Brown, *History of Texas*, vol. 1, p. 421; Francis W. Johnson, *Texas and Texans*, vol. 1; Viener, "Surgeon Moses Albert Levy," *AJHQ*, p. 102.
32. Dr. Levy came to Texas in 1835. After the war he received several land grants. Besides those listed in T.L. Miller, in 1838 he was awarded Headright Certificate #44 — one league and one labor issued by Board of Land Commissioners of Matagorda County. L.W. Kemp Collection, Barker Texas History Center, University of Texas.
33. Herman Ehrenberg, *Fahrten*, p. 86.
34. Ibid., p. 105.
35. Ibid., p. 110; Herman Ehrenberg, *With Milan and Fannin*, p. 101.
36. Ints., Regina (Mrs. H. Lee) Pierce, 1983 and 1987. Mrs. Pierce, a member of Dallas' Temple Emanu-El and a descendant of A. Wolf on her mother's side, stated that Wolf, a native of England, was the black sheep of the family. A. Wolf made several excursions to Texas prior to 1835. See Appendix E. Also, Simon Wolfe, *American Jew as Patriot*, p. 75; Philip Rosenthal, *Roll Call at the Alamo*, p. 43.
37. "In 1978 we personally pursued our search for information on Wolf. Through our interview in the predominantly Jewish London suburb of Hampstead Heath we were able to come up with synagogue records for that region going back to the late 1700s. Since the Jewish population in the era with which we were concerned was relatively small, our quest did not prove to be insurmountable. We found records dating back to 1835 that noted that an Avram (Abraham) Wolf was leaving England for a place in a 'Master A. Sterne's North American colony called Teksis' along with his two sons Benjamin and Michael. In those same records only a few pages before we read of the untimely death and burial of Avram's wife, Sarah, in what is today a Jewish burial ground and crematorium in Hampstead Heath. Wolf an English Jew? Without question." Philip S. Rosenthal, President, Alamo International, Hopatcong, N.J., in a letter dated Dec. 19, 1982, to Charles J. Long, Curator, the Alamo, in archives, Daughters of the Republic of Texas Library at the Alamo. Much of the research for Rosenthal was done by Richard Cloutier, then a member of the staff of the British Museum in London.
38. "ANTHONY WOLFE was among those patriots who were killed in the ALAMO at San Antonio in 1836. CAPT. JOHN W. HALL of old Washington on the Brazos alleged that he resided at his home in the town of Washington some time prior to the time he was killed, where he went through a long spell of sickness, and that he (Capt. Hall) looked after and took care of him. Petition for the administration of his estate was filed in Washington County in 1837, and JOHN W. HALL and THOMAS S. SAUL made bond to secure the proper administration" *Austin Colony Pioneers*, Washington County, p. 254.

    Wolf's sons from his first marriage, according to Enrique Esparza, were "ruthlessly slaughtered" at the Battle of the Alamo. Corres., Charles J. Long, Curator, the Alamo, Dec. 5, 1982, in Archives, DRT Library at the Alamo.

    When Almaron Dickinson, husband of one of the few survivors of the Alamo, jumped from the chapel with a child, the child likely was Michael Wolf, A. Wolf's younger son. "Lt. Dickinson, with a child on his back, leaped from an upper window in the east end of the church; but their lifeless bodies fell to the ground riddled with bullets." Thrall, *Pictorial History of Texas*, p. 246. Wolf was a private. Muster Rolls, pp. 20, 29.
39. Int., Charles J. Long, 1984; C.M. Barnes, *San Antonio Express*, May 12 and 19, 1907.
40. Box 2R237 Kemp (Louis W.) Papers, "Biographical Notebook, Wim-Xi."
41. "Public Debt of the Late Republic of Texas, This is to certify that Anthony Wolf Dec. per D.S. Kaufman, has . . . a claim for Services in the Army 1835 and 1836, amounting to Twenty four Dollars;" July 22, 1851; Texas State Library, Austin.
42. See "An account of the adventures of Moses Rose, who escaped from the Alamo, by Captain W. P. Zuber" in A.J.H. Pennybacker, *History of Texas* (1900), pp. 183-188.
43. The Fredonian Rebellion occurred Dec. 26, 1826 to Jan. 31, 1827. Zuber stated Rose "was an early immigrant to Texas and resided in Nacogdoches, where my father, Mr. Abraham Zuber, made his acquaintance in 1827." Nacogdoches Archives, vol. 80, p. 89; R.B. Blake, "Rose and His Escape," p. 2. Rose dated his residency in Texas from 1826, stating in 1838 in the Chirino case he "knew applicant twelve years, resides here since." Proceedings, Nacogdoches County Board of Land Commissioners, #245.

    The Battle of Nacogdoches Aug. 2-3, 1832, resulted in "the expulsion of Mexican troops from that part of Texas;" McDonald, *Hurrah for Texas*, p. 53. "The 17 Texans who captured the entire Mexican garrison on

Aug. 3rd, 1832, was led by James Carter and piloted by Adolphus Sterne;" Blake, "Rose and His Escape," p. 11.

44. Regarding the Rose ancestry: "My mother-in-law said, 'My Dad told me one time when I was a kid that I was part Jew. I can remember my Daddy telling me when I was a little ole bitty girl that we were part Jew.'" Int. Hazel (Mrs. Paul) Baimbridge, Jr., regarding her mother-in-law's (Ethelyn Rose Baimbridge's) father, Arthur Foster Rose (1890-1927), a railroad engineer who drove a train from Denison, Texas, into parts of Oklahoma. Arthur Rose was the eighth of eleven children, son of Isaac Rose. Arthur presented the Alamo with Moses Rose's gun. Moses bought the gun around 1850, after he left the Alamo.
45. Int., Charles Long, Curator of the Alamo, 1984.
46. Enrique Esparza int. with C.M. Barnes, *San Antonio Express*, May 12, 1907.
47. Survivor Susanna (Mrs. Almaron) Dickinson had stated she recalled a combatant named *Ross* who escaped; she may have meant Rose.
48. L.P. Teer, *Frontier Times*, vol. 39 (Oct.-Nov. 1965).
49. County Courthouse Records, Nacogdoches; R.B. Blake Collection, Stephen F. Austin University; typescript of Rose testimonies, vol. 61, pp. 156, 158, 162-63, 165-66, 204, 225-26; Nacogdoches County Proceedings, Board of Land Commissioners.
50. Blake, "Rose and His Escape," pp. 5-8. R.B. Blake Papers, p. 204. The entry for Rose himself states: "Lewis Rose — James Carter knew him six years ago. 1/3 Leag. Adolphus Sterne states the same." R.B. Blake Papers, p. 204. The Board of Land Commissioners Records, Cert. 266; "FROST THORN, assignee of Lewis Rose, 1/3 League, previous 2nd May 1835." C. Ericson, "Nacogdoches Headrights," p. 8.
51. W.P. Zuber, "The Escape of Rose from the Alamo," *TSHAQ*, (July 1901), p. 1.
52. Ibid., pp. 1-11.
53. Ibid., p. 9.
54. Zuber had been a boy soldier in Sam Houston's army and later became a founder of the Texas State Historical Association. Frank X. Tolbert, *History of Texas*, p. 107.
55. J. Frank Dobie, "Rose and His Story of the Alamo" in *In the Shadow of History*, pp. 10-11. Zuber at age 91 wrote in 1911, "My father, Abraham Zuber, knew Rose and believed him to be a truthful man." Letter, Zuber to Hon. James T. DeShields, San Marcos, Texas.
56. Walter Lord, *A Time to Stand*, p. 202.
57. He was born Louis Rose in Laferee, Ardennes on May 11, 1785; Steven G. Kellman, "The Yellow Rose of Texas," *Journal of American Culture*, vol. 5, no. 2, p. 46.
58. Zuber, "The Escape of Rose from the Alamo," p. 2.
59. Kellman, "The Yellow Rose of Texas," from research he made of records in the French military archives.
60. On June 20, 1837, Rose sold to Frost Thorn his interest in a third of a league of land in the County of Nacogdoches. Thorn later earned the reputation of being the first millionaire in Texas.
61. Sam Reid, Nacogdoches pioneer, was the person who said he heard Rose tell why he did not stay in the Alamo. Blake, "Rose and His Escape," pp. 13-14.
62. Walt Whitman, "Song of Myself."
63. Job I:15.
64. "Political Rights of Jews in United States 1776-1840," *AJA* (April 1955), pp. 51-53.
65. Ehrenberg, *Fahrten*, p. 175.
66. Int. Lawrence P. Johnson, 1981. The Director of the American Jewish Archives confirmed Goliad's Johnson was a Jew, adding that members of the Johnson family continued active in the Ohio Jewish community. Int., Dr. Jacob Rader Marcus, 1975.
67. Cohen, "Settlement of the Jews," p. 146.
68. Ehrenberg, *Fahrten*, p. 160.
69. Ibid., p. 158.
70. James M. Day, "Goliad," in *Battles of Texas*, p. 39; C. R. Wharton, *Remember Goliad*, pp. 43, 55; Carlos Castañeda, *Our Catholic Heritage in Texas*, vol. 6, pp. 297-300.
71. Ibid., p. 45.
72. Ehrenberg, *Fahrten*, p. 194. There is better than a 50-50 chance that the Johnson who set off the explosion was Edward I. Johnson because the list of men "killed by order of General Santa Anna at Goliad, March 27, 1836" includes only two Johnsons, the other being a David Johnson. Walter Prescott Webb, ed., "The Men of Goliad," *SWHQ*, vol. 43 (July 1939-April 1940).
73. Ehrenberg was born Oct. 17, 1816, though other documents give his birth as 1815, 1817, and 1818. He was one of four brothers born in Steuden, near Leipzig, Prussia, coming to New York in 1834 and then to New Orleans. Archives, Arizona Historical Foundation, Hayden Library, A.S.U., Tempe, Az.; Archives, Arizona Historical Society, Tucson, Az. See also Appendix C.
74. Cohen, "Settlement of the Jews," p. 146.
75. Yoakum, *History of Texas*, vol. 2, p. 99.
76. Ehrenberg, *With Milam and Fannin*, p. 204.
77. Ibid., p. 207.
78. The navy added a fourth ship, the *Liberty*, by August 1836, and several more vessels in 1839. Yoakum, *History of Texas*, vol. 2, p. 192.
79. John H. Jenkins, ed., *Papers of the Texas Revolution*, vol. 5, p. 365, item 2628, Thomas to Houston, War Department, Harrisburg, April 7, 1836.
80. K. Gardien, "Kokernot and His Tory," *Texana*, vol. 8, no. 3, pp. 269-294.
81. This was the same ship that had brought Kokernot four years earlier to Texas. "I left New Orleans March 28, 1832, in the schooner Flash, Captain Falwell, for the town of Anahuac on the head of Galveston Bay. We landed on the 6th of April, 1832." Kokernot, "Battle of Anahuac."
82. Albert Emanuel came to Texas in 1834 and had a store in Nacogdoches. At San Jacinto, he served as a private in Captain William Kimbrough's 8th Company, 2nd Regiment, Texas Volunteers. After the war he returned to his business in Nacogdoches for four years, marrying Louisa Hart of New Orleans. In 1840 he moved to New Orleans, where he became a lawyer.
83. D. Lefkowitz, "Jewish Pioneers of Texas," p. 28; H. Cohen, "Early Jewish Settlements in Texas," p. 8; D.W.C. Baker, *Texas Scrap-Book*, p. 569.
84. "[In] the hut on bayshore in which Genl. Sam Houston was placed at Galveztown when his ankle was shattered, Colonel Leon Dyer gave up his blanket, and Colonel W.D.C. Hall applied a poultice of brown sugar and crushed charcoal as an antiseptic. May 5 1836." Unsigned manuscript, Rosenberg Library, Galveston. Col. Dyer did not settle in Texas; int., Susan Dyer Johnson; Ira Rosenwaike, "Leon Dyer: Baltimore and San Francisco Jewish Leader," *WSJHQ*, January 1977, pp. 135-143.
85. Letter of Surgeon Levy, May 5, 1837, and the official report of Lt. J.W. Taylor, April 21, 1837; Yoakum, *History of Texas*, vol. 2, p. 212n. Viener, "Surgeon Moses Albert Levy," p. 103.
86. L.E. Devereaux, *Texas Navy*, p. 4a; J.D. Hill, *Texas Navy*, p. 91.
87. The diary begins in 1840 when Sterne was age thirty-nine and stops in 1846, when he was a member of the Texas Legislature. It resumes in 1850 and continues until his

death in 1852.

88. *Writings of Sam Houston*, vol. 4, p. 342. Houston also wrote, "I have thought [it] proper to nominate the Hon. Adolfo Sterne. . . giving powers as Commissioner, to act on subjects which may be embraced in their instructions from the War Department."
89. Carter, *Scottish Rite Masonry in Texas*, pp. 18, 421.
90. McDonald, ed., *Diary of Adolphus Sterne*, p. xi.
91. *Handbook of Texas*, vol. 1, pp. 972-973.
92. Letter, A. Somervell, Acting Sec. of the Texas Navy, Velasco, 30 June 1836; Jenkins, ed., *Papers of the Texas Revolution*, vol. 7, p. 318.
93. Texas A&M University conferred the Doctor of Agriculture degree on Herbert Lee Kokernot, Sr., of San Antonio on May 26, 1944. Archives, Texas A&M University. When Herbert Lee Kokernot was born in Gonzales Dec. 28, 1867, he was the fourth generation of Kokernots who had lived in Texas. Levi Moses Kokernot, the patriarch, had come to New Orleans in 1817 with David Levi; David's mother, Betsy Van Der Beugel, came in 1820. Stern, *First American Jewish Families*; Int. John Stedman.
94. Int. Ola Mae Renfroe of Marfa, Texas, 1983.
95. The archives of Touro Synagogue in New Orleans contain documents of Kokernot's paternal ancestors' religion, cultural background, and family in "Book of Births and Deaths and Marriages" and "Register of Deaths of the Israelite Congregation Shahari Chasset." However, Kokernot converted to Christianity. Gardien, "Kokernot and His Tory," *Texana*, vol. 8, no. 3, p. 294.
96. *Medical Record and Annals*, vol. 60, no. 8 (August 1967), p. 307.
97. A "List of officers of the Volunteer Army of Texas" names: "Commander in Chief: Col. Francis W. Johnson; Surgeon in Chief: Dr. Albert M. Levy — of N. Orlean's [*sic*] Greys. . . December 17, 1835." Jenkins, *Papers of Texas Revolution*, vol. 3, p. 226.
98. Lewis H. Levy, a descendant, owns the sword. Int., Lewis H. Levy, 1984.
99. Lewis H. Levy had granddaughters named Sara and Rachel, but not until a family reunion in 1984 did he realize these are family names. Levy, a Catholic, is a forester.
100. Rabbi Henry Sandman of Lafayette's Temple Rodeph Shalom.
101. Int., Jessie Levy Foss, 1987.
102. John Henry Brown, *Indian Wars*, p. 81.
103. P. Westmoreland, "Battle of Plum Creek" in *Battles of Texas*, p 106.
104. Brown, *Indian Wars*, p. 81; idem, *History of Texas*, vol. 2, p. 179; John H. Jenkins, *Recollections of Early Texas*, p. 61n.
105. Ehrenberg, *Fahrten*, pp. 264-72.
106. First published as *Texas und Seine Revolution*, 1843; reprinted, *Der Freiheitskampf in Texas im Jahre 1836*, 1844; reprinted, *Fahrten und Schicksale Eines Deutschen in Texas*, 1845; reprinted, *A Translation of Herman Ehrenberg's Fahrten . . .*, 1925; reprinted, *With Milam and Fannin*, 1935.
107. Letter, Ehrenberg to Ashbel Smith, Feb. 9, 1844. Ashbel Smith Papers, Texas State Library.
108. Letter, Barry M. Goldwater to Dr. H. Fuchs, Berlin, Sept. 26, 1940. Goldwater Collection, Arizona Historical Foundation, Arizona State University, Tempe.
109. Diane M.T. Rose, "The Maps, Plans, and Sketches of Herman Ehrenberg," *Prologue*, Fall 1977.
110. Ehrenberg obituary, *Daily Alta California*, Oct. 31, 1866.
111. Letter, Goldwater to Fuchs, Sept. 26, 1940. In 1869 Joe Goldwater was appointed Postmaster at Ehrenberg, where he had one of the earliest Goldwater stores. Leon Harris, *Merchant Princes*, pp. 224, 227.
112. Letter, Goldwater to Dr. B. Sacks, mentioned in typescript article written by Dr. Sacks on Ehrenberg, p. 7. Sacks Collection, Arizona Historical Foundation.
113. Letter, Goldwater to Fuchs, Sept. 26, 1940.
114. Letter, Carlos E. Castañeda to Dr. B. Sacks, Jan. 21, 1955, Sacks Collection, Arizona Historical Foundation.

Chapter 3
The Colonizers

1. *Encyclopedia Britannica* (1957), vol. 5, p. 7; R. Majo Framis, *Vidas de los Navegantes*, vol. 2, pp. 183-191.
2. Castro books on Texas include *Le Texas en 1845*, *The State of Texas* published in Holland in 1946, and *Coup d'oeil Sur le Texas* published in Paris in 1841.
3. Castro colonists settled in what are now counties of Medina, Uvalde, Frio, Atascosa, Bexar, McMullen, LaSalle, and Zavala.
4. Names of ships, captains, ports, and dates are listed in Lorenzo Castro, *Immigration from Alsace and Lorraine*, p. 3.
5. J. N. Waugh, *Castroville*, p. 59.
6. Henry Cohen, "Henri Castro," *PAJHS*, vol. 5 (1897), pp. 1-5; idem., Part 2 of "Early Jewish Settlements" in *One Hundred Years of Jewry in Texas*, pp. 13-15.
7. Letter, Castro to General Houston, July 12, 1844; copy in American Jewish Archives.
8. "The Republic, while it gave what was of no value, land, received what it direly needed, people. Many men considered [the] settlement wholly impracticable." Waugh, *Castroville*, p. 60. The settlement suffered from exposed frontiers to Mexican invaders from the West and Indians from the North.
9. Williams and Barker, eds., *Writings of Sam Houston*, vol. 2, p. 472. Houston wrote Major G. T. Howard Jan. 24, 1842, requesting he "render every aid and service for the accommodation and temporary settlement of the emigrants lately arrived from France . . . until they make a permanent settlement in the colony contracted by Mr. Castro." Ibid., p. 440.
10. Secretary of State of the Republic in 1842 under Houston's second term was Anson Jones.
11. Herbert Gambrell, *Anson Jones: The Last President of Texas*, p. 240.
12. A second tract granted to Castro was never settled. It was on the Rio Grande, commencing at a point opposite Camargo and running to Salt Lake (Sal de Rey), thence in a parallel line to a point opposite Dolores below Laredo. This tract was not colonized by Castro because it was occupied by Mexican troops claiming the territory between the Nueces and the Rio Grande. Waugh, *Castroville*, p. 4; L. Castro, *Immigration*, p. 2.
13. Letter, Castro to Houston.
14. V. Considerant, *European Colonization in Texas*, p. 11. He founded La Réunion near Dallas. Dallas' Reunion Arena is named for this historic settlement.
15. Five years later, an ad for these lands offered "Lands timbered with pecan trees" in the Medina Valley for \$2.50 to \$7.00 an acre; lands on the Hondo, Quihi and Verde Creek, \$1.50 to \$5; lands at San Miguel, \$1.25 per acre.
16. Letter, Castro to Houston, July 12, 1844.
17. L. Castro, *Immigration*, p. 2, gives number of "5,200 people." A source written in 1879 gives the total "485 families and 457 single men;" Thrall, *Pictorial History of Texas*, pp. 522-525. "Twenty-seven boats had brought

2,134 Castro colonists from old Europe to young Texas;" Waugh, *Castroville*, p. 11.

18. Letter, Nov. 2, 1842.
19. Waugh, *Castroville*, pp. 9-11.
20. Williams and Barker, eds., *Writings of Sam Houston*, vol. 3, pp. 418-19. A year later, a letter from Castro to Sam Houston dated July 12, 1844, stated that the ship *Louis Phillippe* from Dunkirk in 1843 was "accompanied by my agent Mr. E. Marlini."
21. His fellow passenger from Liverpool was Prince Solms-Braunfels, head of the German colonization in Texas that bears his name.
22. J. Waugh, *Castroville*, p. 16.
23. Ibid., p. 17.
24. Ibid., pp. 20-21; Diary of Henri Castro, Sept. 11, 1844.
25. Ibid., p. 25.
26. Diary of Henri Castro, Nov. 11, 1844: "I attribute the fact that we had not been molested by Indians to the absence of horses. Informed that the excursions of the Indians had no other end than the stealing of animals." Waugh, *Castroville*, p. 25.
27. Ibid., p. 28.
28. H. Cohen, "Henri Castro," p. 14.
29. H. Castro, *Memorial of Henri Castro to the Senate and House*, pp. 4-5.
30. Ibid., pp. 6-7.
31. *Handbook of Texas*, vol. 1, p. 308.
32. L. Castro, *Republic of Mexico in 1882*, pp. iii-iv.
33. *Texas Almanac 1982-83*, p. 256. Castro County is 500 miles north of Castroville in the Texas Panhandle.
34. H. Cohen, "Henri Castro," p. 15.
35. J. Waugh, *Castroville*, p. 60.
36. L. Castro, *Immigration*, p. 2.
37. R. N. Richardson, *Texas, the Lone Star State*, p. 143.
38. H. Castro, *Memorial of Henri Castro*, p. 2.
39. *Handbook of Texas*, vol. 1, p. 308.
40. De Cordova's map was complied by the draftsman Robert Creutzbaur from records of the General Land Office of Texas, De Cordova, *Texas: Her Resources and Her Public Men*, p. 29. Almost all future Texas cartography was based on this map.
41. John H. Jenkins, *Basic Texas Books*, p. 99. De Cordova published the first edition of *Map of the State of Texas* in 1849. Compilation had taken several years. The University of Texas also owns editions of De Cordova's *New Map of the State of Texas* for 1850, 1857, and 1858. Editions for 1851, 1856, and 1872 are in the Texas State Archives, Austin.
42. Caulfield, "De Cordova Sold Texas to World," *Waco Tribune-Herald*, Sept. 11, 1956.
43. Wayne Gard, "Early Texas Land Merchant," *Dallas Morning News*, n.d. (c. 1962).
44. He served from Dec. 13, 1847 to March 20, 1848. *Members of the Legislature of Texas, 1846 to 1939*, pp. 7, 8n.
45. A. B. Looscan, "Harris County, 1822-1845," *SWHQ*, July 1915, p. 72.
46. H. Cohen, *One Hundred Years of Jewry in Texas*, pp. 16-18.
47. D. Kelley, Intro. to Day, *Jacob De Cordova*, p. vii.
48. Annie Kingsbury (1864-1957), "Jacob De Cordova," typescript, n.d.; Ints. Helen and Gladys Kingsbury, great-granddaughters of the colonizer.
49. M. Stern, *First American Jewish Families*, p. 52. Jon Stedman typescript he compiled on De Cordova genealogy, beginning with year 1641. Rabbi Stern said Stedman supplied him with some De Cordova genealogy. Int., Stern, Dallas, 1982; int., Stedman, Denton, 1982.
50. Kingsbury, "Jacob De Cordova," p. 1.
51. *Kingston Daily Gleaner*, Centenary Issue, Sept. 13, 1934, p. 2; E. Wolf and M. Whiteman, *History of the Jews of Philadelphia*, p. 488. Jacob "moved with his parents to Philadelphia in 1816" at age eight; Walker, *Odd Fellowship*, p. 258. Jacob's half-brother Phineas was born in Philadelphia March 28, 1819; Cohen, *One Hundred Years of Jewry in Texas*, p. 17. Two sources state the family settled there in 1827; *Handbook of Texas*; *Handbook of Waco*.
52. Korn, "The Haham De Cordova," *AJA*, vol. 18, no. 2 (Nov. 1966) p. 146. Korn reports Phineas in an 1890 letter described their father as a strict Jew. The Haham was born in Amsterdam in 1723 and known internationally by philosophers for his writings on the Enlightenment.
53. Stern, *First American Jewish Families*, p. 52. Stephen Birmingham derived much of his data for *The Grandees: America's Sephardic Elite* from Stern.
54. General Gonzalvo De Cordova reportedly was knighted when he intercepted a dagger intended for the King of Spain. Jacob's eldest brother named his first son Gonzalvo (Stern genealogy). The story was repeated by William C. De Cordova, one-time city manager of Livingston, Tx., in Aline Roth int. in *Houston Chronicle Magazine*, July 5, 1953. Gladys Kingsbury said she heard the story from her mother and that the De Cordova coat of arms showed a hand holding a dagger. Ms. Kingsbury and her sister Helen visited the De Cordovas in Jamaica, and also Julian De Cordova at the De Cordova Museum of art in Lincoln, Mass. Int. Kingsbury, 1983. Julian "claimed to have traced his direct descent from Gonzalvo and to have established that he was the true heir to Gonzalvo's title." Letter, Sir Neville (Noel) Ashenheim, Jamaican Ambassador to the United States, to Korn, April 18, 1963. Sir Neville was a great-grandson of Dr. Lewis Ashenheim, coeditor of the first Jewish periodical in the West Indies, *The First Fruits of the West* printed by R.J. De Cordova, 1844. Sir Neville's mother, Eliza De Cordova, was a great-granddaughter of the Haham.
55. E. Eberstadt, *Collection* (catalog of Texana), pp. 43-44.
56. C. W. Raines, *Bibliography of Texas*, pp. ix, xiv.
57. Korn, "Haham De Cordova," pp. 154-56, n32. See Appendix F.
58. Jacob De Cordova moved to Texas *permanently* in 1839. Although earlier dates have been given, he could not have settled there earlier as indicated by census records of a son born in New Orleans. Henry Maxwell De Cordova, according to the Sept. 19, 1850 census of Harris County, is listed as age twelve, born in Louisiana, which makes his birth year late 1838. However, according to Henry's obituary, "Mr. De Cordova was born Jan. 22, 1839, at New Orleans, La." *Times-Record*, Cripple Creek, Colo., Feb. 9, 1921. Jon Stedman archives. Odd Fellows lodge records show Jacob served a one-year term as grand master for Louisiana, his term ending March 1839. He was the "instituting officer" establishing lodges in Houston on July 25 and December 10, 1838; however these were *visits*. When he founded a third lodge (in Galveston) in 1840, "it was altogether correct to speak of him as the Past Grand Master of Louisiana." Walker, *Odd Fellowship*, pp. 122, 127, 128, 130.
59. John Gaines, "Early Texas Land Dealer Once Kept Store on Isle," *Galveston News*, April 1962; Gard, "Early Texas Land Merchant," *Dallas Morning News*, 1962.
60. D. Kelley, Introduction to De Cordova, *Texas: Her Resources and Her Public Men* (1969 ed.), p. vii.
61. "In 1848 he became the agent for lands which General Thomas Jefferson Chambers had sold to John S. Sydnor of Galveston who, in turn, had sold the lands to N.A.

Ware and Jonas Butler. George [W.] [*sic*] Erath persuaded De Cordova to locate a village at the site where the Waco Indians had lived." Kelley, *Handbook of Waco.*

62. L.A. Erath, "Memoirs of Erath," *SWHQ,* vols. 26 and 27 (1922-1924).
63. Merchant Abraham Cohen Labatt moved to Waco as a result of De Cordova's advertising. The name Labatt is inscribed on several nineteenth-century gravestones in Waco. Letter, I. J. Gandler to author, 1984.
64. The dates of his moving to Seguin are listed as 1851, 1852, 1853, depending on the source.
65. The home in Seguin appears in a watercolor painting discovered in 1984 in California inscribed "Eddie's birth place, Wanderer's Retreat, Residence of Mr. J. De Cordova five miles from Seguin, 1852." Courtesy Dorothy Sloan—Books, Austin. The Amon Carter Museum obtained the painting and Wind River Press published it in a collection.
66. The first edition of *Texas: Her Resources and Her Public Men* was published in Philadelphia by E. Crozet. The same year, 1858, also appeared an edition containing a valuable index and the words "First Edition" on the title page, published in Philadelphia by J. B. Lippincott & Co.
67. Jenkins, *Basic Texas Books,* pp. 98-100.
68. Hamilton Stuart, editor, *Galveston Civilian,* 1858.
69. De Cordova, *Texas: Her Resources and Her Public Men,* p. 27.
70. "Texans Have Been Bragging 100 Years," *Dallas Morning News,* Oct. 5, 1958, UPI wire, London dateline.
71. De Cordova, "Texas, Her Capabilities and Resources: Two Lectures"; "Lecture on Texas."
72. Caulfield, "De Cordova Sold Texas to World," *Waco Tribune-Herald,* Sept. 16, 1956.
73. Cohen, "Early Jewish Settlements," p. 17.
74. Caulfield, "De Cordova Sold Texas"; Preece, "He Brought Families to Texas," *Congress Weekly,* p. 11. The Texas Ranger was the grandfather of Preece.
75. Walker, *Odd Fellowship,* 257-58.
76. Ibid., p. 122; "Who Owned It, Called Site for Waco the Most Beautiful Town Location in Texas," *Waco Tribune-Herald,* Oct. 30, 1949, p. 19. De Cordova was "Father of Odd Fellowship in Texas." Walker, *Odd Fellowship,* p. 257. David G. Burnet, first president of the Republic of Texas, and Anson Jones, last president of the Republic, both were members of the IOOF in Texas. Walker, *Odd Fellowship,* pp. 125, 127, 128.
77. "Phineas De Cordova, who was identified with the history and development of the State, died at the home of his son, Mr. Sam De Cordova, 706 Guadalupe St., Austin, May 8, 1903. . . . Rabbi Rosenstein of Temple Beth Israel" officiated. Raines, *Year Book for Texas 1903,* p. 45.

Chapter 4
The Statesmen

1. Texas did not elect another Jewish congressman to Washington until 1979, when it elected Martin Frost, grandson of pioneer San Antonio merchant Joseph Frost, to serve Texas' 24th District covering Oak Cliff, Grand Prairie, and Irving, three suburbs of Dallas.
2. *Congressional Directory 1911,* p. 772; *Biographical Directory of the American Congress 1774-1961,* p. 1144. Boiling Springs is in Middleton Township, Cumberland County, and in this township when Kaufman was age seven resided Abraham Kauffman (*sic*) and John Kauffman (*sic*) as heads of family. Abraham had three males under age ten; John had two. *Census Index, Pennsylvania 1820,* p. 184.
3. Int., archivist, Princeton University, 1978; letter to author Oct. 30, 1978, stated, "The only indication in David Spangler Kaufman's file as to what religion he was is a pencilled note 'of Hebrew extraction.'" Cynthia A. McClelland, archives assistant, Seeley G. Mudd Manuscript Library, Princeton University, Princeton, N.J.
4. Historic Natchez Foundation, 423 Main St., Natchez, Miss.
5. H. S. Thrall, *Pictorial History of Texas,* p. 578; *American Jewish Year Book 1900,* D.S. Kaufman, vol. 2, p. 519.
6. D.G. Wooten, *A Comprehensive History of Texas,* p. 20.
7. D. H. Winfrey, "The Battle of the Neches," *Battles of Texas,* pp. 81, 93, 98. Another historian has a different version: "He was aid [*sic*] to General Rusk in the Kickapoo fight in 1839." Thrall, *Pictorial History of Texas,* p. 578.
8. G. L. Crocket, *History of San Augustine County,* p. 242.
9. Williams and Barker, eds., *Writings of Sam Houston,* vol. 2; L.B. Friend, *Sam Houston,* pp. 88-89.
10. He headed the law firm of Kaufman and Gould. *Handbook of Texas,* vol. 1, p. 939. Sabinetown is "in eastern Sabine County. Its most distinguished citizen was David S. Kaufman. With the collapse of the Confederacy and changes in transportation, it ultimately became a ghost town." *Handbook,* vol. 2, p. 526.
11. *Congressional Directory 1911,* p. 772.
12. D. G. Wooten, *History of Texas,* p. 309.
13. Henry Cohen, "David S. Kaufman," typescript, pp. 4-5.
14. Kaufman represented all Eastern Texas and Timothy Pilsbury represented West Texas. Texas' senators then were Generals Sam Houston and T. J. Rusk.
15. "Speech of Hon. David S. Kaufman, of Texas, on The Territorial relations between the United States and Texas, delivered in the House of Representatives, July 27, 1848." Pamphlet, p. 12.
16. "The Texas Boundary: Speech of Hon. David S. Kaufman, of Texas, showing that Mexico commenced the late War with the United States, by invading territory that belonged to Texas at the period of her annexation. Delivered to the House of Representatives, June 5, 1848." p. 14
17. Ibid., pp. 8-9.
18. D.S. Kaufman, "To the People of the First Congressional District of Texas: printed message from Washington City [D.C.], September 10, 1850." p. 4.
19. Kaufman, "Speech . . . July 27, 1848," pp. 10-11.
20. D. Lefkowitz, "Jewish Pioneers of Texas," p. 27.
21. Kaufman, "Speech . . . July 27, 1848."
22. Kaufman, "To the People of . . . Texas, September 10, 1850," p. 4.
23. Ibid., p. 2.
24. McDonald, *Hurrah for Texas!,* p. 207; H. Cohen, "David S. Kaufman," p. 8.
25. Mary Sexton Estill, "The Education of Anna Kaufman," *Texana,* vol. 4, no. 3 (Fall 1966), pp. 247-257. Ms. Estill, professor of English at Sam Houston State University, was mentor for author, her student.
26. H. G. Schulter and B. F. Toole, "1850 census, Sabine County, Texas: With added family information and corrections," pp. 5-6.
27. Kaufman Street is the main street on the historic square in Rockwall, Tx. A fine portrait of the congressman hangs in the Sam Houston Museum, Huntsville.
28. J. H. Brown, *Indian Wars and Pioneers of Texas,* p. 475.
29. Ibid., p. 474.
30. *National Cyclopaedia,* vol. 35, p. 76; *Who's Who in Texas 1931,* p. 34.
31. *Founders and Patriots of the Republic of Texas,* p. 233.
32. Cohen, "Settlement of the Jews in Texas," p. 145.
33. Brown, *Indian Wars and Pioneers,* p. 475.
34. This is the same town to which Rep. David S. Kaufman

moved in 1842.
35. McDonald, ed., *Hurrah for Texas!*, p. 231, entry for July 28, 1851.
36. Brown, *Indian Wars and Pioneers*, p. 475.
37. *Who's Who in Texas 1931*, p. 34; *New Encyclopedia of Texas*, p. 984.
38. *Beaumont 1908-1909*, p. 71.
39. T.C. Richardson, *East Texas*, vol. 3, p. 1060.
40. *New Encyclopedia of Texas*, p. 653; *Who's Who in Texas 1931*, p. 34.
41. Simon is buried in the family cemetary fifteen miles north of Beaumont on the east bank of the Neches River in southwest Jasper County, where a large obelisk reads: "Sacred to the memory of the Wiess family." His children included Colonel Mark Wiess and Captain William Wiess (twins born in 1840), Captain Valentine Wiess, Napoleon Wiess, Massena Wiess, and Pauline Wiess Coffin. Int., John Stedman,1982; *Southeast Texas Genealogical and Historical Society*, vol. 3, no. 1: p. 32.

CHAPTER 5
THE RANCHERS

1. G.M. White, "Activities of M. Halff," *Frontier Times*, January 1942, pp. 169-75.
2. "The Quién Sabe Ranch, including leased land, comprised over 200,000 acres. They bought the Crouch Ranch of 81,000 acres in Frio County." Int., Betty Halff Llewellyn 1977.
3. Int., Betty J. Stagg; H.B. Levy and C. Murphy, "Halff Genealogy," p. 1.
4. *Liberty Gazette*, 1856.
5. A press account of the hurricane reads: "The steamship *Nautilus* . . . touched at Galveston and left on Friday 8th inst. [Aug. 8, 1856] . . . with the U.S. Mails, 30 passengers, $30,000 in specie, 100 horses and 70 head of cattle."
6. At Liberty, a local citizen who kept a record of cattle crossing the Trinity River by ferry there reported 5,843 head for 1855 and almost 7,000 head the next year. Gard, *Chisholm Trail*, p. 25.
7. Gard, *Chisholm Trail*, p. v. It was abandoned in 1884.
8. Ibid.; Ints., Gard, 1983-84. Travel up and down the Chisholm Trail helped lessen the sectional animosity the Civil War had caused. The trail's cattle trade brought Texas and Northern men in contact with each other, brought down the price of beef, and accelerated the building of railroads.
9. White, "Activities of M. Halff," p. 169.
10. Letter, Bob Beverly, Lovington, N.M., to John H. White, San Antonio, Nov. 23, 1944.
11. Ibid.
12. Henry's brother Alex married Alma Oppenheimer and his sister Lillie married Jesse D. Oppenheimer. Henry moved to the Dallas suburb of Richardson, then ranchland, in 1929, where he died in 1933.
13. Levy and Murphy, "Halff Genealogy," p. 1.
14. C. Wessolowsky, "Letter," April 6, 1879, in *Reflections of Southern Jewry*, p. 81.
15. *Industrial Advantages of Houston, Texas 1894*, p. 39.
16. Ints., Betty J. Stagg, Felix's great-great-granddaughter, 1983, 1985.
17. A.J. Simpson, *Southwest Texans*, p. 92.
18. Ints., Minna Schwarz Susser, daughter of Hattie, fifth child of Charles Weil, 1982, 1984; Ints., Cecelia Weil Cohen, Corpus Christi, and Sarah Weil Kahn, Cincinnati, daughers of Jonah, 1985.
19. *The Cattleman*.
20. Shot and killed was Morris Weil, brother of Charles.
21. Int., Minna Susser. During this era, it was not uncommon for Jewish men to abandon their families in their inability to cope with a culture that lacked traditions, harshness of the frontier, and unknown futures. Int., Bernard Wax, Director, AJHS. The B'nai B'rith Orphans Home in New Orleans cared for many of these children.
22. Hirsch, born in 1834, came to Gonzales in 1854, then settled in Corpus Christi. He worked "with a lavish hand . . . for the welfare of the schools. . . . The teachers have lost a royal ally." "In Memoriam."
23. Int., Minna Susser. Mrs. Adele Gordon had the drum. Int., Edwin Gale, 1985.
24. *Corpus Christi Caller Times*, Oct. 23, 1955, Sunday, March 5, 1972. Charles married Sarah Hymans, a native of Gonzales, who had moved to Corpus Christi when she was orphaned at age nine. She had been reared by Jeanette Weil (Mrs. David) Hirsch, sister of Charles.
25. G.W. Brown, "Jonas Weil — A Horse Breeder, a Scholar, and a Gentleman," *Cattleman*, 1940, pp. 99-100. *Palangana* is a Spanish word meaning basin; one of the pastures was shaped like a basin.
26. Fanny Weil Alexander, "Charles and Sara Weil," p. 12; Int., Estelle Weil Bruck, 1985.
27. Fred Gipson, "It's Round Up Time on Ranch of Jonas Weil," column, c. 1946.
28. All Charles Weil's sons were in the mercantile business except Jonas. Charles' grandson, Alex Weil, Jr., later managed the Weil ranches. B. Isbell, "Weil History Woven Into Growth of City," *Corpus Christi Caller Times*, Oct. 23, 1955.
29. Charles Weil's children: Jonas (named for his great-grandfather Jonas Weil I, born in Surbourg, France, in 1750); Alex (named for his grandfather Alexandre Weil, born in France 1820); Fannie (Mrs. I.H. Alexander), author of family history; Carrie (who married S.J. Lichtenstein, Corpus Christi merchant prince); Hattie, who married Julius Schwarz of Hempstead; Moise; Sylvan; Jeanette (Mrs. Leopold Kaffie); Joseph L.; Simon; and Estelle, who married Edmund Bruck of Waco.
30. B.W. Korn, "A Note on the Jewish Ancestry of Louis Moreau Gottschalk, American Pianist and Composer," *AJHQ*, November 1963, pp. 117-19; E. Wolf and M. Whiteman, *History of the Jews of Philadelphia*, pp. 352, 356, 495.
31. H. Cohen, "Settlement of the Jews in Texas," *PAJHS*, vol. 2, 1894, p. 150; E.W. Fornell, *Galveston Era*, p. 83. Before dying of yellow fever, he requested his body be brought to Galveston for interment in Hebrew Benevolent Cemetery. *Flakes Daily Bulletin*, Oct. 17, 1867; Dreyfus, "Hebrew Cemetery No. 1." Mayor Seeligson's grandson, John Winterbotham, Jr., became a prominent civic leader in Houston.
32. Mayer's mercantile firm was called Mayer and Hagerlund.
33. Handwritten ms., Archives, Institute of Texan Cultures.
34. *Historical Record of Cattle Industry of Texas 1894-1895*, vol. 2, p. 446.
35. Ibid.
36. Institute of Texan Cultures archives.
37. Int., Gladys Mayer, 1983.
38. A. Goodspeed, *History of Texas*, pp. 236-38; V.M. Rose, *History of Victoria*, pp. 89, 90.
39. F.W. Johnson, *A History of Texas and Texans* (1916 ed.), vol. 5, pp. 2338-41.
40. Ibid., p. 2339.
41. Bob Boyd, "Perry Kallison Has Many Neighbors," *San Antonio* mag., June 1972, pp. 51-54.
42. Corres. and int., Frances Kallison, 1984.
43. Nathan Kallison, founder, died in 1945. Besides a com-

plete farm and ranch store, the Kallisons operated Feed and Seed, Ltd., a department store, and Kallison's Trading Post. Associated were Perry, his brother Morris, and Morris' son James. Simpson, *Southwest Texans*, p. 98,

44. He organized the South Texas Polled Hereford Assn. and served as first president.
45. Boyd, "Perry Kallison," p. 54.
46. Simpson, *Southwest Texans*, p. 104.
47. Letter, Frances Kallison to author, 1984.
48. Int., Helen (Mrs. Nathan) Dahlman, 1980.

CHAPTER 6
THE FINANCIERS

1. J. O. Dyer, "Early Banking on Galveston Island," *Galveston News*, Aug. 7, 1921.
2. "Joseph Osterman," typescript, pp. 1, 2, Rosenberg Library.
3. Ibid. Other bankers who made loans on cotton were G.H. Illes of New Orleans, who opened a branch in Galveston, and the Mills brothers who moved there from Brazoria.
4. *Memorial and Genealogical Record*, p. 63.
5. Ibid., p. 64.
6. R. W. Shook, "Abraham Levi: Father of Victoria Jewry," *WSJHQ*, vol. 9, no. 2, p. 149.
7. Abraham Levi gave his children heroic names. Leo's middle name was Napoleon and Charles' middle name was Garabaldi. The family and their dates of birth are Godcheaux, 1852; Fannie, 1854; Leo N., 1856; Rosa, 1858; Charles G., 1860; Melanie, 1861; and Elias, born in 1867 and died after a few months. Fannie married Solomon Halff. Rosa Levi married Moses Haas. *Memorial and Genealogical Record*, p. 66.
8. *Memorial and Genealogical Record*, pp. 63-67.
9. Abraham's sons, Godcheaux Levi and C.G. Levi, in 1879 bought out Levy's interest.
10. V. Rose, *History of Victoria*, pp. 60, 66, 156-59.
11. Int., May Titche, 1982.
12. The Jewish community named a B'nai B'rith lodge for Max Bettin, Victoria merchant who, with a command of four languages, served as chief contact for arriving immigrants to Victoria from the 1880s to after the turn of the century.
13. Godcheaux Levi married in 1877 Theresa Guggenheim, whose family came to Texas from Louisiana in 1854. *Memorial and Genealogical Record*, p. 67.
14. Int., Elaine Levi Lansburgh, 1984.
15. Int., Marie Levi Bitterman, 1984.
16. John Pierson, *Wall Street Journal*, Feb. 5, 1968, p. 1.
17. Int., Daniel Oppenheimer II, 1984, San Antonio.
18. Parents of D.&A. were Joseph and Yetta Oppenheimer. The father was a baker-confectioner in the small town of Burgkundstadt, where Daniel I was born in 1836.
19. Larry Meyer int. with Dan Oppenheimer, School of Business, UT Austin, 1969.
20. The Oppenheimers were in Palestine forty-five years before Hyman Pearlstone came in 1899 and in Rusk thirty-eight years before Fred Florence came in 1894.
21. Daniel was in Ector's Brigade and Anton in Hood's Brigade. Typescript, "History of Daniel Oppenheimer." Dan rose from private to captain.
22. Meyer int.
23. Ibid.
24. Int., Daniel Oppenheimer II, 1984.
25. Ibid.
26. Ibid.
27. Meyer int.
28. Chartered banks were forbidden by the state due to a wave of hysteria that followed the Panic of 1837, and the law lasted most of the nineteenth century.
29. Int., Oppenheimer.
30. Meyer int.
31. Int., Oppenheimer.
32. See chapter 9, The Great Merchants, pp. 141-42.
33. The seven children of Dan and Louisa Goldstein Oppenheimer were Jesse, born in 1870; Alice, 1871 (died early); Henry, 1873; Ida, 1874; Alma, 1877, Frederic G., 1881; and Edna, 1885. *Reform Advocate*, n.d., p. 14.
34. A.J. Simpson, *Southwest Texans*, p. 21A.
35. Pierson, *Wall Street Journal*, Feb. 5, 1968.
36. S. Lytle, "Banking on Tradition," *Dallas Times Herald*, July 24, 1983, pp. A 31, 32.
37. John Gunther, *Taken at the Flood*, pp. 22-24; *Encyclopedia Judaica*, p. 1436.
38. T.C. Richardson, East Texas, vol. 4, p. 418; "Death Comes to Morris Lasker," *Galveston Tribune*, Feb. 28, 1916.
39. Letter, Morris Lasker to Alex Sanger Jan. 1, 1909, in "Letter from a Texas Pioneer, 1909," *WSJHQ*, 15, no. 4, July 1983, pp. 305-16.
40. He served under Col. John S. Ford on the Rio Grande with the 2nd Texas Cavalry and later fought at Sabine Pass and in Louisiana. Lasker, "Letter," p. 310.
41. T. C. Richardson, *East Texas*, vol. 4, p. 419.
42. Gunther, *Taken at the Flood*, pp. 22-24.
43. The six Lasker children: Edward, Albert of Chicago, Harry M. of N.Y., Florina, Etta, and Loula. Etta (Mrs. S.J. Rosensohn of N.Y.) served as national president of Hadassah. *Who's Who in World Jewry* 1965, p. 798.
44. Albert D. Lasker worked as reporter for the *Galveston News* at age fifteen and following graduation from Ball High School in 1895 wrote for the *Dallas News*. Besides his advertising career, he served as Asst. Secretary of Agriculture in 1917, Asst. Chairman of the Republican National Committee in 1920, and Chairman of the U.S. Shipping Board in 1921. He married Flora Warner in 1902 and they had three children: Mary, Edward, and Frances. After Flora's death, Albert married Mary Woodward Reinhardt in 1940. "Ball High: Eight alumni to be inducted into new H. S. Hall of Honor" [on Oct. 7, 1984], *Galveston Daily News*, Sept. 23, 1984, p. D-1.
45. Richardson, *East Texas*, vol. 4, p. 419.
46. Gunther, *Taken at the Flood*, pp. 31, 32.
47. Richardson, *East Texas*, vol. 4, p. 419.
48. Gunther, *Taken at the Flood*, p. 32.
49. Ibid., p. 22.
50. He and his friend B. Adoue paid for and started domestic science and manual training in the Galveston Public Schools.
51. H. Cohen, dedication speech 1918, Temple B'nai Israel archives.
52. I. H. Kempner, "H. Kempner: The First One Hundred Years," *Texas Gulf Coast Historical Assn. Publication*, March 1958, p. 4.
53. He was assigned to Parson's Brigade of Cavalry and was wounded in battle.
54. Kempner, "H. Kempner," p. 4
55. Ibid., p. 4.
56. C. W. Hayes, *History of the Island*, pp. 975-995; I.H. Kempner, "My Memories of Father," *AJA*, April 1976, p. 45.
57. Seven sons and four daughters. Int., Tim Thompson, 1975.
58. Letter, March 24, 1884; J.A. Tinsley (ed.), "Select Letters of Harris Kempner," *Texas Gulf Coast Historical Assn. Pub.*, vol. 1, no. 2 (December 1957), pp. 16, 17.
59. Letter, Kempner to his ranch foreman in Mexia, Texas,

Dec. 15, 1887. Tinsley, "Select Letters," p. 37.
60. Ibid., pp. 19, 20. Letter, May 15, 1884.
61. Ibid., pp. 34, 35. Letter, May 26, 1887.
62. Ibid., p. 15. Letter, Jan. 21, 1884.
63. The Cunningham Sugar Co. was purchased by I. H. Kempner and W .T. Eldridge, Jr., of Sugar Land in 1907. *Fort Bend County Sesquicentennial* 1822-1972, p. 47. G. A. Ulrich later also served as a director. W.R. Johnson, "History of the Sugar Industry in Texas," *TGCHAP*, vol. 5, no. 1 (April 1961), p. 69.
64. The Kempners sold all their stock in Texas Prudential when Stanley died in 1954. Kempner, "H. Kempner," p. 10.
65. After the 1900 Storm I.H. and Bertrand Adoue effected an adjustment of interest on the city's bonded debt, which upheld Galveston's municipal credit. I. H. Kempner served as city treasurer in 1899, finance commissioner 1901 to 1915, and mayor 1917 to 1919.
66. They had five children: Harris Leon, Isaac Herbert, Jr., Cecile, Lyda, and Henrietta Leonora.
67. Int., Gerardo Weinstein, 1975.
68. Kempner, "H. Kempner," p. 12; Int., Tim Thompson, 1975.
69. Ibid., p. 13.
70. Kempner, "My Memories of Father," p. 55.
71. Int., Wayne Gard, 1984.
72. Int., Helen Florence Wineburgh.
73. In 1987, twenty-seven years after his death, Republic and First National merged into First RepublicBank Dallas.
74. H. H. Wineburgh, *Texas Banker*, pp. 234, 235.
75. *Time*, Nov. 10, 1958.
76. Wineburgh, *Texas Banker*, pp. 235-38.
77. Ibid., pp. 239, 240.
78. Int., Helen Florence.
79. The audience was with Pius XII; John XXIII awarded the medal. Bishop Thomas K. Gorman made the presentation at a black tie dinner in Dallas Sept. 15, 1959, presided by Monsignor William F. O'Brien. Baptist minister Luther Holcomb gave the invocation; Rabbi Levi Olan gave the benediction. "Fred was tied in with all the churches," said Helen. Int., Helen Florence. The medal is awarded in gold, silver, or bronze; Florence received the gold medal adorned with the word "Benemerenti" meaning "one deserving well."
80. Its building boom, rail center, and a 45-page booklet touting the town "highest point between Tyler and the Gulf" attracted many families. It later became a ghost town.
81. Richardson, *East Texas*, vol. 4, p. 94.
82. Wineburgh, *Texas Banker*, pp. 14-16.
83. Ibid., pp. 22, 23; *Handbook of Texas*, vol. 1, p. 37.
84. Int., Helen Florence.
85. Wineburgh, *Texas Banker*, p. 48.
86. Dallas patriarchs include Fred Florence, Erik Jonsson, Nathan Adams, R.L. Thornton, and Karl Hoblitzelle. K. Jones, "Dallas Business Legends," *Dallas Times Herald*, Aug. 23, 1984.
87. D. Nevin, *The Texans*, p. 157.
88. Wineburgh, *Texas Banker*, pp. 129, 130.
89. W. L. Perryman, Jr., General American Oil president in the 1960s in Ibid., pp. 131-33. General American prospered and, five years after the death of Meadows, was bought by Phillips Petroleum in 1983. Besides Florence, Robert M. Swesnik, geologist, was another Jew whose talent helped build General American's success.
90. Richardson, *East Texas*, vol. 4, p. 95.
91. Florence also served on the board of directors of Southland Life Insurance Company and the Missouri-Kansas-Texas (MKT) Railroad.
92. D. Nevin, *The Texans*, pp. 173, 174.
93. He was the son of Gabriel and Fanny Bauer Kopperl of Trebitsch, Moravia, where he was born Oct. 7, 1828. H. Cohen, *Early Jewish Settlements in Texas*, p. 19.
94. J. H. Brown, *Indian Wars and Pioneers*, p. 295.
95. "Kopperl, M., married at Cincinnati, Ohio, on Sunday, June 10th at the residence of Wm. B. Symonds, Esq., by the Rev. Dr. Lilienthal to Miss Isabella Dyer, both of Galveston, Texas." *Daily Telegraph*, June 21, 1866. C.L. Greenwood Index: marriages, University of Texas Archives.
96. Isabella Dyer Papers, Rosenberg Library; Letter, Mildred Stephenson, Reference Librarian, Rosenberg Library, to Robert Shosteck, Curator, B'nai B'rith, Washington, D.C., Sept. 29, 1959.
97. Brown, *Indian Wars and Pioneers*, p. 295.
98. Cohen, *Early Jewish Settlements*, p. 20.
99. J. Marshall, *Santa Fe*, pp. 212-14, 216.
100. Author's visit to Hebrew Benevolent Cemetery, 1982; monument verse by Leigh Hunt.
101. *Confederate Veteran*, vol. 10, p. 374.
102. *Handbook of Texas*, vol. 1, p. 973.
103. *Buffalo Banner*, 1899. Int., Henry Ash II.
104. Int., Helen Pearlstone Loeb, 1985; letter Loeb to Ima Joy Gandler, Waco.
105. Int., Lawrence H. Budner, 1985.
106. In the early 1960s Hyman founded the Leon County Hospital in Buffalo in memory of his parents. Int., Helen P. Loeb.
107. Int., Lawrence H. Budner, 1985.
108. Pearlstone served as a director from 1924 to 1962.
109. Typescript biog. from First National Bank, 1936. However, 51 years later InterFirst and Republic merged due to huge real estate losses, and in 1988 the FDIC merged the 41 FirstRepublic Banks and accepted a bid from North Carolina National Bank (NCNB) of Charlotte to purchase the new entity. *Dallas Times Herald*, Aug. 10, 1988.
110. Ints., Lorraine Pearlstone Budner Gordon, Helen Ash Pearlstone Loeb, Marie and Henry Ash Pearlstone.

Chapter 7
The Wildcatters

1. Letter, Paula Krupp Stone, daughter of Haymon Krupp, to author, March 9, 1984; Int., Mr. Leslie Levy of El Paso, who knew Krupp.
2. Owen P. White, "The University of Texas Strikes Oil," *New York Times Magazine*, May 3, 1925, p. 8; "Haymon Krupp is Best Citizen," *El Paso Evening Post*, Aug. 22, 1929, p. 1.
3. "Petroleum Industry Payments to Permanent School and University Funds of Texas." *Texas Almanac 1982-83*, p. 381.
4. Chris P. Fox, "Tribute to Haymon Krupp," *Password*, vol. 15, no. 4 (Winter 1970), pp. 120-24.
5. M. Schwettmann, *Santa Rita*, p. 3.
6. G. Forbes, *Flush Production*, p. 61.
7. Letter, Stone to author, March 9, 1984.
8. They wanted to call their company the Texas Oil and Land Co., but other companies had similar names. Krupp suggested the name "Texon," which was adopted. Schwettmann, *Santa Rita*, p. 7.
9. Burkburnett is located along the Red River separating Texas and Oklahoma. The drilling site was in far West Texas.
10. Schwettmann, *Santa Rita*, p. 8.
11. White, "The University of Texas Strikes Oil," p. 8; Letter,

Stone to author, March 9, 1984.

12. Letter, Haymon Krupp to rancher George B. Hendricks of San Angelo, Dec. 19, 1923. Letter, Frank T. Pickrell to geologist Hugh H. Tucker, Dec. 13, 1923. Schwettmann, *Santa Rita*, pp. 17, 19; Carl C. Rister, *Oil! Titan of the Southwest*, p. 287.
13. Schwettmann, *Santa Rita*, p. 37.
14. The leased land was part of a vast area called the Permian Basin.
15. "Petroleum Industry Payments to Permanent School and University Funds of Texas," *Texas Almanac 1982-83*, p. 381.
16. H.S.R. No. 95, *House Journal*, Austin, Feb. 28, 1949, p. 471.
17. "Best Faculty Money Can Buy?," *Time*, April 26, 1982.
18. Int., Irvin B. Beren, 1983.
19. J.A. Clark and M.T. Halbouty, *The Last Boom*, pp. 151, 152, 160, 161; Rister, *Oil!*, p. 315; D.F. Prindle, *Petroleum Politics*, p. 34.
20. Int., Max A. Morchower of Baytown, 1983.
21. Ints., Irvin Jaffe 1981, 1983.
22. Wynne, Jaffe, and Tinsley.
23. *Texas Almanac 1982-83*, p. 379.
24. Int., I.B. Beren, 1984.
25. Int., Malcolm Brachman 1982; "3 New Trustees Chosen for TCU," *Fort Worth Star Telegram*, March 10, 1950; "Brachman will be honored by Christians, Jews Conference," *Star Telegram*, April 9, 1953; "Sol Brachman Honored for Belief in Brotherhood," *Star Telegram*, May 8, 1953; "Tarrant Man Gets Atomic Fellowship," *Star Telegram*, Sept. 26, 1946. Another Fort Worth oil explorer, I.E. Horwitz, founded the Jewish Welfare Federation of Fort Worth. Int., Gloria Jacobus, 1982.
26. Int., Faye Stein Giller, 1984.
27. Int., M.B. Rudman, 1984.
28. Int., Josephine Davis Rudman, 1985.
29. Ibid.
30. Marcia Smith, "Duke of Anti-Smokers," *Dallas Times Herald*, Dec. 28, 1984, p. D-1.
31. Ruth Goddard, "Wildcatter of Running Duke," *Texas Star*, Jan. 16, 1972, pp. 10, 11.

CHAPTER 8
THE HUMANITARIAN

1. Nathan and Cohen, *The Man Who Stayed in Texas*, pp. 198-200.
2. Int., Rabbi Henry Cohen, 1947; Natalie Moskowitz, "First Citizen of Texas," *Galveston Isle*, vol. 1, no. 6 (December 1947), pp. 6-8, 16.
3. Nathan and Cohen, Man Who Stayed in Texas, p. 282.
4. *Reader's Digest*, February 1939, p. 99.
5. Nathan and Cohen, *Man Who Stayed in Texas*.
6. Webb Waldron, "Rabbi Cohen — First Citizen of Texas," *Rotarian*, February 1939. When the author remarked to Dallas' Dr. Levi Olan, rabbi and philosopher, that she felt Dr. Cohen was as great as the legends about him, Olan replied, "He was greater." Int., Olan, 1977.
7. Nathan and Cohen, *Man Who Stayed in Texas*, p. 122.
8. Author C. Ousley wrote almost an entire page on him in Galveston in 1900 and concluded, "Rev. Henry Cohen . . . as brother to all . . . has been tireless and invaluable. As scholar, writer and preacher, Dr. Cohen ranks with the highest. He enjoys the love and respect of all."
9. See Bibliography for other Cohen writings on Texas history.
10. Stephen Birmingham, "*Our Crowd*," p. 158.
11. G.D. Best, "Schiff's Galveston Movement," *AJA*, vol. 30, no.1 (April 1978), pp. 43-79. Professor Best received a National Endowment for the Humanities grant in 1976 to research this.
12. H. Cohen, "Galveston Immigration Movement," *Federation Review*, March 1908, p. 1.
13. Best, "Schiff's Galveston Movement," p. 51.
14. Birmingham, *"Our Crowd,"* p. 62.
15. Arkansas 155, Colorado 284, Illinois 283, Iowa 1225, Kansas 208, Louisiana 296, Minnesota 997, Missouri 1099, Mississippi 35, Nebraska 611, North Dakota 35, Oklahoma 245, Tennessee 191, Texas 2134, and Wisconsin 48.
16. Galveston Immigration Plan papers, AJHS.
17. Letter, Schiff to Israel Zangwill Nov. 24, 1913, Schiff Papers, AJA; David M. Bressler to Schiff March 31, 1914, AJHS.
18. Nathan and Cohen, *Man Who Stayed in Texas*, pp. 222-25.
19. Int., Henry Cohen, 1948.
20. Archives, Temple B'nai Israel, Galveston.
21. Nathan and Cohen, *Man Who Stayed in Texas*, pp. 262-78.
22. Int., Bess and George I. Moskowitz, parents of the hospitalized boy, 1937.
23. Nathan and Cohen, *Man Who Stayed in Texas*, p. 84.
24. He said he never forgot what it was like to be poor. From age nine to sixteen, he attended Jews' Hospital, a free boarding school for children of the poor. His education was paid for by others. Nathan and Cohen, *Man Who Stayed in Texas*, p. 20.
25. Cong. B'nai Israel (Sons of Israel) minutes of May 13, 1888, record the hiring of young Cohen. The new rabbi (their fourth) was elected for only a one-year term. Leo N. Levi, for whom the national arthritis hospital in Arkansas is named, presided at this meeting. The temple was founded twenty years before Cohen arrived.
26. A Jewish history professor in the East told his students there was no Jewish history nor any Jewish personalities of any consequence west of the Mississippi River.
27. U.T. Librarian Moffit credited Dr. H.J. Leon of the University's Classics Department with helping to get the Cohen collection to Austin. (Professor Leon said he had communicated with Dr. Cohen for advice concerning the library of Houston rabbi Abraham Schecter when the latter's library was willed to the University.) "In addition to the more than 5,000 volumes presented to The University of Texas in 1948, we received at a later date additional books. These were volumes with which he was actively working or wished to keep near him," Moffit recalled. He remembered Cohen saying at the time, "It is difficult to part with old friends." Ints., Moffit, 1964.
28. Letter, Ernest Winkler to author, 1957.
29. Letter, Harry Ransom to author, 1962.
30. H.Y. Benedict, then president of the University of Texas, told Mayor Adrian Levy, "You people in Galveston do not know nor appreciate the true measure of the rabbi's greatness." But this was not true. When Dr. Cohen passed away in 1952 in Houston at the home of his son Harry and daughter-in-law Anne, all flags in Houston and Galveston were at half-mast, and leading places of business were closed the afternoon of his funeral in Galveston. The *Houston Post* wrote, "His humanitarian works were as boundless as humanity itself."
31. Irve Tunick, "An American Ballad," Frontiers of Faith series, NBC, May, 1955.

Chapter 9
The Great Merchants

1. L.E. Daniell, Texas, *The Country and Its Men*. pp. 659-661; H. Cohen, "Settlement of the Jews," p. 139; C. Wharton, *History of Fort Bend County*, p. 17; *Bibliographical Directory of Texas Conventions and Congresses; Handbook of Texas*, vol. 1, p. 896; Genealogy comp. by S.J. Isaacks, 1935. Int., Jack M. Corbin, 1988, whose great-great grandmother was a sister of Samuel Isaacks. Corbin said Samuel's grandfather, called by the family "Samuel the Immigrant," came to Frederick County, Virginia about 1725. He fought in the American Revolution as a private in the South Carolina Line, serving under General Marion. He enlisted in 1776, 1778, 1780, 1781, and 1782. He moved to North Carolina, and about 1800 he settled in Lincoln County, Tenn. Samuel I's son Elijah (a twin) moved from Tennessee to Bevil's Colony in Jasper County, Texas.
2. Ashbel Smith shortly thereafter became Secretary of State in 1844. Smith later helped establish the University of Texas.
3. Ashbel Smith Papers, University of Texas; *Writings of Sam Houston 1843*, vol. 3, pp. 419-20.
4. When Samuel arrived, there were only two wood residences, and his first sleeping place in Galveston was in a tent.
5. Although an obituary lists his arrival in Galveston as 1844, researcher Bob Dalehite of Galveston reported in 1977: "I believe this to be an error as I have documents and letters written by Maas claiming this as his home as early as 1839 (June 24, 1839)." Footnote on Dalehite typescript of Maas obituary, "Death of a Pioneer," *Galveston Daily News*, Jan.11, 1897.
6. Maas was born in Meinbeim in the duchy of Baden, Germany, March 1, 1810.
7. "Death of a Pioneer," *Galveston Daily News*, Jan. 11, 1897.
8. Samuel Maas Papers: letters in English, German, Spanish, French, and Italian, by Samuel Maas. His first two journals (1835-1850) are lively and reflect his adventuresome travels. A third journal covers 1868 in early day Galveston. Deposited by Sam J. Maas, grandson, in archives, Barker Texas History Center, University of Texas at Austin. Partial translation and transcription of Maas journals sponsored by author.
9. Maas Journal entries: "Anvers, 29 April 1844;" "Paris, 17 August 1845."
10. Entry "Paris, Tuesday 23 Jan. 1844."
11. Entry "3rd August 1835."
12. "Death of a Pioneer," *Galveston Daily News*, Jan. 11, 1897.
13. Ints., Harry Levy, Jr., 1978, 1983, 1988.
14. He purchased the home April 16, 1880, from Abraham Kory, Galveston merchant, who moved to Mississippi.
15. Letter, Miriam Maas Holstein, N.Y., to Pat Berntsen, Sept. 9, 1975. (Holstein, then 84, recalled living in the home.)
16. Wm B. Shearer family bought it and lived there in 1911.
17. Dalehite, "The Maas House," p. 1.
18. Deed Records of Harris County, vol. 1, pp. 405-407; K: pp. 138-39, 288-89; N: p. 310; F: p. 704; R: p. 314. A. F. Muir, "Lewis A. Levy: Pioneer Merchant of Houston," p. 3.
19. Probate Records of Harris County, D: pp. 220-25; Deed Records of Harris County, H: pp. 248-49; A. F. Muir, "Lewis A. Levy," p. 4.
20. J. De Cordova, *Texas: Her Resources*, p. 64.
21. Deed Records of Harris County, vol. I, p. 104.
22. Deed Records of Harris County, vol. Q, p. 161.
23. Letter from L.A.L. May 24, 1850, *Asmonean*, vol. 2, no. 10 (June 28, 1850), p. 76. Lewis Levy is buried in Beth Israel cemetery. Mary Levy died May 6, 1888 at the home of her daughter, Mrs. Alex Simon, and is buried in Brenham.
24. "Isle's Firsts: Texas' Oldest," *Galveston Daily News*, Feb. 24, 1985; Int. Etta Mae Kaufman Garon, 1985. A great-grandson of Hirsch's, Paul Burka, became Senior Editor of *Texas Monthly*, winning a Columbia University journalism award in 1985.
25. Ints., Helene (Mrs. Joseph) Levy, 1975, 1985.
26. Int., Julia Baum (Mrs. Louis) Sonnentheil, age 92, Dallas, 1988. Her grandfather was a prominent Jewish pioneer of Meridian, Miss.
27. Restoration work began May 1983. The grand opening took place Feb. 16-17, 1985, with a Mardi Gras celebration, the first in Galveston in more than 50 years, that brought 200,000 tourists to the island. Ints. in Galveston, Feb. 18, 1985.
28. The *Galveston Tribune* was published there from 1923 to 1963. "Historic Blum Building Undergoing Remodeling," *Houston Post*, May 29, 1983, p. E-6.
29. *History of Fort Bend County*, p. 154.
30. "In 1860 Alphonse Levy . . . emigrated from Paris, France, to Galveston, later becoming a partner in the wholesale grocery concern of Leon & H. Blum & Co., remaining with it until after a bad storm, when the concern went out of business." Int. Marguerite Marks, Alphonse's granddaughter, Dallas, 1985.
31. Archives, Rosenberg Library, Galveston; I. Martens, *The Hebrews in America*, p. 169; A. Morrison, *Industries of Galveston*, p. 105.
32. *Galveston News*, August 17, 1899.
33. Ibid.
34. W. M. Kramer, "Pioneer Lawyer of California and Texas: Henry J. Labatt," *WSJHQ*, October 1982, p. 3.
35. Caroline Labatt's brother, H. M. Hyams, became governor of Louisiana. Caroline's father was Samuel M. Hyams of New Orleans, whose sister (Caroline's aunt) was Catherine Hyams, "Marchioness de Solari, First Lady in Waiting on the Princess de Lambelle" and a personal friend of Marie Antoinette. Int. and corres., Richard Torbert, 1984.
36. In New Orleans, Miriam Labatt was Queen of the Mardi Gras. Malcolm Stern, *Genealogies*.
37. *East Texas*, vol. 1, p. 105.
38. General Barnard E. Bee, for whom Bee County is named, served as Secretary of the Treasury for the Republic of Texas. John Edward Weems, *Dream of Empire: A Human History of the Republic of Texas*.
39. "He Died at Ninety-Seven, 'Father' Abraham Cohen Labatt Has Been Gathered to His Fathers; He Attributed His Longevity to Absteminous Habits" (obit.), *Galveston News*, Aug. 17, 1899.
40. J. Friedman, "Jewish Participation in California Gold Rush Era Freemasonry," *WSJH*, pp. 295, 299, 300.
41. E. Sherman, *Fifty Years of Freemasonry in California*; I.O. Whitsell, *One Hundred Years of Freemasonry in California*, III, pp. 86, 949-51.
42. Rabbi Jacob Voorsanger, "Statement," Sept. 11, 1906, Archives, Judah Magnes Museum, Berkeley, Ca.
43. Cemetery date in letter I. J. Gandler, Waco, Texas, to author, Feb. 16, 1983.
44. *Galveston News*, Aug. 17, 1899. Corres. and Int., Richard Torbert, 1984, 1988. Torbert was great-grandson of Joseph and Emily Dyer Labatt; Joseph and Emily's child, Amelia Rosanna was Torbert's grandmother.
45. Architect Alfred Giles designed the store and architect Bartlett Cocke Sr. remodeled it. M. F. Coslett, "Joske's," p. 2; Int. Frederick Joske Oppenheimer, 1985.
46. It was at the end of the railroad. The first Joske store was near the roundhouse of the Southern Pacific Railroad

where engine repairs were made. Joske's in-laws, Sol and Leon Wolfson, also came to San Antonio in 1867 to open a store on Main Plaza.

47. Historic plaque on Menger Hotel.
48. M. F. Coslett, p. 5.
49. Alexander Joske married Blanche Frank of San Antonio. Frank Bros. was a promiment mercantile firm.
50. The store's searchlight guided Lt. James Doolittle to land in San Antonio for re-fueling during his trip around the nation.
51. Meyer, Dan Oppenheimer II int., p. 11.
52. Int. F. J. Oppenheimer, 1985.
53. Int. Bartlett Cocke Sr., 1985.
54. Int. Libby (Mrs. Alexander) Oppenheimer, 1985.
55. Int. F. J. Oppenheimer, 1985.
56. Int. Alex Oppenheimer, 1985.
57. D. S. Hansard, "Dillard to Buy Out Joske's," *Dallas Morning News,* April 14, 1987, p. 1-A.
58. E. Davis and E. H. Grobe, "Men of Texas," *New Encyclopedia of Texas,* vol. 1, p. 820; H. Vandemark, *Makers of Houston.*
59. Houston City Directory 1880, p. 135 shows Abraham "Clk. Wm. L. Foley."
60. Minutes Book of Congregation, February 1925; Anne Nathan Cohen, *Centenary History,* pp. 41-42.
61. Dr. Alexander Sackton, "Shaikevitch," typescript, pp.3-4, based on memoirs of Tobias Sakowitz.
62. Tevye's ancestor had acquired a fortune and owned extensive acreage, mostly in wheat fields. Alex Sackton, pp.1-3.
63. At the turn of the century one of her boarders was Ray Karchmer who became Dr. Ray Daily, prominent Houston physician and civic leader. A. Sackton, p. 6.
64. Int. Alex Sackton, 1985.
65. "Kiam Building," typescript, pp. 70-71, Houston Public Library.
66. Ron Boyd, "Lynn Wyatt," *Dallas Times Herald,* Feb. 15, 1984.
67. Hugh Best, *Debrett's Texas Peerage,* p. 152.
68. *Houston Post,* July 30, 1974, editorial.
69. *Houston Press,* Aug. 25, 1961. Nathan died in 1961 at age 74.
70. Int. Leah Sakowitz Nathan Goren, 1985.
71. Alison Cook, "The Fraying Empire of Bobby Sakowitz," *Texas Monthly,* Dec. 1985, pp. 132-36, 232-46, 258.
72. *Houston Chronicle,* Dec. 23, 1971, pp. 1, 4.
73. George Cohen was elected Chairman of the Board; Max Levine, President; Maurice Lazarus, Vice President; F. J. Matzinger, Treasurer, and Raymond Neilson, Secretary.
74. Survivors included his widow Esther Meyer Cohen of Houston; brother-in-law Leopold Meyer; sister Mrs. Gladys Blum of Galveston; niece Mrs. Marion J. Levy, Jr., of Princeton, N.J.; nephew Robert I. Cohen III of Galveston. *Houston Chronicle,* Dec. 23, 1971, p. 4.
75. *Houston Post,* Dec. 26, 1971.
76. Int., Eugene Kahn Sanger, 1985.
77. Int., Ruth Hexter Kahn, 1985.
78. "Ed Titche Eulogized As Friend of Dallas," *Dallas Morning News,* Feb. 21, 1944.
79. "Ed Titche, Dallas Civic Leader, Dies," *Dallas Morning News,* Feb. 19, 1944.
80. Little known data on Titche's early marriage given in interview by William R. Eliassof, descendant, 1987. Henry Titche Levy long served as Executive Secretary of the Dallas Community Chest (1922-39). Int. Ellis Titche, 1982.
81. Leon Harris, *Merchant Princes,* p. 165.
82. Leon J. Rosenberg, *Sangers: Pioneer Texas Merchants.* Only a few weeks before the first train arrived in Dallas in 1872, eleven persons formed the Hebrew Benevolent Assn. with Alex Sanger, Vice President. Other "first Jews of Dallas" in this group included Moses Ullman, David A. Eldridge, David Goslin, Alex Ortlieb, and Charles Kahn. They arranged the first Jewish service in Dallas.
83. Harris, *Merchant Princes,* p. 160.
84. Ibid., p. 161.
85. Ibid., p. 162; L. Mandelbaum, "Texas Merchants After the Civil War: 1871," *AJA* (April 1960) pp. 71-74.
86. Harris, p. 162; Int. Joseph Sanger Linz, 1985; Int. Eugene Kahn Sanger, son of Sam Sanger, 1985.
87. Int. Joseph Sanger Linz, 1985. Linz's mother was Lois (Bettina) Sanger and his father was Clarence Linz. Philip Sanger's two children were Lois Linz and Jessica (Mrs. Edgar) Pike.
88. Int. Hortense and Morton Sanger, 1985.
89. Harris, *Merchant Princes,* p. xii.
90. Int. Arthur Kramer, Jr., 1984.
91. Int. Charlotte Kramer Hafter, 1985.
92. Stanley Marcus, *Quest for the Best,* 1979.
93. Int. Charlotte Royal Moskowitz, circa 1955.
94. Stanley Marcus, *Minding the Store,* p. 7.
95. Ibid., p. 10; J. W. Rogers, *Lusty Texans of Dallas,* pp. 297, 318.
96. Harris, *Merchant Princes,* p. 177.
97. Marcus, *Minding the Store,* p. 42.
98. Although Stanley Marcus identified minimally with the Jewish community, his daughter Wendy married journalist Henry Raimont and lived briefly on a kibbutz. Robert Kranz, for many years head of the Neiman-Marcus fur workroom, told of how he taught Stanley sufficient Hebrew to get him through his daughter's traditional wedding ceremony. Int., Robert Kranz, 1984. When Temple Emanu-El of Dallas needed a new rabbi, Herbert Marcus and Arthur Kramer were the entire search-and-selection committee. Although each had stated he was an agnostic, each served as president of this congregation.
99. Ints., Harold Cole, Beverly Morgan, Ralph Schnitzer Jr., Ted Strauss, and Stanley Marcus, 1947 and 1948.
100. S. Stewart, *Dallas Morning News,* Sept. 22, 1981.
101. Story told in a newspaper advertisement marking the 100th anniversary, 1977.
102. Don McIver, "Jewelry Firm at 70th Milestone: Prizes Integrity Over Its Gems." *Dallas Morning News,* n.d.
103. John S. Cooper, "The Linz 'Jewelists' Use Prestige to Sell Gems in the Southwest," *Wall Street Journal,* Oct. 8, 1948.
104. Ibid.; Int., Albert Linz Hirsch, 1980.
105. Int., Joseph S. Linz, 1985.
106. Ints., Aron S. Gordon 1982, 1983.
107. Letters Aron Gordon to author, April 11, 1983.
108. Tommy Thompson, "Gordon Brothers 10-year goal: 1,000 jewelry stores nationwide," *Houston Chronicle,* n.d.
109. Int., Morris B. Zale, 1985. Int. Patricia Agostini, 1985.
110. Joe Thompson, "The Ben Lipshy Factor," *Modern Jeweler,* Dec. 1984, p. 46.
111. Libby's Yiddish name was Leeba which means "life." Int. Bert Kruger Smith, 1984.
112. *The Spokesman,* Rotary publication, Wichita Falls, circa 1949.
113. Zale Corporation Annual Report 1984, p. 4.
114. Morris Zale worked also for Max Shain, husband of Freda Shain, Fania Kruger's sister. The Morris Zales lived with them in Wichita Falls nearly five years. Int. Edna Zale, 1987. Fania Kruger became known in her own right as an award winning poet. (See chapter 12) Bert Kruger Smith served for decades as director of the Hogg Foundation for

Mental Health, University of Texas at Austin.
115. Int. Bert Kruger Smith, 1984.
116. Letter Bert Kruger Smith to Ornish, Jan. 22, 1985.
117. March 29, 1924, the first Zale store opened for business.
118. T. Stringer, *NEWS* (Zale Corp. publication), March 1984.
119. David Federman, "Morris B. Zale: The Life," *Modern Jeweler*, Dec. 1984, p. 40.
120. In 1985 Zale Corp. had 1,500 stores and annual sales of over $1 billion. Zale 1984 Annual Report, p. 4.
121. Federman, *Modern Jeweler*, p. 44.
122. Int. Barbara Gutow, 1985.
123. *Dallas Morning News*, Nov. 24, 1986, p. 1-A; *Dallas Times Herald*, Nov. 24, 1986, p. 1-A.
124. Stringer, *NEWS*, March 1984, p. 2; Int., Joy Lipshy Burk, 1985; Int., Barbara Lipshy Marcus, 1987. "Ground Broken for Zale-Lipshy University Hospital," *Newsline*, Fall, 1987, p. 1.
125. Int., Robert Bloom, July 4, 1987.
126. "Rites set for Sam Bloom, advertising firm founder," *Dallas Morning News*, July 19, 1983, p. 21A.
127. David Ritz, "Remembering Bloom," *D Magazine*, July 1975, p. 57.
128. Ibid.
129. Ibid.
130. Int., Evelyn Bloom, July 4, 1987.
131. Ibid.
132. Ritz, "Remembering Bloom."
133. Int., Evelyn Bloom.
134. Ibid.
135. "Rites Set for Sam Bloom."

Chapter 10
The Significant Merchants

1. J. O. Dyer, "Came Here 83 Years Ago, First Experiences of Joe Osterman," *Galveston Daily News*, April 2, 1922.
2. J. O. Dyer, "Life of Early Galveston As Told by Storekeeper," *Galveston Daily News*, Dec. 18, 1921.
3. C. R. Wharton, *Gail Borden, Pioneer*, Joe B. Frantz, Gail *Borden: Dairyman to the Nation*.
4. Dyer, "Life of Early Galveston."
5. Ibid.
6. "History of Southwest Texas," II, p. 145.
7. Int., Beulah Keller, Jan. 5, 1987.
8. Int., Morris Wise, Jan. 5, 1987.
9. Henry Lesinsky, *Letters*, pp. 9-13. Henry was son of Fanny Freudenthal and Leopold Lesinsky.
10. Ibid. pp. 44, 45.
11. Lesinsky, *Letters*, p. 47.
12. Lesinsky, *Letters*, p. 58.
13. "H. Lesinsky, 89, El Paso Pioneer, Dies in New York," *El Paso Times*, Apr. 25, 1924.
14. "Henry Lesinsky, Arizona Copper Miner, Dies Here," newspaper, n.d.
15. S. J. Freudenthal, "El Paso Merchant," p. 8.
16. "Old-Time Houstonian Remembers," *Houston Post*, July 8, 1951.
17. "Family Histories Span Area Growth," *Houston Tribune*, Aug. 23, 1973, pp. 16, 17.
18. Letter, David Westheimer to author, Jan. 8, 1987.
19. "Atwater Exhibit — What It Means to Houston and Texas," *Houston Post*, June 21, 1922. Int., Lisa Rebori, Manager of Collections, Houston Museum of Natural History, 1988.
20. "Growth of Weingartens is One of Greatest Epics of City's Business History," *Houston Post*, Mar. 17, 1935.
21. E. Collier, "Joe, Abe Weingarten Work Way to Riches," *Houston Chronicle*, Mar. 7, 1951.
22. Zarko Franks, "Weingarten Borrowed for Dream, Now Store Sales Top $164 Million," *Houston Chronicle*, Nov. 7, 1965.
23. Int., Bernard Weingarten, son of Joe, May 9, 1987. Joe's nephew, Harold Falik, chaired the United Way drive in 1984.
24. *Who's Who in World Jewry*, 1965, p. 1028.
25. F. Fierman, *Guts and Ruts*, p. 140.
26. Int., Floyd Fierman, 1982; Int., Ruth Zork, 1982.
27. "A. Schwartz, 68, Advises Busy Life," *El Paso Times*, Jan. 1, 1935.
28. Int., Rabbi Robert Kahn, 1988.
29. "Sterling Jewelry started in Brownwood in 1939 in a 15 by 50-foot building on a side street costing $40 a month rent. The store followed the starting of building of an army camp for 20,000 troops." Int., Ervin Donsky, 1984.
30. Etta Levin, *Genealogy of the Levitansky Family*, p. 88. He died in Lithuania in 1919 at the age of 93.
31. *Genealogy*, p. 89. Yonkel carried with him medals he said he had won in the war. Relatives in the North said he fought for the Union Army; int., Dorothy and Moses Levitan (grandson of Yonkel), Chicago, 1980. Genealogist Etta Levin said he never lived in the North and she believed he fought for the Confederacy. Int. Levin, 1983.
32. Meta and Jacob Laib came to Boston in 1873 and then lived in Dallas for four years. They returned to Boston, where Jacob's nephew had the J. Reinertz Steamship Agency.
33. Sadie's cousin, Rosa Levin Toubin, a 1914 graduate of Blinn College, wrote a history of the Jewish community of Brenham.
34. Int., Fannie Levene Ornish, 1985.
35. Int., Bess Shapiro Moskowitz, 1976.
36. One of Moshe's grandsons was Abraham Louis Levin, M.D. (1881-1940), originator of the stomach pump, known as the "Levin Tube." Dr. Levin was helped financially through medical school by cousins in Brenham.
37. She was ordained at Hebrew Union College, Jewish Institute of Religion, N.Y. Int., Dr. Richard and Lois Utay Plumb, 1988.
38. Int., Phil Schepps, 1987.
39. Dave McNeely, "Schepps Always Joined in Any Worthwhile Cause," *Dallas Morning News*, May 26, 1971.
40. Sam Acheson, "Schepps Reached City in 1901," *Dallas Morning News*, n.d.
41. McNeeley, "Schepps Always Joined."
42. The year Julius Schepps died, Rabbi Gerald Klein of Dallas suggested to Schepps' cousin by marriage, Ruth Hohenberg (Mrs. George) Golman, that she interview top civic leaders who knew Schepps. A transcript was given to Dr. Jacob Rader Marcus for the AJA, Cincinnati. Quotes from Cullum, Thornton, and Smith are from these interviews.
43. Felix McKnight, "Julius Schepps: Tall Citizen Who Earned Greatness," *Dallas Times Herald*, May 30, 1971.
44. "Schepps Ready to Help," *Dallas Times Herald*, Feb. 26, 1969.
45. Julius Schepps letter dated Sept. 24, 1965, Phil Schepps papers.
46. R. Compton, "Julius Schepps, Golden Rule His Guide," *Dallas Morning News*, June 22, 1958.
47. "Mourners Crowd Temple for Julius Schepps Eulogy," *Dallas Morning News*, May 28, 1971.
48. The center carried his name from May 8, 1962 to March 17, 1979, then was renamed the Jewish Community Center.
49. Int., Jeanette Ornish (Mrs. Justin F.) Levey, June 3, 1987.

50. Ints., Helen Ann Carb Hurst (Mrs. M.K., Jr.); Meredith Hurst Dalton, 1988.
51. B.B. Paddock, *History of Fort Worth*, II, p. 601; III, p. 31.
52. "Real Estate Board Honors Life Member M. R. Carb Sr." *Fort Worth Star Telegram,*" April 9, 1958.
53. "David Carb, Author, Native of Fort Worth, Dies in New York," *Fort Worth Star Telegram*, Sept. 11, 1952.
54. "Bomber Co-Pilot of 8th Air Force Here on Leave," *Fort Worth Star Telegram,* Jan. 22, 1945. He died in 1976.
55. "HemisFair Exhibit to Tell History of Firm," *Fort Worth Star Telegram*, Aug. 4, 1967; Ints., Mr. Marion Weil, Gloria and Max K. Mayer, Jr., 1988.
56. Int., Ben H. Rosenthal, Sr., of Dallas,1988.
57. Ints., Lloyd Lyman, Sara Alpard, 1987.
58. Paddock, *History of Fort Worth*, III, pp. 132, 324.
59. F. Schiff, "History of the Jews of Fort Worth."
60. Int., Harold Gernsbacher, Sr., 1988.
61. Schiff, "History of the Jews of Fort Worth."
62. "Fort Worth Had 2 Street Railway Systems 20 Years Ago," *Fort Worth Star Telegram*, Jan. 31, 1926.
63. "Sam Rosen Dies, Russian Immigrant 50 Years Ago, Father of Heights Named for Him," *Fort Worth Star Telegram*, Dec. 21, 1932.
64. Sam Hunter, "Immigrant Boy Now North Side Success," *Fort Worth Press*, May 30, 1957.
65. Int., Betty Jo Drescher Silberstein, 1988.
66. Int., Lester Lorch, 1986.
67. "Story of a 'One Horse Peddler,'" privately printed, the Lorch Co.
68. Int., Louis W. Kreditor, Oct. 4, 1987.
69. Int., Irene (Mrs. Ernest) Wadel, May 8, 1987.
70. "Howard B. Wolf, Inc. Background Report," Nov. 1969; Int., Lois C. and Howard B. Wolf, 1987.
71. Renee Wisch, column, *Texas Jewish Post*, Jan. 3, 1980; Jeff Collins, "Luskey's," *Dallas Times Herald,* July 26, 1987, B1, 6.
72. Int., Ruth Rolnick Albert, 1986; int., M.E. Florence, Jr., 1988.
73. "The Saga of Mabel and Edward Byer's Life," brochure; int., Mrs. Arthur Byer, 1986.
74. Int., Henry Bromberg, 1986.
75. Bill Minutaglio, "A Well-Worn Friend: Nine out of nine cowboys choose the hat made in Garland," *Dallas Morning News*, June 14, 1987; "Resistol Hats," *Dallas Times Herald*, July 12, 1981.
76. First Southwest Co. Investment Bankers, Research Dept.
77. "Story of Page Boy Sisters Opens New Chapter Monday," *Dallas Morning News*, Sept. 4, 1949; "When a Designer has a Baby," *Good Housekeeping*, July 1951.
78. Int., Louise Frankfurt Gartner, 1986.
79. M. F. Cavender, "The Frankfurt Sisters," *Dallas,* Aug. 1948.
80. "Battle of the Bulge," *Time*, Sept. 6, 1948.
81. "Yoga Relaxation Break," *Dallas Times Herald* mag., Mar. 1,1964.
82. Int., Bunny Feldman Mayers, 1986.
83. "3 Sisters Rule Unique Firm," *Dallas Times Herald*, Nov. 20,1957.
84. Ints., Sig Badt, 1979, Augusta (Boots) Badt Brin, 1984.
85. Wedding announcement, Lyra Brin Daniels Collection.
86. O. Leonard, "He Saved 600 Sailors," *Americans All;* "Commodore Badt Dies; Commanded FDR Ship," *Washington Star*, Sept. 10, 1967.
87. Int., Rosa Toubin, 1987.
88. C. F. Schmidt, *History of Washington County,* pp. 85, 123.
89. Int., Bette Wolens Miller; Int. Raymond Holbrook.
90. D. C. Kelley, *Handbook of Waco*, p. 112.
91. *Reform Advocate,* Jan. 24, 1914.
92. "I. A. Goldstein Dies," *Waco Times-Herald*, Nov. 19, 1920.
93. I Weiner's father, Avraham Yitzhok, married Chai Sara, whose last name is unknown. Isidore Weiner married Esther Zinman in 1915 in Lithuania. He used "I. Weiner" after he arrived in the U.S. Their children were: Abe I. Weiner, born 1917; Ann Weiner Bell, born 1920; Leon Weiner, born 1924; and Sol B. Weiner, born 1926. Abe I. Weiner died in 1986; Ann Weiner Bell died in 1976. Esther and I. Weiner divorced in 1943, and he married Evelyn Gerson Gaitz in 1944. He predeceased Evelyn Weiner. Int., Leon Weiner, 1988.
94. Int., Sol Weiner, 1985.
95. Ints., Selma Moskowitz Abelman, 1983, Elise Moskowitz Grossman, 1987 (nieces of Ben Greenberg); int., Jerry Klein, 1983.
96. C. H. Moses and M. W. Lowe, Martin Weiss.
97. "The Gugenheim House Restoration Project," privately published by Camp Fire Girls, n.d., Marie Levi Bitterman Collection.
98. Int., Clyde Crockett, age 69, Dallas, May 15, 1988. Ben Gold's manufacturing company operated under the trade name of Nardis, which is Sidran spelled backward. The parent company was founded by Joseph Sidran.

Chapter 11
The Educators

1. Int., Barry Davis, Asst. City Secretary for Dallas, 1988.
2. "Passover in a Texas Town in 1891," *WSJHQ*, vol. 11, 4 (July 1979), p. 324.
3. "From Kempen, Poland to Hempstead, Texas: The Career of Rabbi Heinrich Schwarz," *WSJH*, vol. 19, 2 (Jan. 1987), p. 132.
4. "Rabbi H. Schwarz Dead: Aged Hebrew Litterateur, Had International Reputation as a Writer." Hempstead newspaper, Oct. 18, 1900. E. Gale Collection.
5. "Passover in a Texas Town in 1891," p. 324.
6. Ibid.
7. Mark Seal, "Annette Strauss," *Dallas Morning News*, Aug. 1, 1982; Vivian Castleberry, "Annette Strauss: Dallas' dynamo of civic causes follows path into politics," *Dallas Times Herald*, May 4, 1983; Int., Annette Strauss, March 27, 1987; "Strauss Waltzes to easy victory," *Dallas Times Herald*, April 19, 1987, 1-A.
8. Rabbi Schwarz's great-granddaughter married Dr. Boris Eugene Levine, eminent Los Angeles cardiologist, son of Dr. Max Levine, renowned bacteriologist, a branch of the Texas Levine clan in chapter 10. Int., Felicia S. Levine Zeidenfeldt, 1985. Another great-granddaughter married Harry Battelstein, son of the merchant prince. Rabbi Schwarz's granddaughter married a Weil of the ranching family in chapter 5. The rabbi's brother Sam's wife's maiden name was Hirsch, and she was the sister of A. Harris who founded that department store in Dallas. Letter, Edwin Gale to author, Nov. 25, 1986.
9. Letter Gale to author, Nov. 25, 1986; UTMB brochure, "The Marie B. Gale Professorship in Psychiatry."
10. Int., Ruth Kahn, Feb.11, 1987; Int., Hortense (Mrs. Lawrence) Pollock, 1987; Int., Jerry Bywaters, 1987.
11. C. Wicker, "A Gentleman and a Scholar," *Dallas Morning News*, Feb. 10, 1987, p. 2-C.
12. "The Edmund J. and Louise W. Kahn Chair in History," SMU publication, n.d., p. 19.
13. Int., Ruth Kahn (no relation), 1987; C. Hoppe, "Civic Leader Kahn dies," *Dallas Morning News*, Oct. 31, 1984; "Edmund J. Kahn, philanthropist, dies," *Dallas Times Herald*, Oct. 31, 1984.
14. SMU Publication, p. 19; Robert Miller, columnist, "Team-

work makes Kahn job training center a reality," *Dallas Morning News*, Dec. 11, 1987, 3 D; Int., Louise W. Kahn, 1988.

15. Int., Helene Levy, 1987.
16. Int., Jennie Lovenberg descendant Irvin L. Levy, Dallas civic leader and great-nephew of Cohen; Letter, Irvin Levy to author March 17, 1987.
17. Int., Helene Levy, 1987.
18. *Galveston Daily News*, Oct. 8, 1917, obit.; Lovenberg Papers, Rosenberg Library.
19. Galveston attorney Bleeker Morse, great-grandson of the inventor, drafted the bill for the Texas House and Senate, which was enacted into law and signed by Gov. M.A. Ferguson.
20. Mrs. C. A. Goetting, "Tribute to Olga Bernstein Kohlberg," p. 159.
21. Ernst Kohlberg, *Letters 1875-1877*, pp. 3-8.
22. Kohlberg, *Letters*, p. 4.
23. Ibid.
24. Goetting, "Tribute to Olga," p. 160.
25. "The Late Mrs. Randall," obit. *Galveston News*, Nov. 6, 1888; Henry Cohen, "Settlement" (1895), p. 15.
26. "The Jewish Texans" (1974), p. 7.
27. I. Karniel, "Taubenhaus Memorial," Carmel newspaper, April 12, 1938. Taubenhaus Collec., Texas A&M University Library.
28. Ibid.
29. Ibid.
30. Ibid.
31. Dr. Picard, "In Memory of Haim Taubenhaus," typescript, Texas A&M University.
32. Dr. P. Cohen, "Jacob Joseph Taubenhaus," *Nature and Country*, Jan. 1938; "J. J. Taubenhaus, Plant Pathologist At A&M, Dead: His Studies in Cotton Root Rot Resulted in Finding of Preventive." Associated Press wirestory, Dec. 13, 1937; "Dr. J. J. Taubenhaus," *Dallas Morning News* editorial, Dec. 16, 1937.
33. "Work, Kindness, Tolerance Are Hyman Ettlinger Traits." *Austin American Statesman*, Dec. 10, 1955.
34. Dick Smith, "He's A Phi Beta Kappa All-American," *Daily Texan*, Nov. 6, 1942.
35. "40 Years on Faculty, Rabbis to Honor Ettlinger," *Daily Texan*, March 4, 1953.
36. Wes Hocker, "Versatile Dr. Ettlinger—Ready for 'Next Fifty'," *Daily Texan*, Dec. 14, 1962.
37. Lorraine Barnes, "UT Prof Plays A Paul Revere," *Austin American Statesman*, Oct. 6, 1955; "Interfaith Honor Given Dr. Ettlinger," *Dallas Morning News*, Jan. 29, 1953.
38. Letter, H. J. Ettlinger to author Aug. 15, 1975; "Atomic Physicist To Talk Here As Dr. Ettlinger Honored," *Austin American Statesman*, Jan. 28, 1953.
39. W. L. Gay, "Daniel Sternberg," *Texas Humanist*, May/June 1985.
40. Ints., Paul Lewis 1977, Leah Lewis 1977, Mimi Lewis Barnett 1985.
41. Ints., Sara and Jacob Feldman 1983, 1988; *Who's Who in World Jewry* 1965, p. 244.
42. C. Warnken, "Dr. Schachtel to step down but not out," *Houston Post*, May 17, 1975. p. 8-B.
43. Int., Dr. H. J. Schachtel, Feb. 19, 1987. The song is in the musical "South Pacific."

Chapter 12
The Artists

1. The 1850 Census shows: "Saml MAAS, 38, born in Germany; Isabella, 30, Germany; and four children born in Texas: Maxwell 5, Julius 3, Mary 2, Alfred 1; Henrietta OFFENBACH 24, Germany [probably younger sister of Isabella]; Julia [no last name] 22, Germany." Archives, Rosenberg Library. However, Isabella was age 33 in 1850, and a genealogy of the Samuel Maas family prepared by a descendant, Harry Levy, Jr., lists their four children as Max, Julius, Miriam, and Rosa. Levy did not recall ever hearing of a child named Alfred, who may have died young. Rosa likely was born after the 1850 Census was taken. Mary may have been an incorrect listing by the census taker for Miriam. Miriam married Nathan Spiers and Rosa married M. Redlich.
2. Bob Dalehite, "The Maas House," p. 8.
3. Samuel lived at 1802 Avenue I (Sealy) and Isabella lived at 1727 Avenue I (Sealy). Int. Harry Levy, Jr. 1982.
4. "Death of Mrs. Maas," *Galveston Daily News*, Feb. 20, 1891.
5. Bernard Falk, *The Naked Lady: or Storm Over Adah*; Frank X. Tolbert, "Was the Naked Lady from Nacogdoches?" *Dallas Morning News*, July 13, 1970, p. 21A.
6. Allen Lesser, *The Enchanting Rebel: The Secret of Adah Isaacs Menken*.
7. Llerena Friend, "Adah Isaacs Menken, Texan by Parentage, Preference, or Prevarication?" Texas Collection, *Library Chronicle* of the University of Texas, Spring 1958, p. 58.
8. Falk, *Naked Lady*, p. 23.
9. Leo Shpall, "Adah Isaacs Menken," *Louisiana Historical Quarterly*, vol. 26, no. 1, pp. 162-68.
10. "Alex Simon, Owner of the Grand Opera House," *Brenham Daily Banner Press*, n.d.
11. "Three Generations of Simon Family in Theatre Business," *Brenham Daily Banner Press*, Jan. 18, 1926; Int., Rosanne Leeson, descendant, 1988.
12. Int., Mrs. Selden E. Brin, 1986.
13. "History of the Brin Opera House," printed program, dedication ceremony April 27, 1985.
14. L. E. Daniell, "Mrs. Anna Goodman Hertzberg," *Texas, The Country and Its Men*, pp. 251, 252.
15. Reiter conducted the Waco Symphony ten years, until it disbanded; thirteen years later Daniel Sternberg reorganized it. Int., Sternberg, 1988; Int., Mrs. Harris Oppenheimer, daughter of Pauline and Max Goldsmith, 1987; *Handbook of Texas*, vol. 2, p. 459; W. Heinsheimer, "Bus Stop in Waco," *Reader's Digest*, December 1947; Obit., *San Antonio Evening News*, Dec. 14, 1950; L. Wright, "Culture Club," *Texas Monthly*, June 1987.
16. E. Adams, ed., *New Encyclopedia of Texas*, 1926; "Youth Who Came 22 Years Ago is One of Leading Architects," *Houston Post*, Dec. 29, 1929; "Joseph Finger" typescript, Houston Pub. Library; B. Scardino, "A Legacy of City Halls," *Houston Review*, Fall 1982, p. 160; "Joseph Finger, Architect, Dies," *Houston Chronicle*, Feb. 6, 1953.
17. Int., Fannie Levene Ornish, sister of Gus, 1970; "Ballet Suite by Young Dallasite Written in Conservative Style, to Be on Next Sunday's Bowl Program: Gershun Levene's 'Ballet Suite Exodus' Inspired by Bible, to Have Debut," *Dallas Times Herald*, Sept. 3, 1932; "Suite Written by Dallas Man on Bowl List: Levene's 'Exodus' Accepted for Concert Here on September 4," *Dallas Morning News*, Sept. 3, 1932.
18. John Rosenfield, "Premiere of Levene Work Heard Sun-

day Night," *Dallas Morning News,* Sept. 5, 1932; Int., Gus Levene, Hollywood, 1970; Int., Mrs. Gus Levene, 1985.

19. Bill Warren, "Books," *Austin American Statesman,* May 23, 1971; Alma S. Scarberg, "People," *The Networker,* Austin, February 1985; Ints., Bert Kruger Smith; Letters, Smith to author Jan. 22, 1985, Feb. 5, 1985, Jan. 13, 1988. Fania's older brother Moses was the father of Jacob Feldman, Dallas patron of education.
20. V. Newton, "Word Pictures Flash in Color," *Enterprise-Journal,* Sept. 30, 1973.
21. "Fania Kruger Dies in Austin," *Wichita Falls Times,* July 17, 1977.
22. Int., Frances Mossiker, 1980; Int., A.C. Greene, 1985; Maryln Schwartz, "Frances Mossiker," *Dallas Morning News,* May 30, 1982; Joe Rhodes, "Dallas Author Chronicles Life in Court of Louis XIV," *Dallas Times Herald* , Dec. 21, 1983; M. Brinkerhoff, "Pocahontas," *Dallas Morning News,* Nov. 16, 1976; "Author Frances Sanger Mossiker Dies," *Dallas Morning News,* May 11, 1985.
23. Rosenfield, "Passing Parade." Col., *Dallas Morning News,* Jan. 14, 1935; reprinted in Leon Harris, *Merchant Princes,* p. 358.
24. Harris, *Merchant Princes,* pp. xii, xiii; Int., Leon Harris, 1985; *Dallas Times Herald,* Nov. 24, 1985.
25. Martens, *The Hebrews in America,* pp. 215-16.Steuart, *Gems from the Texas Quarry,* pp. 111-19. In 1989 the author interviewed Grace (Mrs. Charles Lee) Harby, age 92, whose father-in-law, Henry James Harby, was oldest son of Captain Levi Charles Harby and the brother of Jacob De La Motta (Jack) Harby who married Leah Cohen. This author also interviewed in 1989 Mavis Harby Malarek, descendant of Octavia, sister of soldier Julian Harby; and Miss Marianne Swan, then age 76, great-great-granddaughter of Captain Levi Charles Harby.
26. E. Brooks, *Prominent Women of Texas,* pp. 99-100; *Who's Who in America* 1902.
27. G. D. Saxon, "An Oral History Interview" (1982), typescript, p. 9, Rosenfield Collection, Dallas Public Library.
28. Int., G. William Jones, 1985.
29. Int., Claire (Mrs. John) Rosenfield, 1986. Arthur Kramer Sr.'s older sister, Jennie Lind Kramer, marrier Max John Rosenfield, Sr., making Arthur the uncle of John Rosenfield the critic. John's father was`credit manager of Sanger Bros. Int. Ruth Kahn, 1987.
30. Int., Sylvan T. Baer, 1952; John Rosenfield, "Importance of the Fine Arts," speech delivered at Temple Emanu-El.
31. Int., Evelyn Oppenheimer, 1987; Autobiographical typescript.
32. Ints., Patsy Nasher, Raymond Nasher, Ivy Rabinowitz, Ellen Gordesky 1950-1988; D. Fritze and P. Troboy, "She Made Art a Part of Dallas," *Dallas Times Herald,* July 1, 1988, p. 1; J. Kutner, "Patsy Nasher Made an Art of Living," *Dallas Morning News,* July 10, 1988, p. 1; Kutner, "Patsy Nasher Dies at 59," *Dallas Morning News,* July 2, 1988, p. 1.
33. R.D. Nasher, biographical typescript; Bill Marvel, "Nasher Company Wins Arts Award," *Dallas Morning News,* Oct. 7, 1987, 5-C; Colleen O'Connor, "Ray Nasher," *Dallas Morning News,* April 12, 1987, 1-E. In September 1988 the City of Dallas named Nasher ambassador of cultural affairs. "Ambassador Nasher: Great choice for Dallas' international future," Editorial, *Dallas Morning News,* Sept. 8, 1988.
34. Bruce Nixon, "Sculpture of Stature," *Dallas Times Herald,* Jan., 31, 1987, F-1; Ruth Gruber, "Nasher Collection Opens 'in Memoriam'," *Dallas Times Herald,* July 9, 1988, p. F-1; Lee Cullum, "Patsy Rabinowitz Nasher," Editorial, *Dallas Times Herald,* July 2, 1988.

Chapter 13
The Doctors

1. Dr. Levy titled himself "Surgeon in Chief of the Volunteer Army of Texas" in a letter to his sister from "San Antonio de Bexar, December 20, 1835." This was official, as Commander in Chief F. W. Johnson listed Dr. Levy "Surgeon in Chief" on Dec. 17, 1835. J.H. Jenkins, *Papers of the Texas Revolution,* vol. 3, p. 226. Surgeon General of the Texas Army after June 7, 1837, was Dr. Ashbel Smith, a Phi Beta Kappa from Yale who served on the first medical board with Dr. Levy in 1837. L.B. Friend, *Sam Houston,* pp. 17, 88.
2. Int., Jessie Levy Foss, 1986; Dr. S. Kagan, *Jewish Contributions to Medicine,* pp. 5-6; Dr. P. Nixon, *Medical Story of Early Texas,* p. 442.
3. *Medical Record and Annals,* vol. 60, no. 8 (August 1967), p. 307.
4. H. Gambrell, *Anson Jones,* pp. 107-10.
5. Nixon, *Medical Story of Early Texas,* p. 463.
6. Probate Court, Nacogdoches, Estate of Hyman Hertz; H. Cohen, "Settlement of the Jews," *PAJHS,* vol. 2 (1894), p. 143; L. Turitz, *Jews in Early Mississippi,* p. ix.
7. B. Korn, *Early Jews of New Orleans,* p. 327. Land grant to Dr. Lyons' heirs states he died "in the service."
8. H. Cohen, "The Jews in Texas," *PAJHS,* vol. 4 (1896) p. 19; McArthur & Wickes, *Texas Legislature and State Officials,* pp. 47-48.
9. Cohen, "Settlement of the Jews," pp. 153-56; letter Richard Torbert to Faith Nachman Klein, Feb. 22, 1983; Int., Torbert, 1986.
10. Tribute to Rosanna reprinted in *History of Baltimore Hebrew Congregation,* Susan Dyer Johnson Collection. John M. Dyer was congregation's first president in 1830, and his son Leon was president in 1840; letter, Jack and Faith Nachman Klein to author, April 15, 1986.
11. "Dr. Dyer, Physician and Historian, Dies," *Galveston News,* Oct. 3, 1925.
12. "Eulogizes Dyer as Giant in Intellect," *Galveston News,* Oct. 5, 1925.
13. "Hebrew Burial Ground," *Galveston News,* Aug. 31, 1852.
14. Letter, Richard Torbert, grandson of Amelia Rosanna Labatt, to author, May 12, 1986; Barbara P. Warren, "Dr. Isadore Dyer 1865-1920," written for Southern Medical Assn.
15. Int., Susan Dyer Johnson, daughter of the third Isadore Dyer, 1986; letter, Susan Dyer Johnson to author, June 23, 1988.
16. Mulvany, "Dr. Ray K. Daily Reflects," *Houston Chronicle,* May 31, 1970.
17. Int., Dr. Louis Daily, Jr., March 14, 1987.
18. Homer P. Rainey letter to Dr. Daily, Aug. 30, 1943.
19. Int., Dr. Louis Daily, Jr., March 14, 1987.
20. Mulvany, "Dr. Ray K. Daily Reflects."
21. Minutes, Board of Education, HISD, April 30, 1934; Joseph W. Samuels, "Dr. Ray K. Daily: A Woman of Valor," *Jewish Herald-Voice,* Dec. 3, 1975.
22. Carleton, *Red Scare!,* p. 168.
23. Int., Dr. Louis Daily, Jr.
24. Mulvany, "Dr. Ray K. Daily Reflects."
25. "Philanthropist Taub Dies," *Houston Chronicle,* Sept. 10, 1982.
26. Transcript of videotape prepared by Baylor on occasion of the Harris County Hospital District's 20th anniversary, October 1985.
27. Ibid.
28. "Ben Taub," *Baylor Medicine,* July 1981, p. 1; "Ben Taub," editorial, *Houston Chronicle,* Sept. 10, 1982.

29. Broadcast on trauma centers, "Sixty Minutes," CBS-TV, 1986.
30. "City Philanthropist Ben Taub, 93, Dies," *Houston Post*, Sept. 10, 1982, A-1, 15.
31. "Ben Taub," editorial, *Houston Post*, Sept. 12, 1982.
32. Leopold Meyer, *Days of My Years*, p. 267.
33. Ibid., p. 3.
34. I. Immer, "Leopold Meyer," ms. 67 (1981) Houston Public Library.
35. Meyer, *Days of My Years*, p. 205.
36. Adelena's mother was sister of one of the pioneer Levys of Levy Bros. Dry Goods Co. For eight years after her marriage to Leopold, they lived with Adelena's elderly aunt Harriet Levy, "a distinguished grande dame."
37. "Leopold L. Meyer 1892-1982," *Baylor Medicine*, Jan. 1983, p. 2.
38. Meyer, *Days of My Years*, p. 7.
39. Newell E. France, in Meyer, *Days of My Years*, p. xii.
40. "Dr. Bodansky Dies," *Galveston News*, June 15, 1941, p. 1.
41. "Nobel-Prize Winners to Speak," *Galveston News*, Feb. 11, 1952.
42. Int., Samona Bodansky Roddy, 1987. The chemical measurement in Bodansky units (of acid phosphotase in the blood) refers to Aaron's work in New York.
43. "Dr. Bodansky Dies," p. 1.
44. Int., Samona Bodansky Roddy, 1986.
45. Letter, Dr. Irving Graef, NYU, to Bodansky, Nov. 9, 1940; Statement of Boston Committee on Medical Emigres; D.L. Edsall, "A Program for the Refugee Physicians," *Journal American Medical Assn.*, May 13, 1939.
46. "Meyer Bodansky Dies," *New York Herald Tribune*, June 15, 1941, p. 1; Dr. Albert Singleton, "Dr. Meyer Bodansky," *Surgery*, vol. 10, no. 3, Sept. 1941, pp. 489-90.
47. Int., Dr. William Levin, President, UTMB, March 19, 1987.
48. "A Seventy-Five Year History," UTMB, p.120.
49. "Nobel-Prize Winners to Speak, Annual Bodansky Lecture," *Galveston News*, March 6, 1953.
50. Int., Dorothy Whitney Anigstein, 1987. She pronounced his name Lood-vig Ah-nig-steen.
51. Anigstein, "Research Activities," typescript, UTMB.
52. "49th Executive Officer Returns from Special Mission to Poland," UTMB publication, November 1946.
53. *Who's Who in World Jewry, 1965*, p. 26; "Curriculum Vitae, Ludwik Anigstein," typescript, June 3, 1975, UTMB.
54. L. Herz, "Dr. Anigstein Brought UTMB Fame," *Galveston News*, Dec. 5, 1965.
55. Ludwik Anigstein Bibliography, UTMB; Int., Dorothy Anigstein.
56. "Texas, World have Gained," *Galveston News*, Dec. 9, 1970.
57. Int., Donald Vincent Moore, M.D., of Dallas, 1987.
58. "Texas, World have Gained."
59. "Discovery at Med School of Antibiotic Derived from Blood Told Around World," *Galveston Tribune*, Aug. 12, 1950.
60. "Dr. Anigstein Feels Flattered," *Galveston Tribune*, Aug. 17, 1945.
61. Dr. L. Bruce-Chwatt, "Ludwik Anigstein," *Lancet*, Nov. 29, 1975, p. 1103.
62. "Bernhard Gottlieb Passes," *Journal American Dental Assn.*, May 1950, p. 607.
63. Dr. Wm. C. Hurt, Lecture to American Academy of the History of Dentistry, Oct. 19, 1979.
64. W.L. Davis and R.G. Jones, "A New Look at the Gottlieb Collection," *Baylor Dental Journal*, January 1985.
65. Int., Dr. Rose G. Schneider, 1987.
66. "In the News," *Barnard Alumni Magazine*, Winter 1987.
67. Curriculum Vitae, Rose G. Schneider, Ph.D., April 1986.
68. Int., Dr. Rose G. Schneider, 1987.
69. "Schneider Recipient of Sinclair Award," *Galveston News*, May 22, 1975."
70. Letter, Barbara H. Bowman, Ph.D., I.H. Kempner Professor of Human Genetics, to Dr. Gerald Beathard, UTMB, April 4, 1975.
71. Int., Dr. Rose G. Schneider, 1987.
72. Int., Jeanette Lipson, 1985.
73. News release from UTMB, February 1987.
74. Printed program, "The Maimonides Award Dinner: In Tribute to Dr. Joseph Melnick, April 9, 1980."
75. Printed program, "Raymond E. Baldwin Medal, Joseph L. Melnick '36," Wesleyan University 154th Commencement, June 1, 1986.
76. "1965 Awards for distinguished achievement," *Modern Medicine*, Jan. 4, 1965.
77. "Joseph L. Melnick, Distinguished Service Professor and Chairman, Baylor College of Medicine," bulletin, typescript, BCM; "Doctor Says Vaccine," *Houston Chronicle*, July 26, 1961.
78. "Herpes Implicated," *New York Times*, Nov. 18, 1986; "The Joseph L. Melnick Professorship of Virology," brochure, Baylor College of Medicine, 1987.
79. "Better Urinary Test Described by Doctor," *Houston Post*, May 27, 1981.
80. "Brain Damage by AIDS Under Active Study," *Science*, March 27, 1987.
81. "Joseph L. Melnick Professorship of Virology," brochure.
82. Int., Dr. Joseph L. Melnick, 1987.
83. "Melnick Is Honored for 30 Years of Work," *Inside Baylor Medicine*, May 1980, p. 4.
84. Dr. Joseph L. Melnick, Phi Beta Kappa talk, Wesleyan University, May 31, 1986.
85. Letter, Dr. Joseph L. Melnick to author, April 10, 1987.
86. Donald Wayne Seldin, M.D., Curriculum Vitae.
87. Ibid.
88. M. Primeau, "Donald Seldin," *Dallas Morning News*, Jan. 26, 1986, E-1.
89. A.G. Motulsky, "The 1985 Nobel Prize in Physiology or Medicine," *Science*, vol. 231, pp. 126-29.
90. Joseph L. Goldstein, M.D., Curriculum Vitae; Michael S. Brown, M.D., Curriculum Vitae; and bibliographies atached thereto.

Chapter 14
The Lawyers

1. I. Rosenwaike, "The Mussina Family," *AJH*, June 1986, p. 397.
2. H. Cohen, "Jews In Texas History," *Texas Jewish Herald*, April 23, 1936, p. 1; idem., "Settlement of the Jews," *PAJHS* (1894), p. 145.
3. Rosenwaike, "The Mussina Family," p. 399.
4. "Letter to Simon Mussina," *Writings of Sam Houston 1859*, vol. 7, pp. 370-372. Also editors' note by A. Williams and E. Barker.
5. M. Marks, "Philip Eldridge, Pioneer Founder of a Texas Family," *News*, Golden Acres, December 1976.
6. Int., David A. Eldridge, 1987.
7. Int., Ellen Mack, 1986; int., Mrs. Henry Mack II (Norma), 1986.
8. D. Levy, "Letters About the Jews in California 1855-1858," *WSJHQ*, January 1971, p. 19.

9. W. Kramer, "Pioneer Lawyer of California and Texas," *WSJHQ*, October 1982, p. 4.
10. Ibid.
11. Int., Margaret Levi Strauss, 1984.
12. Levi joined Flournoy & Scott, 1876; later he was a partner in Scott, Levi, and Smith. Cohen, Intro. to IOBB *Memorial.*
13. Jos. Hirsh of Vicksburg, Miss., edited the book, which includes a short biography of Levi by Cohen.
14. Leo N. Levi letter in M.L. Strauss collection.
15. Cohen, Introduction to IOBB *Memorial.*
16. The six Hexter brothers and sisters, natives of Baltimore, were: Sarah, J. K., George, Victor, Frances (Brightie), and Avrum. Int. Jean Levi Stein, J. K.'s granddaughter.
17. "J. K. Hexter, Civic Leader, Dies," *Dallas Morning News*, Nov. 18, 1936; "Prominent Dallasite to be buried in Emanu-El Cemetery," *Dallas Times Herald*, Nov. 18, 1936.
18. Int., Ruth Brown Hexter Kahn, 1986.
19. Int., Victor Hexter II.
20. *City of Dallas: Mayors and City Councils*, p. 50. At the turn of the century he wrote letters helping to relocate immigrants during the Galveston Movement. Letter (on Hexter and Kramer letterhead), V. Hexter to immigration agents in New York, 1907. AJHS.
21. They were parents of Victor II and Joan Hexter Warshaw. Ruth later married Lawrence S. Kahn, early Dallas merchant prince.
22. "Louis Hexter Headed Back to Grindstone," *Dallas Morning News*, Aug. 21, 1973, p. 5B.
23. Int., Frederic Tycher, 1984.
24. Int., I. C. Deal, 1984.
25. Int., R. D. Nasher, 1986.
26. Int., John F. Eulich, 1984.
27. Int., Victor Hexter II; "Playwright Louis Hexter Dead at 77," *Dallas Morning News*, Apr. 3, 1977.
28. *Dallas Times Herald*, Sept. 5, 1973, p. 16A. George and Louis died of emphysema; Hexter genealogy.
29. Fifty years later the position of Assistant Attorney General of Texas was filled by Billy B. Goldberg of Houston, a former Texas Democratic Party Chairman.
30. Census of 1900, Rusk County; Ints., Congressman Martin Frost and Shirley Marwil Sanger, 1987.
31. Ints., Frost and Sanger.
32. "Services Held for Charles Brachfield," *IOOF News*, June 1947.
33. Int., Lee Maxwell, 1986.
34. M. Orr, "Old Brachfield Recounted," *Henderson News*, July 4, 1986.
35. Texas State Library, Austin.
36. Int., Florence Rettig, 1987.
37. "Gala Tribute to Gen. Maurice Hirsch," brochure, Houston Symphony Orchestra, June 3, 1980.
38. K. Lewis, "90 Minutes with Gen. Hirsch," *Houston Post*, April 11, 1975.
39. Ibid.
40. "Gen. Maurice Hirsch, civic leader, dies at 93," *Houston Chronicle*, Aug. 5, 1983.
41. Int., Irving L. Goldberg, circa 1955; "Jewish Texans."
42. *Who's Who in World Jewry 1965*, p. 991.
43. C. Lesh, "Hermine Tobolowsky," *Dallas Morning News*, Oct. 19, 1986, p. 1-E.
44. J. Jarvis, "Hermine Dalkowitz Tobolowsky," *Dallas Times Herald*, Aug. 31, 1986, p. 3.
45. Lesh, "Hermine Tobolowsky," p. 2-E.

Bibliography

Source Books

Adams, Ellis A., ed. *New Encyclopedia of Texas.* Dallas: Texas Development Bureau, 1926.

Adler, Cyrus, ed. *American Jewish Yearbook 5661* (1900-1901). 2: 519, Kaufman, D.S.; Philadelphia: Jewish Publication Society.

Alessio Robles, Vito. *Coahuila y Texas en la Epoca Colonial.* Mexico City: Editorial Cultura, 1938.

———. *Monterrey en la Historia y en la Leyenda.* Mexico City, 1936.

Alonso de León. "Historia de Nuevo Leon con noticias sobre Coahuila, Tamaulipos, Texas, y Nuevo Mexico," originally published in Mexico in 1649; reprinted in *Documentos Ineditos o Muy Raros para la Historia de Mexico* edited by Genaro Garcia, 25: 75-77, 90-95; Mexico City: 1909. Translated with commentary by Carl L. Duaine in *Caverns of Oblivion,* Corpus Christi: privately published, 1971.

Anhaiser, Leon and Bettye, eds. *Fort Bend County Sesquicentennial 1822-1972.* Richmond, Tx.: Fort Bend County Sesquicentennial Association, 1972.

Arthur, Stanley Clisby. *Jean Laffite, Gentleman Rover.* New Orleans: Harmanson, 1952.

Austin, Stephen F. *The Austin Papers 1820-1836.* Edited by Eugene C. Barker. 1-3: Washington, D.C.: Government Printing Office, 1919-1922; 4: Austin: University of Texas Press, 1928.

Baker, DeWitt Clinton, ed. *A Texas Scrap-Book: Made Up of the History, Biography, and Miscellany of Texas and its People.* New York: A.S. Barnes, 1875.

Bancroft, Hubert Howe. *History of the North Mexican States and Texas* and *History of Arizona and New Mexico,* 15 and 17 of The Works of Hubert H. Bancroft. San Francisco: A.L. Bancroft, 1889.

Barnstone, Howard. *The Galveston That Was.* New York: Macmillan, 1966.

Barker, Eugene C. *The Life of Stephen F. Austin, Founder of Texas, 1793-1836: A Chapter in the Westward Movement of the Anglo-American People.* Nashville: Cokesbury, 1926. Austin: Texas State Historical Foundation, 1949.

———. *The Father of Texas.* Indianapolis: Bobbs-Merrill, 1935.

———. *Mexico and Texas 1821-1835.* Dallas: P.L. Turner, 1928.

Bedichek, Roy. *Karankaway Country.* New York: Doubleday, 1950.

Benitez, Fernando. *Los Primeros Mexicanos: La Vida Criolla en el siglo XVI.* 2nd ed. Mexico City, 1962.

Best, Hugh. *Debrett's Texas Peerage.* New York: Coward-McCann, 1983.

Biographical Directory of the American Congress 1774-1911. Washington, D.C.: U.S. Government Printing Office.

Biographical Encyclopedia of Texas. New York: Southern Publishing, 1880.

Birmingham, Stephen. *"Our Crowd": The Great Jewish Families of New York.* New York: Harper and Row, 1967.

Bodansky, Meyer, M.D., and Oscar Bodansky, M.D. *Biochemistry of Disease.* New York: Macmillan, 1940.

Bolton, Herbert E. *Texas in the Middle Eighteenth Century: Studies in Spanish Colonial History and Administration.* Berkeley: University of California Press, 1915. Austin: University of Texas Press, 1970.

Brooks, Elizabeth. *Prominent Women of Texas.* Akron, Ohio: Werner, 1896.

Brown, John Henry. *History of Texas 1685-1892.* 2 vols. St. Louis: L.E. Daniell, 1892.

———. *Indian Wars and Pioneers of Texas.* St. Louis: L.E. Daniell, 189[?].

Buck, Samuel M. *Yanaguana's Successors.* San Antonio: privately published, 1949. Reprint, 1980.

Carleton, Don E. *Red Scare!* Austin: Texas Monthly Press, 1985.

Carter, James David, ed. *The First Century of Scottish Rite Masonry in Texas 1867-1967.* Waco: Scottish Rite History Committee, 1967.

Carvajal, Luis de [the Younger]. "Autobiography" and "Letters and Last Will and Testament." In *The Jewish Experience in Latin America* by Martin A. Cohen. 1: 243-312. New York: KTAV, 1971.

———. *The Enlightened: The Writings of Luis de Carvajal, el Mozo.* Edited and translated by Seymour B. Liebman. Coral Gables: University of Miami Press, 1967.

Castañeda, Carlos Eduardo. *Our Catholic Heritage in Texas 1519-1963.* 1-6: Austin: Von Boeckmann-Jones, 1936-1950. New York: Arno Press, 1976.

———, trans. and ed. *The Mexican Side of the Texas Revolution.* Dallas: P.L. Turner, 1928.

Castaño de Sosa, Gaspar. *Journal 1590-1591. See* Schroeder and Matson.

Castro, Henri. *Memorial of Henri Castro, the Founder of Castro's Colony, to the Senate and House of Representatives of the State of Texas.* San Antonio: Ledger, 1855.

Castro, Lorenzo. *Immigration from Alsace and Lorraine: A Brief Sketch of Castro's Colony in Western Texas.* New York: George W. Wheat, 1871.
———. *The Republic of Mexico in 1882.* New York: Thompson and Moreau, 1882.
Cavazos Garza, Israel. *See* Garza, Israel Cavazos.
Chabot, Frederick C. *With the Makers of San Antonio: Genealogies of the Early Latin, Anglo-American and German Families, With Occasional Biographies.* San Antonio: Artes Graficas, 1937.
———. *San Antonio and Its Beginnings 1691-1731.* San Antonio: Naylor, 1931.
Clark, James A. *East Texas Oil Field: The First 25 Years.* Dallas: Texas Mid-Continent Oil and Gas Association, 1955.
Clark, James A., and Michael T. Halbouty. *The Last Boom.* New York: Random House, 1972.
Cohen, Anne Nathan. *The Centenary History of Congregation Beth Israel of Houston, Texas 1854-1954.* Houston: privately published, 1954.
Cohen, Anne Nathan, and Harry I. Cohen. *See* Nathan, Anne, and Harry I. Cohen.
Cohen, Henry, David Lefkowitz, and Ephraim Frisch. *Early Jewish Settlements in Texas: One Hundred Years of Jewry in Texas.* Dallas: privately published for the Texas Centennial, 1936.
Cohen, Martin A. *The Martyr: The Story of a Secret Jew and the Mexican Inquisition in the Sixteenth Century.* Philadelphia: Jewish Publication Society, 1973.
Considerant, Victor Prosper. *European Colonization in Texas.* New York: Baker, Godwin, 1855.
Cox, James. *Historical and Biographical Record of the Cattle Industry and the Cattlemen of Texas and Adjacent Territory 1894-1895.* 2 vols. St. Louis: Woodward and Tiernan, 1895. Reprint, New York: Antiquarian Press Ltd., 1959.
Crockett, George Louis. *Two Centuries in East Texas: A History of San Augustine County and Surrounding Territory from 1685 to the Present Time.* Dallas: Southwest Press, 1932.
Crook, Cornelia E. *Henry Castro and His Homestead.* Castroville, Texas: privately published, 1978.
Cullum, Gen. George W. *Biographical Sketches of Deceased Graduates of the United States Military Academy.* Boston: Houghton-Mifflin, 1891.
Daniell, Lewis E. *Texas: The Country and Its Men.* Austin: privately published, [c. 1924].
Daughters of the American Revolution. *The Alamo Heroes and Their Revolutionary Ancestors.* San Antonio: DAR, 1976.
Daughters of the Republic of Texas. *Founders and Patriots of the Republic of Texas.* Lubbock: DRT, 1963.
Daughters of the Republic of Texas. *Muster Rolls of the Texas Revolution.* Lubbock: Daughters of the Republic of Texas, 1986.
Davis, Edward. *The History of Rodeph Shalom Congregation 1802-1926.* Philadelphia: privately published, 1926.
Davis, Ellis A., and Edwin H. Grobe, eds. *The New Encyclopedia of Texas.* Dallas: Texas Development Bureau, 1926.
Day, James M. "Goliad." In *Battles of Texas.* Waco: Texian, 1967.
De Cordova, Jacob. *Texas: Her Resources and Her Public Men: A Companion for J. De Cordova's New and Correct Map of the State of Texas.* Philadelphia: J.B. Lippincott, 1858.
Dobie, J. Frank. "Rose and His Story of the Alamo: The Line That Travis Drew." In *In the Shadow of History.* 15: 9-15. Austin: Texas Folklore Society, 1939.
Dreyfus, A. Stanley, ed. *Henry Cohen, Messenger of the Lord.* New York: Bloch, 1963.
Duaine, Carl L. *See* Alonso (de León).
Eberstadt, Edward. *Texas: Being a Collection of Rare and Important Books and Manuscripts Relating to the Lone Star State.* Catalog 162. New York: privately published, 1963.
Ehrenberg, Herman. *Texas Und Seine Revolution.* Leipzig: Otto Wigand, 1843. Reprint, *Der Freiheitskampf in Texas im Jahre 1836.* Leipzig: Otto Wigand, 1844. Reprint, *Fahrten und Schicksale Eines Deutschen in Texas.* Leipzig: Otto Wigand, 1845. Translated by Edgar W. Bartholomae, 1925. Condensed and edited by Henry Smith under the title *With Milam and Fannin: Adventures of a German Boy in Texas' Revolution.* Dallas: Tardy, 1935. Reprint of text in English, Texas Heritage Press, © 1989.
Encyclopedia Judaica. Jerusalem: Macmillan, 1971.
Encyclopedia of the New West. Marshall, Texas: Speer and Brown, 1881.
Evans, Eli. *The Provincials: A Personal History of the Jews in the South.* New York: Atheneum, 1976.
Falk, Bernard. *The Naked Lady or Storm Over Adah.* London: Hutchinson, 1934.
Fehrenbach, T.R. *Lone Star: A History of Texas and the Texans.* New York: Macmillan, 1968.
Fierman, Floyd S. *Guts and Ruts: The Jewish Pioneer on the Trail in the American Southwest.* New York: KTAV,

1985.

———. *Roots and Boots: From Crypto-Jew in New Spain to Community Leader In the American Southwest.* New York: KTAV, 1987.

———. *The Schwartz Family of El Paso: The Story of a Pioneer Jewish Family in the Southwest.* El Paso: Texas Western Press, 1980.

———. *Some Early Jewish Settlers on the Southwestern Frontier.* El Paso: Texas Western Press, 1960.

Framis, Ricardo Majo. "Francisco Fernandez De Cordoba." In *Vidas de los Navegantes y Conquistadores Espanoles del Siglo XVI.* 2: 187-238. Madrid: Aguilar, 1950.

Freudenthal, Samuel J. *El Paso Merchant and Civic Leader from the 1880s.* Edited by Floyd S. Fierman. El Paso: Texas Western Press, 1960.

Friend, Llerena Beaufort. *Sam Houston, the Great Designer.* Austin: University of Texas Press, 1954.

Gambrell, Herbert. *Anson Jones: Last President of Texas.* Garden City, N.Y.: Doubleday, 1948.

Garcia, Genaro. *See* Alonso (de León).

Gard, Wayne. *The Chisholm Trail.* Norman: University of Oklahoma Press, 1954.

———. *The First 100 Years of Texas Oil and Gas.* Dallas: Texas Mid-Continent Oil & Gas Association, 1966.

Garrett, Julia Kathryn. *Green Flag Over Texas: A Story of the Last Years of Spain in Texas.* New York and Dallas: Cordova, 1939.

Garza, Israel Cavazos. *History of Nuevo Leon.* Monterrey, Mexico: Gobierno del Estado de Nuevo Leon, Centro de Estudies Humanisticos de la Universidad de Nuevo Leon, 1961.

Gettys, Warner E., ed. *Houston: A History and Guide.* Compiled by workers of the Writers' Program of the WPA. (Sponsored by the Harris County Historical Society.) Houston: Anson Jones, 1942.

Goldberg, Isaac. *Major Noah: American-Jewish Pioneer.* Philadelphia: Jewish Publication Society, 1936.

Goodspeed, W.A. *History of Texas: Memorial and Genealogical Record of Southwest Texas.* privately published, 1894.

Granoff, Albert Leo. *To America, With Love: An Autobiography.* Laredo: privately published [c. 1961].

Greenleaf, Richard E. *The Mexican Inquisition of the Sixteenth Century.* Albuquerque: University of New Mexico Press, 1969.

———. *The Mexican Inquisition and the Enlightenment 1763-1805.* Albuquerque: University of New Mexico Press, 1966.

Gunther, John. *Taken at the Flood: The Story of Albert D. Lasker.* New York: Harper & Brothers, 1960.

Halff, M.H. *My Memoirs.* Edited by B.S. Hendricks. Austin: privately published, 1987.

Hamilton, Charles. *Great Forgers and Famous Fakes.* New York: Crown, 1980.

Hammond, George P., and Agapito Rey. *Rediscovery of New Mexico 1580-1594.* Albuquerque: University of New Mexico Press, 1966.

Harris, Bogardus, and Labatt, comps. *San Francisco City Directory for the Year Commencing October 1856.* San Francisco: Whitton-Towne, 1856.

Harris, Leon A., Jr. *Merchant Princes: An Intimate History of Jewish Families Who Built Great Department Stores.* New York: Harper & Row, 1979.

Hayes, Charles W. *History of the Island and the City of Galveston.* Cincinnati, 1879. Reprint, under the title *Galveston: History of the Island and the City.* 2 vols. Austin: Jenkins Garrett, 1974.

Hill, Jim Dan. *The Texas Navy.* Chicago: University of Chicago Press, 1937.

Horgan, Paul. *Great River: The Rio Grande in North American History.* Vol. 1. New York: Holt, Rinehart and Winston, 1954.

Houston, Sam. *The Writings of Sam Houston 1813-1863.* See Amelia Williams and Eugene C. Barker.

Independent Order of B'nai B'rith, ed. *Leo N. Levi: Memorial.* Chicago: Hamburger, 1905.

Industrial Advantages of Houston, Texas, and Environs. Houston: Akehurst, 1894.

Innes, Hammond. *The Conquistadors.* New York: Knopf, 1969.

James, Marquis. *The Raven: A Biography of Sam Houston.* Indianapolis: Bobbs-Merrill, 1929.

Jenkins, John H., ed. *Papers of the Texas Revolution 1835-1836.* 10 vols. Austin: Presidial/Matthews, 1973.

Johnson, Col. Francis White. *A History of Texas and Texans.* Edited by Eugene C. Barker and Ernest W. Winkler. 5 vols. Chicago and New York: American Historical Society, 1914, 1916.

Johnson, Laurence S. *History of Victoria Bank and Trust Co.* Victoria: privately published, 1950.

Kagan, Solomon R., M.D. *Jewish Contributions to Medicine in America.* Boston, 1934.

Kelley, Dayton C., ed. *Handbook of Waco and McLennan County.* Waco: Texian Press, 1972.

Kenamore, Jane A., and Michael E. Wilson. *Manuscript Sources in the Rosenberg Library, a Selective Guide.*

College Station, Tx.: Texas A&M University Press, 1983.
Kielman, Chester V. *The University of Texas Archives: A Guide to the Historical Manuscripts Collections in the University of Texas Library*. Austin: University of Texas Press, 1967.
Kinnaird, Lawrence, ed. *Frontiers of New Spain: Nicolas De Lafora's Description 1766-1768*. Berkeley: Quivira Society, 1958.
Kohlberg, Ernst. *Letters of Ernst Kohlberg 1875-1877*. Translated by Walter L. Kohlberg. El Paso: Texas Western Press, University of Texas at El Paso, 1973.
Korn, Bertram Wallace. *The Early Jews of New Orleans*. Waltham, Mass.: AJHS, 1969.
Lamar, Mirabeau B. *Papers of Mirabeau Buonaparte Lamar*. Edited by Charles Adams Gulick and Harriet Smithers. 6 vols. Austin: Texas State Library, 1921-27.
Landa, Harry. *As I Remember*. San Antonio: privately published, 1945.
Landis, Charles K. *Carabajal, the Jew: A Legend of Monterrey, Mexico*. Vineland, N.J.: privately published, 1894.
Lane, J.J. *History of the University of Texas, Based on Facts and Records*. Austin: Hutchings, 1891.
Lawler, Ruth Curry. *The Story of Castroville: Its People, Founder and Traditions*. La Coste, Tx.: Ledger, 1974.
Learsi, Rufus. *The Jews in America: A History*. Cleveland and New York: World, 1954.
Lefkowitz, David. "The Jews of Texas." Chap. 24 in *East Texas: Its History and Its Makers* edited by T.C. Richardson, vol. 1. New York: Lewis, 1940.
León, Alonso de. *See* Alonso (de León).
Leonard, Oscar. *Americans All*. New York: Behrman, 1944.
Lesser, Allen. *The Enchanting Rebel, the Secret of Adah Isaacs Menken*. New York: Beechhurst, 1947. Reissue, Port Washington, N.Y.; London: Kennikat, 1973.
Liebman, Seymour B. *The Enlightened: Writings of Luis de Carvajal, el Mozo*. Coral Gables, Fl.: University of Miami Press, 1967.
———. *A Guide to Jewish References in the Mexican Colonial Era 1521-1821*. Philadelphia: University of Pennsylvania Press, 1964.
———. *The Inquisitors and the Jews in the New World*. Coral Gables, Fl.: University of Miami Press, 1976.
———. *The Jews in New Spain: Faith, Flame, and the Inquisition*. Coral Gables, Fl.: University of Miami Press, 1970.
———. *New World Jewry 1493-1825: Requiem for the Forgotten*. New York: KTAV, 1982.
Lord, Walter. *A Time to Stand: The Epic of the Alamo Seen As a Great National Experience*. New York: Harper, 1961.
Marcus, Jacob Rader. *Early American Jewry*. 1-2: Philadelphia: Jewish Publication Society, 1951-53.
———. *Memoirs of American Jews 1775-1865*. 1: Philadelphia: Jewish Publication Society, 1955.
Marcus, Stanley. *Minding the Store: A Memoir*. Boston: Little, Brown, 1974.
———. *Quest for the Best*. New York: Viking, 1979.
Marinbach, Bernard. *Galveston: Ellis Island of the West*. Albany, N.Y.: State University of New York Press, 1983.
Marshall, James. *Santa Fe: The Railroad That Built an Empire*. New York: Random House, 1945.
Martens, Isaac. *The Hebrews in America*. privately published, 1888. Reprint, Arno Press, 1975.
McDonald, Archie P., ed. *Hurrah for Texas! The Diary of Adolphus Sterne*. Waco: Texian Press, 1969.
Memorial and Genealogical Record of Southwest Texas. Chicago: Goodspeed Bros., 1894.
Menken, Adah Isaacs. *Infelicia*. London, Paris, and New York: privately published, 1868.
Meyer, Leopold L. *The Days of My Years: Autobiographical Reflections of Leopold L. Meyer*. Houston: privately published, 1975.
Miller, Thomas Lloyd. *Bounty and Donation Land Grants of Texas 1835-1888*. Austin: University of Texas Press, 1967.
Miller, Townsend. *A Letter From Texas*. Dallas: privately published by Neiman-Marcus, 1944.
Mooney, Booth. *Seventy-five Years in Victoria*. Victoria: privately published, 1950.
Morrison, Andrew. *The Industries of Galveston*. privately published, 1887.
Morrison, Richard. *Index to D.W.C. Baker's A Texas ScrapBook*. Austin: privately published, 1984.
Moses, Carolyn H., with M.W. Lowe. *Hungary Sends a Dallas-Builder: The Story of Martin Weiss*. Dallas: privately published, 1948.
Nathan, Anne, and Harry I. Cohen. *The Man Who Stayed in Texas*. New York: Whittlesey House, 1941.
Nixon, Patrick Ireland, M.D. *The Medical History of Early Texas 1528-1853*. Lancaster, Pa.: privately published, 1946.
Oppenheimer, Evelyn, and Bill Porterfield, eds. *The Book of Dallas*. Garden City, N.Y.: Doubleday, 1976.

Ousley, Clarence, ed. *Galveston in 1900.* Atlanta: William Chase, 1900.
Paddock, Buckley B. *Twentieth Century History and Biographical Record of North and West Texas.* Chicago: Lewis, 1906.
———. *History of Central and Western Texas.* Chicago: Lewis, 1911.
———. *History of Texas: Fort Worth and the Texas Northwest Edition.* Vols. 2, 3. Chicago: Lewis, 1922.
Pennybacker, Anna J. Hardwicke. *A New History of Texas.* Austin: Privately published, 1900.
Prindle, David F. *Petroleum Politics and the Texas Railroad Commission.* Austin: University of Texas Press, 1981.
Ray, Worth S. *Austin Colony Pioneers.* Austin: Pemberton, 1970.
Richardson, Rupert N., et al. *Texas, the Lone Star State.* Englewood Cliffs, N.J.: Prentice-Hall, 1943.
Richardson, Thomas C., and Dabney White, eds. "Henry Cohen." In *East Texas: Its History and Its Makers,* vol. 4. New York: Lewis, 1940.
Rister, Carl Coke. *Oil! Titan of the Southwest.* Norman: University of Oklahoma Press, 1949.
Robles, Vito Alessio. *See* Alessio Robles, Vito.
Rogers, John William. *The Lusty Texans of Dallas.* New York: E.P. Dutton, 1951.
Rose, Victor. *History of Victoria.* Laredo: Daily Times, 1883; reprinted San Antonio: Lone Star, 1961.
Rosenberg, Leon Joseph. *Sangers': Pioneer Texas Merchants.* Austin: TSHA, 1978.
Rosenthal, Philip, and William Groneman. *Roll Call at the Alamo*: New York: Old Army Press, 1986.
Schmidt, Charles Frank. *History of Washington County, Texas.* San Antonio: Naylor, 1949.
Schmier, Louis, ed. *Reflections on Southern Jewry: Letters of Charles Wessolowsky 1878-1879.* Albany, Ga.: Mercer University Press, 1982.
Schroeder, Albert H., and Dan S. Matson. *A Colony on the Move: Gaspar Castaño de Sosa's Journal 1590-1591.* Santa Fe, N.M.: School of American Research, 1965.
Schwettmann, Martin W. *Santa Rita: The University of Texas Oil Discovery.* Austin: Texas State Historical Association, 1943.
Simpson, Arthur J. *Southwest Texans.* San Antonio: Southwest Publications, 1952.
Smith, Edward. *Account of a Journey Through North-Eastern Texas, Undertaken in 1849 for the Purposes of Emigration . . .* London: Hamilton, Adams, 1849.
Speer, William S., and John H. Brown. *The Encyclopedia of the New West.* Marshall, Tx.: U.S. Biographical Pub. Co., 1881.
Stern, Malcolm H. *Americans of Jewish Descent.* Cincinnati: Hebrew Union College Press, 1960.
———. *First American Jewish Families: 600 Genealogies 1654-1977.* Cincinnati: American Jewish Archives, 1978.
Sterne, Nicholas Adolphus. Diary. *See* McDonald, Archie P.
Steuart [Sydnor], Ella Hutchins, ed. *Gems from a Texas Quarry: or Literary Offerings by Leading Writers of Texas.* New Orleans: J.S. Rivers, 1885.
Streeter, Thomas W. *Bibliography of Texas 1795-1845.* 5 vols. Cambridge, Mass.: privately published, 1955-60.
Stringer, Tommy W. *Zale Corporation: From the Beginning.* Dallas: privately published, 1986.
Texas State Legislature. *Members of the Texas Legislature 1846-1962.* Authorized by H.C.R. 30, Third Called Session, 57th Legislature. Austin, 1963.
Thrall, Homer S. *Pictorial History of Texas: From the Earliest Visits of European Adventurers to A.D. 1879.* St. Louis: N.D. Thompson, 1879.
Tolbert, Frank X. *An Informal History of Texas.* New York: Harper & Bro., 1951.
Twentieth Century History of Southwest Texas. 2: Chicago: Lewis, 1907.
University of Texas Medical Branch at Galveston: A Seventy-five Year History by the Faculty and Staff. Austin: University of Texas Press, 1967.
U.S. Congress. House. *Journal.* 1 February, 1851.
Vigness, David M. *The Revolutionary Decades.* Austin: Steck-Vaughn, 1965.
Voorsanger, Jacob. *Chronicles of Emanu-El.* San Francisco: privately published, 1900.
Vorspan, Albert. *Giants of Justice.* New York: Union of American Hebrew Congregations, 1960.
Walker, W.H. *Odd Fellowship in America and in Texas.* Dallas: Von Boeckmann-Jones, 1911.
Waugh, Julia Nott. *Castroville and Henry Castro, Empresario.* San Antonio: Standard, 1934.
Weaver, Bobby D. *Castro's Colony: Empresario Development in Texas, 1842-1865.* College Station, Tx.: Texas A&M University Press, 1985.
Webb, Walter Prescott, ed. *Handbook of Texas.* 3 vols. Austin: TSHA, 1952.
Weber, David J. *The Mexican Frontier 1821-1846: The American Southwest Under Mexico.* Albuquerque:

University of New Mexico Press, 1982.
Weems, John Edward. *Dream of Empire: A Human History of the Republic of Texas 1836-1846.* New York: Simon and Schuster, 1971. Reprint, Fort Worth: Texas Christian University Press, 1986.
Wharton, Clarence R. *Remember Goliad.* privately published, 1931. Reprint, Glorietta, N.M.: Rio Grande Press, 1968.
Who's Who in America 1952-53. Chicago: Marquis Who's Who, 1953.
Who's Who in World Jewry 1965. New York: Pitman/David McKay.
Williams, Amelia W. and Eugene C. Barker, eds. *The Writings of Sam Houston 1813-1863.* 8 vols. Austin: University of Texas Press, 1938-1943.
Wineburgh, H. Harold. *Texas Banker: The Life and Times of Fred F. Florence.* Dallas: privately published, 1981.
Winkler, Ernest W., ed. *Check List of Texas Imprints.* 1: 1846-1860. Austin: TSHA, 1949.
———, ed. *Manuscript Letters and Documents of Early Texians 1821-1845.* Austin: Steck, 1937.
———, ed. *Secret Journals of the Senate, Republic of Texas 1836-1845.* Austin Printing Co., 1911.
———, and Llerena B. Friend, eds. *Check List of Texas Imprints.* 2: 1861-1876. Austin: TSHA, 1963.
Wisehart, M.K. *Sam Houston, American Giant.* Washington, D.C.: Robert B. Luce, 1962.
Wolf, Simon, and Louis Edward Levy. *The American Jew as Patriot, Soldier and Citizen.* Philadelphia: Levytype; New York: Brentano, 1895.
Wooten, Dudley G. *A Complete History of Texas.* Dallas: William G. Scarff, 1899.
———, ed. *A Comprehensive History of Texas 1685-1897.* 2 vols. Dallas: William G. Scarff, 1898. Reprint, TSHA, 1986.
Yoakum, Henderson K. *History of Texas, from Its First Settlement in 1685 to Its Annexation to the United States in 1846.* 2 vols. New York: J.S. Redfield, 1855.

Periodicals, Manuscripts, Archival Materials

Adler, Cyrus. "Trial of Jorge de Almeida by the Inquisition in Mexico." *AJHQ* 4 (1896): 29-79.

Alexander, Fanny Weil. "Charles and Sara Weil." Corpus Christi: privately published, 1959.

Anigstein, Ludwik, M.D. Bibliography. List of 131 articles he wrote. Anigstein Papers, Blocker History of Medicine Collections, Moody Medical Library, UTMB, Galveston.

———. Curriculum Vitae. June 3, 1975. Blocker History of Medicine Collections, Moody Medical Library, UTMB, Galveston.

———. Research Activities. Blocker History of Medicine Collections, Moody Medical Library, UTMB, Galveston.

"Anigstein Services Slated Monday." *Galveston News*, Nov. 2, 1975, p. 1-A.

"Annual Meyer Bodansky Lecture." *Galveston News*, March 6, 1953, p. 12.

Applebome, Peter. "The Wildcatter's Tale." *New York Times*, March 1, 1987, sec. 3, pp. 1, 6-7.

"Archivo General de Indias, Sevilla, Audiencia de Mexico, Informaciones de oficio y parte. Años 1591-1592. Estante 60, Cajon 1, Legajo 3. 1590: Mexico: Ynstruction al Capitan Juan Morlete para yr al Nuevo Mexico en seguimiento de Gaspar Castaño y sus compañeros. Guadalajara." 101 pages. Typescript. Archives, Bancroft Library, University of California, Berkeley.

"Atomic Physicist To Talk Here As Dr. Ettlinger Honored." *Austin-American Statesman*, Jan. 28, 1953.

Atwell, Ben. "Tribute to Julius Schepps." House Concurrent Resolution No. 187, adopted May 28, 1971, Austin.

Aury, Luis. Papers 1803-1821. Barker Texas History Center, University of Texas at Austin.

———. Papers. Humanities Research Center, Harry Ransom Center, University of Texas at Austin.

"Author Frances Sanger Mossiker Dies." *Dallas Morning News*, May 11, 1985.

Austin City Gazette, May 12, 1841, p. 3, col. 3.

"Austin Colony Pioneers." Typescript. DRT Library at the Alamo, San Antonio.

Austin, Mattie Alice. "Municipal Government of San Fernando de Bexar 1730-1800." *TSHAQ* 8 (April 1905): 277-352.

Austin Papers. "Annual Report of the American Historical Association for the Year 1922." Edited by Eugene C. Barker. Vol. 2. Washington, D.C.: U.S. Government Printing Office, 1928.

Axelrod, Ronald A. "Rabbi Henry Cohen and the Galveston Immigration Movement 1907-1918." *Journal* (East Texas Historical Assn.) 15, no.1 (1977): 24-37.

Baker, Karle Wilson. "Following the New Orleans Greys." *Southwest Review* 22 (1937).

"Ballet Suite by Young Dallasite Written in Conservative Style, to Be on Next Sunday's Bowl Program." *Dallas Times Herald*, Sept. 3, 1932.

Barker, Eugene C. "Difficulties of a Mexican Revenue Officer." *TSHAQ* 4 (January 1901): 190-202.

Barnes, Lorraine. "For Science's Sake: UT Prof Plays A Paul Revere." *Austin American-Statesman*, Oct. 6, 1955.

Barnston, Henry. "Houston." *Jewish Encyclopedia* 6 (1901): 486.

Bartholomae, Edgar William. "A Translation of H. Ehrenberg's Fahrten und Schicksale Eines Deutschen in Texas, With Introduction and Notes." Master's thesis, University of Texas, 1925. See also: Ehrenberg.

Bennett, Miles S. "The Battle of Gonzales, the 'Lexington' of the Texas Revolution." *TSHAQ* 2 (April 1959): 313-16.

"Bernhard Gottlieb Passes Away in Dallas, Texas Home." *Journal of the American Dental Association*. 40 (May 1950): 607-08.

Best, Gary Dean. "Jacob H. Schiff's Galveston Movement: An Experiment in Immigration Deflection 1907-1914." *AJA* 30 (April 1978): 43-79.

Bexar County Archives, Bexar County Courthouse, San Antonio.

Blake, Robert Bruce, Papers, X, XII, LXV. Nacogdoches Records.

———. "Rose and His Escape from the Alamo: Together With a Transcript of the Documents Relating to Said Louis (Moses) Rose, Taken from the Records in the Office of the District Clerk and County Clerk of Nacogdoches County, Texas." Typescript. Austin: Texas State Library.

———. "A Vindication of Rose and His Story." In *In the Shadow of History*. Edited by J. Frank Dobie, 10-11.

Bodansky, Meyer, M.D. "The Historical Background of Modern Medical Education." *The Alcalde* (University of Texas publication, Austin) 17 (May 1929). Rosenberg Library, Galveston.

Bolton, Herbert Eugene. "The Spanish Occupation of Texas 1519-1590." *TSHAQ* 16:11-12.

———. Papers. Item 505, 1582-1602. Documents relating to the exploration of New Mexico which include correspondence of Gaspar Castaño de Sosa. Source: AGI, Sevilla. Bancroft Library, University of California at Berkeley.

Boyd, Bob. "Perry Kallison Has Many 'Neighbors.'" *San Antonio Magazine*, June 1972, pp. 51-54.
Boyd, Ron. "Lynn Wyatt: Her international life keeps her at the top of Texas high society." *Dallas Times Herald Unique* magazine, Feb. 15, 1984, pp. 1, 7.
"Brain Damage by AIDS Under Active Study." *Science* 235 (March 27, 1987): 1574.
Bressler, David M. "Results and Significance of the Galveston Movement." *Jewish Herald*, August 6, 1914.
Brindley, Mrs. Paul, Mrs. S.A. Dybowski, Miss Emma Lee, Miss Ruth Nichols, Mrs. Cortes Pauls, and Thomas Rice, eds. "Historic Galveston Homes." Galveston Historical Society, 1951.
"British Med Group Honors Local Doctor." *Galveston News*, July 1, 1956.
Brown, Michael S., M.D. Curriculum Vitae. 1987.
Bruce-Chwatt, Leonard, M.D. "Ludwik Anigstein." *The Lancet* (London, England) (November 29, 1975): 1103.
Carleton, Don E. "A Crisis of Rapid Change: the red scare in Houston 1945-1955." Ph.D. thesis, University of Houston, 1978.
Carr, Marsha E. "The Road Called Westheimer." *Houston* magazine, October 1976, pp. 17-19.
Carvajal Collection. AJHS, Waltham, Mass.
Carvajal, Luis. "Carta a Su Majestad de Don Luis de Velasco haciendo relacion de la entrada de Don Luis Carvajal en el Nuevo Mexico." Archivo General de Indias, Sevilla. 6 Noviembre 1591. Bancroft Library, University of California, Berkeley.
Castañeda, Carlos E., Department of History, University of Texas at Austin. Letter to Dr. B. Sacks, January 21, 1955. Sacks Collection, Arizona Historical Foundation, Tempe.
Castaño de Sosa, Gaspar, Collection. Bancroft Library, University of California, Berkeley.
———. "Memoria del descrubrimiento que Gaspar Castaño de Sos hizo en el Nuevo Mexico, siendo Teniente de Gobernador y Capitan General del Nuevo Reino de Leon." Real Academia de la Historia, Madrid. July 27, 1590. Bancroft Library, University of California, Berkeley.
Castleberry, Vivian. "Annette Strauss: Dallas' dynamo of civic causes follows the path into politics." *Dallas Times Herald Unique* magazine, May 4, 1983, p. 8.
Castro, Henri. Papers 1821-1845. Barker Texas History Center, University of Texas at Austin.
———. "Le Texas: Appercu Historique et Statistique; French Ship Immigrant List 1842." Barker Texas History Center, University of Texas at Austin.
Caulfield, Tom. "De Cordova Sold Texas to World." *Waco Tribune-Herald*, September 11, 1956, Kingsbury Collection.
Chimene, Tillye Braun-Klaben. "The Chimene Family." Typescript. Houston, 1954.
"City Philanthropist Ben Taub, 93, Dies." *Houston Post*, September 10, 1982, pp. A-1, 15.
Cobb, Stanley, M.D. (Vice-Chairman, Boston Committee on Medical Emigres). Letter, February 21, 1939. Bodansky Collection, UTMB, Galveston.
Cohen, Henry. "Biography of the Late Leo N. Levi." *Reform Advocate*, February 1904.
———. "David S. Kaufman." Typescript. n.d. Temple B'nai Israel Archives, Galveston.
———. "Dyer, Isadore," and "Dyer, Leon." *Jewish Encyclopedia* 1903.
———. "Early Jewish Settlements in Texas." *One Hundred Years of Jewry in Texas*. Dallas, 1936.
———."The Galveston Immigration Movement." *Federation Review*, March 1908, pp. 1-8.
———."The Galveston Movement." *B'nai B'rith Messenger* (Los Angeles) March 26 and April 16, 1909. Reprint. *WSJH* 18 (January 1986): 114-19.
———. "Henry Castro, Pioneer and Colonist," *One Hundred Years of Jewry in Texas*, pp. 13-15. Dallas, 1936.
———. "A Historical Sketch of the Jews of Texas" and "History of the Jews of Galveston." *Reform Advocate*, January 24, 1914.
———. "History of a Texas Pioneer [Castro]." *Galveston News*, April 26, 1931.
———. "The Jews in Texas." *PAJHS* 4 (1896): 9-19.
———. "Jews in Texas History." *Texas Jewish Herald* (Houston) April 23, 1936, pp.1-2.
———. "Settlement of the Jews in Texas." *PAJHS* 2 (1894): 139-56.
———. "Texas." *Jewish Encyclopedia* 1901. 12:121.
———. "Texas." *Jewish Encyclopedia* 1906, 12:353.
———. "Texas." *Universal Jewish Encyclopedia*. 1943. 10:203-208.
———. Papers. American Jewish Archives, Cincinnati, Ohio.
———. Papers 1890-1952. Barker Texas History Center, University of Texas at Austin.
———. Papers. The Rosenberg Library, Galveston.
———. Papers. Temple B'nai Israel, Galveston.

["Cohen, Henry"]. *Houston Post,* June 13, 1952. Obituary.
Cohen, Martin A. "The Religion of Luis Rodriguez Carvajal." *AJA* (April 1968): 33-50.
Cohen, P. [Dr.]. "Jacob Joseph Taubenhaus." *Nature and Country* 5 (January 1938).
Collins, Hon. James M. "Julius Schepps-Tall Citizen Who Earned Greatness." *Congressional Record,* 117, no. 81 (1971).
Collins, Jeff. "Store scores success in Western dress: Luskey's follows longtime tradition of fitting cowboys, celebrities." *Dallas Times Herald,* July 26, 1987, pp. B-1, 6.
Colonization Papers. Archives, Texas State Library, Austin.
Cook, Alison. "The Fraying Empire of Bobby Sakowitz." *Texas Monthly* 13 (December 1985): 132-36, 232-46.
Cooper, John S. "The Linz 'Jewelists' Use Prestige to Sell Gems in the Southwest." *Wall Street Journal,* October 8, 1948, p. 1.
Coslett, M. F. "Joske's: 108 Year History, a Tradition Now in Corpus Christi." Typescript.
Cox, I.J. "Early Settlers of San Fernando." *TSHAQ* 5 (October 1901): 142-60.
Curtis, Gregory. "The right way to build something good out of nothing." *Texas Monthly* 13 (December 1985).
Cusachs, G. "Lafitte, the Louisiana Pirate and Patriot." *Louisiana Historical Quarterly* 2, no. 2 (1919): 418-38.
Dalehite, Bob. "The Maas House." Typescript. 18 pages. Rosenberg Library.
Daniell, L.E. "Mrs. Anna Goodman Hertzberg." *Texas, the Country and Its Men,* pp. 251-52.
Darden, Bob. "Waco—Jacob De Cordova's 'beautiful daughter'." *Waco Tribune Herald,* June 6, 1983.
Davenport, Harbert. "The Men of Goliad." *SWHQ* 43 (July 1939): 1-41.
Davis, Walter L., Ph.D., and Ruth Gwendolyn Jones, Ph.D. "A New Look at the Gottlieb Collection." *Baylor Dental Journal* (Dallas) 29 (January 1985): 22-29.
"Death of Mrs. Maas." *Galveston Daily News,* February 20, 1891.
De Cordova, Carl. "The Wanderer: The Life and Achievements of Jacob De Cordova, A Prominent Figure in the Development of Texas." Typescript. Waco: Texas Collection, Baylor University, 1979.
De Cordova, Jacob. "The Cultivation of Cotton in Texas; The Advantage of Free Labour, a Lecture: Delivered at the Town Hall, Manchester, on Tuesday, the 28th day of September, 1858, before the Cotton Supply Association." London: J. King, 1858.
———. "Lecture on Texas delivered by Mr. J. De Cordova, at Philadelphia, New York, Mount Holly, Brooklyn, and Newark. Also a Paper read by him before the New York Geographical Society, April 15, 1858." Philadelphia: Ernest Crozet, 1858.
———. "The State of Texas: Her Capabilities." 114-page pamphlet. Manchester, 1858.
———. Texas, Her Capabilities and Resources: The Substance of Two Lectures Delivered at the Town Hall, Manchester; one on the 28th September, 1858, to the Cotton Supply Association, and the other on the 12th October, 1858, to the Working Classes Generally; with Explanatory Notes and Addition." Manchester, England: Cave and Sever, 1858.
———. "The Texas Immigrant and Traveller's Guide Book." 103-page pamphlet. Austin: De Cordova and Frazier, 1856.
[De Cordova.] *Kingston Daily Gleaner,* September 13, 1934, p.2
"Dedication of the Leo N. Levi Hospital in Hot Springs, Arkansas." *Galveston News,* October 27, 1913, p. 5.
Dillon, David. "Zale's new headquarters fit the firm's informal approach to big business." *Dallas Morning News,* Feb. 13, 1985, p. F-1.
"Dr. Anigstein, Medic College Professor, 'Feels Flattered' When Informed His Name Found on Nazi SS 'Blacklist' in Poland." *Galveston News,* n.d. Blocker History of Medicine Collections, UTMB, Galveston.
"Dr. Bodansky Dies." *Galveston News,* June 15, 1941, p. 1.
"Dr. J.J. Taubenhaus." Editorial. *Dallas Morning News,* Dec. 16, 1937.
Domeier, Doug. "Hexter Acquires Neiman Building." *Dallas Morning News,* Aug. 13, 1972.
Dreyfus, A. Stanley. "Hebrew Cemetery No. 1 of Galveston, Texas." Typescript. 1965. Temple B'nai Israel.
Dyer, Joseph Osterman, M.D. "Dyer Scrap Book." Press clippings of articles on Galveston and Texas history, mostly from *Galveston Daily News,* Dec. 14, 1919-Sept. 19, 1926. Scrapbook compiled in Rosenberg Library in 1932.
"Edmund J. Kahn, Philanthropist, dies." *Dallas Times Herald,* Oct. 31, 1984.
Edsall, David L., M.D. (Chairman). "Boston Committee on Medical Emigres: Statement on the Problem of Refugee Physicians." Typescript. Bodansky Papers, Blocker History of Medicine Collections, UTMB.
———. (Honorary Chairman, National Committee for the Resettlement of Foreign Physicians) "A Program For The Refugee Physician." *Journal of the American Medical Assn.,* May 13, 1939. Bodansky Papers.

Ehrenberg, Emil [Teplitz, Bohemia]. Letter to the "Proprietor of the station 'Dos Palmas' between San Bernardino and La Paz and Ehrenberg, on the Colorado, California." Goldwater Collection, Arizona Historical Foundation, Tempe.

Ehrenberg, Herman. "Letter to Ashbel Smith in Paris, *chargé d'affaires*, Republic of Texas," Feb. 9, 1844. Ashbel Smith Papers, Texas State Archives, Austin.

Erath, Lucy A., ed. "Memoirs of Major George Bernard Erath." *TSHAQ* 26 and 27, 1922-24.

Ericson, Carolyn Reeves. "Nacogdoches - Gateway to Texas: A Biographical Directory 1773-1849." Booklet. Fort Worth: Arrow, 1974.

———. "Nacogdoches Headrights: A record of the disposition of land in East Texas and in other parts of that state 1838-1848." Privately published, n.d.

Esparza, Enrique with Charles Merritt Barnes. "Alamo's Only Survivor." *San Antonio Daily Express*, May 12 and May 19, 1907.

Estill, Mary Sexton. "The Education of Anna Kaufman." *Texana* 4 (Fall 1966): 247-57.

Ettlinger, Hyman J. "Teaching the Understanding of Mathematics and the Accuracy of Mathematics." Typescript. Presented at National Science Foundation Summer Institute, Austin, 1969. Barker Texas History Center.

"Fania Kruger Dies in Austin." *Wichita Falls Times*, July 17, 1987, 6-A.

Federman, David. "Morris B. Zale: The Life." *Modern Jeweler* 83 (December 1984): 36-45.

Fierman, Floyd S. "Samuel J. Freudenthal: Southwest Merchant and Civic Leader." *AJHQ* 57 (March 1967).

———. "The Schwartz Family of El Paso." Monograph 61. Texas Western Press, University of Texas at El Paso.

———. "Some Early Jewish Settlers." *Arizona Bulletin Supplement*, 1903, pp. 29-38. University of Arizona Library, Tucson.

Flake's Bulletin, June 21, 1870, p. 4.

"40 Years on Faculty, Rabbis to Honor Ettlinger." *Daily Texan*, March 4, 1953.

Fretelliere, Auguste. "Adventures d'un Castrovillian." Barker Texas History Center, University of Texas at Austin. Translation in J.N. Waugh's *Castroville*.

Freudenthal, Samuel J. "El Paso Merchant and Civic Leader." El Paso: Texas Western College Press, Southwestern Studies, 3, no. 3, Monograph 11, 1965.

Friend, Llerena. "Adah Isaacs Menken, Texan by Parentage, Preference, or Prevarication?" Texas Collection, *Library Chronicle* (University of Texas), Spring 1958.

Fritze, David, and Pam Troboy. "She Made Art a Part of Dallas." *Dallas Times Herald*, July 2, 1988, p. 1.

"From Kempen, Poland to Hempstead, Texas: The Career of Rabbi Heinrich Schwarz." *WSJH* 19 (January 1987).

Galveston City Directories. R.L. Polk and Co., comps. Houston: Morrison & Fourney, 1891-1940.

"Galveston Plan." *Encyclopedia Judaica*. Jerusalem: Macmillan, 1971, p. 294.

Gard, Wayne. "Early Texas Land Merchant." *Dallas Morning News*, 1962.

Gardien, Kent. "Kokernot and His Tory." *Texana* 8 (1970): 269-94. Waco: Texian Press.

Gay, Wayne Lee. "Daniel Sternberg: Orchestrating Waco's Music with a European Flavor." *Texas Humanist* 7 (May/June 1985): 31-34.

"Gen. Maurice Hirsch, civic leader, dies at 93." *Houston Chronicle*, Aug. 5, 1983.

"Gen. Hirsch, civic leader, dies at 93." *Houston Post*, Aug. 6, 1983.

General Land Office of Texas. "Abstract of All Original Texas Land Titles Comprising Grants and Locations to Aug. 31, 1941." 7 vols. Austin, 1941.

George-Dees, Juliet. "Zachor!" A series of articles on Texas Jewry. *Marshall News Messenger*, 1979.

Gladden, Sanford Charles. "The Durst and Darst Families of America With Discussions of Some 40 Related Families." Typescript. Boulder, Colo.: Johnson Pub. Co., 1969.

Goetting, Mrs. Charles A. "Tribute to Olga Bernstein Kohlberg." *Password*, Quarterly of the El Paso County Historical Society, 17 (Winter 1972): 159-162.

Goldstein, Joseph L., M.D. Curriculum Vitae. 1987.

Goldthorp, Audrey G. "Castro's Colony." Master's thesis, University of Texas, 1928.

Goldwater, Barry M. Letters. Goldwater Collection, Arizona Historical Foundation, Hayden Library, Arizona State University, Tempe.

———. Letter to Dr. H. Fuchs of Berlin, September 26, 1940. Goldwater Collection, Arizona Historical Foundation.

Gordon, Jack. "Show Business Came Into Town on the Stagecoch." *Fort Worth Press*, July 13, 1949.

Greenburg, Rabbi Wm. H. "History of the Jews of Dallas." *Reform Advocate*, Jan. 24, 1914.

Greene, A. C. "Frances Sanger Mossiker." Eulogy delivered at her funeral in Dallas, 1985. Typescript, Mossiker

Collection, Dallas Public Library.

Greenwood, C.L. "Index: Marriages" [card file], Barker Texas History Center, University of Texas at Austin.

Griffiths, Therese. "Baylor's Jewish Institute for Medical Research reflects Jewish community's generosity and support of health care." *Baylor Medicine* (Houston), 1986.

"Ground Breaking for Zale-Lipshy University Hospital." *Newsline* (newsletter, Southwestern Medical Foundation), Fall 1987, p. 1.

"Growth of Weingartens Is One of Greatest Epics Of City's Business History." *Houston Post*, March 17, 1935.

Gruber, Ruth E. "Nasher Collection Opens 'in Memoriam.'" *Dallas Times Herald*, July 9, 1988, F-1, 3.

"H. Lesinsky, 89, El Paso Pioneer, Dies in New York." *El Paso Times*, Apr. 25, 1924, p. 5.

Halff, Henry M. "The Call of the South Plains in Central West Texas." Gregg & Halff, Midland, Texas.

Hansard, Donna Steph. "An insider's view of Zale takeover." *Dallas Morning News*, April 19, 1987, pp. H-1, 7.

Harris County Hospital District. Transcript of videotape for its twentieth anniversary, 1985. Office of Public Affairs, Baylor College of Medicine, Houston.

Herz, Lillian E. "Dr. Anigstein Brought UTMB Fame." *Galveston News*, December 5, 1965, p. 10-A.

Hirsch, Emil G., ed. "Jews of Galveston Number," *The Reform Advocate.* Chicago, January 24, 1914.

"History and Tax Records of the Sabine District and Sabine County, Texas." J.F. Gomer Chapter of Daughters of the Republic of Texas, Hemphill, Texas.

Hocker, Wes. "Versatile Dr. Ettlinger - Ready for 'Next Fifty.'" *Daily Texan*, Dec. 14, 1962.

Hoppe, Christy. "Civic leader, philanthropist Edmund J. Kahn, 80, dies." *Dallas Morning News*, October 31, 1984.

Houston, Sam. "Letter to Simon Mussina." *Writings of Sam Houston 1859* 7: 370-72.

Huhner, Leon. "Jews in the War of 1812." *AJHQ* 26 (1918): 180-81.

Hull, Dorothy. "Castaño de Sosa's Expedition to New Mexico in 1590." *Old Santa Fe* 3 (October 1916): 307-32.

Hurt, William C., D.D.S. Lecture to American Academy of the History of Dentistry, October 19, 1979, Dallas. Typescript. 10 pages. Baylor College of Dentistry Library archives.

Immer, Imrich, ed., "Leopold Meyer." Manuscript 67, p. 1. Houston Public Library, 1981.

"Inquisition in Mexico, Auto de Fe 1590: Trial of Luis de Carabajal, Governor of the Province of Nuevo Leon, for Observing the Law of Moses." Original manuscript and translation. From "Inquisition Vol. 1487" Mexican National Archives, 1927. Translated by A.J. Baker and A.M. Blake for G.R.G. Conway, Mexico City. AJHS archives, Waltham, Mass.

Institute of Texan Cultures. "The Texians and the Texans: The Jewish Texans." Booklet. San Antonio: The University of Texas Institute of Texan Cultures. Principal researcher: W. Phil Hewitt. Contributor: Natalie Ornish. 1974. Reprint, 1984.

"Interfaith Honor Given Dr. Ettlinger." *Dallas Morning News*, January 29, 1953.

"J.J. Taubenhaus, Plant Pathologist At A&M, Dead: His Studies in Cotton Root Rot Resulted in Finding of Preventive." Associated Press, Dec. 13, 1937. Texas A&M University Library archives.

Jarvis, Jan. "Hermine Dalkowitz Tobolowsky." *Dallas Times Herald*, August 25, 1986, *Dallas Inc.* mag., p. 3.

Jewish Herald Voice archives, Houston. 1908-1987.

"Jewish Texans." *See* Institute of Texan Cultures.

Johnson, F., 1st Lieut. "Johnson Statement #32212." Velasco, May 30, 1836. John H. Jenkins, ed., *Papers of the Texas Revolution 1835-1836* 6:419-20.

Johnson, William R. "A Short History of the Sugar Industry in Texas." Houston: Texas Gulf Coast Historical Association Publications. 5 (April 1961):1-83.

Jordan, Charles H. (Secretary, National Coordinating Committee for the Resettlement of Foreign Physicians). "A Memorandum on the Problem of Refugee Physicians." Typescript. Bodansky Collection, UTMB Galveston.

Joselit, Jenna W. "Our Gang: Jewish Crime in New York 1890-1917." *Reform Judaism*, Winter 1984-85, 10-11.

"Joseph Finger, Architect, Dies at 65." *Houston Chronicle*, Feb. 6, 1953.

Kallison, Frances R. "One Hundred Years of Jewry in San Antonio." Master's thesis, Trinity University, San Antonio, 1977.

Kariel, Audrey Daniels. "The Jewish Story and Memories of Marshall, Texas." *WSJHQ* 14 (April 1982): 195-206.

Karniel, I., "R' Meir Taubenhaus: Memorial." Carmel newspaper, April 12, 1938. Taubenhaus Collection, Texas A&M University Library.

Kaufman, David Spangler. Speeches delivered in the U.S. House of Representatives and printed for his First Congressional District of Texas: "Mexican War," June 20, 1846; "Texas Boundary," June 5, 1848; "Territorial Relations between U.S. and Texas," July 27, 1848; "To the People of the First Congressional District of Texas," September 10, 1850.

[Kaufman, D.S.] Letter, Cynthia A. (Mrs. George E.) McClelland, Archives Assistant, Seeley G. Mudd Manuscript Library, Princeton University, Princeton, N.J., to author, October 30, 1978.

Kellman, Steven G., "Remembering the Alamo." *Texas Observer*, Jan. 14, 1983, 15-16.

———. "The Yellow Rose of Texas." *Journal of American Culture* 2 (Summer 1982): 45-48.

Kemp, Louis W. Papers. "Biographical Notebook, Wim-Xi" (Wolf, Anthony), Box 2R237, Barker Texas History Center, University of Texas at Austin.

Kempner, Isaac Herbert. "H. Kempner: The First One Hundred Years." Texas Gulf Coast Historical Association Publications, 2 (March 1958): 1-15.

———. "My Memories of Father." *AJA* (April 1967): 41-59.

Kingsbury, Annie De Cordova (Mrs. Wm.G.). "Jacob De Cordova." Typescript, n.d., Helen and Gladys Kingsbury Papers.

Kohler, Max J. "Incidents Illustrative of American Jewish Patriotism." *PAJHS* 4 (1896):81-99.

Kohut, George Alexander. "The Martyrdom of the Carabajal Family in Mexico 1590-1601." New York: privately published, 1904. AJHS archives.

Kokernot, David Levi. "The Battle of Anahuac: Exciting Engagement of First Texas Navy." *Pioneer, Magazine of Texas*, n.d. Daughters of the Republic of Texas Library at the Alamo.

———. "Reminiscences of Early Days in Texas: An Interesting Narrative of Marvelous Escape in Two Shipwrecks." *Gonzales Inquirer*, June 22, 1878.

———. [Kokernot meets Sam Houston and describes him.] *Gonzales Weekly Inquirer*, August 17, 1878.

———. *Gonzales Weekly Inquirer*, July 19, 1923, pp. C-4, 5.

Korn, Bertram Wallace. "Factors Bearing Upon the Survival of Judaism in the Ante-Bellum Period." *AJHQ* 53 (1964).

———. "The Haham De Cordova of Jamaica." *AJA* 18 (November 1966): 141-55.

———. "A Note on the Jewish Ancestry of Louis Moreau Gottschalk, American Pianist and Composer." *AJA* (November 1963): 117-19.

Kramer, William M. "Pioneer Lawyer of California and Texas: Henry J. Labatt (1832-1900)." *WSJHQ* 15 (October 1982): 3-21.

Krisch, Lucille. ed. "Angelina County Texas 1850 Census and The First Taxpayers." Typescript. Nacogdoches.

"The Krugers: Texas Pioneers." Film. San Antonio: Institute of Texan Cultures, 1975.

Kutner, Janet. "Patsy Nasher Made an Art of Living." *Dallas Morning News*, July 10, 1988, p. 1.

Lamar, Mirabeau B., "Papers of Mirabeau Buonaparte Lamar." 2:18, 38, 152. Texas State Library, Austin.

Landrum, Lynn."Ettlinger." *Dallas Morning News*, January 28, 1953.

Larralde, Carlos Montalvo. "Carlos Esparza: A Chicano Chronicle." R and E Research, San Francisco, 1977.

———. "Chicano Jews in South Texas." Ph.D. diss., University of California, Los Angeles, 1978.

Lasker, Morris. "Letter from a Texas Pioneer, 1901." *WSJH* 15 (July 1983): 305-16.

"The Late Mrs. Randall." Obituary. *Galveston News,* Nov. 6, 1888.

Lefkowitz, David. "Jewish Pioneers of Texas." Dallas, 1936, pp. 26-30.

"Leopold L. Meyer 1892-1982." *Baylor Medicine*, January 1983.

Lesh, Carolyn. "Hermine Tobolowsky: She's a Modern-Day Suffragette who brought about legal equity for women in Texas." *Dallas Morning News*, Oct. 19, 1986, p. E-1, 2.

Lesinsky, Henry. "Letters Written by Henry Lesinsky to His Son." Edited by Albert R. Lesinsky. New York: privately published, 1924.

Levin, Etta Levine. "Genealogy of the Levitansky Family." 107 pages. Typescript. Los Angeles, 1960. AJHS, Waltham, Mass.; Barker Texas History Center, University of Texas at Austin; Natalie Ornish Collection.

"Levy, Dr. Albert Moses, Genealogy." Compiled by members of the family and edited by Rosanne and Daniel Leeson.

Levy, Daniel, "Letters About the Jews of California: 1855-1858." *WSJHQ* 15 (October 1982): 4.

Levy, Helen Blanton (Mrs. Raoul A.) and Claudine Murphy. "A Halff Genealogy." Typescript. 32 pages. Natchitoches, La., 1974.

Lewis, Kathy. "90 Minutes with Gen. Maurice Hirsch, philanthropist, cultural leader and world traveler." *Houston Post*, April 11, 1975.

Lockwood, Frank C. "Native German Early Leader in Southwest: Herman Ehrenberg Was Real Pioneer In Texas and Arizona." *Dallas Morning News*, Feb. 11, 1940.

"Louis Hexter Headed Back to Grindstone." *Dallas Morning News*, Aug. 21, 1973.

Maas, Elaine H. "The Jews of Houston: An Ethnographic Study." Ph.D. diss., Rice University, Houston, 1973.

Maas, Samuel. Two journals written by Maas in English, French, German, and Spanish. Barker Texas History Center, University of Texas at Austin. Partial translations and transcriptions, Ornish Collection, Dallas.
Mandelbaum, L. "Texas Merchants After the Civil War: 1871." *AJA* 12 (April 1960): 71-74.
Marks, Marguerite. "Philip Eldridge: Pioneer Founder of a Texas Family." *News*, Golden Acres, Dallas, December 1976.
Marks, Dr. Samuel. "History of the Jews of San Antonio." *Reform Advocate*, January 24, 1914.
Matagorda [Texas] *Colorado Tribune*, March 1, 1851, D.S. Kaufman obituary.
McDonald, Archie P. "Adolphus Sterne: Mover and Shaker." *Bicentennial Commemorative History of Nacogdoches.* Nacogdoches Jaycees, 1976.
McKnight, Felix R. "Julius Schepps: Tall Citizen Who Earned Greatness." *Dallas Times Herald*, May 30, 1971.
Memorials and Petitions. Archives, Texas State Library, Austin.
Muster Rolls. Archives, Texas State Library, Austin.
"Meyer Bodansky Dies; Professor of Chemistry." *New York Herald Tribune*, June 15, 1941, p. 1.
Meyer, Larry. "History of Daniel Oppenheimer." Int. Jan. 8, 1969. Transcribed 1970. Graduate School of Business, University of Texas at Austin.
Miller, Elton. "Bloom soothed racially troubled city." *Dallas Times Herald*, n.d.
Miller, Robert. "Teamwork makes Kahn job training center a reality." *Dallas Morning News*, December 11, 1987.
Motulsky, A.G. "The 1985 Nobel Prize in Physiology or Medicine." *Science*, 231:126-29.
Muir, Andrew Forest. "Lewis A. Levy: Pioneer Merchant of Houston." Typescript, 1956, AJA.
Mulvany, T. "Dr. Ray K. Daily Reflects on a Full Life as She Nears Her 80th Year." *Houston Chronicle*, May 31, 1970.
Muster Rolls. Archives, Texas State Library, Austin.
Nacogdoches Archives. Robert Bruce Blake Research Collection. 75 vols.
"Nobel-Prize Winners to Speak In Dr. Bodansky Talks Series." *Galveston Daily News*, February 11, 1952.
Oppenheimer, Evelyn. "Autobiography." Typescript, 1987.
Ornish, Natalie. via Associated Press. "Saintly Man of the Isle: Rabbi Cohen Became a Legend in Texas," in *Houston Post*, June 10, 1962, 8-A.
———. "The First Citizen of Texas." *Galveston Isle* 1 (December 1947): 6-8, 16.
———. "Jewish Citizens of Texas Immortalized at HemisFair Exhibit Spotlighting Early Pioneers to Lone Star State." *Texas Jewish Post*, September 19, 1963.
———, contrib. "The Jewish Texans." The University of Texas, Institute of Texan Cultures at San Antonio, 1974.
———. "Jews' start in 'new country' chronicled." *Dallas Morning News*, March 27, 1977, 5-G.
———. "The Legacy of Rabbi Cohen." *Texas Parade, The Business Magazine of Texas* 37 (June 1977): 49-52.
———. "Pioneer Jews of Texas." *Outlook* magazine (New York), Winter 1975.
Orr, Merwyn. "Old Brachfield Recounted." *Henderson Daily News*, July 4, 1976.
Parvin, Bob. "Castroville, Alsatian Colony on a Texas Rhine." *Texas Highways* 28 (March 1981): 22-31.
"Passover in a Texas Town in 1891." *WSJHQ* 11 (July 1979): 324.
"Philanthropist Ben Taub Dies." *Houston Chronicle*, September 10, 1982.
"Philanthropist Ben Taub Given Honorary Degree." *Houston Chronicle*, June 9, 1981.
Picard, Dr. "In Memory of Haim Taubenhaus." Typescript. Texas A&M University Library.
"Playwright Louis Hexter dead at 77." *Dallas Morning News*, April 3, 1977.
Postal, Bernard. "Henry Castro." *Jewish Tribune*, December 27, 1929.
Preece, Harold. "He Brought Families to Texas." *Congress Weekly* 23 (Aug. 20, 1956): 11-13. (Publication of American Jewish Congress)
Primeau, Marty. "Donald Seldin." *Dallas Morning News*, Jan. 26, 1986, 1-E.
"Rabbi H. Schwarz Dead, Aged Hebrew Litterateur, Had an International Reputation as a Writer." Hempstead newspaper, circa October 19, 1900. E. Gale Collection.
"Rites set for Sam Bloom, advertising firm founder." *Dallas Morning News*, July 19, 1983, 21-A.
Ritz, David. "Remembering Bloom." *D Magazine*, July 1975.
Robinson, Linda. "Westheimer: The evolution of a country road." *Houston Business Journal*, n.d.
Romaine, Michael. "Zale's Corporate Child-Care Program." *Texas Business Executive*, Spring/Summer 1982.
Rose, Diane M.T. "The Maps, Plans, and Sketches of Herman Ehrenberg." *Prologue: The Journal of the National Archives* 9 (Fall 1977): 162-170.
Rosenberg, Leon Joseph. "A Business History of Sanger Brothers 1857-1926." Ph.D. diss., New York University, 1967.

Rosenfield, John [1900-1966] Collection 1950-1967. Compiled by Katherine Faust. Dallas Public Library.
———. "The Importance of the Fine Arts." Transcription of speech delivered at Temple Emanu-El, Rosenfield Collection.
———. "Passing Parade." Column, *Dallas Morning News*, January 14, 1935; reprinted in Leon Harris, *Merchant Princes*, 358.
———. "Premiere of Levene Work Heard Sunday Night." *Dallas Morning News*, September 5, 1932.
Rosenwaike, Ira. "Leon Dyer: Baltimore and San Francisco Jewish Leader." *WSJHQ* 9 (January 1977): 135-43.
———. "The Mussina Family: Early American Jews?" *AJH* 75 (June 1986): 397-404.
Rothschild, D.I. "The Story of Westheimer Road." Typescript. Houston Public Library.
Rowe, Edna. "The Disturbances at Anahuac in 1832." *TSHAQ* 6 (April 1903): 265-99.
Ryan, Vincent. "The Murder of Ehrenberg." *Daily Alta California*, Oct. 31, 1866.
Sachnowitz, Sandra Galoob. "The Roots of Temple Emanu-El of Longview, Texas." Typescript. 1986.
Sacks, Benjamin, M.D. Collection. Arizona Historical Foundation, Hayden Library, Arizona State University, Tempe.
———. "Herman Ehrenberg 1816-1866." Typescript. Arizona Pioneers' Historical Society Library, Tucson.
———. "The Riddle of Herman Ehrenberg." Typescript. Sacks Collection, Arizona Historical Foundation, Tempe.
Sackton, Alexander. "Shaikevitch." Based on memoirs of Tobias Sakowitz. Typescript. 7 pages. Leah Sakowitz Nathan Goren Collection.
"Sam Bloom: A Very Special Man." Editorial. *Dallas Morning News*, July 19, 1983.
"Sam Kruger." *Rotary Spokesman*, Wichita Falls, circa 1949.
Saxon, Gerald D. "An Oral History Interview." Typescript, November 5, 1982. Rosenfield Collection, Dallas Public Library.
Scardino, Barrie. "A Legacy of City Halls for Houston." *Houston Review* 4 (Fall 1982): 160-63.
Schachtel, Hyman Judah. "Inaugural Prayer Given at Washington, D.C., January 20, 1965." Schachtel Collection.
Schiff, Flora. "History of the Jews of Fort Worth." *Reform Advocate*, January 24, 1914.
Schlam, Helena Frenkel. "The Early Jews of Houston." Master's thesis, Ohio State University, 1971.
Schluter, Helen G. and B.F. Toole. "1850 Census, Sabine County, Texas."
Schneider, Rose, M.D. "Hemoglobins We Have Known." *Texas Reports on Biology and Medicine* 40 (1980-81): 479-86.
———. "How I became a Harvard person." *Trends in Biochemical Sciences*. Published for the International Union of Biochemistry by Elsevier. 1 (October 1976).
"Schneider Recipient of Sinclair Award." *Galveston Daily News*, May 22, 1975.
Schwartz, Marilyn. "Frances Mossiker." *Dallas Morning News*, May 30, 1982.
Seal, Mark. "Annette Strauss." *Dallas Morning News*, August 1, 1982.
Seivert, Doris Harris. "Louis J. Hexter: The Man Who Helped Build Residential Oak Cliff." *Oak Cliff Tribune*, May 31, 1972.
Seldin, Donald Wayne, M.D.. Curriculum Vitae. 1987.
Shanblum, Moses. "History of Fort Worth Jewry." *Jewish Monitor*, Fort Worth/Dallas, December 11, 1925,
Shook, Robert W. "Abraham Levi: Father of Victoria Jewry." *WSJHQ* 9 (January 1977): 144-54.
Shpall, Leo. "Adah Isaacs Menken." *Louisiana Historical Quarterly* 26:162-68.
Singleton, Albert, M.D. "Dr. Meyer Bodansky (1896-1941)." Editorial. *Surgery* magazine (St. Louis) 10 (September 1941): 489-90.
Slover, Pamela. "Immigrant Becomes Top Banana in Men's Shop Chain." *Waco Tribune-Herald*, October 11, 1981, B-1.
Smith, Ashbel. Papers. Barker Texas History Center, University of Texas at Austin.
Smith, Dick. "He's a Phi Beta Kappa All-American: Math's First Now, But Dr. Ettlinger's Memories of Coaching Days Are Fondest." *Daily Texan*, Nov. 6, 1942.
Smith, Marcia. "The Duke of Anti-Smokers." *Dallas Times Herald*, Dec. 28, 1984.
Stancill, Nancy. "Big H cattle call on tortuous Westheimer." *Houston Chronicle*, Nov. 15, 1981.
Stedman, Jon. Extensive genealogical manuscripts compiled from data he collected from throughout the world, especially on the De Cordova family. Ornish Collection.
Stewart, Susan. "Mr. Stanley: Marcus fine tunes a career in radio." *Dallas Morning News*, September 22, 1981.
"Strauss for Dallas mayor." Editorial. *Dallas Times Herald*, March 8, 1987.
"Strauss Waltzes to Easy Victory." *Dallas Times Herald*, April 19, 1987, A-1.
Stringer, Tommy. *News*, published by Zale Corporation, April to December 1984.

———. "The Zale Corp.: A Texas Success Story." Ph.D. diss., North Texas State University.
"Suite Written by Dallas Man on Bowl List, Levene's 'Exodus' Accepted for Concert Here on September 4." *Dallas Morning News*, Sept. 3, 1932.
Sweeney, Julia. "Writer [Leon Harris, Jr.] had the right grandparents." *Dallas Times Herald*, Nov. 7, 1979.
Talmadge, Candace. "Jewelry firm [Gordon's] plans Growth." *Dallas Times Herald*, Nov. 5, 1981.
"Texans in Action: Work, Kindness, Tolerance Are Hyman Ettlinger Traits." *Austin American-Statesman*, Dec. 10, 1950.
"Texas Merchants After the Civil War: 1871." *AJA* 12 (April 1960): 71-74.
Texas State Gazette, Feb. 24, 1851, p. 206. D. S. Kaufman obituary.
"Texas, World Have Gained from Dr. Anigstein's Work." *Galveston News*, Dec. 9, 1970.
Thompson, Joe. "The Ben Lipshy Factor." *Modern Jeweler* 83 (December 1984): 46.
———. "Morris B. Zale: An Exclusive Interview." *Modern Jeweler* 83 (December 1984): 52-59, 76.
———. "Morris B. Zale: The Achievement." *Modern Jeweler* 83 (December 1984): 63-64, 78.
Thompson, Tommy. "Gordon Brothers' 10-year goal: 1,000 jewelry stores nationwide." *Houston Chronicle*, n.d.
"Three Sisters Rule Unique Firm." *Dallas Times Herald*, Nov. 20, 1957, 2-A.
Tinsley, James A., ed. "Select Letters of Harris Kempner 1837-1894." Texas Gulf Coast Historical Association Publication, 1 (December 1957): 1-47.
Toole, Blanche, ed. "Sabine County Marriages Prior to 1875."
———. "Abstract of Deeds, Sabine County Archives, Hemphill, Texas." Ericson's, Nacogdoches.
Toubin, Rosa Levine. "Colorful Brenham Community Has History of Over 120 Years." *Texas Jewish Post*, September 11, 1980.
Tucker, Chris. "Back to a graceful age with Frances Mossiker." *Dallas Morning News*, March 29, 1981.
Turner, Thomas E. "Waco 100 Years Old But Who Founded It?" *Dallas Morning News*, January 1, 1950.
University of Texas Medical Branch, "The Marie B. Gale Professorship in Psychiatry." Brochure. 1984. Edwin Gale Collection.
Viener, Saul. "Surgeon Moses Albert Levy: Letters of a Texas Patriot." *AJHQ* 46 (December 1956): 101-13.
Waldman, Morris D. "The Galveston Movement." *Jewish Social Service Quarterly* 9 (March 1928).
Waldron, Webb. "Rabbi Cohen—First Citizen of Texas." *Rotarian*, February 1939. Reprint, *Reader's Digest*, February 1939.
Wallis, Gene. "De Cordova Was Publicity Man for an Empire." *Dallas Morning News*, Sept. 18, 1932, IV-6.
Warnken, Charlene. "Dr. Schachtel to step down but not out." *Houston Post*, May 17, 1975, 8-B.
———. "Everyone loved him: Rabbi Cohen was dynamic force in Texas." *Houston Post*, April 24, 1976, 4-B.
Warren, Bill. "Books" Column. *Austin American-Statesman*, May 23, 1971, 31.
Warren, Harris Gaylord, ed. "Documents Relating to the Establishment of Privateers at Galveston 1816-1817." *Louisiana Historical Quarterly* 21 (October 1938): 1086-1109.
Weekly Arizona Miner, August 14, 1869.
Wheeler, C.A. "Address of C.A. Wheeler, Past Grand Master, IOOF of Texas, at the Reinterment of the Remains of Jacob De Cordova and Wife in the State Cemetery, Austin, Texas, Dec. 8, 1935." Typescript. Vann De Cordova Collection.
White, Grace Miller. "Activities of M. Halff and Brother." *Frontier Times* 19 (January 1942).
White, Owen P. "The University of Texas Strikes Oil: Institution, once land-poor, now has income of millions, thanks to Mr. Krupp." *New York Times Magazine*, May 3, 1925.
Wicker, Christine. "A Gentleman and a Scholar." *Dallas Morning News*, Feb. 10, 1987, 2-C.
Winkler, Ernest Wm., "The Cherokee Indians in Texas." *TSHAQ* 7 (October 1903): 97-100.
Wohlbert, Gizelle. "History of the Jews of Waco." *Reform Advocate*, January 24, 1914.
"Youth Who Came to Houston on Borrowed Funds 22 Years Ago Now Is One of Leading Architects." *Houston Post*, December 29, 1929.
Zale, Morris. "Zale's, A Giant and Still Growing." *Jewelers Circular Keystone*, June 1962: 38-41, 54-59.
"Zale Story." *National Jeweler*, November 1958: 54-57, 130-31.
Zollinger, R.O. "Texas Ph.D.s Hold Keys to Many Doors." *Austin American-Statesman*, January 8, 1956.
Zuber, W.P. "The Escape of Rose from the Alamo." *TSHAQ* 5 (July 1901): 1-11.

INDEX

ABOUT THE AUTHOR

Born on the island of Galveston, Natalie Ornish at age 14 enrolled in Sam Houston State University, where she received the B.A. degree in English at age 17. At 18 she was the youngest person to receive a Master's degree from Northwestern University.

She worked for The Associated Press in Chicago and Omaha, Nebraska, doing reporting, editing, and re-write. Galveston's Rosenberg Library sent for her to lead a bond campaign, which proved successful, to make the library — after 50 years of being privately endowed — a public one. She then created Galveston's first historic museum.

She has served as contributing editor for magazines. In Dallas she worked for Rogers and Smith Advertising Agency. She became one of the nation's first female film producers and holds membership in Information Film Producers of America. She is listed in *Who's Who of American Women, Who's Who in World Jewry,* and *Foremost Women in Communications.*